O·C·C·U·L·T

I·N·V·A·S·I·O·N

DAVE HUNT

HARVEST HOUSE PUBLISHERS
Eugene, Oregon 97402

Except where otherwise indicated, all Scripture quotations in this book are taken from the King James Version of the Bible.

Cover design by Koechel Peterson & Associates, Minneapolis, Minnesota

The author's free monthly newsletter may be received by request. Write to:

Dave Hunt
P.O. Box 7019
Bend, OR 97708

OCCULT INVASION

Copyright © 1998 by Dave Hunt
Published by Harvest House Publishers
Eugene, Oregon 97402

Library of Congress Cataloging-in-Publication Data

Hunt, Dave
    The mind invaders / Dave Hunt.
      p.   cm.
    ISBN 1-56507-831-4
    I. Title
PS3558.U46765M56   1998   97-42786
813.54—dc21   CIP

Printed in the United States of America.

00 01 02 03 04 05 /BC/ 10 9 8 7 6 5 4 3

✻ CONTENTS ✻

This book is offered in love and with much gratitude
to the Lord's "seven thousand" who
have not bowed the knee to today's baals
(1 Kings 19:18)
nor yielded to the spirit of ecumenical
compromise and expediency, but have remained
true to their Lord and to His Word—
and with special thanks to all those followers
of Christ around the world
whose discernment, diligence, and generosity
have provided so much of the material which
made this book possible.

We might naturally assume that one of the achievements of science would have been to restrict belief in miracles. But it does not seem to be so . . . the tendency to believe in the power of mysterious agencies is an outstanding characteristic of our own day.
—Max Planck, Nobelist in physics[1]

It no longer seems possible to brush aside the study of so-called occult facts . . . the real existence of psychic forces . . . in which, until now, we did not believe.
—Sigmund Freud[2]

Professor [James] Hyslop . . . admitted that . . . metapsychic phenomena could be explained better by the hypothesis of spirits than by . . . the unconscious. And here, on the basis of my own experience, I am bound to concede he is right.
—C. G. Jung[3]

All these accounts indicate that a vast and mysterious universe— perhaps an inner reality, or perhaps a spirit world of which we are all unknowingly a part—seems to exist.
—Carl Rogers[4]

When the demonic finally spoke clearly in one case, an expression appeared on the patient's face that could be described only as Satanic. It was an incredibly contemptuous grin of utter hostile malevolence. I have spent many hours before a mirror trying to imitate it without the slightest success. . . .

When the demonic finally revealed itself in the exorcism of [another] patient, it was with a still more ghastly expression. The patient suddenly resembled a writhing snake. . . . The eyes were hooded with lazy reptilian torpor—except when the reptile darted out in attack, at which moment the eyes would open wide with blazing hatred. . . . What upset me the most was the extraordinary sense of a fifty-million-year-old heaviness I received from this serpentine being.

Almost all the team members at both exorcisms were convinced they were at these times in the presence of something absolutely alien and inhuman.
—M. Scott Peck as Assistant Chief of Psychiatry
under the Army Surgeon General,
investigating the My Lai massacre[5]

1

* * *

Why This Book?

Fifty years ago World War II had just ended and mankind had awakened to a new hope. The genius that had produced such amazing weapons of destruction could now be directed toward happier pursuits—the preservation of the peace, political stability, and worldwide prosperity. Let us for a moment try to imagine ourselves transported back to that hopeful moment in history. And let us suppose that we were given a selective view through a window of eternity into the future up to the year 2000.

In the unfolding panorama before us we could not see the actual coming events themselves. We were allowed only to see the incredible technological developments that science would produce in the next 50 years. On that basis we were asked to predict the social, moral, and spiritual impact that such unprecedented advances would have upon mankind.

Peering wide-eyed into the future, we saw a new tool of science called a computer. This piece of electronic wizardry would create an explosion of scientific knowledge providing in mere hours far more data than past generations had labored for centuries to uncover. We saw the amazing progress that would come in all fields of science, developments which had once been only fantasy, from the transplanting of human organs and cloning to men walking on the moon and space probes reaching throughout our solar system and beyond.

Given this preview of exploding scientific knowledge, and considering the long-standing antagonism between science and religion, it would have seemed logical to predict a bleak future for any form of spirituality. With science answering all questions and providing seemingly unlimited possibilities, religion would surely be relegated to the scrap heap of history once and for all. No one except a few uneducated religious diehards with misplaced loyalty to past superstitions would have any lingering interest in the realm of the spirit!

A Strange Turn of Events

Reasonable as such a scenario would have seemed to us, it would have been wrong. Science failed us. And there is now an exploding interest not in organized religion but in a generic *spirituality* with a universal appeal.

Most amazing is the fact that the top *physical* scientists (not the *social* scientists) have led this renaissance of interest in spirituality. In a remarkable book, Ken Wilber brought together what the most renowned scientists of this century have had to say about the existence of a nonphysical, or *spiritual*, dimension of reality. He concludes:

> There is no longer any major physical-theoretical objection to spiritual realities. ... This view—which is supported by virtually every theorist in this volume [Einstein, Sherrington, Heisenberg, Schroedinger, Planck, Eddington, et al.]—is probably the strongest and most revolutionary conclusion vis-a-vis religion that has ever been "officially" advanced by theoretical science itself.
>
> It is a monumental and epochal turning point in science's stance toward religion ... [and] in all likelihood marks final closure on that most nagging aspect of the age-old debate between the physical sciences and religion. ... [6]

Instead of building a solid basis for peace, science has brought us to the brink of destruction, with a nuclear sword of Damocles hanging by a hair over our heads and ecological collapse threatening vast areas of our planet. Moreover, scientific materialism has utterly failed to answer the ultimate questions we face and to quench our insatiable thirst for a satisfying purpose and meaning to life. As Nobel laureate Erwin Schroedinger, who played a vital role in developing today's physics, reminds us:

> The scientific picture of the real world around us is very deficient. It gives a lot of factual information ... but it is ghastly silent about all ... that really matters to us. ...
>
> It knows nothing of beautiful and ugly, good or bad, God and eternity. ... Whence came I and whither go I? That is the great unfathomable question. ... Science has no answer to it. [7]

To be sure, science gave us many fascinating insights, the satisfaction of achievement, and a plethora of new toys, but, as Schroedinger says, it couldn't provide even the theoretical answers, much less the substance, of that which *"really matters to us."* There is a longing in the human heart that no amount of scientific achievement or technological gadgetry, prosperity or pleasure, fame or fortune can satisfy.

The Death of Materialism

What was modern man to do? He didn't roll over, pinned to the mat of life by the overwhelming strength of truth. There was no great turning to the God of the Bible. Yes, there was an upsurge of Islamic and Christian fundamentalism, but it never gained general favor, certainly not in political or academic circles, nor with the media. Today's prevailing mood is broad-mindedness, not dogmatism. The only rule is that there are no rules; the only absolute that there are no absolutes—absolutely no absolutes—especially in morals.

"Truth" is "whatever you're comfortable with." Just don't try to push it on anyone else. "If it works for you, or if it feels good," goes the saying, "that's okay, but I've got my own thing." *Spirituality*, yes, but not *one transcendent truth.*

This modern mentality is fostered to a large extent by the misleading term "human potential." Implied in that popular expression is the proud supposition that whatever power exists in the universe, including mysterious spiritual or psychic power, it all belongs to *us;* it represents *human* potential. *We* are free to tap into it and use it to *our own ends.* Such an assumption is not only naive but could foster a dangerous delusion.

That there is "something" beyond the physical universe— that an immaterial universe apparently exists which is not bound by time, space, and physical laws, and that it involves a mysterious power which seems to be unlimited—has become the general consensus. We now know that matter itself is not physical. The electron has no mass. Moreover, as Nobel laureate Sir John Eccles, a neurophysiologist, argues:

> But if there are bona fide mental events—events that are not them-
> selves physical or material—then the whole program of philosophical

materialism collapses. The universe . . . must make (spaceless) room for (massless) entities [i.e. minds].[8]

The existence of a nonphysical dimension inhabited by nonphysical beings is now the generally accepted belief among physical scientists. The only exceptions are a few hard-core atheists and Marxists who still cling to a discredited materialism. Arthur Koestler long ago pointed out:

> The nineteenth-century clockwork model of the universe is in shambles and, since matter itself has been dematerialized, materialism can no longer claim to be a scientific philosophy.[9]

The New Spirituality

As New Age leader Marilyn Ferguson documented nearly 20 years ago in *The Aquarian Conspiracy*, this new paradigm had "already enlisted the minds, hearts and resources of . . . Nobel laureate scientists, philosophers, statesmen, celebrities. . . ."[10] At the same time, however, there is stiff opposition to any attempt to actually define nonphysical or psychic power. The new "spirituality" is strongly ecumenical, and it now dominates not only religion but politics as well.

It is now an apparent advantage for political candidates to profess some kind of spirituality, and the less defined the better. Vice President Al Gore, though a Southern Baptist, worships the mother goddess Gaia and advocates "reliance upon a Higher Power, by whatever name." In his plenary address to the 1990 Global Forum in Moscow, cosponsored by the Soviet Academy of Science (which drew from 83 countries participating scientists as well as religious leaders from among Hindus, Muslims, Buddhists, "Christians," et al), Gore advocated a "new spirituality" common to all religions.

Any number of spiritual leaders, such as Pope John Paul II and his close friend, the fourteenth Dalai Lama of Tibet, wield considerable influence on the world scene. Of the Pope the Dalai Lama says, "Both of us have the same aim."[11] The Pope is sought out by top political representatives from all major countries. Likewise, the Dalai Lama is highly honored in the circles of world power, from the United Nations to the Vatican. Yet he is one of this generation's major purveyors of occultism.

The New "Prince of Peace"

This familiar figure in the saffron robes claims to be Tibet's *God*, the latest *reincarnation* of the original Dalai Lama. Admiration is showered upon him everywhere he appears. He proposes to bring peace to earth by initiating mankind into "Tibetan Tantric Deity Yoga," thereby turning us all into gods capable of creating our own reality with our minds. Does anyone take this fantastic idea seriously? Seriously enough that the Dalai Lama was awarded the Nobel Peace Prize on October 5, 1989!

The front cover of *Whole Life Times* for December 1989 was a replica of a peace poster popular at the time in North America and Europe. The scene offers a magnificent view of the sprawling 11-story, gilt-roofed "Palace of the Gods" in Lhasa, Tibet, ancient residence of the Dalai Lamas—from which the current Dalai Lama (though allegedly God!) fled to escape the Chinese conquerors of his tiny country. Towering in the background are the snowcapped Himalayas overarched with a dazzling rainbow.

Superimposed upon the breathtaking landscape is a head-and-shoulders picture of Tenzin Gyatso, "His Holiness the Dalai Lama of Tibet." His huge image rises out of the palace, dwarfing it and blocking the view of a portion of the majestic mountains behind. In large print at the bottom of the poster/magazine cover are the words "PEACE ON EARTH." The implication is clear: The promise of the angels at the birth of Christ will be fulfilled through the Dalai Lama, Nobel laureate for peace.

This was the *December* issue, but it contained not one syllable about *Christmas* or *Jesus Christ.* The entire magazine was devoted to "PEACE ON EARTH," but how to attain it through the true and only "Prince of Peace" (Isaiah 9:6), through whom alone comes "peace with God . . . by the blood of his cross" (Romans 5:1; Colossians 1:20) was not mentioned even once in its pages. This poster and magazine represent a growing attitude that permeates society and is promoted continually by the media.

Typical of his mission around the world, in Los Angeles in the summer of 1989 (just prior to receiving the Nobel Peace Prize), the Dalai Lama led an audience of 3000 devotees from many countries in a three-day "Kalachakra ritual for world peace" at Santa Monica's Civic Auditorium. Reporting on that conference, *Whole Life Times* explained:

> The Dalai Lama taught in Santa Monica that it was possible for all human beings to eventually become a Buddha, a being of the highest wisdom and compassion and power... [through] a method called Deity Yoga....
>
> Deity Yoga... is a special conscious act of... visualizing the illusion that we are already... god-like... [able] to create our own reality... [that we] are Buddhas.[12]

This is occultism of the highest order. It is also a delusion. Obviously, the Dalai Lama can't create his own reality but shares a common reality with the rest of us. He eats, sleeps, tires, rides the same vehicles, gets wet in the same rain, and uses the same money. If "Deity Yoga" hasn't even changed such simple things for the master who teaches it, then what can it do for the rest of us? Does the world's hope for lasting peace really depend upon such occult means? That increasing multitudes are being seduced with the promise of occult power does not bode well for the future.

The Dalai Lama is everyone's hero because he advocates a "spirituality" acceptable to all. On his first visit to the United States, in 1979, "His Holiness" was welcomed to St. Patrick's Cathedral in New York at what *Time* magazine called "an extraordinary interreligious festival" hosted by Cardinal Terence J. Cooke, archbishop of New York. Declaring that "all the world's major religions are basically the same," the Dalai Lama was given a standing ovation by the overflow crowd of mostly Roman Catholics.[13] In response to the Dalai Lama's speech, Cardinal Cooke (since his death "the Vatican has approved opening the cause for [his] sainthood"[14]) declared:

> This is one of the dramatic movements of the Spirit in our time. We make each other welcome in our churches, temples and synagogues.[15]

There can be no question that we are seeing a dramatic move of *some* spirit; but *what* spirit? It is equally clear that this spirit is *not* the Holy Spirit of the "God of Abraham, Isaac and Jacob" (Exodus 3:6,15, 16; Matthew 22:32; Acts 3:13, etc.), "the God and Father of our Lord Jesus Christ" (2 Corinthians 11:31; Ephesians 1:3, etc.) revealed to us in the Bible. That fact will become clear as we proceed.

The Lust for Power

The secular world is seeking not only' political and military power but spiritual or psychic power. Sadly, the same could be said of much of the evangelical church. John Wimber's book *Power Evangelism* set the tone for a movement that is sweeping the world called the "Third Wave." A new vocabulary was invented for what has more recently come to be known as "the postdenominational church."

In his new book *Confronting the Powers*, Fuller Theological Seminary professor C. Peter Wagner seeks to explain and justify this movement. Wagner calls Wimber "my mentor."[16] He introduces terms that were unknown only a few years ago: territorial spirits, spiritual mapping, Spiritual Warfare Network, A.D. 2000 Movement, ground-level spiritual warfare, occult-level spiritual warfare, strategic-level spiritual warfare, cosmic-level spiritual warfare, praise marches, prayerwalking, prayer journeys, praying through windows, etc. Wagner says that these new concepts and practices (of which Jesus, Paul, and the early church said nothing) hold the key to spiritual breakthrough and worldwide revival.[17] We will examine that claim.

Similarly, and in agreement with Wagner and Wimber, Christian TV and radio and bestselling books persuasively argue that we are in the midst of the greatest revival of Christianity in the history of the world. This revival is characterized, once again, by *power:* power to prophesy, to speak in tongues, to heal the sick, to confront evil spirits, and even to raise the dead. At least that is what we are being told. And there is plenty of apparent evidence of "revival" spreading rapidly throughout the world from such places as the former Toronto Vineyard, the Brownsville Assembly of God in Pensacola, Florida, Benny Hinn's church in Orlando, Florida, and his huge televised crusades. We will carefully examine this evidence as well.

As we will see in more detail later, *power* is the key word involved with the new generic "spirituality" in both secular and religious contexts. Nicky Gumbel, the curate of Holy Spirit Brompton Anglican Church in England, was swept into this new "move of the Spirit" by John Wimber. Gumbel testifies that he felt "something like 10,000 volts" of electricity going through his body when Wimber prayed for him. Prayed for what? For *power.* Said Gumbel approvingly on a teaching tape later:

> The American [Wimber] . . . just said, "More power. . . ." It was the only thing he ever prayed. I can't remember him ever praying anything else. . . .[18]

A Serious Consideration

Thomas Hobbes, seventeenth-century philosopher, could hardly have had church leaders in mind when he said: "So that in the first place, I put for a general inclination of all mankind, a perpetual and restless desire for Power after Power, that ceaseth only in death." Whether or not Hobbes would be shocked by the thirst for power on the part of the Wimbers and Wagners, his statement surely applies today to the top universities in the secular world now involved in psychic research. The CIA, KGB (now the FSB), and other intelligence and military agencies are likewise experimenting with *spiritual* power, which they prefer to call *psychic* power, and which they imagine to be an innate capacity of the human psyche, or mind—i.e. *human* potential.

Is this different from what the church believes to be the power of the Holy Spirit? Or are these equally amazing secular and religious manifestations, as some believe, the same thing but with different labels and packaging? After all, Norman Vincent Peale claimed that his "Power of Positive Thinking" was the same thing as faith.[19] And, anyway, what difference does it make? We will seek to answer such important questions.

Certainly, if biblical prophecies of a coming world government and world religion are to be realized under Antichrist, then the world and the church must come together once again, as happened in the days of the Roman Emperor Constantine. Could the common pursuit of *spiritual power* bring this about? Is that what we are seeing at this critical moment in history?

There was a time when people were easily accused of being witches and were burned at the stake. It was a cruel injustice. Is it possible, however, that we have now gone too far in the other direction? It is no longer credible to believe in a personal Satan or in a personal God. Both have been replaced by a Force with "dark" and "light" sides. Is it not naive, however, to imagine that an impersonal "Force" could bring into existence personal beings with the power of choice and the capability to love or hate, to appreciate beauty and goodness, or to be given over to ugliness and evil?

Just as the physical universe is inhabited by personal beings, some of whom are incredibly evil, could not the immaterial universe next door be inhabited by personal beings, some of whom are every bit as evil as their human counterparts? Could that explain what M. Scott Peck, at that point a total skeptic, apparently encountered and described in the introductory quotation to this chapter? And is it not reasonably possible that these spirit beings could possess even greater power than humans to effect their wicked designs? That possibility ought to have the attention of every inhabitant of this planet. Those who call themselves Christians, however, and know who these beings are, ought to have an even deeper concern.

Last Days "Signs and Wonders"

It should be of more than passing interest to everyone that Jesus Christ and the prophets and apostles, whose words are recorded in the Bible, predicted the burgeoning interest in generic "spirituality" which we are experiencing today. As we shall see, they foretold a time of unprecedented interest in the mysterious and apparently miraculous. Yet they warned that these "last days signs and wonders" would be a great delusion that would prepare the world and a false church for Antichrist.

The fact that Christ and His apostles accurately pinpointed more than 1900 years ago precisely what we are seeing today ought to pique our interest in what else they said, and why. We will examine these prophecies and seek to understand them in the context of today's highly touted "spiritual awakening" that is occurring simultaneously inside and outside the church. Could there be a connection?

Biblical prophets and Jesus Christ Himself warned of a great spiritual delusion and occult seduction in a period of time called the "last days" just prior to Christ's return. The warnings concerned "false prophets" who would perform "great signs and wonders" that would be so convincing that "if it were possible, they shall deceive the very elect" (Matthew 24:24). Paul also warned of a false "signs and wonders" movement in the last days (2 Timothy 3:8). Significantly, nowhere in the Bible do we find a good or legitimate "signs and wonders" movement prophesied for the last days, nor even a hint that it would be needed or helpful.

Today a growing "signs and wonders" movement in the Christian church is literally exploding and is involving not only charismatics and Pentecostals but even evangelicals who only a few years ago were opposed to what they would have characterized at that time as fraud. Today, in spite of the warnings by both Jesus and Paul, there is scarcely any thought that today's signs and wonders might be part of the very spiritual deception which the Bible foretells.

We are also seeing as a part of the "signs and wonders" movement a burgeoning "church growth" movement, a "prayer and fasting for revival" movement, and a "spiritual warfare" movement, all working toward the same goal. Few are those who dare to see any connection between these movements within the church and the false "signs and wonders" which the Bible prophesies for the last-days apostate church. Those who call themselves Christians are just as reluctant to admit the possibility of any satanic involvement in their "miracles" as the secular world is to admit the possibility of such involvement in the human potential and psychic powers it seeks to develop.

It is this author's conviction, based upon more than 50 years of observation and research, that we are in the midst of an accelerating occult seduction of both the secular world and the church. In the following pages we shall present the evidence and arguments on both sides so that the reader may come to his own conclusions regarding the truth behind today's exploding interest in spirituality.

*We must establish in the theological minds the theory of evolution . . .
the doctrine of reincarnation. . . . Our work with modern scientists is of
vital importance. . . .*

—The Occult Digest, January 1931[1]

*We view ourselves as . . . highly evolved animals. If this model is cor-
rect, how can we explain psychic functioning? If we are evolving, we
only evolve what we need at a particular time—we do not develop excess
capability. Perhaps the model is wrong. . . .*

—Astronaut Edgar Mitchell addressing Congress[2]

*In Catholic school here in the Archdiocese of Washington, D.C., we
were taught that Charles Darwin's theory of evolution was gospel truth.*

—Stephen F. Smith[3]

*Evolution . . . is a general condition to which all theories, all systems,
all hypotheses must bow . . . a light illuminating all facts, a curve that
all lines must follow.*

—Jesuit priest Pierre Teilhard de Chardin,[4]
often called the father of the New Age

*The real enemy [of Christianity] is naturalistic, impersonal Darwinism
that deliberately and consciously seeks to set God on the sideline of our
culture.*

—Phillip Johnson, U.C. Berkeley law professor[5]

*The result of these cumulative efforts to investigate [the incredible com-
plexity of] the cell—to investigate life at the molecular level—is a loud,
clear, piercing cry of "design!" . . . so unambiguous and so significant
that it must be ranked as one of the greatest achievements in the history of science. . . .*

*But no bottles have been uncorked. . . . Instead, a curious, embar-
rassed silence surrounds the stark complexity of the cell. When the
subject comes up in public, feet start to shuffle, and breathing gets a
bit labored. In private . . . many [evolutionists] explicitly admit the
obvious but then stare at the ground, shake their heads, and let it go
at that.*

—Michael J. Behe, a Lehigh University biochemist,
in Darwin's Black Box[6]

2

Evolution and Its Role

Far from being a scientific theory of recent origin, evolution was an established religious belief at the heart of occultism and mysticism thousands of years before the Greeks gave it "scientific" status. And the central core of the ancient mystical theory of evolution is the lie of the serpent to Eve in the Garden, the belief that we are evolving ever upward to godhood. Sounding like Pierre Teilhard de Chardin, Masonic authority W.L. Wilmhurst in his book *The Meaning of Masonry* declares:

> This—the evolution of man into superman—was always the purpose of the ancient mysteries [occultisms]. . . . Man, who has sprung from the earth and developed through the lower kingdoms of nature, to his present rational state, has yet to complete his evolution by becoming a god-like being and unifying his conscience with the Omniscient.[7]

New Age leader Robert Muller, for many years Assistant Secretary-General of the United Nations, expresses much the same: "I believe that humanity . . . has a tremendous destiny to fulfill and that a major transformation is about to take place in our evolution."[8] Muller states clearly:

> Decide to open yourself . . . to the potential of the human race, to the infinity of your inner self, and you will become the universe . . . at long last your real, divine, stupendous self.[9]

Evolving Upward to Godhood

The goal of evolution, as portrayed for thousands of years before Darwin, has always been to journey through endless reincarnations until union with the Universal Mind, or All, has once again been achieved. Barbara Brown of UCLA Medical Center declares that we are "evolving to a higher level of mind... [called] super-mind."[10] At Esalen, the New Age center in the Big Sur area south of San Francisco where the Human Potential movement began, Michael Murphy and George Leonard offered a seminar on "The Evolution of Consciousness," which suggested that "a transforma-tion of human consciousness as momentous as the emergence of civilization is underway." Darwin also recognized the spiritual im-plications of his theory. In *The Descent of Man* he wrote:

> Man may be excused for feeling some pride at having risen... to the very summit of the organic scale; and the fact of his having risen, instead of having been aboriginally placed there, may give him hopes for a still higher destiny in the distant future.

Whether Darwin fully realized it or not, the mystical goal of the theory of evolution he championed had always been to be-come "God." In *The Atman Project*, Ken Wilbur lays it out clearly: "If men and women have ultimately come up from amoebas, then they are ultimately on their way towards God."

In *Up from Eden* Wilbur identifies this belief in man's ascension to godhood as the heart of what has been "known as the 'perennial philosophy'... the esoteric core of Hinduism, Buddhism, Taoism, Sufism...." As Jon Klimo in his book *Channeling* summarizes it, the "truth of truths" of the channeled material is "that we are God" and only need to "realize" it. So the serpent's lie to Eve continues to dominate the ambitions of modern man, and evolu-tion is his hope that the lie will one day be realized.

Evolution plays a key role in the occult. Theodore Roszak pointed out that mysticism is "the parent stock from which the theory of biological evolution springs."[11] Anthropologist Michael Harner reminds us that "millennia before Charles Darwin, people in shamanic cultures were convinced that hu-mans and animals were related."[12] Evolution, as the core belief of Hinduism and witchcraft, is at least as old as the theories of reincarnation and karma, in which it is a key element.

Evolution, Reincarnation, and Witchcraft

Of course, evolution must be an essential part of the belief in reincarnation and karma. There is no point in coming back in an endless cycle of death and rebirth unless progress is being made upward. That progress is allegedly accomplished through evolution, not only of the body but of the soul.

Since reincarnation is a belief basic to witchcraft, it is not surprising that it is *amoral.* If a husband beats his wife, the cause-and-effect law of karma will cause him to be reincarnated in his next life as a wife who is beaten by her husband. *That* husband (who will have been prepared by his karma to be a wife-beater) must in turn come back in *his* next life as a wife beaten by her husband; a murderer must in turn become the victim of murder, and so forth endlessly.

The perpetrator of each crime must become the victim of the same crime, which necessitates another perpetrator, who in turn must become a subsequent victim at the hands of yet another, ad infinitum. Rather than solving the problem of evil, karma and reincarnation perpetuate it.

Apropos to our subject of the occult, evolution opens the door to belief in a mysterious "Force" pervading the universe, a Force which evolutionists believe brought life into existence and has directed its astonishing development over billions of years. It is a Force, too, which presumably has even greater heights of evolutionary development in store for mankind. Clearly this force is a substitute for God.

Evolution is a religion without any support in fact. C.S. Lewis wrote: "If minds are wholly dependent on brains, and brains on biochemistry, and biochemistry on the meaningless flux of the atoms, I cannot understand how the thought of those minds should have any more significance than the sound of the wind. . . ."[13] That simple logic destroys Darwinism. If man is the chance product of impersonal evolutionary forces, then so are his thoughts—including the theory of evolution.

A Surprising Development?

Most non-Catholics were surprised when Pope John Paul II, in a formal statement sent to the Vatican's Pontifical Academy of Science on October 23, 1996, announced that evolution was a scientific theory acceptable to the Church. Evangelical leaders such as Charles Colson, Bill Bright, J.I. Packer, Pat Robertson et al., in joining forces with Rome, assured their critics that Catholicism accepts biblical inerrancy. Yet the Canons and

Decrees of the Second Vatican Council (Roman Catholicism's highest authority) declare: "Hence the Bible is free from error *in what pertains to religious truth revealed for our salvation.* It is not necessarily free from error in other matters (e.g. natural science)" [emphasis in original].[14] Evolution is "scientific," and the Bible is not infallible when it comes to science.

Allegedly infallible popes have made dogmatic but embarrassingly unscientific pronouncements based upon false biblical interpretations. Choosing to blame the Bible rather than admit the folly of its leaders, Roman Catholicism denies that the Bible is "free from error" in matters of science. Here is a brief excerpt from the Pope's statement to the Academy:

> I am pleased with the first theme you have chosen, that of the origins of life and evolution, an essential subject which deeply interests the Church.... We know, in fact, that truth cannot contradict truth.... I would remind you that the Magisterium of the Church has already made pronouncements on these matters....
>
> In his Encyclical Humani generis (1950), my predecessor Pius XII had already stated that there was no opposition between evolution and the doctrine of the faith about man.... Pius XII stressed this essential point: if the human body takes its origin from pre-existent living matter, the spiritual soul is immediately created by God.... For my part... [I have said that] the exegete and the theologian must keep informed about the results achieved by the natural sciences....
>
> Today... the theory of evolution... has been progressively accepted by researchers, following a series of discoveries in various fields of knowledge. The convergence... of the results of work that was conducted independently is in itself a significant argument in favour of this theory.[15]

John Paul II was simply reiterating the official position of his Church. In May 1982, on the hundredth anniversary of Charles Darwin's death, the Pontifical Academy of Sciences held a conference of scientists in honor of Darwin and issued this statement: "We are convinced that masses of evidence render the application of the concept of evolution to man and other primates beyond serious dispute."[16] As a further example of endorsements by the Roman Catholic Church, in 1967 the *New Catholic Encyclopedia* had declared confidently:

Evidence ... supports ... the fact of organic evolution. The best judges of the matter are the specialists who, over a period of 100 years, have assembled the necessary evidence. For them the fact of evolution has been established as thoroughly as science can establish facts of the past not witnessed by human eyes.[17]

Deliver Us from Further Embarrassment

The shameful case of Galileo explains why Pope John Paul II warned that "the exegete and the theologian must keep informed about the results achieved by the natural sciences. ..." In enforcement of Church dogma, Pope Urban VIII threatened an elderly and very ill Galileo with torture if he would not renounce his claim that the earth revolved around the sun. On his knees before Rome's Holy Office of the Inquisition, in fear for his life, Galileo recanted of this "heresy"—with his lips but not in his heart. That the sun and all heavenly bodies revolved around the earth remained official Roman Catholic dogma for centuries, with one "infallible" Pope after another affirming it. Only in 1992 did the Vatican at last admit officially that Galileo had indeed been right.

John Paul II's quotation of Pope Leo XIII that "truth cannot contradict truth" is a capitulation to science. Rome's theologians must take care that their interpretation of biblical truth agrees with the latest scientific theories. Yet Peter, who Catholics say was the first Pope, declared that all Scripture was inspired of the Holy Spirit (2 Peter 1:21). Surely the Holy Spirit's knowledge of science is not dependent upon the theories of scientists, who often contradict one another and must revise their theories periodically! If the Bible is not infallible when it comes to science, then why believe it is infallible regarding salvation or anything else?

Nevertheless, Edward Daschbach, a Catholic priest, without any apparent sense of betraying Peter and the Bible, explains the official Roman Catholic position:

> The Church, then, does not accept ... the literal interpretation of the opening chapters of the Book of Genesis that would lead us to think that God, for example, actually made two grown adults suddenly from clay and rib. ... Catholics should be against creation-science for at least three serious reasons:

First: It effectively teaches a distrust of science and ultimately hurts religion as well. By defending a literal understanding of the opening chapters of Genesis . . . creation-science sets itself squarely against the world of true scientific discovery. . . . The myths used by the Genesis authors are simply tools with which they communicate their religious beliefs.

Second: Creation-science is contrary to the method of interpreting Scripture favored universally by scholars and strongly approved by our Church. This favored approach . . . [allows us to] accept the divine revelation contained in Scripture, while accepting at the same time human author's errors in matters of science or history. . . .

Third: Creation-science leads to deep prejudice and bigotry against the Catholic Church. The case in point is the Book of Revelation. When creation-science advocates ply their fundamentalist tools to this final scriptural book, the Church often becomes a target for vehement attack. . . .[18]

Theistic Evolution: A Convenient Compromise

The Pope stands firmly with a theory which contradicts not only the Genesis account of creation but other key portions of the Bible as well. And today's leading evangelical magazine, *Christianity Today* (begun and still backed by Billy Graham), supports the Pope in his endorsement of evolution. An editorial declared:

John Paul II was . . . reminding scientists that if they were to be faithful Christians there were limits beyond which their science could not take them . . . no theory of evolution was acceptable . . . that did not recognize the direct divine origin of the human soul.[19]

This issue was discussed at a gathering of mostly professing evangelicals at Biola University in Southern California in mid-November 1996. There were scientists from various fields, along with journalists, theologians, and educators "representing 58 state colleges and universities, 28 Christian academic institutions, and 18 other organizations." While all agreed that God was involved in the process (which Darwinism denies), there was wide disagreement on the extent of that involvement, all the way from a strict biblical creationist view to the belief that God used evolution to create various species over a period of millions of years and finally infused a pair of them with human souls.[20] The latter theory is called theistic evolution.

In contrast to the intimidation by science and the lack of confidence in the Bible's inerrancy to which both Catholics and many Protestants have succumbed, consider these stirring words from the famous preacher Charles Haddon Spurgeon:

> We shall with the sword of the Spirit maintain the whole truth as ours, and shall not accept a part of it as a grant from the enemies of God. The truth of God we will maintain as the truth of God, and we shall not retain it because the philosophic mind consents to our doing so.
>
> If scientists agree to our believing a part of the Bible, we thank them for nothing: we believe it whether or no. Their assent is of no more consequence to our faith than . . . the consent of the mole to the eagle's sight. God being with us we shall not cease from this glorying, but will hold the whole of revealed truth even to the end.[21]

The Serious Consequences of Theistic Evolution

Genesis lays the foundation for all of Scripture. If its account of creation isn't reliable, then neither is the rest of the Bible which rests upon it; and Christ is proven not to be God and Savior, but a mere man who foolishly took a mythological story of Adam and Eve literally (Matthew 19:4,5). Yet Pope John Paul II, as John Tagliabue, writing for the *New York Times,* reported, "has put the teaching authority of the Roman Catholic Church firmly behind the view that the human body . . . is the product of a gradual process of evolution."[22]

Adam is mentioned about 30 times in nine books of the Bible. Thus to discredit the biblical account of Adam's creation punctures so many holes in the Bible that it can no longer contain a consistent theology. For example, Luke 3:23-38 traces Christ's genealogy to Adam, and Christ is even called "the last Adam" (1 Corinthians 15:45). That title would be demeaning in the extreme if Adam were a prehuman creature that had evolved from lower life forms, as Catholicism officially affirms.

Christianity Today was not the only popular evangelical magazine to favor theistic evolution. So did *New Man,* at that time the official magazine of "Promise Keepers," the men's movement that sprang up a few years ago under the leadership of University of Colorado football coach Bill McCartney and has since grown phenomenally. That periodical expressed its agreement with the

Pope's position on evolution even before he stated it. Furthermore, *New Man* argued:

> Remember, however, that the debate over how God created the world—through millions of years of evolutionary work or through a few words spoken over a few days—is not the central tenet of Christianity.[23]

The truth is that Christianity is not an isolated development of the New Testament but is inextricably linked with all of the Old Testament and therefore stands or falls upon its accuracy or inaccuracy. Paul declared that the gospel which he preached was "the gospel of God" and that it had been foretold by the Hebrew prophets in the Old Testament (Romans 1:1-3) and was the fulfillment thereof. The Bible is one Book. If any part contradicts any other part, then the whole of Scripture is undermined. If the Bible is wrong in its account of man's origin, then why should we trust its teaching about man's redemption?

To support evolution to any degree and in any form is in fact to demolish Christianity. Interestingly enough, the *Satanic Bible* declares, "Satan represents man as nothing more than another animal, sometimes better, but more often worse than those who walk on four paws, because by the pretext of his 'divine intellectual and spiritual development,' he has become the most vicious animal of all."[24] *The American Atheist* knows what is at stake:

> Destroy Adam and Eve and original sin, and in the rubble you will find the sorry remains of the Son of God and take away the meaning of his death.[25]

A Theory That Should Be Discarded

In their desire to be in harmony with science, Roman Catholicism and certain evangelicals are backing a dead horse. Growing numbers of scientists are abandoning evolution as completely untenable because the evidence against it is overwhelming. British astronomer and mathematician Sir Fred Hoyle, though he finds the idea of God creating life distasteful, admits, "The scientific world has been bamboozled into believing that evolution has been proved. Nothing could be further from the truth."[26] Australian biologist Michael Denton, an agnostic and former evolutionist, and author of *Evolution: A Theory in Crisis*, says science has so thoroughly discredited Darwinian evolution that it should be discarded. Mathematics professor Wolfgang Smith says evolution is a "metaphysical myth . . . totally bereft of scientific sanction."[27]

When in 1952 Stanley Miller introduced simulated light into an atmosphere of methane, ammonia, water vapor, and hydrogen and seemingly produced several kinds of amino acids (the building blocks of living creatures), the scientific world was sure it could create life in a laboratory. The pursuit of this chimera, however, has only revealed greater problems. Klaus Dose, a prominent evolutionist, shares his disillusionment:

> More than 30 years of experimentation on the origin of life in the fields of chemical and molecular evolution have led to a better perception of the immensity of the problem of the origin of life on Earth rather than to its solution. At present all discussions on principal theories and experiments in the field either end in stalemate or in a confession of ignorance.[28]

Colin Patterson, Senior Paleontologist at the British Museum of Natural History, confessed: "I had been working on this stuff for more than 20 years, and there was not one thing I knew about it. It's quite a shock to learn that one can be misled for so long." Patterson "started asking other scientists to tell him *one thing* they knew about evolution." Biologists at the American Museum of Natural History in New York had no answer. Continues Patterson:

> I tried that question on the geology staff at the Field Museum of Natural History and the only answer I got was silence. I tried it on the members of the Evolutionary Morphology Seminar in the University of Chicago, a very prestigious body of evolutionists, and all I got there was silence for a long time and eventually one person said, "I do know one thing—it ought not to be taught in high school."[29]

Evolution is taught as fact in Catholic schools, where, as the *New York Times* noted, evolution is "a standard part of the curriculum."[30] Leonard DeFiore, president of the National Catholic Educational Association in Washington D.C., says, "We start with the premise that all creation came from God. Beyond that it's a scientific issue."[31] As cited in the beginning of the chapter, Roman Catholic Stephen F. Smith writes, "In Catholic school here in the Archdiocese of Washington, D.C., we were taught that Charles Darwin's theory of evolution was gospel truth."[32] Lehigh University biochemist Michael J. Behe writes of his days in Catholic schools:

> I don't remember exactly what was said about life, other than it came from God, and that . . . the leading scientific explanation for how He did it was Darwin's theory of evolution.[33]

Nothing could be more in opposition to Christian belief. Oxford University zoologist Richard Dawkins demonstrates that evolution allows atheists to justify their unbelief. Ironically, however, Dawkins, a leading evolutionist, admits in his book *The Blind Watchmaker* that "biology is the study of complicated things that give the appearance of having been designed for a purpose."[34] Isn't it amazing how everything "chance" produces always looks as though it had been designed!

A Clear Mathematical Impossibility

A single cell, the smallest living unit, according to Nobelist Lynus Pauling, is "more complicated than New York City." "The 'simplest' self-sufficient cell has the capacity to produce thousands of different proteins and other molecules, at different times and under variable conditions. Synthesis, degradation, energy generation, replication, maintenance of cell architecture, mobility, regulation, repair, communication—all of these functions take place in virtually every cell, and each function itself requires the interaction of numerous parts. . . ."[35] If any part of this incredibly complex biochemical machinery is not functioning properly the cell will die. Behe provides just one example:

> A single flaw in the cell's labyrinthine protein-transport pathway is fatal. Unless the entire system were immediately in place, our ancestors would have [died]. . . . Attempts at a gradual evolution of the protein transport system are a recipe for extinction. . . .
> At some point this complex machine had to come into existence, and it could not have done so in step-by-step fashion . . . as Darwinian evolution would have it.[36]

The cell doesn't merely "give the appearance of being designed," it could *only* be designed! Dawkins admits that every cell, either of a plant or animal, contains in its nucleus "a digitally coded database larger, in information content, than all 30 volumes of the Encyclopedia Britannica put together."[37] Try to imagine the odds of chance creating a 30-volume encyclopedia! Even if that impossibility somehow occurred, only one cell would have been produced, and there are trillions of cells in the human body, and thousands of different kinds, each working in unbelievably complex relationships with the others!

The mathematical odds against life beginning and developing by chance (even with unlimited time) are so astronomical as to render it logically impossible. Consider some examples. The combinations of just the 26 letters in the alphabet in blocks of 26 is expressed mathematically as 26!, which simply means 26 times 25 times 24 times 23 times 22 times 21 times 20 . . . on down to 2. Thus there are more than 400,000,000,000,000,000,000,000,000 combinations of 26 letters taken together. Yet instead of a mere 26, there could be as many as 3000 proteins strung together in a particular sequence within one cell. Chance could never put them all together in the right order! Furthermore, each protein is itself a long chain of up to 3000 chemically joined amino acid residues folded into precise structures. Try to imagine the odds of having these meticulous sequences happen by chance!

If everything isn't in perfect order it won't work. Thus it would be impossible to "evolve" toward the right combination. The perfect structure must be there to begin with, which could only happen by design. Forget superficial similarities and fossils; evolution can't even get started at the biochemical and cellular level. As Michael Behe reminds us:

> The cumulative [evidence] shows with piercing clarity that life is based on machines—machines made of molecules . . . [which are] enormously complex. . . . The complexity of life's foundation has paralyzed science's attempt to account for it. . . .[38]
>
> Faced with such complexity beneath even simple phenomena, Darwinian theory falls silent.[39]

Sir Fred Hoyle calculated that the odds of producing *just the basic enzymes* of life by chance are 1 in 1 with 40,000 zeros after it.

In comparison, the odds of randomly plucking a particular electron out of the universe are 1 in 1 with 80 zeros after it. Make another universe out of every electron, and the odds of plucking a particular electron out of all those universes by chance are 1 in 1 with 160 zeros after it. Hoyle comments:

> This situation [mathematical impossibility] is well known to geneticists and yet nobody seems to blow the whistle decisively on the theory. . . .
>
> Most scientists still cling to Darwinism because of its grip on the educational system. . . . You either have to believe the concepts, or . . . be branded a heretic.[40]

Obviously Designed by God

The obvious impossibility reveals evolution for the fraud it is. Chance could not even produce the basic enzymes. But enzymes serve astonishingly complex functions, a fact which adds further astronomical odds to the already impossible.

Consider the clotting of blood, in which enzymes play a vital role. Imagine the billions of animals that would have died before this incredible process was perfected *by chance!* In his 1996 book, *Darwin's Black Box,* Behe writes:

> Blood clotting is a very complex, intricately woven system . . . of interdependent protein parts. The absence of, or significant defects in, any one of a number of the components causes the system to fail: blood does not clot at the proper time or at the proper place.
>
> Animals with blood-clotting cascades have roughly . . . 30,000 gene pieces. TPA [Tissue Plasminogen Activator] has four different types of domains. . . . The odds of getting those four domains together is 30,000 to the fourth power. . . . The same problem of ultra-slim odds would trouble the appearance of prothrombin . . . fibrinogen . . . plasminogen, proaccelerin, [etc., each essential to the clotting process]. . . . The universe doesn't have time to wait. . . .
>
> The odds of getting TPA and its activator together [is so small as] not to be expected to happen even if the universe's ten-billion year life were compressed into a single second and relived every second for ten billion years. [Even] worse . . . Darwin's mechanism

of natural selection would actually hinder the formation of irreducibly complex systems such as the clotting cascade. . . .[41]

There are thousands of intricate systems in the body, each of which is incredibly complex. Consider the immune system:

> The internal defense system of vertebrates is dizzyingly complicated. . . . The first problem . . . is how to recognize an invader. Bacterial cells have to be distinguished from blood cells; viruses have to be distinguished from connective tissue.
>
> There are billions of different kinds of antibodies. . . .
>
> The scientific literature has no answers to the question of the origin of the immune system. . . . How the body acquires tolerance to its own tissues is still obscure, but whatever the mechanism, we know one thing: a system of self-toleration had to be present from the start of the immune system. . . .
>
> Whichever way we turn, a gradualistic account of the immune system is blocked by multiple interwoven requirements. . . . The complexity of the system dooms all Darwinian explanations to frustration. . . .
>
> No one at Harvard University, no one at the National Institutes of Health, no member of the National Academy of Sciences, no Nobel prize winner—no one at all can give a detailed account of how the cilium, or vision, or blood clotting, or any complex biochemical process might have developed in a Darwinian fashion.[42]

"Darwin's Black Box"

Behe's book provides example after example of the inconceivable complexity of life at its most basic chemical/cellular level and points out that this "black box," like the inner workings of a computer, cannot even be inferred, much less understood, from the outer visible structure. This inner complexity was completely unknown to Darwin and only discovered recently with the advent of the electron microscope. Behe offers multiple examples to prove that the way life is put together at the molecular level demolishes Darwin's theory because it cannot possibly account for the indisputably intricate design of "irreducibly complex" systems. Such systems *could not have evolved* because, without all parts present and functioning in the right relationship to one another, the system fulfills no function and life cannot be sustained:

What we see [in the cell] is this incredible complexity that no one ever imagined . . . [and] that calls for a conclusion of design. . . .

Biochemistry has, in fact, revealed a molecular world that stoutly resists [Darwinian] explanation. . . . Darwin never imagined the exquisitely profound complexity that exists even at the most basic levels of life.[43]

The typical cell contains about two thousand [mitochondrion compartments]. . . . Each of the little compartments contains machinery necessary to capture the energy of foodstuffs and store it in a chemically stable, yet readily available, form. . . . The system uses a flow of acid to power its machines, which shuttles electrons among a half-dozen carriers, requiring an exquisitely delicate interaction between many components. . . . The cell controls how much and what kinds of chemicals it makes; when it loses control, it dies. . . .

Life on earth at its most fundamental level, in its most critical components, is the product of intelligent activity. The conclusion of intelligent design flows naturally from the data itself—not from sacred books or sectarian beliefs. . . .[44]

Darwin himself said, "If it could be demonstrated that any complex organ existed which could not possibly have been formed by numerous, successive, slight modifications, my theory would absolutely break down."[45] This is precisely what we find at the biochemical, cellular level, a level of life about which Darwin knew nothing. Behe asks, "What type of biological system could not be formed by 'numerous, successive, slight modifications'?" He answers conclusively: "Well, for starters, a system that is irreducibly complex," as explained above.[46] Behe's discussion of DNA provides several further examples:

DNA, the most famous of nucleic acids, is made up of four kinds of nucleotides: A, C, G, and T. The first building block, A, can be in several forms, designated AMP, ADP, or ATP. The form that is first synthesized in the cell is AMP. . . . It is comprised of . . . ten carbons, eleven hydrogens, seven oxygens, four nitrogens, and one phosphorus. . . .

The formation of biological molecules . . . requires specific, highly sophisticated molecular robots. . . . To make AMP . . . we also need very high-tech equipment: the enzymes. . . . In the absence of the enzymes, AMP is simply not made. . . . AMP is required for life on earth: it is used to make DNA and RNA, as well as a number of other critical molecules. . . .

The problem for Darwinian evolution is this: AMP is required for life. Either it immediately has a way to produce or obtain AMP, or the cell is dead. . . .

No one has a clue how the AMP pathway developed . . . [and] no one has written about the obstacle posed by the need to regulate a cell's metabolic pathway immediately at its inception. . . . AMP is not the only metabolic dilemma for Darwin. The biosynthesis of the larger amino acids, lipids, vitamins, heme, and more run into the same problems, and there are difficulties beyond metabolism . . . mountains and chasms that block a Darwinian explanation of life.[47]

An Embarrassing Silence

Had Darwin known of the incredible basic structural complexity of life on the molecular and cellular level he probably would have had enough common sense not to propose his theory. Since the discovery of this "black box," evolutionists right up to the present have maintained a discreet silence on this subject. Behe points out that the prestigious *Journal of Molecular Evolution*, the highest authority in its field, has never "proposed a detailed model by which a complex biochemical system might have been produced in a gradual, step-by-step Darwinian fashion. . . . The very fact that none of these problems is even addressed . . . is a very strong indication that Darwinism is an inadequate framework for understanding the origin of complex biochemical systems."[48]

Between 1984 and 1994 about 400 papers concerned with molecular evolution were published in the *Proceedings of the National Academy of Sciences*. Yet *not one* "proposed [any] detailed routes by which complex biochemical structures might have developed"—nor have any been offered in any other biochemistry journals.[49] It is at this basic level of life (the complexity of which was unknown to Darwin) that Darwinism must now be defended—but evolutionists have avoided the subject for the obvious reason that it cannot be done. In view of the fact that there has *never been* "a meeting, or a book, or a paper on details of the evolution of complex biochemical systems," Behe writes:

"Publish or perish" is a proverb that academicians take seriously. If you do not publish your work for the rest of the community to evaluate, then you have no business in academia. . . . If a theory claims to be able to explain some phenomenon but does not generate even an attempt at an explanation, then it should be banished. . . . In effect, the theory of Darwinian molecular evolution has not published, and so it should perish.[50]

Darwin relied upon similarities in *outward appearances*. He pointed to the great variety of eyes and assumed that they had somehow developed by "natural selection" over great time. Behe's comment is shattering:

Now that the black box of vision has been opened, it is no longer enough . . . to consider only the anatomical structures of whole eyes, as Darwin did in the nineteenth century (and as popularizers of evolution continue to do today). Each of the anatomical steps and structures that Darwin thought were so simple actually involves staggeringly complicated biochemical processes. . . .

Anatomy is . . . irrelevant to the question of whether evolution could take place on the molecular level. So is the fossil record. . . . [It] has nothing to tell us about whether the interactions of 11-*cis*-retinal with rhodopsin, transducin, and phosphodiesterase could have developed step-by-step. . . .

The scientific disciplines that were part of the evolutionary synthesis are all nonmolecular. Yet for the Darwinian theory of evolution to be true, it has to account for the molecular structure of life . . . [and] it does not.[51]

The Bible or Evolution?

Ignorant of the scientific refutation of evolution and of its contradiction of Scripture, Donald Devine, former director of the U.S. Office of Personnel Management, spoke out in support of his Pope: "Prehuman man apparently existed for millions of years. . . . This is not a refutation of the Bible but a confirmation of it—that it took God to breathe in a soul before man could be man."[52] On the contrary, the theory of theistic evolution, involving as it does prehuman ancestors of man (New York's Cardinal O'Connor says Adam and Eve were lower animals),[53] contradicts not only Genesis but the entire Bible.

Rather than God implanting a human soul in prehuman creatures that had evolved from ocean slime, Moses tells us that God formed Adam from "the dust of the ground" and then *later*

God formed Eve from "one of his ribs" (Genesis 2:7,18-23). Prehuman ancestors cannot be reconciled with that account, an account which Jesus Himself confirmed (Matthew 19:4,5).

Christ refers to the Genesis account of man's creation and *quotes directly from it,* placing His stamp of approval on its authenticity. Paul, too, attested to the accuracy of the Genesis account when he declared that "Adam was first formed, then Eve" (1 Timothy 2:13,14; see also 1 Corinthians 15:22,45; Jude 14). Furthermore, Paul says that it was through Adam that sin entered into the world, and *death by sin* (Romans 5:12). If Adam and Eve descended from ancestors who had lived and died during thousands (or millions) of years of prehuman evolution until God finally humanized them, death would have been in effect before Adam sinned. Clearly, such a contradiction would be devastating to Christianity.

Theistic evolution's theory of prehuman creatures as man's ancestors contradicts Genesis, Christ's teaching, Paul's preaching, and the gospel. What the Roman Catholic Church and other proponents of theistic evolution apparently don't realize is quite clear to *The American Atheist:*

> But if death preceded man and was not a result of Adam's sin, then sin is fiction. If sin is fiction, then we have no need for a Savior. . . . Evolution destroys utterly and finally the very reason [for] Jesus' earthly life. . . . If Jesus was not the Redeemer who died for our sins, and this is what evolution means, then Christianity is nothing.[54]

Evolution, that "most bloated of sacred cows,"[55] has persuaded millions that the Bible isn't reliable and that the God of the Bible doesn't exist. As Berkeley law professor Phillip Johnson puts it, "The whole purpose of the Darwinian evolutionary story is to . . . show that you don't need a preexisting intelligence to do all the work of creation."[56]

Facing the Truth

Johnson shocked the academic world in 1991 with his book *Darwin on Trial.* Knowing that it is the unpardonable sin in academia to oppose evolution, Johnson courageously and with the precision of a trial lawyer demolished Darwinism by demonstrating that it would not stand up in court. Johnson indicted his fellow academicians with having "abandoned the truthful and accurate reporting to which science has traditionally been committed in their zeal to extirpate and dismiss religion from public life."[57]

If evolution were true, there would necessarily have been literally billions of intermediary stages filling the fossil record. Imagine the millions of tiny steps it must have taken over millions of years to develop lungs from gills, the stomach and digestive system, eyes, kidneys, the brain and nervous system throughout the body, the heart and bloodstream, sperm and ovum for mammals, the egg and its shell for birds and reptiles, etc. Yet *not one* of these "missing links" has been found!

And what about instinct? Evolution has no answer. Even if the bat's sophisticated radar system suddenly appeared by chance, who taught the first mutated bat to use it? How many millions of Arctic terns drowned before the first one, *by chance,* learned to navigate thousands of miles across the ocean? How many salmon lost their way in the ocean and never made it back to spawn before this uncanny instinct was developed? How many millions of spiders starved before the amazing mechanism for making webs suddenly *chanced* itself into existence—and who taught that unique mutated spider how to make a web? How many eggs of all manner of birds rotted before the instinct to hatch eggs developed, and how was it learned and passed on?

Pursuing a Delusion

Jean Houston, who is both a psychologist and a theologian, presents us with a synthesis of psychology, occultism, and evolution in her workshops and writings. In some of her workshops she leads participants into an alleged awakening of ancient prehuman "memories" as a means of gaining insight into their personalities and working through "emotional blocks." Here is an excerpt from a reporter's account of one such session:

> "Remember when you were a fish," Houston suggested. . . . Nearly a thousand people . . . dropped to the floor and began moving their "fins" as if to propel themselves through water.

"Notice your perception as you roll like a fish. How does your world look, feel, sound, smell, taste?"

"Then you came up on land," Houston recalled, taking us through the amphibian state. . . .

Then Houston suggested, "Allow yourself to fully remember being a reptile. . . . Then some of you flew. Others climbed trees. . . ."

We became a zoo of sounds and movements made by early mammals, monkeys, and apes.

Houston then called us to remember being "the early human" who loses his/her protective furry covering "and . . . evolves into modern human. . . ."

We had become a wriggling sea of bodies—nearly a thousand housewives, therapists, artists, social workers, clergy, educators, health professionals . . . [who] had crawled over and under each other, enjoying ourselves and re-learning what was deep within our memories.[58]

This "exercise in evolutionary memory," as Houston calls it, is patently nonsense. The fact is that no one has such "memories." Nor could such memories exist at some unconscious level (as in Jung's alleged "collective unconscious"), or even at the cellular level, as some argue, inasmuch as evolution is a myth that never occurred in real life. Then what is happening? Obviously, participants are talked into fantasizing in order to play along with the regressive therapy game.

It is amazing to see who is willing to participate in such folly. Houston chaired and organized a symposium for leading U.S. government policymakers entitled "The Possible Society: An Exploration of Practical Policy Alternatives for the Decade Ahead." She tells of guiding about 150 high-ranking officials for about three days. She had these officials on the floor, imagining internal journeys on a search for "the possible society." Such exercises, of course, can lead one into occult contact as surely as the shaman's journey to which it is clearly related.

Evolution, psychology, shamanism: The link is clear, but it is a belief in *evolution* which has led the downward spiral to today's renaissance of the occult. Man's much-vaunted claim to an evolving ascent to perfection has led instead to an inglorious return to pagan superstition.

In its pristine loveliness, there is nothing quite as beautiful as Mystical and Occult lore as handed down through the ages. . . .

The conversion of our great scientists to occult philosophy will perhaps be the outstanding spiritual event of this century. Already many of the leading minds in this field have moved secretly from physics to metaphysics.

—The Occult Digest[1]

A medicine man has . . . spiritual powers . . . to do something supernatural, which cannot be explained by the white man's science. . . . Not only humans can have ton [spiritual power]; animals, plants and stones can possess it . . . the spirit inside a person or thing . . . the power of the universe pervading everything.

—Archie Fire Lame Deer, Lakota medicine man[2]

The team room at the Sheri L. Berto Center is . . . the inner sanctum of the Chicago Bulls—a sacred space adorned with Native American totems . . . I've collected over the years. On one wall hangs a wooden arrow with a tobacco pouch tied to it—the Lakota Sioux symbol of prayer—and on another a bear claw necklace which, I'm told, conveys power and wisdom upon its beholder. The room also contains the middle feather of an owl (for balance and harmony); a painting that tells the story of the great mystical warrior, Crazy Horse, and photos of a white buffalo calf born in Wisconsin. To the Sioux, the white buffalo is the most sacred of animals, a symbol of prosperity and good fortune.

I had the room decorated this way to reinforce in the players' minds that our journey together each year, from the start of training camp to the last whistle in the playoffs, is a sacred quest. This is our holy sanctuary . . . where the spirit of the team takes form.

—Phil Jackson, Coach of the Chicago Bulls[3]

A thread of alternative thought . . . scholars say is working its way increasingly into the nation's cultural, religious, social, economic and political life . . . evidenced by a surge of interest in new metaphysical religions, [spirit] mediums, the occult, reincarnation, psychic healing, Satanism, "spirit guides". . . .

Leaders [in the movement] contend they are ushering in what they call a New Age of understanding and intellectual ferment as significant as the Renaissance.

—New York Times[4]

3

* * *

What Is the Occult?

The word *occult* comes from the Latin *occultus,* which means "concealed" or "hidden." It involves mystic knowledge and magic powers received from the spirit world and dispensed for the benefit of devotees or directed destructively at enemies by those who have been initiated into its secrets. The masters of occult power are known as medicine men (or women), witch doctors, witches, psychics, priests, sorcerers, astrologers, gurus, yogis, shamans, mediums, seers, or healers.

Some of those involved with occult powers attribute them to a variety of deities, others to a "Force" inherent within the universe with a "dark" and "light" side which humans can tap into. Still others claim they are simply using a normal power of the mind which can be cultivated in a special state of consciousness. There are also those who attribute occult powers to the God of the Bible.

Webster's New Universal Unabridged Dictionary defines *occult* as: 1) hidden; concealed: 2) secret; esoteric: 3) beyond human understanding, mysterious: 4) designating or of certain mystic arts or studies, such as magic, alchemy, astrology, etc. In apparent agreement with the dictionary definition, and unabashedly identifying himself with the occult, Archie Fire Lame Deer (quoted on the facing page) boasts that a medicine man has "spiritual powers . . . to do something supernatural which cannot be explained by the white man's science. . . ." An occult connection is no embarrassment to a medicine man or practicing witch, but would be (or should be) to a priest, pastor, or televangelist. Yet many professedly Christian leaders are involved in the occult and are leading their churches into this error, as we shall see.

What Is Going On?

Some years ago, a leading attorney in a city in Florida where I was lecturing, having read some of my books and knowing the type of research I was doing, invited me to breakfast in order to ask me some questions. As soon as we had placed our orders, he launched into an interesting story:

> I was at this party the other night. Someone introduced me to Dr. ____ [he named a world-renowned nuclear physicist]. After some small talk, I asked him a silly question: "Where do you get these brilliant ideas that have made you so famous?"
>
> His reply really dumbfounded me: "Most of them come from the school I attend at night."
>
> "You go to night school?" I asked, not knowing whether to take him seriously.
>
> "Not exactly," he said. "It's like this . . . sometimes after falling asleep at night I find myself . . . well . . . out of my body . . . I don't know where . . . and usually in the company of some other scientists, where we're taught advanced concepts by extraterrestrials of some sort . . . maybe spirit beings . . . I'm not sure."

The lawyer paused for a moment, watching me closely to see how I would react. I said nothing, so he continued. "Was the man drunk, or just pulling my leg? He seemed to be serious. I didn't know how to react. It just blew my mind. What do you think? Have you heard of anything like this?"

I nodded. "You'd be surprised," I told him, "how many medical doctors, scientists, writers, and inventors report similar experiences. The basic concepts for the Xerox photocopying patents came in a similar way. Richard Bach claims that his bestseller, *Jonathan Livingston Seagull,* was all dictated to him by a disembodied spirit. And there's Napoleon Hill. Have you heard of him?"

"He wrote books about success and Positive Mental Attitude, I think. Is that the man?"

"Yes. His books have heavily influenced thousands of top business executives around the world and have changed the whole concept of success/motivation training. Hill claimed to have learned his techniques from 'The Venerable Brotherhood of Ancient India,' a group of highly evolved Hindu Masters who supposedly lived centuries ago and can 'disembody themselves and travel instantly to any place they choose.'[5] They claim to act as spiritual advisers to humans, whom they initiate into the use of their powers. And that's just a sample."

A Host of Questions Arise

"You're not serious," the lawyer responded with a skeptical smile.

"I'm afraid I am. This amazing contact with mysterious beings from a nonphysical dimension has been going on since the beginning of time."

He insisted upon an explanation. Did I think these "beings" which the physicist seemingly encountered were extraterrestrials inhabiting other planets who were able with their superior technology to get to earth? Or were they "spirit beings," as the nuclear scientist suspected? Were they demons, or angels, or something else? Or could it all be explained by some kind of innate power within the human psyche? What about psychics who predict the future or can apparently move physical objects with their minds? Is this all part of the occult? And what exactly is the occult?

Over breakfast that morning I did my best to explain why everything he had mentioned was indeed part of the occult, and exactly how it worked and what was behind it. In the ten years since that conversation, the practice of the occult and its popularity have grown at an astonishing rate.

A Common and Easily Evaluated Example

Logically, a belief in the occult could hardly have persisted for thousands of years unless enough people had convincing evidence that there was something to it. Of course, multitudes in primitive societies would vouch for that. They would swear that the curse of a witch doctor or an "evil eye" could bring not only "bad luck" but death. And we have reliable testimony about these powers, such as that of the Yanomamo shaman from Venezuela who tells his story in *Spirit of the Rainforest*.[6]

In the prestigious *Smithsonian* journal in its January 1996 edition, the explosive growth of dowsing, a very common form of occultism, was documented. Dowsing involves a mysterious power for which there is no possible scientific explanation. Yet its results are verifiable and undeniable.

Dowsing for water with a forked green willow stick held in both hands as one walks back and forth across the ground is an ancient occult technique. Often called "water witching," it is well known in all cultures throughout history. It has been used in the successful location of more than 500,000 producing water wells in the United States alone. How it works, however, is the question.

Dr. Peter Treadwell traveled the world for the multinational pharmaceutical firm Hoffman-La Roche "to dowse for water sources for newly planned factories before they were built." Addressing a group of engineers in Basel, Switzerland, Treadwell declared, "I hope I shall not disappoint you when I say that I am in no position to offer any explanation for the phenomenon of dowsing . . . I have none." In a magazine interview, in response to the question "How is it that Roche, a company based on science, uses a nonscientific method to find water?", he replied:

> That problem has bothered me for a long time, but . . . we keep finding water for our company with a method that neither physics nor physiology nor psychology have even begun to explain. . . . The dowsing method . . . is 100 percent reliable.[7]

Dowsing may be "100 percent reliable" for Dr. Treadwell, but there is a varying margin of error for other dowsers, as in every area of the occult. Dowsers rationalize that the moisture in the green twig is magnetically attracted to the water in the ground, thus causing the twig to bend downward over a good supply of underground water.

However, there is no magnetic attraction of water to water of the magnitude exhibited in dowsing. If the dowser attempts to prevent the stick from turning downward, it will nevertheless do so with such force that the forked portion held firmly in both hands is twisted loose from the bark. Clearly, such force cannot be attributed to an attraction of moisture in the forked stick to water in the ground.

The Crux of the Problem: Information Communicated

More important, for some dowsers the wand or pendulum will, in response to questions, accurately indicate the depth at which the water will be found and the flow of water per minute and even the quality of the water! No impersonal force can transmit information.

Furthermore, many modern dowsers now use dry sticks containing no moisture whatsoever, while others use metal wires and even string and plastic devices. And in addition to water, dowsers have been known to locate oil, deposits of minerals, ancient cities, buried treasure, or any number of other desirable finds. "To dowse," writes one expert, "is to search with the aid of a hand-held instrument . . . for *anything* . . . subterranean water . . . a pool of oil . . . mineral ore . . . buried sewer pipe or an electrical cable . . . an airplane downed in a mountain wilderness . . . lost wallet or dog . . . a missing person. . . ."[8] An editorial in *Gold Prospector* magazine states:

> Dowsing is the easy way to get answers to your questions. You ask nature a question to which she (through your instruments) will answer with a "yes" or "no". . . .
>
> For instance, you need to find . . . gold; the grade of the deposit; ounces per ton; width of deposit; length of vein; and depth of deposit below surface, and the total amount of ore in tons.[9]

Some dowsers are even able to locate these sites for drilling, digging, or diving by dowsing *over maps!* Henry Gross, while sitting in Kennebunkport, Maine, located three well sites on a map of Bermuda and described accurately the depth to drill, the quality of water, and the quantity per minute which each well would produce. At that time Bermuda had gone "three hundred and forty years without drinking water" except for the rain that could be caught by various means. A plaque on a wall in Kennebunkport, Maine, reads:

IN THIS ROOM
OCT. 22ND, 1949, HENRY GROSS
DOWSED THREE FRESH-WATER DOMES
(ROYAL BARRACKS, JENNINGS, CLAYHOUSE)
ON A MAP OF BERMUDA,
AN ISLAND ON WHICH NO POTABLE SPRING-WATER
SUPPOSEDLY EXISTED.
IN BERMUDA, DEC. 7, 1949,
HENRY FOUND THE DOMES AS DOWSED
IN KENNEBUNKPORT. . . .
A DAILY 63,360 GALLONS [FROM CLAYHOUSE]. . . .[10]

Ted Kaufman, a retired public relations executive living in New York, has worked with New York State Rangers using his dowsing abilities to determine whether lost persons were dead or alive and to locate them on a map.[11] The first person to discover that dowsing could be done over maps was Abbe Alexis Mermet, a French priest, around the turn of the century. "Contacted through transatlantic mail by monks desperately seeking underground water for their monastery in the mountains of Colombia, Mermet marked a potential drilling site on a map of the monastery grounds which, when drilled, produced more than the water required. Others have dowsed over maps to locate downed aircraft in remote areas. . . ."[12]

Divination: Another Form of Witchcraft

Of particular interest is the fact that, as the *Smithsonian* article documents, dowsing is now being used to uncover all sorts of information—answers to virtually every question one could ask. Dowsing, then, is simply another form of "divination" (any occult technique for obtaining information and help from the spirit world through a physical device). It is strictly forbidden in the Bible. Other divination devices commonly used include crystal balls, tarot cards, Ouija boards, tea leaves, and pendulums. More occult practitioners in France are licensed to diagnose and treat illnesses by the use of pendulums than there are medical doctors in the country!

That dowsing has always been known as "water witching" is evidence that all cultures have recognized a connection between dowsing and the occult. Yet thousands of those who call themselves Christians, including pastors and other church leaders, have been involved in water witching without apparently being aware that they have been drawn into the occult. Many other beliefs and practices now acceptable within evangelical churches involve the occult. Alan Morrison tells how he was compelled to write *The Serpent and the Cross* because he "became convinced that there was the need [within the church] for far greater understanding and discernment concerning the meaning of the term 'occult.' "[13]

The occult invasion did not begin yesterday. At the same time that the early American colonists were stamping out witchcraft, they were practicing it themselves: "Renaissance esotericism ... astrology, palmistry, and magical healing."[14] We see the same incursions in our day. Having once been involved deeply in the occult, Morrison was staggered to discover that "so many satanic influences which I had renounced on becoming a Christian were gaining increasing popularity within the Church and were upheld as valid Christian experience."[15] This trend is increasing.

Good or Bad?

Occult powers that produce results which cannot be explained by material science are found in the practice of almost every religion, from much that calls itself Christianity to paganism, idolatry, witchcraft, and Satanism. Occultism is present even in religions which are opposed to one another. For example, it is found in the Sufism of Islam and in the Kaballah of Judaism; in aberrant Christian sects as well as in satanic and UFO cults.

Of course, the Roman Catholic Church would argue that the apparitions of "Mary" and other "saints" and the mystical experiences of "saints" in trance have nothing to do with the occult but come from God. The same argument would be made by Pentecostals and charismatics (whether Catholic or Protestant), who attribute their mystical experiences and seemingly miraculous healings to the Holy Spirit. What is the truth? We shall see.

In Christian Science and the other Mind Science religions, where God is "Universal Mind" and the biblical gospel of salvation by God's grace through Christ's death and resurrection is denied, the connection to the occult becomes more obvious. And when it comes to the mysterious powers manifested in voodoo, macumba, Candomble, and other native and nature religions, the occult connection is even clearer

That "spiritual" powers which can neither be affirmed nor denied by materialistic science (because they are beyond its reach) do indeed exist has been amply demonstrated among all cultures, peoples, and religions throughout human history. The acceptance and proliferation of all aspects of the occult are increasingly viewed as perfectly legitimate and desirable in today's world. Whether this is beneficial or detrimental to the best interests of society and the church is another question.

A Widespread and Growing Phenomenon

The proliferation and popularity of psychic networks is evident by the commercials on TV and in newspaper ads. Occultism is one of the growth industries of our time. In November 1996 *USA Today* reported: "Kabbalah is the rage in Tinseltown. . . . 'It's the kind of thing Jews don't talk about,' [TV's] Roseanne [noted]. . . . 'I'm a Catholic shiksa,' actress Diane Ladd says, 'but I'm on a spiritual journey. . . .' She was introduced to Kabbalah by comedian Sandra Bernhard. . . . Jeff Goldblum took the basic course. Barry Diller and Dolly Parton attended a private class. Roseanne explains . . . , '[Kabbalah] is about connection between mind and body, astrology, Atlantis, reincarnation and computers.'"

The universality and persistence of a belief in mysterious powers that exist in a realm beyond the material dimension has been dramatically demonstrated in the former Soviet Union. For more than 70 years, Marxist atheistic materialism was forced on the entire populace. At the same time, believers in any religion, from Christianity to witchcraft, were the objects of relentless persecution.

Once the Iron Curtain came down, and with it the repression of diverse opinions, belief in the occult suddenly exploded. As of this writing early in 1997, one of the most popular television programs in Russia is the "Third Eye," aired each Saturday. Its guests include witches, parapsychologists, healers, and Orthodox priests, who mix their peculiar application of the Bible with crystal balls and all manner of occultism.

One psychic popular on Russian television claims to be able to tell from a photo whether the person pictured is alive or dead, his or her state of health, where the person (or dead body) is located, and other data. A Russian woman "healer" teaches how to use occult power to restore health. Another popular psychic claims to have raised the dead in a mortuary and to be able to lower the level of toxins in food and drink through ritualistic motions of his hands. Then he infuses the food or drink with his occult powers and sells it. Purchasers throughout Russia swear by the benefits they have received in this way.

In America, Daerick and Nedrra Lanakila are the inventors of "energy medicine and quantum healing . . . healing products designed for direct interaction with the body/mind intelligence."

Through their organization, Y.A.T.O. Enterprise, they distribute the "Li.F.E. Energizers System for Vibrancy."[16] It consists of vials filled with "spiritual energy in an aqueous solution of distilled water" designed to "work on all four systems—physical, emotional, mental and spiritual. . . ."[17] Many other examples could be given.

A visit not only to large cities but to small rural towns across America reveals a staggering variety of occult shops, some on the main thoroughfares. There is no denying that in spite of the skepticism one would expect in an age of science, interest and even belief in the mysterious is growing. Nor is there anything new about the occult. "New Age" is a misnomer. In spite of computers and space exploration and communication satellites, neither the gods nor the rituals have changed.

Occultism in Our Modern World Remains Unchanged

Occult practices abound today in every culture around the world. On the roof garden of a fashionable Istanbul hotel, wealthy businessmen (who also regularly pray in Islam's time-honored way) consult a spiritualist at their monthly meeting, while at home their wives "read" the coffee grounds left in their breakfast cups. Both practices are forbidden by Islam. In Romania, former top Communist officials who in Iron Curtain days had Indian yogis brought into the country as part of a circus to be secretly consulted can now practice occultism openly. In Beverly Hills, an attorney and his college professor guest and their wives rest their fingers lightly on an empty, overturned wineglass after dinner and watch expectantly as it is impelled across the table by some unseen power to provide amazing answers to their earnest questions. In New York, driven by the same compulsion, a successful Wall Street trader consults his astrologer to determine when to buy or sell.

In Kenya, after ritual dancing and drumbeating, a Luo tribe witch doctor, with the approval of the United Nations World Health Organization, listens as ancestral spirits speak through patients in deep trance. At the same time, on Long Island, an Episcopal priest and several of his parishioners hold a seance to communicate with dead relatives in order to seek advice from those who had little wisdom upon earth but have somehow become all-knowing since reaching the "other side." In the steamy town of Recife in northern Brazil, Orisha gods and goddesses, imported from Nigeria and Dahomey, and now called by the names of Catholic saints, take violent "possession" of participants in a macumba ceremony.

Meanwhile, at faraway Massachusetts Institute of Technology, a Ph.D. candidate in solid state electronics with an open *I Ching* book on his lap solemnly drops 12 yarrow sticks and studies the resultant pattern. He is seeking guidance for a major decision in his life. Nearby at Harvard, a chemistry professor meditates beneath a mail-order pyramid. And deep in the Amazon jungle, natives drinking *yage* prepared from the *banisteria caapi* vine slip into an altered state of consciousness and begin to describe events taking place in a distant village. The gods, proven to be accurate the next day when a visitor comes from that village, have thus gained the confidence of their followers and thereafter can speak convincingly about the "next life."

In Tibet, lamas exercise ancient secret practices now forbidden by the Chinese Communists: spirit mediums transmit the messages of gods, demons, and the dead, while the *naljorpa* feast on corpses of the enlightened in order to increase their own psychic powers, or engage dead bodies in a mystic dance climaxed by sexual intercourse with the demonically animated corpses. On the Island of Hawaii, a *kahuna* engages in a secret huna ritual to gain control over "life energy" for a wealthy client who carefully keeps his connection with native religion hidden from his business associates and pays the *kahuna* to put curses on his enemies. And in Hollywood, California, in an occult bookstore, a pair of teenage girls, whose parents take them each Sunday to fundamentalist Christian churches, browse among the parentally forbidden witchcraft volumes, eager to discover for themselves the promised powers they became intrigued with through a recent PG-rated movie.

A Legitimate Concern

W. Brugh Joy is a medical-doctor-turned-Eastern-guru. Although he has had enough experience in the occult to be well aware of its dangers, he remains an avid believer and participant in occultism. Nevertheless, he issues this rather alarming warning:

> Tapping these energies is fire, and the consequences . . . can be psychosis, aggravation of neuroses, acceleration of disease processes and suicide.[18]

Such somber pronouncements are rarely heard from those who entice multitudes into occult involvement by trumpeting its benefits. One reads Phil Jackson's book, *Sacred Hoops,* without finding even a hint that there might be dangers hidden within the native spirituality which he touts so highly. His very involvement, on the other hand, serves as a powerful endorsement of what he preaches to his team and readers.

Our concern will be to discover the source and ultimate fruit of occult powers. Unfortunately, the mere display of seemingly miraculous powers is sufficient to cause many people to follow wherever it seems to lead them, as though anything "supernatural" must of necessity be benevolent. It should be clear, however, that evil is very real. Nor is there any reason to believe that evil, so prominent in the natural realm, would not be just as likely to exist in the paranormal.

We will therefore be examining evidence for the reality of these powers, as well as facing some serious and important questions about them. Are they from God or from Satan? Does either God or Satan, or both, actually exist? Or is there simply one universal Force embodying "dark" and "light" sides? Do occult powers and experiences lead ultimately to good or evil, to blessing or destruction? Is it possible to be sure of the source and final disposition of occult powers? If so, how?

Logic Recoils and Begs an Explanation

That someone as well-educated, intelligent, and sophisticated as Phil Jackson (coach of the world champion Chicago Bulls basketball team), along with many team members, believes so strongly in native American spirituality, Zen Buddhism, and other occult powers (as do millions of others equally educated and sophisticated) would seem to negate the idea that such things can be written off as mere superstition. *Something* convincing is going on—but which of the many explanations being offered is true?

That numerous celebrities and even scientists endorse the existence of psychic powers, however, is no excuse for naivete. Logic recoils at Jackson's suggestion that a "bear claw necklace" really possesses occult powers implanted by a medicine man. Common sense also looks askance at Jackson's claim that such powers could be conveyed to beholders. Is it enough just to "behold"? And what of those who "behold" unintentionally or out of historical or anthropological curiosity but with no desire to imbibe spiritual "benefit" from such totems and fetishes?

There can be no doubt that in our day a belief persists in much that modern skeptics have long ridiculed as old wives' tales and childish superstitions. This is true even among some of the world's leading scholars and intellects. Belief and participation in the occult is literally exploding. That fact cries out for a legitimate and definitive explanation—an explanation which we will carefully pursue.

Entering a Forbidden Realm

One would not expect occultism to gain a foothold in the Christian church, since the Bible forbids it in both the Old and New Testaments. Nevertheless, the church has been enticed as well as the world. Much that is now practiced in evangelical circles is the old shamanism (a universally adopted word for witchcraft and other occult practices) under new names.

Anthropologist Michael Harner, himself a practicing shaman, is one of the world's leading authorities on shamanism. A number of the basic elements which he says have been at the heart of shamanism worldwide for thousands of years are widespread within the church: visualization, hypnosis, psychological counseling, Positive Thinking, Positive Confession, and Eastern meditation techniques.[19] To what extent these involve the occult, and why, will be dealt with in the following pages. Multitudes of those who call themselves Christians are involved in the occult, many of them unwittingly.

The Bible provides a far more detailed list of occult practices than the quote from Webster's dictionary at the beginning of this chapter. The Bible lists divination (tarot cards, Ouija boards, crystal balls, pendulums, etc.), observing times (astrology), enchantment (hypnosis), witchcraft, charming (another form of hypnosis), consulting with "familiar spirits" (mediumship, seances, channeling), and wizardry or necromancy (communicating with the dead). The Bible forbids each of these occult practices.

The fact that some people are seemingly healed through occult powers or become successful through occult practices does not prove that the purpose behind them is to bless mankind. There must be *some* bait on the hook or no one would bite. Even if the intent is evil, one would expect *some* apparent good as a means of enticement. Mankind would hardly be drawn to something that was clearly and totally harmful.

In one's enthusiasm for embracing mysterious phenomena, one dare not ignore the question of ultimate purpose. We will attempt to face this vital concern carefully and honestly.

Many people thought that science ... [would] take us away from dependence on a Creator ... [but] modern science actually points strongly toward Him. ... It is only with considerable effort that a person can cling to materialistic views of the universe.

–Michael Behe, Lehigh University Professor of Molecular Biology[1]

The evidence of PK [psychokinesis] along with that of ESP [extrasensory perception] establishes the case for the reality of mind ... [that] mind is what the man in the street thought it was all along. ...

The man in the pulpit too was right in preaching that the human spirit is something more than the material of his body and brain. For the first time, science offered a little support to his view. ...

–Duke University Professor J.B. Rhine,
the father of American parapsychology[2]

There are powers of the mind and powers beyond the mind, which your science could never have brought within its framework without shattering itself entirely ... strange phenomena–poltergeists, telepathy, precognition–which you had named but never explained. ... Any [complete] theory of the universe must account for them.

–Overlords of the Universe to earthlings in
Arthur C. Clarke's *Childhood's End*[3]

That consciousness is ruled by the laws of physics and chemistry is as preposterous as the suggestion that a nation could be ruled by ... the laws of grammar.

– Sir Arthur Eddington, Nobelist in physics[4]

Psychoanalysis ... offers only a partial view of reality, since it overlooks the spiritual dimensions of humanity. That can get you into trouble.

–Professor Charles Tart, University of California[5]

The outstanding achievement of twentieth-century physics is not the theory of relativity ... or the theory of quanta ... or the dissection of the atom ... [but] it is the general recognition that we are not yet in contact with ultimate reality. ..."

–Sir James Jeans[6]

4

* * *

The Death of Materialism

The acceptance of Darwinian evolution in the nineteenth century was the key development in moving the scientific world into hard-core materialism. Nevertheless, increasing numbers of leading physical scientists became convinced of the reality of a nonphysical world. Among them were Nobel laureate Eugene Wigner, one of the greatest physicists of the century, the mathematician and quantum mechanics theorist John von Neumann (sometimes called "the smartest man who ever lived"), and Sir Karl Popper, recognized as the most famous philosopher of science of recent times. Sir John Eccles quotes Popper as saying:

> According to determinism, any theory ... is held because of a certain physical structure of the holder—perhaps of his brain. Accordingly, we are deceiving ourselves ... whenever we believe that there are such things as arguments or reasons. ... Purely physical conditions ... make us say or accept whatever we say or accept.[7]

If materialism and determinism are true, then the theory of evolution itself must be the result of random thoughts and thus could not be true. In fact, the very concept of true and false, good and evil—and all other ideas and beliefs—would simply be the result of random motions of atoms in the brain which all began with a big bang billions of years ago and have proceeded by chance ever since. If so, then our thoughts have no meaning. On the contrary, the fact that the mind must be something other than brain, and that it formulates meaningful thoughts, is demanded by our everyday experience and forms another argument against materialism.

Evolution Destroyed the Soul

As Mortimer J. Adler points out in his book *The Difference of Man and the Difference It Makes,* there is such a vast chasm between animal instinct and uniquely human characteristics (for instance, recognition of good and evil and appreciation of beauty) that there is no way to bridge it by a gradual evolutionary transformation. The human soul stands squarely in the way of evolution. To refute special creation, one would have to show that human personality is simply a quality of organic matter acquired through the evolution of the physical brain and nervous system. Behavioristic and humanistic psychologies provide the rationale for the general acceptance of evolution and materialism. Charles Tart, Professor of Psychology at the University of California at Davis, points out some of the consequences:

> Behaviorism and psychoanalysis make it very clear that the mind is the brain. This means, of course, that when you die you're dead. There is no survival. There's no real spiritual life. . . . Humanistic psychology . . . didn't teach us to question the mechanistic assumptions of the Western world view [it supported them].[8]

Materialistic understanding of man persisted as the *predominant* view in academia well past the middle of this century. Psychology (which we will deal with in more depth in a later chapter) was determined to establish itself as a *science* on a par not only with medicine but with physics and chemistry. This author well remembers the prevailing view when he attended university 50 years ago: Humans were simply complex lumps of protein molecules wired with nerves who made conditioned responses to stimuli bombarding them from the physical world. Human behavior could therefore be reprogrammed through the "scientific" methods of "behavior modification." One day it would be possible, with drugs and therapy, to reprogram the brains of criminals and overly aggressive political leaders and thus turn this world once again into paradise.

A "Ghost" in the Machine

Thoughts were presumed to originate in the brain as the result of chemical and electrical processes. Nothing *nonphysical* could exist. Contrary to common sense, man was the prisoner of whatever his brain cells (for purely mechanistic reasons) "thought." This incredible "fact" of science was taught throughout the academic world.

The great hope was that the laws of physics and chemistry, applied to the brain, would explain human personality. That would allow psychiatrists to manipulate the brain like a mechanic does an engine. Thus all inappropriate behavior could be eliminated. There would be no more wars or crime and this world would become a rhapsody of kindness, pleasure, and prosperity, the Eden no one had believed in.

It was impossible, however, to suppress the evidence that, instead of *producing* thought, brain activity is a *result* of thought. Inasmuch as thoughts originate independently of the brain, they must exist outside the physical dimension. That fact is self-evident on the basis of the many thoughts for which there is no physical counterpart nor any physical stimulus: truth, justice, holiness, perfection, God, ad infinitum. Indeed, consciousness itself exists outside the realm of science. Michael Polanyi argued:

> The most striking feature of our own existence is our sentience [consciousness]. The laws of physics and chemistry include no conception of sentience, and any system wholly determined by these [physical laws] must be insentient [i.e. without consciousness].
>
> It may be to the interests of science to turn a blind eye on this central fact of the universe, but it is certainly not in the interest of truth.[9]

No matter how "intelligent" a computer may be, it can only do what it has been programmed to do. Nor can the brain, though far more complex than any computer, think on its own. If thought were the result of neural activity in the brain, we would all be helplessly dragged along by chemical/electrical processes determining our thoughts and even our morals and emotions. No rational person can accept that hypothesis because we demonstrate our power of choice, and thus control of our brain cells, *countless* times each day. There is a "ghost" in the machine. The human soul and spirit do the thinking and use the brain to communicate these thoughts to the body and through the body to others.

No "Science" of Human Behavior

For materialism to be a valid theory, human personality and behavior would have to be explicable in purely scientific terms and subject to modification according to the laws of physical science. It would therefore be theoretically possible to precisely predict human behavior and to reprogram personality. Otherwise there could be no science of human behavior. Although most psychologists would now recognize that their profession is *not science,* some still cling to that appealing delusion.

It requires little common sense to recognize that there could not possibly be a "science of human behavior." If there were, then for a man to say to his wife or child "I love you" would be no more significant than to say he had an itch or a gastrointestinal pain. Love, an appreciation of beauty, a sense of injustice, and all other uniquely human emotions and understandings would simply be physical reactions within the brain cells, the nerves, and the glands, totally explicable by physical laws, thus as meaningless as a reaction between chemicals in a test tube.

Though behavioristic psychologists such as B.F. Skinner tried for years to convince themselves and others that man is a stimulus-response robot without the power to genuinely make choices—to love or hate, to do good or evil, to be kind or vicious—few retain that opinion today. Apparently one person who still does is Bill Gates, founder of Microsoft and the richest entrepreneur in the world, now worth about 37 billion dollars. Gates "believes that we'll someday be able to replicate intelligence and emotions in a machine. But he admits that the joy of raising daughter Jennifer 'goes beyond analytic description.'"[10] Gates may one day recognize that Jennifer is not a machine.

Mind Distinguished from Brain

If the physical/material universe is all there is, then every facet of occultism (which necessarily occurs in a nonphysical universe) is simply a delusion. There is, however, far too much evidence in support of so-called ESP, telekinesis, precognition, poltergeist activity and other forms of the occult to allow one to accept materialistic dogma. Carl Rogers eventually confessed that "mind is an entity far greater than brain. . . ."[11] Recognizing that consciousness could not be explained by materialism, Rogers realized the consequences and on that basis predicted the imminent practical application of "such paranormal phenomena as telepathy, clairvoyance, precognition . . . healing energies . . . the power of meditation, transcendent forces. . . ."[12]

The famous neurologist Wilder Penfield put it well: "The mind is independent of the brain. The brain is a computer, but it is programmed by something that is outside itself, the mind."[13] Logically, if the mind/spirit/soul is independent of the brain, it could survive the death of the body. Carl Jung, reflecting upon whether the soul, which he called "the psyche," might survive physical death, wrote:

> Total loss of consciousness can be accompanied by perceptions of the outside world and vivid dream experiences. Since the cerebral cortex, the seat of consciousness, is not functioning at these times, there is as yet no explanation for such phenomena. They may be evidence for at least a subjective persistence of the capacity for consciousness—even in a state of apparent unconsciousness.[14]

That some form of consciousness persists even when the brain is not functioning is evident from the many testimonies of those who have been declared brain dead and yet lived to describe in detail what was happening around them while they were being revived. A consciousness that functions independently of the brain is obviously nonphysical. The world of the occult is also nonphysical but it can affect this physical dimension just as our nonphysical minds operate our brains.

Remote Viewing

One of the most powerful occult practices known today is called "remote viewing," to be dealt with in depth in the next chapter. Its practitioners claim that *information of any kind* can be obtained, no matter how far removed from the viewer by space or even *past or future time*. Remote viewing is still being used by both the American and Russian (and other) military and intelligence establishments for espionage purposes. The results, many of them still classified and secret, are mind-boggling and totally inexplicable by science. So accurate have remote viewers become, so they tell us, that governments rely upon them for secret missions when lives hang in the balance.

One of today's premier remote viewers, Major Ed Dames, testifies to having used this occult power in the military. Congress is allegedly well aware of such activities and appropriates funds for this pursuit. Dames heads Psi Tech, a firm which specializes in remote viewing for the civilian world. Still called upon by the military in difficult cases, he claims to have been used to locate chemical weapons that Saddam Hussein was hiding in Iraq from United Nations inspection teams. In all of its remote viewing assignments, Psi Tech guarantees 100 percent accuracy to its customers!

Edgar Cayce many years ago claimed to be able to see "the body" of the patient he was diagnosing in trance and could even describe that person and the bed and room he occupied. Much of Cayce's remote viewing (including his medical diagnoses) proved to be amazingly accurate. Such practices among psychics continue today. *Time* magazine recently reported:

> Rosemary Altea is a spiritual medium and a healer who with her spirit guide, an Apache called Grey Eagle, communicates with spirits to heal, guide and console. . . .
> Writes Altea [in *The Eagle and the Rose*]: "Using mind energy connected with universal God energy, we can give absent or distant healing."[15]

Remote viewers are not so ready to admit the involvement of "spirits." Remote viewing is mentioned briefly here because it has contributed in a major way to the death of materialism. There is no *physical* explanation for the remarkable phenomenon of remote viewing.

Another of today's best-known remote viewers, who also was involved with this technique for the United States military establishment, is Emory University professor Courtney Brown. In the civilian world he teaches and employs what he calls Scientific Remote Viewing (SRV). Says Professor Brown:

> You have to understand that remote viewing is absolute positive proof . . . that we're more than our physical bodies. It was developed in laboratory conditions and now operationalized under laboratory conditions with the strictest of controls.

Remote viewing procedures demonstrate that we have a soul, that we are more than physical beings because the properties of the soul are what we use when we remote view. . . . There is a whole realm of life out there that's not physical.[16]

Science and the Mind

If everything in the universe works according to scientifically defined physical laws, then there are no otherworldly, mysterious, inexplicable powers, and those who believe in them have been badly deluded. On the other hand, if there is a nonphysical dimension, then who knows what astonishing "entities" and "powers" might be out there? And if the mind exists in a nonphysical dimension independent of the brain, then could it not make use of the powers in that dimension and contact entities who reside there?

Obviously it could be dangerous to venture into this realm. Could that be why the Bible forbids occult involvement of any kind? One thing is certain: Whatever understanding or protection one would hope for from the laws of the physical sciences would be left behind on such an adventure.

It is clearly wrong to demand a *physical* explanation for *spiritual* experiences—and if one was not forthcoming, to then deny the reality of a spiritual dimension to life. That would be like denying the reality of the sense of *smell* because odors can't be *felt* or insisting that because *honesty* and *justice* have no *taste* they don't exist. Yet such foolish judgments by science were accepted uncritically until well into this century, when many top scientists finally began to speak out against such nonsense. Referring to the existence of a spiritual dimension, Sir Arthur Eddington wrote:

> The scheme of [the new] physics is now formulated in such a way as to make it almost self-evident that it is a partial aspect of something wider.[17]

That this "something wider" could be nonphysical is, as Eddington believed, suggested by the very qualities of the universe as we know it. The discovery of ghostly particles such as the neutrino makes the existence of discarnate spirits or other nonphysical intelligences much more plausible in a scientific context. With virtually no physical properties—no mass, no electrical charge, no magnetic field—the neutrino behaves very much like a "ghost." Neither gravitation nor electromagnetic force have any effect upon the neutrino. A neutrino zooming in from intergalactic space at nearly the speed of light would almost instantaneously pass through the entire earth without hitting anything. This fact makes the suggestion that "ghosts" can pass through walls seem less fantastic.

"Scientific" Mysticism

Of course, the determined atheist of the past could not accept the existence of soul and spirit and so continued to support materialism even in the face of growing evidence to the contrary. This attitude maintained its dominance in science until very recently. Science has been traditionally given such unquestioned authority that it was virtually worshiped, giving rise to the religion of *scientism*. Scientism is an immensely powerful factor in shaping both secular and religious thought in today's world. Charles Tart defines *scientism* as "the psychological dominance of a materialistic philosophy *hardened* into dogma and masquerading as an authentic science. . . ."[18]

Many scientists, following the lead of Einstein, turned to mysticism. Rather than admit the existence of the God of the Bible, they postulated a universal Force behind evolution, or a universal mind or consciousness. Psychology helped to establish these pseudospiritual beliefs. Carl Jung, who was heavily involved in the occult, had already postulated his "collective unconscious," a concept which he received by inspiration from the demonic realm. Today's remote viewers are convinced that the information they pick up comes from the "collective unconscious." We will examine that claim in due course.

While the development of transpersonal psychologies in the early 1970s brought an almost grudging admission that the realm of the spirit was real,[19] there was a reluctance to admit that science had no jurisdiction over it. Science continued to be regarded as the only way to evaluate the nonphysical as well as the physical. We had been conditioned to revere a "scientific explanation" for all phenomena.

Many of those involved in the New Age were only too eager to pretend they had "scientific" support. When TM (one form of yoga) fell flat as the"Spiritual Regeneration Movement," Maharishi Mahesh Yogi changed its name to "The Science of Creative Intelligence." With that new and deceitful name, TM became a success worldwide.

One of the most ancient *religious* practices in Hinduism and Buddhism is now widely accepted in the West as the *science* of yoga. This new designation gives yoga a respectability which it does not deserve. Among those determined to rebirth religious practices as science was Dr. Walter Yeeling Evans-Wentz, who studied at Stanford University under famed psychologist William James. Evans-Wentz became known as the "scholar-gypsy"; he traveled the world seeking initiation into Hinduism, Buddhism, and other pagan religious practices. His first book involved years of research into the existence of the "wee folk" of Ireland. He wrote:

> We can postulate scientifically, on the showing of the data of psychical research, the existence of such invisible intelligences as gods, genii, daemons, all kinds of true fairies, and disembodied men [spirits of the dead].[20]

If such beliefs sound like old-fashioned superstition, then take a close look at *Touched by an Angel*, one of the most popular television shows today. Many viewers unabashedly take its charming lessons on life and theories about the next life very seriously. Whether there is any connection to a heightened expectation raised by the program itself, accounts are multiplying from those who claim they have encountered angels. Of course, such encounters have been claimed since the beginning of time.

Some of today's most deceptive cults have adopted the word "science" to give their brand of spirituality credibility and authority: Science of Mind, Religious Science, Christian Science, et al. There could be no greater anachronism or delusion, inasmuch as the mind and spirit are outside the realm of science. It would be an equal delusion to insist, upon the basis of any analysis made by physical science, that the occult (which operates in the realm of mind, soul, spirit) was nonexistent. Physical science, by very definition, can make no judgments concerning a nonphysical spirit realm.

The Birth of Parapsychology

Finally, science, after more than a hundred years of being mired in materialism's total denial of a nonphysical dimension, has come around to admitting the reality of a realm beyond the physical universe, and that it could very well be inhabited by spirit beings. After extensive interviews in Europe and America, philosophy-of-science professor John Gliedman wrote "Scientists in Search of the Soul" more than ten years ago in *Science Digest:*

> From Berkeley to Paris and from London to Princeton, prominent scientists from fields as diverse as neurophysiology and quantum physics are coming out of the closet and admitting they believe in the possibility, at least, of such unscientific entities as the immortal human spirit and divine creation.

With the virtual death of materialism, a new "scientific" approach to the occult was born called parapsychology, now taught in most major universities. Inasmuch as a nonphysical dimension of reality is entirely outside the realm of science, the attempt to examine it "scientifically" and to be able to establish how it functions by "scientific controls" could only lead to error. Scientists were set up for a master deception. It would seem that we had reached the point dreamed of by Screwtape and outlined to Wormwood in the famous *Screwtape Letters* by C.S. Lewis:

> We [demons] are really faced with a cruel dilemma. When the humans disbelieve in our existence we lose all the pleasing results of direct terrorism and we make no magicians. On the other hand, when they believe in us, we cannot make them materialists and skeptics. At least not yet.
>
> I have great hopes that we shall learn in due time how to emotionalise and mythologise their science to such an extent that what is, in effect, a belief in us (though not under that name) will creep in while the human mind remains closed to belief in the Enemy [the God of the Bible, the Father of the Virgin-born Savior, Jesus Christ].
>
> The "Life Force," the worship of sex, and some aspects of Psychoanalysis, may here prove useful. If once we can produce our perfect work—the Materialist Magician . . . veritably worshipping what he vaguely calls "Forces" while denying the existence of "spirits"—then the end of our war will be in sight.
>
> But in the meantime . . . the fact that "devils" are predominantly comic figures in the modern imagination will help you. If any faint

suspicion of your existence begins to arise in his mind, suggest to him a picture of something in red tights, and persuade him that since he cannot believe in that (it is an old textbook method of confusing them) he therefore cannot believe in you.[21]

Thus we now have a variety of quasi-materialistic explanations, all of them "scientifically verified," concerning who or what these nonphysical entities might be that seem to be communicating with mankind. They range all the way from splits of the psyche or a force generated by the unconscious to spirits of the dead or extraterrestrials visiting us from distant planets or even secretly living among us. Any suggestion that they might actually be *demons* bent on deceiving and destroying mankind is met with polite smiles, pained incredulity, or outright contempt.

The New "Science" of Consciousness

Professor Courtney Brown directs The Farsight Institute, whose mission, he says, is "to demonstrate scientifically to all of us that we humans are more than our physical bodies, and that life exists on both the physical and subspace (nonphysical) realms."[22] Brown is convinced that some of these mysterious entities with whom psychics make contact are here on planet Earth and that they are actually extraterrestrials (ETIs). He even claims to have made psychic contact with them himself.

Unfortunately, Dr. Brown is relying on his brand of "science" instead of the Bible and has fallen into serious error, which we will discuss in the next chapter. On an Art Bell radio program on November 19, 1996, Brown said:

> In our view, what people really need is the truth about . . . the new scientific understanding of our composite nature . . . soul and body. Finally, people need to know that The Farsight Institute is dedicated to researching and teaching about our essential nature on the level of explorations into consciousness. . . .
>
> We are at a turning point in our human evolution. . . . Finally, one day nearly everyone will recognize that the great debate as to who we are and why we exist has been significantly resolved. This, indeed, is our mission.[23]

Here we have the new "scientific" idea that one must reach a "higher state of consciousness" in order to perceive things as they really are. Yet an altered state of consciousness allows demonic entities to take over and begin to operate the brain to create a universe of illusion. This was obviously a major problem of the "Heaven's Gate" cult, 39 of whose members committed suicide together in Rancho Santa Fe, near San Diego, California, in late March 1997. They imagined they had received "transmissions" from the "next Level" which told them that it was time to "move on" in their evolutionary journey to perfection and that if they left their bodies behind they would be picked up by a giant UFO accompanying the comet Hale-Bopp.

Other UFO groups have been receiving similar data. Dr. Brown published on his website in late 1996 a statement titled "The Interdimensional Portal." It declared that Scientific Remote Viewing "seemed to suggest that there is some type of interdimensional portal or gateway near Earth that is being used for transportation purposes." Whether that statement served to encourage the Southern California cult to make themselves ready for "transport" through suicide will perhaps never be known.

These were highly intelligent people who had tried to follow "science" instead of the Bible in their dealings with what they thought were extraterrestrials. If they actually did receive psychic messages, the entities sending them must have been demons determined to destroy them.

Members of the cult believed that the kingdom they were seeking and to which they thought they were being transported by suicide was "an evolutionary level above human."[24] And they had been deceived into believing that Hale-Bopp's approach to Earth signaled their time of departure. In their position paper on suicide published on their website we see once again the key role that evolution plays in the occult:

> The joy is that our Older Member [the reference is to their understanding of Jesus] in the Evolutionary Level Above Human (the "Kingdom of Heaven") has made it clear to us that Hale-Bopp's approach is the "marker" we've been waiting for—the time for the arrival of the spacecraft from the Level Above Human to take us home to "their World"—in the literal Heavens.
>
> Our 22 years of classroom here on planet Earth is finally coming to conclusion—"graduation" from the Human Evolutionary Level.

We are happily prepared to leave "this world." . . . If you study the material on this website you will hopefully understand our joy . . . [and] may even find your "boarding pass" to leave with us during this brief "window."

We are so very thankful that we have been recipients of this opportunity to prepare for membership in Their Kingdom, and to experience Their boundless Caring and Nurturing.[25]

The obvious sincerity reflected above reveals the power of demonic entities to deceive, entities with whom this group had apparently been in communication through psychic means for more than 20 years. Even some former cult members still hold to its bizarre beliefs. When interviewed by CBS's *60 Minutes,* one former member, whose wife was among those who died, expressed regret that he hadn't been there to "leave this world" with them. He told KQED-FM in San Francisco:

I don't think of them as dead. Well, the bodies, yes. But these are shells behind. I believe they are on a [space] craft somewhere. . . . To move into bodies that had been prepared for them . . . of a finer nature—androgynous, sexless. It's an evolutionary step . . . I don't consider it suicide.[26]

Compounding the Error

Many people who call themselves Christians are drawn into the occult because it acknowledges the reality of the soul and spirit and can even sound biblical in doing so. This apparent agreement with the Bible is a deliberate setup by Satan in order to lead simple souls into deeper deception.

Professor Brown believes that the human soul exists throughout the entire universe at all times. Thus to view anything going on anywhere in the universe is simply to change one's center of awareness from the body to the soul. Here is "The Mission of the Farsight Institute":

The Western scientific paradigm postulates that consciousness is a phenomenon strictly related to brain physiology: when the brain stops functioning, consciousness ceases to exist. This belief has dominated society, and it has inhibited scientific investigation into the nature of the soul. The consequences have been devastating ... [to the] spiritual aspect of life. ....

The Farsight Institute of Scientific Remote Viewing seeks to overturn this flawed paradigm before it is too late. Research at the Farsight Institute demonstrates that consciousness is ... eternal and unbounded ... basic to and permeates all of physical creation ... [making] knowledge of all things ... possible.

At The Farsight Institute, we are dedicated to the practical and benevolent use of Scientific Remote Viewing ... [for] helping humanity to discern that which is real in ... a universe filled with mystery.... Using the controls of modern science ... our goal is no less than to perceive the nature of God. ...[27]

"To perceive the nature of God" by some "scientific" technique operating in the spiritual realm would seem to pave the way for the ultimate delusion. You may be certain that Dr. Brown's god is not the God of the Bible or he would look to His Word for an understanding of God. Science is still on its throne even after the death of materialism. That is a recipe for disaster.

An Unshakable, Universal Conviction

Throughout history and in all cultures, mankind has held a common and unshakable conviction that a nonphysical realm inhabited by spirit beings does indeed exist. That even atheists are not immune to this universal sense of the *noumenal* (a reality beyond the senses) can be easily demonstrated. A suspenseful mystery, for example, or a realistic war movie can stimulate a certain fear in readers or audiences. Horror films or novels about the occult, however, are much more unsettling. Why?

Facing a gun is one thing; facing an unseen "ghost" that is throwing furniture around the room brings terror of a different sort, even to the dogmatic materialist who denies the existence of such entities. As philosopher A.E. Taylor argues:

> The "uncanny" is precisely that which does not simply belong to "this" everyday world, but directly impresses us as manifesting in some special way the presence of "the other" world. ...
>
> It is hard to believe that the most skeptical among us does not know the experience. ...[28]

That sense of the "uncanny" to which Taylor refers is normal. It may be repressed, but it remains, no matter how deeply buried. In the former Soviet Union, even after more than 70 years of enforced atheism and the most severe measures against all religious faith, occultism is rampant. Belief in the supernatural is so much a part of human consciousness that it persists in spite of all the arguments that skepticism can marshal.

Spirit Entities and the Occult

Robert Jastrow (founder and for many years director of the Goddard Institute for Space Studies) theorizes that the evolutionary process could have been going on ten billion years longer on some other planets than on Earth. While the theory of evolution is mathematically impossible, Jastrow's conclusions are nevertheless of interest. He suggests that some entities could have evolved beyond the limitations of space, matter, and time:

> Life that is a billion years beyond us may be far beyond the flesh-and-blood form that we would recognize. It may ... [have] escaped its mortal flesh to become something that old-fashioned people would call spirits. And so how do we know it's there? Maybe it can materialize and then dematerialize. I'm sure it has magical powers by our standards. . . .[29]

Sir John Eccles, Nobel Prize winner for his research on the brain, describes the brain as "a machine that a ghost can operate." As a result of his research, Eccles believes there is compelling evidence to support the traditional religious belief in the existence of a nonphysical soul and/or spirit—and that it is this "ghost" which actually operates the human brain and through it the body. It is certainly reasonable to assume that the "operator" could very well survive the death of the "vehicle" it was operating.

If the human spirit operates the brain, which in turn operates the body, then psychedelic drugs, yoga, hypnosis, TM, and any other technique for altering consciousness could very well loosen the normal connection between the spirit and the brain. That temporary disconnection could allow another spirit to operate the brain and thereby subject that person to occult bondage and delusion.

John Lilly invented the isolation tank, which became the inspiration for the movie *Altered States*. He has devoted himself to exploring "altered states of consciousness." Some of his observations are interesting:

> From certain experiences that I have had of leaving the body while in the isolation tank, I would say that the spirit contains the being that is contained in the brain. . . .
>
> Now, if you work in the tank, what you've done is to shut down all the known senses . . . the gravitational field effect is reduced to the minimum possible. . . .
>
> Once you get the input to the brain down to the minimum possible . . . you're free to go. Some people call it lucid dreaming. . . . It's a lot easier if you have a psychedelic in you, but a lot of people . . . can just meditate and go into these alternate realities. . . . I suspect that a lot of new science can come out of this. . . .[30]

Materialism Is Dead

Lilly was only one of many psychiatrists, anthropologists, and other researchers who realized the connection between drugs and the occult. Here was another powerful factor in the death of materialism. Psychedelic drugs open the doorway to a whole universe beyond the material world. Two generations of Westerners have been set free from materialism by drugs, only to be swallowed up by the occult.

No argument could any longer convince those who had experienced the "altered state" that reality was limited to the physical world. The sights, tastes, smells, sounds, and above all the exhilarating feelings in this strange new land of the *mind* often seemed even more vivid and real than those in the so-called "real world." Ordinary reality seemed drab and tasteless by comparison. The magical door to what Carlos Castaneda called the "sorcerer's world,"[31] a realm surpassing even Alice's Wonderland, had swung open, and America would never be the same. That world was inhabited by entities who would masquerade in any form that best suited their purpose.

Though Harvard professor William James at one time was convinced that human personality and behavior could be explained in materialistic/deterministic terms, he became a supporter of religious and mystical experiences for which there was no materialistic explanation. Unfortunately, he clung to the "scientific method" for understanding the realm of the spirit. As a consequence, James, not unlike the cult members of Rancho Santa Fe, fell victim to the belief that "higher powers exist and are at work to save the world. . . ."

Why should these allegedly "higher powers" be interested in saving the world? Might they not be determined to destroy us for their own selfish reasons? Is it not possible that such evil entities as demons actually exist?

Demonic Possession?

That demonic possession could result from entering an altered state of consciousness is being increasingly acknowledged by scientists and psychologists and other researchers into parapsychology. Jon Klimo, author of one of the most definitive books on channeling, explains:

> If your own mind can affect your own brain, then the similar nonphysical nature of *another* mind might also be able to affect your brain [if it is in a state of receptivity], giving rise to your hearing a voice, seeing a vision, or having the other mind speak or write [through you] by controlling your body the same way you normally control your own body.[32]

Charles Tart admits reluctantly, "There's enough evidence that comes in to make me take the idea of disembodied intelligence seriously."[33] William James, one of the most highly regarded psychologists of this century, wrote:

> The refusal of modern "enlightenment" to treat [demonic] "possession" as a hypothesis . . . in spite of the massive human tradition based on concrete human experience in its favor, has always seemed to me a curious example of the power of fashion in things "scientific."
>
> That the demon-theory . . . will have its innings again is to my mind absolutely certain. One has to be "scientific" indeed to be blind and ignorant enough to suspect no such possibility.[34]

Psychiatrist Stanislav Grof, pioneer researcher into LSD and altered states, reports that some of the LSD subjects he has studied have had encounters with "astral bodies," and in some cases this has led to "the characteristics of spirit possession." Friedrich Nietzsche indicated that the inspiration for *Thus Spake Zarathustra* came as a form of possession. "It invaded me. One can hardly reject completely the idea that one is the mere incarnation, or mouthpiece, or medium, of some almighty power." It takes little thought to realize which "almighty power" inspired this great inspirer of Hitler.

Famed architect Buckminster Fuller, after staying up half the night reading Marilyn Ferguson's groundbreaking book *The Aquarian Conspiracy* (the New Age Bible), suggested that "the spirits of the dead" had helped her to write it. Ferguson laughed and said, "Well, I sometimes thought so, but I wasn't about to tell anybody."[35]

What Does It All Mean?

Materialism is dead. It is no longer the *brain*, a mass of matter, that is credited with thought, but the *mind*, a nonphysical entity that is not part of the brain or any other part of the body and thus could apparently survive the death of the body. The mind could therefore entertain perceptions quite independent of the body and its five senses.

Unfortunately, while the delusionary lie of materialism has been largely discredited, it has been replaced by a new spirituality that still remains tied to this universe and to science. There is a belief in nonphysical "entities," including "angels," but their identity is decided entirely on the basis of what they say about themselves. At the same time, there is an even greater skepticism toward belief in demons, Satan, the God of the Bible, and Jesus Christ as the only Savior.

A major problem with scientific spirituality is its inability to deal with life on a moral basis. It can only promise *power* to supposedly gain control of one's life. The Bible, on the other hand, claims that the problem with the world is *sin* and that it cannot be dealt with by "higher powers." No amount of *power*, no matter how *high*, can solve a moral problem.

Without going outside,
you may know the whole world.
Without looking through the window,
you may see the ways of heaven.

—Lao Tse, sixth century B.C.[1]

Telepathy, clairvoyance, precognition and psychokinesis ... [are] fundamental psi phenomena that, in my opinion, have been established as real beyond the shadow of any reasonable doubt by hundreds of laboratory experiments.

—Professor Charles Tart, long-time researcher
into science and spirituality[2]

Psychic functioning is simply a body of observational data whose scientific description is as yet incomplete.

—Russell Targ and Harold E. Puthoff, senior researchers in the
Electronics and Bioengineering Laboratory of SRI International[3]

Shaman ... is a word from the ... Tungus people of Siberia, and has been adopted widely by anthropologists to refer to persons ... previously known by such terms as "witch," "witch doctor," "medicine man," "sorcerer," "wizard. ..."

A shaman ... enters an altered state of consciousness—at will ... to acquire knowledge, power, and to help other persons. The shaman has at least one, and usually more, "spirits" in his personal service. To perform his work, the shaman depends on special, personal power, which is usually supplied by his guardian and helping spirits.

—Michael Harner, anthropologist and shaman[4]

Then the LORD said unto me, The prophets prophesy lies in my name; I sent them not, neither have I commanded them, neither spoke unto them; they prophesy unto you a false vision and divination, and a thing of nought, and the deceit of their heart.

—Jeremiah 14:14

If there arise among you a prophet or a dreamer of dreams, and giveth thee a sign or a wonder, and the sign or the wonder come to pass whereof he spoke unto thee, saying, Let us go after other gods, which thou has not known, and let us serve them, thou shalt not hearken unto the words of that prophet or that dreamer of dreams; for the LORD your God proveth you, to know whether ye love the LORD your God with all your heart and with all your soul.

—Deuteronomy 13:1-3

5

* * *

Remote Viewing

The age of science, failing to extinguish belief in the occult, inspired many of the brightest minds to attempt either to refute it or to prove it. The British Association for Psychical Research (successor to the Ghost Club at Cambridge University), formally organized in the late nineteenth century, was one of the early groups devoted to this purpose. The American Association for Psychical Research came into existence not many years later. Today numerous major universities and military and intelligence institutes throughout the world (including Russia) are engaged in psychical research, now known as parapsychology. Even Communist China, still stubbornly committed to scientific materialism, engages feverishly in psychic research in competition with the West.

According to Ernest Jones, Freud's biographer, even Freud could not escape what he termed the universal neurosis. Its very universality and persistence defies the atheists' "explanations." Freud's own nagging occult beliefs persisted in spite of his attempted psychological explanations and his scathing ridicule of the religious fantasies held by others.[5] According to Carl Jung, in Freud's later years he finally "recognized the seriousness of parapsychology and acknowledged the factuality of 'occult' phenomena."[6] Before his death, Freud declared that if he had it to do over again, he would devote his life "to psychical research."[7]

A New Respectability

Shamans in primitive societies, and witches in Europe and America, have long demonstrated the apparent ability to "see" events and acquire knowledge separated from them by impossible distances of space and time. Recent laboratory demonstrations by psychics of "remote viewing" have been a major contribution to the acceptance of such powers today.

In 1993 the *Psychological Bulletin*, a journal of the American Psychological Association, published a report by Cornell University social psychologist Daryl Bem and the late parapsychologist Charles Honorton. It reviewed 20 years of research and concluded that subjects were able by mental telepathy to "receive" at a rate far above chance an image being transmitted mentally from a distant location. Nevertheless, many scientists still seek a physical explanation. Some think that Bell's theorem (which allows for correlations between apparently unconnected distant locations and events) together with quantum theory could be the answer.[8] As we shall see, however, such a theory cannot explain the phenomena.

While many scientists were still trying to find some way to maintain their denial of the reality of the occult, a number of enterprising scientists were moving forward in what would become the most amazing development in the entire history of psychic research. In the forefront of this investigation was SRI International, located in Menlo Park, California, south of San Francisco. Formerly known as Stanford Research Institute, SRI now operates independently of Stanford University. It began research involving a new concept called "remote viewing," in which the viewer was able to gather required information without the help of anyone at the distant target site attempting to send a mental image or message.

A Modern Approach

Experiments began in the 1970s in the Electronics and Bioengineering Laboratory of Stanford Research Institute under the direction of two physicists, Russell Targ and Harold Puthoff. Among the principal psychics used were Ingo Swann, Pat Price, and Hella Hammid.[9] These early experiments produced some of the most spectacular results that had yet been seen in the entire area of psychic research. Those results were first reported in a 1977 book by Targ and Puthoff titled *Mind-Reach: Scientists Look at Psychic Ability*.

Margaret Mead wrote the introduction to the Targ/Puthoff volume. Her comments indicate her confidence in remote viewing:

> These particular experiments . . . come out of physics . . . the hardest of the hard sciences; they come out of a respected laboratory; and they do not appear to be the work of true believers who set out to use science to validate passionately held beliefs. Tremendous efforts have been used, which far outstrip the normal procedures, to guarantee scientific credibility. . . .
>
> What they've found is already being duplicated and expanded in laboratories and private organizations around the world.[10]

The Targ/Puthoff remote viewing procedures were adopted and developed further by the military and especially the intelligence branch. Remote viewing has reportedly proved itself repeatedly in successful military and espionage assignments of all kinds. We do not have the space to go into detail, but this important subject must be dealt with at least briefly.

Early Remote Viewing Experiments

The first startling results came through a self-styled "natural psychic" named Ingo Swann, who claimed he was able to "see" distant events and objects. Prior to arriving at SRI, he had just completed some successful psychic experiments with Dr. Gertrude Schmeidler at City College of New York.[11] Here is a condensed description of an early test to which Targ and Puthoff subjected Swann in their Menlo Park laboratory:

> "Ingo," we begin, "a skeptical colleague of ours on the East Coast . . . has furnished us with a set of coordinates, latitude and longitude, in degrees, minutes and seconds, and has challenged us to describe what's there. We ourselves don't know. . . . Do you think you can do it . . . ?"
>
> "I'll try," says Ingo, appearing unperturbed by a request that we, as physicists, can hardly believe we are making. . . . The coordinates indicate a site that is roughly 3,000 miles away, and we have been asked to obtain details . . . such as small man-made structures, buildings, roads, etc.

Ingo closes his eyes and begins to describe what he is visualizing.

... He appears to zero in for a closer view, rapidly sketching a detailed map showing the location of several buildings together with some roads and trees. He goes on: "Cliffs to the east, fence to the north. There's a circular building, perhaps a tower, buildings to the south. Is this a former Nike base or something like that . . . ? I get the impression of something underground, but I'm not sure. . . ."

As we learned . . . when we received a phone call from our challenger . . . Swann's description [was] correct in every detail . . . even the relative distances on his map were to scale![12]

Targ and Puthoff conducted numerous experiments of this nature with other subjects, including at least one jointly with the Soviet Union. This research seemed to yield consistent results which would demonstrate that remote viewing was a reality. The very first try by another subject, Hella Hammid, who made no pretense at psychic ability, was impressive (as were further tests with her).

The tape recording of Hella's first mock experiment begins [long distance walkie-talkies were used inasmuch as the targets were within five miles of the viewer]:

OUTBOUND EXPERIMENTER: I am at my first target location; what do you see?

HELLA: I see a little house covered with red, overlapping boards. It has a white trim and a very tall, pointed roof. But the whole thing feels fake, like a movie set.

Her description turned out to be correct. The actual target was a 15-foot-high model of a little red schoolhouse at a local miniature golf course. A half-dozen mock experiments with surprisingly good results completed the orientation series.

In one experiment, another "natural psychic," Pat Price (a former police commissioner and corporate president),[13] was given coordinates randomly chosen by a computer. It so happened that they pinpointed a secret government installation in the East involved in monitoring satellites of rival governments. Sitting in the laboratory in Menlo Park, California, Price seemingly "walked through" this underground government installation 3000 miles away, described it, and even began to read contents of top-secret files. Fearing they had penetrated government secrets,

Targ and Puthoff halted the experiment and sent the data they had gathered to the appropriate authorities.

What Is Happening?

Remote viewers are convinced they can gather information of any kind whatsoever, wherever it is located in space and time—even in the *future* because time is nonexistent in the nonphysical universe, where the occult operates.

Remote viewers deny that they leave their bodies, even though they "see" remote locations. It is all mental. The results they provide confirm the fact that the mind is not physical, is not tied to the brain, and is therefore outside of space, time, and matter.

It is only to be expected that science, which can only deal with the physical universe, has no explanation for remote viewing. We cannot be content, however, with the inability of science to explain what is happening. We must have an explanation. The potential danger to the soul and spirit is too great to neglect that necessity.

Serious Conflict with the Bible

If remote viewing simply represents (as most remote viewers today claim) the trained utilization of a normal human capability which we all possess, we are faced with a number of serious conflicts with God's Word. For one, the Bible presents a class of men called prophets who wrote the Scriptures. The Bible says that these were "holy men of God" and that they "spoke as they were moved [inspired] by the Holy Spirit" (2 Peter 1:21).

If remote viewing, however, is a normal function of the human mind—and thus all knowledge on any subject, whether it has to do with the past, present, or future, is available to anyone—then the Bible presents a false picture. Biblical prophets were nothing special, they did not need to be "holy men of God," and they were not inspired "by the Holy Spirit," but were picking up information from the "collective unconscious" available to anyone, with or without faith in God. Major Ed Dames claims that these prophets were simply primitive remote viewers. If so, the Bible has deceived us.

Jesus Himself would then be reduced to a remote viewer. For example, when Philip brought his friend Nathanael to Him, Jesus said to him, "Before ... Philip called thee, when thou wast under the fig tree [miles away], I saw thee." If this was nothing more than a normal power of remote viewing that we all possess, then the Bible here again presents a false picture. Nathanael clearly understood this as proof that Jesus was the Messiah ("Rabbi, thou art the Son of God; thou art the King of Israel"). Jesus did not correct him and say, "No this is just normal clairvoyance, the power of remote viewing, that all humans have if they only knew how to use it." He accepted Nathanael's understanding as valid. If the remote viewers are correct, then Jesus dishonestly claimed deity on the basis of powers that are common to all of us (John 1:45-51).

Such is the position taken by Fordham University professor John J. Heaney, a Catholic theologian who received his doctorate in theology at the Catholic Institute in Paris, France. He cites Jesus' having seen Nathanael "under the fig tree" as an example of normal human powers.[14] Heaney even suggests that Christ's ability to still the storm at a word and to walk on water are powers that others have exhibited. He writes:

> It seems to me that Jesus as a human being was blessed and gifted with incredible paranormal and psychokinetic powers. These powers he used at will. Others had such powers occasionally and in a limited way. Jesus seemed to be master over these powers. . . .[15]

Facing Up to a Serious Dilemma

Do we believe the Bible or today's liberal theologians and New Age prophets known as remote viewers? The results which the latter produce, if the reports are true, are impressive. International corporations and governments employ them because of the unusual service they offer. Thus we face a dilemma.

It is a dilemma, however, to which the Bible has already given us the answer. God's Word declares that false prophets do indeed have access to some kind of paranormal power. Some may be able to perform feats that seem miraculous, even foretell the future to a limited extent. One need only cite Balaam or the miracles that Pharaoh's magicians performed in the presence of Moses.

How can we know they are false prophets? The criterion for making that judgment is not their power, no matter how impressive, but *whether they obey the God of the Bible or follow false gods*. We must use that criterion in evaluating today's prophets, whether they are called psychics, channelers, mediums, remote viewers, or by any other label.

The truth is that remote viewers sometimes disagree with one another regarding some very fundamental facts. Two of the men we have named, Professor Courtney Brown and Major Ed Dames, disagree with each other not only as to the theory of remote viewing but even regarding certain "targets." And this in spite of the fact that each heads an institute devoted to remote viewing.

Ed Dames claims to have had a number of very reliable remote viewers target TWA Flight 800, the plane that went down in flames off the East Coast shortly after takeoff from New York in mid-1996. They decided that it was not a missile or bomb or sabotage of any kind, but a mechanical failure, and even located the part that broke down and explained in detail the resultant series of events that brought about the explosions. On the other hand, Professor Brown also claims to have had reliable remote viewers, under strict laboratory conditions, using the same military-derived procedures, target the same event. They concluded that it was sabotage. Said Dames on Gil Gross's radio talkshow:

> TWA Flight 800 we've done under very good controls and the results are available for you to look at right now free of charge on our web site. . . .
>
> Absolutely every one of our professionals gets the exact same stuff . . . they're not told what the target is until after the session is over. . . . It was a terrorist act, it was blown up; we've done deep mind probes of the terrorists, believe it or not we have a very good idea, information about that . . . we have no results at all indicating a mechanical failure. . . .[16]

Where Is God?

Such contradictions demonstrate that remote viewing cannot be of God. The biblical prophets, though living in different cultures and over a span of 1500 years, nevertheless were in perfect agreement in all they said. Two opposing views cannot both be right. Therefore, at least one of these two, Brown or Dames, though claiming impressive results, is dead wrong on important issues. In fact, they could both be wrong.

Most remote viewers make no pretense of relying upon God. Why should they, if theirs is a natural talent of which anyone is capable? Supposedly the very nature of the universe makes remote viewing possible for anyone. If that is so, then once again the Bible has led mankind astray for more than 3000 years. That is a serious charge. If the Bible has deceived us with regard to the nature of prophets and prophecy, then how can we rely upon anything else it tells us?

Logically, if remote viewing is not from God, and is not a normal human power available to all mankind (a fact which we will demonstrate in the next two chapters), then it can only be from Satan, the enemy of God and man.

Protection from the Wrong Side

While Professor Courtney Brown was a guest on Art Bell's late-night radio program, "Coast to Coast" (carried on more than 300 stations), Bell mentioned that international bestselling author Malachi Martin (Jesuit priest and onetime professor at the Vatican's Pontifical Biblical Institute) had called remote viewing "nitroglycerin to the soul." In response, Brown tried to distinguish between the type of remote viewing that the military employs and the Scientific Remote Viewing (SRV) taught at The Farsight Institute (headed by Brown), which allegedly is used only for the good of others. Brown implied that those involved at his Institute are under spiritual protection because all students and instructors engage in Transcendental Meditation (TM) each evening.

Yet TM itself is unquestionably part of the occult. This author has interviewed ex-TMers who, after becoming involved in TM, were invaded by demons or suddenly found themselves apparently "out of their bodies" up on the ceiling looking down upon themselves. Former TM instructor R.D. Scott tells of numerous terrifying occult episodes among meditators during training courses under Maharishi Mahesh Yogi, TM's founder. These experiences could not be figments of the imagination because often more than one person witnessed the same manifestations simultaneously:

> [Meditators] being thrown across the room . . . visions of floating green eyes . . . creatures of light floating above the *puja* table [during initiation ceremonies] as well as demons jumping down meditators' throats and possessing them, ghoulish creatures materializing periodically to stare with terrifying expressions at meditators, or fearful processions of other-worldly creatures appearing suddenly and seen by many witnesses.[17]

On the basis of the testimony of numerous former TMers, including some who had attained high levels in the organization, Transcendental Meditation is not a practice in which to engage for spiritual protection. That Professor Brown believes that TM provides such protection would indicate that he is badly deceived and is receiving his "protection" not from God but from the enemy of his soul. That he could entertain such error and that his entire organization is similarly deceived does not commend remote viewing.

Art Bell later interviewed Fr. Malachi Martin and Major Ed Dames together on his program. Martin has been an adviser to popes and is an exorcist who uses traditional Roman Catholic ritual to confront the demonic. He claims to have seen overwhelming proof of Satan's existence, believes in demonic possession (which he documents in his bestseller, *Hostage to the Devil*), and allegedly has seen many demonized persons set free through the Catholic ritual of exorcism.

A Fascinating Dialogue

The discussion centered around Martin's statement that remote viewing was "nitroglycerin to the soul." Surprisingly, Malachi Martin did not consider remote viewing to be part of the occult, nor was he opposed to it so long as it was done "scientifically." Martin explained:

If it's not done with the proper motivation and . . . scientifically, with the proper methods and checks and balances it can disrupt the soul. . . . We exorcists found that those who did remote viewing or channeling without any of those safeguards that you [Major Dames] just described, that they underwent very severe disturbances and disruptions of their normal persona and also had manifestations that could only be explained in the light of Luciferian intervention in human things.[18]

Martin presented his belief that there are three levels of reality: the supernatural order (God and all that belongs to Him); the natural order (the entire physical universe); and the in-between "middle plateau." Those who enter that plateau can exercise these paranormal "powers of the soul that can apparently be sharpened and developed," but there is also a danger, according to Martin: When someone tries to enter the middle plateau to exercise and develop these powers without "the proper intention or proper controls and checks and balances," he will need the attention of an exorcist. Said Fr. Martin:

> We've found some army officers who came for help as private citizens because they had delved into the middle plateau and came away very disturbed.
>
> Then there are the normal people who use the Ouija board or remote channeling or remote viewing and they entered an area where they were subject to terrible onslaughts from the angel of light [Satan].
>
> The only succor we could give them was through these [Roman Catholic] ceremonies, not therapies but exorcism, a confrontation [with the demonic]. . . .[19]

Dames responded that he was "familiar operationally with the concept of the middle plateau." In his view, channeling was extremely dangerous. He went on to explain:

> The channeler gives up his own identity and turns his identity over to something unknown that has convinced them that it is benign in most cases.
>
> [Martin interjects, "That is very, very, very important. That's where the nitroglycerin aspect comes in."]
>
> That is the essence of channeling, but technical remote viewing is essentially a mind tool where we are fully conscious and fully awake. In the early days, natural psychics employed by the military got involved in an altered state and there were some dangers. . . .

When we would "send"—I use that term loosely—an officer to a remote location, there were instances where in navigating that middle plateau these people . . . ran into these entities on the way and this caused a tremendous amount of grief. We actually had two individuals have heart attacks. . . .

In the case of one of my former students and an army officer . . . these people started to lean toward association with the very entities that they discovered in the middle plateau. . . .

Once something has its hook in you, it's got you and that is why one begins to see behavioral change. . . . We've studied it . . . the hook is in ego . . . the psyche is being pulled along.

[Martin interjects, "That's a very good description of the process."]

[Major Dames continues.] We've had to study it long and hard to discern when we're on dangerous turf . . . the more we give up our own decision-making ability, because that's all we really have is our mind, and our mind is [Martin: "Yes, yes!"] where the basis of whether our soul survives.

[Martin: "Yes, if we forsake that we've forsaken the very essence of us."]

I agree. When these individuals start to give up their decision-making ability and turn their minds over to something else or their minds become completely imbued with ego we lose them.

[Martin: Well, that's the beginning of what is called from my side "possession."]

I'm not familiar that much with possession. I've only seen it once or twice in my career . . . the majority of people who come to me to learn technical remote viewing are . . . balanced . . . interested and enthusiastic and we can spot individuals who are [a risk]. We have to because we've had disasters. . . .

When the disasters occurred in the past, whether on the military team or in the case of one or two civilians, former students, they were real disasters. . . .[20]

Shamanism Under a Modern Name

Art Bell interrupts and asks Malachi Martin whether there would be a relatively safe way to do what Ed Dames does. Martin replies, "Absolutely." He says that Dames "laid out a system of checks and balances" and has "an intimate knowledge of the entities occupying this region in which he enters and works. . . ."

We have already shown that to consider remote viewing as a natural talent (as both Martin and Dames do) completely discredits the Bible. That book claims to be *God's Word,* a unique revelation that could only come through *holy* men specially chosen of God and inspired by His Holy Spirit. But if Martin and Dames are right, then the Bible is at best nothing more than a presentation of information available to anyone by remote viewing. The Bible has lied about its very foundation and therefore should not be trusted in anything else it says.

Martin and Dames agree that in order to gather information through remote viewing, one must enter the "middle plateau." This mysterious realm, they acknowledge, is inhabited by vicious entities which Dames admits are evil and have done great harm to some of his remote viewers. Martin says they cause demonic possession. By their own testimony, then, the information gained by remote viewing comes from the demonic realm!

No wonder the Bible strictly forbids all occult activity. Yet Fr. Martin, the Roman Catholic theologian and exorcist (like Dames, the remote viewer), sees nothing wrong with remote viewing. How is one to be protected? Why, simply by taking a *scientific* approach, with proper checks and balances, and by avoiding too much involvement of one's ego. It is both unbiblical and ludicrous to imagine that Satan and his minions are impressed with, or defeated by, scientific checks and balances.

Remote viewing is simply shamanism under a modern name. For thousands of years, shamans have practiced "out-of-body journeys" to distant places to gather information or to heal or curse an enemy. Remote viewers are not as forthright as the shamans (according to Michael Harner's quote at the beginning of this chapter) in acknowledging the vital role played by the spirit beings. The "angels" to whom Dames looks for "protection" could very well be the same entities whose help the shaman realizes is vital. Are they really angels, or demons?

A Dangerous Delusion

Getting back to the discussion, Dames explains that he has a healthy fear of these evil entities—not a fear of harm to himself, he hastens to explain, because of his "connection with God and angels." He adds, "That is the only reason I can deal in this area." What delusion! Not only does he imagine that he is protected from evil by following scientific protocol, but that God and His angels are with him as he ventures into an area which God has strictly forbidden him to enter.

And what is it that convinces Dames that all is well? Why, it is the amazing results, of course, which he is so careful to use only for the good of humanity. And unlike some others who let their egos get in the way or who surrender their independence to these entities for a price, no harm has come to him and his remote viewers who follow the rules.

Martin commends Dames for his healthy fear of these evil entities and for his trust in "angelic and divine protection." He praises Dames for having classical religious faith and that is why he can "venture into this field without fear . . . you take certain precautions out of respect for your enemy. . . ."

Dames explains further: "I can perceive what these things are. . . . When I was a young man before I learned professional techniques, then I needed . . . faith . . . [in] a higher power . . . my God to protect me from the darkness. But now I can see into the darkness, I can shine this light in there and say, aha, over here is this and over there is that. . . ."

Martin commends Dames, "It seems to me, Major Ed, and I'm speaking as a priest . . . that you are overshadowed by a godliness which I can only ascribe to my Savior. . . ."

"I'm also a simple Christian," replies Dames.

Neither Dames, the remote viewer, nor Martin, the Roman Catholic, seems to have any understanding of biblical Christianity. The delusion is staggering!

A Surprising Conclusion

After some further dialogue Fr. Martin remarks, "I would have illimitable trust in the methods that Major Ed Dames uses and the techniques. I have no qualms whatsoever, I really have not.

"I find that remarkable . . . ," says Art Bell, with obvious pleasure. "Many Christians, people who call this program or send me faxes, would say that what Ed is doing is of the devil."

Ed says quickly, "Art, may I interrupt you . . . ? The head of the Presidential Foreign Intelligence Board, when briefed on the existence of our program, stated, after he went sheet white, that man should not know these things until after he dies!"

"It's a funny inversion of what happened in the Garden . . ." laughs Malachi Martin. "But you see, Art . . . I really do think that a charism [gift of the Holy Spirit, 1 Corinthians 12] has been developed in Ed Dames and his associates, and it is a work of God. . . . I remember being approached by some members of the armed forces in the middle eighties and their complaint was . . . 'Look, we have trained officers in certain techniques and . . . they have now developed symptoms that you describe in your last book about [demonic] possession.' "

A few more words are said and then Art Bell concludes: "I'm surprised at the result we got between the two of you and pleased by it and I would imagine you are too."

"I am very surprised," responds Fr. Malachi Martin, "and I'm very pleased and I've learned so much. And I've been enriched by this. I really want to thank you, Ed Dames."

"It's been nothing but an honor for me, Father Martin."

"May God go with you and give you the grace," are the Jesuit priest's final words of blessing to the "Christian" major.

A Hidden Agenda?

Professor Courtney Brown's book, *Cosmic Journey,* contains unusual information obtained through remote viewing of the alleged presence and activities of ETs on Mars and Earth. As a result, Brown has been in demand on radio talkshows. On the popular "Gil Gross Show" a caller mentioned that in his book Professor Brown had referred favorably to *The Urantia Book* and requested further information. The host of the program, Gil Gross, asked Brown, for the benefit of listeners, to describe *The Urantia Book.* Brown responded:

> [It's] the story of the life on the other side of the physical domain . . . what I call subspace . . . the life that exists after you leave your physical body. And it also has a story of the life of Jesus . . . like the Bible, except it has more recent information. . . .
>
> The military people . . . got *The Urantia Book* and it had some detailed discussions about x, y, and z things that had occurred and

that were not so well spelled out in the Bible. And so they did some targeting on some of these things . . . and they were flabbergasted to find out that a lot of the things that were in *The Urantia Book* actually did occur. . . .

One of the things that was in *The Urantia Book* that we did find out was that the Adam and Eve story that's in the Bible actually had some truth to it . . . a very small amount of truth. The reality was that the ancient prophets were in their own crude way primitive remote viewers and they did actually perceive that there was a couple long ago that were somehow involved in the birth of humans . . . Adam and Eve were project managers of an ET cultural and genetic uplift project that went astray. . . .[21]

Remember, Malachi Martin and Ed Dames both agreed that remote viewing involves entering a realm inhabited by spirit entities. Could it be that the same entities who inspired *The Urantia Book* are now granting the power of remote viewing for their own insidious purposes? That certainly seems likely, given remote viewing's endorsement of Urantia. Could this fact also be a hint of the purpose of remote viewing—to establish its credibility and then use it to destroy faith in the Bible and set up a counter religion?

The Urantia Book goes to great lengths to undermine God's Word, from Adam and Eve as "project managers of an ET . . . project that went astray" to complete rejection of the cross of Christ! It offers a new cosmology of the universe as well as new concepts of God, Christ and salvation. This complex volume of almost 2100 pages contradicts (or perverts) the Bible at every turn. "God" is a trinity of trinities; the higher one (Paradise Trinity) is existential and the lower two (Ultimate Trinity and Absolute Trinity) are experiential. And both are evolving in a 2-billion-year cycle.

There are universes within universes, with millions of "local universes," each formed and thereafter ruled by a "Creator Son," each of whom belongs to the "Order of Michael." Michael of Nebadon (a local universe within which our planet, Urantia, revolves) incarnated to our planet as Jesus of Nazareth. This Jesus was the "personification of the 611,121st original concept of infinite identity of simultaneous origin in the Universal Father and the Eternal Son [whatever that means!]." His headquarters is "a mansion of light on

Salvington" and his evolution has taken him through "all three phases of intelligent creature existence: spiritual, morontial and material."[22]

The deluded remote viewers thought that *The Urantia Book* contained "more recent information" about "the life of Jesus." The Urantia "Jesus" is not the Jesus of the Bible. This ponderous volume, inspired by demons, rejects the very heart of the gospel: that Christ died for our sins. It calls such an idea "a religion wholly puerile and primitive, a philosophy unworthy of an enlightened age of science and truth...utterly repulsive to the [millions of] celestial beings and divine rulers who serve and reign in the universe...an affront to God...that innocent blood must be shed in order to win his favor or to divert the fictitious divine wrath."[23]

Some Further Problems

The person calling the Gil Gross Show presses Professor Brown: "Have you heard from religious leaders about your book? Because in your book there's other things that people might find more shocking...you say that you've communicated by remote viewing with Jesus [and] Buddha...."

"Look, the reason remote viewing works," says Brown testily, "is because we...know under laboratory conditions that we're more than physical blood, meat, bones. We are...a soul inside the body....You don't actually go to the places physically that you remote view but you can accurately describe them down to the finest detail using these very strict military-derived procedures. And when you can do that you say, well, there must be some part of you that is beyond the physical realm. And that part, of course, some people call it the soul, some call it the unconscious...we like to call it the subspace mind....And it's because the soul...can do things that the physical body can't do that we can in fact remote view with tremendous precision...."

The program then moved to a discussion of Dr. Brown's book *Cosmic Voyage* and the secret community of Martians hiding on earth that he discovered through remote viewing. Brown also stated, "On Mars there's a few hundred thousand...who have to leave and they're going to come here in a flotilla. It's an amazing and interesting event. . . ." Dr. Brown has staked his academic reputation on the accuracy of these incredible beliefs which he discovered through remote viewing and which he claims will be revealed as true very soon. We'll come back to that in our chapter dealing with UFOs.

Enter Scientology!

After listening to hours of tapes and trying to follow the charges and countercharges flying back and forth between remote viewers on the Internet, one does not know whom to believe. Nor can we check up on those who claim to have been involved in top-secret government projects that still remain a closed book. The occult involves seduction of the world and the church, so one would expect much confusion.

In our investigation we discovered that a very high percentage of remote viewers are Scientology cult members. Harold Puthoff himself was a high-level Scientologist. So was Ingo Swann. Indeed, the very paper that Swann presented to the First International Congress on Psychotronic Research in Prague, Czechoslovakia, on September 6, 1974, was titled "Scientological Techniques: A Modern Paradigm for the Exploration of Consciousness and Psychic Integration." Much of the funding for early remote viewing came from George W. Church, Jr., another high-level Scientologist, through his Science Unlimited Research Foundation.

The high percentage of Scientologists in the program may explain the obsession with Martians and UFOs among remote viewers. Much of the information they derive through remote viewing sounds like recycled science fiction from the pen of Ron Hubbard, Scientology founder. Scientology involves occultism of the highest order, including all of the lies from the serpent in the Garden.

In brief, Scientology teaches that we are all uncreated, omnipotent, omniscient beings called "Thetans." We Thetans created this entire MEST (Matter, Energy, Space, Time continuum) in which we live. We created creatures as well, then incarnated their bodies. As they died and evolved to higher levels, we repeatedly reincarnated. Finally, having evolved to our present status as humans, we were so far removed from our origin as Thetans that we forgot who we were. Scientology puts one through a process that combines psychotherapy with Eastern mysticism, takes us back through our past lives on the road from Thetan to human, and peels off the "engrams" (traumas) we picked up along the way. When the process is complete we break through to what is called "Clear" and realize who we really are: Operating Thetans [i.e., gods]!

Anyone who believes that scenario and imagines that he is now an omnipotent, omniscient Thetan is clearly under heavy delusion. Psychic research provides the hope of finding ways to demonstrate the power that allegedly lies within us. That this was the motivation for remote viewing research and that the occultism of Scientology aided in its development can hardly be doubted.

While we cannot be certain how much to believe of the reports being given, there can be no doubt that an occult power is at work in remote viewing. There have been some very impressive results produced by remote viewers, results that defy rational explanation. The fact that the lies of the serpent in the Garden undergird the philosophy that comes through in remote viewing provides strong evidence of the identity of the power behind it. The consistent attack upon true Christianity and the attempt to discredit the Bible is further confirmation of that identity.

Whatever one's religious beliefs, the evidence we have reviewed thus far indicates that an occult invasion of this planet is underway. It is gathering momentum at an alarming rate. Whether this invasion, coming at this time in history, is of any significance with regard to biblical prophecies concerning the "last days" is a question that we must face.

For the shaman, all that exists in the revealed world has a living force within . . . like the Polynesian mana *or the Sioux* wakanda *. . . a divine force which permeates all. The knowledge that life is power [positive and negative] is the realization of the shaman. Communion with the purveyors of power is the work of the shaman. Mastery of that power: this is the attainment of the shaman.*

—Joan Halifax, anthropologist[1]

Conjurers or magicians, like anything else, are positive and negative. If positive, they use their secret knowledge to heal the sick. If negative, they use their evil powers to do harm.

—Archie Fire Lame Deer[2]

The "Dark Brotherhood" [loyal opposition to the "White Brotherhood"] act as testing agents for the human race of man, as forces whose task it is to weed out from the human flock the souls . . . [who] are not developed enough to allow them to move forward into the higher ground of spiritual achievement [i.e., evolution].

—"Master Hilarion," channeled through
Canadian businessman Maurice B. Cooke[3]

In a way, we are all bokors [black magicians], we houngan [white magicians/vodoun priests]. The houngan must know evil to combat it; the bokor must embrace good in order to subvert it. It is all one.

—Max Beauvoir, Haitian vodoun priest[4]

Devote yourself to the light side of the Force, Luke. Remember, the light side.

—Obi Wan Kenobi to Luke Skywalker in *Star Wars*

Positive thinking is just another term for faith.

—Norman Vincent Peale[5]

Faith is a force just like electricity or gravity. We have all the capabilities of God. We have His faith.

—Kenneth Copeland, TV evangelist[6]

6

* * *

A Dark and a Light Side?

The basic foundation of occultism is the belief that an infinite Force pervades the universe which those initiated into its secrets can use to their own ends. How one controls this Force varies with each school of occultism. For some, it is essential to make contact with spirit beings or power animals who are the guardians of the Force and who channel it to or through those who become their servants. For others, this Force (which also is believed to be a reservoir of all knowledge—past, present, and future) responds to certain rituals, ceremonies, or secret techniques which can be learned and are passed down to each new generation of initiates.

Of course, the idea of an impersonal Force is enticing. Instead of being accountable to a personal Creator, how much more appealing to become one's own god through mastery of the Force! The personal God of the Bible demands obedience, and there are consequences for disobedience. Forgiveness must be on a righteous basis; i.e., sin's penalty must be paid. A Force, however, being impersonal, knows nothing of morals; it is there for all to use who will follow the laws or rituals by which it operates. One does not need to be a righteous or religious person to use electricity; it is the same with the Force. It is no more moral than gravity, yet it supposedly holds the key to all power and knowledge.

Occultists of all kinds claim that there is a positive and negative side to the "Force"—a "light" side and a "dark" side, as Obi Wan said in *Star Wars*. In witchcraft, similar terminology is used: "white" magic and "black" magic. And so it is in indigenous native spirituality all over the world, in all cultures, and at all times. The famous Lakota Medicine Man, Archie Fire Lame

Deer (so admired by Phil Jackson and other celebrities), quoted at the beginning of the chapter, says exactly that.

A Mysterious, Invisible "Energy Source"?

That there are mysterious forces in the universe no one can deny. A Force beyond human understanding holds the nucleus of the atom together and somehow supplies energy to the electrons in orbit around the nucleus. The universe is filled with mysteries which science is unable to explain.

Although we know that gravity and electricity exist and we can observe and measure them and even put them to use to our own ends, science does not know what these forces are or how they originated. Science tells us that everything is made of energy and that energy can neither be created nor destroyed, but it cannot tell us what energy itself is, how it originated, the source of its power, or why it operates according to certain laws. Physicist Lambert Dolphin writes:

> The nucleus of the atom contains positively charged and neutral particles. . . . Mutual electrostatic repulsion between the like-positive protons would drive the nucleus apart. . . .
>
> There is thus an active force imposed on the universe, which actively holds the very atoms of the material world together moment by moment, day by day, century by century.
>
> Similarly, accelerated electrons circling the nucleus should quickly radiate all their energy away and fall into the nucleus unless there exists an invisible energy source to counteract this.[7]

What is this "invisible energy source"? And what is the "intelligence" behind it? Obviously no "force" has intelligence. That there are many forces productively involved in nature is evidence of an Infinite Intelligence behind all things.

The fact that each force, whether of gravity or entropy, is bound by definite laws (which in turn all cooperate with one another) is evidence enough that no individual "force" is in control. Clearly, all forces are subject to an overriding Intelligence that created them. Nor can anyone sustain a suggestion that one "side" of the Force, either "light" or "dark," is stronger than the other. Thus the situation is hopeless, for neither side will ever triumph. Indeed, "good" and "evil" are meaningless terms.

A Basic Problem: Power Corrupts

Furthermore, if occult power exists innately within all things and all beings, as Archie Fire Lame Deer declares, then far from bringing peace and unity to mankind, the opposite would be true. If "Power corrupts and absolute power corrupts absolutely," the prospect of mankind developing unlimited occult power is frightening rather than encouraging. The temptation to seek greater and greater power in order to outdo the competition would seem inevitably to corrupt everyone, even those ostensibly using the "light side of the Force."

Here we confront a basic problem with the occult: unlimited power to be used for "good" by "white witches" and for "evil" by "black magicians." But who is to define "good" and "evil"? All who master the Force can use it to their own ends, to get what they want out of life in opposition to all others. There is no personal God of infinite love, holiness, impartiality, and authority in charge of the universe—and thus the "Force" could never bring peace to earth. The same would have to be admitted of the entire Human Potential movement. Power brings greater conflict, not peace.

The Bible claims that God is a personal Being of infinite love, wisdom, and power who made man in His moral and spiritual image and to whom man is accountable. Occultism, in contrast, holds out the promise that each person can acquire Godlike powers and thus become his own god. Of course, some occultists believe they must look to the spirit entities who allegedly control these forces. From this concept developed complex rules for obtaining favors from the gods, which were passed on from initiate to initiate in the form of occult rituals.

It is easy to see that the teaching of Positive Mental Attitude in the worlds of business, academia, and psychology is an appeal to call upon the "light" side and avoid the "dark" side of the Force. So it is with Positive/Possibility Thinking, popularized within the church by Norman Vincent Peale and his chief disciple, Robert Schuller. And the same can be said of the Positive Confession (speaking forth the "word of faith") of today's charismatic leaders. Each person's mind (or tongue) can become the channel for this Force so that what one thinks or speaks aloud ("positive" or "negative") will come to pass.

Explaining God Away

Similarly, science has tried to explain the order in the universe as resulting from impersonal laws. Yet consciousness is not subject to any known laws of nature, and its development cannot be accounted for by physical laws. In order to avoid admitting to some "intelligence" behind nature, the hard-core evolutionists hypothesize an "organizing principle" innate within the atom.

Organization requires intelligent planning and direction. This "organizing principle" is credited with all the qualities of God except that of being able to righteously judge those beings which it creates—a capacity which must be vigorously denied in order to escape its awesome consequences. Indeed, the impersonal force becomes personified in man where it resides, mysteriously hidden, as his alleged infinite potential.

Similarly, many modern theologians insist upon "truth" without divine inspiration. Denying that the Bible is God's inerrant Word, they nevertheless appeal to it for lessons contained within its "myths." That "myth" should be revered would seem to require far more gullibility than to believe in truth revealed by God. The famous mythologist Joseph Campbell tells Bill Moyers in their celebrated television series:

> Man's tendency . . . is to personify . . . natural forces. Our way of thinking in the West sees God as the final source or cause of the energies and wonder of the universe. But in most Oriental thinking, and in primal thinking, also, the gods are rather manifestations and purveyors of the energy that is finally impersonal. They are not its source.
>
> The god is the vehicle of its energy. And the force or quality of the energy that is involved or represented determines the character and function of the god. There are gods of violence, there are gods of compassion . . . personifications of the energies in play. . . .
>
> And then do you say, "Well, there must be somebody generating that energy"? Why do you have to say that? Why can't the ultimate mystery be impersonal?[8]

The Serpent's Four Lies

The ultimate mystery cannot be impersonal because the impersonal cannot think, plan, organize, or create, and such capacities are absolutely necessary to bring the universe and especially intelligent life into existence. It takes personal beings even to realize that a mystery exists; and no impersonal "Force" could beget personal beings. It is not a matter of man, as Campbell insists, having a "tendency to personify" the impersonal because of some prejudice or wishful thinking or superstition. The fact is that rational thinking demands a rational explanation for the universe, and rationality must be personal.

Furthermore, the idea of a Force with a dark and a light side is refuted by the personal nature of the revelations received through occult means and upon which the occult is based. It is not merely *power* that is being manifested; there is a consistent *philosophy* accompanying the power that is inevitably communicated. Moreover, as we have already noted, that philosophy can be traced to a personal source: the serpent, or Satan. One of the most striking phenomena encountered by any investigator of the occult is the astonishing similarity between the specific lies which the Bible claims the serpent communicated to Eve in the Garden of Eden (Genesis 3:1-5) and the consistent philosophy underlying all occultism. These lies include the following:

1. *God is not personal but a force.* Although that concept is not stated explicitly, it is implicit in everything Satan said. "Did God say?" challenged the very idea of a personal God who would forbid Adam and Eve to eat of a certain tree. The logic was indisputable. How could the fruit of one particular tree be harmful when the fruit of all of the others was life-sustaining? They all grew out of the same ground. The same force was in all things—in the ground, in the tree, in the fruit and in her as well.

2. *Death is not real; we don't really die.* Because the Force that is in all things resides in us as well, we can't die; we just get "recycled." This lie, of course, has been elaborated as reincarnation in Eastern mysticism and as spirit survival in Western occultism. It is the message that all of the so-called "clinically dead" come back with: Death is not real, and there is nothing to fear—no judgment, just love and acceptance and continued evolutionary progress ever upward.

3. *Man's destiny is to become one of the gods.* We are evolving upward into ever-higher species and ultimately will have reached the pinnacle of evolution: godhood.

4. *The secret is knowledge of good (the "light side" of the Force) and evil (the "dark side" of the Force).* This was surely the serpent's rationale in persuading Eve to partake of the forbidden tree of the knowledge of good and evil. There is nothing wrong with us except the way we think. The power is already within us, but we are ignorant of that fact and need to be "enlightened."

One can easily see the relationship between the serpent's philosophy and the occult. For example, the January 1931 edition of *The Occult Digest: A Magazine for Everybody* offers a book titled *The Serpent Power.* The ad promises 700 pages with detailed instructions in achieving "Serpent Power" through Kundalini Yoga along with "colored photographs of the yoga positions . . . and explanation of Serpent Power." The same issue contains a Rosicrucian advertisement promising the development of a "sixth sense which will make you master of your destiny." Another article, titled "Is Death Necessary?" declares, "Every thinker is agreed that the old world seems to be on the verge of some 'mental' or 'spiritual' discovery or awakening which might very easily upset every so-called fact dealing with life and death."

Surely the obvious parallel with the biblical story of the Garden of Eden is, if nothing else, fascinating. The same 1931 edition of *Occult Digest* contained articles on reincarnation and on obtaining messages from the spirit world as well as articles promising that the development of these occult powers would lead to individual godhood—the same promise with which the serpent enticed Eve.

The story of the Garden of Eden is not myth; it is history. How else can one explain that the very same lies with which the Bible says the serpent deceived Eve have been avidly and gullibly pursued ever since then by her descendants? It is these very lies which make up the foundation of the occult.

What About "Right" and "Wrong"?

Some practicing witches claim that the power they draw upon can only be used in benevolent ways. Then what power do so-called "black magicians" use? Moreover, this claim seems to attribute morals to an impersonal Force. The fallacious concept of a Force innate in the cosmos with a "light" and "dark" side producing "white" and "black" magic has caused much confusion.

The whole idea of a "dark" and "light" side to the Force comes out of Eastern mysticism. It is found in Hinduism, where there is no sin, no right and wrong, each person's *dharma* being an individual matter. It is found in Buddhism and Taoism, in the belief that there is a psychic Force, or *ki*, expressed by the *yin* and *yang*, neither of which is superior to the other, and neither of which is right or wrong, but both must be in balance. Acupuncture, for example, is the attempt to bring the *yin* and *yang* in the body into alignment. As William Devine, chairman of the California Acupuncture Association, has said:

> Oriental medicine is like that. You could bring one patient in, five different practitioners could look at him and come up with five different diagnoses, and nobody's wrong.[9]

On the basis of what "Ramtha" (the 30,000-year-old warrior that J.Z. Knight channels) has said, we can be delivered from the idea of a judgmental God by understanding that "there is no sin, therefore no reason for guilt."[10] Of course, if no one is wrong, then no one is right either. Indeed, the very thought that someone might claim to be *right* is anathema in today's amoral society. As Wade Davis insisted during an interview on the nationally syndicated *Geraldo* talk show, "There is no such thing as right or wrong in religion . . . that's where wars come from."[11] Yet Jesus Christ claimed that all who rejected Him were not only wrong but eternally lost. Clearly a choice must be made between Jesus Christ and the world of the occult.

A Counterfeit Broad-Mindedness

The denial of right and wrong carries the logical consequence that every opinion must be equally valid. This folly masquerades as *broad-mindedness* but is in fact the worst kind of *narrow-mindedness* because it effectively eliminates all other points of view. It is exemplified in the person who purports to agree with everyone and insists that even the widest differences are only a matter of "semantics." Ironically, such professed tolerance of other viewpoints actually destroys them—not by a frontal assault, but by the impolite refusal to take them seriously. An antagonist who disagrees and is willing to discuss the issues is worthy of more respect than the one who, in his broad-minded desire to embrace everything and reject nothing, denies the very real distinctions between opposing views.

To many people such an "everybody wins" attitude is the only way to go, and it has come into the public schools to the detriment of our students. But if "loser" is to be dropped from our vocabulary, then "winner" must go as well. Frustrated with programs put forth by the psychology profession to solve social problems, programs which hold no one accountable for being *wrong*, T.H. Fitzgerald wrote in an *AHP Perspective* article:

> The sense I still get around AHP [Association for Humanistic Psychology] is . . . that everybody is somehow right "from their perspective" because there can be no ultimate arbiter. Dennis Jaffe writes . . . about the Search for Excellence, but if there is to be Excellence, must there not also be Non-Excellence, and what do we say when we meet it on the road . . . ?
>
> Even the language for the discussion of moral issues has been corrupted by psychological cant and the vocabulary of positivist scientism.[12]

One of the most common examples of this absolute intolerance that poses as total tolerance is found in the well-known aphorism, most often used in reference to religion, "We're all taking different roads to get to the same place." While that declaration sounds broad-minded to a fault, it clearly represents the ultimate in narrow-mindedness. Although "different roads" are generously tolerated, they are not allowed to lead to different places, for everyone, no matter what road they take, must go to the *same* place.

So this seemingly broad-minded idea of "all taking different roads" allows for only one destination. In fact, the Bible, in true broad-mindedness, says there are two destinations—heaven and hell—and no one is forced to go to either. The choice is up to each individual. However, for those who want to reach heaven, there is only one way: through Jesus Christ and His death, burial, and resurrection in payment of the penalty that His own infinite justice demanded for sin.

The Embrace That Smothers

It is by such "all roads" sophistry that Hinduism has gained its reputation for tolerance toward all religions. Hinduism does indeed embrace all faiths, but in the process they are absorbed into Hinduism by the "embrace that smothers." Whatever the Hindu in his proverbial broad-mindedness seems to accept loses its former identity and is recast in a Hindu mold. Hinduism is quite willing, for example, to embrace Christ. After all, with 330 million gods, adding one more changes nothing. And unless those who present *The Jesus Film* and other missionary efforts among Hindus clearly point out what is *wrong* with the Hindu approach, and contrast the uniqueness of Christ that distinguishes Him from all Hindu avatars, spurious conversions by the thousands could occur.

Unless the distinction has been made very clear, Hindus who seemingly "accept Jesus" do not accept the Jesus of the Bible, the Jesus who is God become man through the virgin birth and is the *only* "way, truth, and life." The "Jesus" which a Hindu accepts is just one more avatar among thousands. Thus in "accepting Jesus" Hinduism destroys the Jesus of the Bible and creates its own pseudo-Christ.

Such delusion is a major objective of occult entities who communicate with mankind. The words spoken by the "Jesus" who gave Barbara Marx Hubbard a "powerful born-again experience," like those of the "Jesus" who ·dictated *A Course in Miracles* to psychologist Helen Shucman, present a very clever perversion of what the biblical Jesus has to say. Likewise, *The Urantia Book,* allegedly put together by a "commission of twenty-four spiritual administrators acting in accordance with a mandate issued by high deity authorities (the Ancients of Days),"[13] totally perverts the Bible, and especially with regard to Jesus. In all such communications from "higher beings" there is a reinterpretation of meanings which effectively destroys historic Christianity and replaces it with a Hindu/Buddhist, pseudo-Christianity that plays into the hands of the occult. As this attitude spreads, we are seeing the preparation of the coming world religion.

This counterfeit broad-mindedness with its contempt for truth is carried to the masses by today's most popular televangelist, Robert Schuller, who broad-mindedly declares that "we can tell the good religion from the bad religion" by whether it is "positive." He has called upon "religious leaders . . . whatever their theology . . . to articulate their faith in positive terms . . . [in a] massive, united effort by leaders of all religions . . . [to proclaim] the positive power . . . of world-community-building religious values."[14]

The fact that the theologies of Hinduism, Buddhism, Islam, Catholicism, and evangelicalism contradict one another on vital points is apparently nothing to be concerned about so long as each is presented "in positive terms." All religions, Schuller seems to think, represent equally valid "world-community-building religious values." Antichrist himself couldn't improve on that New Age double-talk!

Occultism Invading the Evangelical Church

The occult invasion of evangelical churches is one of the most shocking facts of our day. Ecumenism, with its attempt to avoid the distinction between right and wrong and to accept all views, has been a major factor. It should be clear that the idea of mind power (positive or negative thinking creating one's own reality) is just another form of the dark and light side of the Force. One of that belief's foremost promoters and a major influence in the evangelical church is the well-known and successful Wall Street money manager Sir John Marks Templeton, founder of The Templeton Prize for Progress in Religion.

Templeton and his neopagan views were first introduced to the church in 1986 by Robert Schuller, who continues to endorse him. Schuller's *Possibilities* magazine put Templeton's picture on its front cover, and its major article was an interview with Templeton. In it he expressed his Unity/Religious Science/New Age beliefs: "Your spiritual principles attract prosperity to you . . . material success . . . comes . . . from being in tune with the infinite. . . . The Christ spirit dwells in every human being whether the person knows it or not . . . nothing exists except God."[15] These heresies were promoted by Schuller to his vast audience of readers.

The pantheistic belief that "nothing exists except God" is the foundation of the Mind Science cults. It goes like this: "God is All and God is good; therefore all is good. Thus pain, disease and death do not exist. They are the projection of the negative thinking of those who imagine they experience such things. To be delivered from this delusion one must change one's thinking from negative (the dark side) to positive (the light side)." Such is the theory behind *The Power of Positive Thinking*, Norman Vincent Peale's bestselling book that has powerfully influenced evangelicals for years.

Templeton's beliefs are expressed clearly in his writings. He is an evolutionist, pantheist, universalist, and occultist who rejects the God of the Bible and Christ as the only Savior and claims that heaven and hell are states of mind we create here on earth, that truth is relative, and that Christianity is no longer relevant. Yet this man is highly acclaimed in evangelical circles. He was on the board of Princeton Theological Seminary[16] and for 15 years was on the board of managers of the American Bible Society,[17] in spite of his rejection of the Bible as God's Word. Norman Vincent Peale called Templeton "the greatest layman of the Christian Church in our time."[18]

Templeton's 1994 book, *Discovering the Laws of Life*, is pure occultism. But instead of warning against it, *Christianity Today* devoted the entire back cover of its April 24, 1994, issue to an ad promoting it, and has not apologized to its readers since then. Headlined "WILL INSPIRE MILLIONS OF READERS," the ad contained the same endorsements by five prominent leaders which are on the back of the book jacket: Norman Vincent Peale (who also wrote the foreword), Robert Schuller, Billy Graham, and two prominent Catholic New Age leaders. Here are sample quotes from the book:

> Behind this book is my belief that the basic principles for leading a "sublime life" . . . may be derived from any religious tradition—Jewish, Muslim, Hindu, Buddhist and others as well as Christian. . . .
>
> We have the power to create whatever we need in our life and this power [which] lies within us is the power of the mind. . . . There is a law of life . . . : "Thoughts held in the mind will reproduce in the outer world after their own kind. . . ."

Astronauts travel[ed] into outer space . . . [and] did not bring back any evidence of heaven. And whereas drills had penetrated the earth, they'd found oil, not hell . . . spiritual theorists are inclined to conceive of [heaven and hell] as states of mind. . . .

Through our choices and attitudes we create our own heaven or hell right here on earth . . . the only place we can find heaven is in our own hearts. . . .

Our innate goodness is an essential fact of our existence. . . . When we perceive this truth, we will experience heaven on earth. . . . When our actions arise spontaneously from the goodness of our being, we find peace and the presence of God within us.

Be honest. Be true. Love all parts of yourself . . . the godhood within you . . . is in a state of becoming perfect.[19]

The endorsements by Peale and Schuller, both of whom have promoted the same occult philosophy for years, are not surprising. That *Christianity Today*, Chuck Colson, Billy Graham, and Bill Bright would also praise Templeton is shocking evidence of compromise among leading evangelicals.

A Call for Intellectual Honesty

To reject Christ is every person's right, but it is intellectual dishonesty of the worst sort to insist that His teachings are perfectly compatible with Hindu-Buddhist pantheistic philosophies. This must be so, concludes one writer, because "all the New Agers I've met love Jesus and Buddha and Krishna and anyone, regardless of race or language or religious preference. . . ."[20]

That an unprincipled "love" (which is too weak to bring correction to those whom it loves) somehow renders the question of truth and right and wrong and sound theology irrelevant is a basic fallacy. In fact, genuine love corrects those perceived to be in serious and life-threatening error.

The occult invasion of Western society is a direct consequence of the "scientific" erosion of belief in the transcendent nature of God. Millions in the Western world now practice Transcendental Meditation. The very title *Transcendental* is a fraud. TM is pantheistic and thus denies a transcendent God. It leads one deep within to find the "true self." Our society has become obsessed with self, a self which it is determined to elevate to godhood.

An Important Distinction

The Force is believed to be the guiding power behind evolution. We have seen that evolution is mathematically impossible. Furthermore, it could never account for man's conscience. A sense of moral obligation cannot be explained in physiological terms. As Sir Arthur Eddington wrote, *"Ought* takes us outside chemistry and physics." Man simply cannot be the product of evolutionary forces working on matter. There are no ethics or morals in nature. "Good" and "evil" do not apply to atoms or galaxies or natural forces such as gravity or electricity or psychic power (if there is such a thing).

A Force with dark and light sides allows no difference between a physical law and a moral law. But that distinction is extremely important. A moral law cannot be used for one's own ends, though a physical law could be. Moral laws cannot become the source of personal empowerment, which is the major goal in the New Age movement. Universal moral laws which are binding upon all can only be prescribed by the Supreme God of supernatural monotheism, who Himself in his own character sets the standard of righteousness, love, purity, and goodness.

In contrast to Eastern mysticism, Christianity teaches that the moral laws of God's infinite justice have been violated and that finite man cannot pay the infinite penalty. By his rebellion, man deserves eternal separation from the God who created him. God could pay the infinite penalty demanded by His justice, but it wouldn't be just because He is not one of us. Therefore, in infinite love, God became a man through the virgin birth so that, as God and man in one Person, He could pay the full penalty demanded by His law. This He did upon the cross.

The triumphant cry of Jesus just before He laid down His life—"It is finished"—is an accounting term in the original New Testament Greek (*teleo,* to discharge a debt). The infinite penalty for sin had been paid. According to the Bible, all man needs to do is to admit that as a sinner he deserves what Christ suffered in his place, and to receive the pardon that is offered as a free gift of God's grace and love.

In contrast, there is a palpable emptiness to the occultist's gospel. The only salvation it offers is power to take control of one's life and to fulfill one's desires. Righteousness and truth are missing altogether. The practice of yoga or the attainment of an altered state of consciousness in any other way in order to tap into the Force won't even pay a traffic ticket, much less the eternal penalty for sin. The Force behind Hindu/Buddhist/New Age philosophy lacks the righteous basis for the forgiveness for which every sincere heart yearns. No sin is acknowledged, and even if it were, there is no God who has been sinned against, nor is there a just way for the sinner to be forgiven.

As its answer to man's deepest longings and need, occult philosophy offers a lie. Instead of love, the greatest virtue and highest experience, we are left with a void. *The Star Wars Force* of the occult magician is no better "God" than the impersonal forces at work in the atheist's materialist universe. Sir Arthur Eddington argues:

> When from the human heart, perplexed with the mystery of existence, the cry goes up, "What is it all about?" it is no true answer to ... reply: "It is about atoms and chaos; it is about a universe of fiery globes rolling on to impending doom. ..."[21]

A Conflict Between God and Satan

The Bible presents in great detail the One whom it claims is the true God, the Creator of the universe. It presents Satan as well, the adversary of both God and man. Satan appears as a serpent who entices Eve with the promise that if she will disobey God and follow him she will attain immortality and godhood. This enticer to evil, called "the god of this world" (2 Corinthians 4:4) because he is the inspiration behind the world's false religions, is known throughout the Bible as "the great dragon ... that old serpent, called the Devil and Satan, which deceiveth the whole world" (Revelation 12:9).

Many people today consider themselves too sophisticated to take the story of the Garden of Eden literally. Surely that part about Eve's conversation with a talking snake marks the story as mythology. Such superstition is acceptable only to primitive peoples. Any attempt to teach it today would be an insult to modern man. So the argument goes.

Yet the very skeptics who are too intelligent to believe that Satan used a serpent to speak to Eve embrace native American Indian spirituality. There seems to be no problem in believing that Indian medicine men speak to all manner of animals and birds and even *become* these creatures at times. And are not some of our leading scientists attempting to converse with chimpanzees and even dolphins? Listen to Dr. John Lilly again:

> Dolphins are an example of a high alien intelligence, and I've fought that one out with various people since I published my first book on the subject in 1961, *Man and Dolphin*. But I'm not fighting with them anymore. They're coming around; they're beginning to apply cognitive psychology to dolphins.[22]

The Sioux Indians, whom Phil Jackson looks up to as his mentors and whose spirituality he has adopted, teach that the "sacred pipe" was given to them ages ago by a beautiful woman who used serpents in her magic and who, as they watched, turned into a "young red and brown buffalo calf," then into a "white buffalo," then into a "black buffalo," then disappeared. Black Elk declares that this story "should not only be taken as an event in time, but also as an eternal truth."[23] Jackson, who rejected Christianity and adopted native American spirituality, seems to have no trouble accepting this story as literally true.

The Serpent and the Dragon

The serpent and dragon (identified in the Bible as Satan) are the major benevolent figures both in mythology and in almost all religions. In Haitian voodoo tradition, for example, the Great Serpent is the fountain of all true wisdom and the creator of the universe, who took the Rainbow as his wife and from that union came blood and all creatures. "And then, as a final gift, they taught the people to partake of the blood as a sacrament, that they might become the spirit and embrace the wisdom of the Serpent."[24]

The dragon is found on thousands of temples throughout Asia, while the serpent dominates the religion of India. In Hinduism, Shiva, one of the three chief gods, has serpents entwined in his hair. Yoga is symbolized as a raft made of cobras, and its goal is to awaken the kundalini power coiled at the base of the human spine in the form of a serpent. In the temples of ancient Egypt and Rome the body of the god Serapis was encircled by the coils of a great serpent. Numerous other examples could be given, from the plumed serpent Quetzalcoatl, the Savior-god of the Mayas, to the annual snake dance of the Hopi Indians. Manly P. Hall, one of the greatest authorities on the occult (and himself a practitioner of occultism), has written:

> Serpent worship in some form permeated nearly all parts of the earth. The serpent mounds of the American Indian; the carved-stone snakes of Central and South America; the hooded cobras of India; Python, the great snake of the Greeks; the sacred serpents of the Druids; the Midgard snake of Scandinavia; the Nagas of Burma, Siam and Cambodia . . . the mystic serpent of Orpheus; the snakes at the oracle of Delphi . . . the sacred serpents preserved in the Egyptian temples; the Uraeus coiled upon the foreheads of the Pharaohs and priests—all these bear witness to the universal veneration in which the snake was held. . . .
>
> The serpent is . . . the symbol and prototype of the Universal Savior, who redeems the world by giving creation the knowledge of itself. . . . It has long been viewed as the emblem of immortality. It is the symbol of reincarnation. . . .[25]

In Greek mythology a serpent was wrapped around the Orphic egg, the symbol of the cosmos. Likewise at Delphi, Greece (for centuries the location of the most sought-after and influential oracle of the ancient world, consulted by potentates from as far away as North Africa and Asia Minor), the three legs of the oracular tripod in the inner shrine of the temple were intertwined with serpents. Or, as one further example, consider the Greek and Roman god of medicine, Aesculapius, whose symbol was a serpent-entwined staff from which the symbol of modern medicine, the caduceus, was derived.

In the temples erected in his honor, Aesculapius was worshiped with snakes because of an ancient myth which said that he had received a healing herb at the mouth of a serpent. Here, quite clearly, we have the Genesis story perverted: The serpent is not the deceiver and destroyer but the Savior of mankind, replacing Jesus Christ. At graduation ceremonies at medical schools around the world, where prayers to the God of the Bible or to Jesus Christ would not be allowed, graduates, upon receiving their M.D. degrees, still repeat aloud together the Hippocratic oath. It begins, "I swear by Apollo, by Aesculapius, by Hygeia and Panacea, and by all the gods and goddesses. . . ."

In *Up With Eden,* Ken Wilbur points out that in religions around the world the serpent has consistently been portrayed as the symbol of perennial wisdom and eternal life. There can be no doubt that the serpent, who came to Eve, is identified everywhere (except in the Bible) with the occult and is honored as embodying that mysterious force which occultists of all kinds seek to enlist in the accomplishment of their desires. The Bible, on the other hand, identifies the serpent with Satan and declares that those who seek his occult powers eventually find themselves entrapped as his slaves and lose their souls.

It would seem that in the honor given to the serpent in all cultures and religions we have an admission that the "Force" behind the universe is very personal indeed. Both the Bible and the occult world agree that the serpent is real; they only disagree on whether he is man's friend or foe.

You are in control! . . . God cannot do anything in this earth unless we . . . give Him permission . . . through prayer.

—Frederick K.C. Price[1]

SCIENCE OF MIND teaches that the originating, supreme, creative Power of the Universe . . . is a cosmic Reality Principle . . . present throughout the Universe and in every one of us. . . . Man controls the course of his life. . . by mental processes . . . .

—Ernest Holmes, founder of The Church of Religious Science[2]

Just as there exist scientific techniques for the release of atomic energy, so are there scientific procedures for the release of spiritual energy. . . . God is energy.

—Norman Vincent Peale[3]

You don't know what power you have within you! . . . You can make the world into anything you choose.

—Robert Schuller[4]

When one goes to hear them [Norman Vincent Peale and Robert Schuller] they are giving the New Thought [Science of Mind, Christian Science, Unity et al.] message. Schuller's possibility thinking approach is nothing but New Thought religion, although the leader of the Crystal Cathedral in Southern California doesn't acknowledge it.

—Blaine C. Mays, President of International New Thought Alliance[5]

When I preach on the mind, it frightens some congregations. They immediately think of Christian Science.

—Kenneth Hagin, Positive Confession leader

Primitive cosmologies pictured a creator working in space and time, forging sun, moon, and stars out of already existent raw material.
Modern scientific theory compels us to think of the creator working outside time and space . . . just as an artist is outside his canvas.

—Sir James Jeans[6]

Nowhere in the laws of physics or in the laws of the derivative sciences, chemistry and biology, is there any reference to consciousness or mind . . . its emergence is not reconcilable with the natural laws. . . .

—Sir John Eccles, Nobelist in neurobiology[7]

7

* * *

Naturalism or Supernaturalism?

If we are to understand occultism and recognize the difference between the power of Satan and the power of God (which look the same to uninformed observers), then we must make the very important distinction between naturalism and supernaturalism. In naturalism, all events follow scientifically explicable laws of cause and effect. There are no miracles—only natural occurrences. As we shall see, even many who call themselves evangelicals hold to this pagan belief. It is an ancient heresy that was taught among Christians as far back as St. Augustine, one of the fathers of the Roman Catholic Church. He said:

> God does not act contrary to nature, but only [contrary] to the order of nature known to us.[8]

On the contrary, the God of the Bible exists outside of nature. He created the universe out of nothing and He is totally independent of time, space, and matter. Although God may use natural events as He sees fit, His intervention in human affairs often involves overriding the laws with which He has bound the universe. Were that not the case, no miracle could occur, for a miracle by very definition must violate the physical laws which govern the universe. The very fact that the laws of science have been violated is proof of God's intervention. No one else, including Satan, can do so.

One often hears the statement that "science has proven that miracles are impossible." On the contrary, such "proof" is impossible. A miracle *must be beyond the ability of science to explain,* and thus beyond the ability of science either to prove or to disprove. Inasmuch as science can only deal with *natural* phenomena it can make no pronouncements about *supernatural* events. When Einstein was asked what impact his theory of relativity would have on religion he replied, "None. Relativity is a purely scientific theory and has nothing to do with religion."[9]

Naturalism holds out no ultimate hope of escape from the inexorable deterioration and death of all things. There could be no hope of eternal life for mankind without a God who exists outside of the universe and who can reach into it to bring resurrection life out of the universal death which is an integral part of nature. Indeed, the Force behind naturalism is on its way to extinction.

Doom or Destiny?

The second law of thermodynamics, the law of entropy, declares that this universe is running down like a clock. Inevitably the stars will one day be burned out and the whole universe cooled down far below zero. All human schemes and dreams will have been washed like sand castles into a cosmic ocean of nothingness. *Naturalism* as a religious hope will have proven to be a dismal disappointment.

The God of supernaturalism, however, who is not part of this dying universe, is able to reach in from outside—not with the recycling of reincarnation but with the new life of resurrection. Indeed, the Bible says that He will let go of the atom which He now holds together and create a completely new universe: "The heavens shall pass away with a great noise, and the elements shall melt with the fervent heat; the earth also and the works that are therein shall be burned up. . . . Nevertheless we, according to his promise, look for a new heavens and a new earth, wherein dwelleth righteousness" (2 Peter 3:10,13).

A Question of Morality

Every kind of nature religion (whether called Satanism, Wicca, Hinduism, or whatever) is by very definition amoral. "Good" and "evil" do not apply to atoms or galaxies or natural forces such as gravity or electricity or psychic power. Morals imply responsibility to an ultimate *authority*—something which is entirely lacking in nature. No one can say that atomic power has authority, much less that it is a power "higher" than electricity.

Biblical supernaturalism contends that moral authority derives only from an intelligent personal Creator who exists outside of the universe He has made. Evolution deifies nature. Wolfgang Smith, physics and mathematics professor at Oregon State University, says "evolution has swept the world, not on the strength of its scientific merits, but precisely in its capacity as a Gnostic myth."[10]

Yet evolution reigns in the world of academia, giving scientific credence to naturalism. It says that nature is all there is; there is no transcendent God, no supernatural. But this mysterious force which is allegedly behind evolution is presumed to provide unlimited power to nature and to the human psyche. Human potential is alleged to be infinite; man is potentially a god. All of this in the name of science!

Shamans, Scientists, and Consciousness

The first "scientists" were shamans (witch doctors, magicians, sorcerers, astrologers, etc.). They believed that matter itself was alive, indwelt by spirit beings who controlled it, and that by appeasing these entities through ritual and offerings they could gain favor with the spirits, manipulate the natural world, and harness the forces of nature. The pagan societies suffered every kind of disaster and humiliation at the hands of their gods, yet continued to supplicate them for help. Even more astonishing is the fact that modern man has revived a belief in Gaia (Mother Earth) as a living organism of which we are all a part. This pagan superstition, promoted by Vice President Al Gore, is at the heart of much of today's ecological movement.

In every culture throughout history shamanism has been based upon the belief that the spirit world could be manipulated by thoughts firmly held in the mind, by words repeatedly spoken, and by pictures formed in the imagination. The modern application of these ancient shamanic beliefs is found in the Power of Positive Thinking, Positive Speaking, and visualization. All three of these occult techniques are practiced today in the arenas of education, psychology, business, and within the church.

Modern science was birthed when it was discovered that the physical world of nature is controlled not by elves and gnomes and spirits but by definite *laws*. The ever-more-sophisticated implementation of these laws has produced today's civilization. The discovery of these laws caused materialistic science to imagine proudly that it was capable of uncovering all the secrets of the universe.

Reluctantly, science was forced to admit that consciousness lay outside its province. Thoughts were not physical, nor were the minds which conceived them. Ethics and morality, a sense of truth and justice, and an appreciation of natural beauty, poetry, and music lay outside the natural world of rocks, trees, and even animals and could not be explained in materialistic terms. As humanistic psychology metamorphosed into transpersonal psychology, and parapsychology gained acceptance, it became evident that psychic powers existed which defied the explanations of the physical sciences. Materialism was dead.

A New "Scientific" Paganism

Yet mankind had become so accustomed to the dominance of science that (contrary to Einstein's advice) it continued to look to science for authoritative direction in the new realm of the nonphysical or spiritual. Thus science took on spiritual trappings and became the new paganism. At its altars the world continues to worship human achievement and potential in anticipation of the day when its high priests will have conquered not only space and the atom but will have unlocked every hidden secret of the occult as well. At last mankind will have achieved virtual immortality as master of the universe. This ancient lie of the serpent to Eve, kept alive in pagan religions and the occult, having now donned the mask of modern science is ripening to reap God's wrath upon this world.

The prestige of science backing the new paganism has virtually guaranteed its acceptance by the educated world. Mixing science and religion turns God into an impersonal energy source to be tapped by scientifically applying universal laws. Not only the physical world, but now the spiritual as well, can be controlled "scientifically." Such is the deadly delusion that seduces modern man.

The old occultism, like karma and reincarnation, was based upon a presumed "law of cause and effect." When the witch doctor slits a rooster's throat, sprinkles the blood in a certain pattern, and mumbles a secret incantation, the spirits *must* respond with their magic as part of the bargain. So it is with the new paganism and its new rituals. The only difference is that the formulas are scientific and the priests and priestesses have donned the new robes of laboratory researchers.

Religious Science

Religious leaders began to realize that if they could join in a partnership with science they could sell their particular religion to a wider audience. We saw how successfully this scam was pulled off by Maharishi Mahesh Yogi. When he couldn't sell his brand of yoga in the Western world as "The Spiritual Regeneration Movement," he called it "The Science of Creative Intelligence" and it became a success.

Maharishi was not the first to use this scheme. Long before his day, Mary Baker Eddy had founded the cult of Christian Science. Convinced that multitudes would be attracted to "Christianity" if it were scientific, she turned Jesus into a "scientist" who knew the "mental laws" that allegedly govern this universe. Unfortunately, what Eddy taught was not biblical Christianity based upon the true gospel of Jesus Christ, but an esoteric interpretation of the Bible which only she could explain. In spite of the Bible's declaration that no "Scripture is of any private interpretation" (2 Peter 1:20), Eddy insisted that *her interpretation alone* was the truth, as expressed in her book *Science and Health with Key to the Scriptures*. Mrs. Eddy held that key and had now unlocked a new understanding that all must follow—an audacious and absurd claim.

The absolute authority and infallibility claimed by "Mother Eddy" is now wielded by the "Mother Church," where all except the most minor decisions are made for the branch churches and must be accepted without question. To this day, every Christian Science church around the world must take its Sunday lessons from the Mother Church in Boston, lessons which are based upon the infallible interpretation of Scripture known only to, and revealed only by, Mary Baker Eddy.

Here we have one of the first marks of a cult: that the followers must accept without question whatever the cult leader as the infallible authority decrees. A former Christian Scientist of the third generation explains some of its teachings:

> Mary Baker Eddy declares that there is no sin and no hell, and that death is an illusion. No one needs to be concerned about salvation because everyone will live eternally. . . .
> Jesus was just a man, the perfect example for us to follow. He didn't die for our sins. Instead, he demonstrated the unreality of matter, that all is mind, and that we too can overcome the false beliefs of mortal mind. . . .
> We were warned not to read the Bible without *Key to the Scriptures.* . . . We were always encouraged to repeat the affirmations, "Christian Science is the complete and final revelation" and "Christian Science is a perfect science. . . ."[11]

New Thought—Forerunner of the New Age Movement

Christian Science is part of the New Thought movement that developed during the last half of the nineteenth century. Phineas P. Quimby (1802–1866), whose "studies in mesmerism [early hypnotism], spiritism and kindred phenomena . . . laid the basis for a new structure in the world of thought[12] . . . was regarded as the founder of the [New Thought] movement."[13] New Thought's basic teaching is (like that of Hinduism) that everything is in the mind. We create our own world of good or evil, of health or sickness, of prosperity or want by our thoughts. The practice of hypnosis, which Quimby pioneered in America, seemed to demonstrate this. Mary Baker Eddy was one of the early patients he "healed" and her new interpretation of the Bible was actually based upon Quimby's teachings—a fact which she refused to admit.

New Thought was the forerunner of today's New Age, which has popularized the same delusion under new labels. New Thought was forced out of mainstream Christianity and became the basis for a number of cults, which include (in addition to Christian Science) Unity School of Christianity and

The Church of Religious Science (Science of Mind). Like Unity founders Myrtle and Charles Fillmore, Ernest Holmes patterned his Science of Mind on the same attractive delusion: "Man, by thinking, can bring into his experience whatsoever he desires. . . ."[14] In a proud prophecy that has come to pass, Holmes declared, "We have launched a Movement which, in the next 100 years, will be the great new religious impulsion of modern times . . . [destined] to envelope the world. . . ."[15]

Among today's well-known advocates of Science of Mind are actor Robert Stack and singer Della Reese. This "spiritual philosophy for the New Age" offers a "specific method by which anyone . . . may relate consciously to the Creative Life Force ["God"] of the universe . . . for the purpose of achieving whatever constructive objective is desired. . . . Health, abundance, security, love, peace, and happiness are . . . within the immediate grasp of all who apply . . . principles . . . which the Science of Mind explains."[16] Having reduced God to a Universal Principle that can be utilized according to scientific laws, the creature has become the Creator!

Norman Vincent Peale and Robert Schuller

Norman Vincent Peale, a 33-degree Mason, and his chief disciple, Robert Schuller, kept New Thought alive within mainstream Christianity—so that its tenets are even widely embraced among evangelicals today. Schuller calls Peale "the man who has impacted and influenced my thinking and my theology and my life more than any other living person. . . ."[17] Peale borrowed from Fillmore the phrase "Positive Thinking" (that made Peale famous)[18] and credited Holmes with making him into a positive thinker.[19]

Charles S. Braden's definitive work on New Thought identifies Norman Vincent Peale as the one man "through whose ministry essentially New Thought ideas and techniques have been made known most widely in America."[20] Peale continually spoke of the universe as "mental," of God as "energy," and of "prayer" as the scientific technique for releasing God-energy according to definite "laws." The following statements reveal Peale's basic Science of Mind teaching:

The world you live in is mental and not physical. Change your thought and you change everything.[21]

Your unconscious mind . . . [has a] power that turns wishes into realities when the wishes are strong enough.[22]

Who is God? Some theological being . . . ? God is energy. As you breathe God in, as you visualize His energy, you will be reenergized![23]

Prayer power is a manifestation of energy. Just as there exist scientific techniques for the release of atomic energy, so are there scientific procedures for the release of spiritual energy through the mechanism of prayer. . . . New and fresh spiritual techniques are being constantly discovered . . . experiment with prayer power.[24]

Prayer . . . is a procedure by which spiritual power flows from God . . . releases forces and energies . . . and brings many other astounding results. As in any skill or science one must learn step by step the formula for opening the circuit and receiving this power.

Any method through which you can stimulate the power of God to flow into your mind is legitimate . . . [any] scientific use of prayer. . . .[25]

Kenneth Hagin and "Positive Confession"

Among charismatics, the largest churches and the most popular ministers on radio and TV tend to be those associated with what is known as "Positive Confession," or the "Faith movement." Positive Confession is simply Peale's Positive Thinking carried one step further: expressing the thoughts aloud. Kenneth Hagin is generally credited with founding this latter movement, and his teachings have an authority among his followers almost equal to that of Mary Baker Eddy among hers.

Frederick K.C. Price says: "Kenneth Hagin has had the greatest influence upon my life of any living man . . . his books . . . revolutionized and changed my life." Charles Capps gives a similar testimony: "Brother Hagin was the greatest influence of my life."[26] Kenneth Copeland credits Hagin's tapes with having revolutionized his ministry.[27]

Kenneth Hagin's gospel can be traced back to the writings of E.W. Kenyon, who first taught "the positive confession of the Word of God"[28] and must be recognized as the real founder of today's Positive Confession movement. Kenyon studied at the Emerson College of Oratory in Boston, a hotbed of the emerging New

Thought philosophy.[29] Kenyon's teaching about "the power of words" and his warnings never to make a "negative confession"[30] deeply influenced Hagin and many others who are recognized today as leaders of this movement. Kenyon also taught that man is a little god "in God's class" and therefore can use the same faith-force that God does.[31] We allegedly create our own reality with the words of our mouths: "What I confess, I possess."[32]

Hagin, as quoted at the beginning of the chapter, complains that people often think he is teaching Christian Science. He claims he is not, yet he teaches that the power of God works according to laws. Science is based upon laws. Thus, if what Hagin teaches about God's power being governed by laws is indeed "Christian," then it must be "Christian Science."

"Positive Confession" means to verbalize positive thought and speak it aloud—precisely what shamans have believed and practiced for thousands of years in all cultures. The connection with the Positive/Possibility Thinking taught by Peale and Schuller is acknowledged by Kenneth Hagin, Jr.:

> Somebody will argue, "You're talking about positive thinking!"
> That's right! I am acquainted with the greatest Positive Thinker who ever was: God . . . !
> The two most prominent teachers of positive thinking [Peale and Schuller] are ministers.[33]

The entire "Faith movement" rests upon the occult belief that "faith is a force just like electricity or gravity"[34] which obeys laws, and thus even non-Christians can use it. David Yonggi Cho, pastor of the world's largest church, located in Seoul, Korea, declares: "Think positively and prosper." Cho's brand of Christian Science is based upon "the law of the fourth dimension," a law which both Christians and non-Christians can follow in order to create miracles. He says, "Sokagakkai [a Buddhist sect] has applied the law of the fourth dimension and has performed miracles. . . ."[35] The Sokagakkai are occultists.

The *Wall Street Journal* observed that Cho's Christianity has elements of Korean shamanism in it.[36] Kenneth Hagin also acknowledges that his variety of Christian science (as must be the case with any science) likewise allows non-Christians to obtain miracles by scientifically applying its laws. Hagin writes:

It used to bother me when I'd see unsaved people getting results [miracles], but my church members not getting results. Then
it dawned on me what the sinners were doing: They were cooperat-
ing with this law of God—the law of faith.[37]

A "Law of Miracles"?

The blessings of God's natural order (sun, rain, etc.) fall "on
the just and on the unjust" (Matthew 5:45). His miracles, however, are special blessings of His grace which are reserved for
those who know and love Him. God will not extend His grace
and blessing to those who reject Him. The "laws of faith," however, according to the Positive Confession leaders, work for
anyone, saint or sinner, just like the laws of science.

The teaching that non-Christians can create miracles by following "God's laws of faith" or the "laws of the fourth dimension" is a serious heresy. Tragically, this tempting lie opens the
door into the occult, where evil spirits gladly respond with a
seeming "miracle" in order to deceive and seduce the unsuspecting into further delusions.

Pat Robertson is another Christian leader who has fallen for
shamanism/Christian Science. Founder of the television show
"700 Club," Pat describes his book *Beyond Reason* as "an effort to
teach some of the basic principles that enable you to understand and experience the flow of God's energy . . . and to enter
the world of miracles. . . ."[38] He teaches that miracles work according to laws which "are as valid for our lives as the laws of
thermodynamics or the law of gravity."[39] Robertson says, "The
metaphysical principles of the kingdom [of God], taken by
themselves, can produce fantastic temporal benefits"—and
these benefits, because they follow scientific laws, can be enjoyed by atheists as well as by Christians.[40]

Robertson is teaching naturalism, not Christianity. So enam-
ored is Robertson with the laws of science that he even claims
there is a "law of miracles" which God must always follow in
order to work a miracle.[41] On the contrary, by very definition
anything that can be explained by scientific laws, either in the
physical or spiritual worlds, cannot be a miracle. Only by the
intervention of God overriding the laws which He has imposed
upon nature can a miracle occur.

Charismatic leaders who imagine they have discovered *laws* of faith are promoting a Christianized version of naturalism. Their "God" is not the transcendent Creator who exists outside of the physical universe which He created out of nothing (as Sir James Jeans argues *must* be the case). The "faith God" of Hagin, Robertson, et al. is tied to this physical universe and bound by its laws. John and Paula Sandford, well-known practitioners of "inner healing," profess this irrational heresy as clearly as anyone:

> Miracles happen by the cooperation, union, and interplay of spirit and matter together. . . . Confused . . . men have thought . . . there had to be a violation of principles for miracles to happen. . . . What rot and bunk! Miracles happen by releasing power within matter according to God's principles. . . .
>
> Nature, being filled with the Spirit of God, has immeasurable power, locked within its tiniest cells. . . . Miracles happen by the operation of the Holy Spirit within principles far beyond our ability to comprehend but nonetheless scientific. . . .
>
> I have sometimes been called a Christian Scientist when lecturing on these subjects. . . .[42]

The Charismatics' "Mary Baker Eddy"

The Sandfords studied under Agnes Sanford, the charismatics' Mary Baker Eddy. She is the founder of the Inner Healing movement in the church. Her serious heresies are too numerous to recite here, yet she remains highly honored in the evangelical church to this day. John Wimber, founder of the Vineyard movement, enthusiastically promoted her books until his recent death. Much like Norman Vincent Peale, Sanford calls God "the very life-force existing in a radiation of an energy . . . from which all things evolved."[43] She declares that "God . . . made everything out of Himself and somehow He put a part of Himself into everything."[44] This is pantheism.

To substantiate such heresies, Sanford cites Jesuit priest Pierre Teilhard de Chardin as her authority. Declared a heretic even by the Roman Catholic Church, Chardin was known as the father of the New Age movement. Sanford taught that the "God-force" can be turned on in one's life by simply saying to it, "Whoever you are—whatever you are—come into me now!" What a great invitation to Satan! The true God, who identifies Himself clearly in Scripture and must be known and acknowledged for who He is, would not answer such a call—but Satan and his minions, who hide behind any mask, would gladly accept that invitation.

Bringing occultism into the church, Sanford taught that everything is a matter of thought vibrations which if "negative" make us ill, and if "positive" heal us. Indeed, "positive thought vibrations" projected upon sinners can even turn them into Christians. Sanford wrote, "A new age is being born . . . when love-power [projected] at the command of ministers [and others] is sufficient to change hearts . . . we [have] an inner source of power that can be tapped at will."[45]

Spiritual "Science"

If the power of God is a force like gravity that works according to scientific laws (as Peale, Hagin, Copeland, Cho, Robertson, et al. claim), then anyone (Christian or atheist) who follows these laws scientifically may utilize God's miraculous power. Hagin declares that even non-Christians can receive miracles by applying God's "laws of faith."[46] Charles Capps (a leader in the Positive Confession movement) writes:

> God's Word is *spiritual law*. It functions just as surely as any natural law. . . . Words governed by spiritual law become *spiritual forces* working for you. . . .
> THE NATURAL WORLD IS TO BE CONTROLLED BY MAN SPEAKING GOD'S WORDS. . . . This is . . . *spiritual law*. It works every time. . . . (Emphasis in original.)[47]

That the Positive Confession movement is a form of Christianized science *(naturalism* as opposed to *supernaturalism)* cannot be denied. No one disputes the fact that the laws of science govern the natural world. Anyone may apply the laws of physics and chemistry. It is heresy, however, to teach that God's supernatural power is also governed by laws and can thus be released scientifically.

The Bible teaches that God grants miracles by His grace; and by very definition grace can neither be merited nor elicited as an automatic response to the application of any law. Yet in contradiction to Scripture, David Yonggi Cho writes:

> There are three spiritual forces in the earth. The Spirit of God, the spirit of man, and the spirit of Satan . . . can hover over the material third dimension and exercise creative powers. . . .
>
> The Holy Spirit said, "My son, man still does not realize the spiritual power I have given to him."
>
> Yes, I said, realizing what God was referring to . . . False prophets had power in the realm of the spirit because they had come to realize their potential.[48]

In summary, the so-called "Faith teachers" are teaching a Christianized form of naturalism similar to Christian Science and Science of Mind. Their system works (so they say) by "laws" scientifically applied: God's laws of faith for Kenneth Hagin, the laws of the fourth dimension for Yonggi Cho, the eight laws of the secret kingdom (including the Law of Miracles) for Pat Robertson, etc. They claim to have received such heresies from the Holy Spirit.

Occultism: Satan's Counterfeit "Miracles"

The laws of the physical sciences do not apply in the spiritual realm. So what are these laws to which the Positive Confession leaders refer, laws which govern the realm of spirit and seem to work? We find them in the world of the occult: for example, the "law of manifestation," which declares that thoughts held firmly in the mind, spoken aloud, or visualized will "manifest" in the physical world. This law was taught to Napoleon Hill by the demons who posed as Ascended Masters from a School of Wisdom on the astral plane. Leaders in the Faith movement refer to this law as well.

Occultism counterfeits the power of God. One clear example is found in the confrontation between Moses and Aaron and the sorcerers and magicians in Pharaoh's court. The latter were able, by the power of Satan, to duplicate (but only to the degree allowed by God) what God did miraculously through Moses and Aaron. Thus when God told Aaron to "cast down his rod before Pharaoh, and before his servants, and it became a serpent," we are told that "the magicians of Egypt did in like manner with their enchantments. For they cast down every man his rod, and they became serpents; but Aaron's rod swallowed up their rods" (Exodus 7:10-12).

And so it was with the first two plagues that God brought upon Egypt at the command of Moses and Aaron. Following each one we read, "And the magicians of Egypt did so with their enchantments; and Pharoah's heart was hardened" (Exodus 7:22; cf. 8:7). But following the third plague we read, "And the magicians . . . could not. . . . Then the magicians said unto Pharaoh, This is the finger of God" (Exodus 8:18,19).

The power that Samson evidenced (Judges 14–16) was no display of naturally acquired muscular strength. It could only have been supernatural Holy Spirit power manifested through flesh and blood.

The demoniac in the New Testament "had been often bound with fetters and chains, and the chains had been plucked asunder by him, and the fetters broken in pieces . . ." (Mark 5:4). Again we have the manifestation of a paranormal nonphysical power revealed through flesh and blood for which there is no physical, scientific explanation. We are clearly told by Christ Himself that the power came from unholy spirits invading the physical world and possessing a human body—spirits which Jesus cast out of this enslaved man to free him from their bondage.

The young woman in the city of Philippi "brought her masters much gain by soothsaying" (Acts 16:16). She was a fortune-teller who seemed to have access to a paranormal source of information. Her source of knowledge and power was a "spirit of divination"; and when the apostle Paul, "in the name of Jesus Christ . . . command[ed] [the spirit] to come out of her . . . he came out" and the woman lost her occult powers (Acts 16:16,18).

Beyond Psychic Power

Naturalism seeks to explain all such powers, whether of a Samson or a demoniac, saint or sinner, as within the capabilities of ordinary human beings—if only one can learn the secret. An editorial in *Gold Prospector* magazine suggests that dowsing (which is representative of all occultism) is simply a way of "ask[ing] nature a question to which she (through your instrument) will answer...."[49] One might as well pray to an approaching tornado.

In an earlier chapter we quoted Fordham University professor John J. Heaney, a Catholic theologian. Heaney provides numerous examples of psychic powers and attempts to prove their validity. He then asserts that these powers are innate within everyone, that "certain kinds of paranormal healing ... visions, levitations, stigmata, and in general the manifestation of parapsychological powers ... [are] natural human powers...."[50]

Heaney's naturalism reduces Christ to a psychic. Although Heaney claims that he "accepts the unique God-manhood of Jesus,"[51] he suggests that Jesus manifested "some remarkable powers of telepathy and clairvoyance" such as an exceptional psychic might naturally display.[52] Heaney also suggests that the alleged "telepathic feats of some saints and holy people" and the ability of Padre Pio and others to apparently "read the minds of their penitents" are normal human abilities which do *not* "seem to require any *unique* and *different intervention* by God."[53]

In support of his naturalism, Heaney refers to a number of famous psychics, mediums, psychic healers, and those manifesting psychokenesis whose powers seem to have withstood the scrutiny of science and who are not religious. These psychics claim no spiritual connection. He writes:

> Dr. Dolores Krieger of NYU has trained many nurses in touch therapy. In controlled experiments this technique has been shown to change hemoglobin content in the blood. It has been introduced into many hospitals in the United States.[54]

It is quite apparent that psychic powers are not normal human powers, but spiritual powers that do not emanate from the brain or body. Even the secular researchers admit these are "paranormal" powers. The very investigation of these powers is called "parapsychology" and is related to "transpersonal psychology," which goes beyond the human to something "higher." There are only two possible sources of paranormal power: God or Satan.

According to the Bible, the only legitimate paranormal powers are gifts of the Holy Spirit (1 Corinthians 12:8-10). Clearly distinguishing them from human capabilities, these gifts are distinctly described as "the manifestation of the [Holy] Spirit" (verse 7). These miraculous gifts are attributed to God alone: "All these worketh that one and the selfsame [Holy] Spirit, dividing to every man severally as he will" (verse 11).

That "psychic power," though just as surely not of human origin, is something entirely different from the gifts of the Holy Spirit should be clear. Satan wants to fulfill his ambition to be a god ("like the Most High"—Isaiah 14:14) through humans who have been seduced by the same impossible aspiration. The power he channels through them is the proof he offers that they too can become gods. In fact, "psychic power" enslaves those through whom Satan manifests it.

Multitudes today are captivated by the delusion of limitless human potential. Having swallowed that bait, they are trapped in the endless pursuit of paranormal powers. Fueling that pursuit is the belief that some secret key will unlock unlimited potential, that there is some ritual or technique or state of consciousness which will by some "law" bring forth this supranormal knowledge and energy.

The Supernatural Working of God

That the manifestations of the Holy Spirit displayed through human flesh are called "gifts" has caused some confusion. They are not gifts in the sense of being given to any individual to possess and thereafter use as he or she sees fit. If genuine, the gifts of the Spirit are under the direction and control of God and are provided by His grace exclusively for His purposes and to His glory.

No one can heal, do a miracle, raise the dead, or prophesy anytime he so desires. Not even Jeremiah, Isaiah, Ezekiel, or any of the other prophets could do so. When Jeremiah desired to prophesy to the people he had to wait upon God: "And it came to pass *after ten days* that the word of the LORD *came* unto Jeremiah" (Jeremiah 42:7). Clearly, miracles come only by the empowerment and direction of God, and not by human initiative.

Nor can the gifts of the Spirit be taught for a fee and learned in a seminar, as the late John Wimber led people to believe. Peter declared: "For . . . prophecy came not in old time by the will of man, but holy men of God spoke as they were moved by the Holy Ghost" (2 Peter 1:21). No one can initiate, mandate, or activate the moving of the Holy Spirit!

Whatever the "gift of the Spirit" may be, it is given in specific instances to effect God's purpose *at that time;* it does not become a power possessed by an individual which he can wield at his discretion. If someone lays hands upon a sick person and prays, and the person is instantly healed, that is a manifestation of the "gifts of healing" according to God's will. The person who prayed does not now possess the gifts of healing like some magic wand which he can wave at will. To imagine that to be the case is one of the basic errors in the charismatic movement.

It is a great delusion for anyone to imagine that he possesses any gift of the Spirit in the sense that he can exercise it whenever he so desires. And that includes the gift of tongues—a gift which multitudes imagine they "possess" and can "practice" when they please and, thereby, have been led astray.

Beware of any alleged "gift" that is initiated or possessed by the human spirit! It is a grievous error to promise a "miracle service" at a particular time and location and to purport to do "miracles," or to offer seminars that teach how to do "signs and wonders." Whatever purports to be the manifestation of a "gift of the Spirit" and is not initiated by Him, but is under man's control, is not of God but from the occult.

Christianity Requires Miracles

With the observation that the Creator must be separate from His creation, Sir James Jeans has eliminated pantheism/naturalism as a viable theory. On the other hand, if naturalism is true, then there are no miracles caused by God's intervention and overriding the laws of science. And if that is the case, then Christianity is a lie, for Christianity requires miracles. It promises resurrection, the greatest miracle of all. Indeed, Christianity is founded upon the resurrection of Jesus Christ:

If Christ be not risen [from the dead], then is our preaching vain, and your faith is also vain . . . ye are yet in your sins. . . .

In a moment, in the twinkling of an eye . . . the dead [who believed in Christ] shall be raised incorruptible, and we [who are still alive] shall be changed . . . death is swallowed up in victory. . . . Thanks be to God, which giveth us the victory through our Lord Jesus Christ (1 Corinthians 15:14,17,52,54,57).

Resurrection, the only hope for life out of death, is a miracle. It is not a phenomenon governed by natural laws that can be brought into play by those who know the secret of the limitless potential allegedly residing in all of us. No, it is God reaching into a fallen universe from the outside.

Salvation is the same kind of miracle: eternal life as a gift of God's grace out of the eternal death which His own infinite justice has pronounced upon a rebellious and sinful mankind. That gift is given freely to all who acknowledge they can't merit it and humble themselves to receive it *as a gift*. Moreover, the miraculous power of Christ's resurrection is the only means by which we can possibly live the victorious Christian life which the Bible presents as the standard for all believers.

The Great Difference

Nowhere is the difference between naturalism and supernaturalism seen more clearly than when it comes to God and Jesus Christ. Naturalism sees an impersonal Force behind all existence, a Force that is in all things and thus may be experienced and utilized by looking within one's own being. The God of the Bible, on the other hand, is totally other than the universe and all He made, including man. According to the Bible, Jesus Christ is God who came to this earth through a virgin birth to become a man in order to reveal Himself to us and to die in our place for our sins.

There is no procedure or ritual that can cause a sinner to pass from death to life. The new birth is a miracle of God's grace that only He can accomplish. Unlike the scientific application of laws to release spiritual energy, we must approach the God of the Bible as unworthy sinners trusting in His grace and mercy. There are no formulas that we can think, speak, or visualize that will require Him to respond to us.

Here is the great difference between psychic power and spiritual power. The former presumably comes from some force inherent within the human psyche, or perhaps within the mind, producing the fabled "mind over matter" that psychics boast of and is being pursued in laboratories. True *spiritual* power comes from God and is miraculous, overriding the laws of physics and chemistry. God's power also exerts a moral influence, which is entirely lacking in any natural force.

The Bible asserts that this moral power flows to believers in Christ through their faith. Norman Vincent Peale claimed that Positive Thinking was the same as biblical faith. Of course that is not true. An atheist could teach Positive Thinking seminars, and some do. Faith is not a power we aim at God to get what we want.

Biblical faith is not some power of the mind, but simple trust in God alone and in Jesus Christ, who is God come to this earth as a man through the virgin birth. Faith in Christ must include who He is and what He has done. The fact that He died for our sins and rose again to live His life in those who open their hearts to Him is the source of an entirely new moral power over sin. That power is unknown in nature.

I became fascinated by Sioux culture and its proud warrior heritage.
Lakota warriors had a deep reverence for the mysteries of life. That's
where their power, and sense of freedom, came from. . . . Crazy Horse,
the greatest Sioux warrior, was first and foremost a holy man.

To the Lakota, everything was sacred, even the enemy, because of
. . . the interconnectedness of all life. As one seer put it: "We are earth
people on a spiritual journey to the stars. Our quest . . . is to look
within, to know who we are, to see that we are connected to all things,
that there is no separation, only in the mind."

—Phil Jackson, Chicago Bulls' coach[1]

Peace . . . comes within the souls of men when they realize their relation-
ship, their oneness with the universe and all its powers, and when they
realize that at the center of the Universe dwells the Great Spirit, and that
this center is really everywhere. It is within each of us.

—Black Elk, Medicine Man[2]

An upsurge of critical scholarship has suggested that the primal [indige-
nous] cultures . . . were not just agrarian-based neolithic societies, but,
indeed, were highly sophisticated cultures of partnership between men
and women as well as partnership with spiritual powers.

—Jean Houston in *Life Force*[3]

The meager available native records contain abundant evidence that the
later civilizations of Central and South America were hopelessly domi-
nated by the black arts of their priestcrafts. . . .

None could achieve to the greater Mysteries until a human being had
suffered immolation at his hand and the bleeding heart of the victim
had been elevated before the leering face of the stone idol . . . the man-
made demon.

—Manly P. Hall[4]

O Wakan-Tanka *and all the winged Powers of the universe, behold us!*
This tobacco I offer especially to You, the Chief of all the Powers, who
is represented by the Spotted Eagle who lives in the depths of the heav-
ens, and who guards all that is there!

—Lakota Holy Man Slow Buffalo[5]

There is no possibility . . . that Vodou will ever be eradicated from
Haitian society, because . . . it is interwoven so completely within the
fabric of Haitian life.

—Professor Leslie G. Desmangles[6]

8

* * *

Native, Indigenous, and Nature Religion

One of the surest and most acceptable paths leading into the occult is today's back-to-nature movement in the name of ecological preservation of our planet. Earth has suffered much harmful damage due to mankind's carelessness and greed. While the industrial nations must bear their share of the blame, some of the worst pollution and destruction has occurred in Communist lands and also in developing countries of the Third World. Furthermore, pollution (such as that caused by volcanic eruptions) and destruction (such as blight and insects, forest fires started by lightning, or plagues) are an integral part of nature itself.

Nevertheless, the popular delusion has gained unchallenged acceptance that anything "natural" must be beneficial. It seems to be overlooked that nothing is more natural than disease, suffering, death, and *natural disasters* (hurricanes, earthquakes, drought, and floods, to name a few). In fact it is against such destruction regularly wrought by nature that humanity has desperately struggled to protect itself, and in so doing has arrived at the present degree of civilization.

It seems more than ironic that after mankind has fought for centuries against the often antagonistic and sometimes deadly forces of nature, there should now be a popular and growing movement calling for partnership with these same forces. Such ideas sound appealing, but would have afforded no comfort to the Donner Party starving in the impossibly deep snow in the Sierra Nevada mountains. To them (and to other victims of wind, ice, and storm) nature could not have been more cruel, vicious, and unmerciful!

A Call to Reason

It was the unnatural act of reason opposing the natural processes of nature that brought under control a host of formerly fatal diseases, that lowered the death rate in infants, and that has extended the average life expectancy. The repeated unnatural act of taking out an appendix or transplanting a kidney or removing a tumor has saved countless lives. Such realities ought not to be forgotten in the rush to worship a mythological Earth Mother.

Only a relentless battle *against* nature has achieved the many comforts and benefits unknown in earlier times and taken for granted today. *None* is a product of nature. There is nothing *natural* about computers, television, space travel, dams, bridges, books, or even such basic necessities of human life as weaving, food processing, plowing, planting, weeding, or cooking. Then why the cry to "get back to nature"?

Moreover, it was Western science that brought these benefits to mankind. These blessings would never have resulted from Hinduism's pantheistic philosophy or Eastern mysticism. Nor would medical science ever have blossomed from the beliefs of the North American Indians, which the West is now embracing in its pursuit of "oneness with nature." What irony, that indigenous peoples who still find themselves appealing to unheeding spirits against the diseases which ravage them in nature's own undeveloped territory (diseases which modern medicine has cured) are now being exalted as examples for universal emulation!

This is not to deny that some plants and roots with healing qualities have been discovered by native peoples or that they have something to teach us. Nor is it to deny that ecological destruction has been unnecessarily wrought by the human folly and avarice of "civilized" peoples. At the same time, however, charges against science and technology must be made on reasonable grounds. It is a quantum leap from respecting and protecting our environment (which we should do) to deifying "Mother Earth."

A Selective Favoritism

Nor should we overlook, much less condone, today's rampant prejudice against Christianity. Biblical faith has become taboo in American society, while anything else, including witchcraft and voodoo, is accepted without question. A great hue and cry is being raised across the country to prohibit any public display of crosses or manger scenes. At the same time, totem poles are immune from comparable criticism or objections. Even the United Nation's World Health Organization (WHO) has given its approval to a revival of witchcraft under the popular euphemism of "traditional medicine" or "native cures."

Whatever is native or "indigenous" is indiscriminately praised, and woe to those who have the temerity to point out any flaws in native cultures or religions. We must all emulate what the natives of Africa or of a South Pacific island or our own native American Indians believe and practice! Such is the propaganda line which is promoted in the media and goes virtually unchallenged.

On Sunday evening, November 17, 1996, the popular *A&E* channel aired "America's Mysterious Places." It presented witchcraft in Salem and early New England along with voodoo in New Orleans as benign. Spokespersons for voodoo said, "We are descendants of those slaves carried here from Africa who brought voodoo with them." The purpose of voodoo was explained as simply serving the spirits and worshiping the gods and goddesses. Not a word about the curses which terrify the populace where voodoo is practiced. The program showed favorable depictions of the serpent god. A voodoo priestess explained that she was the equivalent of a Catholic priest or a Jewish rabbi. Such erroneous statements left viewers misinformed—duped, in fact.

Pagan religions are even being introduced into public schools in the United States in spite of the prohibition on school prayer or any favorable reference to Christianity. Of course these religions are classified as "culture," which is simply a deceit. The same is true in community programs. Consider, for example, Carolee Nishi, "the creator and volunteer director of a unique after-school program sponsored by the YMCA of

Honolulu that teaches Hawaiian Studies to children ages 4–14." The word *religion* is not to be found in the full-page promotional piece about Nishi in United Airlines' *Hemispheres* magazine. Instead, it is said that she teaches "hula dancing . . . Hawaiian history and culture."[7] Occultism escapes mention.

Even the United States government promotes native American spirituality in spite of the "separation of church and state" which is enforced so strictly against anything Christian. The National Park Service has promoted Indian animist/spiritist religion—including the worship of nature spirits—while blaming the Bible for the destruction of the West! For example, Gary Hathaway, Acting Superintendent of Lava Beds National Monument, in an official newsletter which was handed out to park visitors in 1993, stated:

> Native Americans had a spiritual tie to their land. . . . [White men] used the resources for their own commercial gain, and the timeless spirituality of the land was disrupted. . . . Their spiritual viewpoint, recorded in Genesis, called for them to dominate the land and subdue it . . . vast areas of the West were destroyed.
>
> Today the spirituality of the land at Lava Beds is undergoing an awakening . . . throughout the monument the presence of spirits can be felt . . . you can [even] see them when they choose to appear in their visible forms. . . .
>
> Enter the medicine circle reverently, as you would enter your own church. Let the spirits of the winds, the rocks, and the animals speak to you. . . .[8]

The Changing of the Gods

Western nature enthusiasts are adopting Native American fetishes. While some wear these occult objects (imbued with power by the spirits) as jewelry, Phil Jackson honors and displays them in the inner sanctum of the Chicago Bulls. This is the fullest rejection possible of the Christian faith in which Jackson's parents hoped to raise him, and a surrender to paganism. Walter Yeeling Evans-Wentz, in his encyclopedic work on paganism—not as a critic but a sympathetic believer—explains the origin of the power which Jackson and other admirers of native amulets and charms believe resides in the objects they venerate:

Dr. Taylor has brought together examples from all parts of the globe of so-called fetishism, which is veneration paid to natural living objects such as trees, fish, animals, as well as to inanimate objects of almost every conceivable description, including stones, because of the spirit believed to be inherent or resident in the particular object: and he shows that idols originally were fetishes, which in time came to be shaped according to the form of the spirit or god supposed to possess them. . . .

The divine virtue residing in the images of the gods [or fetishes] was thought to be . . . transmitted by the imposition of hands and by magic passes . . . [and] extraordinary curative properties were attributed to it.[9]

Native Americans still pray to the trees and rocks and other inanimate objects. This is the superstition of animism, against which all experience and logic cries out in protest. Phil Jackson praises Crazy Horse as a great holy man. Black Elk claims that "our great chief and priest Crazy Horse . . . received most of his great power through . . . visions of the Rock, the Shadow, the Badger, a prancing horse (from which he received his name), the Day, and also of *Wanbli Galeshka,* the Spotted Eagle, and from each of these he received much power and holiness."[10] A prayer in the steam lodge cries out to the rocks:

O you ancient rocks who are sacred, you have neither ears nor eyes, yet you hear and see all things. Through your powers this young man has become pure . . . worthy to go to receive some message from Wakan-Tanka.[11]

How amazing that Jackson and so many others like him would reject the God of the Bible, who has so fully proved His existence and love, and in exchange turn to pagan idolatry! How astounding that so many who have been raised by Christian parents would renounce the salvation which Christ offers and embrace instead the superstitious hope of some mysterious power within fetishes! One is reminded of God's lament over His people Israel:

Hath a nation changed their gods, which are yet no gods? But my people have changed their glory for that which doth not profit.

Be astonished, O ye heavens, at this, and be horribly afraid; be ye very desolate, saith the LORD.

For my people have committed two evils: they have forsaken me, the fountain of living waters, and have hewed out cisterns, broken cisterns, that can hold no water (Jeremiah 2:11-13).

Those who deny the miracles of Jesus recorded by legitimate eyewitnesses in the Bible willingly accept the hearsay and myth passed on by native "holy" men and women. Black Elk tells how Slow Buffalo received his power from a buffalo in a "vision":

> I saw a great people who were breaking camp . . . suddenly . . . I was there with them . . . they all turned into buffalo. . . .
>
> They showed me a large buffalo bull and said that He would be my Grandfather . . . a younger buffalo . . . would be my Father; then they pointed to a buffalo cow . . . She was my Grandmother . . . a younger cow . . . would be my Mother.
>
> They said that with this fourfold relationship, I should return to my people and that I should teach them what I had been taught there. . . .
>
> Slow Buffalo then began to sing another of his holy songs.
>
> > *These people are sacred;*
> > *From all over the universe they are*
> >   *coming to see it.*
> > *White Buffalo Cow Woman Appears is sitting*
> >   *here in a sacred manner;*
> > *They are all coming to see her.*[12]

An Undeniable Common Source of "Power"

Shamans among the natives of North, Central, and South America, as Slow Buffalo's account demonstrates, believe that they receive their power from animals and birds. At times they experience becoming these creatures, and the power animals likewise become humans. Black Elk's biographer, Joseph Epes Brown, explains the native American's deification of self—the lie from Eden:

> The Indian actually identifies himself with, or becomes, the quality or principle of the being or thing which comes to him in a vision, whether it be a beast, bird, one of the elements, or really any aspect of creation. In order that this "power" may never leave him, he always carries with him some material form representing the animal or object from which he has received his "power . . ."

In wearing the eagle-feathered "war bonnet," the wearer actually becomes the eagle, which is to say that he identifies himself, his real Self, with Wakan-Tanka [the Great Spirit which Wanbli Galeshka (the Spotted Eagle) represents].[13]

Even skeptics who have studied them around the world acknowledge a malevolent power behind pagan religions. The *Times Literary Supplement* (London, England) in its review of Evans-Wentz's book declared: "The author . . . after examining the evidence, concludes that . . . there is a residuum, an x, which nothing can account for except the hypothesis that . . . immaterial beings really do exist and occasionally manifest themselves in certain places to people who bring a certain psychic equipment to the perception of them. . . ."[14]

Clearly paganism is not an accident of the human imagination but a system designed by some intelligence which is timeless and has always had access to mankind worldwide. The same practices are found everywhere. Even when cultural practices are diverse and there has been separation from other peoples by natural barriers of oceans and vast land distances, the same occult practices persist. The identity of the intelligence behind these native religions is betrayed by paganism's anti-Christian qualities.

In every culture, those who spent their lives learning the secrets of occult power were honored as the priests, priestesses, witches, witch doctors, medicine men, sorcerers, magicians, gurus, and masters. All are so basically similar that they are now included by anthropologists under the one term *shaman,* the title given by the Tungus tribe in Siberia to its witch doctors or medicine men. Siberian shamans practice the same sorcery that Carlos Castaneda calls "a religious and philosophical experience that flourished [in America] long before the white man came to this continent, and flourishes still."

The universal involvement of pagan religions with animals supports the biblical account of the serpent appearing as a "power animal" or "guardian spirit" to speak with Eve. Moreover, shamans worldwide receive basically the same information from their "power animals" as Eve received from hers. There is only one difference: The Bible identifies this teaching as the great lie of Satan, while native religions embrace it as the truth. The comments by anthropologist Michael Harner, one of the world's leading authorities on shamanism and a practicing shaman himself, are very revealing:

> The connectedness between humans and the animal world is basic in shamanism.... The shaman has to have a particular guardian in order to do his work ... [and] the guardian spirit is sometimes referred to by native North [and South] Americans as the power animal. ...
>
> The capability of the guardian animal spirits to speak to a human or to manifest themselves sometimes in human forms is taken as an indication of their power. ... The belief by shamans that they can metamorphose into the form of their guardian animal spirit or power animal is widespread and obviously ancient. ...
>
> In the course of the initiation of a shaman of the Wiradjeri tribe in Australia, he had the nonordinary experience that feathers emerged from his arms and grew into wings. Then he was taught to fly.[15]

A Question of Morals

The picture being painted for us of the idyllic life of perfect harmony with nature and with one another supposedly lived by indigenous peoples before the evil white man came along is not true. Concerned by such lies, Jungleman, once a powerful shaman of the Yanomamo Indians of the Amazon, told the bitter truth about the lives of indigenous peoples in *Spirit of the Rainforest*. It is a tale of continual sexual perversion and abuse, warmongering, brutality, living in terror of human and spirit enemies; of curses, suffering, and death. It is a story, too, of deliverance through Jesus Christ into a whole new life of peace and joy and hope for eternity.

There is a chasm of morality between animals and man which cannot be bridged by any natural process. Historian/philosopher Herbert Schlossberg reminds us: "Animals do not act morally or immorally; they only act naturally. A system of ethics that says human beings ought to base their behavior on nature therefore justifies any behavior, because nature knows no ethic."[16] In full agreement, Nobelist Sir John Eccles points out that any nature religion must of necessity be amoral:

> The concepts of injustice, unfairness, and perverseness—like the obligations to honor, to respect and to permit—are intelligible only within a moral context and to moral beings.
>
> In the mindless universe of mere nature . . . there is neither justice nor mercy, neither liberty nor fairness.[17]

If there is one basketball player in the NBA whom even the secular press holds out as lacking the basic moral behavior expected of human beings, that man is Dennis Rodman. When Phil Jackson interviewed Rodman for possibly joining the Bulls, Jackson claims that his spirit connected with Rodman's because Rodman was also into native American spirituality. Jackson writes:

> He [Dennis] smiled and looked around and checked out the Native American artifacts on our wall and asked me about them. He told me that he had a necklace that was given to him by a Ponca from Oklahoma, and showed me his amulet. I sat for a long spell in silence with Dennis. I felt his presence. . . . We had connected by our hearts in a nonverbal way, the way of the spirit.[18]

The immorality and cruelty of indigenous people is never mentioned—only their "closeness to nature." Phil Jackson sanitizes the evil practices of native religions. He tells how Lakota warriors loved to "sneak into an enemy camp and make off with ponies."[19] No hint that this is stealing, or that they took slaves as well. A few pages later he talks of the emphasis he puts upon good character in his coaching! In his oft-repeated high praise for Indian warriors, Jackson fails to mention that they scalped and tortured their victims and had been doing so for centuries before the white man invaded their continent.

Jackson refers respectfully to the "path of the warrior"; the subtitle of his book is "Spiritual lessons of a hardwood warrior." Never does he acknowledge the bloodthirsty nature of their warfare and their brutal treatment of their captives, and even of their own wives and women. Such glamorization of native American culture is the context in which we must evaluate Jackson's boast: "Over the next few years, I quietly integrated Lakota teachings into our [basketball] program."[20] In fact, it is a badly skewed view of Native American teachings and practices which Jackson has foisted on his team and the many readers of his book.

A Fashionable Blindness

The current simplistic "black is good, white is bad" attitude in the West partakes of a similar fashionable blindness. It denies the biblical teaching that there is no difference between the races—that all are sinners equally in need of salvation. The media continually emphasizes that the great conflict is black against white and that it is primarily the fault of the whites because blacks always lived in peace until the white man arrived on the scene. The truth, however, is that blacks fought and killed and enslaved and tortured blacks in Africa before the white man came along—and are doing so today.

It is astonishing that Louis Farrakhan could talk any blacks into becoming Muslims. It was the Muslims (Arabs) who were the first suppliers of slaves (from their well-supplied warehouses on the West African coast) to Europe and America. Moreover, it was the blacks themselves who captured and sold their own people—from other tribes, of course. All through Africa the tribes had their territories and fought their wars, as they do even today. Actually there was more peace in Africa, as distasteful as that fact may be for Africans to swallow, when the colonialists were in control than there was before or has been since the Africans have achieved independence. Lack of space prevents the enumeration of the conflicts of centuries between the many native tribes in Africa. The example of only two of those tribes so much in the news of late must suffice.

The Hutus and Tutsis have been killing one another for 400 years. The Hutus were the first to populate the area now known as Rwanda and Burundi, preceding the Tutsis by about 500 years. They were farmers. The Tutsis, who raised cattle, were the ethnic minority but held a higher place in the occupational hierarchy and had more wealth and received preferential treatment by the colonialists. As an aftermath of the Hutu riots in 1959, however, the Belgians ceded Rwanda to the Hutus, who immediately massacred Tutsis by the tens of thousands. In Burundi the Tutsis gained control and proceeded to slaughter Hutus. The present bloodbath began in 1994:

> Rwandan Hutus went on a rampage and massacred between 500,000 and 1 million Tutsis. The Rwandese Patriotic Front, an exile Tutsi army based in Uganda, struck back and seized control

of Rwanda. Two million Hutus, terrified of Tutsi vengeance, fled to Tanzania and Zaire ... [and] aid officials estimate that as many as a million displaced Hutus face death from hunger and disease.

In a worst-case scenario, the very heart of Africa could implode, sucking the 30 million people in the region ... into a vortex of violence.[21]

A Plea for Honest Evaluation

God declares that "*all* have sinned and come short of the glory of God" (Romans 3:23). It is dishonest to treat native cultures as though they were immune to that indictment. Consider two young sisters, survivors of Oatman's wagon massacre in 1851. Their captivity by Apaches and sale into slavery to another tribe is recounted in agonizing detail. The two girls spent some years with their Native American captors performing slave labor. The younger sister died from starvation. Most interesting was the reaction of the girls' fellow "slaves" (the Indian squaws). Great was the women's amazement when they learned how civilly the white man lived with his wife. They expressed the vain hope that they might escape and join so kindly a society.[22]

Or who could forget the cruel massacre at the Marcus Whitman Mission in the State of Washington? Entirely unprovoked, it reflected the Indians' tragic superstition that the god of these gentle missionaries had malevolently caused the deaths of some of their people. Indigenous peoples are as fallen and as prone to sin as are the rest of mankind. We cannot honestly sanitize any segment of society in our fallen world.

Margaret Mead's book *Coming of Age in Samoa* sold millions of copies in numerous languages, was the recognized standard in anthropology for decades, and provided a key "scientific" justification for the sexual revolution which is still perverting today's world and much of the church. The book, however, was a fraud put forth to justify her own adultery and lesbianism. More recent research in Samoa has shown that Mead's representation of an idyllic native society unspoiled by sexual restrictions was totally false. The facts about Samoan life are exactly the opposite, yet the lie continues to provide "scientific" excuse for immorality worldwide.

In the Hawaiian Islands a revival of native religion, hailed as the recovery of lost tradition, has brought into the open witchcraft practices that survived in secret under a thin veneer of professed Christianity. One follower of native Hawaiian religion, who had been responding openly in an interview, suddenly clammed up when asked about the current use of "evil spells." After a long, uncomfortable pause, the one being interviewed exclaimed:

> I cannot! I'm terrified of it. Nobody talks about the religion. Hawaiians are still being prayed to death by other Hawaiians.[23]

A Stark Contrast

In spite of the facts to the contrary, the favorable treatment of indigenous religions, the dishonest cover-up of the evil inherent in their societies, and the libelous opposition to Christianity persist. The Bible is carefully examined by critics in an attempt to find any flaw; and it has withstood that test, as we document in *In Defense of the Faith*. When it comes to native/ nature religions, however, any myth will do, no matter how absurd. Truth and verifiability are irrelevant. That a religion or cultural practice is indigenous answers all questions.

Bill Moyers' television series have done much to promote this propaganda and anti-Christian bias. He allowed Joseph Campbell to pitch the lie that our salvation comes from returning to nature, and to misrepresent Christianity.[24]

Some Christian missionaries have mistakenly identified Christianity with their own Western way of life and have imposed that lifestyle upon other cultures. On the other hand, paganism has brought fear and death, while true Christianity has brought freedom and life. A missionary to the Philippines writes:

> Prior to our coming to these people they . . . were animistic, and the spirits that they worshiped had warned them that they were never to allow any other religion to come into their area. If they did, their children would die, crops fail, and other tribal people would war against them and overcome them.
>
> Their [religion] . . . involved the worship of trees, rocks, and their dead ancestors, which acted as mediators between the living

and the spirits that ruled over them. Needless to say, they lived in great darkness and continually tried to maintain their relationship with the spirits through offering blood sacrifices, which included chickens, pigs, and the ultimate sacrifice for the whole village was human sacrifice . . . their own children.

Praise God, much has changed for the Higaonon people since the Lord opened a door . . . for us to minister His Word to these people. . . . When the time came that we understood their language well enough we began to teach them from God's Word, beginning in Genesis . . . [and] it was exciting to see the people realize their sinfulness and their inability to deal with their own sin. . . .

Over the next few days and weeks most of the people . . . told us that they understood . . . that Jesus died for their sin and they were trusting in His blood for their salvation. . . . The first believers have a vision to reach all of the Higaonon people and have sent out their own . . . missionaries and have established believers in seven other villages. . . .[25]

In *Natural History*, Shoefoot (Koshiroteri), who had spent his life as a shaman among the Yanomami Indians of Venezuela, reveals the evil behind indigenous religions: "Shamans often tell their people that the cause of a relative's illness or death is a malevolent spirit sent [from] a neighboring village. Wars of retaliation are commonly carried out with clubs and bows and arrows . . . people are afraid to venture out of their villages, even to hunt or draw water from the river." The former shaman writes:

As the years went on, the responsibilities of a shaman weighed heavier and heavier upon me. I was tired. So many sick and dying. I could not cure them, no matter how hard I tried. So many threats to my village. People were raiding and killing one another. I could not protect them. Often there were food crises.

I took more *ebene* [hallucinatory drug used by the Yanomami shamans] to get assistance from the spirits, but . . . my spirits left me with nothing but worry and fear. . . . Some men [shamans] got lost in the spirit world when they took the drug; many ran into the jungle and were never heard from again. Now and then, one of them was found dead. . . . I wasn't strong enough to go on like this.

A visitor from another village told me about foreign people, nabas, who had come to live on the river . . . [and knew] a big spirit which could help us. This spirit was different from the big super-spirit [*yai pata*] of the Yanomami; it was friendly and not desiring death and destruction. I went to these naba, and they told me of their spirit and his peaceful ways . . . soon my spirits . . . said [if] . . . I would abandon them . . . they would kill me. . . .

I stopped taking *ebene* and turned to the spirit of the naba . . . it was stronger than my forest spirits. They became afraid and went away. . . . [Instead] of telling me to kill people or lead raids . . . the new spirit told me to stop fights whenever I could.

I became calm in my mind and my fear went away. I no longer hated anyone or wanted to cause their death. My old spirits were happy whenever someone died and they kept telling the shamans to stir up more violence. We thought we had power over these spirits, but they really had the power over us. . . . Even when we shamans were chanting and taking *ebene*, and we looked content, there was turmoil inside, for our spirits kept telling us to kill. Some men [shamans] lost all control and sense when they took the drug, sometimes even killing their own wives and children.

Today I no longer live in fear and . . . I have talked with people in the neighboring villages; we have ended our feuds and stopped the killing . . . we are able to devote ourselves to growing more food and we have better homes to protect ourselves from the mosquitos. The *nabas* told us that malaria comes from mosquitos, not from evil shamans, and we have changed our belief. . . .

Our population at Honey Village is growing while many others are decreasing in number. The new spirit has made me free from the fear I had all the time of so many wars. Today my people are better off and at peace.[26]

Ritualism and Nature Religion

A basic error of nature religion is the worship of created things and creatures instead of the God who created them. Even though these religions often seem to honor a "great spirit" over all, this god is only the greatest power in a pantheon that is always identified with various aspects of creation. The Bible (and common sense) declares that the universe was brought into existence and is sustained by a Creator. His moral laws have been written in every conscience so that we all know we are morally accountable to this one true God, have violated His laws, and must look to Him alone for salvation. The biblical indictment could not be clearer:

For the wrath of God is revealed from heaven against all ungod-liness and unrighteousness of men, who hold the truth in unrigh-teousness, because that which may be known of God is manifest in them [mankind], for God hath showed it unto them.

For the invisible things of him from the creation of the world are clearly seen, being understood by the things that are made, even his eternal power and Godhead, so that they are without excuse.

Because that when they knew God [from creation around them], they glorified him not as God, neither were thankful, but became vain in their imaginations, and their foolish heart was darkened.

Professing themselves to be wise, they became fools, and changed the glory of the uncorruptible God into an image made like corruptible man, and to birds, and to fourfooted beasts, and creeping things.

Wherefore God also gave them up to uncleanness through the lusts of their own hearts, to dishonor their own bodies between themselves, who changed the truth of God into a lie, and wor-shiped and served the creature more than the Creator, who is blessed forever. Amen (Romans 1:18-25).

In all pagan/nature religions there is a presumed cause-and-effect relationship between the ritual or ceremony performed and the obtaining of the power or healing or other blessing sought. The whole idea of pagan ceremonies—the rites of shaman or witch, the burning of candles, the making of potions, the use of fetishes, etc.—is that they will (if done correctly) elicit a response from the gods or spirits.

Just as the laws of science require an automatic response in the natural order, it is imagined that the gods can be made to re-spond as well. So it also is in Roman Catholicism and Eastern Orthodoxy. To make this absolutely clear, The Council of Trent (the highest authority in Catholicism) decreed:

If anyone says that by the sacraments of the New Law grace is not conferred *ex opere operato* [by the very act itself], but that faith alone in the divine promise is sufficient to obtain grace, let him be anathema [excommunicated and thereby damned].[27]

As we have seen, this cause-and-effect relationship suggests Christianized science, for which there is absolutely no biblical support. In the Old Testament there were many sacrifices and ceremonies commanded by God, but *never* was it suggested that any ceremony or sacrifice had an efficacious effect by itself. There was no thought that God was impressed by the act, much less that it brought about an automatic response from God that followed certain spiritual laws. On the contrary, because the hearts of priests and people were not right, God rejected the sacrifices of Israel, even though they followed the ceremonial procedures according to the letter of the law:

> To what purpose is the multitude of your sacrifices unto me? saith the LORD. I am full of the burnt-offerings of rams and the fat of fed beasts, and I delight not in the blood of bullocks or of lambs or of he goats. . . .
>
> Bring no more vain oblations: incense is an abomination unto me. . . . When ye spread forth your hands, I will hide mine eyes from you; yea, when ye make many prayers, I will not hear; your hands are full of blood.
>
> Wash you, make you clean; put away the evil of our doings from before mine eyes; cease to do evil; learn to do well: seek judgment, relieve the oppressed, judge the fatherless, plead for the widow (Isaiah 1:11-17).

Ceremonialism: Some Important Distinctions

This basic error of paganism is repeated in all ritualism: the belief that by performing certain ceremonies divine favor may be obtained. One finds such rituals everywhere in paganism and nature religions: the vestments the priests wear, the swinging censors filled with incense, the incantations, the elaborate ceremonies performed to obtain favors from the gods. So it is in Roman Catholicism and Eastern Orthodoxy.

Beginning in the fourth century, with the influence of Emperor Constantine, Roman Catholicism became a mixture of paganism and Christianity. Augustine himself testified:

> The man who enters [a church] is bound to see drunkards, misers, tricksters, gamblers, adulterers, fornicators, people wearing amulets, assiduous clients of sorcerers, astrologers. . . .
>
> The same crowds that press into the churches on Christian festivals also fill the theatres on pagan holidays.[28]

There were those within the Church and even among the kings and emperors the popes installed who realized the evil in the old pagan practices and from time to time forbade them. Roman Emperor Charlemagne decreed: "With respect to trees, stones, and fountains, where certain foolish people light torches or practice other superstitions, we earnestly ordain that that most evil custom detestable to God, wherever it be found, should be removed and destroyed."[29]

At the same time, however, similar pagan practices were being "Christianized" and absorbed into the Church, where they remain part of Catholicism and Eastern Orthodoxy to this day. The priesthood and ceremonies of Israel commanded by God in Old Testament times are often cited as justification for the sacramentalism within professing Christianity. The New Testament, however, makes it clear that the redemption we have in Christ made the Old Testament priesthood and sacrificial system obsolete.

An important distinction must be made between the rituals of pagan religions and Roman Catholicism and Eastern Orthodoxy (which presume to obtain favor from God through sacraments), and the specific ceremonies of the Jewish priesthood. The latter were symbolic of the redemption that would be effected through Christ. All of the Old Testament sacrifices looked forward to the Lamb of God, the true sacrifice, God Himself come to earth as a man, to give His life in payment of the penalty for our sins:

> Which [the tabernacle/temple] was a figure for the time then present, in which were offered both gifts and sacrifices that could not make him that did the service perfect as pertaining to the conscience; which stood only in meats and drinks, and diverse washings, and carnal ordinances, imposed on them until the time of reformation.
>
> But Christ being come an high priest of good things to come, by a greater and more perfect tabernacle, not made with hands. . . .
>
> Neither by the blood of goats and calves, but by his own blood he entered in once into the holy place, having obtained eternal redemption for us (Hebrews 9:9-12).

The entire Bible testifies that God is neither bound by, nor does He respond according to, any alleged "spiritual laws."

There is no automatic response that can be gotten from Him through certain rituals.

The Present Trend

The pagan beliefs which oppose God's plan of redemption now permeate Western society, undermining the strong influence which the Bible once had. And it is that biblical influence to which much of the credit for the West's scientific, technological, and economic advancement must be given. The resultant prosperity stands in marked contrast to the abject poverty of the Third World, where paganism has reigned, and Communist countries, where materialistic atheism has been the religion.

Technological benefits, however, affect only this life. The question of what lies beyond this brief sojourn on earth has haunted mankind since the dawn of history. This is where *religion* enters in: to offer something beyond death—the happy hunting ground of the American Indian, the celestial harem of the Moslem filled with beautiful maidens . . . a land to which spirits go, but a land of shadow and fear. Hope of life after death is vain, however, without a resurrection.

Not Buddha, not Confucius, not Mohammed, nor any other religious leader rose from the dead. Christ alone, after giving His life to save sinners, came back from the grave. The apostles gave their lives to bring this good news of redemption, "the gospel of the grace of God" (Acts 20:24), to the lost. Martyrs by the millions have died to keep that message pure. Today that truth is mocked—and in the name of Christ! In a fine display of *mea culpa,* the United Church of Canada confessed to the native American Indians, "Our Christian image of God is twisted and blurred. We were closed to the beauty of your spirituality. Please forgive us."

Representatives of the Roman Catholic, Lutheran, Episcopalian, American Baptist, United Church of Christ, United Methodist, and Presbyterian churches have apologized to American Indians for giving them the gospel:

> Dear Brothers and Sisters: This is a formal apology . . . for the destruction of traditional Native American spiritual practices. We ask for your forgiveness and blessings. The spiritual power of your religion could have been a great gift to us.[30]

In the same spirit, the World Christian Gathering on Indigenous Peoples met in Rotorua, New Zealand, in mid-November, 1996. Richard Twiss, representing the Lakota nation from the United States, said that his people's way of life and culture (religion) "were gifts of God." Twiss is "a consultant on racial reconcilation for Promise Keepers,"[31] the fast-growing Christian men's movement. The Gathering embraced indigenous religions and called for incorporation of some of their rituals into the worship in Christian churches. Elijah Harper, a Canadian MP representing the Cree nation, declared that "the spiritual awakening of the world would come from indigenous peoples all over the globe."[32]

Try to imagine Christ apologizing for dying for the sins of the world and being the only Savior, or the apostle Paul apologizing to Jewish, Greek, and Roman converts for winning them to Christ! The stakes are too high—the eternal destiny of souls—to compromise truth. Unfortunately, compromise, as we shall see, is coming from the highest levels of Christian leadership.

Everyone is free to accept or to reject Christ. But it is dishonest to call oneself a Christian while misrepresenting what Christ taught and accomplished. By the same token, native and nature religions must be honestly evaluated for what they truly are, including the beliefs behind them and the results they produce.

A medicine man . . . must have the power to communicate with the spirits and be able to speak the shaman's secret language—Hambloglaka. . . . [A] ceremonial rattle and drum . . . are pleasing to the spirits and invoke their help.

—Archie Fire Lame Deer, Lakota Medicine Man[1]

Each shaman generally has at least one guardian spirit in his service. . . . The guardian spirit . . . is the fundamental source of power for the shaman's functioning. . . . The shaman frequently sees and consults with his guardian spirit, travels with it on the shamanic journey, has it help him and uses it to help others. . . .

In addition to the guardian spirit, a powerful shaman normally has a number of spirit helpers. . . . In some cultures, shamans take mind-altering substances. . . . Some degree of alteration of consciousness is necessary to shamanic practice.

—Anthropologist/shaman Michael Harner[2]

Whatever the method of channeling, it is the content [of the message given] that is most important, and here there is remarkable agreement, even unanimity, among the various channeled entities.

—Australia's *New Age News*[3]

The feeling one gets when a good medium is in trance and talking as though she were the spirit of someone biologically dead is frequently very convincing. It can feel so real that it curls your hair.

—Lawrence LeShan, past president of the Association for Humanistic Psychology (AHP)[4]

Communication with creatures and spirits . . . is effected in the shamanic seance; the sacred medium in trance is possessed by gods or spirits who use him or her as a means of divine transmissions.

—Joan Halifax, New Age anthropologist[5]

By the favor of the Gods, I have since my childhood been attended by a semi-divine being whose voice from time to time dissuades me from some undertaking. . . .

—Socrates, quoted by Plato[6]

There is a deep need in the world just now for guidance—almost any sort of spiritual guidance.

—C.G. Jung[7]

9

* * *

Spirit Communication
and Possession

The attempt to communicate with spirits of the dead is
absolutely forbidden by God (Leviticus 19:31; 20:6,27;
Deuteronomy 18:11). Nevertheless, it has been practiced in all
cultures since the beginning of time. Of course, there was also
the belief that the gods and other guiding spirits could be
contacted for their help as well.

In the Western world spiritualism attracted many prominent
people, such as abolitionist orator William Lloyd Garrison, writers James Fenimore Cooper and William Cullen Bryant, and
journalist-publisher Horace Greeley. Queen Victoria routinely
consulted mediums. Thomas Edison spent years trying to devise
an electronic means of communication with departed spirits. The
Ouija board was developed specifically to communicate with the
spirits of those who had died in World War I.

Seances and Mediums

Seances, in which contact was made with alleged discarnates,
were held in the White House while Abraham Lincoln, a
professing Christian, was President. Powerful manifestations of
poltergeist activity, including the levitation of a grand piano,
were claimed to have been witnessed by Lincoln and Cabinet
members during these seances. MacKenzie King, prime minister of Canada, secretly engaged in necromancy and believed he
was in touch with his dead mother. Unlike King, the famous
W.E. Gladstone and the first Earl of Balfour, two of England's
prime ministers, were very open about their spiritualist beliefs
and frequent attendance at seances. It was through attending

spirit seances with his wife, Helen, that Carl Rogers became convinced of the reality of the spirit world.

Many professed mediums are undoubtedly frauds, as is the case with astrologers, palm-readers, psychics, and fortune-tellers. The existence of organized, mediumistic fraud has been documented in *The Psychic Mafia.* Ex-spiritualist M. Lamar Keene confessed that for 13 years he was part of a nationwide network of 2000 phony mediums who traded information about clients and conspired to cheat countless people out of millions of dollars. He claimed that massive card files on "believers" were kept at Camp Chesterfield, Indiana—known as "the hub of world Spiritualism"—for the use of mediums "on the inside."

There is, however, solid evidence that communication with spirit entities does take place. Ruth Montgomery was one of the most highly honored women journalists of her day when she was assigned by an editor to investigate the strange phenomenon of communication with alleged spirits of the dead. Surprisingly, she found herself confronted with more than enough evidence to overcome her seasoned journalistic skepticism. Eventually "spirit entities" began writing books through Montgomery, and she became known as "the Herald of the New Age."[8]

California's Episcopalian Bishop James Pike, a former lawyer, rejected most of what the Bible said. After the suicide of his son, Pike was convinced that he had made contact with his son's discarnate spirit through a medium in London, England: Enna Twigg. Pike's skepticism was overcome when the spirit speaking through Twigg mentioned numerous details of private life that only he and his son knew.

"Proof," But of What?

A most unusual case involved the well-known psychologist William James and Columbia University professor of logic James Hyslop. The latter was a psychic investigator and friend of Carl Jung. Hyslop and Jung had together concluded that "spirits" from a nonphysical dimension of reality were communicating. Hyslop and James agreed that whoever died first would try to make contact with the survivor. James died in 1910. Hyslop lived another ten years.

Some time after James' death, Hyslop received a letter from a husband and wife (whom he had never heard of) in Ireland (a country he had never visited). They had been playing with a Ouija-board-like device and were bombarded by messages from the discarnate spirit of someone named William James telling them to contact a Professor James Hyslop, of whom they had never heard. The message they delivered was "Remember the red pajamas?" It was an apparent reference to a trip Hyslop and James had taken together in which, upon arriving in Paris, their luggage was missing. They shopped for a few necessities. The pajamas Hyslop bought were bright red and James had teased him about them at the time.[9]

While it would seem that only the surviving spirit of William James could have sent such a message, there is another possible explanation: A demon who knew of the red pajamas incident could very well have sent that message in order to encourage faith in the satanic lie that death is only an illusion. There are many other remarkable cases like this one.

Contact with the Dead—Or with Demons?

Fordham University theologian John Heaney summarizes in his book a number of convincing cases involving alleged communication from the dead through famous mediums. The cases that cannot be explained away after lengthy scientific investigation are accounted for by something called "Super-ESP." That amazing talent would supposedly enable one to pick up any information from anywhere and anyone at any time.

As a Catholic, Heaney of course believes in communication through prayer with the "saints" and that the "saints" (no one is made a "saint" by the Roman Catholic Church until long after death) sometimes appear on earth to assist the living. Heaney does his best to find an ordinary explanation but cannot rule out the involvement of spirit beings.[10] He concludes that "apart from genuine contact with the dead, there is no other rival theory [than "Super-ESP"] to explain the data."[11]

In fact, contact with the dead would hardly explain anything—certainly not the cases (and there are many) where accurate information is given by the alleged discarnate which was beyond that person's intellectual capacity to comprehend before his or her death. Yet such seeming omniscience is manifested in some cases. For the alleged spirit of Aunt Jane, who had been a simple soul, to speak intelligently of quantum mechanics, for example, would hardly prove that it was Aunt Jane speaking from beyond the grave, but rather that it was not! Nor is it reasonable that the spirits of the dead should have *unlimited* knowledge after death.

The apparent communication from an alleged discarnate is taken as evidence to support the serpent's lie that death is nothing to fear. Having "proved" its identity, the alleged discarnate invariably proceeds to present persuasively the rest of the lies the serpent told Eve in the Garden.

Once Bishop Pike was convinced he was indeed speaking with the spirit of his dead son Jim, that entity proceeded to debunk Christianity. The spirit proceeded to say, "Don't you ever believe that God can be personalized...he is the central Force." It went on to explain that Jesus was *not* the Savior, but only one of many enlightened beings existing on a higher plane. Likewise, the entity that dictated *A Course in Miracles* through Helen Schucman said: "The name of Jesus Christ as such is but a symbol ... [of] love that is not of this world ... a symbol that is safely used as a replacement for the many names of all the gods to which you pray.... This course has come from him."[12]

Why the Biblical Prohibition?

To prevent such deception being embraced, the Bible forbids any attempt to contact discarnate spirits. Not because such contact is possible, but because it is impossible—and demons take advantage of this human desire as they impersonate the dead in order to promote their lies. The case of Samuel's spirit coming back (1 Samuel 28:7-20) would seem to be an exception allowed by God in order to pronounce final judgment upon King Saul for his disobedience. (The shock expressed by the witch of Endor and her sudden identification of Saul would seem to argue that it was indeed Samuel who appeared.)

Heaney, though a Catholic theologian, contradicts the Bible by referring to "a deceased person who remains 'earthbound'

... in a confused or bewildered or malicious state...."[13] On the contrary, no deceased persons are "earthbound," hanging around to haunt or help the living. Those who die as Christians are instantly "absent from the body and ... present with the Lord" in heaven (2 Corinthians 5:8). As for those who have rejected the gospel, their fate is given to us by Christ through the "rich man": "In hell he lifted up his eyes, being in torments" (Luke 16:23).

Heaney frankly admits that both the Bible and his Church condemn consulting the dead (except the alleged "saints," of course). Nevertheless, he tries to justify the practice by saying that "the biblical prohibitions apparently were directed against aims and motives which are quite different from the aims and motives of modern researchers."[14] He quotes Protestant clergyman Donald Bretherton of London University, who agrees:

> "Seeking after the dead" in ancient times was designed to show Yahweh as either incompetent or untrustworthy, whereas modern mediumship seeks to show the reality of the claim that "underneath are the everlasting arms."[15]

In fact, it is a delusion of liberal theology to imagine that the messages that come through mediums support belief in the God of the Bible. Instead, they undermine such faith by speaking of God as a "Force" and of Jesus Christ as an ascended Master who exists on a higher plane than most of the discarnate souls. *All* channeled material parrots the lies of the serpent in the Garden of Eden. Indeed, it is through this occult invasion of demonic beings impersonating the dead that a host of error has entered the world and even polluted the church.

Communication with the dead implies that souls and spirits are free to flit about on the astral plane and have become the communicators of an "ancient wisdom" to mankind. One cannot believe in communication with the dead and at the same time believe God's Word: ". . . it is appointed unto men once to die, and after this the judgment" (Hebrews 9:27).

Was the Ancient "Muse" a Spirit?

In Greek mythology the arts were under the direction of the nine daughters of Zeus by Mnemosyne. These nymphs, or lower deities, also known as muses, inspired writers and artists. The Muse Euterpe was the inspirer of lyric poetry; the Muse Terpsichore inspired music and dancing. Johannes Brahms felt that at times when composing he was "in tune with the Infinite." Although he believed that his inspiration came from God, the fact that he admitted having to be "in a semitrance condition ... [with] the conscious mind ... in temporary abeyance,"[16] as with a spirit medium, betrays another source. God does not inspire trance mediums. Tchaikovsky confessed that under similar inspiration he "behaved like a madman."[17]

Richard Strauss was sure that at least some of the music he wrote was "dictated" to him by "Omnipotent Entities" not of this earth.[18] The great opera *Madame Butterfly*, Giacomo Puccini was convinced, was dictated to him "by God."[19] Gustav Mahler claimed that he was compelled by other powers to compose · what he hadn't chosen to write. George Gershwin testified that *Rhapsody in Blue* came to him suddenly, that he heard and saw as though on paper "the complete construction of the *Rhapsody*, from beginning to end." Of his hit song "The Blizzard," country-western composer Harlan Howard said his pencil just kept on writing, surprising him as it went, and he wondered, "Did some great songwriter in the sky use me as a medium?"[20] Operetta composer Rudolf Friml said:

> I sit down at the piano, and I put my hands on the piano. And I let the spirit guide me! No, I never do the music. I never compose it; oh no, no!
>
> I am a tool. I am nothing. I am being used. It comes from someone, a spirit perhaps, using me.[21]

We can only conclude that, just as they all believed, some entity or entities not of this world have guided these composers. But who are these entities? And what about Benny Hinn, Kenneth Copeland and other charismatic leaders who claim that the Holy Spirit inspires them to speak forth some prophecy that proves to be false? And what of the claims that Christ has even appeared to some of them?

Would Jesus really appear to Yonggi Cho in a red fireman's uniform, or to Oral Roberts in a form 900 feet tall, as these men claim? And could the countless apparitions around the world really be the Mary who gave birth to Jesus, when they speak forth so many lies and continually contradict Scripture? Who or what are these beings? What is their purpose? The question of the identity and purpose of these entities requires a careful answer.

Identifying the Modern "Muse"

Music has had a key role in the occult as far back as history records. The pulse-beat of drums and rattles is vital in voodoo and most shamanism, to which rock music is closely related. "Christian rock groups" mimic the beat that shamans have long used to call up demons. Ray Manzarek, keyboard player for the rock group *The Doors*, explains the relationship between shamanism and modern rock:

> When the Siberian shaman gets ready to go into his trance, all the villagers get together . . . and play whatever instruments they have to send him off [into trance and possession]. . . .
>
> It was the same way with The Doors when we played in concert. . . . I think that our drug experience let us get into it . . . [the trance state] quicker. . . .
>
> It was like Jim [Morrison] was an electric shaman and we were the electric shaman's band, pounding away behind him . . . pounding and pounding, and little by little it would take him over. . . .
>
> Sometimes he was just incredible. Just amazing. And the audience felt it, too![22]

Many rock stars have been involved in the occult and admit to a mysterious source of inspiration. John Lennon told of mystical experiences as a young teenager: "I used to literally trance out into alpha . . . seeing these hallucinatory images of my face changing, becoming cosmic and complete."[23] Of his songwriting Lennon said, "It's like being possessed: like a psychic or a medium."[24] Much credit for fomenting rebellion and turning millions of youth against God and the Bible belongs to the many rock stars beginning with Elvis Presley. The Beatles' own press agent, Derek Taylor, confessed:

> They're completely anti-Christ. I mean, I am anti-Christ as well, but they're so anti-Christ they shock me. . . .[25]

According to Keith Richards of the Rolling Stones, "The Stones' songs came spontaneously like an inspiration at a seance. The tunes arrived 'en masse' as if the Stones as songwriters were only a willing and open medium."[26] Of the Beatles Yoko Ono has said, "They were like mediums. They weren't conscious of all they were saying, but it was coming through them."[27] Of the inspiration process Marc Storace, vocalist with the heavy-metal band Krokus, told *Circus* magazine:

> You can't describe it except to say it's like a mysterious energy that comes from the metaphysical plane and into my body. It's almost like being a medium. . . .[28]

"Little Richard" said, "I was directed and commanded by another power. The power of darkness . . . that a lot of people don't believe exists. The power of the Devil. Satan."[29] Jim Morrison called the spirits that at times possessed him "The Lords," and wrote a book of poetry about them.[30] Folk rock artist Joni Mitchell's creativity came from her spirit guide, "Art." Nothing could detain her when he "called."[31]

Contemporary musicians offer the same consistent testimony regarding inspiration by otherworldly entities that we find among the most famous composers from the past. Today's musicians, however, admit that much of their inspiration comes from an *evil* source. Why should we doubt their testimony? David Lee Roth, who wrote "Running with the Devil" and called himself "toastmaster for the *immoral majority*," admitted that the goal in the world of rock was to conjure up *evil* spirits and surrender to them:

> I'm gonna abandon my spirit to them, which is actually what I attempt to do. You work yourself into that state and you fall in supplication of the demon gods. . . .[32]

Superstar Jimi Hendrix was not so eager to be possessed but seemed rather to have been a victim. Called "rock's greatest guitarist" and known as the *Voodoo Chile of the Aquarian Age*, Hendrix "believed he was possessed by some spirit," according to Alan Douglas. His former girlfriend, Fayne Pridgon, has said:

He used to always talk about some devil or something was in him, you know, and he didn't have any control over it, he didn't know what made him act the way he acted . . . and songs . . . just came out of him. . . .

He was so tormented and just torn apart . . . and he used to talk about . . . having . . . somebody . . . drive this demon out of him.[33]

Steven Halpern, one of the best-known New Age composers, testifies, "I started recording what I received in trance or altered states. . . . I ended up being guided."[34]

This type of spirit guidance is widespread. In Chapter 1 we referred to the nuclear scientist who was taught advanced concepts by spirit beings. We noted that Chester Carlson, inventor of the Xerox photocopying process, received guidance for his invention from the spirit world.[35] Medical scientist Andrija Puharich, holder of more than 50 patents, gave his opinion about these strange inspirations:

I am personally convinced that superior beings from other spaces and other times have initiated a renewed dialogue with humanity. . . .

While I do not doubt [their existence] . . . I do not know . . . what their goals are with respect to humankind.[36]

Enter the Ouija Board

A Ouija board demonstrates the ease with which anyone can be caught up in the world of the occult. Scientific tests with a Ouija board have proved beyond dispute that an intelligence independent of the persons using the board is guiding the planchette. Sir William Barrett conducted experiments in which the operators were blindfolded and the alphabet around the board was scrambled without their knowledge. In addition, an opaque screen was held between the sitters and the Ouija to make doubly sure that those using the board could not see the letters. Under these rigorously controlled conditions the planchette moved faster than ever. In his report to the American Society for Psychical Research, Barrett said:

For we have here, in addition to the blindfolding of the sitters, the amazing swiftness, precision and accuracy of the movements of the indicator spelling out long and intelligent messages . . . without halting or error . . . messages often contrary to and beyond the knowledge of the sitters. . . .

Reviewing the results as a whole, I am convinced of their supernormal character, and that we have here an exhibition of some intelligent discarnate agency . . . guiding [the sitters'] muscular movements.[37]

It was through a Ouija board that Carl Rogers (at the time a complete skeptic) became convinced he had contacted the spirit of his dead wife, Helen, and received a consoling message from her.[38] Many channelers first made contact with their spirit guides through a Ouija board. The Ouija has been implicated by investigators in numerous cases of apparent demon possession. Nevertheless, it overtook Monopoly in 1967 to become America's most popular parlor game.

The Ouija board first put Pearl Curran, a St. Louis housewife, in contact with a spirit entity which called itself Patience Worth. Patience claimed to have lived in Dorsetshire, England, in the seventeenth century. During a 20-year period Patience dictated through eighth-grade-educated Pearl Curran "more than one-and-a-half million words in poems and historical novels." One literary piece of 70,000 words was analyzed by Professor C.H.S. Schiller of London University, who found it to contain "not a single word [which] originated after 1600." He stated:

When we consider that the authorized version of the Bible has only 70% Anglo Saxon, and it is necesary to go back to Lyomen in 1205 to equal Patience's percentage . . . we realize we are facing a philological miracle.[39]

Miracle? That hardly sounds scientific. How much more rational to admit that Curran was indeed possessed by a spirit that had perfect knowledge of pre-1600 English and of events in early England. We are faced with a phemonenon which cannot be explained away and demonstrates the reality of occultism.

According to Dr. Raymond Moody, who has spent many years investigating alleged encounters of the living with the presumed spirits of deceased loved ones, "Science can't distinguish . . .

[whether] this is purely a phenomenon of consciousness or some entity beyond one's consciousness."[40] It is beyond the capacity of science to deal with spirits. Nor do we need any help from science to face the evidence. New York City clinician Armand DiMele, though skeptical of most channelers, acknowledges that in some cases accurate information has come through a medium that could not be known by any normal means:

> I have spoken to "spirit voices" who have ... told me things about my childhood. Specifics, like things that hung in the house [that he hadn't thought of for years so the medium wasn't "reading his mind"]. There's some undeniable evidence that something happens, something we don't understand and can't measure.[41]

They Are "Teaching Us Something"

One of the most powerful evidences we have of the reality of these spirit entities and of their continued contact with mankind is found in the consistency of the messages which they provide through those who claim to be in touch with them. The *same message* comes independently through persons widely scattered around the world and who have never been in contact with one another. That fact has been noted by all of the investigators.

Parapsychologist D. Scott Rogo defines channeling as "bringing through some sort of intelligence, the nature undefined, whose purpose is to promote spiritual teachings and philosophical discussion."[42] Terence McKenna, who has replaced Timothy Leary as America's drug guru, notes that one of the experiences common to psychedelic trips is contact with spirit beings who have a *message:* "Unless I'm completely crazy, they're trying to teach us something." Their message is amazingly consistent and, as Rogo says, involves *spiritual* teachings.

Quoted at the beginning of this chapter, Australia's *New Age News* notes the "remarkable agreement, even unanimity, among the various channeled entities." That fact is emphasized repeatedly by Jon Klimo in his definitive book on this subject. The major theme, as Klimo points out, is our alleged oneness with God, our ignorance of this oneness, the necessity to realize this oneness through "enlightenment," and our return to earth through reincarnation many times in this long evolutionary process of attaining our true or higher self.[43] It is the religious philosophy with which the serpent "enlightened" Eve.[44]

It was shattering for atheist Helen Shucman when she began hearing a voice saying, "This is a course in miracles; take it down!" As well as teaching medical psychology at Columbia University, Shucman was Assistant Head of the Psychology Department at Presbyterian Hospital in New York. Far from diagnosing her as suffering from delusion, her equally atheistic colleagues told her to follow the instructions. When the dictation finally ended, the "Course" ran to an astonishing 1100 pages and has been acclaimed for its brilliant insights by psychologists and theologians alike.

The voice dictating *A Course in Miracles* claimed to be Jesus Christ Himself, intent upon correcting errors in the Bible that have offended unbelievers because of their "narrow-mindedness." The *Course* explains that "forgiveness" is simply recognizing that sin does not exist and therefore there is nothing to forgive. The *Course* is popular with those who want to call themselves Christians while rejecting sound biblical doctrine. It has been taught at Robert Schuller's Crystal Cathedral.

The dictating "Jesus" contradicted nearly everything the Bible says about Him. That fact is admitted by Kenneth Wapnick, head of the foundation that publishes the *Course*.[45] Not surprisingly, what this "Jesus" said was in perfect agreement with the messages being communicated by a wide variety of entities through thousands of "channels" around the world. Yet Shucman was ignorant of the phenomenon of "channeling" until it suddenly happened to her.

When insurance supervisor Jach Pursel tried Eastern meditation at the prompting of his wife, he thought he kept falling asleep. She found herself, however, talking with the strangely accented "Lazaris" when Jach was in this state. "Lazaris'" themes echo *A Course in Miracles*, "Seth" (recorded in numerous books over a 24-year period through Jane Roberts), "Ramtha," and many other channeled entities: All is One and we are reincarnating, evolving, spiritual, immortal beings, all part of God but unaware of that great fact and on a journey of enlightenment to realize who we really are.[46]

The "higher Self" of Meredith Lady Young, a New Hampshire publisher, channeled through her *Agartha: A Journey to the Stars*. Once again the message was positive thinking, evolutionary advancement to perfection, the oneness of all, that "God" is an energy, and that man is God: "We [channeling spirits] are multidimensional beings from another more spiritually evolved plane. Our aim is one of positive reinforcement to further man's development. . . . The human race must recognize its deeply buried bond with Universal Energy or no significant spiritual growth is possible."[47]

A Monotonous Echo from Eden

When genuine contact is made with the spirit realm, the communications that come through are inevitably anti-Christian. The "God" of the channeled materials contradicts God's Word and even holds God up to ridicule. One of the boldest, latest, and most popular examples is found in *Conversations with God: An Uncommon Dialogue*, which Neale Donald Walsch claims just "happened" to him and is "God's latest word on things."[48] In an obvious put-down of Jesus, this "God" says:

> There was once . . . a new soul . . . anxious for experience. "I am the light," it said. "I am the light. . . ." *Every* soul was grand . . . and every soul shone with the brilliance of My awesome light. And so the little soul in question was as a candle in the sun.[49]

The blasphemy continues with this "little soul" coming to earth to discover its true self. Like Buddha and many others, Jesus eventually "attained mastery. . . . What Jesus did . . . is the path of the Buddha, the way of Krishna, the walk of every Master who has appeared on the plane. . . . So who said Jesus was perfect?"[50] Yet we're born as gods and goddesses and there is neither sin nor judgment.[51] There are no morals; God has no opinions and makes no judgments; we are free to do whatever makes us feel good.[52] It is all very comforting to those who, like Phil Jackson, want to justify their rejection of the Christ of the Bible and replace Him with "another Jesus" (2 Corinthians 11:4) and "another gospel" (Galatians 1:6,7).

This "God" (who claims to be the author of *A Course in Miracles*)[53] also tells Walsch that Satan and demons are nonexistent: "You have created in your mythology the being you call 'devil.' You have even imagined a God at war with this being. . . . Of course, a real devil does not exist. . . ."[54] Of course "God" says we are all evolving through many lifetimes ever higher to oneness with God. Walsch has been on earth during many lifetimes and may have as many chances to do it over again and again as he wants or needs.[55] "God" says:

> This "be Who You Really Are" business . . . [is] the most challenging thing you'll ever do. . . . You may never get there. Few people do. Not in one lifetime. Not in many . . .
> You are immortal. You never do die. You simply change form. [Concerning Adam and Eve,] there were more than two. [Life] evolved over billions of years . . . the evolutionists are *right* . . . !
> Using psychic ability is nothing more than using your sixth sense . . . not trafficking with the devil . . . there is no devil. . . . Each to his own without judgment.[56]

It is the amazing unity of the channeled material and the fact that its basic message consistently reflects the four lies of the serpent in the Garden that both proves its reality and identifies its source. Enlightenment involves recognizing the illusion of our daily entranced experience and awakening to the true reality lying behind it.[57] Jean Houston declares:

> These [channeled] "entities" as we call them—are essentially *"goddings" of the depth of the psyche*. They are personae of the self that take on acceptable form so that we can have relationship and thus dialogue.[58]

Goddings of the depth of the psyche so we can *dialogue* with ourselves? Jean can't even tell us what that means! How much more reasonable to accept the evidence that demonic entities are deceiving mankind.

How Spirit Communication Works

We have already quoted Nobel-Prize-winning brain researcher Sir John Eccles that the existence of "consciousness or mind . . . is not reconcilable with the natural laws as at present understood."[59] According to Eccles' fascinating research, the mind cannot be part of the physical universe (including the brain) but is nonphysical/spiritual and uses the brain to operate the body. Eccles calls the brain "a machine that a ghost can operate." Normally one's own spirit is the "ghost" that operates the brain—but under the right circumstances another "ghost" might take over. This possibility must be taken into account in our investigation of the occult.

If our minds are independent of our bodies and could therefore survive the death of the body, then, as Robert Jastrow argues, there could be other minds out there without bodies. And if the hypnotist's mind can control a subject, another mind could do that also and perhaps interfere with the hypnotherapy process used by so many therapists today. Such "ghosts" could introduce into the patient's brain false memories or other delusions, even of having lived a previous life. The consistent theme of channeled material argues persuasively that all of it is being inspired by the same "ghosts."

Here we are confronted with a form of "possession." Of course, a more benign form of this "possession" could be the very inspiration attributed to the muse in the past and still experienced by musicians, artists, scientists, and other creative persons today. In his classic work on channeling, Jon Klimo points this out:

> The argument is that mind operates brain (and the rest of the body) at all times in a basically psychokinetic manner. . . .
>
> Yet, the argument goes, if your own mind can affect your own brain, then the similar nonphysical nature of another mind might also be able to affect your brain, giving rise to your hearing a voice, seeing a vision, or having the other mind speak or write by controlling your body the same way you normally control your own body.[60]

That these entities can "take over" has been demonstrated countless times. So has Christ's ability to deliver those possessed. A TM instructor sent to a South American country to inaugurate Transcendental Meditation there began to see "Satan" every time she looked at the picture of TM's founder, Maharishi Mahesh Yogi. Attempting suicide, she was confined to an insane asylum, where Christ rescued her.

After being initiated into yoga by Swami Rama (one of the prize subjects of biofeedback research at the Menninger Clinic), a Chicago housewife was tormented by psychic visitations from Swami and committed to a hospital psychiatric ward. There she was led to Christ and delivered.

Using the Silva Method techniques that she had been taught, a schoolteacher visualized her mentally handicapped pupils improving. She was commended for the remarkable results. Then one night her brother received a frantic call at about 2 A.M.: "My God, George! *Something's* in my apartment— something *evil*, and it's after me! Please come and help me!"

These and many similar cases can only be explained as an invasion of the person by evil entities. In each case that invasion resulted from entering an altered state of consciousness through forms of hypnosis and Eastern meditation. In spite of the testimony of countless persons who have been terrorized, driven insane, and even driven to suicide by these entities, John Lilly denies their reality. Of the evil entities which he acknowledges one meets in altered states, he declares:

> You can meet up with entities there that you feel are going to eat or absorb you. Well, this turns out to be nonsense. This is your projection . . . the evil in you. Evil is what you project.[61]

Many refuse to accept the existence of Satan and demons in spite of the evidence. Parapsychologist Loyd Auerbach writes: "To set the record a bit straighter, let me say that the only demons we, as scientists, deal with are one's own 'demons' that may be conjured up by the subconscious and the imagination."[62]

Auerbach is mistaken in calling himself and his fellow psychologists "scientists." Psychology is not a science. Furthermore, science has nothing to say about spirits. Nevertheless, his sweeping statement is believed by multitudes. With a healthy fear of evil spirits neatly debunked by psychologists, occult experimentation becomes enticing. "Demons" are merely fragments of one's own personality. All that is needed is to accept the *new understanding*.

Demonic Possession

Nevertheless, increasing numbers of psychologists and psychiatrists—former doubters such as M. Scott Peck—are now, like Freud, Jung, and James before them, admitting their belief in the existence of *evil spirits*. A former doubter, psychiatrist Ralph B.

Allison, says, "I have come to believe in the possibility of spirit possession . . . by demonic spirits from satanic realms, and that's an area I don't care to discuss or be part of. . . ."[63]

A host of psychologists and researchers could be quoted who have come to the same conclusion. In *The Unquiet Dead,* psychologist Edith Fiore tells how the failure of psychotherapy to treat, and psychological theory to explain, certain behaviors led her on a search that resulted in her belief in demonic possession. In Maya Deren's *Divine Horsemen: Voodoo Gods of Haiti,* the stark terror of possession is described:

> I have left possession until the end, for it is the center toward which all the roads of Vodoun converge. . . .
>
> Never have I seen the face of such anguish, ordeal and blind terror as at the moment when the loa [spirit] comes.[64]

Wade Davis is a young scientist with degrees from Harvard University in anthropology and biology and a Ph.D. in ethnobotany. He has explored not only the physical world but the "spirit world" of a number of indigenous religions. He has ventured where few white men have ever gone—into the inner sanctum of the secret societies of the Haitian vodoun masters who hold the power of life and death over that tortured island.[65] As an eyewitness, Davis writes:

> For the nonbeliever, there is something profoundly disturbing about spirit possession. Its power is raw, immediate and undeniably real, devastating. . . . The psychologists who have attempted to understand possession from a scientific perspective . . . come up with some bewildering conclusions. . . .
>
> These wordy explanations ring most hollow when they are applied to certain irrefutable physical attributes of the possessed . . . [such as] the ability of the believer to place with impunity his or her hands into boiling water. . . .[66]
>
> [I watched] a woman in an apparent state of trance carry a burning coal in her mouth for three minutes. . . . She did it every night on schedule. In other societies believers affirm their faith . . . by walking across beds of coals, the temperature of which has been measured at 650 degrees Fahrenheit. . . .
>
> Western scientists have gone to almost absurd lengths to explain such feats . . . citing the effect that makes drops of water dance on a skillet. . . . To my mind, it begs the question entirely. After all, a water droplet [bouncing] on a skillet is not a foot on a

red-hot coal, nor lips wrapped about an ember. I still burn my wet tongue if I place the lit end of a cigarette on it. . . .

The woman had clearly entered some kind of spirit realm. But what impressed me the most was the ease with which she did so. I had no experience or knowledge that would allow me either to rationalize or to escape what I had seen.[67]

The Medium Who Gave Herself to Science

There is considerable data to support the belief that "possession" involves the invasion of the person by another independent entity. Eileen Garrett was so uncomfortable with being possessed by "spirit controls" who spoke through her that she gave herself to every possible scientific test in order to prove to herself that it was all a figment of her imagination. But the tests, in fact, confirmed her worst fears: that she was indeed possessed by entities she could not escape.

One series of rigorous medical tests was conducted in New York by Dr. Cornelium H. Traeger, a specialist in arthritis and heart disease. When he began the tests, Dr. Traeger held firmly to the common opinion of psychologists that the entities allegedly speaking through Garrett were simply splits of her psyche and not separate entities with their own minds. While Garrett was possessed by different "control" spirits, Traeger tested her "blood count, bleeding time, clotting time, respiration, pulse, heart pressure and cardiac reaction by an electrical cardiograph, as well as by the injection of various drugs."[68] According to an associate, Dr. Elmer Lindsay:

> The results were . . . so surprising that Dr. Traeger hesitated to show them to his colleagues. No human heart could show records so diametrically opposed and divergent. . . .
>
> When the bleeding time . . . blood counts [etc.] were checked the results suggested an actual change in the physical composition of the medium's blood when she was [controlled by different entities]. . . .[69]

Other elaborate tests were administered to Mrs. Garrett and her "controls" by Hereward Carrington, director of the American Psychical Institute. Again the results were startling. When Carrington tested Mrs. Garrett and the various entities speaking through her with a lie detector, the polygraph confirmed that each entity differed fundamentally from the medium and from each other. Referring to cases where "possession" is suspected, SRI senior scientist Willis Harman points out:

> Physiological and biochemical changes . . . can include brain-wave patterns, chemical composition of bodily fluids, immune status, allergies, skin electrical responses, and others [which differ depending upon which "personality" is in control]. . . .
>
> This development leaves little doubt that in some important sense the alternate personality "really exists" as surely as does the usual personality.[70]

Not surprisingly, the entities controlling Eileen Garrett presented the same lies right out of the serpent's mouth. They claimed to be gods who represented "the God principle which is within us all." Their message agreed with that coming through all the other channels: that there is no death and no judgment—only acceptance as the departed ones move on from this life to another level of existence and continue to learn their lessons and advance ever higher.

The evidence is overwhelming that intelligent entities exist independent of mankind and that they are able, when given entrance, to use the human body to their own ends. The consistent message they present betrays their true identity and purpose.

Our trip has always existed. . . . All through the dark ages there were the Sufis, the Kabbalists, the Brotherhoods and Sisterhoods and the witchcraft groups and the Knights of Malta, and the Masonic orders. . . .

—Drug guru Timothy Leary in a speech at the 22nd Annual Convention of the Association for Humanistic Psychology

In time, I suspect we will come to discover that modern psychopharmacology has become, like Freud in his day, a whole climate of opinion under which we conduct our different lives.

—Peter Kramer in his bestselling *Listening to Prozac*

The brain is made up of several hundred billion neurons and trillions of synapses. Each individual human brain is more complex than the entire physical universe with all its stars and planets, and . . . forces . . . at work in it.

Unlike the physical universe, the biochemical activities that run the brain remain almost wholly shrouded in mystery. We have no idea, for example, how the brain makes a thought or an emotion. . . .

[Psycho-pharmacology] does not reflect an . . . understanding about how the brain and mind function. At the root lies a dangerous assumption that it is safe and effective to tamper with the most complex organ in the universe!

Curiously, in light of so much psychiatric concern about the dangers of biochemical imbalances, all known psychiatric drugs produce widespread chemical imbalances in the brain, usually involving multiple systems of nerves. Prozac is no exception. . . . It seems foolhardy to imagine that blocking one of the brain's biochemical functions would somehow improve the brain and mind.

—Peter R. Breggin, M.D.[1]

I will praise thee, for I am fearfully and wonderfully made; marvelous are thy works, and that my soul knoweth right well.

Search me, O God, and know my heart; try me, and know my thoughts, and see if there be any wicked way in me, and lead me in the way everlasting.

—Psalm 139:14,23,24

One door opens to the world of the spirit: imagination. . . . To follow Christ we must create in our minds God's unseen world, or never confront it at all. Thus we create in our minds the Christ. . . .

—Calvin Miller, author of many Christian books[2]

10

* * *

Drugs, Imagination, and the Occult

The religious use of mind-altering drugs has a long history going back to the Oracle at Delphi and beyond. The coca leaf was used by the Incas in their religious rituals just as the sacred mushroom has been used by other indigenous peoples in theirs. These substances ushered the users into another dimension inhabited by the "spirits" that empowered and guided them. Because it has been traditionally "sacred" to them, native American Indians have had the right (under the American Indian Religious Freedom Act) to take peyote for religious purposes—unless they were on active duty with the armed forces. That restriction has now been removed provided certain guidelines are followed.[3]

By the mid-1800s, the coca leaf had become popular in Europe for its alleged medicinal qualities. In 1883 cocaine was advertised by Parke-Davis in the United States as a remedy for alcoholism and morphine addiction. Sigmund Freud used it to treat his recurring depression and prescribed it for some of his patients. Freud's biographer, Ernest Jones, quoted Freud as saying that cocaine produced a feeling of "exhilaration and lasting euphoria, which in no way differs from the normal euphoria of the healthy person." He denied it was addictive and seemingly couldn't praise it enough. It was not until 1914 that cocaine was identified as a "narcotic" and was subjected to the same controls as morphine and heroin.

A Major Beachhead for the Occult Invasion

In the 1960s, Timothy Leary, the Pied Piper of Harvard, led mesmerized youth into *spiritual* experiences that materialistic science had told them did not exist. Leary's LSD (and other psychedelics) turned out to be the launching pad for *mind trips* beyond the physical universe of time, space, and matter to a strange dimension where intoxicating nectars were abundant and exotic adventures the norm. For millions it was a "mind-blowing" experience that forever changed their lives.

Rock musicians played a key role in leading two generations of youth into drugs. Often the music was written under the influence of psychedelics and the concerts became one huge drug party. Leary called the Beatles "the four evangelists." Listening to the Beatles' album *Sergeant Pepper's Lonely Hearts Club Band,* Leary said, "The Beatles have taken my place. That latest album—a complete celebration of LSD."[4]

The drug movement of the '50s, '60s, and '70s established a major beachhead for the occult invasion of Western civilization. Alan Morrison writes:

> At that time, a new counter-culture was formed which opened up the youth of that period to a massive infestation of demonic influence and extreme sinful behavior. Central to this was the use of hallucinogenic and mind-altering drugs such as Marijuana, Cannabis resin, Lysergic Acid Dithylamide (LSD), di-Methyl Tryptamine (DMT), Mescaline, Peyote and other fungal concoctions.[5]

Millions subsequently discovered that they could get as "high" or even "higher" through various techniques of Eastern mysticism (TM and other forms of yoga, visualization and hypnosis). Thus was born something called "New Age." Hindu and Buddhist occultism penetrated every area of Western society, from psychology and medicine to education and business. Numerous yogis and gurus, such as Vivekananda, Yogananda, Maharaj Ji, Maharishi Mahesh Yogi, Baba Muktananda, and others quickly realized that drugs had opened the Western mind to their message, and they invaded our shores.

Sorcerers and sorceries are condemned in the Old Testament (Exodus 7; Isaiah 47; Jeremiah 27; Malachi 3). In the New Testament sorcery and sorcerers are again denounced

(Acts 13:6,8; Revelation 9:21; 18:23; 21:8; 22:15). Today's word for sorcerer is shaman; and the Greek word translated sorcery in the New Testament is *pharmakeia*. The shaman must enter an altered state of consciousness to obtain his spirit guide and effect his sorcery, and often the means of doing so is through mind-altering drugs.

The popular use of psychedelics and the accompanying involvement in Eastern religions is in the process of transforming Western society. The effect upon two generations was summarized in the following story in the *Los Angeles Times:*

> Joyce [Lyke], the granddaughter of a Southern Baptist preacher, is studying under a Sufi mystic in Berkeley. Her husband [Brian], a former Presbyterian minister, laughingly calls himself an evangelical Taoist. Brian stops laughing when asked what religion he is passing on to his children. . . .
>
> Said Brian, "I don't know about the kids. I'm not indoctrinating them in anything, really. We don't go to church. . . ."
>
> At Carmel High School, where Karina [Lyke] goes to school, some of her friends are starting to experiment with LSD and purportedly hallucinogenic psilocybin mushrooms. Her parents see psychedelic drugs as a key to their own spiritual awakening and cannot see themselves advising their daughter to "just say no."[6]

Prescription Drugs

Medical science has increased the average lifespan remarkably, for which we are all grateful. It cannot, however, escape responsibility for the discovery, proliferation, and oversubscription of drugs. We are an evil and unrepentant society, and (just as the Bible foretells for the last days) a large part of that evil is due to drugs: "Neither repented they of their murders [including abortions?], nor of their sorceries . . ."(Revelation 9:21).

Even young children are being caught in the drug web. If Johnny misbehaves, mother increases his Ritalin dose; and to keep herself on an even keel, she takes Prozac. A large percentage of Americans no longer know how to stand up to adversity and thereby develop strength of character. Instead of facing their problems and working through to a solution, they insist upon a wonder drug to assist them with every difficulty.

The United States Department of Justice Drug Enforcement Agency (DEA) classifies Ritalin in "Schedule II," along with cocaine and other addictive drugs such as PCP. The Indiana Prevention Resource Center warns that "snorting or injecting Ritalin" for its "cocaine-like stimulant effects . . . is just the latest trend . . . that recalls the 'Speed Freak' era of the late 1960s."[7] In fact, "all branches of the armed forces reject potential enlistees who use Ritalin or similar behavior-modifying medications."[8] Says Marine recruiter Master Sergeant Cruz Tores:

> Unfortunately, there's nothing we can do if the person has been using Ritalin. Its considered to be a mind-altering drug. Because of that, the [armed] services look at it as a very, very serious drug.[9]

Influential psychoanalyst Elizabeth Zetzel considers a person's endurance of anxiety and depression essential to proper emotional growth. She warns that to artificially improve mood with a pill could deny the person the very strengthening experience needed for a real solution. Christians who take the easy way out through a drug miss the lesson of endurance and faith that God wants to teach them! Psychiatrist Peter Breggin, a leading expert on psychoactive drugs, warns:

> The moral and psychological dangers posed by Prozac [and other similar drugs] are ultimately more threatening than its physical side effects. But this is not the first time that America has fallen unabashedly in love with a prescription medication. Until the danger of addiction became obvious, Valium enjoyed an escalating reputation as "mother's little helper." Housewives got through their daily chores by remaining in a drug-induced fog. . . .[10]

There are more cells in the brain than stars in the universe; and these cells make up hundreds of billions of neurons and trillions of synapses in perfect balance. Moreover, the mysterious link between the spirit of man (which was made in God's image) and his brain and body is forever beyond the grasp of science. Yet that connection is being tampered with by drugs in order to adjust man's behavior. How could there be a *chemical* solution? Yet millions take drugs such as Prozac, Effexor, Benzedrine, Dexedrine, Ritalin, Zoloft, Paxil, etc. to adjust mood and behavior.

The brain is far too complex to be precisely "adjusted" with drugs. There are more than 500 different neurotransmitters in the brain and no one knows exactly how they work or the consequences of "adjusting" them with drugs. As *Time* recently pointed out in a research article:

> So far, the tools [drugs] used to manipulate serotonin in the human brain are more like pharmacological machetes than they are like scalpels—crudely effective but capable of doing plenty of collateral damage. Says Barry Jacobs, a neuro-surgeon at Princeton University, "We just don't know enough about how the brain works."[11]

Dr. Breggin reminds us: "If depression . . . has a biological or genetic basis, it has not been demonstrated scientifically. . . . Biopsychiatric theory remains pure speculation and runs counter to a great deal of research and clinical experience, as well as common sense. . . ."[12] Breggin continues:

> The biochemical imbalance theory has replaced Freud's psychological theory as the most widely accepted explanation for emotional pain and suffering. Freud's theory in turn had replaced more religious and philosophical explanations, such as original sin, the devil, and moral degeneracy. . . . The biochemical imbalance theory is merely the latest biopsychiatric speculation, presented to the public as a scientific truth. . . .
>
> The ironic truth is this: The only known biochemical imbalances in the brains of nearly all psychiatric patients are those caused by the treatments. Those rare exceptions who have known hormonal disorders . . . are almost always treated as medical rather than psychiatric patients.[13]

Some Words of Caution

The awesome implications of tampering with the brain are not generally being faced by the medical profession or told to the public. *All* psychiatric drugs produce their effect by causing brain dysfunction. The same drugs which American psychiatrists prescribe for *treatment* were used by Soviet psychiatrists for *torture*. It is sometimes mistakenly suggested that taking drugs to change the brain's function is no different from taking insulin. There is one huge difference: Insulin operates below the neck, while psychoactive drugs affect the brain. And remember, no one knows exactly what these drugs do to the brain nor how harmful they may be even beyond the many cases of violence, including suicide and murder, which court cases claim were caused by various prescription drugs.

A word of caution: We are not advocating that anyone now taking medication should abruptly stop. Psychiatric drugs can be addictive, and to stop suddenly after taking them could have serious consequences. *Any* change in medication should only be under the supervision of a physician. We are simply pointing out that *no one really knows* how drugs work nor the full range of their effects. Many drugs prescribed by doctors were highly praised for years before the damage they produced was properly assessed and they were removed from the market.

Even LSD was touted by many psychiatrists as a "miracle drug" and was in use for years before it was banned by the government in 1966. Some M.D.s still petition for its restoration. In April 1990 the United States General Accounting Office reviewed all drugs approved by the FDA between 1976 and 1985:

> It found that 102 of 198 approved drugs turned out to have "serious postapproval risks"—adverse reactions that could lead to . . . severe or permanent disability, or death.
>
> The rate was even higher for psychiatric drugs: Nine of fifteen recently approved medications developed serious postapproval risks, including one that had to be withdrawn from the market.[14]

For a physician to prescribe Prozac (or Ritalin, or other similar drugs) is not like a mechanic fine-tuning an engine. The prescription is not based on a diagnosis of the brain but on a behavioral profile. Prozac is not given to "balance" the brain, but rather to artificially improve one's feelings about oneself.

Breggin is not the only psychiatrist to criticize "biological psychiatry"—i.e., the use of drugs to adjust mood. There are many others. There have been critical articles in professional journals of psychiatry and psychology. The efficacy of these drugs is open to question, a question that has not been settled.

In pursuing a *chemical* solution, science ignores what ought to be the first priority: getting right with God through Jesus Christ. His incarnation united God and man in His own Person; and He brings that reconciliation and union within the human spirit when He is received as Savior. Christianity is not a set of rules for one to follow. Only Christ can live the Christian life, and He will live it in and through those who believe in Him. Paul said: "But when it pleased God . . . to reveal his Son in me" (Galations 1:15,16). Christianity is the revelation of Christ in our lives through the power of God!

To those who trust Him and obey His Word, Christ becomes their very life. As the apostle Paul declared: "I am crucified with Christ; nevertheless I live: yet not I, but Christ liveth in me" (Galatians 2:20). Obviously, the Spirit of Christ within needs no help from psychotherapy or drugs. Nor does Christ promise an easy path. The Christian life is beset by trials and temptations and conflicts allowed by God to test us to see whether or not we will really trust and obey Him.

Two Generations of Sorcerers

The *moral* and *spiritual* consequences of tampering with the brain and nervous system through drugs could be far worse than the *physical* dangers. Remember, the brain is "a machine that a ghost can operate." The normal connection between the brain and the human spirit is loosened by drugs, allowing a demonic spirit to operate the brain. That fact is being completely ignored by the entire field of psychopharmacology.

Already two generations of youth have been led unwittingly into sorcery. They thought they were just having fun on "recreational" drugs, only to be ushered seductively into the sorcerer's world. As a result, they developed a basically Hindu philosophy of life that totally transformed them.

We have already quoted Terence McKenna that the entities one meets on drug trips "are trying to teach us something." Brad Green is only one of multitudes who stepped into the occult through the psychedelic door. His experience is typical of many which have been related to the author in interviews around the world. Here are his own words:

When I first took acid [LSD], I took weak enough doses just to have fun and see colors and psychedelic patterns . . . but when I started taking really heavy doses . . . I got a spirit guide.

After that, whenever I took psychedelic drugs, I was always guided by spirit beings. I had spirit teachers showing me lessons, making diagrams right in front of me. . . . One of the first times I took a strong dose of LSD, I had a lesson in astrology. . . . I saw all the signs of the zodiac . . . the whole thing was laid out in living color, big charts . . . information being printed right in front of me by spirit beings. . . . I heard their voices, but I didn't see any of them at that time.

On another LSD trip, the spirit guides taught me about Hinduism. . . . They taught me the highest Hindu vibration, OM [pronounced AUM]. I saw the whole universe dissolve into vibrations and started seeing vibrations of energy coming out of phone wires . . . and the spirits showed me that everything came down to one basic vibration, the OM. I saw "vibes" in people. . . .

I had quit high school and devoted my life to taking drugs. . . . With spirits teaching me, I thought I'd entered into a higher education . . . more worthwhile than just dull stuff in school.

One of my friends was taught Transcendental Meditation by spirits on an LSD trip. He never had any teaching from Maharishi. By the time he was 18, just following what the spirits had taught him . . . he had reached Cosmic-consciousness.

Later on we were heavily influenced by the Beatles. They had a record called "Revolver" that I'd heard but didn't understand until I heard it again . . . when I was stoned. The song was teaching meditation. It said, "Turn off your mind, relax and float downstream, listen to the voices, are they not speaking . . . !" It was about spirit beings guiding you into Cosmic-consciousness.

A lot of stuff the Beatles put into their albums . . . had all kinds of enticement to get kids into LSD . . . then later they advocated Maharishi Mahesh Yogi after they'd . . . gotten into TM. The Beatles, I think, were largely responsible for initiating hundreds of thousands of kids . . . into the Eastern way of thinking. . . .

I accepted everything the spirits taught me because it had to be truth coming from the Universal Self. I began to believe that was what God was. I started to believe that God was the OM and that the universe was just maya, an illusion. . . . [Later] I began to realize that the spirits had been teaching me Hinduism. I accepted it as truth—I didn't care what it was called.[15]

Such experiences cannot be attributed to imagination or coincidence. There is a very clear purpose and a unity to what is taught to those who enter the sorcerers' world. It is the same worldwide in all cultures and in all periods of history. Unquestionably, contact has been made with nonhuman intelligences that have a definite agenda.

A Modern Revival of Neoshamanism

McKenna is very high on drugs. He suspects that they have been put here by extraterrestrials, and even that the sacred mushrooms may be intelligences themselves. He is convinced that a partnership between hallucinogenic plants and mankind will shape our future:

> In 1975 we underwent something like a second neolithic revolution . . . [through] the invention of home fungus cultivation. Suddenly, twenty or thirty species of psilocybin containing mushrooms, which were previously rarely-met forest endemics . . . have become ubiquitous. Stropharia cubensis . . . was, before the invention of human cultivation, a rare tropical mushroom. Now it grows from Nome to Tierra del Fuego in every attic, basement and garage. . . . My brother and I wrote the book *Psilocybin: Magic Mushroom Growers' Guide* in 1975. It sold [more than] 100,000 copies. . . . Bob Harris . . . wrote a book called *Growing Wild Mushrooms.* Jonathan Ott wrote a book. Spore companies sprang up . . . it's very hard to imagine how many people are doing this. . . .
>
> I think that a true symbiosis is happening between humans and hallucinogenic plants. LSD was a *thing* of the laboratory. Psilocybin is a *creature* of the forests and fields. When man propagates it, when we spread it, when it intoxicates us, there is a reciprocal relationship and transfer of energy and information . . . it may be smarter than we are. . . .
>
> What a long, strange trip it's been, from the cave paintings at Alta Mira to the doorway of the starship. And now we stand on that threshold, hand in hand with this strange new partner. . . .[16]

McKenna refers to an "unresolved problem in botany: why there is such a tremendous concentration of plant hallucinogens in the New World" and considers that to be the reason why "hallucinogenic shamanism is so highly developed" in North, Central, and South America. Noting that "millions of people were touched by LSD," he adds, surprisingly, "I don't think that mass drug-taking is a good idea." He then makes an interesting suggestion:

> But I think that we must have a deputized minority—a shamanic professional class . . . whose job is to . . . perform for our culture some of the cultural functions that shamans performed in preliterate cultures.[17]

After having told the world how to grow the sacred mushroom and being so enthusiastic that "everyone" is getting into it, how does he propose that only a "deputized minority—a shamanic professional class" be the ones through whom the new revelations will officially come? In fact, one need not take hallucinogens to become a shaman—many shamans do not. All one needs to do is to activate the imagination through certain techniques, the most powerful of which is visualization. Far more people in the world and also in the church have bought into this "harmless" method than into drugs.

Jean Houston reminds us, "Throughout history human beings have invented or discovered many ways to alter consciousness as a gateway to subjective realities, heightened sensitivity, and aesthetic, creative, and religious apperceptions. Ritual drumming, dancing, chanting, fasting, ingesting mind-altering plant substances, yogas, and meditative states—such means have helped to suspend the structural givens and cultural expectations of a certain reality construct—the conditioned mindscape —so that alternative realities and solutions can be perceived."[18]

Imagination and Visualization

Occultism has always involved three techniques for changing and creating reality: thinking, speaking, and visualizing. The first one is the most familiar, having been promoted in the world and the church as "Positive Thinking" by Norman Vincent Peale and as "Possibility Thinking" by Robert Schuller. The second is mostly known among charismatics. It is the "Positive Confession" (or Positive Speaking) of the Faith movement to which we have already referred as well.

The third technique is the most powerful. It is the fastest way to enter the world of the occult and to pick up a spirit guide. Shamans have used it for thousands of years. It was taught to Carl Jung by spirit beings, and through him influenced humanistic and transpersonal psychology. It was taught to Napoleon Hill by the spirits that began to guide him. Agnes Sanford, of whom we will have more to say later, was the first to bring it into the church. Norman Vincent Peale was not far behind her, and his influence was much greater. He wrote:

> Suppose a trusted friend . . . said, "There's a powerful new-old idea . . . a concept available to all of us that can shape and change human lives for the better in an astonishing way. . . ."
> You'd say, "Tell me about it!" wouldn't you.
> That's what I want to do in this book—tell you about it.
> The concept is a form of mental activity called imaging. It consists of vividly picturing, in your conscious mind, a desired goal or objective, and holding that image until it sinks into your unconscious mind, where it releases great, untapped energies. . . .
> The idea of imaging . . . has been implicit in all the speaking and writing I have done. . . . But only recently has it begun to . . . be recognized by scientists and medical authorities. . . .[19]

This occult technique has invaded the church. Certain leaders have been teaching visualization for years. In his booklet, *The Power of the Inner Eye,* Robert Schuller (like Yonggi Cho and others) perverts Scripture by claiming that it advocates the occult technique of visualization. He writes:

> In the May, 1985, issue of *Psychology Today,* there was a wonderful article entitled "In the Mind's Eye." [It] deals with . . . visualization. . . . This is the vision that the Bible is talking about in the verse, "Where there is no vision the people perish.". . .
> I have practiced and harnessed the power of the inner eye and it works. . . . Thirty years ago we started with a vision of a church. It's all come true.

On the contrary, Solomon (Proverbs 29:18) is not encouraging the occult practice of visualization! Does Schuller really credit what his church is today to harnessing "the power of the inner eye" through visualization? What did God have to do with it? And if God was involved at all, was it because the practice of visualization somehow compelled Him to do it?

Destroying True Faith in God

Michael Harner declares that primitive shamanism is being revived in the Western world through the use of ancient occult techniques under modern names and for modern purposes: in medicine and psychology, in mind dynamics courses, and in motivational training in the business world. As one professional journal noted, "Ancient shamanic practices are currently being adapted for contemporary use in healing illnesses. . . ."[20] The major shamanic practice, of course, is visualization.

We now have an "American Association for the Study of Mental Imagery" (visualization). The "First World Conference on Imagery," presented by Marquette University and the Medical College of Wisconsin, was held in San Francisco during June 20–23, 1985. Others have followed. These conferences cover the use of visualization in medicine, psychology, education, business, and other areas. Yale University Professor of Medicine Bernie Siegel said years ago, ". . . applied to physical illness, the most widely used and successful [technique] has been . . . imaging or visualization."[21] Says Phil Jackson, "Visualization is an important tool for me. . . ."[22]

Visualization has become an important tool among evangelicals as well—which doesn't purge it of its occult power. Yonggi Cho has made it the center of his teaching. In fact, he declares that no one can have faith unless he visualizes that for which he is praying. Yet the Bible states that faith is "the evidence of things not seen" (Hebrews 11:1). Thus visualization, the attempt to "see" the answer to one's prayer, would work *against* faith rather than help it! Yet Norman Vincent Peale declared, "If a person consciously visualizes being with Jesus that is the best guarantee I know for keeping the faith."[23]

The quote at the beginning of the chapter by Calvin Miller, one of the most highly regarded evangelical authors today, that we must create the only Christ we can know in our *imagination,* is blasphemy. Richard Foster and many others teach basically the same occultims, which we will deal with in a later chapter. Listen to Miller again:

> Still, imagination stands at the front of our relationship with Christ . . . in my conversation with Christ . . . I drink the glory of his hazel eyes . . . his auburn hair. . . .

What? Do you disagree? His hair is black? Eyes brown? Then have it your way. . . . His image must be real to you as to me, even if our images differ. The key to vitality, however, is the [imagined] image.[24]

Once more, this is contrary to Scripture. Of Christ, Peter said, "Whom having *not seen,* ye love; in whom, though now ye *see him not,* yet believing, ye rejoice with joy unspeakable and full of glory" (1 Peter 1:8). In the previous verse he refers to a future "appearing of Jesus Christ." John likewise speaks of "when he shall appear" (1 John 3:2), and Paul speaks of loving "his [future] appearing" (2 Timothy 4:8). Visualizing Jesus would seem to be an unbiblical attempt to have Him appear before the proper time—unless, of course, one insists that it is only imagination. Yet those who are involved attribute results to this process that could scarcely be explained as resulting from fantasy conversations with oneself.

Furthermore, a "Christ" who would take on any color of hair or eyes and any form to suit the visualizer is not the real Lord Jesus of the Bible and history. Then who is this entity that appears in response to this occult technique to deceive Christians?

More Than Imagination?

As we have noted repeatedly, a major evidence that something more than the imagination is involved in occult phenomena is found in the consistent undergirding philosophy communicated by the visualized entities. Another evidence is found in the fact that the same entities make contact repeatedly around the world and throughout history with individuals who have never heard of them nor had any contact with one another, as well as with individuals who were not seeking contact through visualization. The number of times the Great White Brotherhood or the Tibetan Djwhal Khul or various "saints" and "Mary" and even "Jesus" have appeared to those who were not seeking them at all cannot be coincidence.

Consider, for example, the case of Will Baron. He had lost his confidence in the Bible in high school through the teaching of evolution. Later, through drugs and Eastern mysticism, he had become part of the New Age movement. He was, in fact, a board member of the New Age cult Lighted Way. On this special day Will had been doing his usual morning meditation for only a few minutes when, as he reports:

> Suddenly, a physical force that I had never felt before seemed to come upon me. Brilliant light filled my whole being . . . permeating every cell of my body. My brain, especially, was flooded with light, as if a thousand-watt bulb had been switched on inside of my head. . . .
>
> I felt a deep sense of peace. . . . My mind, my rational thinking was still functioning normally, with clear and precise, logical thoughts. I had not taken any kind of drugs whatsoever.
>
> Suddenly, a man radiating intense golden-white light stood before me. My first perception was that the mysterious, shining figure looked just like Jesus Christ. Immediately a strong intuitive thought . . . surfaced that told me this person was Djwhal Khul, the high-ranking member of the White Brotherhood of Masters . . . who had dictated to Alice Bailey the contents of the metaphysical books she had published. . . .[25]

The director of the New Age cult to which Will belonged was a spirit medium. She had an experience similar to his but with a different entity. At least, whatever it was took a different form. Will remembers vividly her excitement as she told the group:

> I was awakened in the middle of the night. To my amazement a man stood right in the middle of my hotel bedroom. I was shocked. . . . He was about six feet tall and had a dignified bearing of great authority. He said to me, "Get down on your knees! . . . I am Jesus Christ, and I am going to heal you. . . ."
>
> He is power-r-r-ful. He touched my head . . . blessing me [then] walked straight through the solid, locked door of my hotel room. . . .[26]

That this was not Jesus is clear to anyone who knows the Bible. Moreover, one need not wait until this "Jesus" decides to come for a visit. He can be made to appear at any time, according to the teaching introduced by Peale and Sanford that has been seducing the church for more than 50 years and is still gaining momentum. Just as shamans visualize their spirit guides, so Christians now by the millions are visualizing "Jesus," and He is literally appearing to them—or so they think. We will deal with this occult invasion of the church in a later chapter, but one example will be given now. A pastor tells of his first experience in the occult practice of "healing of the memories," which Agnes Sanford brought into the church:

> I began to visualize myself as a boy of eight . . .
> "Now see if you can imagine Jesus appearing," [the seminar leader] instructed. "Let Him walk toward you."
> Much to my amazement . . . Jesus moved slowly toward me out of that dark playground. He began to extend His hands toward me in a loving, accepting manner. . . .
> I no longer was creating the scene. The figure of Christ reached over and lifted the bundle from my back. And He did so with such forcefulness that I literally sprang from the pew.[27]

That this was more than imagination is clear. The one who originally visualized the image of "Jesus" was *surprised* when it suddenly took on a character of its own and he realized that he was no longer creating the image. This "Jesus" had its own life and personality. There can be no doubt that real contact had been made with the spirit world. We may be equally certain that this being was not the real Jesus Christ. No one can call Him from the right hand of the Father in heaven to put in a personal appearance. The entity could only have been a demonic spirit masquerading as "Jesus."

The Classic Case of Napoleon Hill

In Chapter 1 we briefly mentioned Napoleon Hill. He was not seeking contact with spirit beings when he was suddenly confronted in his study by an unexpected and uninvited intruder. Hill claims that an emissary came across the astral plane. In a voice that "sounded like chimes of great music," this visitor from another dimension declared: "I come from the Great School of Masters. I am one of the Council of Thirty-Three who serve the Great School and its initiates on the physical plane."

Hill was informed that he had been "under the guidance of the Great School" for years and had been chosen by them to give the formula of success, the "Supreme Secret," to the world: that "anything the human mind can believe, the human mind can achieve."[28] Here again is the same lie that turns one from God to the alleged power of the human mind. Peale and Schuller try to link this occult power with prayer and faith. Hill was not praying, but was introduced to a mysterious source of "guidance" claiming to inhabit a spiritual dimension ("a region beyond the power of our five senses to know") from which "unseen, silent forces influence us constantly."[29]

Although he spoke and wrote a great deal about "mind power" and "positive mental attitude" (a phrase he was inspired by these entities to coin), Hill was convinced that behind these forces were "unseen watchers" guiding the destiny of those who were willing to submit to their leadership. There was no limit to the success and wealth which these allegedly higher beings would give in exchange for following their principles. Hill claims to have gotten these secrets from contact with "The Great School of Masters," of which he wrote:

> Sometimes known as the Venerable Brotherhood of Ancient India, it is the great central reservoir of religious, philosophical, moral, physical, spiritual and psychical knowledge. Patiently this school strives to lift mankind from spiritual infancy to maturity of soul and final illumination.[30]

Still a perennial bestseller even after 60 years, Hill's best-known book, *Think and Grow Rich,* has been credited with changing the lives and influencing the careers of a large percentage of America's top business executives. Its 1941 edition contains endorsements from United States Presidents Theodore Roosevelt, Harding, Wilson, and Taft; and from some of the world's greatest scientists and founders of America's leading corporations: Thomas A. Edison, Luther Burbank, John D. Rockefeller, F. W. Woolworth, William Wrigley, Jr., George Eastman (of Eastman Kodak), Robert Dollar (of Dollar Steamship Lines), and others.

The Venerable Brotherhood of Ancient India taught Hill the power of visualization. Following their advice, Hill visualized nine famous men from the past sitting around a table as his "advisers." And their advice proved to be remarkably sound and profitable for Hill to follow.

As a result, Hill became very successful, and millions of other people (including many of America's leading business, professional, and political leaders) adopted and proved the astonishing power of this ancient shamanic technique in every area of their lives. Though he clung to the idea that it was all imagination, from what Hill wrote it is clear that visualization had opened the door to the world of the occult:

> These nine men were Emerson, Paine, Edison, Darwin, Lincoln, Burbank, Napoleon, Ford and Carnegie. Every night . . . I held an imaginary council meeting with this group whom I called my "Invisible Counselors."
>
> In these imaginary council meetings I called on my cabinet members for the knowledge I wished each to contribute, addressing myself to each member. . . .
>
> After some months of this nightly procedure, I was astounded by the discovery that these imaginary figures became apparently real. Each of these nine men developed individual characteristics, which surprised me. . . .
>
> These meetings became so realistic that I became fearful of their consequences, and discontinued them for several months. The experiences were so uncanny, I was afraid if I continued them I would lose sight of the fact that the meetings were purely *experiences of my imagination* [emphasis in original].
>
> This is the first time I have had the courage to mention this. . . . I still regard my cabinet meetings as being purely imaginary, but . . . they have led me into glorious paths of adventure . . . [and] I have been miraculously guided past [scores] of difficulties. . . .
>
> I now go to my imaginary counselors with every difficult problem which confronts me and my clients. The results are often astonishing. . . .[31]

Carl Jung also tried to deny the reality of the entities that visited and guided him. Jung finally was forced to admit their objective reality. Surely Hill could not really believe that his *imagination* gave each one of his nine counselors "individual characteristics," characteristics which he confessed surprised him. And whence the wisdom that proved so beneficial on so many occasions when problems beyond his ability to solve were presented to his "imaginary" advisers? Of course, it is much more comfortable to believe in the power of imagination than to accept the fact that one has become the victim of an occult invasion.

Playing a Dangerous Game

Psychologist/theologian Jean Houston and her husband, Robert Masters, brought shamanism into the parlor. In their book *Mind Games* they give detailed instructions for a "guide" to lead a group into "an altered state of consciousness together. . . . One ever-deepening trance." (The guide is instructed to be careful to retain normal consciousness in case it becomes necessary to rescue the other players from their altered states.) The climax comes in the form of an encounter with an entity called the "Group Spirit," which will appear to be very real to the entire group. Here are some of the instructions from Houston and Masters to be read by the guide to the group:

> We are gathered here in this circle . . . creating a pool of consciousness. . . . And we are going to cause to rise now, out of that pool, the entity we have called the Group Spirit. . . . You will be aware . . . of the Group Spirit's location [in the center of our circle] . . . we can and must materialize the Group Spirit, endowing that entity with a sufficiently material being that it can appear to us all. . . . We will be able . . . to see it, and hear it, and we even could touch it, were it not necessary to take certain precautions. . . .[32]

"Precautions" for what, one must ask? Does the "Group Spirit" not like to be touched, and might it cause harm? This sounds very real, and so it must be in order for the participants to "see it, and hear it" and even to "touch it" if that were allowed.

One need not join a group to pick up a spirit guide. The shamans have always done it alone. Los Angeles physician Art Ulene, a popular television medical consultant and a TM graduate, was introduced to "guided imagery" while making "a film of relaxation techniques with Dr. David Bresler, a psychologist at UCLA." Ulene, who has his own spirit guide, tells others how they too may pick up a similar life companion. He leads them into an altered state of consciousness, has them visualize a "relaxing scene," and then tells them:.

> Slowly look around your relaxing scene until you spot a living creature. Don't be surprised by what you find. . . . Move in closer on the creature. Ask it to move a little closer to you. . . .
>
> Now . . . it's time for the two of you to get acquainted. . . . Talk to your creature. Tell it your name. Ask its name. Believe it or not, you'll get an answer. . . .
>
> When you and your creature have said all there is to say, it's time to return to this world again. Say goodbye and promise you'll return again. Then slowly open your eyes. . . .

We all have this inner diagnostician, a creature advisor who can
come to us in time of need. Our creatures may not have the proper
degrees, but their brand of medicine works. . . .[33]

Is this madness—or something more insidious and dangerous? Those who get involved definitely make contact with *something* that began as imagination but becomes an entity with its
own personality and functions independently of the one who visualized it. Yale University medical professor Dr. Bernie Siegel
was shocked when it happened to him. He said:

I didn't believe it would work, but if it did I expected to
see Jesus or Moses. . . . Instead I met George, a bearded, long-
haired young man wearing an immaculate flowing white gown and
a skullcap. It was an incredible awakening for me. . . .

George was spontaneous, aware of my feelings, and an excellent
advisor.[34]

Trust Badly Misplaced!

"An excellent advisor"? Sounds like Napoleon Hill again. And
don't be surprised to discover that the advice given by "George"
was exactly like that which came from Hill's nine famous men.
One of the indications that this is not just "imagination" is
found in the "advice" which the inner advisor or spirit guide
provides. It offers knowledge and wisdom unknown to those
who originally visualized the creature or creatures; and that
counsel, as we continue to emphasize, always presents in slightly
different form the same lies with which the serpent, according
to the Bible, seduced Eve in the Garden of Eden. That fact
should provide evidence of who or what is the source of the
"wisdom" being offered.

Masters and Houston suggest that the "altered state of consciousness" is the best way to contact occult entities. The reason
they give is rather interesting:

[Perhaps] within that range of states we think of as normal,
conscious contact with these other life forms has been made impossible by some kind of shielding against it. . . .

By altering consciousness we sometimes drop the shield, and
the contacts become possible.[35]

Indeed, it seems that the various occult techniques for altering consciousness, like consciousness-altering drugs, have been specifically designed and developed to open one to the occult by knocking down a "shield." Might it not be that this "shield" has been put in place by God to prevent an invasion of the human personality by demonic entities? The best advice would be, "Don't drop that shield!"

Yet the very techniques which tear down that shield are being recommended and taught not only by Masters and Houston and other New Age gurus but are being promoted in the church. The door of the human spirit is deliberately being opened to an occult invasion! Here is what a former leader in the New Age movement, speaking from years of experience, has to say:

> After lengthy observation [from inside, as a leader] of the entire New Age scene, I am convinced that these techniques (rebirthing, yoga, TM, visualization of inner guides, etc.) have an intrinsic power in themselves. They work because they are designed specifically to *blow open doors and knock down barriers that God has placed in the human spirit to prevent a takeover by demonic beings that I came to realize are real and very destructive.*[36]

Rather than being representations of the collective unconscious (one of the lies taught to Carl Jung by these deceiving entities), the preponderance of evidence indicates that the entities encountered through shamanic techniques are forms taken by demonic spirits intent upon deceiving and destroying mankind. Yet Masters and Houston (along with many others involved in the occult) promise that if you "trust the guide and have confidence in the ability of the guide to protect you, then you will be safe from harm." It sounds hauntingly like something which the disguised wolf might reassuringly whisper in the ear of Little Red Riding Hood.

How Do We Know What Is Real?

In 1996 the media had great fun with the story that First Lady Hillary Clinton had made contact and carried on conversations with a former First Lady, Eleanor Roosevelt. There were disclaimers by Hillary that the conversations had been "imaginary." Was she then just talking to herself? Surely it had to be more than that! In fact, Hillary had been led by Jean Houston into the ancient occult technique of visualization.

On the one hand, it all sounds ludicrous, conjuring up in the imagination some mysterious entities which then seemingly become "real," whatever that means. On the other hand, it would be insulting to accuse all of these highly intelligent and well-educated persons of a common madness. Indeed, the very fact that so many people all over the world at all times of history have had the same experience puts the stamp of reality upon it. The fact, however, that these entities are not physical raises the question of how "real" these spirit guides are—and here we confront the question of what is meant by "real."

One result of the transformation taking place in our world through drugs and other shamanic practices is the confusion about "reality" that now plagues so many people who were once quite certain of the answer to that question. Is what is experienced on the drug trip or in the "higher consciousness" achieved through Eastern mysticism the "real" state of affairs, or is reality found in ordinary consciousness? It has become popular to claim that we create our own universe with our minds, so reality is in a state of flux and differs for each of us. This is patent nonsense that comes from the Hindu belief that all is *maya*, an illusion.

Logically, the mere fact that the universe existed long before Homo sapiens came along to "create" reality with his imagination should have ended the kind of delusion that Jean Houston and others like her have foisted upon a gullible following. Yet this theory persists. To demolish this fantasy, that we are all dreaming a common dream we call "reality," and to establish the fact of a *real* universe independent of our minds, Sir James Jeans pointed out that there are three criteria which are essential for objective reality: *surprise, continuity,* and *change.* Here is what he meant.

Twenty million people are suddenly awakened from sound sleep by an earthquake in Mexico City which kills many of them by collapsing the homes and apartments they occupy. The fact that they were *surprised* by this event—indeed awakened by the shaking and roaring of an earthquake that they certainly were not even dreaming of—is evidence enough that an objective reality imposed itself upon its victims. It would be madness to suggest that a hurricane that destroys homes or a fire that guts a hotel were simply part of a common dream which the victims had all agreed upon. Yet the new-consciousness gurus who are so popular continue to promote techniques for getting out of this "ordinary" but delusionary state of consciousness into a new reality created by the mind in a so-called "higher state of consciousness"—which is supposedly the *real* world.

Sir James Jeans' second criterion to establish objective reality, *continuity,* is as easily understood. After a 20-year absence you return to your high school for a reunion. The same rooms in which you once attended class are there, complete with desks, blackboards, and cracks in the ceiling—everything that you had scarcely even remembered during the 20-year interval. All has remained in place without one thought from you. Those young trees you remember have grown large without any help at all from your mind.

Obviously, your old school and its surroundings, like the rest of the world and universe, are not some dream you have dreamed, but an objective reality that exists entirely independent of you and the rest of mankind. Imagine the chaos if reality were in fact the product of billions of individual minds of independent and forgetful (or even insane) makeup. Whose "reality" would be dominant, and how often would one person's self-created "reality" suddenly be overturned by another's imposing itself? And by what logic could it be imagined that the billions of people on this earth somehow got together and managed to create the universe we all experience, from the interior of the atom to the farthest star—a universe that was here long before we even arrived?

There have also been *changes* at your high school during your absence. The old crackerbox gymnasium has been torn down and a new and much larger one stands in its place. *Change* such as this, coming without our knowledge in places we have forgotten, clearly has occurred without our minds creating it. This too demonstrates the objectivity of the physical universe about us. These three criteria—*surprise, continuity,* and *change*—also prove the reality of occult experiences for the same reasons.

When scientists such as Sir James Jeans state, as he did, that the universe is "like a great thought," they do not mean a thought in human minds but, as Jeans said, "in the mind of some Eternal Spirit," who alone could be the Creator of the universe. Far from mentally creating reality, mankind has been struggling to discover a reality that exists independently of his thoughts and imagination and that was obviously created by a mind far beyond his comprehension or abilities. The only sensible thing to do is to stop trying to manipulate reality and allow that Creator to have His way in your life.

At the root of all the world's great spiritual traditions lies the aboriginal pulse of shamanism, the archaic spiritual heritage of humankind stretching back 40,000 years or more into the mists of pre-history. . . .

This ancient wisdom is still preserved and practiced by shamans in native cultures. . . . It is precisely this ancient wisdom, which has been lost within our own Western culture, that we so urgently need at this time in order to correct the condition of extreme imbalance, disease, and destruction we find on the planet today.

—The Ojai Foundation[1]

Only the recognition on a worldwide scale of the oneness of creation can provide the critical global consciousness necessary to chart a new course for a sustainable future.

—World Council of Churches[2]

We are living through one of the most fundamental shifts in history— a change in the actual belief structure of Western industrial society . . . allowing us to recapture the insights of thousands of years of exploration of human consciousness [i.e., shamanism]. . . .

—Institute of Noetic Sciences[3]

Shamans—whom we in the "civilized" world have called "medicine men" and "witch doctors"—are the keepers of a remarkable body of ancient techniques. . . . These shamanic methods are strikingly similar the world over, even for peoples whose cultures are quite different in other respects, and who have been separated by oceans and continents for tens of thousands of years.

—Michael Harner[4]

The Earth is mandating that the human community assume a responsibility never assigned to any previous generation. We are being asked to learn an entirely new mode of conduct and discipline. This is preeminently a religious and spiritual task.

—Thomas Berry, Adjunct Associate Professor
Emeritus, Fordham University[5]

Increasingly, it is realized that any efforts to safeguard and cherish the environment need to be infused with a vision of the sacred.

—Carl Sagan in an appeal for joint commitment in science and religion to a group of scientists in Moscow in 1996[6]

Who changed the truth of God into a lie, and worshipped and served the creature [creation] more than the Creator, who is blessed for ever. Amen.

—The apostle Paul in Romans 1:25

11

* * *

Ecology, Shamanism, Science, and Christianity

With the end of the Cold War easing the threat of all-out nuclear battle, the emphasis is now upon reversing the pollution that threatens us everywhere. Here in America, more than 30 states have adopted laws requiring environmental issues to be taught in schools. The National Environmental Education Act, originally passed in 1970, then repealed in 1981, was reinstated in November 1990.

Some of the theories which have been put forth to generate international support for the environmental movement—such as whether the hole in the ozone layer is a cyclical natural phenomenon or man-made and worsening—are debatable. Is the globe actually warming or cooling? In the '60s and '70s, scientists were warning about global cooling, not global warming. As late as 1977, the U.S. Academy of Science warned of a coming new ice age. Now we're being warned of global warming in spite of record-breaking cold—a threat which some scientists have called "just a lot of hot air."

In mid-December 1993, *U.S. News and World Report* carried a major exposé titled "The Doomsday Myths." It named and examined false alarms sounded by environmentalists. Nevertheless, the environmental movement is gathering considerable momentum and has the attention and backing of most government, scientific, and religious world leaders.

A Nature Religion for Today

While it calls primarily upon scientific data for support, the ecological movement is a *religion* with its own *ecotheology*. Georgetown University professor Victor Ferkiss approvingly says that ecological concern "starts with the premise that the Universe *is* God." [7] Carl Sagan, the recently deceased high priest of cosmos worship, declared with the authority of academia behind him: "If we must worship a power greater than ourselves, does it not make sense to revere the Sun and stars?"[8] No, it does not. Reverence does not pertain to *things* but to *persons*.

One can hardly escape the similarity between a native bowing before a stick or stone which he credits with some occult power, a witch worshiping "Mother Nature," and scientists and university professors crediting mystic evolutionary forces with producing the human brain. It is a perversion to give reverence to the impersonal creation instead of to the personal God who created us, a perversion entertained in order to escape moral accountability to our Creator. Therefore the Bible indicts in the clearest terms those who, like Sagan and many of his fellow scientists, worship the creation instead of its Creator; and it warns clearly of the consequent perversion of morals and behavior.

Underlying the environmental movement is the belief that mankind is the product of evolutionary forces inherent within the universe. Based upon that theory we must therefore get back in tune with nature, our Mother, rather than with the Creator. New Agers (and they include increasing numbers of scientists) have adopted the view long held by shamans and Eastern mystics that the universe is a living entity of which we are all an integral part. What is needed, therefore, is to recognize our essential oneness with nature or "the Universal Mind" and to experience this oneness through "higher states of consciousness."

This growing pagan spirituality with its worship of creation instead of the Creator is an ideal vehicle for joining in partnership science and religion. As early as 1988, Willis Harman, president of the Institute of Noetic Sciences (founded by astronaut Edgar Mitchell), was giving speeches on "The Immanent Reconciliation of Science and Religion,"[9] a reconciliation, of course, which could not include true Christianity. Nevertheless,

Christians are being drawn into this coalition. The ecological crisis is used to justify that process.

Increasingly, scientists are adopting the shamanistic view that Mother Earth is a goddess named Gaia. This belief is promoted at high-level gatherings of scientists. Conferences of the Dallas-based Isthmus Institute regularly draw leading scientists and religionists together to discuss "science and spirituality." Usually held at a University of Texas campus, typical conferences include discussions of the "spiritual" aspects of ecology and of "Gaia."[10] Of course, their meaning of "spiritual" is pagan/pantheistic and anti-Christian.

Honoring the Goddess

As one would expect, the belief in Gaia is very appealing to feminists and even to those among them who call themselves Christians. A growing movement within the Christian church resulted from the "Re-Imagining God, the Community and the Church" conference held November 4–7, 1993, in Minneapolis, Minnesota. One of the plenary speakers was Chung Kyun Kyung, a South Korean Presbyterian. In her plenary address to this *Christian* gathering, Chung declared:

> I want to share three images of God so striking in Asia and how these images of God transformed my Christianity and my theological understanding of God. The three goddesses I want to share with you are Kali, Quani, and Enna. These three are my new Trinity . . . I claim Kali as the goddess of justice. . . . Kali is usually located in India and Sri Lanka, a Hindu image. Quani is Buddhist image of god. . . . Enna means mother and Enna means earth. It is the indigenous goddess of the Philippines. . . ."[11]
>
> The Christian church has been very patriarchal. That is why we are here together, in order to destroy the patriarchal idolatry of Christianity. . . .[12]

Instead of being excommunicated from her church and shunned by the Christian community for her blatant blasphemy, Chung is highly honored. Eighteen months before the Minneapolis conference, she had also given a plenary address at the Seventh World Council of Churches (WCC) international conference, February 7–20, 1992, in Canberra, Australia. One trembles to repeat her angry, hateful words against the God of the Bible and her wicked perversion of Christianity and the Holy Spirit. Yet the WCC delegates gave Chung a standing ovation. Ecumenical Press Service reported:

> Combining verbal fireworks with a performance by Korean and aboriginal dancers, Chung rendered a dramatic evocation of a female Holy Spirit. She linked that spirit to that of Hagar, the Egyptian slave woman in Genesis, who Chung said was "exploited and abandoned by Abraham and Sarah."
>
> Chung then burned bits of paper bearing the names of other exploited spirits—which she said were full of "han," the Korean word for anger—and identified them as Holocaust victims, freedom fighters, murdered advocates of non-violence, struggling Korean women, the poor, and women in Japan's "prostitution army" during World War II.
>
> Chung said, "I also know that I no longer believe in an omnipotent, Macho, warrior God who rescues all good guys and punishes all bad guys. . . ."[13]

In that same WCC plenary address, Chung said of the Holy Spirit, "Don't bother the Spirit by calling her all the time. She is working hard with us." Eighteen times Chung summoned the spirits of the dead who have suffered injustices in the past. She claimed that "without hearing the cries of these spirits, we cannot hear the voice of the Holy Spirit." After calling on the spirits of the dead, Chung said, "I hope the presence of all our ancestors' spirits here with us shall not make you uncomfortable." [14] It is these very demonic spirits with which the shaman works.

Most of those involved in the environmental movement are anti-Christians who blame the Bible and Christianity for the ecological crises we allegedly face. In their celebrated television series, Joseph Campbell tells Bill Moyers, "The Christian separation of matter and spirit . . . has really castrated nature. And the European mind, the European life, has been, as it were, emasculated by this separation. The true spirituality, which would have come from the union of matter and spirit, has been killed. . . ."[15] Yet Campbell rejects the greatest "union of matter and spirit" possible: the incarnation of Christ, when God was born into the world and became a man.

Christians Come Aboard

Christians are joining an anti-Christian ecumenical movement, and the Christian media is reporting it favorably. One of the early organizations formed was the North American Conference on Religion and Ecology (NACRE). Its first international conference was held May 16–19, 1990, at the Washington (D.C.) National Cathedral. In his role as president of the World Wide Fund for Nature, His Royal Highness Prince Philip, Duke of Edinburgh, was a prime organizer of what he hoped would be an "Assisi Event for North America"—an ecological conference patterned after Pope John Paul II's gathering in Assisi, Italy, in 1986, of world religious leaders to pray for peace.[16] The climax of the four-day program came with an "Interfaith Ceremony and Religious Perspectives on Nature: Buddhist, Jewish, Muslim, Sihkh, Lummi Indians, and Christian beliefs regarding conservation and the environment, followed by an inter-faith blessing of the Cathedral and the oak grove."[17]

In March 1991 the Southern Baptists' Christian Life Commission, directed by Richard Land, "held its first environmental seminar. Later that fall, the United Church of Christ convened an environmental summit for minorities. . . ." The largest black denomination, the National Baptist Convention USA, involved itself in environmentalism at about the same time.[18] Also in 1991, Evangelicals for Social Action (Ron Sider, executive director) helped to organize a gathering of scientists and religious leaders to discuss rescuing the environment. Several mainline Protestant denominations, along with leaders such as Robert Schuller, World Vision's president Robert Seiple, and Asbury Theological Seminary president David McKenna, were enthusiastic about lending support to what is largely a pagan movement.[19]

In an example of Christian media support for this unabashedly heathen movement and the top-level Christian involvement therein, *Christianity Today* reported happily upon this conference. No mention was made of the fact that it arose out of Moscow's occult/New Age "Global Forum" at which Carl Sagan suggested that earth should be "regarded as sacred" to encourage treating it with "care and respect"—not because God made it, but because it (Gaia) made us.[20]

In May 1992, leading evangelicals again joined a coalition of science and religion sponsored by the "Joint Appeal by Religion and Science for the Environment."[21] Sagan was its cochairman, along with James Parks Morton, dean of the Cathedral of St. John the Divine in New York City. "More than 150 scientists, theologians and ... politicians ... [met] in Washington ... with congressional leaders. ... Among the participating religious groups were the National Council of Churches, the National Conference of Catholic Bishops, the Consultation of the Environment and Jewish Life, and World Vision...."[22]

"Joint Appeal" is based at New York's huge Episcopal Cathedral of St. John the Divine, a bastion of New Age/ecumenical/antichrist deception, where a female "Christa" was displayed on a cross. Its blasphemous dean, James Parks Morton, declares, "We are increasingly being called to realize that the body of Christ is the earth—the biosphere—the skin that includes all of us."[23] Out of the May 1992 meeting came an environmental consortium, "The National Religious Partnership for the Environment," which included the U.S. Catholic Conference, the National Council of Churches, the Evangelical Environmental Network, and the Consultation of Jewish Life and the Environment.[24]

Yet another similar organization, the National Religious Partnership for the Environment (NRPE), was founded in 1993 by Vice President Gore, who also takes an active part in "Joint Appeal." NRPE, too, is based at St. John the Divine and has distributed tens of thousands of packets containing ecologically oriented prayers, sermon ideas, and Sunday-school lessons to Catholic, Protestant, Jewish, and evangelical congregations across the country. Beside World Vision, other evangelical organizations involved include Sojourners and InterVarsity Christian Fellowship. NRPE's director is likewise convinced that the ecocrisis will transform "what it will mean to be religious [and "Christian"] in the 21st century."[25]

Redefining Christianity Through Ecology

Richard Austin (one of the speakers at the EarthCare '96 conference) declared: "Christ is fully God and fully Earth. . . . He came to save the world." Austin added that saving the earth is our job, too: "I hear the Bible calling us to redeem from destruction the Creation."[26] Yet Christ said, "Ye are from beneath, I am from above; ye are of this world, I am not of this world" (John 8:23). Furthermore, this world is "kept in store, reserved unto fire against the day of judgment . . . in which the heavens shall pass away with a great noise and the elements shall melt with the fervent heat; the earth also and the works that are therein shall be burned up" (2 Peter 3:7,10).

Thomas Perry, a Catholic priest, says the ecocrisis calls for "a new sense of what it means to be human [and] a new story of how things came to be." What the Bible says about man's origin in Genesis must be revised, along with the very meaning of mankind. Emphasis must shift from a possible heaven to caring for Earth, and ethics and morals must involve the rights of the natural world. Larry Rasmussen, Union Theological Seminary professor, calls for a "biospiritual faith" in which man is a part of the natural order of things "with no special claim on its resources and no special claim on God's love." [27]

Such pagan folly is gaining an increasing following among evangelicals, who now claim that Christ's command to preach the gospel includes rescuing the environment. Such is the message of a course titled "Environmental Stewardship: A Biblical Perspective" taught at Youth with a Mission's University of the Nations at their headquarters in Hawaii. Thus Christians enter compromising partnerships with the ungodly and expend their time and efforts on caring for the earth instead of preparing souls for eternity.

Yes, we ought to be prudent with natural resources. Many of the warnings about ecological problems, however, are alarmist exaggerations for promoting humanist solutions. Moreover, most of the problems are due to the selfishness of sinful man and the corruption of godless governments. Christ did not call us to *reform* society. Men need to be *regenerated*—born again through faith in Christ. While there are legitimate concerns involving this *time* on this earth, the great concern should be for *eternity* and heaven.

"Joint Appeal's" executive director, Paul Gorman, has said that caring for the earth "is part of what it will mean to be religious in the future."[28] Indeed, the environmental movement is redefining what it means to be a Christian.

A Growing Science/Religion Coalition

This new partnership between religion, science, and politics began with the "Global Forum of Spiritual and Parliamentary Leaders on Human Survival" in 1985. Spiritual and political leaders from five continents and the world's five major religions gathered to plan ecological salvation and world peace. Conferees issued a joint declaration: "We are entering an era of global citizenship.... This new consciousness transcends all barriers of race and religion, ideology and nationality.... We hold up the vision of a new community, where... human violence gives way to an age of mutually assured welfare and peace."[29] Beware when mankind thinks it has achieved "peace and safety..." (1 Thessalonians 5:3)!

That pact led to the 1988 five-day Global Forum conference at Oxford, England. Religious and political leaders (joined this time by leading scientists) from 52 countries met again to "join all faiths with all political attitudes." Participants included U.S. senators and leading scientists, members of the Supreme Soviet and the Soviet Academy of Sciences, the U.N. Secretary General and the Archbishop of Canterbury, the late Mother Teresa and the Dalai Lama, cabinet members, cardinals, swamis, bishops, rabbis, imams, and monks.[30] The "Final Statement of the Conference" declared:

> We have [been] ... brought together by a common concern for global survival, and have... derived from our meeting a vivid awareness of the essential oneness of humanity... [and] the realization that each human person has both a spiritual and a political dimension....

> Each of us has been changed by our Oxford experience . . . and
> [we] have undertaken commitments that are irrevocable.[31]

Next came the January 15–19, 1990, Global Forum (with more than a thousand participants from 83 countries) held in Moscow, to which we referred earlier. It was cohosted by the first freely elected Soviet parliament, all Soviet religious bodies, the USSR Academy of Sciences, and the International Foundation for the Survival and Development of Humanity. In his plenary address, Senator (now Vice President) Al Gore, a Southern Baptist who worships the mother goddess Gaia, declared that ecological problems could be solved only through a "new spirituality" common to all religions.

Participants signed "The Moscow Declaration." That conference called for "a global council of spiritual leaders"[32] and the "creation of an interfaith prayer . . . a new spiritual and ethical basis for human activities on Earth."[33] The Declaration itself stated, "Humankind must enter into a new communion with Nature. . . ."[34] Obviously, such a declaration is meaningless if humankind is the evolutionary offspring of nature. Must animals, trees, and plants be urged to find a "new communion with Nature"? Then why mankind? The declaration was in fact an unwitting admission that man is not part of nature.

The Greening of Christianity

Mikhail Gorbachev, still President of the Soviet Union at the time, was of course one of the plenary speakers at the 1990 Global Forum in Moscow. In his speech, as an atheist, Gorbachev called mankind to reconciliation with nature rather than with the God who created nature. He said:

> Humanity is a part of the single and integral biosphere. . . . ecologization of politics requires . . . molding a new contemporary attitude to Nature . . . returning to Man a sense of being a part of Nature. No moral improvement of society is possible without that.[35]

No longer President of Russia, Gorbachev is now more influential internationally than ever. His richly endowed Gorbachev Foundation USA has its offices in the Presidio (former U.S. military base) overlooking the Golden Gate Bridge. A consultant on closing other U.S. military bases, Gorbachev is also president of the ecological watchdog, Green Cross International, a Global Forum offspring headquartered in the Hague.

Green cross? What right does Gorbachev or his organization have to turn the bloodstained cross, red with Christ's blood shed for our sins, into something *green!* Yet this is exactly what is happening to the message of the cross through the environmental movement. The green movement is a humanistic attempt to restore the lost paradise of Eden without acknowledging that the problem is man's rebellion against his Creator.

Yes, the pollution and wanton exploitation and destruction of the environment are foolish and wrong. But the folly and evil of worshiping Mother Earth and treating each species as sacred and having the same rights as humans is even more wrong—yet that is the philosophy being espoused by present world leaders. Nor is there any turning back of this tide.

At conferences on environmentalism one finds papers and speeches being delivered with such topics as "The Greening of a Great City" and "The Greening of the Church." The former referred to "the role of the Cathedral of St. John the Divine in New York." The latter was described as "developing an environmentally informed theology, spirituality and ecological practice within the Christian Church." Yes, the church has joined a *Green* movement and Christian leaders echo its philosophy.

Richard Foster, whom we will discuss in more detail in a later chapter, became a new guru to evangelicals with his 1978 bestseller *Celebration of Discipline*. It opened many Christians to the occult by instructing readers in occult techniques (including visualization of Christ). Foster advocated "centering down" through Eastern mystical techniques and meditating upon nature:

> After you have gained some proficiency in centering down, add a five- to ten-minute meditation on some aspect of the creation. Choose something in the created order: tree, plant, bird, leaf, cloud, and each day ponder it carefully and prayerfully. . . . We should not bypass this means of God's grace. . . .[36]

Science, Evolution, and Religion

The pagan worship of nature was extolled at the "Re-Imagining God" conference attended by many professing evangelicals.

Along with summoning "the spirit of Earth, Air, and Water," Chung Kyun Kyung declared:

> For many Asians, we see god in the wind, in the fire, in the tree, in the ocean. We are living with god, it is just energy. . . .
>
> We believe that this life-giving energy came from god and it is everywhere, it is in the sun, in the ocean, it is from the ground and it is from the trees. We ask god's permission to use this life-giving energy for our sisters and brothers in need.
>
> If you feel very tired . . . you go to a big tree and ask tree, "Give me some of your life energy!" [37]

The coalition between religion and science for the ecological rescue of Earth is gaining momentum. We hear blasphemous statements regarding Earth from conservative "Christian" leaders, especially within the Roman Catholic Church. Before his death, Carl Sagan, an atheist and leading anti-Christian, began making favorable comments about religion. He had clearly joined the new coalition. He enthusiastically quoted the following from Pope John Paul II:

> Science can purify religion from error and superstition; religion can purify science from idolatry and false absolutes. Each can draw the other into a wider world, a world in which both can flourish. . . .
>
> Such bridging ministries must be nurtured and encouraged. Nowhere is this more clear than in the current environmental crisis. . . . It has the potential *to unify and renew religious life* (emphasis in original).[38]

Science will be a major ecumenical influence in creating a world religion. We have already explained why the Roman Catholic Church is especially intimidated by science and thus eager to find itself in agreement with whatever science seems to propose.

Arriving to attend the June 3–14, 1992, Earth Summit in Rio de Janeiro, the Dalai Lama, a close friend of the Pope, was welcomed warmly by Cardinal Eugenio de Araujo Sales.[39] The Roman Catholic Church was the only church which had the right to attend the conference because Vatican City is recognized as a sovereign state on the same level as the United States, Great Britain, etc.[40] Addressing the 1992 Rio Earth

Summit, the United Nations Secretary-General called the world back to the pagan worship of nature:

> Over and above the moral contract with God, over and above the social contract concluded with men, we must now conclude an ethical and political contract with nature, with this Earth to which we owe our very existence and which gives us life.
>
> To the ancients, the Nile was a god to be venerated, as was the Rhine, an infinite source of European myths, or the Amazonian forest, the mother of forests. Throughout the world, nature was the abode of the divinities that gave the forest, the desert or the mountains a personality which commanded worship and respect. The Earth had a soul. To find that soul again, to give it new life, that is the essence of Rio. [41]

Gorbachev says that the main purpose of Green Cross is "to bring nations together . . . to stimulate the new environmental consciousness . . . returning Man to a sense of being a part of Nature." To require man to act like he is "part of Nature" is an admission that he is not. Nature's creatures need no such urging. Yet Gorbachev admitted that "conflict with nature is fundamental to our technologies."[42]

Radios, TV, cars, planes, computers, operas, and art are not natural. Nor are ambulances, doctors, hospitals, and compassion—and right there we confront a major contradiction within the ecological movement and the evolutionary theory upon which it is based. Sir John Eccles writes, "The facts of human morality and ethics are clearly at variance with a theory that explains all behavior in terms of self-preservation and the preservation of the species."[43]

Irrationality of Environmental Causes

The human conscience stands as a firm witness against Darwinism and the entire ecological movement which is based upon it. Even the most fanatical defenders of evolution contradict it in their daily lives. To be consistent, evolutionists ought to shut down all hospitals, cease all medications, and let the weak die. After all, evolution requires that only the fittest survive. But man is compelled by conscience to be compassionate because he is made in the image of a God who "is love."

Medically prolonging the lives of those with genetic disabilities or diseases works against evolution, for it allows such persons to reproduce and pass on their defects to subsequent generations and thereby weakens the race. If evolution is true, then we must stop trying to find a cure for AIDS, stop treating those with the HIV virus and let them die. Since AIDS is largely a homosexual disease, it must be nature's way of wiping out those who practice what is undeniably *unnatural* sex and do not reproduce. The sooner those with deficiencies of every kind die, the better for the survival of our species!

If stopping all assistance to the ill so that only the "fittest survive" sounds harsh, then blame nature—that's *her* way. Don't blame the personal, loving, and gracious Creator who has given us the capacity to be compassionate. Nor would letting the weak die without any assistance seem harsh if we were a product of nature. The evolutionist's attempt to have it both ways— denying a personal Creator yet insisting upon morals and compassion which can't come from nature—betrays the lie that is taught as fact in public schools.

On their TV series, Joseph Campbell tells Bill Moyers that "the impulses of nature are what give authenticity to life, not the rules coming from a supernatural authority. . . ."[44] On the contrary, the "impulses of nature" give us the tooth and claw law of the jungle. The personal Creator commands us to love one another. If evolution were true, then whatever man did, from muggings to murder to war, would be a natural act against which no complaint could be raised. Police, courts, prisons, and criminal accusations would have to be eliminated. If man is a highly evolved animal, then no complaint can be made on moral grounds against anything he does any more than against any other animal.

A Plea for Some Rational Thinking!

There is no right or wrong in nature. Clearly it is not "wrong" for a volcano to spew forth poisonous gases. Whatever nature and her offspring do is simply "natural." If man is a product of nature through evolution, then whatever he does must likewise be natural. Therefore it cannot be wrong for a man-made factory or aerosols to spew forth pollution, and if we were part of nature we wouldn't make rules against pollution. There would be no concern for the ecology and no environmental movement whatsoever if man were really the product of evolution.

As for all the furor that is raised over the possible extinction of a species, such as the spotted owl, hasn't evolution been doing away with species for millions of years? Nor has any species ever tried to rescue another species from extinction. Then why should man be the first to do so? By destroying creatures standing in his way, man, as the ultimate predator, would only be fulfilling his evolutionary purpose as the "fittest" species which is able to "survive" at the expense of all others.

To stop loggers from felling trees because it might cause the spotted owl to become extinct is to work against the natural forces of evolution! In fact, it would be interference with nature to prevent a hunter, if he is truly part of nature, from shooting a buffalo or another man. Why should a man be prevented any more than a wolf or coyote or lion from killing his prey?

Honest logic discredits the environmental movement and the evolutionary theory behind it. One cannot believe both in evolution and ecological preservation of species or habitats. There should be concern neither for "endangered species" nor for the ecological well-being of this planet. If evolution is a fact, then if man, as a result of the evolution of his brain and nervous system and psyche, destroys the Earth in a nuclear holocaust or some other ecological disaster, in the big picture of the evolving universe that must be accepted as progress, since it was brought about by evolution.

On the other hand, the mere fact that man can reason about ecology and survival of species, including himself, indicates that he is not the product of such forces, but, having the power to interfere with them, must have a higher origin. Obviously he didn't make himself.

Clearly, man is not the evolutionary offspring of nature but was created in the image of God. Only an intelligent Creator could have brought mankind into existence. That being the case, the solution to human problems is not in getting back to nature and listening to the earth, as we are being told, but in getting in touch with the God who made us and in submitting to His will.

The Occult Connection

On January 23, 1997, at 17:30 to 17:35 Greenwich Mean Time, "The Gaia Mind Project" held a "Simultaneous Global Meditation and Prayer." The goal was, at the moment of an "archetypically appropriate planetary alignment," to have millions of people around the world involved in "simultaneous meditation and prayer" with the intent to "advance the evolution of consciousness."[45] Once again we see evolution at the heart of the occult—and the use of visualization, the most powerful occult technique. The newsletter organizing this event declared:

> We hope that by joining together we may initiate a shift in our understanding or our relationship with Gaia . . . in which we recognize ourselves as the living Earth's emergent self-reflexive consciousness. Our intention is to use this astrological mandala to identify one moment for people to join together in a resonant expression of unified global consciousness. Perhaps through the power of intentional synergy we may help catalyze the evolution of consciousness and potentiate global healing.
>
> Participation is simple. On January 23rd, meditate, pray or do whatever brings you into closer contact with the Divine for five minutes starting at the local equivalent of 17:30 GMT. Then, at 17:35 GMT, join in a minute of focused visualization. White light seems to be the most universal spiritual archetype, so we suggest envisioning white light in unison as a way to bring ourselves into resonance at the moment the astrological star pattern becomes exact in New York City. . . .
>
> Astrologically, this particular date represents the first of a series of exceedingly rare multiple conjunctions in the first degrees of Aquarius spanning several weeks. Archetypically, the major planets involved represent the benevolent expansion of spiritual liberation. . . .
>
> Your help is crucial to spread awareness of this opportunity to catalyze the transformation of global consciousness.

Here we have all the elements of the occult which we have thus far considered: our oneness with the universe, the power of the mind, the evolution and transformation of consciousness, astrology, spirituality, and liberation.

The titles and descriptions of the Pre-Conference Institutes at a typical environmental conference provide further evidence that to whatever extent the ecological movement is supported by science it is science mixed with occultism:

USING EXPRESSIVE ART TO EXPERIENCE OUR CONNECTEDNESS TO ALL LIFE FORMS

By sensing and being receptive we can listen to our inner voice and the voices of nature. As we journey inward delving into the mysteries and vitality of our own nature we connect to those energies in all life forms. . . .

EARTH AND SPIRIT IN PUBLIC EDUCATION

[Spirituality is brought into the public classroom under the guise of dealing with environmental issues. Thus in spite of the alleged separation of church and state that prohibits any promotion of Christianity in the classroom, the old pagan religions of nature worship and indigenous spiritualities are allowed entrance.]

EARTH ALIVE: A JEWISH EXPERIENCE

Judaism is rooted in a powerful awareness of the unity of all life. Jewish practices offer daily opportunities for honoring and celebrating our relationship with the Earth. In this workshop we will explore Jewish ways of connecting with the Earth.

RE-OPENING THE CHRISTIAN MYSTERIES: PERSPECTIVES FROM THE NEW COSMOLOGY

This institute will be concerned with redefining and rethinking the main themes in Christianity. . . . [Again we have the greening of Christianity.]

THE SACRED SYMBOLS OF THE GODDESS

Drawing on her years of research into ancient goddess reverence . . . Merlin will lead this exploration into the wisdom and power of the goddess tradition. She will look at its contribution to the growing Earth-honoring spirituality, the evocation of magical powers. . . .

DEEP TIME AND THE HEALING OF OUR WORLD

Here the concept of our planet as a living system moves to an experiential level that is intimate and empowering . . . [by shifting] one's sense of identity from a small, separate selfhood, to one of interexistence with all beings.[46]

We Are the Earth and Cosmos

Deepak Chopra exemplifies naturalism's failure to distinguish matter from mind and spirit, mass from morals. He goes so far as to suggest that human relationships are affected by the relationships between atoms and particles "at the quantum level."[47] Such mystical foolishness flies in the face of common sense and experience. It is the natural outcome of the belief that "all is one," that the earth is a living creature called "Gaia," that the entire universe is one living being with a universal consciousness of which we are each integral parts. Says Chopra:

> Everything in the universe influences everything *else* in the universe. . . . When you remember that every electron that vibrates causes the universe to shake, you become struck by the realization of the power inherent in your choices. And when we apply these insights to our personal and professional lives, we are making positive evolutionary change . . . that extends through the world.[48]

There is no evidence that the vibration of a single electron shakes the universe or that each choice of every individual has universal repercussions. Yet Chopra declares that we are each "holograms of the universe . . . all of the qualities in *any* relationship are also part of our *own* psyche."[49] Though this delusion contradicts common sense, it has gripped the imagination of those in the ecological movement.

This mystical belief of the connection between all things furthers the shamanic fantasy that human consciousness can change the environment. Based upon that belief, there have been a number of attempts to heal our planet through enlisting millions of persons around the world to visualize peace and meditate upon ecological wholeness. We mentioned a current attempt above, but these attempts go back more than a decade. *Science of Mind* magazine for November 1986 carried the following announcement:

> On December 31, 1986, from 12 noon to one p.m. Greenwich Mean Time, millions of people around the world will gather in spirit and simultaneously send out their love and light in meditation, prayer, song or whatever form of worship is most meaningful for them. They will visualize the world as peaceful, harmonious, and balanced, with everyone having all they need to live a productive and fulfilling life. . . .
>
> It is our opportunity as individuals, and as a world body, to begin to heal and bring our planet back into harmony and balance—a worldwide nondenominational, nonpolitical, cooperative effort that will unite people in a common bond with a common goal: PEACE ON EARTH. . . .
>
> Turn within and seek and find and know the only Presence, the only Power, the only Cause, the only Activity of your eternal life. Be a totally open channel for the glorious expression of this infinite YOU. We at Science of Mind magazine hope that you—our readers—will join this Healing Meditation. We remind you that it deals with real energy, real power, and real possibilities for contributing to a more peaceful world.

In spite of the allegedly "real energy, real power" generated by this and many similar events, conditions on earth have not gotten better but have steadily worsened. Nevertheless, these absurd efforts continue up to the present. Worse than abused, the God who created us is denied and "this infinite *you*" is deified in His place.

The Shamanic Connection

University of Texas Health Science Center professor Jeanne Achterberg points out what we all know: that shamanism is being embraced in the West. Part of the reason, she says, is that "something is generally felt to be lacking in the training and demeanor of the practitioners [psychiatrists]. . . ." She adds that "shamanism has much to teach us, especially in regard to that most difficult lesson for those of us in the helping professions: learning to honor the uniqueness of each individual's path."[50] Again, Jesus Christ as *the* way is rejected.

Hillary Clinton has long promoted shamanism, including public endorsement. Placing her on its front cover with the caption THE MOST POWERFUL WOMAN, *Time* magazine declared, "Just by being herself, Hillary Rodham Clinton has redefined the role of First Lady." Inside was a picture of this "most powerful woman" (who claims to be a Christian), head reverently bowed, being "blessed" by a North American Indian spiritual healer (shaman) in Montana.[51]

The practice of shamanism, which often is called New Age these days, is intertwined with the environmental movement. As we have already seen, shamanism involves contacting nonphysical entities in order to gain special knowledge and power. Robert Vetter, an anthropologist, tells the story of John Tallhorse, alleged to be the last Comanche medicine man alive. Having been diagnosed with incurable cancer and having spent all of his money on hospital and medical bills, he "turned to the traditional ways of his people . . . [and] resolved to go on a vision quest."

Alone at night in an isolated place in the mountains, after fasting all day and having "smoked and prayed four times, following the ritual belief that tobacco smoke carries one's prayers heavenward," he was approached by something that terrified him. Tallhorse claims it was the spirit of Auannah Parker, a famous Comanche war chief, whom he recognized from his portrait. Says Tallhorse, "He breathed fire on me and paralyzed me. I was just lying there, dead, until he talked to me." He continues:

> He looked at me and said, "Son, what are you doing here? Nothing's the matter with you."
> I said, "I'm sick."
> He said, "No . . . Morning is coming here, son. There's a man out there that they say is real sick. They told me to visit him too before I go. . . . This whole world stands still for just a little while toward morning. . . . That's when spirits come out."[52]

This is an interesting case because John Tallhorse knew nothing of the use of visualization (the very heart of shamanism) for meeting a "spirit guide." The spirit (impersonating demon) came to him uninvited and unexpected. The surprise element, as we have seen, is one of the marks of a genuine experience. What occurred, including the cure of cancer, was spontaneous and could not have been a hallucination created by his expectations.

For the shaman, these spirit entities encountered on the vision quest are connected with the Earth. Eagle Man, a modern shaman, commends the Native Americans for the great gifts they allegedly gave to the world as "a result of their deeply spiritual relationship with nature." He then adds, "Getting back to nature will be the key to saving the planet." [53]

The return to nature is a basic message that comes through in almost all communications from the occult world. Marilyn Ferguson says that "the new paradigm sees humankind embedded in nature."[54] Ramtha channels through J.Z. Knight the same message of harmony with nature. It is the common message of the entities that communicate through channelers, mediums, Ouija boards, and other occult means.

Billions of people around the world watched the opening ceremony of the 1994 winter Olympics in Oslo. They heard environmental concerns expressed in the speeches. Actors and actresses in exotic costumes played the parts of scores of traditional Norwegian nature spirits emerging from under the snow. The TV announcers casually remarked that Norwegians don't build on a property without the approval of the nature spirits. It was suggested that communing with such entities would facilitate correct ecological decisions.

Down the Primrose Path

Although contact with such entities is claimed universally, their true identity, location, and purpose—whether "nature spirits," "space brothers," "Ascended Masters," deceased loved ones, "power animals," gods and goddesses, etc.—is always beyond verification. This ought to be disturbing, yet it seems not to be. Medical scientist Andrija Puharich writes:

> Considering that I have had two years of intermittent experience [of contact with them], I am remarkably ignorant about these beings.
>
> On the other hand I have complete faith in their wisdom and benevolent intentions toward man and living things on earth. My

lack of hard knowledge about them is the kind of deficiency that does not erode my faith in their essential pursuit of the good, the true, the beautiful and the just.[55]

Such trusting naivete from a scientist is astounding! Yet one finds similar trust to be universal regarding the imagined forces of nature and the spirits which allegedly control those forces. In contrast, the Bible is rejected, even though its integrity is fully demonstrated internally and externally. The message the Bible brings is not the one mankind wants to hear.

We have mentioned Bill Moyers' television series with Joseph Campbell, the world-renowned expert on mythology. In it Campbell referred to the remarkable "commonality of themes in world myths."[56] To Campbell, mythology was "the song of the universe."[57] That mystical view that the universe is a living creature has a winsome appeal, but it fails to explain the impersonal violence of nature's destructive forces—or man's moral conscience. In fact, the evidence overwhelmingly proves that there are evil entities who are leading mankind down a destructive path of delusion.

It is impossible to progress along the spiritual path except through the practice of [Eastern] meditation.

—Djwal Kul, ancient Tibetan Master[1]

The most accomplished psychics in the world seem to be those steeped in mysticism, so we should not discard lightly what they say. It is not anathema to me, as to many scientists, to speak of the spiritual realm.

—Edgar Mitchell, astronaut[2]

The basic model of man that led to the development of [Eastern] meditational techniques is the same model that led to humanistic psychotherapy.

—Lawrence LeShan, past President, Association for Humanistic Psychology[3]

Emergence of the Mystical *by Henry C. Clausen, [33rd degree Mason]* . . . *is a gleaning from* . . . *teachings imbedded in the ancient mysteries of Egypt and of Greece,* The Bhagavad-Gita *of the Hindus, the lessons of Buddha, and the inspiring tenets of modern Theosophy* . . . *[with] sections under the heading of "Mysticism, Key to Knowledge"—"Seeking Inner Light."* . . . *The volume should be in the hands of every Mason.*

—Masonic review of book authored by the Scottish Rite Sovereign Grand Commander and published by Masonic headquarters in Washington D.C.[4]

There is a growing missionary spirit in Hinduism. . . . *A small army of yoga missionaries is ready to go to the West. They may not call themselves Hindu, but Hindus know where yoga came from and where it goes.*

—From an editorial in *Hinduism Today* titled "An Open Letter to Evangelicals," by its editor, Reverend Palaniswami, a Hindu monk[5]

America is on the verge of a breakthrough in Buddhadharma, *a flowering of the wisdom that has enlightened billions of souls on the other side of the world.*

—Tracy Cochran, a consulting editor of *Tricycle: The Buddhist Review*[6]

YOGA HELPS BENNETT STOP SMOKING

—Caption of news release across the country concerning former Education Secretary, William J. Bennett[7]

No, I don't have to have faith, I have experience.

—Joseph Campbell[8]

12

* * *

The Influence of
Eastern Mysticism

In 1974, Stanford Research Institute (now SRI), with funds from the Charles F. Kettering Foundation, undertook a study to determine how Western man could be deliberately turned into an Eastern mystic/psychic. Directed by Willis W. Harman (who later became president of Edgar Mitchell's Institute of Noetic Sciences), the project was called *Changing Images of Man*. The scientists involved sincerely believed that a turn to Eastern mysticism was the only hope for human survival.[9]

The task of persuading the public to accept this new direction fell to one of Dr. Harman's friends and admirers, Marilyn Ferguson. She fulfilled her assignment with the publication in 1980 of her groundbreaking bestseller, *The Aquarian Conspiracy*. In it she said:

> A great, shuddering irrevocable shift is overtaking us . . . a new mind, a turnabout in consciousness in critical numbers of individuals, a network powerful enough to bring about radical change in our culture.
>
> This network—the Aquarian Conspiracy—has already enlisted the minds, hearts and resources of some of our most advanced thinkers, including Nobel laureate scientists, philosophers, statesmen, celebrities . . . who are working to create a different kind of society. . . .
>
> The [Eastern mystical] technologies for expanding and transforming personal consciousness, once the secret of an elite, are now generating massive change in every cultural institution—medicine, politics, business, education, religion, and the family.[10]

Eastern mysticism has penetrated every area of Western society. Children's comic books that once offered Charles Atlas courses in body building now advertise courses in mind power, which teach how to control the minds of others. Movies such as the *Star Wars* and *Star Trek* series, TV series such as "Kung Fu," "Highway to Heaven," and "Touched by an Angel," and TV cartoons by the dozens ("Mutant Ninja Turtles," "Power Rangers," "Masters of the Universe," etc.) have made Eastern mysticism the normal way of thinking. Across America, YMCAs offer classes in yoga, and churches of all denominations follow the trend. According to Palaniswami, the editor of *Hinduism Today,* yoga and other forms of Eastern meditation "were too sophisticated for public consumption 30 years ago, but today they're the hottest item on the shelf."[11]

Universities now offer courses in Yoga Psychology, Metaphysics, Hatha Yoga, The Origins of Salem Witchcraft, Eckankar, Tarot Card Workshops, Psychic Development and Techniques, Astrology, Self-Awareness Through Self-Hypnosis, and similar subjects. A *Washington Post* article about a Maryland grammar school was titled "Meditation Comes to the Classroom,"[12] while the *Seattle Times* reported that inmates at Walla Walla State Penitentiary were learning "stress management" through the regular practice of Hatha Yoga.[13] A nationally syndicated columnist wrote:

> Instead of singing hymns, they're sitting in the lotus position chanting "omm" at America's oldest school of theology [Harvard Divinity School].
> The Nave's [school paper] calendar reminds students that March 20 is . . . "a special time to listen to the Buddha and meditate on the perfection of enlightenment. . . ." There's no mention of Palm Sunday or Passover, reflecting their insignificance at an institution where all is venerated, save Western religion. . . .
> Harvard . . . is an elite institution, training the next generation of mainline church leadership. Its degrees are passports to power in the Protestant establishment. . . .
> Will the last graduating Christian please collect the Bibles and turn out the lights?[14]

The Evangelists of Eastern Mysticism

How did this transformation overtake a "Christian" America? The drug movement in the '60s and '70s opened the West to the cosmic gospel of the invading Eastern gurus. Most Westerners find it difficult to think of these smiling and bowing yogis, swamis, and lamas as *missionaries* determined to win us with their mystic gospel. It comes as a great surprise that the largest missionary organization in the world is not Christian but Hindu—India's Vishva Hindu Parishad (VHP).

Yes, *missionary* organization. Nearly 20 years ago, in January 1979, at the VHP-sponsored second "World Congress on Hinduism" in Allahabad, India (attended by about 60,000 delegates from around the world), a speaker declared, "Our mission in the West has been crowned with fantastic success. Hinduism is becoming the dominant world religion and the end of Christianity has come near." By law, no Christian missionary activity is allowed among Hindus in India, but Hindus aggressively evangelize the West, and with great success. Among the primary goals listed in VHP's constitution are the following:

> To establish an order of missionaries, both lay and initiate, [for] the purpose of propagating dynamic Hinduism representing... various faiths and denominations, including Buddhists, Jains, Sikhs, Lingayats, etc. and to open, manage or assist seminaries or centers for spiritual principles and practices of Hinduism ... in all parts of the world. . . .[15]

Interestingly, the 1979 World Hindu Conference was chaired by the Dalai Lama, who publicly proclaims tolerance for all religions. Hinduism and Buddhism infiltrate our society, government, and even public schools as science, while Christianity is banned as a religion.

Phil Jackson is applauded for turning the Chicago Bulls' headquarters into a sacred repository of fetishes and totems and introducing his entire team to Eastern mysticism. *Newsweek* referred favorably to Jackson as the man "who brought Zen principles to bear in coaching the Chicago Bulls to three consecutive NBA championships." The article lauded Jackson for accomplishing "one of the more daunting challenges in the history of religion."[16] It would be another story had he indoctrinated his team with Christianity.

Of all the gurus who have come to the West, none has done more to establish the credibility of Eastern mysticism than Tenzin Gyatso, the Dalai Lama, spiritual leader in exile of Tibet's Gelugpa, or Yellow sect, of Mahayana Buddhism. He claims to be the fourteenth reincarnation of the original Dalai Lama, a god on earth with the power to initiate others into their own godhood. Here we have again the persistent occult theme of human deification echoing the serpent's lie in the Garden of Eden.

In August 1996, Hollywood elite such as actor Richard Gere and MGM President Mike Marcus honored the Dalai Lama at a fund-raising dinner for the American Himalayan Foundation. The thousand guests contributed about 650,000 dollars. Harrison Ford introduced the self-proclaimed god. Of course, Shirley MacLaine was on hand, along with Leonard Nimoy and many other well-knowns. Late in 1996 two major films were in production about the Dalai Lama's life.[17]

A Worldwide Deceit

As part of the most massive missionary effort in history—aimed directly against Christianity—every guru who has come to the West (from Maharishi Mahesh Yogi to Bhagwan Shri Rajneesh to Baba Muktananda) was sent here by his guru specifically to win converts to the Hindu/Buddhist pantheistic faith. Yogananda, for example, founder of the Self-Realization Fellowship (SRF) and one of the forerunners of this massive evangelism campaign, personally initiated more than 100,000 disciples into *kriya yoga*. Maharishi has initiated millions into his TM brand of yoga. Yet the missionaries from the East all protest that they are teaching the *science* of yoga, health, and higher states of consciousness, not *religion*.

We can register no legitimate complaint against those who seek to persuade others of what they sincerely believe to be important truth. However, they should not lie about their product or their purpose. And that is exactly what the gurus from the East have done. "Yoga" is a Sanskrit word meaning to "yoke," and its aim is to yoke with the Hindu concept of God through self-realization: to achieve the enlightenment of realizing that *atman*, the individual soul, is identical with *Brahman*, the universal soul—i.e., that one's true self is God. Yet yoga instructors solemnly swear that yoga has nothing to do with religion, when in fact it is the very heart of Hinduism.

The magnitude of the deceit is comparable to the Pope claiming that, instead of heading a church, he represents a group of nonreligious scientists. India has banned foreign missionaries since shortly after it gained independence. All the while, India's missionaries travel the world converting millions to Hinduism and Buddhism while protesting their tolerance for all religions and denying the religious nature of their mission.

There has been much criticism, some of it no doubt justified, of Western missionaries who have gone to Africa, China, and India with the gospel of Jesus Christ and attempted to westernize other cultures. That goal cannot be justified. Western culture is not Christianity. In fairness, however, we must ask why there has been little or no criticism of Buddhist, Hindu, and Muslim missionaries who have aggressively pushed their religion and way of life upon an unsuspecting Western world.

Life Is an Illusion—So Make Up Your Own!

Much credit for bringing Eastern mysticism into Roman Catholicism and the West goes to Jesuit priest Pierre Teilhard de Chardin. As a young girl, psychologist Jean Houston (who led Hillary Clinton into "contact" with former First Lady Eleanor Roosevelt) was heavily influenced by de Chardin.[18] Houston claims that the techniques she teaches for activating the imagination open the person to a new reality. Echoing de Chardin's Eastern mysticism, she claims that this alternate reality is more real than the "cultural trance," known as "normal waking consciousness . . . in which we all dream the same dream, more or less, and call it: reality."[19]

Carl Jung wrote introductions to some of the first Western editions of books on yoga and Eastern mysticism. Reflecting the Hindu view that life is but a dream, Jung was obsessed with dreams and their interpretation. In one dream he saw himself in yogic meditation representing his "unconscious prenatal wholeness. . . ." In commenting upon the dream, Jung declared:

> In the opinion of the "other side" [i.e., the communicating spirit guides] our unconscious existence is the real one and our conscious world a kind of illusion . . . which seems a reality as long as we are in it. It is clear that this state of affairs resembles very closely the Oriental conception of Maya.[20]

Jung claimed to have received multiple communications from the "other side." The messages he received were consistent with the vast majority of such communications—proving again a common source and identifying it beyond dispute. Over and over, Eastern mysticism rears its serpentine head. Ramtha's message is no exception: "You are God, and therefore capable of creating any reality you desire, if not now, then in a later incarnation."[21] Again it is Hinduism's belief that all is *maya,* or illusion. Houston's goal is to deliver us from this common delusion so that

> . . . we will one day look back astounded at the impoverished world of consciousness we once shared, and supposed to be the real world—our officially defined and defended "reality."[22]

Yoga was developed to escape from this unreal world of time and sense and to reach *moksha,* the Hindu heaven. With its breathing exercises and limbering-up positions, yoga is promoted in the West for enhancing health and better *living*—but in the East it is understood to be a way of *dying.* Yogis claim the ability to survive on almost no oxygen and to remain motionless for hours, free of the "illusion" of this life.

The Deceit and Danger of the "*Science* of Yoga"

In a classic flimflam, one of the world's most ancient *religious* practices is being sold as the "*science* of yoga." The average Westerner is not aware that yoga was introduced by Lord Krishna in the *Baghavad Gita* as the sure way to Hindu heaven, or that Shiva (one of the most feared Hindu deities) is addressed as *Yogeshwara,* or Lord of Yoga.

That yoga is Hinduism is usually denied. Hearing occasional references to Patanjali's second-century B.C. *Yoga Sutras,* the

Westerner assumes that Patanjali was an early Indian Plato or Einstein. In fact, Hindus regard him as one of their greatest religious leaders. Thinking they are buying *health,* millions are unwittingly getting involved in *Hinduism.* Believing they are being taught *scientific* practices, yoga enthusiasts are led unaware into Eastern *religious* beliefs and rituals which are designed to open them to the occult.

Hatha Yoga, known as *physical* yoga, is alleged to be devoid of the mysticism in other forms. Not so. Yoga is yoga, and all of the positions and breathing exercises are specifically designed for yoking with Brahman, the universal All of Hinduism. If the goal is physical fitness, one should adopt an exercise program designed to that end, not one designed for reaching godhood. In one of the most authoritative Hatha Yoga texts, the fifteenth-century *Hathayoga-Pradipika,* Svatmarama lists Lord Shiva (known by Hindus as "The Destroyer") as the first Hatha Yoga teacher. No wonder yoga can be so destructive!

The average yoga instructor does not mention the many warnings contained in ancient texts that even "Hatha Yoga is a dangerous tool."[23] In an unusually frank interview in *Yoga Journal,* Ken Wilber (practicing mystic and yoga enthusiast, often called today's "Einstein of consciousness") warns that any form of Eastern meditation, even done "correctly," involves "a whole series of deaths and rebirths; extraordinary conflicts and stresses . . . some very rough and frightening times."[24]

David Pursglove, a therapist and transpersonal counselor for 25 years, lists some of the "transpersonal crises" common to people who get involved in Eastern meditation:

> Frightening ESP and other parapsychological occurrences . . . [spontaneous] out-of-body experiences or accurate precognitive "takes" . . . profound psychological encounter with death and subsequent rebirth . . . the awakening of the serpent power (Kundalini) . . . energy streaming up the spine, tremors, spasms and sometimes violent shaking and twisting. . . .[25]

"Such experiences," admits the *Brain/Mind Bulletin,* "are common among people involved in Yoga, [Eastern] meditation and other [pagan] spiritual disciplines. . . ."[26] These crises have reached such epidemic proportions that Johns Hopkins University School of Medicine professor Stanislav Grof (a leading

LSD authority) and his wife Christina (a Hatha Yoga teacher) organized the "Spiritual Emergency Network" (SEN) in 1980. SEN coordinates numerous regional centers throughout the world involving more than a thousand professionals who "understand the nature of 'spiritual awakening...'"[27] and can, hopefully, advise those experiencing these spiritual terrors.

Transcendental Trickery

Transcendental Meditation (TM), one of the most popular forms of yoga in the West, exemplifies the deliberate misrepresentation that characterizes so much of today's New Age scene. As already mentioned, Maharishi Mahesh Yogi at first introduced TM to the West as a Hindu religious practice. He openly taught that its purpose was to produce "a legendary substance called *soma* in the meditator's body so the gods of the Hindu pantheon could be fed and awakened."[28] But when TM was excluded from public schools and government funding as a religious practice, Maharishi quickly deleted all reference to religion and began presenting TM as pure *science*.

Such deliberate deceit says much about Maharishi's integrity. Nothing was changed except the labels. This deception has been furthered by the many celebrities, who have practiced and then enthusiastically promoted TM. Bob Kropinski, a former TM instructor, explains:

> In 1957 they [Maharishi] started an organization called Spiritual Regeneration Movement... for religious and educational purposes only....
> In 1974 [he] ... completely renamed all the corporations... [under] a new set of Articles of Incorporation, deleting everything that said "spiritual" and "religious" ... to legitimize the teaching of Hinduism.
> For example, Maharishi ... began calling God "the vacuum state." He instructed [TMers] in the deception.[29]

Subsequent advertisements dishonestly declared that TM "is not a religion, not a philosophy, not yoga... involves no change of belief system...." In fact, TM involves all of these. According to Kropinski, Maharishi told those on the inside:

It doesn't matter if you lie teaching people . . . [because] TM is the ultimate, absolute spiritual authority on the face of this Earth.

[TMers] are the only teachers and upholders of genuine spiritual tradition. . . . They're running the universe.

They are controlling the gods through the soma sacrifice.[30]

Former TMers have filed lawsuits asking millions of dollars in damages because of the trauma they suffered through TM. Kropinski (who won such a lawsuit) relates that people experienced violent shaking, hallucinations, murderous impulses, and suicidal thoughts "as a result of the TM practice." At teacher-training sessions distraught TMers would complain of flying into uncontrollable rages in the midst of meditation, smashing furniture, assaulting their roommates, and trying to commit suicide. Some have committed suicide and others have gone insane.

Another former TM instructor, R.D. Scott, tells of numerous "spirit manifestations" among meditators. These included "visions of floating green eyes . . . creatures of light floating above the *puja* table [TM initiation-ceremony altar]." Ghoulish creatures materialized periodically to stare with terrifying expressions at participants.[31]

Refuting the claim that these experiences were merely hallucinations, Scott points out that often more than one person saw "the same procession of spirit creatures simultaneously and without any advance warning. . . ."[32] Such possibilities are not mentioned in the ads and brochures promoting the alleged benefits of TM and other forms of yoga.

Beachheads of Occult Invasion

The proliferating centers where yoga and other forms of Eastern meditation are taught become focal points of the occult invasion. Channeled messages describe such centers as "the first beachheads secured by the approaching forces . . . to prepare the human species for its collective awakening."[33] This so-called "awakening" into "higher consciousness" is actually the demonization of mankind in preparation for Antichrist and his world religion. For a fuller documentation of that fact, see *The New Spirituality* by this author.

Consider the case of Maurice B. Cooke. A respected Toronto businessman, Cooke became one of today's most popular channelers through dabbling in Eastern mysticism's Raja Yoga. Learning to "still" his conscious mind, he began to receive telepathic messages "dictated from a nonphysical source" which identified itself as Hilarion.[34] Yoga opened Cooke to the spirit realm exactly as it is designed to do.

The incidence of such "contact" with spirit entities is increasing. Although Cooke did not seek to become a channeler, thousands of others have pursued various forms of Eastern mysticism with the deliberate purpose of entering into what they believe to be a dialogue with the spirit world and with allegedly higher entities. Lyssa Royal relates her story:

> I was trained formally by a highly respected channel in Los Angeles. . . . In 1986 I began the deliberate choice of developing my channeling ability in order to access the quality and depth of information that is presented in our books, *The Prism of Lyra, Visitors from Within,* and now *Preparing for Contact.*
>
> The channeling process is simple. I put myself into a[n Eastern] meditative state. . . . Another consciousness (or entity) links . . . telepathically with my brain and then uses it as a translation device. . . .
>
> While in trance, the entities through me are questioned by author Keith Priest and/or various other individuals attending the private or public gathering.[35]

The communications consistently received in this manner by numerous channels have been recorded in thousands of books and videos and are influencing the thinking of an entire generation in the West. The transmissions which Lyssa Royal receives from "several entities who are channeled for our research" fit the usual pattern. While acknowledging that she is not certain of the true identity of the communicating entities, Lyssa trusts the information they provide. She writes:

> In no way is it necessary for the reader to believe the entities are who they say they are. . . . Use the material presented to stimulate your own search for truth. [Yet it always echoes Satan's lies!]

> I have often been asked if I really believe that I chan-
> nel extraterrestrial entities. I have answered that it is not a
> matter of belief or disbelief. Instead, the importance lies in
> where the information and the channeling process takes me in my
> understanding. . . .
> The more I channel her [Sasha, one of several entities], the
> more real she becomes. If she is simply the product of some un-
> discovered ability within the human consciousness, then I still
> consider my relationship with her to be a gift. She has opened
> doors to the universe for me . . . ![36]

It is astonishing that millions of otherwise intelligent and
well-educated Westerners can be so easily persuaded to accept
as "truth" information transmitted by mysterious entities whom
they are unable to identify. Yet this fact offers further proof of
the Genesis account of Satan's seduction of Eve and confirms
the universal appeal of his lies.

The practice of yoga and other forms of Eastern meditation
creates the same altered state as do drugs, hypnosis, drumming, dancing, visualization, and other shamanic techniques
now so widely used in the West. The door is opened to demonic
seduction of mankind. Incredibly, yoga is now widely practiced
and promoted within the church. Robert Schuller gave it his
early endorsement:

> A variety of approaches to meditation . . . is employed by many
> different religions as well as by various nonreligious mind-control
> systems. In all forms . . . TM, Zen Buddhism, or Yoga . . . the medi-
> tator endeavors to overcome the conscious mind. . . .
> It is important to remember that meditation in any form is the
> harnessing, by human means, of God's divine laws. . . .
> Transcendental Meditation or TM . . . is not a religion nor is it
> necessarily anti-Christian.[37]

Reincarnation

Yoga was developed as an escape from endless reincarnations.
The theory of reincarnation is continually promoted by the
deceiving spirits "channeling" to mankind. In Eastern mysticism,
as in Christian Science, death is an illusion. Existence follows an
endless cycle of birth, death, and rebirth through reincarnation.

There is no such thing as resurrection, but a "transmigration of souls" into one body after another.

Reincarnation has become a widely accepted belief in the West to replace the biblical declaration that it is "appointed unto men once to die, but after this the judgment" (Hebrews 9:27). In the East, however, reincarnation is viewed as a means of punishment. Gandhi called it "a burden too great to bear"—returning to this life of suffering and disappointment, spinning forever upon a never-ending "wheel of reincarnation"!

One cannot believe in both reincarnation and resurrection. Each new reincarnation leaves one more body in the grave, overcome by death. In contrast, the Bible promises complete victory over death through Christ's sacrificial death and resurrection for our sins. Jesus Christ was *resurrected*, not reincarnated. The Antichrist, lacking the marks of Calvary, will likely claim to be the latest *reincarnation* of the "Christ spirit."

Professing Christians go to astonishing lengths in attempting to reconcile the anti-Christian doctrine of reincarnation with the Bible and even to find it taught there. Elijah is a favorite because "Malachi prophesies the return of Elijah, and Jesus says John the Baptist is Elijah returned."[38] Yet Elijah was taken to heaven without dying and appeared with Moses in conversation with Jesus (Matthew 17:3), so he could not have been reincarnated into John the Baptist's body, as it is claimed. Clearly, John the Baptist came "in the spirit and power" of Elijah (Luke 1:17), not as Elijah himself.

Some who teach reincarnation pose as born-again Christians. Reincarnationist Herbert Bruce Puryear says, "I love Jesus, and I know Him as my personal Savior."[39] Yet he admits that "most of Christian theology must be reexamined and rewritten in the light of this new truth." It is not surprising that Puryear claims to have experienced in prayer "the radiant white light"[40] so common in the occult.

Reincarnation and Scientific Evidence

Yes, some scientific evidence is claimed for reincarnation. There are the studies of clinical psychologist Helen Wambach. She hypnotically regressed hundreds of subjects into "past lives" and found them to be more than 99 percent accurate in descriptions of life and surroundings. Hypnosis, however, involves a highly suggestible state in which one is controlled by the hypnotist. It is entirely reasonable to believe that a demon would take advantage of this passive state to interject its influence as well. Hypnosis is one of the oldest occult practices. No one should ever submit to hypnosis.

Another respected researcher in this area is psychiatrist Ian Stevenson. He has investigated and documented a number of cases of young children who, in the process of spontaneously expressing memories of past lives, gave so much factual data that there seemed to be no other explanation except reincarnation. Once again, of course, a demon could have implanted such "memories" of past places and events.

Yet in the scientific evaluation of the data, the possibility of demonic interference in an altered state is not even considered. Nor is there any "scientific" way to know whether or not a demon was involved. Yet that possibility alone is sufficient to undermine what few examples reincarnationists can offer. Reincarnation can be refuted by simple logic, but the Bible, which contradicts reincarnation, is fully verifiable in every point (see *In Defense of the Faith* by this author). One cannot believe in both the Bible and reincarnation.

Amoral, Senseless, and Hopeless

Reincarnation is *amoral, senseless,* and *hopeless.* It is *amoral* because (as noted earlier) it perpetuates evil. If a husband beats his wife, the cause-and-effect law of karma will require him to be reincarnated in his next life as a wife who is beaten by her husband. That husband will have to return in his next life as a wife beaten by her husband and so forth endlessly. The perpetrator of each crime must become the victim of the same crime, thus necessitating another crime, the perpetrator of which must in turn become a subsequent victim at the hands of yet another criminal, ad infinitum.

Reincarnation is also *senseless* because no one recalls the many past lives he or she has supposedly lived nor the previous mistakes and lessons supposedly learned. What then is the point of living again and again, only to bear the burden of bad karma due to misdeeds one can neither remember nor correct? It is argued that *subconsciously* we have such memories and are thus benefiting at an unconscious level. If that were true, we should see evidence that mankind has gradually progressed morally. Obviously, this is not the case.

Evolution, the essential partner of reincarnation, claims that man is the result of hundreds of thousands of years of gradual advancement to an ever-higher order of being. The Bible, however, says that man is degenerating into ever-more-immoral behavior. One need only read the daily papers and study history to know which of these opposing views is correct.

That reincarnation is also *hopeless* follows logically. The karma built up in the present life must be worked off in a future reincarnation. In that process more karma is accumulated, which must be worked off in a subsequent life, and so it continues endlessly. The cycle offers no release. As for escaping through yoga, there is no explanation of how that practice could abrogate the immutable law of karma nor any proof that anyone has ever effected such an escape.

A further moral dilemma is presented. Suffering by an individual could never make right his past misdeeds. Nor would living a perfect life in the future (even if that were possible) make up for past wrongs. Somehow the penalty must be paid or God Himself could not forgive us.

In Christianity alone the penalty for breaking God's laws is paid by God, who became a man through the virgin birth. He never ceased to be God and will never cease to be man. Jesus Christ is the one and only God-man, who as perfect and sinless could represent the human race, taking the penalty it deserved, and could fully pay that penalty. Only on that basis can pardon justly be offered to all who repent and receive Christ as Savior.

What a difference there is between an impersonal law of karma which can only perpetuate evil and suffering, and the personal God who loves us so much that He became one of us to pay the penalty we deserved, which alone could end evil and suffering!

The New Panacea: Eastern "Meditation"

Harvard University has long been among the leaders in promoting the occult through psychic research. One of its projects involved experimentation with Buddhist monks' psychic powers. The results have been convincing. For example, a Harvard film crew, dressed for the Arctic, set out in zero-degree-Fahrenheit weather from a 17,000-foot-elevation monastery, accompanying ten monks wearing only sandals and light cotton wraparound cloths. At 19,000 feet, on a rocky cliffside ledge, "the monks took off their sandals and squatted down on their haunches . . . leaned forward, put their heads on the ground, and draped the light cotton wrappings over their bodies." Harvard professor Herbert Benson reported:

> In this position, being essentially naked, they spent the entire night practicing a special type of gTum-mo meditation called Repeu. . . . A light snow drifted down over them during the early morning hours.
>
> No ordinary person could have endured these conditions. We're sure of that. Yet the monks . . . simply remained quietly in their meditative positions for about eight consecutive hours. . . .
>
> Finally, at the . . . sounding of a small horn, they stood up, shook the snow off their backs, put their sandals on and calmly walked back down the mountain again."[41]

Paramahansa Yogananda attempted to explain such amazing abilities of certain monks: "Lord Krishna pointed out the holy science by which the yogi may master his body and convert it, at will, into pure energy. The possibility of this yogic feat is not beyond the theoretical comprehension of modern scientists, pioneers in an atomic age. All matter has been proved to be reducible to energy."[42]

In fact, there is no evidence that any atomic conversion of any part of a yogi's body takes place. If that were the case, yogis would not need to eat, drink, or sleep for days at a time and could duplicate the feats of Superman. Yogis have definite limitations far below the level of atomic energy. The possessing demon is obviously limited in what it can manifest through a human body.

The scientists at Harvard and elsewhere accumulate data which show that something paranormal is going on. But science cannot explain it because the source behind psychic power is not atomic but demonic, a source which science can neither identify nor evaluate. Eastern meditation, having been credited with miraculous power, has become increasingly popular in the West. It is another door into the occult.

The Old "Shell-Game Switch"

It is essential to understand the vastly different meanings given to the word "meditation" in the West and in the East. Meditation in the West has always been synonymous with *contemplation,* or thinking deeply about something. Christian meditation involves seeking deeper insights into God's Word (Psalm 1:2), pondering God Himself (Psalm 63:6), reflecting upon God's works (Psalm 77:12), and considering what our responsibility is and what our response should be (1 Timothy 4:15).

In contrast, Eastern meditation (in spite of Robert Schuller's endorsement) involves ceasing to think, and emptying the mind. It is a prelude to possession. Through repeating over and over a word or phrase (a mantra) or focusing on a candle or upon one's breathing, the mind goes blank and one enters an altered state of consciousness. An Eastern meditation instructor tries to explain this induced state as natural:

> If you're new to [Eastern] meditation, remember that all of us naturally meditate. We have ordinary experiences . . . that regularly put us in a meditative state: watching the sun as it sets, listening to soothing music, or just being at the water's edge.
>
> Our mind slows down, our body relaxes, and our consciousness changes. Our brain shifts into the slower frequency known as the alpha state. And that's it—we are meditating.[43]

What he describes is, of course, the opposite of the contemplation which has always comprised meditation in the West. But the switch has been made and the West has taken the bait. Phil Jackson has involved the entire Chicago Bulls team in Eastern meditation, a practice which he picked up in college. He writes,

"The first time we practiced meditation, Michael [Jordan] thought I was joking. Midway through the session, he cocked one eye open and took a glance around the room to see if any of his teammates were actually doing it. To his surprise, many of them were."[44] Jackson, who rejected Christianity, explains what he found in Eastern mysticism:

> What appealed to me about Zen was its emphasis on clearing the mind. . . . One of the fundamental tools for doing that is a form of sitting meditation known as *zazen.* The form of *zazen* I practice involves sitting completely still on a cushion with eyes open but directed downward and focusing attention on the breath. . . . Over time your thoughts calm down . . . and you experience moments of *just being* without your mind getting in the way . . . keeping your mind open and directing it at nothing."[45]

Buddhism offered Jackson an escape from the God of the Bible whom, as a young boy, he once feared and desired to please. Says John Daido Loori, abbot of Zen Mountain Monastery in upstate New York: "Buddhism is a . . . religion without a God or (depending on the school) an afterlife. . . . [It is] the search for the nature of the self, which ends in the realization that there is no self, that all the beings and objects . . . are manifestations of the same underlying reality."[46]

The Delusion of Cosmic/Unity Consciousness

The feeling of being part of everything else in the universe is known as "unity" or "cosmic" consciousness. It is common on a drug high and very appealing to those who have rejected a personal Creator. In contrast to the delusion of a mystical union with an impersonal universe, God's love is experienced by Christians in a personal relationship with Him.

Astronaut Edgar Mitchell, commander of Apollo 14, had the mystical experience of cosmic consciousness on his return trip from the moon. So profoundly was he affected that he abandoned the outer space program to explore inner space. He describes that experience and the transformation it made in his life in his recent book, *The Way of the Explorer: An Apollo Astronaut's Journey Through the Material and Mystical Worlds:*

It wasn't until after we had made rendezvous ... and were hurtling earthward ... that I had time to relax in weightlessness and contemplate that blue jewel-like home planet suspended in the velvety blackness. . . . [I felt] an overwhelming sense of universal *connectedness* . . . an ecstasy of unity.

It occurred to me that the molecules of my body and the molecules of the spacecraft itself were manufactured long ago in the furnace of one of the ancient stars. . . .

We needed something new in our lives, revised notions concerning reality and truth. Our beliefs were, and still are, in crisis.[47]

What do the material molecules of one's body, a spacecraft, and stars have in common with one's soul and spirit? To fail to distinguish between inanimate matter and consciousness and personality is a delusion of colossal proportions.

The irrationality of Mitchell's experience was overlooked in his delight at having achieved the Hindu's "*savikalpa samadhi*—a recognition of the unity of things while still perceiving them as separate."[48] Many people within the Christian church, as we shall see, are having equally powerful mystical experiences which have brought them into occult delusion and bondage.

Like Phil Jackson, Edgar Mitchell was raised in a devout Christian home. Jackson's was Pentecostal, Mitchell's was Southern Baptist. Neither man understood true Christianity, and thus each rejected his own *misconceptions* rather than the truth.

Fantasies from "Inner Space"

Returning from the moon, with his experience of *samadhi* fresh in his memory, Mitchell founded the Institute of Noetic Sciences, "dedicated to advancing our understanding of consciousness. . . ." That organization, he says, spends "hundreds of thousands of dollars and many thousands of staff time hours investigating man's inner experiences. . . ."[49] Mitchell writes:

I would like to close with a saying that those of you who have heard me speak have heard many times in the past. It helps me convey the notion that seems to be permeating our thinking at this point. . . . It is that "God sleeps in the minerals, awakens in plants, walks in animals, and thinks in man."[50]

It is astonishing that anyone could believe in a "God" who originally had no consciousness but "awakened" in plants and was finally able to think in man. Man's thoughts, from base trivialities and petty selfishness to grandiose delusions and the monstrous evil of a Himmler and Hitler, do not reflect well upon Mitchell's "God"!

Once a professing Christian, Mitchell has even exceeded the pagans by attributing evil thoughts and lusts and wickedness to his god who "thinks in man." Such is the deluding power of mystical experiences in furthering the occult invasion.

The same delusion is current within the church. Consider the book *Journey to Inner Space: Finding God in You.* Written by a guru from the East? No, by the pastor of the First Baptist Church in Seattle, Washington. More of that later.

Shaktipat and the Charismatics

Professor Michael Ray of the Stanford Graduate School of Business came to a new view of human potential and its application to the business world after being introduced by his psychotherapist to the Siddha Yoga of Swami Muktananda. At that time the Swami (since deceased) was the guru to many business leaders and Hollywood stars. Ray's life was transformed when an assistant to Muktananda ran a peacock feather across the "third eye" in the center of his forehead. Says Ray:

> I saw a bolt of lightning, like a pyramid of light. I began literally bouncing off the floor and trembling. I cried. I felt tremendous energy, love, and joy.
>
> What I had experienced, I later learned, had been shaktipat, or spiritual awakening of kundulini energy inside me [the serpent force coiled at the base of the spine and awaiting release in an altered state]. . . .[51]

As we shall see, Ray's experience was much like that of thousands of charismatics who are convinced they have received a "special touch from the Holy Spirit" at a John Wimber or Benny Hinn "miracle" service or at the former Toronto Airport Vineyard, or perhaps from the worldwide "revival" flowing out of the Brownsville Assembly of God in Pensacola, Florida, or elsewhere. One cannot escape the similarity between *shaktipat* and what the charismatics, both Catholic and Protestant, call being "slain in the Spirit."

At the touch of the evangelist, usually on the forehead, the subject falls backward into the arms of "catchers" standing by. In this trancelike state he has a variety of occult experiences, from flashes of light to a sense of well-being and love; from uncontrollable weeping or laughter and violent shaking to "speaking in tongues." It was evangelist and healer Kathryn Kuhlman who made "slaying in the Spirit" a household term among charismatics in the '60s and '70s. Televangelist Benny Hinn claims to be Kuhlman's successor, having picked up "the anointing," which he says still lingers at her grave.

As a further example of the similarity between "slaying in the Spirit" and *shaktipat*, consider what happened to Gerald Jampolsky. He has become famous for his use of *A Course in Miracles* in his psychiatric practice and in his books and lectures around the world. Jampolsky believes he was prepared for the message of the *Course* through *shaktipat*, administered by Muktananda:

> It seemed as though I had stepped out of my body and was looking down upon it. I saw colors whose depth and brilliance were beyond anything I had ever imagined.
>
> I began to talk in tongues. A beautiful beam of light came into the room and . . . I was filled with an awareness of love unlike anything I had known before.
>
> And when I [later] started reading the *Course*, I heard a voice within say, "Physician, heal thyself; this is your way home," and there was a complete feeling of oneness with God and the Universe.[52]

As a result of such mystical experiences, Ray and Jampolsky and thousands like them have adopted the views of Eastern mysticism. We are in the midst of an occult invasion.

Eastern Mysticism and Ecumenism

Many Christians assure themselves that there is real virtue in trying to see all the good they can in everyone and that in so doing they are showing Christ's love. After all, isn't love the most important virtue (1 Corinthians 13)? But love is meaningless without truth. Showing the influence of Eastern mysticism, a recent poll revealed that 71 percent of Americans, 64 percent of those who claim to be "born-again," and 40 percent of self-described evangelicals do not believe in absolute truth.

That denial of God's truth is promoted in all communications from entities claiming to be spirits of the dead, Ascended Masters, space brothers, "Jesus," or whoever is most appealing to the particular recipient. Judith Skutch, the publisher of *A Course in Miracles,* attests to the fact that "the same perennial philosophy or ancient wisdom" is expressed consistently through "different voices."[53] The message of the 500,000-word *A Course in Miracles* is no exception. Dictated to an atheistic psychologist by "Jesus," the *Course* reflects the same promotion of Eastern mysticism that Edgar Mitchell embraced on his moon journey:

> The world you made . . . is only in the mind of its maker . . . by recognizing [this] you gain control over it. . . . The oneness of the Creator and the creation is your wholeness . . . your limitless power . . . it is what you are.
>
> God would never decide against you, or He would be deciding against Himself. . . .
>
> Forgiveness . . . does not pardon sins . . . it sees there was no sin.
>
> All guilt is solely an invention of your mind . . . in understanding this you are saved . . . how simple is salvation! It is merely a statement of your true identity.

The lie is so obvious that it requires no explanation. Every child has conscience enough to know that he is morally accountable for his deeds and that sin has separated him from God. Yet the lie is so appealing that intelligent adults by the millions embrace it in their desperate flight from truth and God.

Embracing the Wildest Tales

It can hardly be coincidence that "Ramtha," who channels through J.Z. Knight, preaches the same cosmic gospel from the East. Those who have rejected the Bible as "myth" turn right around and swallow the wildest tales—and there is none wilder than Ramtha's.

Having allegedly lived in mythical Atlantis 35,000 years ago and having "ascended into the Seventh Heaven, where he and God became one . . . [Ramtha] is now part of an 'unseen brotherhood' of superbeings who love us and hear our prayers."[54] The top business leaders of the world accepted Napoleon Hill's story of a Temple of Wisdom run by a school of Masters on the astral plane, so why not Ramtha's delusion as well? Indeed, Ramtha's followers include some of America's brightest and most highly educated.

Ramtha's teachings even influenced "managers and executives of the Federal Aviation Administration (FAA) whose decision-making and judgments have the greatest impact on the agency. . . ." Ramtha's influence came through a stress management course for FAA executives over a period of years at a cost of 1.4 million dollars to taxpayers. The bizarre training, which resulted in lawsuits against the FAA, was given by a California psychologist who is reportedly a follower of Ramtha and has even conversed with him.[55] The amoral nature of the training and its relation to the rejection of sin and absolute truth reflects Ramtha's blatantly anti-Christian teachings, which echo to a large extent *A Course in Miracles* and have been summarized as follows:

> God is neither good nor bad. . . . He is entirely without morals and non-judgmental. There are no divine decrees. Is-ness is his only business. Hell and Satan are the "vile inventions" of Christianity, a product of "your insidious Book [the Bible]," which Ramtha advises his listeners *not* to read.
>
> There is no such thing as evil. Nothing you can do, not even murder, is wrong. . . . I AM . . . "does not even have the ability to judge you." There is no forgiveness of sins because there are no sins to forgive.
>
> Every vile and wretched thing you do "broadens your understanding. If you want to do any one thing, regardless of what it is, it would not be wise to go against that feeling. . . .
>
> "Everyone . . . whether he is starving, or crippled . . . has chosen his experience for the purpose of gaining from it. . . ." Why condemn the Holocaust? Every murdered Jew *chose* to be killed, and Hitler was merely undergoing a learning experience.[56]

That seemingly sane and well-educated people by the tens of thousands have become the followers of Ramtha (and of other entities who speak the same lies through various channels) makes the Heaven's Gate suicide cult members seem rational by comparison. India, Tibet, Burma, Sri Lanka, and other countries where Eastern mysticism has been practiced for thousands of years are among the poorest countries in the world and the most blinded by superstition. Yet Westerners, having rejected the Bible, are looking for enlightenment in the very Eastern religions which destroyed and impoverished these countries.

In one of her rare accurate insights, the late psychic Jeane Dixon foresaw this massive turning to the East. The story is reminiscent of the Garden of Eden. Dixon relates how a serpent crawled up on her bed and wrapped itself around her:

> Its eyes were gazing fixed toward the East.... The serpent turned its head and our eyes met. Its eyes reflected all the wisdom and suffering of the ages, but also an unspoken plea for trust and understanding. It moved its head again, facing the East once more, as if to tell me that I must look to the East for wisdom and understanding. Somehow I sensed that it was conveying to me that if my trust and faith in it were great enough, I would be able to partake of its unlimited, unearthly wisdom. The serpent looked back, and while I gazed deeply into its eyes, it withdrew and vanished.[57]

Later reflection convinced Dixon that this serpent had been Satan appearing to her and that he was going to deceive the world on a massive scale.[58] Who better would know the role that Eastern mysticism would play than the very instigator of that delusion! Yet Dixon thought she saw in the serpent's eyes "all the wisdom and suffering of the ages." How seductive is the occult invasion!

. . . The number of people entering the mystical stage of development . . . seems to have increased a thousandfold in . . . a mere generation or two. . . . One wonders if the explosion in their numbers might represent a giant leap forward in the evolution of the human race . . . toward . . . global consciousness and world community. . . . Perhaps the greatest prophet of this leap was Teilhard de Chardin.

—M. Scott Peck[1]

There is no doubt in my mind that there will be a rapprochement between the spiritual values that New Age people hold so dear and . . . science.

—Karl Pribram[2]

There is a pop religiosity going on right now, a kind of childish interest in ghouls and devils and vampires. But . . . also uncertainty and a longing for truth. . . .

—Jason Epstein, Random House editor[3]

Whereas in previous generations "altered consciousness" was considered a mark of bohemian depravity if sought voluntarily or one of madness if involuntary, nowadays a "high" is the essence of psychologic sophistication.

—Walter Bromberg[4]

There is a great awakening sweeping over the world today. There are times when one fully believes that we are entering a new and more complete age . . . into the sunlight of "Old knowledge made new."

—*The Occult Digest*[5]

At Stanford University's well-regarded Graduate School of Business the syllabus for a seminar on "Creativity in Business" includes meditation, chanting, "dream work," the use of tarot cards and discussion of the "New Age Capitalist."

—Robert Lindsey, *The New York Times*[6]

Barnes and Noble has increased the number of religious titles it carries by 35 percent since 1993 . . . holy is both very hip and very profitable.

The New York Times News Service[7]

One of the biggest advantages we have as New Agers is, once the occult . . . terminology is removed, we have concepts and techniques . . . acceptable to the general public. So we can change the names and . . . open the New Age door to millions who normally would not be receptive.

Dick Sutphen, New Age leader[8]

13

* * *

New Respectability
in a New Age

It is now 20 years since housewife J.Z. Knight exploded onto the New Age scene as the channel for Ramtha, that mythical warrior fugitive from Atlantis. In 1988, "amid a barrage of negative press . . . she withdrew from public view." Nevertheless, in spite of another messy divorce in 1992 from a husband who accused her of promoting a cultlike atmosphere, more than a thousand of Knight's followers have moved to Yelm, Washington, to buy property and build homes near her 3-million-dollar estate and to attend her "Ramtha School of Enlightenment." About 2000 others reportedly "descend on Yelm to attend twice-yearly retreats . . . [paying] a minimum of $1350 a year to encounter Ramtha via Knight; to learn a blend of Yoga, quantum physics and mental exercises they say enhance spiritual awareness and psychic abilities; and to seek spontaneous healing of everything from corns to cancer."[9]

In February 1997, Knight paid the expenses of a group of 14 scholars, headed by J. Gordon Melton, religion researcher from University of California, Santa Barbara, to visit her to determine whether she and Ramtha are legitimate. The results of their investigation will be included in a book Melton is writing about the Ramtha phenomenon. That Knight invited them demonstrates her sincerity and willingness to be tested.

Earlier, Knight had welcomed psychic researcher Stanley Krippner of San Francisco's Saybrook Institute. Krippner was accompanied by a neurophysiologist who gave Knight a battery of tests while she channeled Ramtha. The tests revealed "increases in heart rate, muscle tension and skin moisture and decreases in blood volume, pulse and skin temperature that . . . could not be faked." As with other mediums, such as Eileen Garrett, who submitted to every conceivable scientific test, it is clear that a spirit entity at times takes possession to speak through Knight. Krippner told her after the tests:

> I don't know who you are, JZ, but I do know you are not a fraud.[10]

Rejection and Rebellion

Knight claims her spiritual odyssey began when, as a teenager ostracized by "a stepfather who loathed her," she "fell in love with God" and "talked to Him incessantly," and eventually "God began to talk back to her." This "talking with God" to obtain new insights and revelations independent of the revelation that God has given us in His Word is characteristic of the occult and of much that claims to be Christian. Knight's "god" is certainly not the God of the Bible.

Ramtha's concept of God—one of the many lies that Knight channels and along with her followers has embraced—has been expressed by many other entities through other channels. So has nearly everything else Ramtha says.

> God is a mind composed of consciousness and energy, birthed from the void. And the power of God is to transform [energy waves] into particles of experience.
> We'll make a New Age of superconsciousness possible, in which new kinds of energy coexist with the old.[11]

To imagine that "the void" could birth anything is obviously the same delusion as Edgar Mitchell's unconscious god awakening in plants. That intelligent people by the millions accept such lunacy while rejecting the God of the Bible testifies again to the self-delusion which grips those who imagine they can escape moral accountability to God. It reflects, too, the growing respectability of occultism in today's world.

The rejection of the God of the Bible by the "flower children" of the '60s resulted in rebellion against all authority. They concealed their self-centeredness with talk of peace and love. No rules would be needed in their brave new world. Everyone would be free to take dope, listen to groovy music, enjoy free sex, and "make love instead of war." On drug trips they experienced the same cosmic consciousness as Edgar Mitchell had in space and Michael Ray and Gerald Jampolsky had through *shaktipat*.

The fantasy of cosmic unity doesn't work in real life. Camelot was a farce. One could, however, keep on dreaming the impossible dream—through yoga or drugs or both. The flight from reality and reason continues with the growing popularity and acceptance of "pot" and other consciousness-altering drugs (and now heroin) along with Eastern meditation. Gene Edward Veith painted the grim picture well:

> Fashion magazines such as *Vogue* and *W* have been featuring a new look for the '90s: gaunt, emaciated women with hollow eyes sprawled on a bathroom floor, holding out their arms for a needle. Glamorous models cultivate a zoned-out look, shuffling down the runway like semi-conscious zombies. The fashion world is calling it "heroin chic"... [and] teenage drug use is skyrocketing... [up] 78 percent from 1992....
>
> "I believe in drug use," confesses the head of a major record label, quoted anonymously in *The Los Angeles Times*. "It's part of growing up and the creative process...."
>
> The psychedelic '60s turned on with LSD; the strung-out '70s... [on] amphetamines; the hard-charging '80s got its kicks from cocaine. Today's pop culture is cultivating a dark, depressed mood.... Young people, dressed in black, indulge themselves in bleak, moody introspection, and their music wallows in cynicism, anger, and despair. Their drug of choice, increasingly, is heroin.
>
> Jonathan Melvoin, keyboardist for the Smashing Pumpkins, recently died of a heroin overdose. So did Shannon Hoon of Blind Melon. So did Hole's Kristen Pfaff, Skinny Puppy's Dwayne Koettel, and Replacement's Bob Stinson. Nirvana's Kurt Cobain, hailed as the spokesman for his generation, killed himself after a long struggle with heroin addiction....
>
> Secular drug treatment agencies boast success rates only in the single digits... Teen Challenge cures 70 to 86 percent of the addicts it serves. Other Christian groups and churches are meeting with similar success. Bondage to drugs, like other bondage to sin, is best dealt with by the gospel of Christ.[12]

We have already noted the relationship between drugs and the occult. The New Testament refers to the occult as "sorcery," the English translation of the Greek word *pharmakeia.* And now a new dimension has brought further respectability to occultism: the "potheads" and "dropouts" of the '50s and '60s are the doctors, lawyers, politicians, psychologists, social workers, university professors, and scientists of the '90s.

The consciousness revolution is no longer spearheaded by a bunch of scraggly young freaks; it's being fed to us from the top down. Its occult fruit is ripening for a horrible harvest. Again, as Veith put it, "The upsurge of drug use during President Clinton's administration is probably due less to his cutbacks in the drug czar's office and interdiction efforts than to the permissive culture he embodies and represents...joking on MTV about wishing he had inhaled. . . ."[13]

New Respectability in the Church

One can hardly blame the world for embracing the occult when the church (including evangelical leadership) is doing the same. Church leaders increasingly jump onto a bandwagon with little regard for where it came from and where it is going. Evangelical acceptance of M. Scott Peck and his heretical bestselling books is a case in point. By December 8, 1993, when Peck appeared on the Oprah Winfrey Show, his first book, *The Road Less Traveled,* had been on *The New York Times* bestseller list a record-breaking 500 weeks (now more than 600). He told Oprah that he had been "divinely led" to write it. Yet he had earlier admitted that he was not a Christian at that time. The anti-Christian teachings in that book ("the collective unconscious is God," etc.)[14] refute any claim to divine involvement.

In his next book, *People of the Lie,* published after his alleged conversion, Peck's heretical pronouncements continue unabated. Peck says he "would not exclude from the [exorcism] team any mature Hindu, Buddhist, Muslim, Jew, atheist, or agnostic who was a genuinely loving presence."[15] In *The Different Drum,* Peck declares that "the salvation of the world" would come "through communities . . . nothing is more important." No mention of salvation through Christ. Peck's position on the faculty of the Omega Institute, which offers courses in "Zen, magic, witchcraft, altered states of consciousness, and various other occult arts,"[16] belies his professed Christianity.

When New Age Roman Catholic priest (now Episcopal priest) Matthew Fox published *The Coming of the Cosmic Christ,* in which he equates fundamentalist Christianity with fascism[17] and separates Jesus from the "Christ" that dwells in us all (a common occult theme), there was M. Scott Peck's glowing endorsement on the back cover. Nevertheless, Peck and his books continue to be praised by leading evangelicals, even in Moody Bible Institute's *Today in the Word.*[18] The following comments by authors Brenda Scott and Samantha Smith are a shocking reminder of the new respectability which the occult has gained even within the evangelical church:

> If New Agers recognize Peck as one of their own, and if he is content to be so identified, then why can't Christians have the [same] discernment . . . ? Instead, he conducts seminars . . . teaching Christian pastors his Zen methods of "community."
>
> Dr. Calvin Van Reken, assistant professor of moral theology at Calvin Seminary, recommended *The Road Less Traveled* in the January 24, 1992 issue of the campus periodical. David Mains spent several days reading from Peck's book, *The Different Drum: Community Making and Peace,* on nationwide broadcasts of "The Chapel of the Air." David Mains never told his listeners that Peck considers his books New Age or that *The Different Drum* . . . mocks the sinlessness of Christ and teaches Zen Buddhism.
>
> We wrote to the "Chapel" . . . , explaining Peck's New Age doctrines and affiliation, and enclosed a copy of his article from *New Age Journal.* We were concerned that the "Chapel's" endorsement of Peck might lead many astray. Our letter was never acknowledged, and *The Different Drum* continued to be aired. . . .[19]

Evangelical Leaders and the Occult

Matthew Fox insists that "Christianity has been out of touch with its 'core,' its center, its sense of mystical practice and cosmic awareness."[20] David and Karen Mains have done their part to correct that alleged deficiency. In her eighteenth book, *Lonely No More,* Karen advocates acquiring a personal spirit guide and other occult practices which Fox promotes.

A bestselling author and popular speaker at women's conferences, at the time that book was published Karen was "chairperson of the trustee board for InterVarsity Christian Fellowship/USA."[21]

Karen Mains approvingly quotes and takes the advice of modern mystic Thomas Merton, who was as much Buddhist as Roman Catholic monk.[22] She equates tremors and violent shaking of her body with a mysterious power from God that rushes through her hands (common occult manifestations), which she calls a "charism of healing."[23] She feels the oneness of her self with the molecules of her body and the universe of things and creatures, seemingly experiencing and commending the cosmic or unity consciousness of an Edgar Mitchell or yogi.[24] She is convinced that at "the insistent initiation of the Holy Spirit" she is "being forcefully guided to make rapprochement" with Jung's unconscious.[25] This book is an incredibly self-centered and self-absorbed account by a Christian leader who has been led inadvertently into occult bondage.

Karen Mains goes into great detail about her dream life, to which she attaches a Jungian interpretation, seemingly unaware that Jung's theories came from demonic inspiration. She says that a tall, dark, and handsome man "in his early thirties" had been appearing to her in dreams "six or eight times a year for the last four or five years." Looking earnestly into her eyes, he has told her, "You are everything I have ever wanted spiritually."[26] He has clung to her, head on her breast, and wept.[27] Karen's "spiritual director," a Catholic nun and Jungian psychotherapist, explained that her "male-self" (Jung's animus) has been "wooing" her. Karen accepts that "this is indeed my male-self, the animus that I need to complement my female being, the anima." She considers this theory which Jung learned from the demonic world to be "exceptionally scriptural."[28]

Submitting to a "spiritual director" opens the door to the occult, especially in view of the methods which those trained in this growing profession employ. According to Spiritual Directors International, "about 350 Christian-based spiritual-director training programs exist in the United States," most of which are Roman Catholic and ecumenical. One network based in San Francisco listed "2600 members who are trained spiritual directors." A typical training program "mixes psychology, sociology, theology and spirituality in classes, lectures, discussions and hands-on exercises."[29]

At Cenacle, a Catholic contemplative center, Karen's alleged "male-self" from her dreams, through the occult technique of visualization, turns into an "idiot-child sitting at a table." She sees its "totally bald" head "lolled to one side . . . drooling . . . emaciated and malnourished . . . a little skeleton of a ragamuffin . . . [with] sad, huge eyes. . . ." Under the guidance of her Catholic/Jungian "spiritual director," Karen is convinced that this visualized "idiot-child" which has now come alive to her is, in fact, the "Christ child" within, that part of herself "that is Christ" and has been attempting to woo her![30]

Secular psychology's delusion of the "inner child" invaded the church through "Christian psychology" and is now taught in seminaries and promoted by leading pastors. This author watched in distress on Sunday morning, June 8, 1997, as Charles Stanley, a solid evangelical pastor, spent much of his sermon advising listeners concerning "the child within." Karen Mains has gone more deeply into this delusion. Hers is no ordinary child, but Christ Himself!

"The Christ child within me," she calls it. Was Christ not a mature man in His thirties when He died on the cross for our sins, and is He not now at the Father's right hand in a resurrected, glorified body? Does He not come to live within us *by His Spirit* as the Lord of life and glory who conquered death? How then can He still be a child—and such a child as He never was, "emaciated and malnourished . . . a little skeleton of a ragamuffin . . . [with] sad, huge eyes . . ."? What delusion is this, and from what source?

In a valiant effort to hear no evil, see no evil, speak no evil, *Christianity Today* (*CT*) defended the heresies of Karen Mains in an article which castigated those whom it labeled as "self-appointed heresy hunters . . . arbiters of legalism sitting in judgment . . . [in a] modern-day witch-hunt."[31] The article was an illogical and unbiblical attack against anyone who would bring correction in the church, and a denial of the responsibility of each Christian to be a Berean (Acts 17:10,11). The scolding complaint that David and Karen Mains were misunderstood and harshly judged contained no documentation either of their teachings which had been questioned or of the supposedly unfair criticism lodged against them. Instead, readers were expected to believe whatever *Christianity Today* said.

A Scandalous Cover-Up

In a *CT* follow-up article two months later titled "Christian McCarthyism," Philip Yancey denounced as "McCarthyism" any attempt to bring correction in the church.[32] That accusatory label succeeded 50 years ago in protecting Communists in influential positions (who were betraying the United States from within) by ridiculing anyone who exposed Communist infiltration. We now know that McCarthy was right! In like manner, those who stand against heresy and desire correction in the church today are also ridiculed. Will the church likewise awaken too late?

Yancey said that Karen Mains had merely "written about her dream life," and quoted neither her nor her critics. Such a cover-up of heresy and occultism in a leading evangelical magazine is unconscionable! He argued, "It is time for us to remember that Jesus named *love,* not theological or political correctness, as the identifying mark of Christians." Political correctness has nothing to do with Christianity, but doctrinal soundness is its safeguard. Yancey seems to have forgotten that love's language is "the truth" (Ephesians 4:15) and that Christ Himself said that love causes Him to correct those who fall into error (Revelation 3:19).

Christianity Today has played a major role in giving credibility and respectability to the occult. Yancey says, "Richard Foster dares to use words like meditation . . . which puts him under suspicion as a New Ager." In fact, Foster advocates and gives instructions on how to practice Eastern meditation so that the visualized image of Jesus comes to life: "You can actually encounter the living Christ in the event, be addressed by His voice and be touched by His healing power . . . Jesus Christ will actually come to you."[33]

What Foster advocates is the most powerful occult technique known. Yet he has the backing of Christian leaders around the world, and many of them have joined his Renovare movement for reviving Eastern mysticism in the church. Yancey and *CT* suppress anything that would reflect badly upon well-regarded Christian leaders, and present Foster as having become the target of false charges.

Tony Campolo is also depicted as unfairly criticized, as though his blatant heresies were nonexistent. Like Sir John Marks Templeton, Campolo says that Christ dwells in everyone whether they know it or not. In a recent book, in a chapter titled "Embracing the Feminine Side of God," Campolo declares: "There is that feminine side of me that must be recovered and strengthened if I am to be like Christ. . . . And until I feel the feminine in Jesus, there is a part of Him with which I cannot identify."[34] Yet it is "Christian McCarthyism" to point out that such ideas are unbiblical!

Christianity Today seems more concerned with defending error than correcting it (which it does, selectively, at times). Nor is *CT* the only such magazine that has drifted away from the truth. Writing in the magazine of the Evangelical Covenant Church, North Park Theological Seminary professor Richard W. Carlson decries the "paranoid responses" on the part of critics of the New Age movement. "All is clearly not bad in New Age," he writes, and some "aspects may even be healthy for the church. . . ."[35] No wonder such statements as the following could be uttered triumphantly by a professor lecturing at Harvard Divinity School:

> The environmental movement, in conjunction with New Age spirituality and the rediscovery of the native American worldview, is assaulting the arrogant domination of nature that has brought the planet to the brink of ecocatastrophe. . . .
>
> *All* life is sacred and must be protected from the ravages of the species ironically titled Homo sapiens. And so, more recently, there has been the revelation of Gaia, the entire earth as a living entity. The Great Goddess has had many names and this is but the latest. . . .
>
> It is above all the Bible that must be blamed . . . ! The repressive, racist, phallocratic and hierarchical heritage of biblical religion has deformed Western culture. The Christian churches, of course, have been the chief vehicle of this monumental deformation. . . .
>
> What is on the decline is the tattered residue of the Judeo-Christian tradition in the churches and synagogues. . . . This

particular god is dying if not yet quite dead. But other, more ancient, gods are alive and stirring.[36]

The Role of Freemasonry

Occultism has also gained a new respectability both in the world and the church through its acceptance and promotion by numerous business and civic leaders and pastors. Among the latter, none was more influential than Norman Vincent Peale. A prolific and popular "Christian" author, Peale's writings have introduced millions in the world and church to the occult. There are at least two sources of Peale's occultism: the writings of occultist Florence Scovel Shinn (documented later in this book), and Freemasonry.

A 33° Mason, Peale was pictured on the cover of the Masonic magazine, New Age. He was inducted into the Scottish Rite [Masonic] Hall of Honor on September 30, 1991, and his portrait now hangs in the Washington D.C. Masonic Temple.[37] He was often held up by Masons as an example of Masonic character. Yet instead of honestly acknowledging the truth about Masonry, Peale perpetuated its deceits.

According to its own documents, Masonry involves occultism. Its influence permeates both the world and the church. Although many professing Christians are Masons, Masonry is an anti-Christian religious cult rooted in paganism. Masonry contains much of the mysticism of Hinduism and Buddhism, and is Luciferian. Yet Peale declared, "I have never seen the slightest word or expression [in Masonic rituals] that is anything a Christian could not endorse."[38]

Such an obviously false statement sheds further light upon Peale's perversion of Christianity. No one who has reached the 33rd degree could be so ignorant. Declarations by Masonic authorities expose Peale's dishonesty on that subject. Albert G. Mackey, coauthor of *Encyclopedia of Freemasonry*, is one of Masonry's highest authorities. In *Manual of the Lodge*, Mackey traces Masonic teaching back to "the ancient rites and mysteries practiced in the very bosom of pagan darkness. . . ."[39]

Albert Pike, Sovereign Grand Commander of the Southern Supreme Council of Scottish Rite Freemasonry in the USA, was "an honorary member of almost every Supreme Council in the world."[40] He authored *Morals and Dogma of the Ancient and Accepted Scottish Rite of Freemasonry* for the Supreme Council of the Thirty-Third Degree, which was published by its authority. This compendium of official Masonic lore traces Masonry to Hinduism, Buddhism, Zoroastrianism, and other Eastern religions. In that volume Pike declared:

> Masonry, like . . . all the Mysteries, Hermeticism and Alchemy, conceals its secrets from all except the Adepts and Sages, or the Elect, and uses false explanations and misinterpretations of its symbols to mislead those who deserve only to be misled. . . .[41]
>
> Part of the symbols are displayed [in the Blue Degrees] to the Initiate [Mason], but he is intentionally misled by false interpretations. It is not intended that he shall understand them, but . . . that he shall imagine he understands them.[42]

Secrecy and occultism go hand in hand. At the heart of Masonry is a secret Luciferian doctrine which a Mason comes to understand only when he reaches the higher levels. Manly Palmer Hall, another of the greatest authorities on Masonry, writes, "When the Mason . . . has learned the mystery of his Craft, the seething energies of Lucifer are in his hands. . . ."[43] Nevertheless, Masonry is highly respected in today's world and Masons constitute a high percentage of those in leadership both in the world and in the church.

Those who deny that Jesus is the only Christ and that He came once-and-for-all in the flesh have embraced the spirit of Antichrist (1 John 4:1-3). Such is the teaching of Eastern mysticism and the mind science cults: that Jesus had attained to the state of "Christ consciousness" available to all mankind. Masonry declares the same:

> Jesus of Nazareth had attained a level of consciousness, of perfection, that has been called by various names: cosmic consciousness, soul regeneration, philosophic initiation, spiritual illumination, Brahmic Splendor, Christ-consciousness.[44]

An Anti-Christian Religion of Salvation by Works

Masonry has its own anti-Christian gospel, which assures members that through good works and obedience to its tenets they will reach the Celestial Lodge in the Sky presided over by the G.A.O.T.U (Great Architect of the Universe), or "God as you conceive him to be." Masonic authority Carl H. Claudy writes: "Masonry . . . requires merely that you believe in some deity, give him what name you will . . . any god will do, so he is your god."[45]

In the initiation into the very first degree, the Lambskin represents "that purity of life and conduct which is necessary to obtain admittance into the Celestial Lodge above [i.e., heaven]. . . ." In the 19th degree of Scottish Rite Freemasonry the initiate is told that attachment to Masonry's "statutes and rules of the order" will make him "deserving of entering the celestial Jerusalem [heaven]." In the 28th he is told that "the true Mason [is one] who raises himself by degrees till he reaches heaven" and that one of his duties is "to divest [him]self of original sin. . . ." These and other rituals of Masonry fly in the face of the many declarations in the Bible that salvation is "not of works" (Ephesians 2:8-10) nor by "works of righteousness" (Titus 3:5).

In the ritual for "Knight of East and West," the Master, after anointing the candidate with perfumed ointment, declares that his body has "this day been made holy!" In a further mockery of the blood of Christ shed for sin, the Senior Warden, after taking a drop of blood from the candidate's arm, declares that he has washed his robe in his own blood. He is then given the "sacred word, Abaddon," which, according to Revelation 9:11, is the name of the leader of the hordes of hell.

Similar blasphemy is found in nearly all Masonic rituals. How then could Peale declare that there is nothing a Christian "could not endorse"? Albert Pike declares, "Masonry . . . is the universal, eternal, immutable religion. . . . [It] sees in Moses . . . in Confucius and Zoroaster, in Jesus of Nazareth and in the Arabian Iconoclast [Mohammed] Great Teachers of Morality . . . and allows every brother of the Order to assign to each such higher and even Divine Character as his Creed and Truth require."[46] But no Mason may declare that the God of the Bible is the only true God or that Jesus Christ is the one true Savior of sinners, for such statements would undermine Masonry's ecumenical embrace of all religions. Thus in Masonry's "Maundy Thursday Ritual of the Chapter of Rose Croix" it is stated:

> We meet this day to commemorate the death of Jesus, not as inspired or divine, for this is not for us to decide.[47]

Joseph Fort Newton, another authority on Masonry, writes, "Masonry is . . . a worship, in which men of all religions unite.[48] . . . It invites to its altar men of all faiths, knowing that, if they use different names for the nameless one of a hundred names, they are yet praying to the one God. . . ."[49] In full confirmation of this astonishing and impossible ecumenism, Albert Pike also wrote: "Masonry [is the religion] around whose altars the Christian, the Hebrew, the Moslem, the Brahman [Hindu], the followers of Confucius and Zoroaster, can assemble as brethren and unite in prayer. . . ."[50] And again Manly P. Hall declares:

> The true disciple of ancient Masonry has given up forever the worship of personalities. . . . As a Mason his religion must be universal: Christ, Buddha or Mohammed, the names mean little, for he recognizes only the Light and not the bearer [person]. . . .[51]

The quotes we have given above demonstrate beyond dispute the anti-Christian nature of Masonry. Yet more than a million Southern Baptist laymen and clergy are in Masonry's "brotherhood," and defend it as "Christian." In a stunning demonstration of Masonry's power (and the number of Masons present), the 1993 annual convention of Southern Baptists voted that Masonic membership was "a matter of personal conscience." The vote followed the report delivered to the convention by the Interfaith Witness Department that many "tenets and teachings of Freemasonry are not compatible with Christianity and Southern Baptist Doctrine" and that much "undeniably pagan and/or occult" was involved in Masonry.[52] How astonishing that anti-Christianity is an option in the largest Christian denomination in America!

New Age, Old Lie

For many years the magazine of Scottish Rite Freemasonry in the United States was called *New Age*. That title accurately described Masonic beliefs and rites. In order to hide that fact (because the truth about the New Age is becoming known), the name has been changed to *Scottish Rite of Freemasonry Southern Jurisdiction USA*, or *The Scottish Rite Journal*.

There is a remarkable center of occultism known as Findhorn on the east coast of Scotland. Sometimes called "the Vatican of the New Age movement," Findhorn was founded upon the specific instructions of alleged "spirit guides." Cofounder Eileen Caddy was apparently the first to receive this guidance through an "inner voice" that said, "Be still . . . and know that I am God. . . . Listen to Me, and all will be well. . . . I am closer than your breath, than your hands and feet. Trust in Me." An inner voice is a major tool of the occult. We will later see the prevalence of this delusion within the church and the devastation it is creating.

All of the original adult members of this unique community of Findhorn were "channels" for a variety of entities that had brought them all together by similar "guidance." Harmony with nature and communion with the spirits inhabiting nature were the common theme. Even the alleged spirits of "transformed" Russian prisoners that channeled through Anne Edwards preached the familiar gospel of naturalism/pantheism: that everything is "God" and that each person's "Higher Self," as a part of "God," can create its own reality.[53]

This appealing message, again so similar to what the serpent told Eve in the Garden, is being repeated through literally thousands of "channels" as the phenomenon of contact with "spirit guides" explodes around the world. Satan has been the source of this lie since the beginning and continues to instill it in minds that are open to his inspiration. Psychiatrist and LSD researcher Stanislav Grof notes with approval the consistent thread running through the world of the occult:

> In these LSD experiments, people were . . . moving into what we call transpersonal realms . . . which include past-life memories,

mythological encounters, experiences of oneness with nature, one-ness with the cosmos, and so on. . . .

When I met Swami Muktananda who invited me to a seminar on Kashmir Sivaism, a system of Indian Philosophy, I discovered . . . that this ancient philosophical system was extremely similar to the system that has emerged spontaneously from the non-ordinary [altered] states of consciousness of modern Westerners.

To find such a convergence was a very interesting thing . . . that people are discovering the same perennial truths [in] these non-ordinary states as the ancient mystics had discovered. . . .

The most advanced developments in science are returning to this ancient knowledge that comes from the mystical traditions.[54]

This consistency cannot be the result of imagination. Will Baron, however, was reluctant to believe that the visualizations and meditation he was being indoctrinated into were anything more than imagination. Yet the experiences were so surprising and powerful that he was convinced. He describes the first experience:

As one of the group members was channeling a message, all of a sudden the inside of my forehead lighted up . . . as if someone had switched on an electric light bulb inside the front of my brain.[55]

Further convincing evidence came when a new member gave psychic readings to the group after they had visualized her "in the center of a triangle of golden light . . . this Christ light . . . aligned to her higher self." She told Will things about himself that she couldn't possibly have known. Says Will:

I was absolutely stunned. . . . With excitement I told Rosie . . . that everything channeled had been 100 percent accurate.

At the end of the class, I . . . [asked her], "Rosie, have you been involved in this kind of channeling activity for a long time?"

"No, not at all," she replied. "In fact this is the first class that I have attended. . . ."

"Wow," I exclaimed. "You have incredible psychic ability!"[56]

Selling the Lie

Demonstrations of apparent "psychic power" such as Will encountered give credibility and respectability to the occult in our day. The testimonials coming from excited individuals on the television commercial for the "Psychic Network Hotline" create new believers. The belief that alleged psychics are simply tapping into a power that we all have is supported by supposed authorities, as in this statement by Joseph Campbell in his Bill Moyers interview:

> We are at this moment participating in one of the very greatest leaps of the human spirit to a knowledge . . . of our own deep inward mystery. [In fact], the greatest ever.[57]

The occult invasion is gathering momentum. Much of that growth is due to the new respectability granted to "spirituality," and nothing seems so spiritual as the occult. Writing for the *New York Times News Service*, Mary Tabor said:

> In the last few years readers have begun gobbling up an even broader range of books on religious and spiritual topics. Religious and quasi-spiritual books are creeping onto mainstream best-seller lists . . . [riding] a groundswell of interest in spiritual and theological matters. . . .
>
> Publishers and booksellers say the upswing in reader interest stems partly from a desire for spiritual and moral guidance, and partly from disillusionment with a computer-driven and increasingly violent society.[58]

One of those bestselling books is *The Celestine Prophecy*. Although it is fiction, its alleged "insights . . . and the uncanny accuracy" concerning "the quantum leap forward humankind is preparing to make as we approach the new millennium" are being taken seriously by a wide range of readers. The author recites in a different and exciting manner the same lies one hears consistently from the proliferating channels, lies echoing the serpent in Eden and by now familiar to every reader. Nor can there be any doubt, as the book states, that a "spiritual renaissance [is] occurring on our planet today."[59]

The new respectability granted to "spirituality" opens the door to the clever deceit that a person may be "spiritual" but not "religious." When he first encountered the New Age cult in which he became entangled, Will Baron asked what "religion" it represented. In response to his inquiry, the leader replied,

"No, we are not a religion. We are spiritual."[60] Even Sears, that bastion of conservatism which has the trust of millions, in its very first newsletter to women promoted occultism in the reprint of an article condensed from *New Woman* magazine:

> **First, relax.** Make your mind still and quiet—an absolute blank. . . .
> **Meet your inner adviser.** With your quieted mind, invite a very loving, wise figure into your awareness. It could be an old man or woman, a plant, a dog. Sit patiently and let an image emerge. Then talk about whatever is troubling you. . . .[61]

As earlier noted, "spirituality" has become the great delusion. It doesn't matter what kind of "spirituality" one espouses. Just being "spiritual" is sufficient for the New Age mentality. "Spirituality" has taken on a generic and ecumenical meaning divorced from truth. In fact, to suggest that truth exists and that all else is a lie brings immediate antagonism. This new spirituality is Satan's net in which he snares multitudes.

Marina Raye is a "spiritual motivator, seminar leader and president of High Performance." She teaches "Sacred Sexuality" based upon the belief that "everything is God . . . the pitcher of water, the floor, the fly that buzzes around . . . it's all God . . . [so] we can greet our fellow humans as divine beings, Goddesses and Gods. We recognize the interconnectedness of all life. . . ." Raye says, "A hopeful sign of the shift in consciousness is that many churches are willing to sponsor my workshops. . . . What better place to normalize Sacred Sexuality than in a church sanctuary!"[62]

An Astonishingly Broad Acceptance

Celebrities are the leading promoters of occult "spirituality." Merv Griffin promoted Maharishi Mahesh Yogi and TM in the '70s. Ten years ago Oprah Winfrey revealed that the "secret of her incredible vitality and energy [and] success . . . is her personal relationship with God." The illegitimate daughter of a Mississippi Baptist minister, her mother couldn't handle her and sent her to her father. "He drove the devil out of this hellraiser," says Oprah. Unfortunately, her idea of the devil and God is unbiblical. Her "god" is Phil Jackson's god of the occult. Winfrey "has embraced *A Course in Miracles* and on her show has agreed that 'all religions lead to God.'"[63] Says Oprah:

> I center myself each morning by trying to touch the God light I believe is in all of us. Some people call it prayer, and some call it meditation. I call it centering up. I get boundless energy from that. . . . It is because of this God-centeredness that I am where I am.[64]

In her embrace of the occult, Oprah is joined by many other celebrities. As earlier noted, Robert Stack and Della Reese are involved in Science of Mind. Actress Demi Moore follows the occultism of holistic-medicine guru Deepak Chopra. John Travolta, Tom Cruise, Nicole Kidman, and Kirstie Alley are involved in Scientology. And the psychic hotline is promoted by Dionne Warwick who thereby "encourages people to consult mediums to determine the future."[65] The list goes on and on, from ex-Beatle George Harrison and the late John Denver to Elizabeth Taylor and Shirley MacLaine.

Governments, too, pursue the occult! Ingo Swann, one of the founders of the remote-viewing program, explains that the United States became involved in psychic research because "the amount of money and personnel involved in the Soviet psychotronics clearly confirmed that they were serious about it and had already achieved breakthroughs which justified the increases in expenditures and tightest security." He continues:

> Several quite respectable sources have informed me that two major nations are making advances in psychoenergetics applications. . . . [and] a third smaller nation, with well-known hatred of the American way of life, is also making progress.
>
> I know that liberated Russia sold for big bucks the Soviet psychic secrets three times over in order to acquire needed foreign exchange. . . .
>
> Remote viewers did help find SCUD missiles, did help find secret biological and chemical warfare projects [in Iraq], did locate tunnels and extensive underground facilities and identify their purposes.[66]

There has also been apparent cooperation between the United States and the Russians in the field of psychic experimentation, much of it sponsored by Esalen,[67] the New Age center south of San Francisco where the Human Potential movement was spawned in the 1960s. The Pentagon has had its own Meditation Club headed by Edward Winchester. He talked the Soviets into jointly "visualizing peace" during the height of the Cold War, and on a goodwill tour he meditated "inside the Kremlin...and distributed...meditation kits...to peace committee officials in Moscow, Kiev, and Leningrad...." On a TV program "allegedly seen by 150 million Soviets, Winchester ran a public meditation in front of the Kazan Cathedral" in Leningrad.[68]

Military and Government Involvement

It would take several books to report on the occult invasion of the U.S. military. *Psychic Warrior* by David Morehouse lifted the lid of secrecy on the military's remote-viewing program. Morehouse reveals the intensive training involved for America's psychic spies and warriors and some of their exploits. Contrary to the CIA's claim that it has abandoned the program, Morehouse believes that "Star Gate is as active as ever but has gone further undercover...[and that] the government is taking this technique into the realm of weaponry...." Though officially retired, he can't sleep at night "without the TV blaring, just to shut out all the internal data."[69]

The Monroe Institute in Faber, Virginia, founded by Robert Monroe, which teaches out-of-body trips (OBEs), has been a favorite with military and government officials and business leaders. After the death of his wife in 1992, Monroe claims to have taken an OBE to visit her, but couldn't handle the emotion of it, so swore off OBEs for fear that if he took another one he might not come back. Recently deceased, Monroe is truly out of his body and now knows what a lie this all was. Monroe received three patents for audio signals to induce an altered state of consciousness. Even Buddhist monks use the tapes "as a training tool." As the *Wall Street Journal* reported:

> Retired General Albert Stubblebine, former director of the U.S. Army Intelligence and Security Command, confirms that the Army sent personnel to the institute in the 1980s...[while] investigating the potential military applications of psychic phenomenon....
> The bestselling co-author of *Beyond IBM*, Katie McKeown, visited the institute...after the unexpected death of Louis Mobley, her

friend and collaborator on the book.... Mobley communicated with her through James R. Hoover, a DuPont manager—and skeptic—attending the institute at company expense.

Mr. Hoover, who had never met Mr. Mobley... [was] skeptical until... Ms. McKeown... said that certain remarks could only have come from Mr. Mobley. That "scared the daylights out of me," says Mr. Hoover. "I still get chills thinking about it."[70]

Nearly ten years ago Representative Charles Rose claimed that "At any given time, about one fourth of congressmen are engaged in exploring psychic phenomena...."[71] As a result of Orange County, California Treasurer Robert L. Citron's reliance upon the investment advice of a psychic and an astrologer, the affluent county "lost $1.7 billion in risky investments... [and] declared bankruptcy December 6, 1994."[72] The *New York Times News Service* recently reported, "Washington [D.C.] rings with the opinions of futurists and spiritualists... 'gurus' to [Newt Gingrich]...."[73] *U.S. News & World Report*, referring to the "spiritual dimension" in the nation's capital, said that it is "unsettling that the speaker of the House drinks deep from the advice of spiritualists.... The Clintons have met with Marianne Williamson, the bestselling author who promotes the power of miracles...."[74]

Lack of space prevents us from reciting the occult involvement at the highest levels of government and business around the world. We must at least mention its occurrence in the world of Islam. In Saudi Arabia, where the holiest Muslim shrines are located, the occult is rampant. King Fahd is so deeply in bondage to the occult that he avoids spending time in the royal capital city of Riyadh because of a psychic prophecy that he would die there:

> The habit of consulting witches and wizards has spread like an epidemic... every prince has his own witch or wizard living with him....
>
> It is widely believed in the kingdom that one of Fahd's nephews has a room in his palace dedicated to the black arts.... Blind belief in supernatural powers extends beyond the royal family and is linked to a series of recent tragedies.[75]

The Broad Road to Destruction

No one explains the basis of the new spirituality better than psychology professor Charles Tart. He lets us know in the clearest terms that it represents a rejection of the Bible and of biblical Christianity. The new spirituality is based entirely upon one's personal experience in an altered state of consciousness. No criteria can be used to evaluate whether such experiences are real; but reality, as in the case of Karen Mains and so many others (like those caught up in the "Toronto Blessing," the "Pensacola Revival," and the new "Spiritual Warfare," as we shall see) is defined by the experience itself. Says Tart:

> When you believe a prescribed doctrine, you tend to become rigid, and rigidity is hard to hold onto in a world where change is the norm. So what the spiritual psychologies offer people is a chance to explore the transpersonal realm for themselves. People can directly experience themselves as entities connected with the universe. That's a lot to offer. . . .
>
> The notion that science or psychology can make such a distinction [between a genuine spiritual experience and a bogus, self-delusionary one] doesn't hold up very well. . . . Lots of techniques exist throughout the world for inducing religious experiences—from fasting, to meditation, to dance. . . . Perhaps transpersonal psychology can increase the efficiency of progress on the spiritual path. . . .
>
> I . . . advise people to shop around [for a suitable technique]. To just "jump in" and get totally involved with the first or second path you find could be dangerous, if not wasteful. But don't shop around casually. Give some energy to a particular path. Give it a month or two to see where a given practice is leading you. . . . When you find a spiritual path with real heart for you, you might think of making a commitment to it. See where it leads you. . . .
>
> I'm hoping that the study of transpersonal psychology will gradually give rise to spiritual practices that are more effective and less cluttered with outdated cultural baggage. Then people can embark on the spiritual path without risking their mental health, or having serious problems during their journey.[76]

Amazing! Here is an intelligent, highly educated, and sophisticated man, a university professor, who advocates taking a "spiritual path" that could go anywhere or nowhere, which he admits could be dangerous and which science and psychology can't evaluate. "See where it leads you," he suggests, ignoring the possibility that one could find out too late that it leads, in fact, to eternal destruction. Of course, he doesn't believe in heaven or hell. All that matters is how it suits one's fancy.

Such a mentality is the basis of the new spirituality: the idea that there is no truth, no right or wrong, just "experience." This delusion comes from Eastern mysticism and is gaining increasing acceptability and credibility in the West.

A Tragic Rejection of the Truth

This embrace of an "anything goes" spirituality has been in process for some time. Going back to August 1987, the annual conference of the Association for Transpersonal Psychology was titled "Spirit in Action." Pittsburgh psychologist Jon Spiegel, writing in the Association for Humanistic Psychology (AHP) Newsletter, declared, "AHP has always held spiritual concerns close to its heart... [remaining] open to spiritual practices both east and west. We have championed the return of spirit to therapy."[77]

One can only wonder what humanists mean by *spirit, spiritual concerns,* and *spiritual practices.* In fact, they are willing to accept *almost* any "spirituality"—Buddhism, Hinduism, witchcraft, or any form of shamanism. There is one "spirituality," however, which is not acceptable, and that is Christianity. Why? Because it claims to be the truth, a claim that is intolerable for those who must remain open to anything—except, of course, Christianity.

The new spirituality maintains that "right" is what is "right for you," which may be different from what is "right for me." But that doesn't matter because we're both "right" in our own way. Truth is whatever one chooses to believe because the source of truth lies within each of us.

The new respectability given to the occult in the 1990s reflects at least in part an upsurge in interest in religion. The nation's Christian bookstores, numbering more than 2500, had about 3 billion dollars in sales in 1995, three times the total in 1980. Nor do Christian books any longer come exclusively from religious presses as they did a few years earlier, but many now come from the large secular publishers. Early in 1997 the Lily Foundation gave a 5-million-dollar grant to WNET-TV, New York's public television station, to produce 39 weekly half-hour feature programs about religion and ethics to premiere in the summer of 1997. "Religion Newsweekly," as the program is to be called, "will cover a variety of religious viewpoints and . . . will not 'proselytize' for any particular religion. . . ."[78]

Once again there is no right and wrong, no truth. One religion is as good as another. Yet the many important contradictions between religions render that view impossible.

Common sense cannot refrain from protest. This "truth doesn't exist" or "it doesn't matter" approach would be disastrous if it were adopted in real life. Imagine an airline pilot practicing that philosophy. He certainly wouldn't reach his intended destination, nor would he and his passengers live very long. Then why should intelligent people imagine that just any road will lead to heaven? Wouldn't the God who has imposed such definite laws on the physical universe (without which there could be no science) have equally definite moral and spiritual standards as well?

"Spiritual" Is Where You Find It

Phil Jackson considers basketball to be a very "spiritual" pursuit. He writes of the "link between spirit and sports." By "spirit" or "spiritual" he obviously means something entirely different from biblical Christianity. And his *new spirituality* with its new acceptability by the world has opened up to him seemingly infinite possibilities that have liberated him from the narrow-mindedness of his youthful upbringing.

Jackson acknowledges that there is a spiritual dimension to existence. He has experienced it, and it works, even to the extent of producing championship basketball teams! No longer, however, is true spirituality defined by the Bible. The very concept of something being true and something else false has been discarded. Spirituality, for Jackson, is a vast realm to be explored and experienced. He refers to "my two greatest passions: basketball and spiritual exploration."[79]

Yes, exploration! What possibilities that thought opens for wandering wide-eyed through exotic landscapes along a variety of paths made possible through the rejection of the Bible as

God's Word and infallible guide! And who cares where one path or another may lead? The excitement is in the discovery. All that matters is the experience of limitless exploration.

This new respectability which the world grants to a generic *spirituality* (so long as it isn't Christianity) has allowed Phil Jackson (like multitudes of others) to reject what he thinks is Christianity without any sense of guilt. His embrace of all religions has clouded any understanding he may ever have had of Christianity.

Jackson equates faith in oneself with faith in God. In the occult we are each god. Declaring that the Bulls "certainly had faith in themselves in 1991-92," he writes, "You have to trust your inner knowing." *Amazingly*, he confuses one's inner knowing with "what St. Paul called faith: 'the substance of things hoped for, the evidence of things not seen' (Hebrews 11:1)."

On the contrary, Paul specifically said that he had no confidence in himself or in anyone else (Philippians 3:3). Repeatedly the Bible warns against trusting in any man, including one's own self. Solomon wrote, "Trust in the Lord with all thine heart, and lean not unto thine own understanding" (Proverbs 3:5). Jeremiah warned, "Cursed be the man that trusteth in man . . . and whose heart departeth from the Lord" (Jeremiah 17:5). Jesus said, "Have faith in God" (Mark 11:22).

A Serious Delusion

Jackson has been able to convince himself that he hasn't really rejected Christianity; he has simply broadened his horizons to realize that the Bible is only one of many religious books, all of which he treats with equal respect. Thus he can rationalize that he has actually become *more spiritual* through embracing *all spirituality*, including native American spirituality and Zen Buddhism and Hindu concepts, together with anything else that seems to work. He writes with no sense of irony:

> The day I took over the Bulls, I vowed to create an environment based on the principles of selflessness and compassion I'd learned as a Christian in my parents' home; sitting on a cushion practicing Zen; and studying the teachings of the Lakota Sioux. . . .

Even for those who don't consider themselves "spiritual" in a conventional sense, creating a successful team—whether it's an NBA champion or a record-setting sales force—is essentially a spiritual act.[80]

The greatest example of "selflessness and compassion" he could have learned from his parents was Christ's giving of Himself on the cross to die for our sins—but Jackson has rejected Christ for Zen and native American spirituality. Phil Jackson's new spirituality is completely at odds with the Christianity he once espoused, as are the native American spirituality, Zen Buddhism, Eastern meditation, and other religions to which he is now "open."

Jackson is not alone in his trashing of Christianity. He is joined not only by other NBA coaches such as Miami's Pat Riley, but by many pastors and seminary professors. A London, England, newspaper recently noted, "Liberal Anglican and Catholic clergy will today address a meeting of pagans and witches in an attempt to establish 'common ground.'"[81] The Salem, Massachusetts Religious Leaders Association "officially welcomed a high priest witch to its ranks. An Episcopal priest said nobody in the interfaith clergy group could think of any compelling reason to exclude the witch."[82]

As the 20th century draws to an end, there is a growing disenchantment with one of its greatest achievements; modern, high-tech medicine. . . . Can prayer, faith and spirituality really improve your physical health? A growing and surprising body of scientific evidence says they can!

—Time magazine[1]

Indeed, more and more medical schools are adding courses on holistic and alternative medicine with titles like "Caring for the Soul."

—Dr. Wallace Sampson, Stanford University[2]

We are comprised of at least four aspects—the physical, the emotional, the mental and the spiritual. In order to be complete, a healing system must include all aspects. An energy block in any of these levels can create disease. So the balance of the entire person is necessary . . . .

—Yonina Jacobs, clinical psychologist and healer
well known throughout the U.S., Europe, and Israel[3]

Disciplines like yoga and tai ch'i are more than exercise regimens: They're mind-body empowerment techniques that have developed over thousands of years.

—Dr. Sarah Sallon, Director of the Natural
Medicine Research Unit, Jerusalem's Hebrew
University-Hadassah Medical Center[4]

I got more from mind-body medicine than I bargained for. I got religion. Now I know there is a consciousness that transcends science, a consciousness toward which our species is sputteringly evolving . . . spurred ironically by our . . . rendezvous with mortality.

—Marty Kaplan, Harvard *summa* in biology, former
speechwriter for Vice President Mondale[5]

The holistic health movement has served as a platform for disseminating the world view of the New Consciousness and promoting occultism as an approach to health.

—Paul Reisser, M.D.[6]

Spirit is seeping into medicine.

—Joan Borysenko, Harvard Medical School[7]

Il est bon de connâitre les délires de l'esprit humain. Chaque peuple a ses folies plus ou moin grossieres.

—Millot[8]

14

* * *

Holistic Medicine

According to the *New England Journal of Medicine,* about one-third of Americans are involved in "unconventional medical treatments" in any given year. *Time* magazine reported that "Americans spend an estimated 30 billion a year on 'alternative therapists and faith healers.'"[9] In 1990 Americans made "425 million visits to providers of unconventional therapy, contrasted with 388 million visits to all primary care physicians. . . ." To keep up with this trend, Harvard Medical School began offering a month-long course in "unconventional techniques."[10] Most unconventional treatments are New Age methods involving Eastern meditation, yoga, visualization, acupuncture, iridology, homeopathy, biofeedback, and other mystical techniques. For example, Jon Kabat-Zinn "has applied Zen concepts to stress reduction at the University of Massachusetts Medical Center, which he directs."[11]

One obvious danger is the absence of regulations. "Anyone who wants to put on a course can do it," says Stanford University School of Medicine professor Wallace Sampson. "There's close to zero quality control."[12] Outside the USA there is even less. Some patients are convinced they have found help; but for many it is a disaster. When doctors in Los Angeles told Pat Paulsen his colon cancer was beyond their ability to cure, he went to "one of about 35 alternative clinics just across the border in Tijuana [Mexico]." After injections "from the embryo of a blue shark," Paulsen felt so much better that he was going to write a book. Instead, like many others, he died.[13]

Far worse than possible harm to the body is the danger of occult bondage that can result. Chanting accompanies the preparation of some herbal concoctions in order to enhance their occult power. "Faith" in the mysterious can bring a response from the demonic world. Nevertheless, as *USA Weekend* recently reported:

> With 1 in 3 Americans turning to alternative healers, a government panel has prescribed a change in doctors' training. Now more MDs-to-be are studying cures from herbs to prayer. ...
>
> In 50 of the USA's 135 medical schools, anatomy and biochemistry are being supplemented with acupuncture, homeopathy, nutrition, massage and prayer. ... A panel ... at the National Institutes of Health recommended all medical and nursing students be exposed to alternative theories and techniques. ...
>
> "We're not saying every medical student should learn how to be an acupuncturist or a guided imagery leader," says Allen Neims, a Florida physician who was chairman of the NIH panel. "But they should learn enough about these techniques that they can communicate reasonably with their patients and other practitioners about them. ..."[14]

Holistic Means Wholistic

New Age "holistic medicine" is sometimes spelled "wholistic" because it supposedly deals with the whole person: mind, body, and spirit. Three simple questions need to be asked of any practitioner of holistic medicine: 1) What kind of "medicine" do you give to a *spirit*? 2) Were you really trained in medical or nursing school to diagnose and treat a *spirit*? 3) Isn't "spirit" really a *religious* term? What *religion* are you practicing on your patients in the name of *science*? In fact, holistic medicine is shamanism revived in the West.

While the field of medicine is not without its problems and abuses due to the greed of manufacturers and the incompetence of some practitioners and regulating bodies, that subject is outside the scope of this book. We are dealing only with the occult. Holistic medicine purports to apply and manipulate mysterious nonphysical forces. Therefore, holistic treatments have no medical or physiological explanation to support them. The alleged "scientific" basis is simply that in some cases they have been found to "work." In addition to those named above, other holistic methodologies include reflexology, radionics, vitamin kinesiology, crystal healing, and therapeutic touch. Lack of space prevents us from dealing with each of these.

Consider homeopathy. Anyone can set up shop as a homeopath. The original solution of whatever substance is supposed to effect a remedy is diluted repeatedly until there is no detectable trace of that element remaining. Such repeated dilutions give homeopathy its unique power: a mysterious "force" in the solution that no chemist or physicist can identify. The *UC Berkeley Wellness Letter* recently warned: "Except for the ghostly molecules, homeopathic solutions may contain nothing more than water or alcohol. Thus they are not likely to harm you. But can they do you any good? Be wary of anybody—and any product—that promises to cure what no one else can."[15]

A Successful Invasion

A *Jerusalem Post* feature article recently explained: "We live in remorselessly stressful societies. . . . Our diet is heavy on hormone-injected meat, devitalized white bread, and chemical-filled fruits and vegetables." The article goes on to explain the result of widespread dissatisfaction with this state of affairs:

> The pendulum started its swing back some 30 years ago, with . . . "alternative" medicine. At first largely the preserve of the faddish and . . . weird, alternative medicine has grown increasingly respectable. . . . It's now dispensed by MDs in university and general hospitals in North America, Europe and all over Israel.
> Israel's first Department of Integrated Medicine opened at Assaf Harofeh Hospital in 1991, and treats up to 14,000 patients a year. . . . Says its head, Dr. Shay Pintov . . . "It's part of a trend throughout the Western world: People today are increasingly aware of their own health, and tired of chemical solutions. . . ."
> In the US, over 400 universities now offer some level of behavioral [alternative] medicine training. . . . Research into natural and folk-healing techniques is a growing field worldwide. . . .
> Integrated or natural medicine . . . has a major role to play. . . . Its emphasis on mind-body control and relaxation can answer the relentless stress of post-industrial living. Its insistence on healthy non-processed foods speaks for itself.[16]

We can only commend the trend toward better nutrition and away from the oversubscription of drugs. However, through its reliance upon mysterious, nonphysical forces for holistic purposes, Western health care has been invaded by the occult.

Acupuncture, for example, was designed in China to realign in one's body the universal force called the *tao*, made up of *yin* and *yang*. Yes, a needle piercing the skin could conceivably cause a beneficial reaction in a nerve, but that is not the original theory behind it. According to anthropologist Michael Harner (who praises the holistic movement), the word "holistic" is a euphemism for witchcraft, now known as shamanism:

> The burgeoning field of holistic medicine shows a tremendous amount of experimentation involving . . . techniques long practiced in shamanism, such as visualization, altered states of consciousness, aspects of psychoanalysis, hypnotherapy, meditation, positive attitude [Positive/Possibility Thinking], stress-reduction, and mental and emotional expression of personal will for health and healing [positive confession].
>
> In a sense, shamanism is being reinvented in the West precisely because it is needed.[17]

A recent *Los Angeles Times* article was titled "Alternative Care Edges into Medical Mainstream."[18] Occult techniques such as visualization of inner guides (the most basic and powerful shamanic practice) and "touch for health" (the attempt to convey "love and well-being" and to realign the psychic force within through meditatively passing one's hands over the patient a few inches from the body) are being openly practiced in major hospitals across America.

This movement, which brings "spirituality" into medicine, is gathering astonishing backing and momentum. Harvard psychologist Joan Borysenko, quoted above, carries the message everywhere. The ad for a lecture at the University of Alberta, Canada, described her as having been trained in "the great spiritual traditions of the world" and as "a spell-binding lecturer . . . who blends science, psychology, and spirituality in a unique and powerful way . . . equally at home presenting in hospitals, synagogues, churches, and civic settings . . ." Dr. Borysenko tells of her first attempt to interest members of the medical profession in the idea that "spiritual well-being can actually make the difference between our life and our death . . .":

> I spoke to a group of gynecologists and obstetricians at a formal professional meeting . . . screwed up my nerve and started talking

about the nature of mind and consciousness, prayer, near-death experiences, miraculous healing. . . . I had no idea how they'd react, and I was . . . nervous, but it turned into an incredible experience.

I've never had so many people wait around afterward to share their stories with me, and it carried on all through the day. At the reception that evening, I heard them trading stories with each other on every side.[19]

Establishing the "Scientific" Benefit of "Prayer"

A mid-1996 poll found that 82 percent of Americans believed in the "healing power of personal prayer" and 77 percent believed that "God sometimes intervenes to cure people who have a serious illness," while only 28 percent believed in the "ability of faith healers to make people well through their faith or personal touch."[20] Prayer, being a "spiritual" practice, is also included in the holistic approach—but not biblical prayer to the one true God.

On "Larry King Live" for May 31, 1997, Robert Schuller said that Positive or Possibility Thinking was a form of prayer. Unfortunately, Schuller was promoting holistic, or occult, prayer. Followers of *any* religion—and even atheists—can be positive thinkers. As Harner points out, shamanism involves positive affirmations intended to activate a universal force. Such "prayer" may therefore be directed to any god or force or alleged "higher power" of one's choosing, or even to one's own inner power or higher self.

Religion and spirituality of *any kind* seem to be helpful. As a result, "faith" has become a scientific term that has nothing to do with truth or the one true God in whom alone genuine faith may be placed. A 1995 study at Dartmouth revealed that one of the "strongest predictions of survival after open-heart surgery is the degree to which patients say they draw strength and comfort from [any] religion. . . . People who regularly attend religious services [of any kind] have . . . lower blood pressure, less heart disease, lower rates of depression and generally better health than those who don't attend."[21] According to data gathered by Dr. Nicholas Fortuin, internationally known cardiologist at Johns Hopkins

Hospital, "People with faith recover about 70 percent quicker" than those without it.[22] And it seems that *any* faith will do.

William Dempsey, Jr., an emergency department physician, believes that doctors "should consult with the clergy" and that the time has come "to bring down the wall between science and religion. . . ."[23] (We have already seen the destruction of true faith which that process creates.) Dr. Dale Matthews, a professing Christian and member of John Marks Templeton's "Humility Theology Information Center Advisory Board,[24] agrees: "Scientific knowledge has demonstrated the positive benefits of religion. I can say, as a physician and scientist . . . that, scientifically, prayer is good for you. The medical effects of faith on health are not a matter of faith, but of science."

One of Dr. Matthews' patients who "did not consider herself religious" nevertheless "found Matthews' attention to the spiritual dimension extremely helpful." She said, "If it weren't for the spiritual progress, I probably wouldn't be alive today."[25] To be opened to a spirit which is not the Holy Spirit of God may provide temporal benefits but with ominous consequences for eternity.

Harvard's Herbert Benson questions whether there is a God who really answers prayer. Jeffrey Levin insists: "I can't directly study that, but as an honest scholar, I can't rule it out."[26] Benson, however, points to the placebo effect:

> Decades of research show that if a patient truly believes a therapy is useful—even if it is a sugar pill or snake oil—that belief has the power to heal. . . . Faith in the medical treatment . . . [is] wonderfully therapeutic, successful in treating 60% to 90% of the most common medical problems. But . . . faith in an invincible and infallible force carries even more healing power. . . . It is a supremely potent belief.[27]

Refuting Christ's Unique Claims?

Inasmuch as religious faith of *any* kind—and in spite of serious contradictions between religions—produces the same benefits, logically the results cannot be attributed to the efficacy of *any* religion. Any such "faith" healing must be due to the placebo effect, which is caused not by some power in the religion but by the *belief* that it has such power. According to psychiatrist Peter Breggin, it has been "repeatedly demonstrated that up to 50 percent or more of depressed patients improve on the sugar pill. In some studies, nearly 90 percent have improved on placebo."[28]

What or in *whom* one believes (whether in Buddhism or Hinduism, in Mohammed or in Christ) is apparently not important for some healing effects. Rather, *belief itself* seems to trigger some inner power that does the healing. This is only true, however, of psychosomatic problems. Logically, a firm belief in an alleged remedy should cure what depression or a fear of getting ill has caused. Most ailments plaguing Americans—and most "healings" by "faith healers"—fall into that category. "Anywhere from 60% to 90% of visits to doctors are in the mind-body, stress-related realm," according to Dr. Herbert Benson, president of the Mind/Body Medical Institute of Boston's Deaconess Hospital and Harvard Medical School.[29]

The Bible itself supports this finding: "A merry heart doeth good like a medicine, but a broken spirit drieth the bones" (Proverbs 17:22). This statement, however, does not suggest an unlimited power or potential within man. It limits the efficacy of the connection between mind and emotions and body to the kind of healing help one might obtain from a good medicine. The simple fact is that a relaxed, happy, optimistic attitude can assist the body's normal ability to heal itself.

In a *Christianity Today* feature, evangelical leader and theologian J.I. Packer writes, "Statistics suggest that any form of prayer by anybody, Christian or not, helps patients recover. . . . Patients who have asked whatever God they pray to to watch over and heal them, and who are trusting [their] God to do it, relax inwardly in a way that, being natural, is actually therapeutic."[30] With obvious approval, *Christianity Today* reported:

> Foundations, government agencies, teaching hospitals, and universities are now sponsoring numerous studies testing scientific evidence for the efficacy of prayer. This past July . . . researchers from Georgetown, Duke, and Harvard universities, the National Institutes of Health, and the National Institute for Healthcare Research (NIHR) convened to "stimulate an explosion of research in religion in health." The conference was designed specifically to "determine the viability and mechanism of placing 'the faith factor' into mainstream medical care."

> Academics are developing ... studies aimed at establishing a sci-
> entifically discernible link between prayer and healing. ... The
> landmark study that began generating new interest was conducted
> by Randolph Byrd in 1984 ... [involving] approximately 400
> patients at San Francisco General Hospital. ...[31]

The enthusiasm of *Christianity Today* is difficult to understand. We have already seen the deception and denial of truth
that result when science is mixed with Christianity. Furthermore, evidence that generic prayer to *any god* aids healing
would undermine the very faith in the God of the Bible which
Christianity Today upholds. Why trust in Jahweh, who demands
holiness, when any libertarian god will do? The article quotes
several authorities (presumably Christians) to the effect that
the establishment of the efficacy of any "prayer" deals a death-
blow to the God of the Bible:

> Siang-Yang Tan, associate professor of psychology at Fuller
> Theological Seminary and author of *Managing Chronic Pain* [says]:
> "We can't, on the basis of Byrd's study, say that prayer offered
> through Jesus is better than a Muslim's prayer offered to Allah
> ... [only] that some prayer is better than no prayer. ... You will
> never be able to prove that the Judeo-Christian God is the true
> God. That can only be known through faith. ..."[32]

"Faith" and "Proof"

On the contrary, we can and must *prove* "that the Judeo-
Christian God is the true God." If Tan is right, then why should
anyone have faith in the God of the Bible rather than in the
Star Wars Force—or in Christ any more than in Buddha or in
some witch or witch-doctor? True faith is not a leap in the dark
in order to "believe in *something*." There must be a solid *reason*
for one's faith. As Peter exhorted Christians:

> But sanctify the Lord God in your hearts: and be ready always to
> give an answer to every man that asketh you a *reason* of the hope
> that is in you ... (1 Peter 3:15, emphasis added).

As we have shown in a number of recent books *(In Defense of
the Faith, A Cup of Trembling,* and *A Woman Rides the Beast),* there
are hundreds of clearly stated biblical prophecies concerning

Israel and her Messiah. Their indisputable fulfillment in Israel's history and in the life, death, and resurrection of Jesus Christ has been witnessed by the world. The prophecies are too numerous and specific for chance or coincidence to explain their precise fulfillment. Here is conclusive proof that the God of the Bible is the one true God, that the Bible is His Word, and that Jesus Christ is the true and only Savior of mankind. If there were not such proof, faith would be folly. To trust one's eternal destiny to *any* religion, church, or leader without sufficient proof is to commit spiritual suicide. Nor is any such proof found in any scriptures but the Bible or for anyone except Jesus Christ.

Yes, Christ lives in the Christian's heart (Romans 8:9-11; Colossians 1:27), and His Spirit bears witness with our spirits that we are His children (Galatians 4:6). But non-Christians need objective proof, and the Bible provides it. Jesus went to great lengths to *prove* that He was alive (Acts 1:3), and Paul *proved* from the Old Testament that Jesus was the Christ (Acts 9:22), as did Apollos (Acts 18:28). We must do the same.

Once such proof has been understood, the choice can be made to trust in the Lord Jesus Christ as one's personal Savior for eternity. Thereafter, God often gives faith to believe in Him for healings that can be instantaneous and far beyond anything a placebo effect could produce. Many undeniably miraculous healings, fully established by medical examination, are on record. It is both unnecessary and outside the scope of this book to provide that documentation here.

Dr. Tan is pleased that "people are becoming more open to religion," but he is concerned that they are "becoming open to all religion, including New Age varieties."[33] Indeed they are. And without the proof that Dr. Tan denies exists, there is no reasonable basis for choosing one religion or alleged "savior" over another.

Faith in Faith—Or in God?

Many people who call themselves Christians have come to that decision on a purely subjective and emotional basis. Their

Christianity is self-centered and dependent on feelings. They go from church to church seeking signs and wonders, always hoping for a new experience and fleshly excitement. As Paul said, they "will not endure sound doctrine" (2 Timothy 4:3), which alone provides a solid foundation for the Christian life. Many think they are Christians because they had a seemingly miraculous experience of being healed, of falling into a trance-like state when touched by a faith healer, of feeling warmth or electricity in their bodies, of shaking violently or of voicing strange and involuntary sounds.

For such Christians (if such indeed they are), prayer is a religious technique for getting what they want. They pray mightily to persuade God to fulfill their desires. "Faith" becomes the struggle to believe that what they are praying for will happen. Obviously, however, if things happen because they *believe* they will happen, they don't need God. Indeed, they have become their own gods, able to create reality with their minds by "believing."

Multitudes have been taught (by authors and televangelists) to seek personal acquisition of "supernatural power." John Wimber and the Vineyard Christian Fellowship have been foremost in promoting this delusion. While Christian terminology is used and Bible verses are sometimes cited in supposed support, the healing movement within much of today's church is a mixture of heresy and occultism more akin to the holistic movement than to Christianity. This "Christian occultism," a subject to which we will return later, is described by former Vineyard pastor John Goodwin:

> Wimber talks about healing as though this is a technique that someone can learn. . . .
> He goes on to say in this healing video, "As I'm praying for somebody, in evaluating them and taking in information with my five senses . . . I also send up my antenna into the cosmic reality and begin to gather information. . . . When you feel that heat in your hands you know somebody is going to be healed."
> This is dangerous stuff. It's important that you understand the connection . . . between what we see happening in the Vineyards, and in the occult and in the New Age movement. . . . They are all related because they have the same source.[34]

What then is true faith? Jesus said, "Have faith *in God*" (Mark 11:22). Faith is believing that *God* will answer prayer—but only according to His will, in His time, and in His way. Faith does not attempt to bend God's will to its own ends by some prayer technique. Instead of mentally trying to create the fulfillment of his wishes by Positive or Possibility Thinking, or by a Positive Confession or some other technique, the true believer, in submission to God's sovereignty, love and wisdom, sincerely prays as Jesus Himself prayed: "Nevertheless not my will but thine be done" (Luke 22:42).

In contrast, holistic medicine involves no concern for truth or for God's will, but only for something that will *work*. And it relies upon techniques which contradict conscience and the Bible. Holistic medicine attempts to tap into an occult force; and that very attempt rejects the grace of the one true and personal God whose very existence and sovereignty it denies. The appealing magic of the occult produces just enough results to keep its victims nibbling the bait.

A New International Delusion?

Most of mankind think primarily of their own comfort and welfare. Obsessed with a self-centered concern for their own health and well-being, many become the gullible victims of "faith healers" and/or of the entrepreneurs of the latest "alternative" therapies and miracle cures. Seeking perpetual youth, they spend their time and money responding to seductive ads promising incredible results. Such was the case with Will Baron, who says, "psychotherapist Peter Blythe completely changed my life. But I have never met him." It all came about, says Baron, through Blythe's book, *Stress Disease:*

> It introduced the New Age "holistic" concept, the idea that body, mind, and spirit are inseparable, and that each needs to be in harmony in order to produce total health. . . .
>
> I was fascinated to read of . . . acupuncture, homeopathy, psychic surgery, chakra balancing, rebirthing, primal therapy, reiki, crystals, and bioenergetics. Descriptions of these treatments talked a lot about "energies," "balance," and "wholeness." Being

seduced into the New Age through . . . alternative healing techniques seems to be a common occurrence.[35]

One of today's most popular holistic gurus is Deepak Chopra, whom *Time* has admiringly called the "emperor of the soul."[36] The *London Daily Telegraph* calls his *New York Times* bestseller, *Ageless Body, Timeless Mind*, "brilliant and exhilarating." The *Washington Post* calls it "dazzling"; the *San Francisco Chronicle*, "enlightening."[37] Yet the book is simply a rehash of Eastern mysticism in pseudoscientific and medical terms, a clever presentation of Hinduism in a way that appeals to Westerners:

> In unity consciousness, the world can be explained as a flow of Spirit, which is awareness. Our whole goal is to establish an intimate relationship with Self as Spirit. To the extent that we create this intimacy, the experience of ageless body and timeless mind is realized. . . .
> When you get in touch with your own inner intelligence, you get in touch with the creative core of life. . . . We are made victims of sickness, aging, and death by gaps in our self-knowledge.[38]

"Gaps in our self-knowledge" cause "sickness, aging, and death"? So we are simply ignorant of our own godhood and immortality? The entire book, so highly celebrated (more than a million hardcover copies have been sold), is an attempt to prove that the serpent's lie to Eve is really the secret truth and that Chopra can demonstrate it. The seductive subtitle is *The Quantum Alternative to Growing Old.* Yet Chopra himself is aging like the rest of us. With proper diet and exercise he may live longer than many people, but very soon death will take its toll. Still, his followers believe such folly as this:

> This possibility [of living above disease and death] has always been accepted as fact in the East. In India and China, some spiritual masters are believed to have lived hundreds of years as a result of achieving a state of timeless awareness. . . .
> When the spell of mortality is broken, you can release the fear that gives death its power . . . when you see yourself in terms of timeless, deathless Being, every cell awakens to a new existence. True immortality can be experienced here and now . . . the experience of timeless mind and ageless body that the new paradigm has been preparing us for.[39]

So we are each a "deathless Being" deceived by "the spell of mortality"? And intelligent people continue to believe this lie? No one need fear death, says Chopra, because, as parts of the universal energy field, we are all immortal. Multitudes take hope in this fantasy.[40] "We are not individual beings at all," says Chopra, "but merely local expressions of an infinite, universal field of energy."[41]

Energy is impersonal and unconscious and therefore has nothing to do with the human spirit and individual personality. Energy takes many forms, including the molecules which make up the cells of plants, animals, and our bodies. It is no comfort to know that when our bodies die and decay, the energy is not destroyed but takes other forms. The issue is the destiny of the eternal soul and spirit, not of the energy which comprises temporal bodies.

While Chopra offers much valid advice for living a more healthful life, he holds out unrealistic hopes. The holistic movement is driven by an astonishing gullibility fueled by self-centered interests.

A Measure of Public Gullibility

Deepak Chopra's November 1996 newsletter contains an interview with Christiane Northrup, M.D. This "pioneering holistic physician" promotes Eastern mysticism and declares that "the way the universe works is that we attract to us whatever we are vibrating." John Marks Templeton teaches much the same thing.[42] Tell that to victims of rape, robbery, and murder! They were "vibrating" the violence they suffered and thus attracted it to themselves?

Northrup goes on to say, "Deepak talks about the field of absolute bliss and beingness . . . that's our birthright. That's who we are."[43] Really? Then why must we go into an altered state of consciousness to *experience* "who we are"? The magnitude of the delusion is exceeded only by the monumental pride that accepts it. Yet the willingness to embrace such folly has made Chopra a household name and a multimillionaire. His books have quickly sold more than 7 million copies and the fees for his seminars are 300 dollars or more per couple.

Chopra is a Hindu who believes that individual self (atman) is identical with universal Self (Brahman). Strange that we don't act like it and have to delude ourselves into "realizing" what we allegedly already are! He tries to explain our less-than-Brahman experience by suggesting that "toxic accumulations . . . impair the free flow of energy throughout the body, mind, and spirit." This delusion permeates holistic medicine. His recommendations are a mixture of Hinduism involving Agni (the Hindu god of fire) and *pranayama* (yoga breathing techniques), along with common-sense suggestions about diet and promotion of Hinduism's Ayurvedic teachings. "Balance in Ayurvedic medicine is the foundation of health," says Chopra.[44] Many of his medical colleagues would dispute that statement.

Chopra was named in a lawsuit by the widow of a man suffering from leukemia who, after adopting Ayurvedic practice, was allegedly pronounced cured, then died shortly thereafter. The suit was eventually dismissed and Chopra claimed only minimal involvement. Yet the man who "allegedly pronounced the 'cure' . . . [is] described in Chopra's books as 'perhaps the greatest . . . Ayurvedic physician alive today.' "[45]

Chopra suggests that in order to experience optimum health one should "let go of guilt." Yet neither Chopra's Hinduism nor his New Age beliefs offer any basis for real forgiveness. He says that guilt, "of course, is simply blame directed at yourself."[46] On the contrary, man has sinned against God and that is the cause of his guilt. Chopra's philosophy is amoral as well as anti-Christian.

The *Los Angeles Times* has called Chopra a "New Age superstar. . . ." Chopra and two other Indian-born doctors published an article in the *Journal of the American Medical Association (JAMA)* "that discussed ayurvedic medicine in glowing terms. . . . Months later a *JAMA* editor published a lengthy, exhaustively documented article that, in effect, accused the trio of . . . peddling warmed-over transcendental meditation with no scientific basis. . . . Chopra struck back at *JAMA* with a lawsuit . . . [which] has since been dismissed."[47]

Deepak Chopra claims, "We have a new science. . . ."[48] In fact, Chopra is offering not science but religion. Tragically, those who follow Chopra's advice often succumb to occult delusion and embrace Hinduism as well.

Marty Kaplan, Hollywood studio executive, screenwriter, and producer, was "a cultural Jew, an agnostic, a closet nihilist. . . ." He took up meditation from a Deepak Chopra book and embraced the generic false god of the occult—Self as "God." Such is his delusion that he believes this was the God of Jesus. In an article titled "Ambushed by Spirituality," Kaplan enthusiastically tells of his tragic entrapment in the occult:

> What attracted me to meditation was its apparent religious neutrality. You don't have to believe in anything; all you have to do is do it. . . . The spirituality of it ambushed me. Unwittingly, I was engaging in a practice that has been at the heart of religious mysticism for millennia. . . .
>
> The God I have found is common to Moses and Muhammad, to Buddha and Jesus . . . what the Cabala calls Ayin, nothingness . . . Spirit, Being, the All.
>
> I used to think of psychic phenomena as New Age flimflam. I used to think of reincarnation as a myth. I used to think the soul was a metaphor. Now I know there is a God—my God, in here, demanding not faith but experience. . . ."[49]

The Maharishi/TM Connection

In 1983, tired of smoking and drinking to hold himself emotionally together as a busy physician and hospital chief of staff, Chopra visited the Indian headquarters of Maharishi Mahesh Yogi. He became an almost fanatic convert to TM, traveling the world pushing Maharishi's patented Ayur-Veda Products. Until 1987 Chopra was "chairman and sole stockholder of Maharishi Ayur-Veda Products International. He was a millionaire to whom, in 1989, Maharishi awarded a title translatable as Lord of Immortality." Although he has since broken with Maharishi,[50] the following excerpt from a newspaper article eight years ago helps us understand Chopra today:

> The man currently most responsible for disseminating the great sage's [Maharishi's] ideas is . . . Deepak Chopra, former chief of staff of New England Memorial Hospital and now president of the American Association of Ayurvedic Medicine. . . .

Under Maharishi's guidance, Chopra has helped open 60 Ayurveda Medical centers in 23 countries . . . introduc[ing] the ancient Indian healing art to the Western world. . . .

Chopra, 42, who meditates twice a day for 40 minutes, routinely prescribes it [TM] for his patients. He got into meditation eight years ago . . . he and his wife, Rita, both took instruction. . . .

It changed his life. . . . He cut out cigarettes, coffee and alcohol and became "10 times more efficient. . . ."

Meanwhile . . . from materials Chopra passes out at his quantum healing seminars:

"How I view my body, how I perceive it, determines my experience of it. My experience of it determines my reality of it. My interpretation of my body determines its reality, its very molecules. . . .

I am now ready to reinterpret my body as a field of changing patterns that in fact I control."[51]

It is clear that Chopra's views of health and the body are derived from his practice of TM and from Hinduism's doctrine of *maya:* that there is no objective world out there; we each create and control our own reality with our minds. We have already seen the absurdity of that belief. Chopra no more controls the molecular composition and function of his body than he can dispense with food and drink. He doesn't even know the molecules of his body.

For any person to declare that his thoughts create "the very molecules" of his body—molecules which he can neither see nor his thoughts comprehend—betrays a psychotic delusion. That multitudes believe Chopra and hope to achieve this state for themselves bears witness to the delusionary power of the occult. The utter folly of Chopra's statement cannot be denied. The molecules of his body are composed of electrons and subatomic particles some of which science hasn't even discovered yet. And he controls them? Nonsense!

We have earlier seen the heavy occultism associated with TM. Chopra's deep involvement in TM could explain his delusion. The very name "Transcendental Meditation" is dishonest. There is nothing transcendental about it. Through TM one does not come to know the true God who transcends all. Instead, one looks within to realize that one's self is God. Consider the following testimony of two additional former TM instructors, Joan and Craig:

JOAN: The initiation everyone must go through is a Hindu worship ceremony honoring the Hindu gods and Ascended Masters, including Maharishi's own dead guru Dev.

As a teacher of TM I was told to lie . . . to tell them [initiates] that the mantra we gave them was a meaningless sound, the repetition of which would help them to relax—whereas it was really the name of a Hindu deity with tremendous occult powers behind it.

For those who really got into it, TM was like taking a rocket ship into another state of consciousness. . . . They would eventually believe that . . . they could become God.

CRAIG: I was deeply involved in TM for several years before I began to realize that I had joined a Hindu cult. By that time, however, I was too committed to . . . back out. . . .

Several hundred of us from around the world studied for a month with Maharishi in Europe to become teachers of TM . . . and the effect it had was at times very frightening.

Some would see grotesque spirits sitting next to them when they meditated. Some were attacked by the spirits. Others [were] . . . overcome with blind rage, even with the urge to commit murder. . . . Maharishi explained that bad karma was being worked out from past lives—a necessary part of our journey into "higher consciousness."

I finally achieved Unity Consciousness. . . . However, the initial euphoric feeling that I had "arrived" . . . soon gave way to panic. I had lost the ability to decide what was "real" and what wasn't.

Maharishi told me to stop meditating. Gradually I returned to a semblance of normality—but I suffered from frequent lapses into Unity Consciousness, much like a flashback from LSD.

After coming back to the United States, I worked at Maharishi's International University. My roommate there committed suicide, and I was committed to a mental institution.[52]

Beyond the Placebo Effect

Psychologist Albert Ellis, President of the Institute for Rational Emotive Therapy, is not impressed with "scientific evidence for prayer." He believes that "patients who get better after praying do so because faith bolsters their immune system, not because a personal God actually intervenes. Echoing Sigmund

Freud, Ellis has quipped that religion is 'equivalent to irrational thinking and emotional disturbance.'"[53]

Ellis cannot be disputed in those cases which can be explained by the placebo effect. Not all healings, however, fall into that category. There are instantaneous organic healings that could not possibly result from the power of suggestion.

Furthermore, we have controlled experiments where neither the researchers nor the subjects knew which group was the object of prayer. Thus no placebo effect could be involved. One recent study conducted by psychiatrist Elisabeth Targ, clinical director of psychosocial oncology research at California Pacific Medical Center in San Francisco, involved "20 severely ill AIDS patients randomly selected. . . ." Half were "prayed for" by "20 faith healers. . . ." No one knew who was being prayed for, yet the results were encouraging enough "to warrant a larger, follow-up study with 100 AIDS patients."[54]

Typical of the "healers" used in the study was Eetla Soracco, who "draws on Christian, Buddhist, and Native American traditions." Obviously, what she calls "Christian" is not biblical or she would find it to be in serious conflict with "Buddhist and Native American traditions." With such a mixture of beliefs on the part of the "faith healers" involved, any resultant benefits could not be attributed to any particular "god" or religion.

Clearly the results could not be attributed to the patients' "faith." Nor could the results have come from a power projected by those who prayed, since they knew neither the identity (other than names) nor location of those for whom they prayed. There had to be intelligent direction, and from a non-human source.

Harvard Medical School professor Joan Borysenko says: "We're already whole. Our own core self, our higher nature . . . has always been complete and always will be. What we need to do is use our struggles as a pathway back to that most important part of ourselves. . . ."[55] Borysenko's explanation doesn't ring true. Why must we struggle to get back to what we already are? And why were only those patients selected for prayer involved in such a struggle?

Searching for an Explanation

In a recent conference at Harvard Medical School, "spirituality" was linked to health, and speakers referred to a "patient's spirituality" as an "untapped resource."[56] Harvard's Herbert Benson writes in his latest book, *Timeless Healing:*

> Our genetic blueprint has made believing in an Infinite Absolute part of our nature. Evolution has so equipped us in order to offset our unique ability to ponder our own mortality. To counter this fundamental angst, humans are also wired for God.

Again we are confronted with the most astounding nonsense from a university professor: Although God does not exist, it is beneficial to humans to believe in a nonexistent "god." Therefore, the "force" behind evolution, knowing that belief in this imaginary "god" would have a powerful placebo effect, introduced this fantasy into our genetic makeup. What ludicrous fantasies people will concoct in an attempt to escape moral accountability to the God who created them!

Yet for the placebo effect to work it doesn't matter what or in whom one believes. *Belief* itself activates some inner power. Evolution needn't have wired us to believe in a "god" at all. Wouldn't it have been better to wire us to believe in ourselves so we wouldn't have to attend seminars designed to build up our self-image and practice yoga to realize that our true self is god?

Nevertheless, in apparent full agreement with Benson, Rhawn Joseph, a neuroscientist at the Palo Alto VA Medical Center in California, declares, "The ability to have religious experiences has a neuro-anatomical basis." How amazing that this fantasy belief in a nonexistent "god" works in conjunction with neurological mechanisms which evolution has developed to accompany it! And those who promote this shameless malarkey ridicule faith in God! Surely Christ's words apply equally to today's scientific pharisees: "Ye blind guides, which strain at a gnat and swallow a camel" (Matthew 23:24).

Beware of the Frauds

Although we are warning of the occult (demonic power) behind much in the holistic movement, it is not all occultism. There are also many frauds who rely upon deceit while pretending to have some mysterious power. This is true of many of the so-called psychic surgeons, notably in the Philippines and Mexico. Trickery is likewise used by witch doctors in the jungle, where one would imagine it would not be needed because Satan would have unchallenged power.

In 1930, Franz Boas published a partial autobiography of Giving-Potlatches-to-the-World, a Kwakiutl shaman. He tells how his initiation into shamanism came about through observing the healing techniques of the shamans in his tribe. During the healing ceremony, Making-Alive, assisted by four other shamans, locates the place of sickness on a patient's chest, sucks out of it something that looks like a bloody worm, declares he has extracted the sickness, and sings his sacred song. He vomits blood and a piece of shining quartz which he throws into the air. As it "vanishes" he declares that he has shot it into the stomach of Giving-Potlatches-to-the-World. At that point the latter is invited to become a shaman and decides to accept the offer.

The four-year course includes techniques for deceiving patients and witnesses into believing that magic was being performed when in fact it was a fraud. The "bloody worm" was simply a bit of eagle down placed in the mouth before the "healing" and soaked in blood drawn by biting the tongue. Perhaps the most interesting part of his story was the fact that his techniques were so convincing that people seemed actually to be cured because they were convinced he had removed the sickness or evil.[57] It is the placebo effect once again.

This is not to say that all shamans are frauds. Some are indeed the servants of Satan, and demons work through them in astonishing ways to keep their devotees in bondage to their false religion. Wade Davis explains something of holistic medicine in Haiti's vodoun society. It all has a familiar ring:

> In vodoun society, the physician is also the priest, for the condition of the spirit . . . determines the physical state of the body.

Good or bad health results . . . from the proper or improper balance of the individual. . . . Health is a state of harmony . . . something holy . . . for the gods. . . .

To restore the patient's health may involve a number of techniques. At the material level these include herbal baths and massage . . . and perhaps most importantly, a sacrifice, that the patient may return to the earth a gift of life's vital energy.

But it is intervention on the spiritual plane that ultimately determines the patient's fate, and for this the houngan is but a servant of the loa. The spirit is called into the head of either the houngan or an assistant, and like an oracle the physical body of man dispenses the knowledge of the gods.[58]

There are many holistic practitioners who are sincere but who have themselves been deceived into learning techniques which have no efficacy. We have named a few. Let the reader do his or her own research and remember that if there is no physiological/medical explanation, then either the treatment is a fraud or, if it works, it may well be due to an occult power.

Holistic medicine is clearly a major beachhead of the occult invasion. It seems to provide evidence for the existence of a mysterious healing power available to anyone's "faith." It gives support to Al Gore's thesis that what this world needs is "faith in a higher power, by whatever name. . . ." Holistic medicine is but one more giant step for mankind toward the coming world religion of Antichrist.

[The founding of Alcoholics Anonymous in Akron, Ohio, on June 10, 1935] was the greatest event of the twentieth century.

—M. Scott Peck, psychiatrist[1]

[The 12-Step Program is] a way of spiritual healing and growth that may well be the most important spiritual model of any age for many contemporary Christians.

—Keith Miller, best-selling Christian author[2]

[We] came to believe that a Power [whatever we conceived it to be] greater than ourselves could restore us to sanity.

—Step 2 in the 12-Step program of Alcoholics Anonymous

Every man's conception of God must vary with his mental cultivation and mental powers. The Mason does not pretend to dogmatic certainty, nor imagine that certainty attainable. . . .

—From the lecture for the 14th Masonic degree

Why should we attempt to confine the idea of the Supreme Mind within an arbitrary barrier, or exclude . . . any conception of the Deity . . . ?

—From the lecture for the 28th Masonic degree

The 12 Steps are a package of Christian practices, and nothing is compromised in using them. . . . We ought to use them gladly. . . . They are doing tremendous good.

—Pastor Tim Stafford in *Christianity Today*[3]

For years Alcoholics Anonymous quietly did its work. But within the last ten years we've seen best-selling books on all sorts of addiction. Twelve-Step programs now seem to be popping up all over the place. . . . The 12-Step movement has tapped a profound need in people.

—*Christianity Today*[4]

It is the Christian community that is the source of the 12 Steps. So to the extent that we have this strategy today, it was Christian instincts and values that nurtured that and made it possible. The dilemma is that the sort of Christian wisdom that's embodied in the 12 Steps got separated off institutionally from the mainstream of the church.

—Dale Ryan, former Baptist pastor, now executive director of the National Association for Christian Recovery[5]

15

* * *

Twelve Steps with "God As You Conceive Him"

Eastern mysticism's influence in the West goes back further than one would suspect, even predating the drug movement and the invasion of the gurus from the East. We have already seen that Napoleon Hill received the basic philosophy of the PMA and success/motivation movements from spirit entities who deceitfully posed as ancient Ascended Masters known as the "Venerable Brotherhood of India." At about the same time that Hill was introducing the business world to the occult, Agnes Sanford was bringing it into the church. A hundred years before either of them, however, occultism had established a major beachhead in the West through Masonry. Then in the 1930s and '40s the occult invasion was expanded greatly through Alcoholics Anonymous (AA).

The influence of AA's 12 Steps has been enormous. One can scarcely keep track of the many 12-Step groups which have been formed as a result. In their excellent book, and one that every Christian ought to read (*12 Steps to Destruction*), Martin and Deidre Bobgan point out: "Thousands of groups across America use Wilson's Twelve Steps, and most codependency/recovery programs utilize the Twelve Steps in one way or another. . . . All seem to merge the philosophy, psychology, and religion of the Twelve Steps into whatever treatment program they happen to have devised."

The new terms "addiction" and "recovery" now include anything one can imagine. There are even "recovery" Bibles, notably *Serenity for Every Day*. Alcoholics Anonymous has spawned groups such as Adult Children of Alcoholics, Debtors Anonymous, Emotions Anonymous, Gamblers Anonymous, Narcotics Anonymous, Overeaters Anonymous, Sex-Addicts Anonymous, Smokers Anonymous, Shoplifters Anonymous, Workaholics Anonymous—and even Fundamentalists Anonymous. The Dallas Center for Religious Addiction and Abuse sees parallels between families that produce Christian fundamentalists and those that allegedly produce alcoholics, and it targets mainline Christians for "recovery." Of course, the anti-Christian groups are very comfortable with a "higher power" that can be anything one chooses to trust—and delivers them from the God of the Bible!

A Perfect Front for Satan and Demons

AA's 12-Step program (and the others patterned after it) opens the door to the occult by introducing members to a generic "god." Step 2 says, "Came to believe that a Power greater than ourselves could restore us to sanity." Step 3 continues, "Made a decision to turn our will and our lives over to God as we [Hindu, Buddhist, Christian, Mormon, Catholic, agnostic, et al.] understood Him." As in Masonry, any false god will do. Obviously, a willingness to submit to and trust in Al Gore's Higher Power "by whatever name" provides Satan and his minions with a perfect front for their influence and activity.

Satan is not an atheist. He knows that God exists and he wants to take His place and to be worshiped by mankind. To that end, he encourages belief in a "higher power" in order to turn men from the true God to himself. Satan knows that all people have a sense of alienation from God and that the Holy Spirit is wooing mankind to Himself. What better way for Satan to prevent such reconciliation with the true God through Christ than to effect a pseudoreconciliation with a counterfeit higher power?

Such was the case with Bill Wilson himself, the founder of Alcoholics Anonymous. Though Wilson studied under Sam Shoemaker, Episcopalian pastor in Boston, and studied for a year under Bishop Fulton J. Sheen (the closest thing the Catholic Church has had to a televangelist), he never received the Lord Jesus Christ as his Savior.

In *Christianity Today* (*CT*), Tim Stafford says, "The 12 Steps are Christian."[6] Yet none of the 12 Steps contains a mention of Jesus Christ, much less of the gospel. How then could they be Christian? Even Stafford admits that Wilson "never pledged his loyalty to Christ, never was baptized, never joined a Christian church. . . ."[7] The Christian church, however, has joined AA.

Rechristianizing the Unchristian

Stafford and *CT* are pleased with AA to the point of suggesting that Sam Shoemaker "may have made his greatest contribution through Wilson."[8] Yet Stafford also writes, "AA is pluralistic, recognizing as many gods as there may be religions, any of which can work."[9] How can such a destructive concept be considered a great contribution to mankind? Moreover, how can Stafford say that "nothing is compromised in using them [12-Step programs]"?[10] Such comments are typical of *CT*'s long-standing record of theological ambivalence, ecumenism, compromise, and outright support of error.

Stafford also approves of 12-Step programs patterned after AA which have come into the church. He attempts to justify this posture by suggesting that the church's adaptation of AA's methodologies involved "re-Christianizing the 12 Steps."

If the 12 Steps, as Stafford says, are Christian, what need could there be to "re-Christianize" them? If, as is the case, they embody concepts designed to be acceptable to anyone, including atheists, then to speak of "re-Christianizing" them is a delusion. The truth is that AA's 12 Steps are anti-God and anti-Christian. To adapt them into the church is wicked.

The embrace of any form of the 12 Steps within the church implies that God, the Bible, and Jesus Christ offer no solution (or at least an inadequate one) for the sins of drunkenness and other "addictions" and that AA has at last filled that void. Yet thousands of churches across America are doing precisely that. The Willow Creek Community Church of South Barrington, Illinois, pastored by Bill Hybels, is a particularly instructive case inasmuch as it has been called "the most influential church in North America"[11] and a model of the church for the next century. In an exhaustive study of "the Willow Creek phenomenon" for his Ph.D. dissertation, G.A. Pritchard writes:

One of the first staff members I spoke with proudly told me how more than five hundred individuals met at the church each week in various self-help groups (e.g. Alcoholics Anonymous, Emotions Anonymous, Sexual Anonymous). Upon investigation I discovered that these programs were not actually the church's. Although many church attendees were participating in the programs, the actual meetings were being run according to outside organizations' policies.

One of the requirements of these organizations was that individuals could not evangelize or otherwise teach other participants about God.[12]

An Intolerant Tolerance

So we have come to the point where evangelical churches are sponsoring and recommending to their members programs for overcoming sin in their lives by techniques and a higher power which replace (or at the very least supplement) God and the power of the Holy Spirit! Stafford commends 12-Step groups for allegedly being "tolerant."[13] Should we commend tolerance regarding the identity of God and the difference between God's truth and Satan's lie? As for the alleged "tolerance," consider the rules of 12-Step programs at Willow Creek:

> One official code of instruction explains:
> The Steps suggest a belief in a Power greater than ourselves, "God as we understand Him." The Program does not attempt to tell us what our Higher Power must be.
> It can be whatever we choose, for example, human love, a force for good, the group itself, nature, the universe, or the traditional God (Deity).
> The code instructs, "We never discuss religion."[14]

In Scripture we are commanded to "earnestly contend for the faith . . . once [for all time] delivered to the saints" (Jude 3). How then can we be tolerant of promoting higher powers that take the place of God? In support of the tolerance he commends, Stafford says, "Christians [in AA groups] can express their convictions." What convictions? That Jesus is *the* Higher Power? That is neither allowed nor is it biblical.

AA's concept of a higher power is pagan. It would therefore be an insult to Christ to associate Him with it in any way. Christ is not a power but a person. Stafford notes that Christians may not say anything that would "undermine the pluralistic assumptions of the group by suggesting that others' views of God are misguided."[15] So this commended "tolerance" has its limits and is in actual fact intolerant of the gospel!

What Stafford really means—and this is all that AA allows—is that a Christian (like a Mason) is free to say that Jesus is *a* or *his* Higher Power, but not *the* Higher Power. Why then commend this intolerant tolerance?

Moreover, how could anyone express the gospel truth about Jesus ("I am *the* way, *the* truth, and *the* life; no man cometh to the Father but by me"—John 14:6; "There is no other name under heaven given among men whereby we *must* be saved"—Acts 4:12; etc.) without thereby declaring that all other views are false? The truth, then, is that the false gospel of AA suppresses the true gospel of Jesus Christ; and the tolerance it professes is only of error, while it remains intolerant of truth. Pritchard comments on the Willow Creek 12-Step programs:

> Even church members could not talk about Christian truth in these meetings at Willow Creek. Although the programs give lip service to a "Higher Power," they function as practical atheism, teaching the categories of the contemporary psychological world-view. Yet the lack of theological content did not stop the church from advertising these programs each week during . . . services.
>
> That Willow Creek would sponsor and advertise these programs illustrates the church's lack of priority for . . . Christian truth.[16]

A Tragic Ecumenical Indulgence

An official AA publication says, "Alcoholics Anonymous does not demand that you believe anything. . . . AAs tread innumerable paths in their quest for faith. If you don't care for the one I've suggested, you'll be sure to discover one that suits. . . . You can, if you wish, make AA itself your 'Higher Power.'"[17] It could not be clearer that any false god will do. Hell for eternity becomes the cost of sobriety in this life.

It was psychologist William James and his book, *The Varieties of Religious Experience,* which encouraged Wilson to believe that any god would do. That was also the source from which Wilson derived justification for the mystical and ecumenical religious experience which he claims alcoholics must seek for deliverance from their affliction:

> [William] James gave Bill [Wilson] the material he needed to understand what had just happened to him—and gave it to him in a way that was acceptable to Bill. Bill Wilson, the alcoholic, now had his spiritual experience ratified by a Harvard professor, called by some *the* father of American psychology![18]

In keeping with *CT*'s longstanding tolerance toward the errors of psychology, toward the false gospel of Roman Catholicism, and toward ecumenism, Stafford writes, "Christians can and do use AA or other 12-Step groups . . . there is no harm in getting help where it is available."[19] From yoga? From TM? Why not from Christian Science? And why turn to any 12-Step program unless Christ and His Word are not sufficient?

The issue is not whether an alcoholic receives some help. There are fantastic testimonies of changed lives through everything from hypnosis and psychotherapy to an alleged UFO abduction. The tragic truth, however, is that temporal help through AA's "higher power" leads the recipients away from Jesus Christ and eternal salvation. Moreover, AA gives very little real help even in overcoming alcohol. Christian groups which rely solely upon Christ have a far better record.

Like so many other groups that have fallen into the occult, AA reflects the mentality with which John Wimber infused the Vineyards: If it "works," then go for it. Yes, AA "works" for some people, sometimes. The Bible, however, warns against seeking help from false gods. The consequences are tragic in the destruction of lives in this present world as well as eternally. Although AA is very rigid in its opposition to alcohol, other immoral behaviors may be condoned and even encouraged to fill the void left by the denial of alcohol.

Stafford writes with approval, "The 12 Steps penetrate every level of American society." Is this good? On the contrary, that penetration is all the more reason to sound the alarm against AA's false god and gospel. Yet instead of sounding that alarm, Hybels and Willow Creek and countless other churches support and promote this deadly delusion. Stafford and *CT* ought to give a clear warning against a system which, though it kept the founder from drinking, left him firmly in Satan's clutches for eternity. Of Bill Wilson, Stafford admits that after deliverance from alcohol, "the rest of his life was morally erratic." Yet Stafford and *CT* say, "The 12 Steps are a package of Christian practices and nothing is compromised in using them."[20]

A False Foundation

In simple and honest terms, Bill Wilson, founder of Alcoholics Anonymous, was a drunk. The terms "alcoholism" and "alcoholic" had not yet become acceptable as they are today. Martin and Deidre Bobgan pick up the story: "After years of struggling with the guilt and condemnation that came from thinking that his drinking was his own fault and that it stemmed from a moral defect in his character, Wilson was relieved to learn from a medical doctor that his drinking was due to an 'allergy.' Dr. William D. Silkworth had hypothesized that 'the action of alcohol on . . . chronic alcoholics is a manifestation of an allergy.' "[21] AA's official biography of Wilson relates:

> Bill listened, entranced, as Silkworth explained his theory. For the first time in his life, Bill was hearing about alcoholism not as a lack of willpower, not as a moral defect, but as a legitimate illness. It was Dr. Silkworth's theory—unique at the time—that alcoholism was the combination of this mysterious physical "allergy" and the compulsion to drink; that alcoholism could no more be "defeated" by willpower than could tuberculosis. Bill's relief was immense.[22]

Dr. Silkworth's erroneous theory might have remained in obscurity had not Bill Wilson founded Alcoholics Anonymous upon it, and millions of drunks, as happy as Wilson to be relieved of moral accountability for their abuse of alcohol, turned that theory into an almost universally accepted axiom. The fact is, however, that the theory which led to the founding of AA— that alcoholism is a disease—is false. One of the world's leading authorities in this field, University of California professor Herbert Fingarette, has written an entire book[23] as well as numerous articles against this delusion.

Fingarette refers to "a mass of scientific evidence accumulated over the past couple of decades . . . which radically challenges every major belief generally associated with the phrase 'alcoholism is a disease.'" He explains that this mistaken concept "has never had a scientific justification."[24] Writing for Harvard Medical School, Fingarette said, "This myth, now widely advertised and widely accepted, is neither helpfully compassionate nor scientifically valid."[25]

As for the alleged efficacy of AA and other recovery programs, Dr. Fingarette says that "treatments for alcoholism as a disease have no measurable impact at all."[26] Stanton Peele, author of *Diseasing of America: Addiction Treatment Out of Control*, agrees and offers research to show that multitudes have been persuaded by "brainwashing" that they have the disease of alcoholism, and that the overall result has been to impede the normal recovery which otherwise would take place.[27] The Harvard Medical School published a paper which refuted AA's claim that its program is needed because alcoholics rarely recover "on their own resources."[28] In fact, said Harvard:

> Most recovery from alcoholism is not the result of treatment. Probably no more than 10 percent of alcohol abusers are ever treated at all, but as many as 40 percent recover spontaneously.[29]

The facts are in stark contrast to Stafford's and *CT*'s assurance: "We [Christians] ought to use them [12-Step programs] gladly. They belong to us originally. They are doing tremendous good."[30] In fact, 12-Step programs are doing great harm by turning people from the true God to a false higher power, and by denying the sufficiency of God's Word and robbing multitudes of its transforming power. It is reprehensible for *Christianity Today* or any Christian organization or church to encourage participation in 12-Step programs. Tragically, with such misguided encouragement, multitudes have embraced not only an anti-Christian pagan system but an outright fraud.

Alcoholics Anonymous and the Occult

Turning from the true God to false gods of any kind opens the door to occult manifestations, deception, and bondage. Such is the legacy of AA. Bill Wilson and his close friend, Bob Smith, were both heavily involved in the occult even before they conceived of AA. Nor did that involvement cease after AA's founding.[31] The official AA biography of Wilson reveals, without embarrassment, that for years after AA's founding regular seances were still being held in the Wilsons' home and other psychic activities were being pursued, including consulting the Ouija board.[32] The biography declares:

> [T]here are references to seances and other psychic events in the letters Bill wrote to Lois [his wife] during that first Akron summer with the Smiths [Bob and Anne], in 1935. . . .
>
> Bill would lie down on the couch. He would "get" these things [from the spirit world] . . . every week or so. Each time, certain people [demons impersonating the dead] would "come in . . . long sentences, word by word would come through. . . ."[33]
>
> [In 1938] as he started to write [the AA manual], he asked for guidance. . . . The words began tumbling out with astonishing speed. He completed the first draft in about half an hour. . . .
>
> Numbering the new steps . . . they added up to twelve—a symbolic number; he thought of the Twelve apostles, and soon became convinced that the Society should have twelve steps.[34]

So it was through mediumship that Wilson received the manual for Alcoholics Anonymous from the demonic world. It is not surprising, then, that the effect of AA upon many of its members is to lead them into direct occult involvement. Wilson even experimented with LSD in the hope of reaching a higher mystical state and proving survival of the spirit after death.[35] In 1958, Wilson wrote to Sam Shoemaker:

> Throughout AA, we find a large amount of psychic phenomena, nearly all of it spontaneous. Alcoholic after alcoholic tells me of such experiences . . . [which] run nearly the full gamut of everything we see in the books.
>
> In addition to my original mystical experience, I've had a lot of such phenomenalism myself.[36]

The "original mystical experience" to which Wilson referred was his alleged "conversion." It came about in a classic occult encounter with a "white light," rather than by faith in Jesus Christ through the gospel. Wilson had fallen into a deep depression and in desperation cried out, "If there is a God, let Him show Himself! I am ready to do anything, anything!" He had demanded something that God was under no obligation to provide. It was an opportunity for Satan to respond with a "spiritual experience" that set the stage for the seduction of millions. Wilson testified that in response to his cry:

> Suddenly the room lit up with a great white light. I was caught up into an ecstasy. . . . It seemed to me, in the mind's eye, that I was on a mountain and that a wind not of air but of spirit was blowing. And then it burst upon me that I was a free man. . . .
>
> All about me and through me there was a wonderful feeling of Presence, and I thought to myself, "so this is the God of the preachers!" A great peace stole over me. . . .[37]

This was *not* the "God of the preachers" but the one who transforms himself "into an angel of light" (2 Corinthians 11:14)—a light that is reported over and over by those involved in the occult. How can we be sure of this? Because God does not lead anyone to trust in false gods, as did Bill Wilson as a result of this experience. Nor does God dictate 12 Steps which comprise a false gospel to keep those who follow them from trusting Christ for their soul's salvation.

The experience was so profound that Wilson never touched alcohol again. Satan would be more than willing to deliver a man from alcoholism in this life if thereby he could ensnare him for eternity. And what greater triumph than to inspire this man to lead millions into the same delusion! Wilson now had an appetite for more spiritual experiences and immediately became actively involved with the best-known group in his day that offered them: the Oxford Group.

The Oxford Group

It had been through his attendance at an Oxford Group meeting held in a Manhattan rescue mission that Wilson had been motivated to demand that God "show Himself." Now he became a regular at the group's Sunday evening meetings at Calvary Church, pastored by Episcopalian Sam Shoemaker. Wilson would later write that Shoemaker had provided "the spiritual keys by which we [alcoholics] were liberated."

The Oxford Group had been founded by Frank Buchman (a Lutheran minister) who seemed to have a testimony in his early days of truly knowing Christ. Whether that is true or not, his creation, the Oxford Group, soon departed from any semblance of biblical Christianity. The Oxford Group was almost from the very beginning ecumenical. Terminology was adopted which would not offend unbelievers and therefore lacked the essentials of the gospel which alone can save the soul. That compromise having been made for allegedly good reasons, from then on it was steadily downhill.

The Oxford Group would later become Moral ReArmament (MRA). This metamorphosis came about through the mystical "guidance" that was a large part of Buchman's life, and would carry over both into MRA and AA. "It was while walking in the Black Forest [in 1936] that the idea of 'Moral Rearmament' came to him [Buchman]."[38] Five years later, Shoemaker officially broke with Buchman. He explained: "Certain policies and points of view . . . have arisen in the development of Moral Rearmament about which we have had increasing misgivings."[39] English author and former MRA member Roy Livesey writes:

> It must be said that I look in vain in around one hundred Oxford Group and MRA publications on my shelf and find little help to point the way of salvation. . . .
> Involvement with what seems to be the good in MRA often leads to something quite devastating in the spiritual realm. For example, three Indian leaders at Caux [MRA headquarters in Switzerland] impressed me, and their evident peace aroused interest in the Eastern life.
> MRA had been a stepping stone for me into the occult. The meetings at Caux had served only to encourage me still further.[40]

In spite of Shoemaker's apparent concern that the gospel was being compromised in MRA, it was his soft approach which had influenced Buchman in the first place. Instead of clearly declaring the gospel of which Paul was not ashamed, the gospel which "is the power of God unto salvation to everyone that believeth [it]" (Romans 1:16), Sam Shoemaker would urge his hearers to "accept God however they might conceive of him. . . ."[41] Here was the origin of Wilson's desperate prayer. It was the origin as well of the concept expressed in Step 3: "Made a decision to turn our will and our lives over to the care of God *as we understood him.*"

God does not answer to just any name, nor does He respond to those who, when they call upon "God," have in mind a false god. Jesus said, "This is life eternal, that they might know thee, the only true God, and Jesus Christ, whom thou hast sent" (John 17:3). Paul felt it necessary to identify the One whom the Athenians worshiped as "the unknown God" and to declare to them the gospel (Acts 17:22-31). We are warned that God's judgment comes upon them "that know not God, and that obey not the gospel of our Lord Jesus Christ" (2 Thessalonians 1:8). Our eternal destiny will be determined by our relationship with the one true God of the Bible. Obviously a belief in false gods prevents one from believing in the true God alone.

The Making of Mediums and Channelers

Even before it became MRA, the Oxford Group emphasized a daily "Quiet Time with the Holy Spirit" during which a pencil and notebook would always be at hand to record "every God-given thought and idea." Why should God be giving any thoughts apart from His Word—and how would one distinguish such thoughts from one's own? This is a dangerous procedure and one which is widely practiced (under the label of "journaling") even by evangelicals today. Members were cautioned to check their subjective "guidance" against the Bible and "with others who are also receiving guidance in quiet times."[42] Such safeguards, however, only encourage error since such "guidance" itself is unbiblical. Nowhere does Scripture even hint that this kind of extrabiblical "guidance" is to be expected from God.

Buchman and his teachings were warmly received by various churches and groups of Christians. Some, however, had the discernment to recognize the occultism which was developing. The Christians at Cambridge University accepted Buchman's challenge to live more "Christlike lives." Eventually, the Cambridge Inter-Collegiate Christian Union (CICCU) cooled to his "guidance" and Buchman turned to Oxford, the university which gave his movement its name. Dr. Oliver Barclay, a former CICCU president, wrote:

> Buchman was at first received warmly by CICCU.... As time went on, however, disturbing features emerged. He spoke of the Quiet Time, but it was less and less a time of Bible study and prayer and increasingly a time of "listening to God." This members did with their minds blank and with pencil and paper in hand, writing down the thoughts that came to them.
>
> In this way men received entirely irrational guidance... regarded as authoritative.... They tended to lose their concern for doctrine and to end up less definite about the gospel....[43]

The influence of this concept of a quiet time in which one receives direct communication from the spirit realm (kept alive in the church today through Richard Foster and others) can be seen in Step 11 in AA, which calls for "meditation to improve our conscious contact with God as we understood Him...." Dick B, one of the biographers of the movement, writes:

> The [AA] Big Book's Eleventh Step discussion at pages 85–88 ... references to "meditation," "prayer," asking "God to direct our thinking," asking "God for inspiration, an intuitive thought or a decision"... and "morning meditation," hearken back to the Akron days when Bill and Dr. Bob and Anne had Quiet Time with scripture reading and prayer [and also seances].[44]

The emphasis in AA is purely upon the "experience" of recovery. In contrast, Christ offered deliverance through truth as revealed in His Word: "If ye continue in my word ... ye shall know the truth, and the truth shall make you free" (John 8:31, 32). Satan hates the truth and uses mystical experiences for persuading men to believe his lies. Tragically, as we shall see in more depth later, the occult has managed to invade a large segment of the church through the growing reliance upon experiences rather than upon the Word of God. Alan Morrison reminds us:

> Former Quaker and rock guitarist John Wimber, founder of the ... Vineyard ministries ... openly advocates a "paradigm shift" away from thinking with Western logic into the exclusively experiential

way of oriental thinking.... He also claims that "first century Semites did not argue from a premise to a conclusion; they were not controlled by rationalism."[45]

This is a highly erroneous and mischievous statement. Not only is it historically inaccurate but it...denigrates logic...[and] epitomizes the considerable confusion in the Charismatic Movement in its failure to identify the difference between (unhealthy) *rationalism*, whereby the miraculous is denied and the supernatural work of the Spirit is blasphemed, and (wholesome) rationality, whereby the Christian exercises necessary discernment....

The ultimate first century Semite was surely the Lord Jesus Christ; yet He continually used the most devastating logic to demolish His opponents....

Never before [today] has a "sound mind" been so necessary in the life of the Church.[46]

The Central Role of Guidance

The emphasis upon religious experiences rather than truth, and the power of such experiences to convince recipients that they have been touched by God, is a common denominator in most cults (Mormonism's "burning in the bosom," for example) and especially in the occult. It matters little whether the mystical experience comes from drugs, from yoga, from channeling and mediumship, from hypnosis, or from near-death experiences involving the "white light." The results are almost always the same: blindness to the gospel of Jesus Christ, and eventual immorality, exactly as foretold in Romans 1:21-32.

Seeking guidance, not from the Bible but from God Himself allegedly speaking with an inner voice, became a major part of the Oxford Group, then MRA and finally AA. It is clear that such "guidance" is meant in AA's Step 11: "Sought through prayer and meditation to improve our conscious contact with God as we understood Him, praying only for knowledge of His will for us and the power to carry that out."

It was out of the Oxford Group that *God Calling* came. It is one of the bestselling "Christian" books of all time and one of the most deceptive. Written by "two listeners," it purports to be the words of Jesus Christ dictated to them as they placed themselves in the proper passive trance state and wrote them down.

What this "Christ" says in *God Calling*, however, could not possibly come from the true Jesus Christ of the Bible because it contradicts the Bible repeatedly. Roy Livesey gives a summary of the occult teachings of the demon impersonating Christ which is presented in *God Calling*. Here is a partial list:

> The visible realm is a manifestation of God's thought or Divine Mind. The invisible "spirit world" is superior to and more real than the physical realm. The creation . . . operates according to unbreakable laws, which even God must keep. . . .
>
> Our deliberate imagining of something with the intention of making that thing come into existence will produce the desired result. God is within every man and can be found within. Man needs only to quieten all sense-distraction and turn inwards to commune with the "god within." By means of thought-power, word-repetition, and visualization, it is possible to contact and feel Christ's presence on earth beside us.[47]

"Guidance" As a Vehicle of Satanic Deception

God Calling repeats the same lies found in *A Course in Miracles*, which also purports to be Christ's words today. There are other similar channeled materials. One of the more recent is titled *The Jesus Letters*. Like *God Calling*, it was allegedly "received" from Jesus Christ by two women. The principal channeler was Jane Palzere. The means by which they received these *Letters*, again like *God Calling* and *A Course in Miracles*, was the well-known occult technique of automatic writing. Of these demonic *Jesus Letters*, which are filled with the most blatant heresy, Norman Vincent Peale (betraying again his perversion of Christianity) gave the following glowing endorsement:

> It little matters if these writings come from Jesus of Nazareth or Jesus of Jane [Jane Palzere]; they are all the same consciousness and that consciousness is God. I am a part of God, and Jane and Anna are part of that same God.[48]

A.J. Russell, who published *God Calling*, had earlier written *For Sinners Only*, in which he recommended the Oxford Group.

Russell had claimed a "religious conversion" in 1924, following which he "had a number of strange mystical experiences in which the air around him seemed to crackle as though charged with electricity, and ... he would hear a voice guiding him." Here we have the occult invasion once again, and its influence very clearly runs through the Oxford Group into MRA, then AA, and on into the church of today.

Through *For Sinners Only*, "the Oxford Group became known worldwide."[49] Russell continued to be led by the voices of spirit entities which he considered to be "divine guidance." Any investigation of the occult invasion of the world and church leads down a maze of interconnected pathways revealing the influence of a few key figures. Russell is undoubtedly one of them. He published Agnes Sanford's books and promoted her occultism. Sanford, in turn, led a multitude of others astray through her influence upon church leaders such as John and Paula Sandford, Rita Bennett, Richard Foster, Bill Vaswig, and John Wimber. And always we find that "listening to the Spirit" in order to receive "guidance" plays an important part.

MRA and the New Age Movement

The influence of Moral ReArmament can be seen in the New Age movement in the world and is also very evident within the church. Frank Buchman, the Lutheran pastor who wanted so badly to change the world that he compromised the gospel and embraced new revelations through occult guidance, was a forerunner of today's new spirituality. One of his disciples, a close associate during the '40s and '50s, has written:

> MRA was est and TM. It was *consciousness* raising and *sensitivity*. It was *encounter* and confrontation. Frank Buchman was drying out drunks before AA's Bill W had his first cocktail. He was moving hundreds of people in hotel ballrooms to "share" with each other before Werner Erhard was born. He inspired thousands on all continents to meditate for an hour upon arising decades before Maharishi Mahesh Yogi left India. He was indeed Mr. Human Potential, ahead of his time. . . .

A prominent New England churchman . . . wondered out loud to the writer one day how much the whole encounter-sensitivity movement owed to Buchman and his sharing groups. Werner Erhard's est carries identifiable similarities. Brother Roger Shultz who founded the Taize Community in Burgundy, France, south of Paris, in 1940, attributes important elements of his inspiration to his association with the Swiss Oxford Group in the thirties. Paul Tournier was identified with the same fellowship in Switzerland from 1933 to 1939 and he has frequently expressed his debt to Buchman for much of his own approach to counseling. . . .[50]

There are other connections between Buchman and the New Age. We have mentioned Findhorn, on the coast of Scotland, and the fact that occult communication with various spirit entities (nature spirits, devas living in plants, etc.) was a daily part of Findhorn life. It was principally through the guidance received by Eileen Caddy that Findhorn came into being. And as Livesey points out, "Like A.J. Russell . . . Eileen Caddy first learned about guidance when she was in MRA."[51] Eileen's first husband, Andrew, was obsessed with MRA, but she disliked it and at first was unsuccessful in obtaining the coveted "guidance."

She began to receive that guidance when she left Andrew and with her friend, Peter Caddy, went to Glastonbury, England. The voice told her, "I have brought you and Peter together for a very special purpose, to do a specific work for me."[52] She still had enough conscience to be bothered by her adultery, but in the end, the voice won out. She eventually was divorced from Andrew, married Peter, and together they founded Findhorn. Later they too were divorced.

Changing the World

Many Christian groups which started out well have departed from the faith because they didn't want to be perceived as narrow-minded and felt that softening their language would help them reach a wider audience. The initial compromise, to reach "key people," only gets worse. Such was the case with YMCA and YWCA, and we will later see that it has afflicted some of today's major Christian organizations. Already by the early 1940s, in his zeal to "change the world," Buchman had become so blind to the truth that he declared that MRA was "the full message of Jesus Christ."[53] The comments of former MRA member Roy Livesey are instructive:

> Buchman was now poised to integrate people of other religions and faiths into MRA and to reach out to leaders and politicians like [Mahatma] Gandhi in India, Adenauer in Germany and many others.
>
> MRA was now more involved with the "universal religious experience" rather than Christianity and it was leading supporter Rajmohan Gandhi, grandson of the Mahatma, who declared that MRA was the one thing on which Eastern and Western countries can unite.[54]

This broad-minded and ecumenical promotion of generic "spirituality" has a strong appeal and contributed greatly to Buchman's vast success. Of course, success in this life does not automatically translate to success in the life to come. One piece of MRA literature was "believed to be the largest, simultaneous, global distribution of any single literary publication in history . . . 75 million copies."[55] An MRA film, *The Crowning Experience*, with endorsements from leaders such as a former prime minister of Japan and boxer Sugar Ray Robinson, was credited with playing a major role in "bringing a solution to [discrimination in] Little Rock [Arkansas]."[56]

Buchman had a notable impact on diplomacy during the Cold War. The United States Ambassador to Moscow, Admiral William H. Stanley, declared, "The choice for America is Moral Re-Armament or Communism."[57] MRA's worldwide influence caused the Communists to strike back. Moscow radio said,

> Moral Re-Armament is a global ideology with bridgeheads in every nation in its final phase of total expansion throughout the world. It has the power to capture radical revolutionary minds. It is contaminating the minds of the masses. . . .[58]

MRA became active in more than 50 countries and achieved NGO (Non-Governmental Organization) status with the United Nations, which it enjoys today. Its principal conference center, located in Caux, Switzerland, is a mecca to which world leaders are drawn. The setting high above Lake Geneva and the beautiful lakeshore city of Montreux is exceptionally magnificent even for Switzerland. The large hotels and property exude affluence, elegance, and power.

While living in the area, this author and his family made several visits to Caux in 1966 and 1967. Buchman had died on August 8, 1961, but MRA's worldwide influence had not diminished. On one of those visits, we met Gandhi's grandson, who was there with an "Up with People" (an MRA offshoot) singing group from India. There was never a shortage of wealthy and influential visitors who were staunch supporters of MRA. It was our first encounter with MRA, and we found it confusing to speak with those whose lives had been "transformed" through impressive spiritual experiences, young people who had a compelling zeal to "change the world" but who didn't seem to know Christ or His Word, though they used "Christian" phrases. Livesey tells of his visits to Caux:

> I could not fail to be impressed by the ex-Mau Mau leader who stood on the platform with a white woman. Thirty years previously he had been responsible for the burial-alive of the woman's father . . . in Kenya. There had been forgiveness and the two had become friends under the umbrella of MRA. . . .
>
> At Caux the number of parliamentarians and members of government seemed endless. They came from all over the world. They were hosted by experienced MRA workers who . . . endeavored to give them the maximum exposure to MRA.
>
> There was an African President and several members of his cabinet. There was a Roman Catholic Archbishop. There was a King and Queen, recently returned from the Charles and Diana Royal Wedding. . . .[59]
>
> [At a Health Conference in 1984] everything but the Bible seemed to be quoted. . . . This conference did not even have a hint of Christ. . . .
>
> In the introductory session, a Moslem exhorted, "Don't fall into the trap of seeing only one God. . . ." Dr. Paul Campbell, an MRA leader, led the large assembly in a standing ovation.[60]

"Guidance" Gone Astray

Behind the apparent success of this movement lies the entrapping delusion of occult guidance. Its worldwide triumphs hide tragic stories of confusion, immorality, and ruined lives. A new magazine produced by David Belden, *Forum on MRA*, has become a medium of expression for those who wish at long last to tell the hidden truth. Livesey writes:

> After more than thirty years when this writer has heard only the plus side of MRA, at least from those in the movement, MRA people are exploring honestly and sensitively through *Forum on MRA* the problems they have known. . . .
> They are being confessed both by the 1930s generation and by their MRA children.[61]

Forum on MRA publishes letters from former MRA activists and their children as well as those still loyal to that organization. We now quote at length from one of those letters. Written by a woman to whom Livesey gave the pseudonym "Bertha," it gives a rare insight into Buchman and his MRA from the inside.

"[My] parents met Frank Buchman about 1939 and committed themselves to MRA. My young memories are intensely happy. . . . Guidance, MRA, the team meetings in our home, the dinners given to 'change' someone. . . .

"One day in a team meeting I got up and announced how I had given my life to God and was going to save the world . . . my father was on stage and I wanted to be just like him. . . .

"In November 1957, when I was 14, Dad had guidance to go on a trip in a small airplane with two other men. The plane crashed in the mountains and everyone was killed. . . . There were hundreds gathered at the Club for Dad's memorial service . . . there was no body; just pieces and parts in the snow. . . .

The Oppressive Fruit of Occult "Guidance"

"That summer our whole family went to Mackinac. A few weeks after we arrived Mom, with red-rimmed eyes, asked us three children to sit with her at a big round table. . . . It had been the team's 'guidance' that Mom had to tell us how she and Dad had tried to live absolute purity [one of MRA's four absolutes] and for a three-year stretch of time they had not had sex, but Dad confessed he had an affair with our grandmother. . . .

"The tone, the accusatory eyes that came with this meeting killed my childhood for me. In a moment's time I lost my father in a way the plane crash hadn't taken him. . . . I lost all I knew to be true in life . . . the warm memories of my grandmother. . . .

"My 12-year-old sister, Helen, came apart . . . and all alone hitchhiked as far as Chicago. . . .

"Mom was sat down in a meeting with her friends, people she had shared her life, her goals, been vulnerable with, and they said it was because of her impurity and failures that Dad was killed. . . . On the night before Dad had left on his trip they had sex without having team guidance about it. With the viciousness of a feeding frenzy of sharks they attacked her. Mom never recovered. . . .

"There was no savings, no insurance. . . . Dad and Mom had given their time, their money, their commitment to MRA. . . . With one exception, I don't remember anyone in MRA offering this 37-year-old widow any help. . . .

"That summer of 1958, when Mom left Mackinac in her shattered state, I had my clear profound moment of epiphany when I felt God's presence . . . [and] gave my life to God. . . . With cynical eyes I look back at that experience. What was deep and real at 15 I now view as the only option left in my destroyed world. . . .

"The next summer at Mackinac . . . I was smarter at 16, seeing the way people were used, the power structure, the manipulation, yet I remained deeply, totally committed. If it were Jonestown I would have drunk the Kool-Aid. . . . I truly got the global picture, the vision of the ideology. . . . I worked seven days a week . . . used all my time for changing the course of history. . . .

"I miss the truly wonderful people who were kind to me . . . some of the finest minds and giving personalities. . . . How did it go so wrong with as much talent and ability and wholeness of its individuals . . . ?

"I was the only family member left in MRA. . . . I worked all spring after school saving money for my trip to Mackinac. The summer of 1960 was hell. . . . I was noticeably shunned, leaving me feeling like the group leper. I worked double shifts. . .

I nibbled as I cooked and slept about four hours a night. I went home to my senior year in high school exhausted.

"Someone at the [local MRA] Club had guidance that I would look like a more committed, disciplined person if I lost 15 pounds. . . . Every Saturday I would go to the Club and be accused of not succeeding to lose weight. I was so nervous I ate more, then took more Dexedrine pills thinking maybe by the next Saturday someone would finally approve of me . . . say they were glad I was part of God's perfect plan for the world.

"From the exhaustion of 16-hour workdays all summer, then the Dexedrine high for three months, my body crumbled. I got German measles in January of 1961. . . . Encephalitis followed and I was hospitalized in a coma which lasted about ten days. I had significant neurological damage. Two years were spent in and out of the hospital. It took another two to return to relearn to read, walk, regain fine motor skills. . . .

"I don't remember even one phone call or visit from those in the team I considered my friends. . . . For five years I worked for MRA, gave every cent I was given or earned, gave all my heart and teenage passion, and when I was no longer well I was meaningless to the group. . . .

"When I was 23 I met John, who had been full-time with MRA and left Caux in 1961 to go to college. . . . John and I talked for hours like war comrades must when they meet. . . . We fell in love right away and married in 1966 before he went to Vietnam. . . . We lost contact with MRA and left it behind in our lives. When I read the *Forum* I realize how alive all the pain still is. . . ."[62]

A Telling Contrast

The greatest tragedy of this story is that "Bertha" and her family apparently never really knew the God they thought was giving them "guidance." There is not a word about Christ in her story. "Bertha" still seems to be under occult bondage, still imagining that MRA could yet change the world.

Roy Livesey also left MRA and became a genuine Christian. More than ten years later he returned with a Christian friend and former MRA member for a visit to an MRA center in

England. They were warmly received, but everything was different now. Livesey recalls:

> Like true Christians, the people in MRA have a burning desire to communicate the truth as they believe it. . . . [But there was a] gulf separating us from our old friends . . . a gulf clear to those who are in Christ. A man "remade" along MRA lines is not the same as a converted man who has new life in Christ.
>
> Our conversations were difficult. . . . My old friend soon told me we were arguing. The Bible speaks of contending for the faith. . . .
>
> When I was involved in MRA I didn't know that even as I had some success taking the yardstick of absolute standards, in God's eyes I was a sinner. . . . I did not know that the only answer was to be found in Jesus Christ. I didn't know that the Bible says I was without excuse and that I needed Christ . . . that Jesus Christ is God . . . that He shed His blood and paid the price for my sin . . . that I needed to be saved. . . .
>
> David Belden's *Forum on MRA* had brought to light the testimonies of many like Bertha who were "in" MRA. These included some who are truly the insiders, who have given many years in the service of the MRA idea only to find that it hasn't satisfied the real desires of their hearts. They have sought after the truth and not found it.[63]

There is nothing so deadly as religion. Every false concept of God (from the Star Wars Force to AA's higher power) provides a front for Satan and demons. The counterfeit miracles and false guidance are enticements along the path to occult bondage for those who refuse to submit wholly to God's Word. Tragically, MRA and AA and their offshoots are accepted even within the church. The same compromise that began in the Oxford movement is corrupting Youth with a Mission, Inter-Varsity Christian Fellowship, Campus Crusade for Christ, and other Christian organizations in their equal zeal to "change the world for Christ." The compromise of ecumenism opens the door to what seems at first to be only a tiny trickle of error far outweighed by the "good" it produces. The trickle has become a flood, as we shall see.

The media are concerned about a threat to education from the so-called religious right. There was no such outcry when the left began its pervasive brainwashing.

—Thomas Sowell[1]

My alienation from Christian values intensified in high school, where my teachers exposed me to fascinating ideas such as the theories of evolution, reincarnation, and extrasensory perception.

—Will Baron[2]

There should and must be [occult] mind games for persons of all ages, including small children, and in the future such mind games will be routine in education at all levels.

—Robert Masters and Jean Houston, *Games*[3]

The humanist revolution is proceeding full tilt ahead in our time, and the "congregation" for the new religion is a captive student audience. . . .

—John Steinbacher

At present I'm in a real battle. I'm training to be a Secondary School teacher. The syllabus includes "stilling" or mystic meditation, introducing children to [power] animals and ancient spirits. The school is a mainstream state school and the... [administration] is endorsing this shamanistic initiation technique.

—Letter from England on file[4]

The CIA did not go out of the mind control experiment business altogether. They only became more secretive. Two such projects were nicknamed BLUEBIRD and MKULTRA. These tests were conducted primarily on unsuspecting human guinea pigs. . . .

—From *Psychiatrists: The Men Behind Hitler*[5]

We envision a revolution of the mind, a new way of thinking. . . .

—Mikhail Gorbachev, State of the World Forum, 1996[6]

I have many friends who are gay and I never condemn them from the pulpit.

—Billy Graham[7]

As a society, we've become inured to shame. . . . Millions tune in to an endless parade of vice and weirdness on daytime television. . . . We glorify violence in music and films. We idolize foul-mouthed entertainers and transvestite sports figures. We re-elect public officials caught smoking crack cocaine and seducing boys. . . . We've . . . done away with concepts of right and wrong. . . .

—Linda Chavez in "Counterpoints," *USA Today*[8]

16

* * *

The Seduction of Youth

Robert Muller, former Assistant Secretary-General of the United Nations and known as "the philosopher of the United Nations and its prophet of hope,"[9] is one of today's leading figures in global education. He is the chancellor of the University of Peace in Costa Rica and founder of The Robert Muller School in Arlington, Texas, as well as the author of its *World Core Curriculum Manual,* which is widely used by educators in many countries. Muller considers himself a good Catholic, as does his church. One of his prized possessions is a "golden crucifix given to him by Pope John Paul II."[10]

Muller is a major contributor to the occult invasion. His "god" is a "mysterious force which rules the universe" and is acceptable to all religions.[11] To save the world, he would indoctrinate youth with a universal *spirituality* (i.e. the occult) for which he has developed the curriculum. Former U.N. Secretary-General U Thant, a dedicated Buddhist/atheist, is one of Muller's spiritual mentors.[12] In his farewell address to the United Nations in December 1971, U Thant let it be known that global education must be *spiritual* but not religious:

> I would attach the greatest importance to spiritual values. . . . I deliberately avoid using the term "religion." I have in mind . . . faith in oneself, the purity of one's inner self which to me is the greatest virtue of all. With this approach . . . with this concept alone, will we be able to fashion the kind of society we want. . . .
>
> The need for global education must transcend material, scientific, and intellectual achievements and reach deliberately into the moral and spiritual spheres.[13]

How does "faith in oneself, the purity of one's inner self" work for those who are not pure? Both the Bible and everyday experience agree that all people are sinners. How can anyone,

much less a world leader, trust the future to an inherent goodness in mankind which history denies? Nevertheless, those in
control are determined that global education for the next generation of youth will embody a *spiritual* development of the god
within.

This theme was prominent at the Second Annual State of the
World Forum in October 1996. Organized by the Gorbachev
Foundation, the Forum drew more than 600 leaders from
around the world to discuss the new world order. In his plenary
address, Rabbi Arthur Hertzberg singled out religions as "the
cheerleaders of hatred." The Forum praised Buddhism while
denigrating Christianity.[14] Much of what was said echoed
author Duane Elgin's assertion that "knowing our connection
with the consciousness of the living cosmos . . . [provides the]
foundation for the global culture."[15] Speaking for the youth
leaders present, Harvard student Bill Burke-White said:

> This community [of today's students] . . . has no tolerance for
> dogmatism and fundamentalism . . . we were born into an awaken-
> ing Earth. . . . Imagine . . . a world which has realized the Youth
> summit's vision of building a Global Youth Alliance . . . a network-
> ing of the many youth organizations that share these heart-felt
> visions for the new millennium. . . .[16]

Global Spirituality in Education

What could U Thant, Muller, Gorbachev, and other leaders
mean by spirituality? U Thant's spirituality denies the God of
the Bible and comes from an occult force. Muller explains:

> Of course, the question arose immediately: how can one speak
> of a global spirituality in a world of so many religions and atheists,
> besides there being religions like Buddhism, Jainism and Sikhism
> which have no God? However, there is a common denominator
> when humans see themselves as part of a very mysterious and beau-
> tiful universe. From that awe emerges a spiritual approach to life.
> Everything becomes sacred . . . and miraculous . . . regarding the
> mysterious force which rules the universe.[17]

No force, no matter how mysterious, can be the source of any
"spiritual" qualities. We have spiritual qualities only because we
were created in the image of the God who "is a Spirit" and who

requires that we "worship him in spirit and in truth" (John 4:24). This madness—that an impersonal force could produce personal beings—is embraced and defended as *science* in man's attempt to escape moral accountability to his Creator.

Muller's spirituality—with which he is determined to indoctrinate the world's youth—coincides with that espoused by Norman Vincent Peale and John Marks Templeton. He is convinced that belief, especially when visualized, causes what we deeply desire "to materialize."[18] Muller's spirituality comes from a seducing spirit claiming to belong to a long-dead Tibetan Master well-known in the occult as Djwhal Khul. In the preface to Muller's *World Core Curriculum* we read:

> The underlying philosophy upon which The Robert Muller School is based will be found in the teachings set forth in the books of Alice A. Bailey by the Tibetan teacher, Djwhal Khul . . . [19] and the teachings of M. Morya as given in the Agni Yoga Series Books. . . .
>
> The Robert Muller School was fully accredited in 1985. . . . The school is now certified as a United Nations Associated School providing education for international cooperation and peace.[20]

Muller was awarded the UNESCO Peace Education Prize in 1989. In 1990, delegates from 155 countries met in Thailand at the World Conference of Education for All in order to continue plans toward a world curriculum, much of it adapted from Muller's ideas. Other conferences have followed with the cooperation of Republican and Democratic administrations: Bush's America 2000, Clinton's Goals 2000, leading to Project Global 2000. Dr. Dennis Laurence Cuddy, former Senior Associate in the U.S. Department of Education, explains:

> UNESCO AND UNICEF, which are partners with Global 2000, are putting into action [worldwide] the initiatives developed at the World Conference of Education for All [Thailand, 1990], the largest educational conference ever held.[21]

Educating for Global Citizenship

A major goal of America 2000 and Goals 2000 is to establish educational and testing standards throughout the country, placing control of all education under the Federal government through the establishment of "Outcome Based Education"

(OBE). OBE has little to do with what parents expect of education and much to do with indoctrinating children into "politically correct reactions" to situational ethics. As *The Iowa Report* puts it, OBE and Mastery Learning (ML) are designed for "manipulating students through behavior modification, based on B.F. Skinner's methods . . . open[ing] the door to destroying their traditional and religious values. . . . In such a [OBE/ML] program traditional Christian values are not acceptable. . . ."

This national program is already set up to monitor "outcomes"—that is, to determine whether the student's behavior measures up to the expected transformation. The National Assessment of Educational Progress (NAEP) evaluates programs in state schools. If the "outcomes" don't meet standards, material is distributed to the schools by the National Diffusion Network (NDN) to "remediate" the deficiencies.

The program is international. Jean-Francois Revel refers to the same process taking place in France.[22] We are seeing the culmination of well-laid plans going back many years, involving even the Soviet Union. In 1934 the Carnegie Corporation funded a study on education which made reference to "Western civilization merging into a world order . . . a new age of collectivism [socialism] is emerging."[23] In 1958 President Eisenhower signed the first United States-Soviet agreement involving education.[24] The transformation in education accelerated with the historic *General Agreement* signed by President Ronald Reagan and Mikhail Gorbachev in Geneva, Switzerland, in November 1985.

The *Agreement* "traded US technology for USSR psycho-social strategies used to indoctrinate children, modify behavior, and monitor the people to ensure compliance."[25] It called for "joint studies on textbooks" which would result in a joint curriculum "for all grades of primary and secondary education, as well as college and university studies." Malachi Martin warned:

> One day soon, one assumes, schoolchildren in Gorbachev's birthplace of Privolnoye and schoolchildren in Reagan's birthplace of Tampico, Illinois, will all learn the same materials.[26]

The many organizations working together to unify world education, and the progress they have achieved down to the local level across America, is a story outside the scope of this book.

Our concern is the occult and anti-Christian spirituality and accompanying immorality influencing youth. The occult invasion of the public schools, which necessarily must destroy Christianity, did not happen overnight. In 1972 Harvard University Professor of Education and Psychiatry Chester M. Pierce stated in his keynote address to the Association for Childhood Education International:

> Every child in America entering school at the age of five is insane because he comes to school with certain allegiances toward our founding fathers, toward his parents, toward a belief in a supernatural being. . . .
> It's up to you, teachers, to make all of these sick children well— by creating the international children of the future.[27]

A Calculated Brainwashing Process

Closed to Christianity as too dogmatic, public schools became the experimental laboratories for the latest psychological theories and all manner of occultism, from Native American spirituality and yoga to witchcraft. Universities became the proving grounds of the revolution against not only democracy but the conventional family and all Christian values.

It was Phil Jackson's brother Joe, older by four years, who had also "lost his faith" in spite of "speaking in tongues" for a time, who led Phil into self-hypnosis and also introduced him to Zen Buddhism. Joe, in turn, had learned the latter from a professor at the University of Texas. College had the same effect on Phil. His roommate, a former Lutheran, encouraged Phil "to take a detached look at the [Christian] belief system . . . and explore life more freely. It was a heady feeling. The sixties were in full swing, and I immersed myself in the counterculture. . . ."[28]

In Phil's senior year (1967) he married, and he and his wife had a daughter. He writes that the great appeal of the '60s for him "was the emphasis on compassion and brotherhood, getting together and loving one another *right now*. . . ."[29] Yet he and his wife, having pledged their love to each other, were divorced. Jackson explains that the youth were "trying to escape from their parents' archaic views and reinvent the world."[30] And the schools themselves were deliberately encouraging that "escape," especially from Christianity.

The ultimate goal, of course, is to control the thinking of the world's citizens—and Christianity stands in the way. Most of the world's governments have been involved in experiments with covert hypnosis, secret administration of drugs, electric shock treatments, and electrical stimulation of the brain in attempts to control human behavior. Thousands have been tortured in these experiments, not only in Nazi Germany and the Soviet Union, but today in Muslim countries and the West. The United States is no exception. Two of the CIA's programs which have been reported upon to some degree by others were BLUEBIRD and MKULTRA.[31] Space limitations prevent further comment.

Educators, psychologists, and psychiatrists (beginning with Dewey, Skinner, Pierce, et al.) are determined to control the minds of our youth by seemingly legitimate means. The government has been passing laws which make manipulation of the mind possible through the public schools. Evangelical Christianity (which stands in the way of the coming world religion) must be destroyed. In its place, Native American spirituality and the occult techniques of shamanism (such as visualization of inner guides) are being introduced.

Holistic Education

The new agenda for worldwide education involves the same holistic concepts that are taking over the health-care field. *Holistic Education Review* editor, Jeffrey Kane, admits that "holism refers to what is holy." What does "holy" mean to humanists? And what does "holy" have to do with public education in the United States, where supposedly we have a separation between church and state? When Kane says that the goal of holistic education "will enable the child to unfold spiritually,"[32] we know he is not referring to anything compatible with Christianity. Indeed, as *Humanist Magazine* stated:

> The classroom will and must become the area of combat between . . . the rotting corpse of Christianity . . . and the new faith of Humanism.[33]

Humanism is the religion of man as his own god possessing infinite power and having his own "values" within himself.

It is the religion of the Human Potential movement, the occult religion of the psychic powers which man hopes to develop through supposedly higher states of consciousness. Imagination is the major vehicle of holistic education, the means of achieving this state most easily and of encountering the entities which inhabit the occult dimension. Donald A. Cowan, President Emeritus of the University of Dallas, has said:

> What will take the place of logic, fact and analysis in the coming age? The central way of thought for this new era will be imagination. Imagination will be the active, creative agent of culture, transforming brute materials to a higher, more knowable state. . . .[34]

In her book *Growing Up Gifted,* Barbara Clark of the California State University system advocates yoga and visualization and the development of psychic powers. "Transcendence" is to be achieved through establishing a sense of unity consciousness among the students by "transpersonal communication," creating confidence in U Thant's purity within:

> Transpersonal communication is designed to help people learn to trust the validity of their personal experiences and accept what they learn from these experiences as their best source of wisdom and truth.[35]

While he was governor of Arkansas, Bill Clinton and Hillary established The Governor's School in a "restructuring" of that state's public schools. Foul language was encouraged as part of a brainwashing procedure designed to strip students of biblical morals. There was blatant promotion of gay lifestyles, free sex, New Age beliefs and practices (including the worship of self and the universe as God), rebellion against authority, and alienation from parents as preparation for leadership in the New World Order. The Clinton administration aims to restructure the entire American public school system, bad as it already is, along these same lines.

It is in this atmosphere of open hostility to the Christian faith that our children and grandchildren must be raised. To compromise is to be destroyed inch by inch.

When "Values" Replace Biblical "Virtue"

The denial of the God who created us for a purpose and set moral standards for our conduct has left man adrift in the universe with only his imagination as a guide. Years ago "Values Clarification" destroyed morals by teaching grammar-school children to establish their own "values" from within themselves. Today it is "Consensus Building," in which individual values, however learned or established, are torn down through "group thinking" and the new global standard becomes what everyone agrees upon "for the good of the whole world."

Society now recognizes "homosexual values" as well as "family values." Homosexual values are deemed to be broad-minded and thus acceptable; family values are deemed to be narrow-minded and "negative" toward homosexuality and other immorality, and are thus unacceptable. Such is the amoral atmosphere of the classrooms in which our youth are being "educated" globally. Malachi Martin put it succinctly:

> "Good" will no longer be burdened with a moral or religious coloring . . . [but] will simply be synonymous with "global. . . ."
> The emphasis is upon homogeneity of minds, on the creation and nourishing of a truly global mentality.[36]

Bruce Logan, director of the New Zealand Education Development Foundation, has decried the departure from the certainty of biblical virtues decreed by God, and their replacement by the uncertainty of "values." The latter, says Logan, "can be beliefs . . . feelings . . . preferences . . . whatever any person, group or society happens to value, at any time, for any reason . . . thus Michael Jackson and [the late] Mother Teresa both have 'values' to which each is faithful . . . [with] some sort of moral equivalence thereby suggested. . . ."[37]

Anglican priest David Guthrie, administrator of Auckland's Holy Trinity Cathedral, rebutted Logan. He praised the new liberty from biblical injunctions and even claimed this immorality was *Christian*. Wrote Guthrie:

> Whatever it means to be a Christian in today's world, it does not entail the acceptance of a legislating God. . . . As the world of global culture settles on its new tack, there will be a new set of

"virtues" ... virtues that the human community chooses in that moment of time to espouse and adopt, not because they are legislated by divine authority ... but because the community chooses them to be so.[38]

In fact, it is not "the community" that decides, but *part* of the community over the objections of the rest. Is a 51-percent-to-49-percent vote sufficient for determining right and wrong? Opinions also change, so that today's virtue could become tomorrow's vice. "Good" and "evil" would have no meaning. With regard to homosexuality, a tiny minority through intimidation has imposed its will on society as a whole.

A Calculated Destruction of Morals

A recent *Reader's Digest* poll across the country shows that the courts, media, and public schools are forcing upon children humanistic values to which their parents and an overwhelming majority of American citizens are opposed. For example, 80 percent disapprove of the U.S. Supreme Court ruling that it is unconstitutional to offer prayer at a high school graduation, while only 18 percent approve. As for prayer in public schools (voluntary and personal, not regimented), 75 percent favor it and only 19 percent are opposed. William J. Bennett, Secretary of Education from 1985 to 1988, declared:

> The Founding Fathers intended [Christian] religion to provide a moral anchor for our democracy. ... Yet again and again as Education Secretary ... I was attacked as an "ayatollah" when I supported voluntary school prayer—and the posting of the Ten Commandments in schools.[39]
>
> There is a fight in this country for the minds of our children.[40]

Tragically, the public education system in the United States is devoted to destroying Christian beliefs and replacing them with evolution, witchcraft, Hinduism, Buddhism, or Native American religion. In most schools in the Western world, *teaching* provides the excuse for *indoctrination*. Jean-François Revel makes that point about his native France:

> The abuse of trust and the betrayal of the teacher's moral duty shine forth here in ignominious fashion. ... Right up until 1967 all

French school textbooks provided an idyllic vision of the USSR, in accordance with the most optimistic propaganda cliches. . . .

Teaching gave way to militant preaching. Thus, in a teachers' guide, the author (Vincent, Bordas, 1980) gave his colleagues the following instructions:

Two camps exist in the world: one imperialist and antidemo-cratic (USA) one antiimperialist and democratic (USSR). . . .

[Even as late as 1987, when there was no excuse for not knowing the horrible truth] the achievements of the Soviet economy were described in [glowing] . . . terms . . . not in partisan newspapers . . . but in school textbooks imposed on children. . . .[41]

Parents who object to the gross breach of trust on the part of the educational system and to its calculated destruction of their children's morals are denied the right to "interfere" in (and often even to know) what public schools are doing to their own children. For their legitimate concern, they are scorned as "fanatical fundamentalist Christians," now the most demeaning of epithets. Writer Tom Robbins expressed today's contemptions defiance of God and His word:

Our purpose is to consciously, deliberately evolve toward a wiser, more liberated and luminous state of being, to return to Eden, make friends with the snake and set up our computers among the wild apple trees.[42]

The Psychologizing of Society

To enforce the remolding of youth into the world citizen of the future, the government professes its concern for the psycholog-ical well-being of the child. In *The Psychological Society*, Martin L. Gross laments:

The schoolhouse has become a vibrant psychological center, staffed not only by schoolteachers trained in "educational psy-chology" but by sixty thousand guidance workers and seven thousand school psychologists whose "counseling" borders on therapy. . . .[43]

What has psychology's dominant influence in our public schools wrought? Fifty years ago the worst problems faced by schoolteachers and administrators were 1) talking in class; 2) chewing gum; 3) making noise; 4) running in halls; 5) cutting in line; 6) dress code violations; 7) littering. Today they are:

1) drug abuse; 2) alcohol abuse; 3) pregnancy; 4) suicide; 5) rape; 6) robbery; 7) assault. A *Reader's Digest* article commented:

> Americans learned that Magic Johnson had contracted the AIDS virus, New York City schools were handing out condoms to adolescents, and a nephew of President John F. Kennedy had had sex with a woman he picked up in a bar. Each news event was about something altogether alien to contemporary culture: sin.
>
> Sin isn't something many people spent much time worrying about in the past 25 years. But . . . sin . . . at least offered a frame of reference for behavior. When the frame was dismantled during the sexual revolution, we lost the guidewire of personal responsibility. . . . The United States has problems with drugs, high-school sex, AIDS and rape. None of these will go away until people in positions of responsibility come forward and explain, in frankly moral terms, that some of the things people do nowadays are wrong.[44]

The new "values" instilled in public schools are also reflected in the amoral, evil heroes and heroines which today's youth admire. Marilyn Manson's album *Antichrist Superstar* "was the third top-selling CD in its first week of release [in the fall of 1996]. With his stage name taken from suicidal sex symbol Marilyn Monroe and serial killer Charles Manson, this ordained satanist priest and his head-banging band openly defy every moral principle. Wearing T-shirts that read 'Kill God, Kill Your Mom and Dad, Kill Yourself,' the band celebrates hate, racism, sexual depravity, violence and blasphemy . . . as they mock God and rant against Jesus. Marilyn [Manson] said: 'I'm on my way down now, I'd like to take you with me.' "[45]

Only upon the ruins of Christianity could psychology's theologians build their occult religion. Carl Rogers admitted, "Yes, it is true, psychotherapy is subversive. . . . Therapy, theories and techniques promote a new model of man contrary to that which has been traditionally acceptable."[46] In *Psychology Today* (*PT*) Rollo May exulted, "We have bid goodbye to the theologians at the wake for our dead God." Already in 1969, *PT* declared that we must "face our own inner experiences without the guidance of traditional . . . foundation stones of Judeo-Christian experience. . . . We are compelled to erect our own morality, arrive at our own faith and belief. . . ."[47]

Today's Blameless Human

Right and wrong have lost their meaning because, according to modern psychology, none of us is responsible for anything we do. We are all victims, driven to do whatever we do by the traumas we suffered as children, traumas which have created hidden motives and urges buried in the unconscious and are thus unknown to us and beyond our control. Many of today's parents, convinced of such lies, will not discipline their children for fear of damaging their psyches. As Gross points out:

> Before Freud, no educated adult could find a plausible reason to avoid responsibility for his actions. It was left to psychoanalysis and psychodynamic psychology to create a blameless . . . man. It is not done by covering up his faults, but by tracing them back to his childhood, when he was morally innocent. . . .
>
> Freud once explained this blamelessness to a patient ashamed of his cowardliness. "I pointed out to him that he ought logically to consider himself as in no way responsible for any of these traits in his character . . . these reprehensible impulses . . . were only derivatives of his infantile character surviving in his unconscious; and . . . moral responsibility could not be applied to children."
>
> It is the *perpetual-child theory*. Not only neurosis, but unhappiness or inability to find love or friendship have been lifted from our adult shoulders and thrust back onto the sagging breast of mother. . . .
>
> Unhappily married forty-five-year-olds may not seek the answer in their own selfishness or immaturity. . . . "My mother (or father) did such and such . . ." is the litany of the Psychological Society.[48]

Sin has been redefined as sickness and the list of "mental illnesses" grows almost daily. Instead of being held accountable and called upon to repent, the sinner is given "therapy." Everything from disobedience to murder is excused as some syndrome or addiction. Adulterers are now "sex addicts" whose insurance covers lengthy "treatment" at secular and even "Christian" psychiatric hospitals.

The explosion of youth's rebellion, crime, and immorality has coincided with the exponential growth of psychology since the early 1950s. There was a 43-percent increase in the number of Americans in the 10–19 age bracket who were committed to psychiatric hospitals from 1980 to 1987, while the number of private psychiatric beds per 100,000 persons more than doubled in the five years from 1983 to 1988. What a growth industry! Psychology has been rightly called the only profession that "creates the diseases which it claims to cure."

The firm discipline which children need and the Bible commands (Proverbs 13:24, 22:15; Hebrews 12:6; etc.) is now called "child abuse" and children have been taken by government agencies from Christian parents who lovingly applied the corrective rod. What was once disciplined as laziness, disinterest, stubbornness, or rebellion is now excused as a mental "disorder." The number of children diagnosed as having "learning disabilities" nearly tripled from 1977 to 1992! Children are placed on Ritalin after they and their parents have been convinced by some therapist of their abnormality—a stigma (and excuse) which will likely be with them for life. In spite of its addictive nature, the lack of evidence of its helpfulness, and the many incidents of violence and suicide brought on by withdrawal from it, Ritalin is being given to about a million American children.

A Raging Epidemic of Mental Illnesses?

To increase their power over society, psychiatrists and psychologists constantly invent new kinds of "mental illness." Americans now suffer by the millions from alleged maladies that were unknown a few years ago. These are defined in the "Bible of mental illness," the American Psychiatric Association's *Diagnostic and Statistical Manual for Mental Disorders (DSM)*. When first published in 1952 it listed 112 mental disorders, compared with a half-dozen 100 years earlier. DSM-II in 1968 listed 163. There were 224 in DSM-III, published in 1980. DSM-IV came out in 1994, and the list of disorders had grown to 374! Whence this raging epidemic of new mental illnesses—or are we being duped? One newspaper editor wrote sarcastically:

> Does your 10-year-old dislike doing her math homework? Better get her to the nearest couch because she's got No. 315.4, *Developmental Arithmetic Disorder.* Maybe you're a teenager who argues with his parents. Uh-oh. Better get some medication pronto because you've got No. 313.8, *Oppositional Defiant Disorder.* . . . I am not making these things up. (That would be *Fictitious Disorder Syndrome*). . . .

I know there are some cynics out there who . . . wouldn't be caught dead on a psychiatrist's couch. . . . Your unwillingness to seek professional help is itself a symptom of a serious mental problem. It's right here in the book: 15.81, *Noncompliance with Treatment Disorder.*[49]

A CBS-TV special reported that uppermost in the minds of the youth interviewed were nagging doubts about mental health."[50] In trying to show the folly that has overtaken America one author has written:

For eons some children, like adults, have always been more active than others. Perhaps they play harder or wander mentally because of a short attention span . . . [and] parents simply dealt with this as a fact of life. . . . And the wise parent saw that children, like adults, learn to change their behavior for the better . . .

However, psychiatry has deemed there is something wrong. . . . The child and parents thought he was normal when they walked into the psychiatrist's office. They think he is abnormal when they walk out. . . . As a normal child he would have been tolerated, endured, disciplined . . . whatever parents have done for thousands of years. And in all likelihood, he would have grown out of it with little significance made of the situation.

As an abnormal child, however, he would have been treated much differently by his parents, his teachers, and possibly his classmates. He would have been "special" . . . on years of medication. . . . He himself would, of course, think he had something inherently wrong with him. . . . Most likely this sense of "abnormality" would be with him the rest of his life. . . . [51]

Occultism in Public Schools

An article titled "Guided Imagery in Education" in the *Journal of Humanistic Psychology* declares, "From Delphi's 'know thyself' through scripture's 'you shall be as gods!' we are left with the certitude that we are, indeed, multidimensional beings capable of works beyond our imagining and that our primary purpose in life is to discover who we are and who we can become." The author seemingly doesn't know that "you shall be as gods" is Satan's major lie. The article introduces transpersonal education and states that "meditation and guided imagery are the core of the curriculum."

The techniques taught to children in public schools are similar to those used by witch doctors for contacting the "spirit guides" (demons) that give them their power. Schoolchildren are taught to visualize themselves under water, see DUSO the dolphin coming to them, focus on it until its image becomes clear, then talk to it. *It will talk back.* Contact has been made with a spirit entity. Thereafter, DUSO need only be visualized and will come to one's immediate aid. The nationwide language-arts curriculum READ includes the following visualization exercise:

> Close your eyes and breathe deeply to relax. . . . Picture in your mind a place . . . become acquainted with your surroundings . . . ask to meet a guide. An animal, person or being will accompany you and give you whatever power you might need. . . .
>
> Watch what this new companion does or shows you. Listen to what it says. Go wherever this guide wants to lead you. You are safe. . . . [52]

Third-graders in California were taught to visualize a personal spirit guide in the form of an animal, then had to write about their occult experience with this creature for a public bulletin-board display. Oregon students were seated in the order of their astrological signs for a Winter Solstice celebration as the "sun god" and "moon goddess" entered the auditorium accompanied by chanting and the beating of drums. "Celebrating Winter Solstice with 'dance around the Solstice tree' is one of the *Anti-Bias Curriculum's* suggested alternatives to Christmas."[53]

Those who bring the occult into education are highly honored. Occult psychologist Jean Houston was named "Educator of the Year" in 1984-85 by the National Teachers Education Association (NEA) and by the National Catholic Educators. Lamar Alexander, Education Secretary under President Bush, confessed that the book that influenced his thinking the most in the last ten years was *A God Within,* by Rene Dubos, in which Dubos says that "our salvation depends upon our ability to create a religion of nature . . . suited to . . . modern man."[54]

A Montana mother discovered that her fourth-grader's class was to pretend it was part of a mythical Indian tribe. The children were to imagine themselves going on a quest "alone in the wilderness . . . to prove to their tribe that they are worthy of being considered adults." Concerned that these quests would be used to encounter spirit guides, she studied the lessons. In one, the children were introduced to a mystical youth "from the Modat Tribe, 'known to have great shamans.'" They were to follow him (in their minds) to a "deep canyon ... [where] you feel many spirits rising ... calling you to visit this incredible place." The students were to write a paper describing their adventures there.[55] These are only a few of the examples of occultism being taught to young children in public schools.

Toys, Games, and Films

Many of the games, toys, videos and films most popular among children and youth involve the occult. Games such as "Dungeons and Dragons" (there is even a "Christian" counterpart called "Dragon-Raid") involve the players in nonstop occultism. These "fantasy role-playing games" are extremely dangerous because of the use of the imagination, which is the quickest way into the occult. Lack of space prevents us from naming and analyzing these. Parents need to study these games for themselves.

Children's cartoons on TV and videos provide both enticement and initiation into the occult. Parents need to be aware of the purpose and meaning behind them. America's children have become obsessed with the occult through the media. There is a parallel between the creatures who have become the heroes and heroines of today's youth and the ancient pagan gods and goddesses—both in their appearance and in their powers.

Among the most popular heroes are the Teen-Age Mutant Ninja Turtles, who maintain their special powers through Eastern meditation learned from their guru, Splinter the Rat. She-Ra is the head of a group of sorceresses and goddesses who rule the universe from Crystal Castle, the center and source of all power. Then there are the half-human, half-animal Thunder Cats whose eyes light up with an inner occult power. Many more could be named.

More than one Sunday school or vacation Bible school teacher has asked the children in the class what they would do in danger or trial, only to hear some respond that they would cry out not to God or Christ but to She-Ra, Princess of Power, to He-Man, or to the Power Rangers.

The *Star Wars* film series started a trend 20 years ago. George Lucas promoted witchcraft by introducing the Force with a dark and a light side (black and white magic). The Jedi knights were the followers of the "old religion," another name for Wicca, or witchcraft. The laser sword was not a weapon but a divination device which only those initiated into its powers could use. Luke Skywalker couldn't make it work until he learned to go into an altered state and "let the Force take over." Obi Wan Kenobi became Luke's spirit guide, communicating with him from the other side. Darth Vader, who seemed the embodiment of evil, turns out to have U Thant's inner perfection and joins Obi Wan on the other side of death, thus revealing the oneness of all. Yoda is a yogi who teaches Luke the power of positive thinking. For millions of young children the occult Force took the place of God.

Star Wars was followed by other films openly promoting the occult. There were *Close Encounters of the Third Kind, Poltergeist, Ghost,* and a host of others. Through films and videos today's youth are being seduced into the unholy trinity of sexual immorality, rebellion, and the occult. One of the hottest films during 1996 was *The Craft.* This story of four girls who became involved in witchcraft was aimed at teenagers.

"Wizards" is a game that has been used in Southern California public schools, supposedly to teach spelling. However, it promotes demonology and sorcery and humorously portrays Satan as a great achiever and leader. Other occult books include Deborah Rozman's *Meditating with Children: A Workbook on New Age Educational Methods,* which has received wide praise. Referring to the effects of this book, the *San Jose Mercury* newspaper declared enthusiastically, "Educators who once turned to Ritalin and other drugs for hyperactive children . . . are now turning to daily meditation exercises—with positive results."

A book presenting Christianity would not be allowed in public schools because of the selectively-enforced separation of church and state. But this book is accepted widely, even though it teaches basic Hindu religious practices and is dedicated to "Paramahansa Yogananda for some of the exercises and much of the inspiration for writing this book [and] above all . . .to The One. . . ." Its basic premise is "the Divine Nature of Childhood," and its stated purpose is to help "Children everywhere

... evolve towards their spiritual destiny." The book is a compendium of blatant Hindu religious symbols and practices,
from chanting the OM and yoga exercises to self-realization.
Yet *East-West Journal* says, " ... the absence of a religious point
of view in the book makes this volume an excellent learning
vehicle."[56]

A Deadly Evil, A Destructive Conspiracy

Occultism is always associated with immorality and sexual perversion. Against the wishes of parents, condoms are given out
and "safe sex" taught to young children in school. To suggest
abstinence from premarital sex as a preventive is excluded as a
religious idea. Yet even secular studies have demonstrated that
having sex before marriage increases the likelihood that the
marriage will end in divorce—exactly the opposite of today's
propaganda and of what those who engage in this practice
imagine.

One of the deadliest sexual practices is homosexuality and
lesbianism. A person who lives an exclusively homosexual
lifestyle is *one thousand times more likely* to contract AIDS than
a heterosexual. Lethal health hazards such as "fisting" and
ingestion of feces are common homosexual practices. Sado-
masochism is practiced by 37 percent of homosexuals.

Those who oppose homosexuality are denounced as bigots.
Yet the raw statistics alone should cause anyone to oppose it.
The national outcry against this deadly habit ought to be far
greater than against tobacco. The median age of death for married heterosexual men is nearly twice that of homosexuals: 75
compared with 39. Only 1 percent of homosexuals live beyond
the age of 65. The average age of death for married women is
79 compared with 45 for lesbians. Homosexuals are 87 times
more likely to commit suicide and 23 times more likely to die
from heart attacks. Based on the facts, it is reprehensible for
anyone to encourage the practice of homosexuality!

The facts, however, are suppressed. Politicians are cowed
into submission by the voting power of gays and cater to
them. This has been especially true of the Clinton administration. Religious leaders, Catholic and Protestant, are increasingly legitimizing homosexuality. Billy Graham has called

it a sin, yet otherwise remains virtually silent on the subject. During his September 23–27, 1992, Portland, Oregon crusade, Graham (pleading neutrality in political issues) refused to comment on that state's Proposition 9, which would have prevented the government "from promoting, encouraging or facilitating homosexuality."[57]

Concerned conservatives call for a "return to traditional moral values." Yes, but *what* "tradition" and by *what* authority? By the mutual consent of decent society? Who defines these terms? We desperately need to heed the counsel of God! Christ said, "As many as I love, I rebuke and chasten. Be zealous, therefore, and repent" (Revelation 3:19). It is far more loving to reprove homosexuals than to "accept them." One who truly loves these misguided souls will point them to Scriptures which call their perversion a sinful abomination to God—and will urge them to cease from a practice which can only bring a premature and painful death to themselves and to their "lovers."

AIDS enjoys a status never before granted to a *highly contagious and deadly disease.* Instead of being treated like the fatal plague it is, AIDS has become a civil right that gives those carrying it a privileged status and even the prerogative to keep their infection secret. Health laws prevent anyone with such diseases as hepatitis from working in a restaurant, yet those with AIDS may do so. To bar them, which common sense would demand, is forbidden as "discrimination," even though it means certain death to those who may as a result of this insane policy accidentally contract the HIV virus.

Such criminal folly threatens us all with unprecedented catastrophe. The contamination of blood supplies due to ignorance and carelessness resulted in large numbers of hemophiliacs dying of AIDS. Arthur Ashe is only one of many "transfusion" casualties. In spite of current precautions, medical personnel treating HIV patients have contracted AIDS. Recently an entire family (parents and children) were wiped out by AIDS, though they were heterosexuals. How it was contracted remains a mystery.

The latest studies released late in November 1997 reveal new strains of HIV developing which are far more difficult to detect, and an epidemic raging faster than previously estimated, with 30 million (1% of all sexually active adults) now infected. The cry is for a vaccine in spite of the scientific evidence that none can ever be found.

Homosexuals and Lesbians: The New Privileged Class

Pressured by that militant and tiny minority (about two or three percent, according to polls), both the media and public schools present homosexuality as natural and acceptable. The doors of public schools, closed to Christian speakers, are opening wide to those who through misrepresentation and outright lies advocate homosexuality. "Project 10" is only one public-school program designed to open up America's young children to homosexuality. Children are being taught to experiment in order to learn their sexual "orientation" or "preference."

First-grade readers being used across the country include *Daddy's Roommate* (promotes homosexuality as normal and wholesome), and *Heather Has Two Mommies* (relates the story of a child born through artificial insemination to two lesbians living together). A third-grade reader includes *Gloria Goes to Gay Pride*. The *Philadelphia Gay News* boasted:

> If the religious right wing was upset about *Daddy's Roommate*, Michael Willhoite's ground-breaking children's book about a boy living with his gay father and the father's lover, Willhoite expects them to go ballistic when he completes work on the sequel, *Daddy's Wedding*. He already refers to himself and colleague Leslea Newman, who created the equally controversial *Heather Has Two Mommies*, as the "Antichrist Twins.". . .[58]

Calling themselves the "Antichrist Twins" is an admission of the antichrist nature of this perversion. That the homosexual community is determined to pervert the youth of America is admitted. Says Willhoite, "*We may not be able to change their minds* [the parents'], *but at least we can take a shot at changing their children's minds.*"[59] Here is an inadvertent admission that, contrary to their claims, no one is *born* a homosexual; individuals are enticed into that sin.

Homosexual propaganda spreads numerous lies. The homosexual is portrayed as far more loving and kind than the average citizen. If that is the case, why do homosexuals persist in behavior which may be deadly both to their "lovers" and to the population as a whole? Another lie is the claim that AIDS is not really contagious. Then why do we have an epidemic of it? In fact, Dr. John G. Bartlett, head of infectious diseases at Johns Hopkins Hospital, has called AIDS "history's most lethal epidemic."[60] Then there is the clever use of statistics that more sexual child abuse is committed by heterosexuals than by gays. Yes, the 98 percent of the population which is heterosexual accounts for more child abuse than the 2 percent which is homosexual. However, that 2-percent tiny minority consistently accounts for *one-third to one-half of all sexual child abuse,* which it *considers to be normal behavior.* The most extensive study done to date of male sexual child abusers reveals that the average homosexual victimized 7.5 times as many boys as the average heterosexual did girls.[61]

A primary goal of the National Gay Task Force is the removal of all age-of-consent laws. The shocking fact is that NAMBLA (North American Man–Boy Love Association), outspoken advocate of pedophilia, was formed in a church with a number of "Christian" leaders, both Protestant and Catholic, participating and voicing their approval of this perversion. Sadly, a significant percentage of pedophiles are Roman Catholic priests.

Disney World in Orlando held its seventh annual Gay & Lesbian Day during May 29–June 1, 1997. Advertisements showed Mickey Mouse and Donald Duck walking hand in hand past a sign reading "Gay Day at Disney." The event drew more than 60,000 "gay men, lesbians, bisexuals and families," compared with 30,000 the year before. How evil to commend to children a sexual perversion which cuts life expectancy in half!

As a part of the festivities welcoming the Clinton administration to Washington D.C. in January 1993, our nation's capital hosted a Homosexual Inaugural Ball sponsored by the President's Inauguration Committee, with invitations carrying the President's official seal. Above the dancing, celebrating homosexuals, a giant video screen ran clips of all the statements favorable to homosexuals from Clinton's speeches—to the cheers of the gays. Clinton has appointed numerous homosexuals and lesbians to key positions in his administration.

For Your Children's Sake

Not long after Bush and Quayle lost the election to Clinton and Gore, the *Atlantic Monthly's* cover story was titled "Dan Quayle Was Right." It pointed out what even the sociologists are now admitting, after a two-decade study: that the effects of family disruption are devastating and pervasive. Havoc has been wreaked in millions of lives by the growing ridicule aimed at stable families headed by a mother and father committed to a loving and faithful union at any cost. Flouting biblical sexual morals not only causes divorce, single parenthood, and births out of wedlock, but it is at the root of most of today's most vexing social problems. No amount of money can heal America's crime-ridden cities and broken families, and the "new morality" and "alternative lifestyles" championed by liberal government only make matters worse.[62]

Many Christian parents have believed the lies of psychology and have failed to discipline their children lovingly and biblically. Without that protection, the world more easily makes its inroads. The faith of the parents is not being passed on to the children in many cases.

One of those who was caught up in drugs and rebellion but saw the evil and fled, writes:

> I was a child of the 60s, part of the flower-child movement. I recall how exciting it seemed to be . . . part of a global confederation of youth, given a new vision of peace, love and brotherhood, bonded by drugs and music.
>
> It all seemed so new and wonderful going in. Coming out was another story. I was fortunate to get out with my mind intact, though it took me years to recognize and to be freed of the spiritual bondage I'd entered. Other friends were not so lucky. Deaths, broken minds and spirits were the order of the day. I wasn't even a full-fledged hippie—just a straight Baptist kid dabbling in fun like drugs and forms of Satanism I didn't recognize then. . . .
>
> I . . . am amazed at how I was deceived. . . . I've talked with . . . friends and we have mused about that era . . . looked back on it in disbelief, as though we'd been hypnotized for a time. . . . [Beside the] drugs . . . there was another potent force . . . the rock groups were our heroes, our gurus. . . . Music certainly helped turn the tides of America toward mysticism, drugs, and the spirit of Antichrist. Our beloved Beatles turned on to Eastern religions and drugs—and so did we.[63]

In spite of all the protests that parents may voice, the change agents are determined to prevail and will continue to press their *spiritual* agenda. Parents need to 1) have family devotions daily and make certain that their children know Christ personally and are fully committed to Him; 2) see that their children are believers in and followers of the Lord out of genuine choice and not due to parental or church pressure to conform; 3) see that their children's honest questions are answered and that they know what they believe and why, on the basis of God's Word; 4) know fully what they are being taught at school (public or Christian), arm them to stand against what is wrong, and, if necessary remove them from classes or programs calculated to undermine their faith and morals; 5) carefully supervise friendships, activities, and other influences upon their lives, which can be as deadly as public school influences; and 6) pray earnestly to God for wisdom, love their children fervently, and be ready at all times with godly counsel, patiently and lovingly given.

Youth should be fully persuaded that what God thinks of them and what He will say to them when they appear before Him one day is all that matters. As Jim Elliot, one of the martyrs of Ecuador, said when, as a young man, he chose the mission field over more lucrative careers: "He is no fool who gives up what he cannot keep to gain what he cannot lose."

I will be like the most High [God]....

—Lucifer, Isaiah 14:14

Today I lay claim to all the attributes of God ... [and] as a Divine being ... I rejoice in my Divine nature.

—Science of Mind, December 1986[1]

As the Haitians say ... the vodounist dances in the hounfour to become God.

—Wade Davis, anthropologist and world explorer[2]

In the Holy Scriptures ... we read of a unique call directed to us. ... : "You are gods ... all of you" (Psalm 82:6; John 10:34). ... As human beings we each have this one, unique calling, to achieve theosis ... we are each destined to become a god, to be like God Himself. ...

—Christoforos Stavropoulos, Orthodox scholar
explaining the heart of Eastern Orthodoxy[3]

For the Son of God became man so that we might become God. The only-begotten Son of God, wanting to make us sharers in his divinity, assumed our nature, so that he, made man, might make men gods.

—Catechism of the Catholic Church, quoting St. Athanasius
and St. Thomas Aquinas[4]

Man is called to cooperate with God ... [in] his salvation and divinization. ... The divinization of man comes from God.

—Pope John Paul II[5]

Man will not play junior partner in a firm he thinks he can run better himself. That is why I killed God.

—A Roman Catholic Dominican priest[6]

Man was created in the God class. ... We are a class of gods. ... God Himself spawned us from His innermost being.

—Kenneth Copeland with Paul Crouch on TBN[7]

We were created to be gods over the earth, but remember to spell it with a little "g."

—Charles Capps, Positive Confession leader[8]

Eventually ... all perspectives lead us ... to return to the truth of truths ... that we are God.

—Jon Klimo, summarizing channeled messages[9]

*Prince, Subject, Father, Son, are things forgot,
For every man alone thinks he hath got
To be a Phoenix, and that there can be
None of the kind, of which he is but he.*

—John Donne, English poet, 1611

17

* * *

Playing God:
The Lust for Power

Nothing is quite so appealing to a child as tales of magic powers. Yet as one leaves childhood behind, one does not entirely outgrow one's childish dreams. Their pursuit has provided much of the motivation behind science and technology, from alchemy to nuclear physics and everything in between.

Human ambition and desire have no limit. Those who believe in God try to usurp His power as their own (as Satan did) or to persuade Him to dispense it to their own ends (the avaricious goal of most prayer). In Science of Mind and Religious Science, faith is not trust in and submission to the God who created us, but "the key to the God-Power within ... the active instrument which takes my every thought and manifests it in the world of form and experience."[10] The business world follows the Pied Pipers of success whose seminars promise the same mind techniques for personal power.

Harold Bloom, author of *The American Religion*, suggests that "for the American, god is none other than himself."[11] The serpent's lie from the Garden (the very heart of the occult invasion), that man can become a god in his own right, still rules the human soul. And how better to prove that man *is* God than by demonstrating godlike, psychic powers?

The belief that some gifted individuals have already mastered such powers keeps palm readers, psychics, and gurus in business. According to *Psychology Today*, "Dionne Warwick's Psychic Friends Network logs 4 million minutes a month at $3.99 a minute and last spring [1996] celebrated its 10-millionth caller.[12] The hope for magic remedies fuels the alternative health craze and causes thousands diagnosed with terminal illnesses to seek the "miracle cures" promised through mysterious products, foreign clinics, and psychic surgeons. As we have seen, no one trumpets the delusion of infinite potential more persuasively than Deepak Chopra. His monthly newsletter is titled *Infinite Possibilities for Body, Mind & Soul. Infinite?* Only God is infinite. So man is God.

Nor does the fervent longing ever die that these unlimited powers will become commonplace within one's lifetime. Norman Vincent Peale claimed that man's empowerment could be realized by visualizing God as energy ("God is energy," said Peale) and by breathing this "energy" in.[13] If God is the energy behind the universe, then man can be his own God by learning to control that energy—precisely what the serpent told Eve. David Spangler, cofounder of Findhorn, declares with no sense of irony or shame:

> The being that helps man to reach this point [of godhood] is Lucifer . . . the angel of man's evolution. . . .[14]

The delusionary hope persists that somewhere within each of us infinite powers lie hidden. That fantasy created the New Age movement with its insistence that human potential is limitless—if only we can escape the bondage of negative, fundamentalist thinking that prevents us from reaching that fabled state of "higher consciousness" for fully utilizing all of our innate powers. According to the Dalai Lama:

> From the Buddhist point of view, our consciousness has the potential to know every object. Because of obstructions we are, at present, unable to know everything. However, by removing these obstructions gradually, it is ultimately possible to know everything.[15]

This is pure nonsense, which the Dalai Lama himself has never been able to demonstrate—even though he claims to be God. Yet millions continue to believe him.

A Key Question

From its very beginning in alchemy and sorcery, science has pursued unlimited power. Magic gradually gave way to materialism in the West, and science tried unsuccessfully to deliver mankind from its superstitions. Seventy years of forced atheism and materialism in the Soviet Union failed to remove the innate belief in something beyond matter. No sooner had the Iron Curtain come down than the liberated citizens in the Communist countries of Eastern Europe went on a spiritual binge and opened themselves to every cult and religion. Heretofore unthinkable programs such as "Thoughts on the Eternal: Sunday Moral Sermon" were instant successes on Soviet TV, as were psychics and healers.[16]

Science has now returned to the belief that an immaterial universe exists, a universe inhabited by spirit beings and containing powers beyond our finite imagination. Exploration of this new frontier is carried on in earnest through psychic research (parapsychology) at top universities (University of Nevada's Consciousness Research Laboratory, Princeton's Engineering Anomalies Research Lab, etc.) and independent laboratories such as SRI and the Institute of Noetic Sciences.

Altering consciousness is believed to open the doorway to that "other universe" and to be the key to developing psychic powers. To assault that door with consciousness research, the government has authorized experimentation once again with psychedelic drugs such as LSD, MDMA (ecstasy), DMT (a drug occurring naturally in the human brain), peyote (from the cactus bud) and psilocybin (from the sacred mushroom).[17] Physician Larry Dossey, author of *Prayer Is Good Medicine*, is convinced that "when the history of consciousness in the twentieth century is written, the current laboratory studies on mind over matter will mark the most important turning point."[18]

"Mind over matter" and "mind control" over other minds have been the dream of occultists for thousands of years. Science is now giving apparent support to that possibility. *Psychology Today* admits that it now "seems that human intention alone can influence machines—even at a distance, when no influence seems possible." Dean Radin, director of University of Nevada's consciousness research, contends: "The movement of mind does affect matter. It influences everything you can imagine, including mind itself."[19]

Is a *human* mind actually influencing matter and other minds? Or could it be a *nonhuman* mind, perhaps a demonic manifestation under the guise of human potential? Could it all be a ploy in order to convince man that Satan's promise of godhood is the truth—in order to enslave him?

Finding the "God Power" Within

One of the leaders of the occult invasion in the West was Alice A. Bailey. Before her death some 40 years ago, she was the chief channel for Djwhal Khul, the Tibetan Master, who dictated through her about 20 books and whose teachings are followed by Robert Muller and many other leaders. Amazingly, Khul's dictations through Bailey present a precise blueprint of the occult invasion exactly as it has been proceeding. Bailey's writings were originally published by the Lucifer Publishing Company, now known as Lucis Trust, which works closely with the United Nations. Its *World Goodwill Newsletter* declared:

> Avante-garde psychology is affirming amazing human potentials which, when cultivated, lead to states of consciousness which have always been called divine.[20]

Could these states of consciousness make it possible for demonic entities to take over and deceive those involved? Ignoring that possibility, psychic research seeks to establish scientific verification of a godlike power of the *human mind* which can clairvoyantly diagnose and heal diseases, shut down electronics, "see" what is happening at remote, secret, and hidden locations, and even move physical objects at a distance. Beginning at Duke University in the 1930s with J.B. Rhine, the father of American parapsychology, numerous laboratory experiments (which have been repeated around the world) verified that *mind* is separate from the physical brain and is *apparently* able to influence physical forces and objects in a manner that defies physical laws.

We have made passing reference to the fact that the U.S. and other governments have avidly pursued the development of psychic powers for intelligence gathering, national defense and even offensive capabilities. The full truth about these programs remains a closely guarded secret. David Morehouse, who was involved in a CIA program, claims to have "spent eight months, eight hours a day, being trained . . . to transcend space and time to access people, places, and things remote from [him] . . . to go forward and backward in time . . . etc."[21] *Psychology Today* commented:

> Though the CIA claims it has abandoned the program [Star Gate] . . . Morehouse and his remote viewing colleagues believe . . . the government is . . . training individuals in "remote influence"—accessing another human mind to inflict harm on it. . . .
>
> Morehouse says remote influence was used against Saddam Hussein in the Gulf war. "Later, on CNN, I saw him accuse the U.S. of using psychics to attack him."[22]

Though skeptics call spoon-bending psychic Uri Geller a fraud, SRI and other scientists expended much time and effort testing his powers and decided that some inexplicable force was involved. "Under scientists' scrutiny, he erased video tapes [with his mind], increased the mass of gram weights, and called eight of 10 dice throws." Shamans and mediums would say that such powers come from spirits, but differ as to the identity of these entities. Like most psychics, Uri Geller believes these are normal powers of the human mind and that "we once had full power over our minds, but . . . we have forgotten many of the abilities we once had."[23]

John Randolph Price founded the Quartus Foundation for Spiritual Research "on the divinity of man." Price unabashedly declares the Foundation's goal to be:

> To continually document the truth that man is a spiritual being possessing all the powers of the spiritual realm . . . God individualized, and that as man realizes his true identity, he becomes a Master Mind with dominion over the material world.[24]

Becoming "God" Once Again

Scientology, like Hinduism, teaches that we are gods who have forgotten who we are and need to rediscover the magic powers we possess. So it is with yoga: Its goal is "self-realization"— to reach that state of consciousness where we realize that we are gods who have simply forgotten our identity. Of course, if we are gods who have forgotten who we are, what good would it do to "remember" our true identity? Wouldn't we likely forget it again?

At her seminars to packed audiences, when she was at the height of her New Age popularity, Shirley MacLaine would tell her gullible followers, "Just remember that you are God, and act accordingly." Common sense immediately protests: There is no way mere humans can act like God—something which Shirley herself has been unable to do. If we're God, why aren't we already acting the part? And why does God have to pay to attend a seminar to find out who He is? Wouldn't He know it without being told? The lie is so preposterous!

The magnitude of this incredible delusion is matched only by the Himalayan pride that promotes and wants to believe it. We have already referred to psychiatrist M. Scott Peck, his pretense of becoming a Christian, and his endorsement by and popularity with evangelical leaders who ought to know better. In his *Playboy*, *Newsweek*, and *New Age Journal* magazine interviews and his appearance on the Oprah Winfrey show, Peck has made statements that certainly contradict any alleged Christian faith. Moreover, Peck also promotes the serpent's lie:

> To put it plainly, our unconscious is God. God within us.... Since the unconscious is God ... we may further define the goal of spiritual growth to be the attainment of Godhood by the conscious self ... to become totally, wholly God ... a new life form of God....
>
> God wants us to become Himself (or Herself or itself). We are growing toward godhood. God is ... the source of the evolutionary force and ... the destination.[25]

Similarly, Norman Vincent Peale declared that in prayer we commune not with the God who created us but with "the great factor within [one]self, the deep subconscious mind.[26] Psychologist Carl Rogers called self "the god within" and advocated worshiping at its altar. Spirit guides have been pushing this fantasy ever since Satan introduced it to Eve, and it is the heart of Eastern meditation and mysticism. Alan Watts, Episcopal-priest-turned-Zen-Buddhist Master, declared:

> The appeal of Zen, as of other Eastern philosophy, is that it unveils ... a vast region ... where at last the self is indistinguishable from God.[27]

Ramtha declares: *"We* created the universe. *We* made the stars . . . [but] after thousands . . . of incarnations, we, the great gods of light, have forgotten who we are! We no longer remember that we created the universe. . . . We must stop worrying about right and wrong . . . and love God by loving ourselves. . . . We have the power to reverse aging and live forever in our present body . . . to heal any disease, even to grow a new limb if one is cut off. What prevents us from doing these things? It is our 'altered ego,' the 'Antichrist' within us who keeps telling us we are not God."[28] Behold the Bible turned inside out!

The "God" who dictated the recent bestseller *Dialogue with God* tells Neale Donald Walsch that we are all "Gods and Goddesses at birth. . . . What I am, you are. . . ."[29] The stupidity and blatant blasphemy of this *Dialogue* is exceeded only by the egos willing to embrace such lunacy. Walsch, the "God" who doesn't know he is "God," is told by "God" that, oddly enough, it is going to take a lot of effort to realize who he really is:

> Let's be clear that . . . [you must dedicate] your whole mind, your whole body, your whole soul to the process of creating Self in the image and likeness of God. This is the process of Self realization about which Eastern mystics have written.[30]

Rama, one of Hollywood's favorite gurus in the 1980s, charmed his followers with this absurdity: "Whenever you make a mistake, remember that you are God. God doesn't make mistakes. God only has experiences."[31] J.Z. Knight declares, "God is inside each individual . . . everyone is divine. This outrageous realization creates a human being who . . . [lives] according to what *feels* right.[32]

That professing evangelical Christians have also embraced this lie is astonishing, but such is the case. And that gullible acceptance is rampant in the "faith" and charismatic movements.

"Ye Shall Be as Gods"

Like Finis Dake in *God's Plan for Man*,[33] televangelist Benny Hinn claims that Adam and Eve were super beings who could fly faster and higher than birds, even into space, and outswim the best fish under water: "Adam was . . . the first Superman . . . with one thought he would be on the moon . . . he could swim [under water] and not run out of breath and so did his wife . . . they were both super beings."[34] Consider the following from other Positive Confession leaders:

Man was designed or created by God to be the god of this world (Robert Tilton, Kenneth E. Hagin, Charles Capps).[35]

You have the same ability [as God has] dwelling or residing on the inside of you (Charles Capps).[36]

We have all the capabilities of God (Kenneth Copeland).[37]

Creative power was in God's mouth. It is in your mouth also (Charles Capps).[38]

We are in God; so that makes us part of God (Kenneth Copeland).[39]

God has made us . . . the same class of being that He is Himself. . . . God took something of Himself . . . and put it into man. . . . Man was master. Man lived on terms equal to God. . . . This is the end of the weakness message! (Kenneth E. Hagin).[40]

Did you know that from the beginning of time the whole purpose of God was to reproduce Himself . . . ? Who are you . . . [but] the expression of all that God is. . . . And when we stand up here, brother, you're not looking at Morris Cerullo; you're looking at God! (Morris Cerullo).[41]

Satanist leader Michael Aquino stated with conviction on the "Oprah Winfrey Show," "We are not servants of some God; we are our own gods!"[42] In at least partial agreement, Kenneth Copeland and Paul Crouch (like Shirley MacLaine) insist on TBN that they are indeed gods. "You are a little god," declare Copeland and Benny Hinn on TBN. "I am a little god!" exults Paul Crouch on international television, and condemns to hell the "heresy hunters" who say this teaching isn't biblical.

Rodney R. Romney, pastor of Seattle's First Baptist Church, embraces and teaches almost the entire spectrum of occultism that we are exposing. In his book *Journey to Inner Space: Finding God-in-Us* Romney writes, "To know God, to love God, and to understand God is finally to realize one's own godhood."[43] The book has been republished with all its heresies intact since we exposed it in *The Seduction of Christianity*. In that part of the book which he says he "received" from "the higher source" by "listening"[44] (like the "two listeners received" *God Calling*), Romney records these words from "God":

> Through prayer and meditation the individual divinity of your being unites with omniscience, and the microcosm becomes one with the macrocosm . . . this sacred place of your inner knowing . . . is the stepping-stone to the stars.[45]

To teach that man is God, a god, or equal to God, and that faith is a force that works according to certain laws, differs little from atheism. Either way, there is no being in the universe who is man's superior. So it is in the New Age movement.

Freemasonry, too, in its secret rituals, promotes this central lie of the serpent. In his explanation of the 18th degree, Rex R. Hutchens, 33rd degree, states with approval, "The most ancient mythologies speak of men made gods." In the lecture for the 23rd degree, Albert Pike commends Pythagoras for having taught "the necessity of personal holiness to qualify as man for admission to the society of gods." The ritual for the 31st degree determines whether the candidate "deserves to dwell among the gods." The candidate's escort is the Egyptian god Horus. Isis, Horus' mother, is the first to speak. Eventually the god Thoth "reports that a majority believe the man worthy to dwell with the gods." Osiris "renders the final judgment," giving his approval as well.[46]

The Mormon Church has its own variation on this theme: "As man is, God once was; and as God is, man may become." Mormonism's "God" is an exalted man who, like the candidate in Masonry, attained to godhood through much effort—and every Mormon male hopes to do the same. In 1974, the late Mormon President Spencer W. Kimball declared:

> In each of us is the potentiality to become a God. . . . Man can transform himself . . . he has in him the seeds of Godhood that can grow. He can lift himself by his very bootstraps.[47]

Following the Serpent

The serpent's promise of godhood to Eve, as we have seen, is the foundation of occultism, paganism, Hinduism, and the

New Age movement. The January 1931 edition of *The Occult Digest: A Magazine for Everybody* contained an article titled "Awakening the Divine Self." Readers were assured, "Within you is every power of the universe—all love, all wisdom, all life." The magazine referred to this power as "serpent power," which indeed it is.

The same lie is a major theme running through much science fiction. Gene Roddenberry, the now-deceased creator of the *Star Trek* movies and TV series, was "brought up in a Baptist household ... went to a Baptist young people's Christian Association ... [but] spoke negatively about all religions, especially Christian[ity]." Roddenbery was convinced "that the human race is an infant God ... [and] that he was God."[48]

Nowhere is the serpent's lie professed more openly or honored more highly than in Mormonism. From the pulpit of the Mormon Tabernacle in Salt Lake City on June 8, 1873, Mormon leader Brigham Young declared: "The devil told [Eve] the truth [about godhood] ... I do not blame Mother Eve. I would not have had her miss eating the forbidden fruit for anything in the world...."[49] In apparent agreement, psychologist Rollo May called Eve's sin *felix culpa,* or "fortunate fall."[50]

Joseph Smith founded his cult upon the delusionary aspiration after godhood. Smith taught that matter and intelligence have always existed and the ascent to godhood has been pursued forever. There must, therefore, be an infinite number of gods in Mormonism, though Mormons claim they only deal with "the God of this world"—which, incidentally, is how the Bible refers to Satan (2 Corinthians 4:4). The secret rituals in Mormon temples are the first step for Mormon males in following their gods on this long road to "exaltation."

Recently deceased Mormon President Spencer W. Kimball said that Christ has given Mormons "a code of laws and commandments whereby we might attain perfection and, eventually, Godhood...."[51] How long is "eventually"? Joseph Smith indicated it could take eons of time:

> When you climb a ladder, you must begin at the bottom and ascend step by step until you arrive at the top; and so it is with the

principles of the Gospel; you must begin with the first, and go on until you learn all the principles of exaltation [to godhood].

But it will be a great while after you have passed through the vail [of death] before you will have learned them all.[52]

Mormonism had the approval of Norman Vincent Peale, who was the keynote speaker at President Kimball's 85th birthday celebration in 1980. He called the Mormon leaders "men of God . . . [who] are doing God's work . . . by their fruits ye shall know them. . . ." Because Kimball was "so deeply spiritual," Peale asked him, "Will you bless me?"[53]

Perhaps Peale, who was a 33rd-degree Mason, favored Mormonism because it is so much like Masonry. Each state in the U.S.A. has a Supreme Grand Lodge of Freemasonry and most Grand Lodges publish a *Monitor* for the guidance of members in the official doctrines and practices. Consider the following from the *Kentucky Monitor:*

> The three really great rituals of the human race are the Prajapati ritual of ancient Hinduism, the Mass of the Christian [Roman Catholic] Church, and the Third Degree of Masonry.
>
> Together they testify to the profoundest insight of the human soul: that God becomes man that man may become God![54]

Power, Power, Who Has the Power?

Instead of the eons of effort and initiation which the Mormon expects to endure in order to reach godhood, yoga offers self-realization (the arousal of the Kundalini serpent power) in this life. Parapsychologists hope to demonstrate in the lab that the powers of godhood already reside within us all and only need to be released. *World Goodwill* is confident that "we can experience ourselves as we really are . . . our divine inner self . . . we must believe in the divinity of humanity."[55]

Experimental psychologist and parapsychologist Lawrence LeShan, after many years of careful research, concluded that psychic powers are demonstrable under laboratory conditions but that they are beyond scientific explanation. He wrote:

As we continue our exploration . . . of consciousness, we find that the methods of logic and of mathematics . . . cannot be used here. They simply do not apply. [56]

Sir Arthur Eddington agreed. This "greatest of the British astronomers" said, "Natural law is not applicable to the unseen world. . . . All attempts to prove that these powers come from the human mind or psyche have failed."[57] Could that be because they do not originate from man but from another source?

It is comforting to believe that a God of love, justice, mercy, and infinite wisdom and power is in charge of the universe. It would be terrifying indeed if instead there were billions of self-centered gods, each with infinite power. The hope of realizing the alleged infinite human potential is exciting for oneself, but the thought that everyone else could have the same power turns the dream into a nightmare. Life would become a ghastly struggle of a world of sorcerers competing with each other.

Consider the terror that grips members of thoroughly shamanized primitive cultures. These exist not only in the Amazon jungles today but in "civilized" countries such as Haiti, where voodoo is an ever-present terror in spite of the claim that it is used only for benign purposes. What a frightful place this world would be if every Tom, Dick, and Harry, as well as every Jane and Joan, had infinite God-powers to use as each pleased!

Wonderful Truth or Cruel Hoax?

The goal of parapsychology is to prove that people do indeed have such powers—that they are gods who create their own universe with their minds. Any child knows that is not true. Who walks in sunshine while the "negative thinkers" about him are in the rain? Who continues to fly safely through the air on a plane that the other passengers and crew, because of their negative thinking, have conspired to "imagine" is falling from the sky? And if faith is a belief which creates by its own power, then the patients in mental hospitals ought to be giants of faith. They surely believe their delusions as strongly as the human mind can believe, yet their belief fails to produce the "alternate reality" of their madness.

Far from mentally creating reality, mankind has been struggling to discover the incredible secrets of a universe which is at once so awesome in size and yet so intricate in minutest detail that it reflects the genius of a Designer whose mind and creative power is infinitely beyond human capabilities. How could *we* possibly have created galaxies we don't even know exist and black holes and an internal depth of unnumbered atoms about which we are equally ignorant? The simple truth is that natural events proceed on their course quite independently of the thoughts of puny man. To think otherwise is such folly that its persistence can only be the product of a delusion driven by the same blind pride that fueled Lucifer's mad ambition to be "like the Most High."

How cruel to tell Calcutta's million beggars who are born and live out their miserable lives and die in its streets that their running sores, gnawing hunger, and poverty do not really exist, but have been created by their own "negative" thinking! There is no suffering, disease, or death; one merely imagines it is there. All one needs to do to change one's experience of life is to change the way one perceives it. This is surely the cruelest hoax of all time.

Bringing God Down to Our Level

Most of those who teach that we can each create our own reality also theorize a Universal Mind as the source of infinite power and knowledge. Oddly enough, this infinite Mind has no mind of its own but mirrors what *we* think. Most appealing of all, it does not reprove us for sin. No one expressed this delusion more clearly than Ernest Holmes, founder of the Church of Religious Science:

Man, by thinking, can bring into his experience whatsoever he desires. . . .[58]

We are co-partners with the Infinite . . . a Universal Creative Mind which receives the impress of our thought and acts upon it.

Because of Its very nature, this [Universal] Mind cannot act without an image of thought [supplied by man].[59]

"Channeled entities," no matter who they claim to be, consistently teach that we create our own reality with our minds.

"Seth" (channeled through Jane Roberts), for example, declares: "You are given the gift of the gods; you create your reality according to your beliefs. . . ."[60] Ramtha tells us, "Love yourself, you are God. . . . We create our own realities within which to express ourselves . . . and in which to evolve." Again, Klimo reminds us that this view "is virtually identical with . . . many other channeled materials."[61]

Consider the spontaneous ease with which lightning blacks out a city, a snowstorm closes roads and airports, or a tornado tears off rooftops—all of this and more not only without any help from human minds but in spite of both curses and positive affirmations. Then contrast this with the hours of seminars and self-hypnosis and subliminal suggestion tapes, the meditation and yoga, the positive declarations endlessly repeated—all of this intense effort aimed at "creating a new reality," yet with so little visible effect. When a power failure blacked out one of her seminars, Shirley MacLaine led her audience of about a thousand in earnestly visualizing the problem being cleared up. The attempt failed to produce a demonstration of what Shirley teaches, and the crowd of would-be gods, unable to dispel the darkness, had to go home.

Playing God Through Visualization

We have referred to visualization, the major occult technique for allegedly creating reality. Phil Jackson learned it in college, and it became a very important part of his "spirituality" as well as a technique which he has taught to the Chicago Bulls team.[62] Yonggi Cho teaches that God created the universe through visualizing it first in His mind and then manifesting it through the power of thought,[63] and that we, through the laws of the "fourth dimension," can do the same.

Cho insists that one cannot have faith except through visualizing that for which one is praying, and that through visualizing we bring this goal or object into being.[64] However, as we have seen, we can only visualize the gross outline of a person or thing. The actual composition of cells and atoms is beyond our imagination. Our visualization could hardly be responsible for bringing into existence what we can't visualize!

Of course, some forms of visualization (an architect visualizing the structure he is drawing, a reader visualizing the scene described in a novel, etc.) are legitimate. One enters the occult through using visualization to create reality or to contact spirit entities, including Christian attempts to visualize Jesus, or God.

Phil Jackson says that during "forty-five minutes of visualization at home" before the game, "I usually call up images of the players in my mind and try to 'embrace them in the light,' to use the Pentecostal parlance that has been adopted by the New Age."[65] Again Phil reveals his ignorance of Christianity. The idea of being embraced by the white light comes neither from the Bible nor from "Pentecostal parlance" but from the occult.

Is the Universe a Hologram?

The modern development of holograms has supplied one of the major "scientific" arguments in support of the belief that we are infinite beings possessing infinite powers. A holographic image can hang in the air and be seen from all sides. Primitive ones were used in the *Star Wars* film series. The remarkable feature of a hologram is that no matter the number of pieces into which it is cut, each one contains the entire image.

Some theorists claim that the basic structure of the universe and all in it is holographic. If so, each of us is a tiny holographic image of the whole, containing within ourselves all wisdom, power, and knowledge that ever was or ever will be. Deepak Chopra declares, "If you examine yourself, you realize that we are all holograms—everything in the outside world is inside us."[66] It certainly does not follow from self-examination that we contain the universe within ourselves. On the contrary, it takes little reflection to recognize this idea as a delusion.

Nevertheless, the holographic theory has been embraced even by such top scientists as Brian Josephson, Nobel laureate in physics. On that basis, Josephson expects to explore the entire universe from the innermost depths of the atom to the farthest reaches of the cosmos by looking within himself through yoga. He has held this belief for many years now, but we still await the evidence.

What About "Ye Are Gods"?

What then did Jesus mean when He quoted Psalm 82:6, where God says, "I have said, Ye are gods"? Because He was testing the Pharisees' comprehension of Scripture, Jesus didn't quote the next verse: "But ye shall die like men." It sounds as though being a god and death are related. Clearly, in reminding them that God had said they already were gods, Jesus was not calling men to *become* gods. We must go all the way back to Genesis 3:22 to find when and where God called men gods. There God says, "Behold, the man is become as one of us."

It was Satan, not God, who had promised godhood to Eve—and not that she would be *God*, but "as [the] *gods*" (Genesis 3:5). Ah, there was the catch! There is only one true God. The gods are all false. They are the pretenders after godhood, the followers of Satan, who have believed his promise of godhood. These demonic beings are worshiped through idolatry. Speaking of "that which is offered in sacrifice to idols," Paul writes that "the Gentiles . . . sacrifice to devils, and not to God" (1 Corinthians 10:19,20).

Every problem in the world today can be traced to Eden, when mankind became a race of godhood-seekers. Today we have nearly 6 billion such seekers on earth, all in conflict with one another, all seeking for the power to enforce their will upon others. Unless we abdicate the throne of our "godhood" and are reconciled to God through the sacrifice of Christ on the cross, we remain under God's judgment for joining Satan's rebellion. God warns:

> But the Lord [Jahweh] is the true God. . . . The gods that have not made the heavens and the earth, even they shall perish from the earth, and from under these heavens.[67]

God puts His finger on the root of every earthly problem: rebellious man, pretending to be a god, and claiming he can create with his mind. And He exposes the lie very simply: Obviously we have not created the heavens and the earth, but He has. The one true God declares unequivocally that all who claim to be gods but have not created the heavens and the earth shall perish! Yet Paul Crouch declares:

> If we are not "little Gods," we will apologize to you in front of ten thousand time ten thousand before the Crystal Sea![68]

Orthodox Christianity?

As in Catholicism, the very heart of Eastern Orthodoxy is the call to become gods through Church ritual and good works. Orthodox theologian Daniel B. Clendenin explains that in Orthodox theology, "Deification . . . is the ultimate purpose of God's creation." He quotes Orthodox saints to the effect that we "become god through union with God by faith."[69] These "saints" further declare that "The 'science of stillness,' contemplation, and the interiorization of prayer through constant invocation of the name of Jesus are also of chief importance [in reaching godhood]."[70] We must also "participate faithfully in the sacraments." Moreover, "Keeping the commandments of God is indispensable: 'In the end they make a man god . . . the deification' for which we were created."[71]

Deification is a lengthy process in which the Church and its priesthood are absolutely essential. Salvation by grace through faith is vigorously opposed. Showing Roman Catholicism's agreement on this point with Eastern Orthodoxy, Pope John Paul II, in his celebrated book *Crossing the Threshold of Hope* (highly acclaimed by evangelical leaders), explains that "salvation and divinization" are the "ultimate purpose" of man's life. "With God, man 'creates' the world; *with God, man 'creates' his personal salvation.* The divinization of man comes from God."[72]

Campus Crusade for Christ has long accepted Roman Catholicism and Eastern Orthodoxy as true Christianity. A former staff member who became an Orthodox priest testifies, "During my two-and-a-half years on staff [at Crusade headquarters] . . . I fully participated in the nearby Greek Orthodox parish, Saint Prophet Elias. . . . Campus Crusade encouraged my active participation. . . ."[73] Frank Schaeffer (son of Francis and Edith Schaeffer) dedicates the story of his conversion to Orthodoxy to several former Campus Crusade staff members who are now Orthodox priests and who introduced him to the Orthodox Church.[74]

Schaeffer makes it abundantly clear that the evangelical faith in which his famous parents raised him had to be renounced as a false religion in order for him to embrace the Catholic/Orthodox faith. He now calls being "born again" the Protestant's "meaningless . . . magical instantaneous 'silver bullet' solution to sin." He says we are not saved by "believing that Christ died on the cross for us [but] *by struggling to become like Christ.* . . . We are gradually saved as we are deified" (his emphasis).[75]

Independence and Power
from "The God of This World"

Satan's primary tactic in opposing God is not to foster atheism but false religion. Satan's boast, "I will be like the most High" (Isaiah 14:14), admits God's existence but exalts self to the same lordly level. Satan became, in fact, "the god of this world" (2 Corinthians 4:4). He damns far more souls with the prideful lure of power and success than by dragging them into the gutter. He didn't tempt Eve with alcohol or bestiality but with the ambition to become one of the gods. Satan's purpose is not to prove that Christ never existed. It is to have his man, Antichrist, worshiped as Christ. A perverted "Christianity" is Satan's ultimate weapon.

It is humbling to admit that we are sinners heading for eternal judgment at the hands of God and are totally unable and unworthy to save ourselves or to do anything to merit salvation. We must accept salvation as a free gift of God's grace. So says the gospel. Far more humanly appealing, however, is the following concept adopted by numerous groups which are networking millions of people together as global citizens of a new world:

> Those who are looking for a savior can find one by looking in the mirror. Do your part in helping people grow by teaching practical spirituality, and they will realize that the redeemer and deliverer lives within each heart.
> And then, as each one releases the radiant energy to go forth on wings of Love, all things will be made new. That is the practical way of salvation.[76]

The words *savior* and *redeemer* are borrowed from Christianity. They have been given a meaning, however, which is diametrically opposed to the biblical gospel of Jesus Christ. Margaret R. Stortz, Science of Mind Practitioner, writes: "The task of the practitioner in the lives of those who feel powerless is . . . to help them realize their *own* power ... to begin to discover that they can indeed 'decree a thing and it shall be established. . . .'"[77]

The prophet Jeremiah, however, declared: "Who is he that saith, and it cometh to pass, when the Lord commandeth it not?" (Lamentations 3:37). Nowhere does the Bible teach that any man or woman can decree whatever he or she desires and make it happen by adherence to some universal law, by Positive Thinking or speaking it forth in a Positive Confession. That delusion, however, is shared by all occult systems, and is taught dogmatically by the Hagins, Copelands, Chos, and other Positive Confession leaders.

"I want to be independent of people ... and circumstances. I want my reality to be orchestrated from within me," says Deepak Chopra.[78] But even he, the expert who teaches such delusion to others, cannot make his theories work for himself. Far from creating his own reality from within, Chopra, like everyone else, is threatened from without by problems which irritate him. He filed a 10-million-dollar lawsuit against parties he claimed had conspired to defame him. He later said, "Maybe I should be enlightened enough to say it doesn't matter."[79]

What Is the Source of Power?

Lawrence LeShan worked "with the psychic Eileen Garrett and repeatedly observed her producing paranormal phenomena under the most careful scientific conditions. . . ." He was convinced that she was genuine, but he didn't know what that meant—nor did she.[80]

Garrett submitted to tests by scientists in Paris and Rome, at Cambridge and Oxford, at Columbia University and Johns Hopkins Medical School, and by J.B. Rhine at Duke, desperately hoping for proof that the spirit entities which controlled her in trance were simply splits of her own psyche. All the evidence indicated, instead, that they were independent personalities, separate from her. Said LeShan:

> Here was one of the greatest psychics ever known to science, a deeply serious woman who spent the last thirty years of her life trying to understand what her mediumship was all about, a woman

who, during those thirty years, worked almost entirely under experimental conditions with any scientist who would work with her, saying that she did not know whether her paranormal information was derived from spirits of the dead or telepathy.[81]

Ira Progoff, the celebrated psychotherapist (and great champion of the kind of "journaling" that produced *God Calling*), submitted Garrett to numerous tests. He psychoanalyzed both "Uvani" and "Abdul Latif," her two principal "controls" (who had taken possession of Garrett under hypnosis and continued to speak through her against her will), and carried on lengthy dialogue with two "god figures," Tahoteh and Ramah, who also possessed Garrett. Progoff concluded that he had reached "the God principle which is within us all."[82]

Eileen Garrett was *possessed* by a number of spirit entities who even used her vocal chords to speak forth in ancient languages of which she had no knowledge. We believe, on the basis of the lies they promoted, that they, like all of the other entities channeling satanic delusion, were demons. The classic horror film *The Exorcist* was based on a true story involving demonic possession which came about through a Ouija board, which J.B. Rhine investigated and declared to be "the most impressive" poltergeist phenomenon he had seen.[83] That possibility, however, is one which the parapsychologists don't want to face.

The demonic entities who seek to gain control of mankind through the offer of "psychic" power will pose as anything from spirits of the dead to Ascended Masters to the Universal Mind to one's own Higher Self. In the end, however, they want everyone to believe that these are powers of the human *mind*. Earlier we mentioned the torment that plagued Jimi Hendrix and his concern that he was possessed by a demon. Nevertheless, he couldn't escape the lie that it was really his own mind. He said:

> Things like witchcraft, which is a form of exploration, and imagination, have been banned by the establishment and called evil.
> It's because people are frightened to find out the full power of the mind.[84]

Of course, no parapsychologist imagines that the human mind acting on its own has infinite power. There must be a partnership. Even LeShan or Progoff would admit that Garrett had to draw from some universal Mind or Consciousness such as Jung proposed, or some universal Force. What is it? Why not a demon?

The manifestation of psychic powers has led even atheists to believe in some "higher power" or "universal consciousness" of which the human mind is a part or can tap into and use as it pleases. Psychiatrist and psychic researcher W.E.R. Mons called it "the Psychic Power."[85] It existed, he believed, beyond the human mind but was responsive to the mind. Mons was convinced that this Power was "not the heavenly monarch of the Church or the Creator-God of the Old Testament . . . God did not create man, but mankind [created] God."[86]

The psychics and researchers have some amazing successes mixed with failures; they cannot get a handle on the power they seek. Obviously psychic power will never be under the psychic's control but is controlled by someone else. We believe that entity (on the basis of conclusive evidence) to be Satan and that he dispenses paranormal power only to advance his agenda.

Satan does not care whether man believes he has this power in partnership with some universal Mind—or with spirit entities. Any theory that denies the true God of the Bible is acceptable. Nor does man, in his lust for power, care what the explanation is, so long as he can play at being God.

Many of the best scientific minds . . . suppose that intelligent life exists . . . throughout the universe . . . that some of these life forms . . . can communicate with us. . . .

The very best way and perhaps for the present the only way [of contact with these entities] is within the context of an altered state of consciousness.
—Robert Masters and Jean Houston[1]

We are on the threshold of a major breakthrough in interplanetary communication. . . . It is no more a matter of wondering if there could be somebody out there, but how to establish the first interplanetary dialogue. . . . We are working around the clock to sift data.
—Soviet astronomer Mirzoyan[2]

In April 1996, Nevada governor Robert Miller "renamed State Route 375 the Extraterrestrial Highway, supposedly because of the frequency of UFO sightings."[3]

From the public's perspective the government policy in these areas [UFOs] for nearly fifty years appears to be one of silence, secrecy and disinformation. . . . There is a great individual spiritual challenge. . . .
—From the Introduction to Conference papers,
When Cosmic Cultures Meet[4]

I have listened to a general who headed up an agency of the U.S. Air Force and who told me about his own contact [with aliens]. I have had dinner with an ex-CIA pilot who assured me the aliens were actually here, alive and in large numbers, working secretly with our scientists. And another man, a former Naval Intelligence officer, assured me he had once been assigned the mission to brief three admirals on the nature of the secret treaty that linked the U.S. government to these aliens, who lived inside our most secret military bases.
—Jacques Vallee, astrophysicist and
one of the most credible UFO investigators[5]

Military remote viewers . . . noticed a certain group of Martians who . . . seemed like . . . shamans . . . ominously, they seemed to have an ability to detach their subspace [spiritual] aspects from their physical bodies in order to attend gatherings of others similar to themselves. Quite honestly, this spooked the U.S. military.
—Professor Courtney Brown, Ph.D., remote viewer

We couldn't be happier about what we're about to do. Doubt was never an issue. It's just the happiest day of my life. I've been looking forward to this for so long.
—Members of "Heaven's Gate" cult, speaking on farewell suicide tape[6]

18

* * *

UFOs, ETIs, and Near-Death Experiences

If man is the product of universal evolutionary forces, then there could theoretically be intelligent life on numerous other planets throughout the cosmos. If life began on Earth by chance, it might have begun elsewhere by chance as well. A recent letter to the editor of *Time* said, "Common sense and mathematics dictate that in a universe of trillions of star systems, the conditions for life could be rare and still occur millions of times. If it could happen here, we can be sure it has happened elsewhere."[7] However, as we have shown, the mathematics prove that life couldn't happen by chance here or anywhere.

Evolution was central to the religion of the Heaven's Gate cult members. These intelligent and talented people were convinced that suicide would allow them to be reincarnated into new bodies on a higher evolutionary level. If the theory were true, higher life-forms must exist elsewhere. Evolution could have been in progress on some other planets 10 billion years longer than on Earth.

Robert Jastrow (past director of the Goddard Institute for Space Studies) suggests that some extraterrestrial intelligences (ETIs) could have evolved as far beyond man as man is beyond a worm. Their incredible powers would make them seem like gods to us, compelling us to fall down and worship them. If, or when, they find us here on Earth, will they be friendly? That question should terrify evolutionists.

President Reagan suggested that a direct threat from alien forces could unite Earth's inhabitants for mutual protection.

Obviously, however, any beings able to travel the vast distances to Earth must be so far beyond our capabilities that we could not defend ourselves. Thus the film *Independence Day*, which depicted Earth's forces winning the battle, was ludicrous.

It would take our spacecraft about 90,000 years to reach Earth's closest stars! Our galaxy is about 100,000 light years across, with the next closest galaxy about 1.5 million light years beyond that. To penetrate only 1 percent of our galaxy would take Pioneer or Voyager 2 million years! Jacques Vallee claims that "space-time could be folded to allow almost instantaneous travel from one point of our universe to another. . . ."[8] That is unproved theory, and certainly beyond human capabilities. ETIs reaching Earth by any means would have to be so far beyond us that they could do with us as they pleased.

An international conference, "When Cosmic Cultures Meet," was held in Washington, D.C. during May 27–29, 1995. It dealt with how to handle the expected contact with ETIs. This author was the only speaker to point out the absurdity of thinking that we would have anything to say should such an event occur. We would have no defense against the weapons of such creatures, no basis for negotiation, and no reason to hope for mercy, but much reason to fear.

Why should such "highly evolved" beings act toward us mere "worms" in any way other than in their own selfish interests? There is no evidence that evolution produces kindness, even in its highest forms, but exactly the opposite. A species doesn't survive long enough to reach godlike status by dealing fairly and compassionately with others. They would likely be even more self-serving than we are. They might keep some of us as pets or slaves, but their robots would be more efficient and cheaper to maintain, so most earthlings would be destroyed.

The Vastness of Space— And a Nonphysical Dimension

Even if evolution were true, the incredible distances involved make it highly unlikely that *physical* beings in *physical* spacecraft could ever reach Earth. Furthermore, as Jacques Vallee points out, UFOs are able "to appear and disappear very suddenly, to change their apparent shapes in continuous fashion and to merge with other physical objects."[9] Clearly, they are not physical, though (like poltergeist demons) they can affect the physical world. UFOs have been tracked on radar at 7000 miles per hour making a 90-degree turn without slowing down—an impossibility for a physical object. A SWAT team in Atlanta, Georgia observed a giant UFO hovering directly over them at close range. It moved away suddenly at incredible speed, passing through the sound barrier without a sound—again, impossible for a physical object.

If UFOs are not physical, what are they and who operates them? Jastrow suggests that some beings could have evolved, beyond the need of bodies, to become "spirits." That idea is now acceptable to many top scientists. Vallee says: "The entities could be multidimensional, beyond space-time itself."[10] Being unhindered by space and time, nonphysical ETIs could contact us here on earth by mental or psychic means.

In fact, as Masters and Houston suggest, only telepathic/psychic communication is practical. Again the vast distances demand that conclusion. It would take 1000 years for Earth's radio signals to penetrate a mere 1 percent of our galaxy and another 1000 years for a reply to reach us—and millions of years to reach even the fringes of the universe. Therefore, present attempts to make radio contact with ETIs are as foolish as the theory of evolution behind them.

Of a highly evolved nonphysical creature, Jastrow says, "How do we know it's there? Maybe it can materialize and then dematerialize [as UFOs seem to do]. I'm sure it has magical powers by our standards. . . ."[11] We are at a serious disadvantage. Our materialistic science provides no means of evaluating spiritual entities or events, much less of identifying them or their motives. Why couldn't they be demons?

Unwittingly, Jastrow, though an agnostic, is echoing the Bible's description of Satan and demons: spirit entities able to appear and disappear, masters of deception, which fits Vallee's conclusions regarding UFOs. Paul warned, "Satan himself is transformed into an angel of light. Therefore it is no great thing if his ministers also be transformed as the ministers of righteousness . . ." (2 Corinthians 11:14,15). Seemingly unaware of this possibility, or unwilling to face it, Andrija Puharich, though a brilliant scientist, wrote that while he was "remarkably ignorant about these beings," he had "complete faith in their wisdom and benevolent intentions toward man. . . ."[12] Likewise, author Whitley Strieber, after years of contact, still doesn't know who or what these entities are, but he wants us to trust them. Why?

It took Strieber years to admit that his own bizarre experiences were real—and he doesn't yet understand them. Highly intelligent, well-educated, and already a bestselling author with a reputation to maintain, Strieber seems an unlikely candidate for repeated hallucinations, nor need he lie to sell his books. In *Communion*, he meticulously describes what he calls "a shattering assault from the unknown . . . an elaborate personal encounter with intelligent nonhuman beings."[13] Do they come to Earth from other planets, or from another dimension? Strieber still doesn't know.[14]

Strieber is angry and confused. He feels violated. "The visitors," he tells us, "marched right into the middle of the life of an indifferent skeptic without a moment's hesitation." At first he thought he was going crazy. Eventually, being diagnosed as insane would have been preferable to believing that what he was experiencing was *real*. But the "three psychologists and three psychiatrists" who gave him "a battery of psychological tests and neurological examination" declared him to be "normal." He also passed a lie detector test given "by an operator with thirty years' experience." In his search for truth, Strieber also consulted space scientists, physicists, and an astronaut, only to be told: "To the scientific community, the nature of this phenomenon remains an unresolved question."

A Perfect Setup for Demons

Serious international efforts have been underway for decades to contact ETIs. In this country the program was titled Search for Extraterrestrial Intelligence (SETI) and was connected to NASA. In 1993 Congress cut government support to SETI and it was succeeded by Harvard University's "Project Phoenix," an intense, continuing effort to make radio contact with ET civilizations. Other nations, too, are sending radio signals into space and listening for some coherent message from "out there." As part of this search, the Voyager spacecraft carried a message on a gold record affixed to its exterior:

We cast this message into the cosmos. . . . Of the 200 million stars in the Milky Way galaxy, some—perhaps many—may have inhabited planets and spacefaring civilizations. If one such civilization intercepts Voyager . . . here is our message.

This is a present from a small, distant world, a token of our sounds, our science, our images, our music, our thoughts and our feelings. We are attempting to survive our time so we may live into yours. We hope someday, having solved the problems we face, to join a community of galactic civilizations. This record represents our hope and our determination, and our good will in a vast and awesome universe.

Jimmy Carter
President of the United States of America
THE WHITE HOUSE, June 16, 1977

As a professing Christian, Carter's hope should have been eternity with Christ in heaven. Instead, he proposed a glorious future with a galactic community in a universe which the Bible says will be destroyed at the end of the millennium: "The heavens shall pass away with a great noise, and the elements shall melt with fervent heat . . . all these things shall be dissolved . . . we, according to his promise, look for new heavens and a new earth, wherein dwelleth righteousness" (2 Peter 3:10-13).

Professor Courtney Brown claims that remote viewers have identified ET civilizations which are visiting Earth and that "we are about to enter the realm of galactic life as fully participating members in the community of worlds."[15] Syrian President Hafez Assad, in an interview with *Time* magazine, expressed the belief that *only* an extraterrestrial power could bring real peace to this world.[16] Even leading Christians have spoken favorably of this unbiblical and impossible event.

Jastrow and Vallee are not the only scientists who acknowledge the possibility that ETIs may be nonphysical. Unfortunately, Earth's science offers no protection against such entities. That we are now trying to make contact with nonphysical beings provides the perfect setup for demons.

Unresolved Contradictions

Sightings of strange flying objects have been recorded as far back as human history can be traced. The modern UFO era began on June 24, 1947, when businessman and veteran pilot Kenneth Arnold, flying near Mount Rainier, sighted nine "flying saucers" moving at about 1600 miles per hour. Two weeks later "an Army Air Force colonel announced that officers of Roswell's 509th Bomb Group had captured a flying saucer and some dead alien creatures at a crash site on a farm 75 miles northwest of Roswell [New Mexico]. A few hours later, Air Force officials denied that the report had ever been made."[17] Today, Roswell is a mecca for UFO enthusiasts who come to visit the International UFO Museum and nose about town for information.

After 50 years, rumors still persist that the government is covering up the truth and that wrecked spacecraft and preserved bodies of the dead aliens (along with up to 600 live ones working with us) are supposedly secreted at Nevada's top-secret "Area 51," an underground complex as large as Manhattan hidden beneath Nellis Air Force Base. When this was reported to Vallee by "informants," they had no answer to his logical question of "who takes out the garbage" and his comment that "the base would . . . stick out like a sore thumb on infrared satellite imagery . . . there is no such thing as a hidden underground base of that magnitude anymore."[18]

On the other hand, Jacques Vallee admits that his interest in UFOs dates from the time he "witnessed the destruction of tracking tapes of unknown objects at a major observatory."[19] A *Newsweek* poll conducted in 1996 revealed that 48 percent of Americans believe that "the government is hiding proof of UFOs from the public."[20] Recently some of the mystery surrounding the cover-up was dispelled:

With growing hysteria over alleged UFO sightings in the 1950s, the Air Force repeatedly concocted false cover stories to hide the fact that their super-secret spy planes had been spotted. . . . Concern lest the public learn of the secret spy planes [U-2s] "led the Air Force to make misleading and deceptive statements . . ." [historian Gerald K.] Haines wrote [in the spring 1997 issue of *Studies of Intelligence,* an unclassified CIA journal].[21]

Frank Kaufman, now 80 years old, still maintains that he and several other men "stationed at the Roswell Army Air Field [in 1947] stumbled onto . . . the wreckage of a spaceship northwest of town. . . . Kaufman, a retired government intelligence agent, said he watched soldiers put five dead aliens into body bags and haul a damaged spaceship . . . to the post. Glenn Dennis, a Roswell mortician, said he got a call from the Army post to send out several small, hermetically sealed caskets."

The Air Force insists that the wreckage was of a high-altitude balloon from a top-secret program monitoring the atmosphere for signs of Soviet nuclear tests.[22] Vallee admits (as John Keel suggests) that it might have been "a Fugo balloon."[23] On June 24, 1997, the Air Force issued a 231-page full report titled "The Roswell Report, Case Closed," which attempted to lay it all to rest: "The 'bodies' were not aliens but dummies used in parachute tests between 1954 and 1959."[24]

Is Kaufman so confused that his memory of seeing the wreckage of some "balloon" in 1947 became associated with dummies that crashed ten years later? Is Dennis confused also? Would caskets be needed for damaged dummies? It seems impossible to reconcile conflicting accounts. Daniel Ross writes:

When the spaceships appeared in the late 1940s, and sighting reports began to number in the thousands . . . an almost impenetrable security lid came down. . . .[25]

It has even been suggested by some informants with "inside knowledge" that Navy Secretary James V. Forrestal "jumped to his death from a sixteenth-story hospital window" after having seen terrifying aliens "shaped like praying mantises, and who were more advanced than us by perhaps a billion years."[26] There is no lack of lunacy in the rumors about UFOs.

A Persistent, Unexplained Phenomenon

The UFO craze is fueled by sightings of UFOs worldwide. There were a great number in the Soviet Union beginning in April 1989, with the largest concentration coming in the city of Voronezh (population about 1 million), 300 miles southeast of Moscow. Newspapers around the world carried the story of witnesses observing a UFO land in a park, and its giant occupants get out and walk around. There were so many sightings and witnesses that Vallee went to the USSR accompanied by an investigative reporter from *Le Figaro* to check the story for himself. He concluded:

> The USSR was in the grip of one of the most massive UFO waves to come along since the French wave of 1954 ... [leaving] a clear message: the UFO mystery is as vivid and as puzzling as ever. ... But of its physical reality there cannot be any doubt.[27]

More recently, numerous UFO sightings in Israel have been reported in the Israeli press. " 'The Great Invasion,' headlined one story in the *Maariv* daily, in which 16 examples of UFO sightings in the past three months were reported. ... "

Israeli radio has even aired reports of alien abductions. A certain Uri Sakhov said his captors were green, only reached his chest in height, and made unintelligible sounds. "Scientists found that dust on Sakhov ... was different from soil in the area."[28] At about the same time (revealing the hysteria that surrounds this subject), "hundreds, if not thousands of panicked Spaniards collapsed TV and radio switchboards with frantic calls ... [in response to] a 'news alert' showing aliens hovering over New York ... [and] New Yorkers fleeing in the streets." It was all actually an ad (at the bottom of the TV screen was the word "advertisement") for the U.S. film *Independence Day* opening in Spain.[29] Shades of Orson Welles!

The vast majority of the thousands of UFO sightings reported annually have some ordinary explanation. Many reports are crackpot inventions, such as Louis Farrakhan's assertion that he was "carried by a beam up into an unidentified flying object called the Mother Plane where the voice of the long-dead Elijah Muhammad announced that Reagan and the Joint Chiefs of

Staff were planning a vast and bloody war."[30] Equally ludicrous are the claims of abductions for medical examinations and impregnation of women for crossbreeding and the many supposedly witnessed crashes of UFOs. Surely any civilization billions of years ahead of us wouldn't need to make so many clumsy attempts at such procedures, nor would its space vehicles navigate light years of space only to crash on earth.

It is beyond the scope of this book to document the many cases of seemingly valid UFO sightings. Those may be studied from other sources. This author is personally acquainted with reliable witnesses who have carefully observed UFO phenomena at very close range. These are not "lights dancing across the sky" as were seen across Arizona in March 1997 by many witnesses and recorded on video and which remain unexplained.[31] These were daylight encounters lasting several minutes at such close range that there was no mistaking the reality of what was seen, and no earthly explanation for it.

Not of This World—And Nonphysical

FBI files include numerous reports of mysterious flying objects seen in many parts of the country by competent observers, including Air Force pilots and instructors as well as FBI personnel. The incredible speed and maneuverability of the objects (impossible for earthcraft) indicate an origin beyond this planet. The reports also include observations of physical evidence on the ground, such as indentations as well as burned and radioactive areas where the object had apparently landed. A CIA memorandum from the Deputy Director (DDCI) to the Director of Central Intelligence (date obliterated) states:

> At this time, the reports of incidents convince us that there is something going on that must have immediate attention. . . . Sightings of unexplained objects at great altitudes and travelling at high speeds in the vicinity of major U.S. defense installations are of such nature that they are not attributable to natural phenomena or known types of aerial vehicles.[32]

There is no doubt that some UFOs are real. Airline and fighter pilots and even astronauts (Ed White, first American to walk in space, James McDivitt, James Lovell, Frank Borman, et al.) have seen them. Vallee says, "We have met too many truthful witnesses, we have seen too many cases of actual traces... unidentified flying objects do exist." He returns to the element of mystique, however, adding, "They are astounding... have the ability to affect the perception of time and space and the consciousness of those who come close to them."[33]

That UFOs are "real," however, does not necessarily mean "physical." All of the evidence indicates that they are intruders from another *dimension* of reality. Vallee says:

> I speculate, although I cannot prove, that a non-human form of intelligence is involved... that manipulates space and time in ways we do not understand... the UFO phenomenon [is] far more complex, stimulating, awesome and ultimately important and mysterious than... [physical spacecraft].[34]

Something *nonphysical* is visiting us for unknown reasons. Arthur C. Clarke said, "One theory that can no longer be taken very seriously is that UFOs are interstellar spaceships."[35] According to Vallee, who knew leading ufologist J. Allen Hynek very well, the latter said:

> I have come to support less and less the idea that UFOs are "nuts and bolts" spacecraft from other worlds. ...
>
> To me, it seems ridiculous that super intelligence would travel great distances to do relatively stupid things like stop cars, collect soil samples, and frighten people. ...[36]

For the many reasons given above and the biblical ones which follow, we do not believe that any spacecraft crashed near Roswell or anywhere else or that any bodies were recovered. We do not doubt the sincerity of those "witnesses" who are convinced otherwise and we have no explanation for the confusion involved. However, there is no question that *physical* wreckage and *physical* bodies are not part of the UFO scene.

Why Humanoid ETIs Don't Exist

That life could develop by chance *anywhere* is mathematically impossible. This has been proved beyond dispute. With electron microscopes opening up *Darwin's Black Box* (see Chapter 2) to reveal the inconceivable complexity of life at the molecular level (and with computers calculating the impossible probabilities involved in putting the elements together by chance in the right sequences) we can state dogmatically that evolution is a fraud.

If intelligent life exists anywhere (as on earth), it was created by God and put there for a purpose. Of course, God *could* have created intelligent life on other planets, but the Bible makes it clear that He did not. Everything Scripture tells us of God's plans for the entire universe for all eternity involves planet Earth. It is to this Earth that Satan came to spread his rebellion, and it is to this Earth that Christ came to die for man's sin, and thereby defeated Satan on the cross.

It is here to Earth that Christ will return to destroy Satan's kingdom and reign for 1000 years. And it is to the new Earth in the new universe that the heavenly Jerusalem will descend (Revelation 21:1,2); and it is from that new Jerusalem that Christ will rule for all eternity. Christ's sacrifice on the cross on this planet purified heaven itself (Hebrews 9:23), having fully dealt with sin for the entire universe.

There are no physical ETIs "out there" to visit Earth. The only intelligent life in addition to man is in spirit form: God, holy angels, Satan, and demons (fallen angels). Spirits, however, whether angels or Satan and his minions, are able to invade the physical realm and to perform feats impossible by our standards—and to leave physical evidence. There is no evidence, however, that they can have sex with women and produce offspring, as is speculated by some.

Satan put boils on Job, caused Sabeans and Chaldeans to rob Job and kill his servants, and caused a "great wind" to destroy Job's house and kill his children. Satan took Christ to the top of a mountain and to the pinnacle of the temple. Jannes and Jambres (2 Timothy 3:8), the magicians in Pharaoh's court, were able to duplicate by the power of Satan many of the miracles that Moses and Aaron did by the power of God. UFOs seem to manifest a similar power.

The delusionary power of the entities which manifest themselves in UFOs was demonstrated in the tragic "Heaven's Gate" suicides in March 1997. One of many UFO cults, it was founded in the mid-70s by Marshall Applewhite and Bonnie Lu Trusdale Nettles, known as "Bo and Peep." Bonnie died in 1985 and Applewhite carried on as the cult's leader. Its beliefs centered in reincarnation, evolution, and UFOs. Members were told to get ready to be taken from this Earth to the next evolutionary level by a giant UFO. The quote at the beginning of this chapter reflects the incredible power of the UFO delusion.

Redemption for ETIs?

Any intelligent created beings with the power of choice (a necessity for worship and love), being less than God, would make less-than-perfect choices. Sin is defined as coming "short of the glory of God" (Romans 3:23). God does not need to experiment ("Man rebelled, but let's try again on another planet"). If there are other sinners scattered throughout the universe, God must have created them. But why? Surely one planet of rebels is enough!

Our own compassion and conscience (as well as Scripture) tell us that a loving God would want to forgive sinners and reconcile them to Himself. To do so *righteously*, however, the penalty for having broken God's laws must be paid. Finite beings (as all created beings must be) could never pay the infinite penalty required, so God Himself would have to do so by becoming one of them. The Bible declares that God did this for Earth's inhabitants, becoming a man through the only virgin birth and dying for our sins upon the cross.

For beings on other planets to be redeemed, God would have had to become one of them and die for them as well. But the Bible indicates that "the man Christ Jesus" (1 Timothy 2:5) is "the same yesterday and today and forever" (Hebrews 13:8). To suggest that Christ also took other forms at other times, is an antichrist doctrine (1 John 4:1-3).

The Bible clearly says, "The wages of sin is death" (Romans 6:23) and "without shedding of blood is no remission [of sin]" (Hebrews 9:22). The Bible also states that Christ died only *once*, and here on Earth as a man. Therefore, there is righteous reconciliation to God for man alone. There is no redemption for any other creatures. Christ's sacrifice could not have been repeated on any other planet nor could it be perpetuated in the Roman Catholic "Sacrifice of the Mass," as that Church claims. The Bible declares:

> ... by his own blood he entered in *once* into the holy place [heaven], having obtained eternal redemption for us ... [and] now *once* in the end of the world hath he [Christ] appeared to put away sin by the sacrifice of himself. ...
>
> But this man, after he had offered *one* sacrifice for sins forever, sat down on the right hand of God. ... For by *one* offering he hath perfected forever them that are sanctified. ... There is *no more offering for sin* (italics added for emphasis) (Hebrews 9:12,26; 10:12,14,18).

For sinners to escape God's judgment, the infinite penalty for their sins must be paid, which finite beings could never do. That Christ fully paid that penalty is attested to earthlings by irrefutable proof: testimony of eyewitnesses, archaeological and historical evidence, and prophecies fulfilled on this Earth. That other beings would have a savior who had died on a distant planet is in complete contradiction to all that the Bible teaches.

The Final Conflict

It is possible that UFOs and belief in ETIs may play an important part in convincing mankind to follow the Antichrist. Surely if contact were made with "friendly" ETIs offering their godlike powers for mankind's good, Earth's leaders would jump at the chance. Again, what a setup for a takeover by demons!

Much of the channeled material tells of a coming encounter with ETIs and encourages us to welcome them as friends. Having received many transmissions through channeling various entities, Lyssa Royal writes:

> We are entering an age ... [which] requires us to be participants of contact [with ETIs]. This ... phenomenon ... will enter the life of every human ... we must accept and acknowledge our own evolution by entering species adulthood and becoming responsible galactic neighbors. ...

By willingly engaging the extraterrestrials in open contact, we as a planetary species send out a beacon to the universe proclaiming our . . . coming of age into a galactic community. . . .[37]

What limits there may be upon satanic "power and signs and lying wonders" (2 Thessalonians 2:9) we don't know; but the manifestations will be sufficient to cause the whole world to worship Antichrist as "God" (Revelation 13:8). And the fact that mankind is now open to contact and to receive advice and help from ETIs (even nonphysical ones, who can only be masquerading demons) sets the stage for the "strong delusion" (2 Thessalonians 2:11).

Jacques Vallee, an agnostic, is convinced that a major purpose of UFOs is to manipulate human consciousness for some ultimate deception. He links UFOs to the occult:

> A few investigators—notably Ray Palmer, John Keel, and Salvatore Freixedo—have suggested . . . that there may be a link between UFO events and "occult" phenomena.
>
> At first view, the very suggestion of such a link is disturbing to a scientist. However . . . the phemomena reported by [UFO] witnesses involve poltergeist effects, levitation, psychic control, healing and out-of-body experiences . . . familiar [themes of] occult literature . . . which have inspired not only the witchcraft revival, but also . . . "psychic" writers and . . . "scientific parapsychologists. . . ."
>
> Furthermore, there is a connection between UFOs and occult themes in their social effects. . . .[38]

A Fascinating Common Thread

From the very beginning in the Garden of Eden Satan has communicated an unvarying lie to the human race to prevent mankind from believing in Christ and from receiving the pardon that Christ freely offers. The ideas of evolution and of life on other planets further that goal. Moreover, the messages being channeled from alleged ETIs are the same as those received in yogic trance, under hypnosis, on drugs, through mediums in seance, or in any other altered state of consciousness.

"Contact" with UFOs or alleged ETIs, as Vallee points out, is of an occult nature and involves altered states of consciousness in which delusion is at its greatest. It was Shirley MacLaine's dabbling in the occult that opened her, like so many others, to the belief that extraterrestrials were in contact with earthlings to guide them into a "New Age." One well-known contactee admitted to Vallee that aliens "provided much [data] on the occult side. They claimed they had a lot to do with our religion. They spoke about witchcraft and cults. . . ."[39]

Furthermore, the effect of repeated "contact" (which "contactees" themselves describe) sounds like demon-possession as the Bible presents it. Whitley Strieber, in *Transformation*, claims he can call ETIs into his life at any time. He simply turns himself over to these "visitors," even though he admits that he still struggles with the fear that they are evil and he doesn't know what they really represent. Again it sounds like Eileen Garrett and the spirits that controlled her when she went into trance.

At one point Strieber came to the conclusion that the visitors were probably the gods who created us. UFOs and ETIs are clearly contributing to an ecumenical, worldwide religion which opposes the biblical message and resembles the ancient polytheistic pagan religions condemned by God. In fact, these entities seem to resemble the ancient gods of the pagans. As only one example, an entity identifying itself as Ashtar (Ashtoreth, Astarte, Ishtar, etc.?) has been in communication with numerous contactees.

Ashtar has lied continually. George Van Tassel was given instructions for building an "Integratron" that would reverse aging. Van Tassel is dead. Thelma Terrell, under the name Tuella, also channels Ashtar, who declared that the "great prophecies" from the space brothers would all be fulfilled in the early 1980s—another lie. Ashtar gave much other misinformation through T. James (about the earth being hollow, that George Adamski, who "published two books with obviously faked photographs,"[40] was genuinely in touch with ETIs, that Lemurians still have cities in Antarctica, etc.). Of course, Ashtar's main lies are about Jesus Christ, denying all that the Bible says about Him and creating "another Jesus" (2 Corinthians 11:4).

Altered Consciousness: Occultism's Master Key

Professor Courtney Brown was involved in TM at its highest Siddhis level. He also trained to have out-of-body experiences

(OBEs) at Robert Monroe's Institute in Virginia before he got into remote viewing. The key to all three is the altered state of consciousness in which, Brown says, "logic" ceases and we become part of a "field of consciousness."[41] Robert Monroe developed a patented technology called "Hemisync" that "makes one's mind resonate mechanically like that of a great seer or mystic who has spent a lifetime exploring the boundaries of consciousness." At that point, says Brown, one enters "subspace," where "an aspect of each of us exists . . . as do other beings."[42]

Says Brown, "I have personally remote-viewed an insignia on the uniform of an ET . . . I have had extensive experience with a variety of extraterrestrials. Most of this contact has been through remote viewing."[43] In the same manner, he claims to have contacted "Jesus" and "God" (the latter is still evolving!), and Buddha, who, says Brown, "sits on the Federation Council that helps monitor the affairs of humans on earth. To this day, he watches over us."[44] As always in occultism, Jesus and God are lowered to Buddha's level.

If Brown were not a Ph.D. still actively teaching in a university, one would think he had gone mad. He has *talked* to "Jesus" and "God" and "Buddha"? He has been in touch with Martians and other races of ETIs? And a major publisher, Dutton/Penguin, prints this incredible occult fantasy?

Clearly, the altered state essential for remote viewing opens one to demonic influence. Satan feeds remote viewers bits of valid information to keep them involved, then slips in his lies along with signs and wonders. And enough pseudoscientific support is published for multitudes to be convinced. Daniel Ross writes in *UFOs and the Complete Evidence from Space:*

> The interplanetary visitors watched all our space developments, and particularly our trips to the Moon. . . . Scientific specialists advising government and military authorities believed that Venus and Mars were the origin of the spacecraft.[45]

The story of how Brown's wife (a TM instructor) was visited by one of the "Greys" (alleged species of ETIs which Brown had never described or discussed with her) at a crucial time, and how a "luminous being" that appeared to Brown led him into contact with the military remote viewer who trained him in this technique, follow the pattern of demonic guidance. His experiences in "subspace" of meeting the usual "bright light," dead relatives, and ETIs are similar to encounters experienced by the clinically dead in near-death experiences (NDEs). Here we have the whole occult picture as we have been documenting it.

ETIs, Spirit Communications, and NDEs

Not only ETIs inhabit subspace and may be viewed there, according to Brown, but also spirits of the dead. Says Brown, "People who no longer reside in our physical space 'live' in subspace. It's not accurate to say that these are 'dead' people, since they are very much alive."[46] Here we go again with the serpent's denial of death! Brown's story confirms the connection between all occult phenomena.

It was during an OBE at the Monroe Institute, says Brown, that "a remarkable thing happened that greatly changed my views about extraterrestrials."[47] He tells how he met the spirits of several long-dead relatives, but his recently deceased Aunt Elsie was missing. When he inquired about her he suddenly encountered "the brightest light I had ever experienced . . . like looking right into the sun," and was confronted by "hundreds of thousands of Greys." The dead aunt's voice was heard to say, "These are the beings whom you want to help."[48] Here ETIs are associated with discarnates.

It should be no surprise to learn that Norman Vincent Peale, who brought more occult delusion into the church than anyone in this century, also claimed to have been in touch with discarnates on several occasions. Of one encounter, Peale wrote:

> I was seated on the platform of a large auditorium. . . . Some ten thousand persons . . . were singing hymns. . . . Then I "saw" him, my father who had died long before at age eighty-five. He came striding down the aisle . . . about forty years old. . . .
>
> I was spellbound . . . [by] what I was "seeing." The huge auditorium faded away. I was only with him. Getting closer, he smiled that great smile of his. He raised his arm in the old-time gesture. . . .

I arose from the chair, advanced to the edge of the platform, reaching for him. Then he was gone, leaving me shaken, somewhat embarrassed by my actions, but happy at the same time. . . .

The bishop [on the platform] . . . when I told him of the incident . . . said, "Why shouldn't we believe your father was here? He would like a meeting like this, wouldn't he?"[49]

The altered state of consciousness essential for such experiences can come in a variety of ways. That Peale could have had such an unbiblical encounter is not the main problem, but that he would accept it as from God. Fighter pilots can have similar experiences under the stress of G-LOC (the loss or near-loss of consciousness suffered when subjected to several times the pull of gravity). In an Arthur C. Clarke TV special, pilot Rob McConell tells of coming into a bright light and a euphoric feeling under such conditions.[50] On the same program, Jim Whinnery, chief aeromedical scientist at the Naval Air Warfare Center, describes G-LOC's effect:

Dreamlets that include seeing family, friends, loved ones, a sense of not wanting to be disturbed because it's a pleasurable experience . . . extremely vivid. . . .

Just after I had left the centrifuge and . . . was walking down the hall . . . I found that I was . . . up behind myself, looking down at myself. . . .[51]

As we have seen, altered states of consciousness allow an alien spirit to operate the brain. Under those conditions one experiences implanted "memories" of prior lives, visions of the future, floating out of the body, cosmic or unity consciousness, contact with a being of light as well as with ETIs, etc. Altered consciousness would surely include the coma of a person who appears to be clinically dead.

Near-Death Isn't Death

One of the most obvious pieces of misinformation promoted by Satan through so-called "clinical death" is that those who return can tell us what it means to die. The very name given to this phenomenon (*near*-death or *clinical* death) indicates that these people haven't really died and come back—that would be a resurrection. Therefore, they don't have anything to tell us about death, a state which they haven't yet experienced.

That Satan is using this altered state of consciousness to his own ends is quite apparent from the fact that those who "come back" almost invariably promote a major lie from the serpent: that we don't really die. Swiss psychiatrist Elisabeth Kübler-Ross, who interviewed more than 20,000 survivors of clinical death and who has become deeply involved in the occult, claims that "death does not exist."[52] According to Raymond Moody, a medical doctor whose 1976 book, *Life After Life*, sold millions of copies and began the NDE craze, a major effect of the NDE upon almost all who experience it is that they no longer fear death.[53] Dr. Moody, too, has gotten deeply into the occult, contacting spirits of the dead through mirror gazing.[54] One news report said:

> "Even my two wonderful kids (ages 22 and 19) were a little worried this time," Moody admitted. . . . But the doubting off-spring have now become believers, as have thousands of people who watched a recent Oprah Winfrey Show featuring Moody. The nation's top-rated talk show sent two skeptics to visit the former grist mill in Alabama that Moody has converted into a place to experience encounters with dead loved ones. . . .
>
> There was a Harvard professor of medicine and a WTBS sports producer. . . . Both were to attempt encounters in the space of one day, without the sort of careful preparation with subjects that Moody has used in the past. . . .
>
> The Harvard professor . . . [saw] a vision of her dead mother; the TV producer . . . a vision of his dead father, all to the surprise of many in Oprah's audience of 14 million. . . .
>
> "Mirror gazing will be accepted again, absolutely," Moody insists. "I have no question in my mind it will be verified as valid . . . that process has already started."[55]

To be able to see and communicate with those who have died is taken as proof that we don't die. That lie is repeated frequently by alleged discarnates in seances. The supposed spirit of Bishop James Pike's dead son stated was that his *mission* was to show that there is no death. He went on to say that God is not personal but "the central Force," and that Jesus was *not* the Savior but merely a highly evolved man.

Those who return from clinical death almost unanimously deny death and judgment as the Bible presents it. The experience of apparently slipping out of this body and moving on to the next level of existence is so beautiful (so they say) that most of those involved have no desire to return to Earth. They testify that there is *no judgment* to face after death—only a "being of light" who accepts everyone without question, then restores them to life. For example, Ken Vincent writes of his experience:

> The white Light was wonderful! It was just love. I knew my life would be reviewed. . . . I knew I had done things that I was not proud of, but there was total acceptance.[56]

A rash of bestselling books with similar stories followed *Life After Life.* The accounts of those who "died" and came back to tell about it are still popular on talkshows. One of the most popular yarn-tellers was Betty Eadie, who assured listeners and readers that everyone goes to heaven, as she did when she was clinically dead and was "literally embraced by the Light, Jesus." Her book, *Embraced by the Light,* quickly made the *New York Times* bestseller list and sold well in Christian bookstores because it presents the lie which most people want to believe.

Eadie passes herself off as a Christian, dedicating her book "To the Light, my Lord and Savior Jesus Christ, to whom I owe all that I have." In fact, she is a Mormon whose "Jesus Christ" is not the Jesus Christ of the Bible, and her book and lectures contain considerable Mormon doctrine, including almost the entire spectrum of occultism and satanic lies:

> I learned that we are all divine . . . each and every one of us is divine, perfect.[57]
> The LDS Church is the truest Church on the earth.[58]
> [I] watched as our spirit brothers and sisters entered physical bodies for their turns upon earth.[59]
> There are many paths to God. . . . All religions upon earth are necessary because there are people who need what they teach.[60]

Damion Brinkley had two "near-death experiences" which Dr. Raymond Moody calls "probably the most remarkable in the world." His story is told in two books, *Saved by the Light* and *At Peace in the Light.* Fox Television made his experiences into a movie. In the following summary by a reviewer, notice the same anti-Christian occult elements, from the "white light" and human godhood to no death and no judgment:

> Struck by lightning and pronounced dead for 28 minutes...
> [Brinkley] had the usual out-of-body experience in which he watched his wife and paramedics try to save him. . . . He encountered a council of 13 beings of light, who . . . gave him a mission to return to Earth and build centers where people could heal emotionally and spiritually [with a false gospel]. . . .
>
> Brinkley . . . argues that . . . there is no heaven or hell as described in Christian terms. . . .
>
> God is light, pure love and energy all at once . . . and the realm where God resides . . . is fantastic . . . filled with . . . "beings of light," where a city of crystal cathedrals emanates with powerful love. We were all beings of light once; some . . . courageously decided to come to Earth in order to co-create with God. . . .
>
> "We are not poor, pitiful humans trying to have a religious experience. We're great, awesome and mighty spiritual beings trying to have a human experience," he says. . . .
>
> Faith is not a requirement, there is no judgment . . . just the life review serving as a reminder that love is the most powerful force in the universe.[61]

To Heaven/Hell and Back?

Through opening himself to the "guidance" of his quiet time and "journaling," Frank Buchman was prepared to embrace any demonic deception so long as it was a "spiritual experience." The ultimate delusion came through a near-death experience resulting from a stroke. Buchman told friends:

> I saw the glory of the other world. I saw the outstretched arms of Christ. . . . It was better than anything I had ever seen, the vision of the life beyond. . . . I am going to stick to that vision. The unfathomable riches of Christ. It was glory. . . .[62]

Of course in near-death experiences Hindus see visions of their gods and Buddhists see the void. Is that because the brain is creating the vision from one's belief, or do demons paint a picture within the person's belief system? Visions are a poor basis for faith. Nevertheless, visions are held in high regard by many Christians. Some of the most popular speakers on the charismatic circuit are those who have allegedly been to heaven—and hell—and come back to tell about it.

The stories told are unbiblical at best and fraudulent in at least some cases. The End-Time Handmaidens, headed by Gwen Shaw, offer at least a dozen books featuring trips to heaven and hell. Betty Maltz's book *My Glimpse of Eternity* (it sold about a million copies) tells of her meeting Jesus in heaven. Her story was published by Catherine Marshall in Norman Vincent Peale's *Guideposts* magazine. The validity of her story was later questioned when her six additional books, as well as verbal accounts, added to or contradicted her earlier account.[63]

Percy Collett allegedly spent five-and-a-half days in heaven and told his story to appreciative Full Gospel audiences. He claimed that "dogs in heaven do not bark, but the horses praise God . . . God the Father is bigger than Jesus and has feathers on his left hand."[64] One of the speakers most in demand for several years at Full Gospel Business Men's Fellowship banquets and many churches was Dr. Richard Eby. His books (*Caught Up into Paradise* and *Didn't You Read My Book?*) and accounts in meetings and over TBN are unbiblical and self-contradictory.

In contrast to the vast numbers of the clinically dead who return telling of beautiful experiences, medical doctor Maurice Rawlings, in two books, *Beyond Death's Door* and *To Hell and Back*,[65] tells how he became a Christian through resuscitating a heart-attack patient who was screaming that he was in hell. He has resuscitated others who similarly thought they were in hell. Rawlings explains that Kübler-Ross, as a psychiatrist, interviews days or weeks after their experience those who have recovered from clinical death and that they remember only what was pleasant. In fact, the patient who came back screaming about hell later denied having had such an experience.

There is no indication that anyone who was resurrected, either in the Old or New Testament, went about telling what it was like to be dead—and these were persons who had been genuinely resurrected from death. Paul was "caught up to the third heaven" (2 Corinthians 12:1-4) but told nothing of that experience. Only John, in the Revelation, was authorized to describe that scene.

Those who claim they have been taken to heaven and/or hell and told by God to come back and report what they have seen are either lying or deluded. When the rich man in hell asked Abraham to send Lazarus back to warn his five brothers, Abraham declared: "They have Moses and the prophets . . . if they hear not Moses and the prophets [God's Word], neither will they be persuaded though one rose from the dead" (Luke 16:29,31). Clearly God sends no one on such a mission.

Contact with UFOs, communication with ETIs and discarnate spirits, the experience of so-called clinical death—all contradict the Word of God. Indeed, to contradict God's Word and the gospel of Jesus Christ is their obvious purpose. Jesus Christ alone has come from heaven to earth to tell us of His "Father's house" of "many mansions" (John 14:1-3). He alone has come back from the dead to tell us the truth. We do well to heed His Word.

On July 16, 1843, and again on the same day in 1881, the Virgin Mary appeared on the top of a palm tree near the village of Ville Bonheur in . . . central Haiti . . . [near] a sacred vodoun pilgrimage site. . . . For the peasants, the apparition . . . was none other than Erzulie Freda, the goddess of love, and her presence . . . only added to the reputation of the sacred [vodoun] waterfall.

—Wade Davis, anthropologist[1]

God wishes to establish in the world devotion to My Immaculate Heart. . . . To whomever embraces this devotion, I promise salvation.

—Our Lady of Fatima, June 13, 1917[2]

Today I am with you in a special way, holding little Jesus in my lap . . . I am your Mother.

—Our Lady of Medjugorje, December 25, 1996[3]

Whenever I see an image of Mary, I feel that she represents love and compassion. She is like a symbol of love. In Buddhist iconography, the goddess Tara occupies a similar position.

—The Dalai Lama[4]

I am a lawyer. Yes, lawyers have Guardian Angels like everyone else. . . . I went to sleep before my surgery and woke up 58 days later with . . . a man standing immediately to my left in clerical collar and a fedora hat. He stood there constantly for hours. It was my Guardian Angel.

—Robert W. Morgan, 33rd-degree Mason[5]

When I feel confused . . . [and] I've come up with a solution, I feel like I've gotten spiritual input from my father [murdered in 1993].

—Michael Jordan, NBA all-time great[6]

I urge you to ask everyone to pray the Rosary. With the Rosary you will overcome all the troubles which Satan is trying to inflict on the Catholic Church.

—Our Lady of Medjugorje, June 25, 1985[7]

Already the Rosary alone can do miracles in the world and in your lives. . . .

—Our Lady of Medjugorje, January 25, 1991[8]

In speaking of the disasters predicted in the . . . "Third Secret of Fatima" . . . the Pope [John Paul II] referred to "oceans flooding entire continents, people annihilated suddenly, by the millions. . . ." The Pope then "reached into his pocket and . . . pulled out his Rosary. 'Here is the medicine against this evil!' he exclaimed. 'Pray, pray, and don't ask any more questions. Leave everything else up to the Madonna!' "[9]

19

* * *

Apparitions of Angels, Ghosts, and Mary

A further indication of the occult invasion is the large number of people seeing not only UFOs but angels, Marian apparitions, and discarnate spirits. Nona Coxhead advertised in newspapers in her native England for those who were willing to share personal mystical experiences. Says Coxhead, "So many mystic experiences came pouring in to me that I had to stop advertising—fast!"[10] A.J. Russell, who published *God Calling* and promoted the Oxford Group, was a firm believer in appearances of the dead.[11]

As the quote opposite indicates, Michael Jordan, one of the greatest basketball players of all time, believes he receives guidance from his dead father. Is this just a "feeling" generated by wishful thinking and affected by the occult influence of his coach, Phil Jackson? Or is it something more than that?

Even cadets at the military academy at West Point have reported seeing "ghosts." Plebes swear that they witnessed several appearances of a ghostly soldier about five feet, three inches tall, dressed in full Jackson-era regalia. The "ghost" repeatedly appeared and dematerialized in Room 4714 of the 4th Division barracks. West Point has had a number of such "appearances."[12]

Researchers have noted the same occult influence present in appearances of ghosts, UFO encounters, and apparitions of angels and Mary. In contrast to UFOs, which are witnessed in normal consciousness, Marian apparitions (with some exceptions) are "seen" only by certain "visionaries" who are in an altered state of consciousness.

Nevertheless, multitudes (without "seeing" the "virgin") are convinced by rosary beads changing color, apparent healings, and changed lives. Investigative reporter Michael H. Brown (who exposed the Love Canal toxic waste debacle) is one of many converted through the apparitions. Having investigated a number of them, Brown writes:

> During . . . the last ten years, we . . . have been experiencing a major supernatural episode. . . . In Europe and Asia, in Nicaragua and the Middle East, in Africa and America, are accounts of an apparitional woman calling herself the Blessed Virgin Mary who appears to visionaries and gives them inspiration, instructions, and messages, including warnings about the future of the world. . . .
>
> The reports of . . . the apparitions of a saintly woman whom Catholics call Our Lady or the Queen of Heaven are remarkably consistent. . . .[13]

Angelic Visitations and the Bible

Unlike UFOs and Marian apparitions, biblical angels usually appear as ordinary human beings, even touching and conversing with witnesses who are in normal consciousness. And unlike UFOs and Marian apparitions, there is solid biblical support for appearances of angels as "ministering spirits, sent forth to minister for them who shall be heirs of salvation" (Hebrews 1:14).

The Bible records many instances of angels ministering to God's people. In the Old Testament, angels appeared to Abraham (Genesis 18), to Moses (Exodus 3), to Balaam (Numbers 22), to Gideon (Judges 6), to David (2 Samuel 24), to Daniel (Daniel 9), and to others. In the New Testament, angels appeared to Zacharias and Mary (Luke 1), to the shepherds (Luke 2), to Cornelius (Acts 10), to Peter (Acts 12), to Paul (Acts 27), and to John in the book of Revelation.

Nevertheless, the biblical warnings of last-days deception would seem apropos of today's exploding interest in angels. They are now showing up as often as UFOs. About half of Americans believe they have their own guardian angels, and 48 percent believe UFOs are real.[14] *Newsweek* reported, "Angels are appearing everywhere in America."[15] That same week, *Time*'s cover stated, "The New Age of Angels—69 percent of Americans believe they exist. What in heaven is going on?"[16]

During an intense 11-day session in 1979, a young Missouri farmer claimed to have received from a being called Raphael *The Starseed Transmissions,* which Jean Houston called "perhaps the finest example of 'channeled knowledge' I ever encountered."[17] Once again we see the clear opposition to Christianity. The following from "Raphael" is a diabolically clever perversion of what the biblical Christ taught:

> I am the Christ. I am coming this day through the atmosphere of your consciousness. I am asking you to open the door of your reason, to allow me into your heart. . . .
>
> I came to you first through a man named Jesus . . . the bridegroom returns. Whoever will come after me will have to die to all definitions of self, take up my spirit, and follow along the lines of my vibrational field.[18]

Evaluating Angelic Appearances

Two things stand out from the Bible record: Angelic appearances are rare and are only for a special purpose. Thus those who claim multiple and purposeless appearances of angels are under occult delusion. Popular televangelist Benny Hinn alleges that angels have appeared to him repeatedly (and without purpose) from childhood. On TBN Hinn testified:

> I'll never forget 1974. . . . I'm telling you the truth, I'm not lying—every night for a whole year angels appeared in my room.[19]

Hinn's claim is at best ludicrous. God's powerful messengers dropped in for 365 consecutive nightly visits? Hinn even enthusiastically predicts such angelic visitations for others: "It's going to happen . . . get ready to know the activity of angels. . . . Each of you can have 6000 angels at your disposal. . . ."[20] On another occasion he prophesied "many visitations of angels that will come as young men knocking at your door."[21]

Even *Touched by an Angel* (one of the most-watched shows in America) at least has angels (actresses Roma Downey and Della Reese) showing up on some definite mission, which Hinn's daily appearances lack. Executive producer Martha Williamson "hopes her one-hour homilies are ecumenical: 'I've never believed that God was a specific denomination.' " Says Williamson:

One of the reasons I believe angels are so popular today is because angels are nonthreatening. So you get angel cookbooks . . . it becomes an angel religion. . . .[22]

That program offers a generic god who forgives apart from Christ, no matter what one may have done. In a *TV Guide* interview, "angel" Della Reese explains, "We deal in spirituality [that anyone can accept]. That's a God [as you conceive him to be] thing."[23] Catholicism's major newspaper, *Our Sunday Visitor,* praises this program,[24] while secular *Time* pointed out:

> These mighty [angelic] messengers and fearless soldiers have been reduced to bite-size beings, easily digested.
> The terrifying cherubim have become Kewpie-doll cherubs. For those who choke too easily on God and His rules . . . angels are the handy compromise, all fluff and meringue, kind, nonjudgmental . . . available to everyone like aspirin. . . .[25]

In contrast to *Time's* discerning criticism, TBN's Paul Crouch gushes, "Reports are coming in from around the world through prophetic words of knowledge, dreams, visions, appearances of angels and apparitions of Jesus and *other heavenly visitors.* . . ."[26] *Other heavenly visitors?* Who or what could *they* be? Crouch claims that a beautiful woman (an angel or Mary) appeared to him and Jan several times to encourage them. Says Crouch:

> She handed Jan a *perfect pink rose.* . . . Jan thanked her. . . . We had turned our head for only a moment or two, but when we turned back, our lady was gone! She could not possibly have made it back across the large empty plaza, *the size of a football field,* without our seeing her leave . . . five credible witnesses will testify that this had to be a *heavenly visitor!* Jan saw this remarkable lady *two other times* . . . !
> Naturally, our Catholic brothers and sisters believe this person to be Mary. . . . I do not know. . . . In the 1980's, David Duplessis, father of modern Pentecostalism, visited Medjugorje . . . and concluded what *he* experienced was . . . a revival, the likes of which he had given up seeing in his lifetime, and he spotted no "bad fruit." The heavenly apparitions, concluded the great Charismatic leader, were "*of God*". . . (emphasis in original).[27]

As we have documented elsewhere,[28] this "father of modern Pentecostalism" was deceived by the Roman Catholic Church in its bid to draw Protestants back under the Pope. That David

Duplessis, like the Crouches and millions of others, was badly deceived by Marian apparitions, will become clear as we proceed.

Angels, Ghosts, Discarnates, and the Occult

In *A Book of Angels* (1990), author Sophy Burnham tells how a skiing angel saved her life on the slopes. In the next five years, more than a hundred books about angels were published by various authors.[29] Even atheistic psychiatrist Elisabeth Kübler-Ross claims to have "spooks ... guardian angels, whatever you call them" who speak to and guide her.[30]

G. Richard Fisher, an astute cult watcher, notes that "The book *Ask Your Angel* ... blatantly admits that conversing with angels is ... 'divination,' a practice strictly forbidden by God (Deuteronomy 18:10-12) that can have disastrous consequences (1 Chronicles 10:13).... Islam and Mormonism sprang from purported angelic visitations. And as for seeking involvement with angels (Colossians 2:18), Paul says, 'Off limits ... !' Today's angel mania is a direct violation of Scripture."[31]

One of Satan's most useful tools and Roman Catholicism's greatest modern heroes (soon to be canonized by Pope John Paul II as the first step to sainthood) was Padre Pio. As a novice monk, he asked and was granted permission by his superior to suffer for the sins of the world—a clear denial that Christ fully paid for our sin by His suffering on the cross. Pio manifested the stigmata (bleeding) from hands and feet for 50 years.[32] He testified that multitudes of spirits of the dead came to visit him on their way to heaven to thank him for paying for their sins with his sufferings so they could be released from purgatory. Other monks testified that they heard multitudes of voices talking with Padre Pio at night.[33] And this anti-Christian flaunting of occultism is praised by the Vatican!

Catholicism teaches that Christ's suffering on the cross was not sufficient to get anyone to heaven.[34] The suffering of good Catholics or a Padre Pio will do what Christ's suffering failed to accomplish.[35] Here we have a major contradiction not only between Catholicism and the Bible but within Catholicism itself. Vatican II declares that, in addition to Christ's suffering, each person must also suffer for his own sins. That is the reason for purgatory.[36] Yet Catholicism also declares that indulgences reduce or eliminate that suffering and that others can suffer in one's place—so one doesn't have to suffer after all.[37]

The Padre's heavy occultism also involved "angels." Typical is the following:

> Padre Pio . . . "met" his own guardian angel as a youngster and occasionally received counsel from him. . . .
>
> Padre Pio frequently sent his angel to someone who needed help [and others' angels came to him]. For example . . . an Italian girl . . . sent her angel to ask for good health for her Uncle Fred. The girl then decided to visit Padre Pio for the first time. When she approached him, he joked with her, "Your angel kept me up all night, asking for a cure for your Uncle Fred!"
>
> The mother of a desperately ill infant also sent the baby's angel to ask Padre Pio for prayers. As soon as she did so, she saw her tiny child shiver as if something had touched her. Although the doctors were mystified, the baby quickly improved. . . .[38]

Trapped by "Guardian Angels"!

Lenny and Diana Goldberg learned to contact their very own "angels." "We were looking for the next step in our [spiritual] growth," says Lenny, "when we found a book that . . . [contained] step-by-step directions for communicating with one's 'guardian angels.'" He continues:

> We obtained the materials called for . . . a Ouija board and . . . pure white candles, and set to work in the hopes of speaking to angels who would have all of the answers we were seeking. We said a prayer that only the highest angels should respond and we asked for protection against any "lower entities" as we lit the candles. In a very short time, each of us was communicating, via the board, with our very own angels . . . as spirit channelers. . . .
>
> [We] soon found out that we could communicate with . . . fairies, "ascended masters" such as "Michael the Archangel" and even "car angels" that protected us while in our Camry.
>
> The Ouija board soon became too slow . . . so the guides taught Diana and later me to communicate by automatic writing.[39]

Lenny Goldberg was told by his "guardian angels" that he had been chosen to have a book channeled through him about the coming "New Age" and life on other planets. The main theme of the book would be "unconditional love and how to achieve it." Such a theme assured Lenny of the benevolent nature of the entities now guarding and guiding him. He continues his story:

> When it came time to write the book... the "highest spirit"... entered me to begin dictation. His name was "the christ."...
> Over time... the voices of my invisible "friends" became... threatening that they would stop their communication if I did not obey their increasing demands. . . . The "miracles" that were taking place in my life assured me that I must persevere.[40]

Lenny awakened to the awful reality when, as he says, "One day... 'the christ' informed me that it was time to take the next step in my evolution. I was to join them where they were." Lenny's story begins to sound like Heaven's Gate:

> "In heaven?" I asked. "Wouldn't I have to be dead to go there?"
> The spirit answered affirmatively and offered some creative suggestions as to how to kill myself. At this I fell on my knees in tears and pleaded that there might be some other way that I could serve God and remain with my family.
> And then I did something that as a Jew I'd never done before. Somewhere I had heard that Jesus... could help. . . . I found myself praying to this unknown Jesus, ". . . please show me how I can live and serve God. . . ."
> Suddenly I heard a different voice telling me... that the spirit I was channeling was Satan . . . ! I felt confused, scared, angry, and dirty. I called for my "guardian angel" who had told me he would always protect me. And he said, "Yes, I am Satan. Certainly you knew all along that you were serving me."

Two days later Lenny met with a local evangelical pastor who explained the gospel and led him in a prayer to receive Christ. He began to read the Bible. When he came to 2 Corinthians 11:14 ("Satan himself is transformed into an angel of light") he understood it clearly. Lenny ends his story, "In June of 1989, Jesus was my 'way out' of Satan's 'new age.' "[41]

The Power of Apparitions

Nancy Fowler, a 48-year-old Conyers, Georgia housewife, who lives on a 180-acre farm 23 miles east of Atlanta, has been called "an unlikely visionary."[42] She claims to have been speaking privately with "Mary" and "Christ" since 1988. Larger crowds are being attracted to Conyers than to any of the other 200 current sites of purported apparitions around the world.[43] As many as 80,000 pilgrims have gathered there at one time to hear the "visionary" relay the latest "message from Mary." Pilgrims testify to changed lives, healings, and other miracles.[44]

One of the most-visited Marian shrines in the world is that of Our Lady of Guadalupe. She allegedly appeared as an Indian woman to Juan Diego, an Indian peasant, near Mexico City, at a sacred hill dedicated to the Aztec mother goddess, Tonantzin, mother of all Indian deities. Catholic Indians identify "Mary" of Guadalupe with Tonantzin. She is called "Mexico's Symbol of Unity, the Patron Saint and Protectress of Mexico," under whose banner the Mexicans fought the Spaniards for independence in 1910. She impartially provides miracles and protection to everyone, from Chicano gang members in Los Angeles to drug runners or devout South American peasants.[45]

One of the most powerful stories comes from a Fr. Barham, descended from a long line of pastors and leaders in the Assemblies of God, and now a Catholic priest. He tells of a man who converted to the Assemblies of God and hated his former Catholicism with a passion. Furious at finding a book about Medjugorje in a Bible bookstore, he bought every copy and took them home to destroy them. He heard a woman's voice, "Would you pray with me?" He found himself on his knees. Fr. Barham continues the story:

> And when he knelt . . . he began to sob . . . [and] . . . began to think, "Could this be Satan trying to deceive me . . . [to] believe that my mother who has died is speaking to me?"
>
> He was to become an official in the local Assembly of God Church that weekend. But . . . Sunday morning he heard the voice saying, "Would you pray with me?"
>
> He answered, "If you are from Satan and if you're trying to make me believe you're my mother . . . I plead the blood of Jesus over you and I command you to leave . . . !"

The voice said, "I am your Mother, but I'm . . . the one that Christ gave you at Calvary."

He said, "Are you the woman of Medjugorje?"

"Yes," she said.

"Well, I have questions for you . . . what about that Catholic belief that Jesus is present on the altar at the Catholic Mass . . . ?"

She said, "It is my Son, Soul and Divinity, who becomes present on the altar. . . . Now, would you go outside . . . ?"

I knelt in my yard and Mary said, "Look at the moon." When I did . . . I saw Mary holding the Body of her Son, taken from the cross at Calvary . . . [and] sobbed at what I was seeing. . . .

I did not go to the Assembly of God Church. Instead, I sought out [a] Catholic Church [that] had confession open to me. I was reconciled with the Church I had hated. . . .

Now . . . I am back where I belong. . . . I've been able to bring many people back to the Catholic Church that once I pointed away from it. I have found Christ more alive in my heart and in my life. And I have found Mary as my mother.[46]

Convincing? Yes, but no more so than the appearance of Djwhal Khul to Will Baron. Radiating an almost blinding golden light and a soothing presence that filled him with peace, this demonic "Ascended Master" drew an eager Baron deeper into the occult. Will writes:

When I first saw him, my own initial thought was, He looks just like Jesus Christ. . . .

Any lingering doubts in my mind . . . were now demolished forever. The dramatic visitation by Djwhal Khul relegated the philosophies of materialistic atheism to the level of absurdity.[47]

Medjugorje

Medjugorje, Yugoslavia, is unusual in that apparitions of "Mary" have supposedly been occurring *daily* to four visionaries since 1981. Some experts who have visited this site to investigate remain skeptical. Others have been convinced of the validity of the apparitions. Such was the case with a team from the University of Montpellier, France, led by Henri Joyeux, member of the French Surgeons' Academy and recipient of international medical awards. Another group was led by Marco Margnelli (a skeptic and avid Marxist at the time), Italian specialist in investigating visions. So convinced was Professor Margnelli of the validity of the apparitions that he converted to Catholicism.[48] The Roman Catholic Church, however, has not given its approval to Medjugorje.

"Mary's" image is appearing everywhere, even in such unlikely places as on the glass exterior of a Clear Water, Florida bank, and on the floor of one of Mexico City's busiest subway stations, where an image of Our Lady of Guadalupe began creating chaos early in June 1997. Although about 20,000 Marian apparitions have been reported through the centuries, "less than a dozen...have been officially recognized by the Church."[49]

Some Catholics charge that the Medjugorje phenomenon is being exploited by the Franciscan Order.[50] The Franciscan University of Steubenville (with which the Promise Keepers men's movement has been closely involved) is a major sponsor of trips to Medjugorje, where more than 16 million pilgrims now visit annually.

Pope John Paul II reportedly said to the Superior General of the Franciscan Order, "All around Medjugorje bombs have been falling, and yet Medjugorje itself was never damaged. Is this not perhaps a miracle of God?"[51] *Inside the Vatican* considers the site to be—

> the scene of an exceptional spiritual revival. More confessions are heard in Medjugorje than in any other parish of the entire world; more than 150 confessors work without interruption here every day. In the year 1990 (before the outbreak of civil war), 1,900,000 people took Communion; 30,000 priests and bishops have visited the site. Many conversions are reported.... In the USA 600 Medjugorje prayer groups have been formed; in Austria 500; and several hundred in Italy.[52]

Mary or Sophia?

One of the most spectacular apparitions of Mary was seen not by the usual visionaries in an altered state, but by multitudes of ordinary people—and in a suburb of Cairo, Egypt:

> It was...witnessed by at least a million Egyptians...and yet the Western press...and Christianity in particular all but totally ignored it.... Scholars and government leaders saw her...!

Mary [had] appeared in a dream to a devout Egyptian named Khalil and told him to build a church on his land . . . [and] she'd return in fifty years to bless it.

Khalil did as he was told, and exactly five decades after, on April 2, 1968, at about 8:30 P.M., several women pedestrians and a group of Moslem workmen . . . noticed movement up on the dome of the church Khalil had built. . . .

"I heard some people shouting in the streets," recalled Farouk Mohammed Atwa. "I ran to them. I saw a lady dressed in white on the church dome at the north. . . ."

Atwa and his colleagues thought the woman, who was kneeling at the cross on top of the dome, was ready to commit suicide. "Lady, don't jump! Don't jump!" A rescue team was summoned. . . .

As the newspaper *Watani* later reported, "They all saw her dressed as if in a bright gown of light in a view similar to that associated with the Virgin Mary. . . .

The apparition returned a week later and soon was seen up to three times a week . . . on occasion visible for hours. Huge crowds formed around the church . . . at times the crowds swelled to an estimated 250,000 . . . and for the first time in Egyptian history, Catholics, Orthodox, and Moslems prayed together in public. The Moslems chanted from the Koran, "Mary, God has chosen thee. And purified thee; He has chosen thee. Above all women."

Witnesses saw Mary emerge from a blinding glove of light. . . . The main message seemed to be ecumenism.[53]

In Eastern Orthodoxy, icons are the counterpart to apparitions of Mary and other saints. As one scholar says, "Icons are absolutely central to Orthodoxy, distinguishing it from both Catholicism and Protestantism. In the . . . first Sunday of Lent . . . liturgy is an anathema on all those who reject icons. . . . Icons are . . . a source of revelation."[54] Icons are considered to be windows to heaven. The Orthodox prostrate themselves before icons and kiss them. To attribute such power to a physical object opens one to the occult.

One of the most influential figures in Russian Orthodoxy (he greatly influenced Tolstoy) was theologian, philosopher, author, and mystic Vladimir Sergejevich Soloviev. At age nine he had his first vision, not of "Mary" but of the goddess Sophia. This pagan deity remained the guiding figure in his life. One of her appearances came when he fainted while passing from one car to another on a train and would have fallen under the wheels had she not rescued him. This moved him to write, "Only now do I understand that there is God in man, that goodness exists, along with true joy in life. . . ."[55]

Is Mary or "Virgin Mary" Appearing?

All over the world thousands of shrines stand as testimony to the seeming reality of "Marian" apparitions and to the "miracles" reportedly accompanying them. As is the case with UFOs, while many alleged appearances of "the Virgin" may be explained away, there are many for which the testimony of witnesses can hardly be denied.

The Bible makes it clear that Mary remained a virgin only *until* "she had brought forth her firstborn son" (Matthew 1:25) and that she had other children by Joseph (Matthew 13:55; etc.). Therefore, any apparition claiming to be the *"Virgin Mary"* is not of God. Nevertheless, Mary must remain a virgin to merit the exalted position that Catholicism gives her. Consider the following from Pope John Paul II (note that "faith" is in Mary and the Church, not in Christ or His gospel):

> All those who have at some time prayed to the Most Holy Virgin, even though they may have strayed from the Catholic Church, conserve in their hearts an ember of faith which can be revived. The Virgin awaits them with maternal arms open wide.[56]

More than a hundred million devotees annually visit the thousands of Marian shrines around the world to beg miracles from "Our Lady." There are only a handful of shrines to Jesus, and these are visited by very few people. It is not unusual to see Roman Catholics, especially elderly women, crawling "on their bare knees going around a statue of Mary . . . getting up from this show of devotion with blood on their knees."[57] This demonic *"Virgin* Mary" keeps her followers looking to her and to their good works for salvation and thus missing the assurance they would have of eternal life if they trusted in Christ and His full payment of the penalty for their sin upon the cross.

There is neither example nor teaching in the Bible to indicate that God allows or has any purpose for a Peter, a Paul, an Abraham, a Mary, or any other dead person to appear to the living. Even a leading Catholic magazine describes Medjugorje and other apparitions not officially approved by the Church as a "very subtle con-game. . . ."[58]

Much that "Mary" says, however, is not subtle but openly blasphemous. For example, on December 25, 1996, Our Lady of Medjugorje declared, "I am your Mother."[59] Devotees of the apparition at Conyers, Georgia, have formed a group called "Our Loving Mother's Children."[60] True Christians, however, are the "children of God by faith in Christ Jesus" (Galatians 3:26), not the children of Mary. Yet Catholicism teaches that Mary's followers become her children and that "no true child of Mary is ever lost."[61] Where can that be found in the Bible?

The "Mary" who appears promises what only God could do: to be with her millions of followers simultaneously around the world.[62] The parish priest at Medjugorje, Fr. Slavko, writes: "Mary's presence and proximity to us . . . is the main message of Medjugorje. The fact that people feel her presence and then, through her, God's presence . . . [is] the strength of Medjugorje. We should at all times continue thanking God for her presence and become yet more conscious that she is with us. . . ."[63] Omnipresence is one of God's unique qualities and it is blasphemy to attribute it to "Mary."

"Mary's" words are often repetitious and shallow, certainly unworthy of a special visitation to earth. "Mary" even makes childish errors, such as this from Our Lady of Medjugorje: "Pray, little children, for the health of my beloved Son, who suffers and whom I have chosen for these times."[64] Mary is concerned for the *health* of the resurrected and glorified Christ? And *she* has chosen *Him*? Catholics, who believe that Jesus Christ (body, soul, spirit, divinity, etc.) is simultaneously millions of tiny wafers in the Mass, have no problem accepting the equal fantasy that Jesus is a baby, a child, or even in bad health.

A Demonic Impersonation and False Gospel

Wherever this "Mary" appears she promotes the serpent's lies and teaches the false doctrines of Roman Catholicism. "Mary" makes promises which she would have to be God in order to fulfill and offers a salvation which Christ alone can give and assistance not needed by those who trust Christ. She repeatedly denies the sufficiency of Christ's sacrifice upon the cross. For example, "Our Lady of Fatima" declared, "Make sacrifices for sinners, for many souls perish and go to hell because there is no one to make sacrifices and pray for them. . . ."[65] In fact, the one and only sacrifice that can save souls has already been made on the cross.

These demonic apparitions have been encountered for centuries. In 1251 "Our Lady of Mount Carmel" allegedly appeared to St. Simon Stock and gave him the Great Promise ("Whosoever dies wearing this scapular shall not suffer eternal fire"), and to Pope John XXII in 1322, giving him the Sabbatine (Saturday) Privilege. Confirmed by Popes Alexander V, Clement VII, Pius V, Gregory XIII, and Paul V,[66] that demonic lie has seduced untold millions:

> I promise to assist at the hour of death, with the graces necessary for salvation, all those who, on the first Saturday of five consecutive months, shall confess, receive Holy Communion, recite five decades of the Rosary, and keep me company for fifteen minutes while meditating on the fifteen mysteries of the Rosary, with the intention of making reparation to me . . . for the sins committed against [my] immaculate Heart . . . [and die wearing my brown scapular].[67]

The Bible clearly says that "all have sinned and come short of the glory of God" (Romans 3:23). Mary acknowledged that she needed a "Savior" (Luke 1:47) like any other sinner. Her heart was not "immaculate." Furthermore, as David declared, sin is only against God (Psalm 51:4) and could not be against Mary. Yet the Roman Catholic Church supports such heresies presented by the apparitions. Every Pope since 1930 has given his wholehearted approval and backing to "Our Lady of Fatima." A priest writes enthusiastically (and unbiblically):

> The promise which the Mother of God makes in establishing the devotion of the Five First Saturdays is among the most powerful ever made. With the full assent and cooperation of Her Divine Son, Our Lady offers all Her children on Earth the absolute certainty of salvation and a place in Heaven for all eternity!

It is indeed a measure of Our Lady's celestial influence and a monument to Her Heart overflowing with love that She asks so little of us in return for fulfilling this great promise of salvation. To those who piously perform this holy devotion of Reparation, She solemnly pledges the gift of Heaven, saying in clear and certain terms: *"I promise salvation."* [68]

The apparition's promise of salvation is not only blasphemy, but its obvious purpose is to prevent those who rely on it from receiving the true salvation which Christ offers to all who believe on Him alone. And why would anyone look to "Mary" when Christ, the Savior who died for our sins, offers salvation freely? It is a denial of the true salvation Christ offers for this demonic "Mary" of Roman Catholicism to promise salvation in exchange for devotion, prayer, or other good works.

That Roman Catholics are taken in by "Mary's" false promises is sufficient evidence that they have not believed Christ's promise through the gospel. Instead, they have believed the false gospel of Rome, which is in full agreement with the lies of the apparitions. Those who believe this "Mary" have embraced a lie which will finally damn them.

The Fatima Crusader, which for years has been in the forefront of promoting the message of Fatima and devotion to Our Lady of Fatima and her Immaculate Heart, asks the disconcerting question "Could we ever know if we had sufficient devotion so that Our Lady would be bound to keep Her promise to us?" [69] The *Crusader* responds enthusiastically, "It is here that we are wonderstruck by the limitless Divine Mercy, and the profoundly Catholic character of the revelations of Fatima." This attempt to give assurance falls short, however, as additional conditions are added, such as the following from the alleged "Child Jesus" to Lucy on February 15, 1926. One is left wondering how much "fervor" is enough and exactly what it means to be "lukewarm and indifferent" while reciting the Rosary:

> It is true, My daughter, that many souls begin, but few persevere to the very end . . . to receive the graces promised. The souls who make the Five First Saturdays with fervor and to make Reparation to the Heart of your Heavenly Mother, please Me more than those who make fifteen, but are lukewarm and indifferent. [70]

"Mary" and a "Baby Jesus"?

One investigator writes, "Often there is a babe—the Christ Child—in her matronly arms."[71] At Fatima the "Child Jesus," floating on a luminous cloud, appeared with the Virgin on July 13, 1917, to declare that there would be no peace until the world was dedicated to the Immaculate Heart of His Mother in reparation of the sins committed against her. A similar apparition of "Mary" and "Jesus" appeared to Lucy, the only survivor of the original three visionaries, in her convent cell at Pontevedra on December 10, 1925:

> The Most Holy Virgin appeared . . . and by Her side, elevated on a luminous cloud, was the Child Jesus . . . [who] said, "Have compassion on the Heart of your Most Holy Mother, covered with thorns, with which ungrateful men pierce It at every moment, and there is no one to make an act of Reparation to remove them."[72]

On February 15, 1926, "the *child* Jesus" again urged Catholics to "spread this devotion of [and] reparation to the Immaculate Heart of His Holy Mother," declaring that *reparation must be made to the Immaculate Heart of Mary for mankind to be saved!*[73] What a blasphemous denial of the simple gospel of salvation by grace through faith in Christ and His redemptive work, yet it is embraced within the Roman Catholic Church.

That the *babe* or *child* "Jesus" often appears with "Mary" only adds to the proof that these apparitions are demonic. Jesus Christ was a mature man in His thirties when He died on the cross for our sins. He rose from the dead and ascended to His Father's right hand (Mark 16:19; Acts 2:33; 5:31; 7:55; Romans 8:34; Colossians 3:1; Hebrews 10:12; 12:2; 1 Peter 3:22; etc.), where He "ever liveth to make intercession" for us (Hebrews 7:25). His resurrected, glorified body is so glorious that John fell at His feet as dead when He was given a glimpse of Him (Revelation 1:17). The idea that He is still appearing as a babe in Mary's arms or as a small child is a blasphemous fiction invented and maintained by the Roman Catholic Church in order to exalt Mary as Queen of Heaven above Jesus Christ. Yet even some evangelical leaders (such as Jack Van Impe) refer to the apparitions as though they were from God.

Imagine parents carrying around baby pictures of a son who is now a grown man and speaking of him as though he were still an infant. Yet Catholicism, in its art and images, continues to present Christ as a babe, or child. Roman Catholicism honors continual alleged appearances of Christ in infantile form and offers devotion to innumerable doll-like images of the infant Jesus as though they were Himself. At Christmas 1996, *Our Sunday Visitor* devoted an entire two-page article to "The Holy Infants of Mexico"—images which differ in appearance from each other, yet are all supposed to be of the "Christ Child." As this popular Catholic paper says, "In Mexico, devotions to the Christ Child are widespread and abundant. . . . Devotion to *Santo Nino de Atocha,* the 'Holy Child of the Atocha,' although centered in Mexico, has spread widely, and has a special niche in the hearts of many North Americans." The article goes on to explain:

> During World War II, soldiers of the New Mexico National Guard fought bravely . . . [at] Corregidor, and turned to the little Jesus for protection. Approximately 2000 survivors of this campaign and their families walked in procession to the little shrine of the Atocha near Santa Fe, N.M., to give their thanks.[74]

Notice that it was not the Lord Jesus Christ glorified in heaven, the mature man who conquered sin and Satan on the cross, rose triumphant from the grave, and is now at the Father's right hand, Lord of the universe, to whom these soldiers looked for protection, but to "the little Jesus"! In fact, the *little* Jesus no longer exists, but this fiction turns multitudes away from trust in the true Lord Jesus Christ. Whatever "power" protects Catholics who trust and honor this "Baby Jesus" is surely not of God. The very act of trusting in a power other than God opens one to the occult. Satan is happy to oblige and thereby seduce those trusting in this counterfeit "Jesus."

Other images of the infant "Jesus" to whom Catholics pray for protection include "The Doctor of the Sick," through which many sick people have allegedly been healed; "the Holy Child of Good Fortune," whose blessing supposedly brings good luck; and "*El Nino Cieguito,* the Blind Child Jesus," who is "venerated in the Capuchin church in the city of Puebla." A *blind* Jesus? He who opened the eyes of the blind is Himself blind?

It is amazing to read the claim that the tiny image of "the Holy Child Jesus, Doctor of the Sick, continues to radiate comfort and blessings." Similar claims are made for the other lifeless images.[75] The Roman Catholic is convinced that some real power is involved. Inasmuch as that power cannot be from either the "Child Jesus," who doesn't exist, or from a lifeless idol, it can logically only be from Satan—or a placebo effect.

After Jesus Christ ascended to heaven at the end of the 40 days in which He presented Himself to His disciples following His resurrection (Luke 24:50,51; Acts 1:1-11), we have no account of Him coming back to this earth to appear to anyone. He is present among His own in Spirit but not physically or visibly. If anyone sees Him it must be through a vision of Him in heaven such as that by the church's first martyr, Stephen:

> But he, being full of the Holy Ghost, looked up stedfastly into heaven . . . and said, Behold, I see the heavens opened, and the Son of man [not a "Child Jesus"] standing on the right hand of God . . . (Acts 7:55-59).

Another Major Contradiction

In 1854, Pope Pius IX declared the "Immaculate Conception" to be a dogma which all Roman Catholics must believe. The claim that Mary was conceived without sin began to be taught by the apparitions. For example, "Our Lady of Lourdes" identified herself to Bernadette Soubirous in 1858 as the "Immaculate Conception." Author Michael H. Brown writes, "This was . . . the first affirmation . . . that Mary was conceived without original sin." [76]

If Mary did not sin, and death (as the Bible says) comes by sin, then logically Mary would not have died. Following that reasoning, Pope Pius XII made it an official dogma in 1950 that Mary had been taken bodily to heaven without death. Here we are confronted with a glaring contradiction within Roman Catholicism and the apparitions of "Mary" which it honors.

Marian apparitions frequently claim to be the "woman clothed with the sun, and the moon under her feet, and upon her head a crown of twelve stars" seen in Revelation 12 in conflict with the Red Dragon. For example, "Mary" appeared in this form to Catherine Laboure in Paris in 1830. This same "Mary" allegedly told Stefano Gobbi, an Italian priest, "You are in the period in which the struggle between Me, the Woman Clothed With the Sun, and my adversary, the Red Dragon, is moving toward its conclusion. . . ."[77]

The Roman Catholic Church supports this identification of Mary as the woman clothed with the sun. Yet of that woman we are told, "And she being with child cried, travailing in birth, and pained to be delivered" (Revelation 12:2). Pain (specifically that associated with childbirth) is because of sin (Genesis 3:16). A sinless Mary could not have suffered pain in childbirth, but the woman clothed with the sun in Revelation 12, whom the Church says is Mary, suffers pain. If that woman is Mary, then she could not have been immaculately conceived and lived without sin and been assumed bodily to heaven. The Roman Catholic Church cannot have it both ways.

"Mary" the Savior, Queen of Peace

The "Mary" of the apparitions consistently warns that her Son is angry with the world and that she is trying to restrain Him from pouring out His wrath upon mankind. In November 1991, at Conyers, Georgia, she said, "Please, children, unless you amend your lives, my Son's hand is about to strike."[78] To prevent His judgment, "Mary" offers her peace plan for the world. On August 6, 1981, our Lady of Medjugorje identified herself as "the Queen of Peace." In fact, the Bible says that Christ is the "Prince of Peace" (Isaiah 9:6) and that He "made peace through the blood of his cross" (Colossians 1:20). What blasphemy for this "Mary" to present her "peace plan for the world"!

"Mary" is the Savior who stands in the way of Christ's wrath and appeases Him, but needs the prayers and devotion of her followers in order to continue to do so. Here we obviously have another satanic ploy to turn Catholics from confident trust in Christ to trust in Mary. He is depicted as our adversary, from whom "Mary" must rescue us. And the ploy has worked. Consider this well-known prayer to Mary:

O Mother of Perpetual Help . . . in thy hands I place my eternal salvation, and to thee do I entrust my soul. . . . For if thou protect me, dear Mother, I fear nothing; not from my sins, because thou wilt obtain for me the pardon of them; nor from the devils, because thou art more powerful than all hell together; nor even from Jesus, my Judge himself, because by one prayer from thee, he will be appeased.

But one thing I fear; that in the hour of temptation, I may neglect to call on thee and thus perish miserably. Obtain for me, then, the pardon of my sins. . . .[79]

On February 5, 1954, the Virgin of Balestrino warned Caterina, the visionary, "*My Son Jesus is very disgusted. . . . He wants to send a punishment, but I, His Mother, will try to find a way to keep you under my mantle.*"[80] Such was also the blasphemous message received from an apparition in Argentina north of Buenos Aires by stigmatist Gladys Herminia Quiroga de Motta. Accompanying "Mary," a little "Jesus" allegedly declared: "*Before the world was saved by means of Noah's Ark. Today the Ark is My Mother. Through her, souls will be saved, because she will bring them toward Me. He who rejects My Mother rejects me!*"[81]

"Mary" and Fatima

"According to a documentary aired on Iranian television, what occurred in Fatima, Portugal, was not a Christian miracle but a Muslim one. In fact, Iranian TV affirms that it was not the Virgin Mary who appeared to the three shepherd children, but Fatima herself, daughter of Muhammed, the prophet of Islam. The program recounts how the apparitions occurred and how Fatima has become a place of pilgrimage for faithful from around the world. Among other images are scenes from the pilgrimages to Fatima of Paul VI and John Paul II."[82]

The Lefebvrist bulletin, *Si Si No No*, of July 1996 claims "the Iranian television program reflects an Islamic strategy to 'co-opt for Islam' the Madonna's prophecy that Russia will be converted." It says, "Several years back, not long before he died, the Ayatollah Khomeini, ruler of Iran, sent a letter to President [Mikhail] Gorbachev, then leader of the Soviet Union, inviting him . . . to convert to Allah. Shiite Iran is in competition with

Sunnite Turkey to win over the vast Turkish-Moslem populations of Central Asia. . . . To present to these masses the conversion of Russia to Islam as . . . 'predicted' in a vision in 1917 by the 'daughter of the Prophet' . . . would have its advantages in propaganda terms."[83]

Bishop Fulton J. Sheen, based upon the same "Our Lady of Fatima" prophecy, predicted that Islam would be converted to Christianity "through a summoning of the Moslems to a veneration of the Mother of God":

> The Koran . . . has many passages concerning the blessed Virgin. First of all, the Koran believes in her Immaculate Conception and also in her Virgin Birth. . . . Mary, then, is for the Moslems the true Sayyida, or Lady. The only possible serious rival to her in their creed would be Fatima, the daughter of Mohammed himself. But after the death of Fatima, Mohammed wrote: "Thou shalt be the most blessed of all the women in Paradise, after Mary."[84]

Sheen considers it remarkable that "Our Lady" appeared in the Portuguese village of Fatima (named after Mohammed's daughter during the Moslem occupation) and thus became known as "Our Lady of Fatima." When a statue of "Our Lady of Fatima" is carried through Moslem areas of Africa, India, and elsewhere, Moslems turn out by the hundreds of thousands to worship her. In two days an estimated 500,000 came to give their respects to this idol in Bombay, India.[85]

"Our Lady of Fatima" allegedly appeared to Pope John Paul II during his convalescence from the assassination attempt, telling him that she had saved his life because of a special mission she had for him and that she would give the world a sign causing mankind to bow to his spiritual authority. In gratitude the Pope has made several visits to Fatima and brought one of the bullets taken from his body to be placed in a diamond crown that graces the statue. The Pope has given his "Apostolic Blessing to Father Nicholas Gruner for his . . . very important apostolic work with *The Fatima Crusader.* . . ."[86] The Pope has said:

> Could I forget that the event in Saint Peter's Square [the assassination attempt] took place on the day and at the hour when the first appearance of the Mother of Christ to the poor little peasants has been remembered for over 60 years at Fatima in Portugal? For

everything that happened to me on that very day, I felt that extraordinary Motherly protection and care, which turned out to be stronger than the deadly bullets.[87]

The content of the appeal of Our Lady of Fatima is so profoundly rooted in the Gospel and in the whole of Tradition, that the Church feels Herself summoned by its message. . . . This message contains a truth and a call, which in its fundamental context, are the the Truth and the Call of the Gospel itself. . . . I want to renew my appeal that the Message of Fatima be listened to.[88]

That the Pope and the Catholic Church are in perfect accord with the demonic apparition and their antibiblical theology and false gospel says it all. And one would not expect it to be otherwise, considering Catholicism's deep involvement in the occult.

The Pagan and Occult Connection

Carol Damian, art historian, author, and professor at Miami's Florida International University, is also a Catholic. A visit to a Roman Catholic convent museum in Cuzco, Peru, mile-high capital of the ancient Incan Empire, opened her eyes to an apparent connection between apparitions of the Virgin Mary and those of another "virgin mother and child" known to the natives of Peru long before the Spanish arrived:

> Gazing up at a larger-than-life image of . . . what I thought was . . . the Virgin Mary, the guide [a nun] reverently described the painting as that of Pachamama, the Earth Mother and patroness of the Andes. . . .
>
> "Please explain again, slowly, why you called the Virgin Mary Pachamama," I asked her. "Who is Pachamama? She looks like the Virgin Mary of my Catholic experience. . . ."
>
> Returning to one painting that was particularly endearing to the people from Cuzco . . . she began to tell her story and the Virgin Mary was transformed. The painting . . . inspired me to pursue the legend of Pachamama. . . .
>
> Every year I returned to Cuzco, paid a visit to her first, and looked at every painting of the Virgin that I could find within about a 50-mile radius of the city. . . . The Virgin Mary took on different titles, wore different costumes and headdresses . . . but she was an Andean virgin. She was Pachamama, the Earth Mother . . . the Moon Goddess . . . the Inka [sic] Queen. . . .

Beneath her gorgeous finery, they were able to hide their sacred Inka [sic] stones and other magical objects, and continue to revere their own special deities. . . .[89]

Former New Ager Alan Morrison reminds us that some occultists have claimed "Mary" as one of the Ascended Masters. That is not surprising, inasmuch as they claim "Jesus Christ" as one of them as well. One New Age prophetess, Elizabeth Clare Prophet, foretold that "Mary" would "transmit messages of peace" with increasing frequency at the dawning of the Age of Aquarius. Is it just a coincidence that the Roman Catholic "Mary" has accelerated her appearances as we move toward the close of this century and millennium? Morrison continues:

> The pictorial form in which this "Ascended Master," Mother Mary, is represented in the occult literature is virtually identical to the form of the Virgin Mary which appears in Roman Catholic visions and apparitions. The Neo-Gnostics refer to this spirit-entity as the *"Archetypal New Age Woman,"* and it is difficult to avoid the conclusion that for centuries Roman Catholics have been hoodwinked into regarding a demonic discarnate deception as a genuine vision of the mother of Jesus Christ. In other words, the Virgin Mary of the visions is an evil spirit.[90]

On the threshold of the Third Millennium, just as technology and science are facilitating greater understanding and control of our physical world, miracles, supernatural events and apparitions are multiplying at a dizzying rate. And it is making some Catholic intellectuals a bit uncomfortable.

—Inside the Vatican[1]

From somewhere . . . the smoke of Satan has entered the temple of God.

—Pope Paul VI (1972), who closed Vatican II[2]

Anybody who is acquainted with the state of affairs in the Vatican in the last 35 years is well aware that the prince of darkness [Satan] has had and still has his surrogates in the court of St. Peter in Rome.

—Malachi Martin, former Jesuit and professor at the Vatican's Pontifical Biblical Institute[3]

The devil within the Church today is actually protected by certain Church authorities. . . .

—Archbishop Emmanuel Milingo, Rome[4]

"Traditional Indian medicine may be the art of nursing, not just the science. Native holistic practices are not alternative. They're part of the whole practice." This according to Ann Hubbert, director of patient care at St. Mary's Hospital in Tucson, Arizona. This Roman Catholic hospital was "the first hospital in the nation to officially incorporate Indian healing with modern medicine. . . ." The practice was initiated when the hospital hired Edgar Monetatchi, Jr., a medicine man, in 1984.

—Brain/Mind Bulletin[5]

"We're moving toward the integration of the East and West, and it's happening through health care," says Sister Breitenbach, a Poor Handmaids of Jesus nun, director of the Healing Arts Center in Mishawaka, Illinois. A fan of [Deepak] Chopra's, she sees no conflicts between the new and the old age: "People are so uptight about this kind of thing. We used to call it trust in God."

—Time[6]

Jesus is the fulfillment that the great mystics of the world have looked for for centuries.

—John Michael Talbot, popular musician and founder of the Roman Catholic Brothers and Sisters of Charity[7]

I've worn a Scapular [relying upon its promise: "Whosoever dies wearing this Scapular shall not suffer eternal fire"] since I was a child.

—Pope John Paul II[8]

20

* * *

Occultism and the
Roman Catholic Church

The Roman Catholic Church claims to be the true Christian church founded by Peter, who it claims Christ chose to be the first Pope. Supposedly, as the Bishop of Rome, Peter established that city as the hub of Christianity. Headquartered there since its beginning, the *Roman* Catholic Church claims to have been the only valid Christian church throughout history. All other Christian churches are alleged to be false and (except for Eastern Orthodoxy) to have originated in the sixteenth century with the Protestant Reformation. History, however, says something else.*

In fact, there were millions of Christians who, for a thousand years before the Reformation, refused allegiance to the Church of Rome because of its pagan/occult practices and apostasy. These true followers of Christ were persecuted and killed by Rome. Tragically, the false accusations of heresy and immorality made by the Inquisition against these martyrs to justify their extermination are still the official view found in encyclopedias today.

Far from succeeding Peter, the popes (as history testifies) were the successors of Constantine and other Roman emperors. They laid claim to imperial authority through a fraudulent document they circulated in the Middle Ages known as *The Donation of Constantine.* To impose "Christianity," the popes acquired their own armies and navies and enough military might to rule the world. As one Catholic historian admits:

---

*For a full discussion of these issues, see *A Woman Rides the Beast,* by this author, published by Harvest House.

From the *Donation*, it is plain that the Bishop of Rome [Pope] looked like Constantine, lived like him, dressed like him, inhabited his palaces, ruled over his lands, had exactly the same imperial outlook . . . lord[ing] it over church and state.

Only seven hundred years after Peter died, the popes had become obsessed with power and possessions. Peter's [alleged] successors [had become] . . . the masters of the world. They . . . dress in purple like Nero and call themselves Pontifex Maximus.[9]

Historian R.W. Southern declared: "During the whole medieval period there was in Rome a single spiritual and temporal authority [the Papacy] exercising powers which in the end exceeded those that had ever lain within the grasp of a Roman emperor."[10] One eighteenth-century historian counted 95 popes who claimed divine power to depose kings and emperors. Historian Walter James wrote that Pope Innocent III (1198–1216), who abolished the Roman senate, "held all Europe in his net."[11] He "murdered far more Christians in one afternoon . . . than any Roman emperor did in his entire reign,"[12] confessed a Catholic historian. Of this pope, who never lost a battle, historian R.W. Thompson wrote:

[Kings] Philip Augustus and Henry IV quailed before him, and Peter II of Aragon and John of England ignominiously consented to convert their kingdoms into spiritual fiefs and to hold them in subordination to him . . . paying an annual tribute.[13]

Christ had said, "My kingdom is not of this world; if my kingdom were of this world, then would my servants fight . . . (John 18:36). Yet those who claimed to be Christ's vicars commanded armies in His name that looted and massacred, that sacked cities and deposed kings. Waving what they claimed was His cross, these tyrants wrested the kingdoms of the world from their rulers, amassed great personal wealth, and often lived lives of unrestrained debauchery and evil. With good reason the thousand-year period of history preceding the Reformation was called "the Dark Ages."

Paganization of the Church

Most of the corruption of the church can be traced to the supposed conversion of Constantine to Christianity. This remarkable event could only have been a master strategy of Satan. Constantine married Christianity to paganism and opened the door of the church to a massive occult invasion. In fact, Constantine's "conversion" itself involved two classic occult events:

> On the afternoon before the battle [against Maxentius at the Mulvian Bridge] . . . Constantine saw a flaming cross in the sky, with the Greek words *en toutoi nika*—"in this sign conquer." Early the next morning, according to Eusebius [who says Constantine personally swore the truth of this account to him] and Lactantius, Constantine dreamed that a voice commanded him to have his soldiers mark upon their shields the letter X with a line drawn through it and curled around the top. . . ."[14]

This perverted "cross" so closely resembled the Mithraic "cross of light" that the followers of the god Mithras in Constantine's army were not offended. Under this ecumenical blend of paganism and Christianity, this "first Christian emperor" slaughtered his enemies in the name of the Christ who had said, "Resist not evil; but whosoever shall smite thee on thy right cheek, turn to him the other also" (Matthew 5:39). The popes would even exceed Constantine in their bloody conquests and perversion of Christianity.

By A.D. 380 (43 years after Constantine's death) Christianity had been made the official religion of the empire. Paganism *as a separate religion* was outlawed—a futile gesture, since it had already been absorbed into the church. Eventually, failure to give allegiance to the Pope was considered treason against the state, punishable by death. As Islam would be a few centuries later, a paganized Christianity was imposed upon the entire populace of Europe under threat of torture and death. Even a Catholic historian admits that Roman Catholicism became "the most persecuting faith the world has ever seen . . . [commanding] the throne to impose the Christian [Catholic] religion on all its subjects."[15]

The great secular historian Will Durant writes candidly:

> Compared with the persecution of [alleged] heresy in Europe from 1227 to 1492, the persecution of Christians by Romans in the first three centuries after Christ was a mild and humane procedure.[16]

That Constantine was used by Satan to paganize Christianity is proved by what followed. St. Augustine remarked, "The man who enters [a fourth-century church] is bound to see . . . people wearing amulets, assiduous clients of sorcerers, astrologers. . . . The same crowds that press into the churches on Christian festivals . . . fill the theatres on pagan holidays."[17] [Pope] Julius II "would not leave Bologna till his astrologer marked the time as auspicious; Sixtus IV and Paul III let their stargazers fix the hours of their major conferences."[18]

The First "Vicar of Christ" and His Successors

In Constantine's day, the emperor, as the head of the pagan priesthood in Rome known as the Pontifical College (now headed by the Pope), was called *Pontifex Maximus*. Constantine headed the church, as would the emperors after him for five centuries. He called himself *Vicarius Christi* (Vicar of Christ). Yet he continued to officiate at pagan celebrations and to endow pagan temples even as he built Christian churches! The popes eventually claimed the emperor's titles, *Pontifex Maximus* and *Vicar of Christ*, as their own. True Christians separated themselves from an increasingly apostate church and began to call the popes Antichrist.

Constantine never renounced his loyalty to the pantheon of pagan gods. He abolished neither the pagan Altar of Victory in the senate nor the Vestal Virgins; and the sun-god rather than Christ continued to be honored on imperial coins. Throughout his "Christian" life Constantine mixed pagan and Christian rites and continued to rely upon "pagan magic formulas to protect crops and heal disease."[19] Historian Philip Hughes, a Catholic priest, writes:

> In his manners he [Constantine] remained, to the end . . . the Pagan of his early life. His furious tempers, the cruelty which . . . spared not the lives even of his wife and son, are . . . an unpleasing witness to the imperfection of his conversion.[20]

Under Constantine, pagan practices were given a Christian veneer and adapted by the Church to satisfy the multitudes joining its ranks. Pope Leo I (440–461) boasted that St. Peter and St. Paul had "replaced Romulus and Remus as [Rome's] protecting patrons."[21] Will Durant writes:

> Paganism survived [within the church] . . . in the form of ancient rites and customs condoned, or accepted and transformed, by an often indulgent Church. An intimate and trustful worship of saints replaced the cult of pagan gods. . . . Statues of Isis and Horus were renamed Mary and Jesus; the Roman Lupercalia and the feast of purification of Isis became the Feast of the Nativity; the Saturnalia were replaced by Christmas celebration . . . an ancient festival of the dead by All Souls Day, rededicated to Christian heroes; incense, lights, flowers, processions, vestments, hymns which had pleased the people in older cults were . . . cleansed in the ritual of the Church . . . soon people and priests would use the sign of the cross as a magic incantation to expel or drive away demons. . . .
>
> [Paganism] passed like maternal blood into the new religion, and captive Rome captured her conqueror. . . .[22]

Since the days of Constantine, Roman Catholicism has always and everywhere accommodated itself to the pagan religions of those peoples which it Christianized. In his monumental study of paganism, Evans-Wentz makes this interesting comment:

> Perhaps most of us will think first of all about the ancient cults [worship] rendered to fountains, rivers, lakes, trees, and . . . stones. There can be no reasonable doubt that these cults were flourishing when Christianity [Roman Catholicism] came to Europe. . . .
>
> It was too much to expect the eradication of the old cults after their age-long existence, and so one by one they were absorbed by the new religion. In a sacred tree or grove, over a holy well or fountain, on the shore of a lake or river, there was placed an image of the Virgin or some [Catholic] saint, and unconsciously the transformation was made as the simple-hearted country-folk beheld in the brilliant images new and more glorious dwelling-places for the spirits they and their fathers had so long venerated.[23]

Roman Catholicism and Voodoo

Images, holy water, and Catholic rituals cannot be found in the Bible, but have all been adapted from paganism. Their counterpart is found today in voodoo and related cults. Haiti, which is said to be "eighty-five percent Catholic and one hundred and ten percent Vodoun,"[24] is one of many modern examples of Catholicism's adaptation to pagan occultism. Latin America (which is 90 percent Catholic) is similar. A Catholic newspaper describes religion there as "a synthesis of [native American] Indian and European cultures. . . ."[25]

Voodoo is only one of several pagan religions that slaves brought to the West from Africa. The frightening spiritist cult of Santeria, imported from Cuba and exploding in barrios across America, is another blend of African paganism and Catholicism involving "gods" who front for demons passed off as Catholic saints. In Brazil and Cuba, spiritism and voodoo-related African religions (such as Macumba and Candomble) blend with Catholicism. Most Latin Americans are active both in Catholicism and indigenous or imported occultism.

An article in *Our Sunday Visitor* titled "In the Temple of the Voodoo" asks this question: "Why is New Orleans, one of the world's most Catholic cities, caught in the bewitching spell of an ancient cult?" The author provides many examples of Catholicism's comfortable relationship with Voodoo:

> Celeste Champagne [says], ". . . my mother taught me about the *voodoo*—and the spirits. . . . The voodoo is part of my life to this day—just like Holy Communion. . . ."
>
> Andy Antippas, a former professor of English who now devotes his time to studying the history of religion . . . says, "Africans . . . sold into slavery . . . brought their voodoo religion with them. Christianity [Catholicism] was forced on them. So, to appease the masters, the slaves prayed through the icons and statues of Christianity [Catholicism] to their own voodoo gods. . . ."
>
> On a clear day, the line . . . snakes through the front gate of the Lafitte Cemetery. Why? So men and women of every description and background can scratch the traditional X on the late Voodoo Queen Marie Laveau's tomb, giving impetus to their invocations for good for themselves and ill for their enemies. . . .
>
> Priestess Ava Jones [is] a graduate of Xavier Prep Catholic High School and Loyola University School of Law . . . [and] has foregone a career in law to devote her life to voodoo. . . . She lectures frequently on voodoo and African religions to such diverse groups as the American College of Surgeons and the American Academy of Cardiology. . . .

A call to her will often be met with, "I'm with a client now. Can I call you back?" And she will . . . as soon as she returns from daily Mass, and Communion.[26]

In Haiti, as elsewhere where Rome was in control, baptism into the Roman Catholic Church was compulsory. The converted slaves continued to practice their pagan religions under the appearance of Catholicism by disguising their African gods with the names of Catholic saints. In 1790, Moreau de Saint-Mery observed that "African slaves used their Catholic faith as a scheme under which 'primitive' religious practices could be performed."[27]

Religion-and-international studies professor Leslie G. Desmangles reports that Catholicism and voodoo are so intertwined in Haitian religious life that Catholic and voodoo objects can be seen on the same altars. Voodoo is the dominant force in Haitian political and social life, and its *oungans* and *mambos* are powerful and influential figures. Voodoo and Catholic ceremonies are commonly performed consecutively in conjunction with one another for the same event, such as funerals, weddings, and sacred pilgrimages to the waterfalls of Ezili and Damballah.[28]

Professor Desmangles explains:

> Catholic ritual performed by the pret savann [Catholic priest] and those performed by the oungan [Vodou priest] coexist . . . to make the whole of the Vodou ritual. . . . Vodou baptisms . . . entail ritual performances by both the pret savann and the oungan. Vodou fills important . . . civic as well as political functions . . . Catholicism too is integral to Vodouisants' lives. . . .[29]

The blending of voodoo into Roman Catholicism is not merely at the parish level. It goes to the top and involves more than mere tolerance. Newspapers around the world carried the following story of the Pope encouraging voodoo priests to make a Constantine-like "conversion":

> Pope John Paul II sought common ground with believers in voodoo Thursday, suggesting they would not betray their traditional faith by converting to Christianity. On the second day of his 10th African pilgrimage, the Pope held a dramatic and

emotional meeting with priests of the *vodun*. . . . The Pope told the voodooists that just as they draw on their ancestors for their religion, so do Christians [Catholics] revere their "ancestors in the faith, from the Apostles to the missionaries. . . ." Voodoo priests at the meeting warmly welcomed the pontiff.[30]

"Gods" and "Saints"

Desmangles tells of "attending Mass at one prominent provincial parish" where "the curate poured libations of water at the four cardinal points before the celebration of the Eucharist, as if to acknowledge the presence of God, the saints, and all the lwas [Vodou gods] in the cosmos."[31] There are so many lwas in Vodou that they have been categorized into families depending upon their characteristics and functions. The lwas are believed to inhabit a mythological island under the sea known as the city of Vilokan. At the beginning of the ceremony the oungan invokes Legba, the keeper of the gates to Vilokan (while the devotees sing a chant of praise to him), in order to make contact with the gods.[32]

A major purpose of the voodoo ceremony is to be possessed by one of the lwas. This demonic possession is the "quintessential spiritual achievement in a believer's religious life . . . a direct engagement with the spirit world."[33] Apart from the frightening act of "possession," the function of the lwas in voodoo is little different from that of the so-called saints in Catholicism. A letter from a former Catholic (with a few names changed) could be about voodoo gods:

> I'm 37 years old and before this year I never had a relationship with God. I come from a large Catholic family. I went to Catholic schools until I reached college.
>
> I can tell you the patron saint for a golfer or the patron saint for mothers or even one for hopeless cases. If the saint for hopeless cases grants your request, you must have his prayer printed in your local newspaper. I can teach you how to say a Rosary. I can show you my beautiful statue of the "Blessed Mother." . . .
>
> I have a scapular medal which if I die while wearing it, I will go straight to heaven. There is my miraculous medal, which if worn gives special graces from the Virgin Mary. . . . I can find a little pamphlet with special prayers to whatever saint you want to

intercede for you. . . . And . . . you can borrow my catalog to send away for a medal of that saint to wear around your neck. . . .

You don't have to ever waste time looking for something you have lost. I will give you a little prayer for St. Anthony. ["St. Anthony, St. Anthony, please come around. There's something lost that's got to be found."] He's the patron saint of lost articles. In no time at all, whatever you have lost will turn up. . . .

And I have some Mass cards handy. For just $25–50 a priest will say a special Mass for the soul of the dead person to move them in purgatory closer to heaven. Who knows, the one you buy might just be the one that pushes them through the gates!

Oh! The last thing I need to tell you . . . get your baby baptized immediately after it is born. . . . I lost my first child at five months and he was not baptized. I remember the pain I felt in the hospital when the priest told me that he could not baptize a dead baby, that my child would not go to heaven . . . [but to] Limbo . . . not a bad place, but you can never see God there. I cried for a long time . . . thinking I would never see my child . . . so, don't wait for the baptism!

These are all things I may have told you before I was born from above . . . saved by the blood of the Lord Jesus Christ.[34]

One need only turn to the Eternal Word TV Network (EWTN) to learn of the many "saints" (and their tombs and images) who are held up for veneration and to whom Catholics are encouraged to look for help and even salvation. This Catholic network was founded and is directed by an enterprising nun who calls herself Mother Angelica. Numerous priests appear on the programs, along with various lay Catholic leaders and enthusiasts. EWTN offers a continual procession of the most obvious superstition and occultism.

Bob and Penny Lord, bubbling with enthusiasm for what the "saints" can do, take viewers on exciting trips to trace the holy lives and learn of the miracles performed by "Visionaries, Mystics & Stigmatists." The tomb of Sister Margaret Mary, seventeenth-century mystic, was visited early in 1997. Viewers were told that she lost her voice while singing in a choir and only regained it when "the baby Jesus appeared in her arms." At Jesus' special request, Margaret Mary was able to make reparation for the sins which wounded Him.

Obviously, this apparition was an occult invasion from the demonic. Jesus Christ is not a baby. And only Satan would suggest human suffering as "reparation" for another person's sin. The Bible repeatedly assures us that Christ alone could and did suffer the full penalty for sin: God "laid on him the iniquity of us all" (Isaiah 53:6). To suggest otherwise is the most serious heresy.

John the Baptist hailed Christ as "the Lamb of God which taketh away the sin of the world" (John 1:29). All others (including so-called saints), being sinners ("all have sinned"— Romans 3:23) could not pay for another's sins. Peter declared that Christ "suffered for sins, [He] the just [sinless one] for [us] the unjust [sinners], that he might bring us to God [to heaven, not purgatory]" (1 Peter 3:18).

Yet on EWTN, Michael Freze, author of *They Bore the Wounds of Christ*, glorifies the saints who, supposedly in response to Christ's request, "offer themselves up to suffer in union with Christ for the sins of the world" and as a result bear the stigmata. He calls them "other Christs among us."

Freze goes on to explain why neither the saints nor anyone else could be sure of their salvation. In a shocking denial of Christ's triumphant cry "It is finished!" (John 19:30), Freze tells us it wasn't really finished. Boldly, this young expert on the stigmata informs EWTN's viewers:

> A lot of people, Catholics and others, say, "What about the crucifixion, wasn't that our salvation once and for all?"
>
> No, it wasn't. It was the *beginning* of salvation . . . the redemption plan is ongoing. God chooses people to participate in Christ's passion . . . Jesus is always offering Himself. . . .

Prayers to the "Saints" and Their Images

Images entered the Church when Constantine accommodated the pagans joining it by retaining their idols under Christian names. In Eastern Orthodoxy (which only split from Catholicism in A.D. 1054), icons have intrinsic power. Catholic apologists insist that veneration is not of the *image* but of the saint it represents. Yet John Paul II, speaking at St. Peter's Basilica, says images have power:

> A mysterious "presence" of the transcendent Prototype seems as it were to be transferred to the sacred image. . . . The devout

contemplation of such an image thus appears as a real and concrete path of purification of the soul of the believer . . . because the image itself . . . can in a certain sense, by analogy with the sacraments, actually be considered a channel of divine grace.[35]

The images in Catholic churches are mostly of Mary and other "saints" who constitute an elite corps of the dead (not unlike lwas, spirit guides and Ascended Masters) that appear to and assist the living from beyond the grave. In the Bible, however, all of God's people, while still living on earth, are called saints, both in the Old Testament (Psalm 30:4; 85:8; 149:1; etc.) and in the New (Romans 1:7; 15:25; 1 Corinthians 1:2; etc.). The New Testament epistles were written to the saints then living at Rome, Corinth, Ephesus, Colosse, and so on.

Each Christian is a saint and has equal access to God through the Lord Jesus Christ. The idea that someone who has lived a particularly holy life and to whom miracles have been attributed is voted to be a saint by a church hierarchy many years after his or her death (and thereafter can be petitioned for help) is absolutely foreign to Scripture. This is pagan occultism. For many Latin American Catholics (even in the United States), "a *curandero*, or shaman-healer, is also called a saint."[36]

On EWTN, again early in 1997, we find two enthusiastic priests, Fr. George W. Kosicki and Fr. Harold Cohen, offering a "Marian Helpers" booklet. They can scarcely contain their excitement as they commend to viewers Sister Faustina, who "shared so fully in Christ's death and resurrection . . . and continues that ministry in heaven now." Jesus supposedly said to her, "Distribute graces as you will, to whom you will, and when you will!" The priests urge viewers. "Get in touch with her!"

While it is biblical to ask friends on earth to pray for us, there is no example in Scripture of asking a dead person to do so, nor any means given for contacting the deceased. God repeatedly warns against attempted contact with discarnate spirits (Deuteronomy 18:9-12; etc.). Nowhere in the Bible is prayer directed to Abraham, or to Moses or Daniel or Mary. All prayer is to God alone. The Holy Spirit Himself intercedes for us (Romans 8:26), Christ is our advocate at the right hand of the Father (Romans 8:34; 1 John 2:1), and He is the "one mediator between God and men" (1 Timothy 2:5).

Yet millions of Roman Catholics not only ask the so-called saints (who can't hear them) to intercede for them, but also pray to them directly as though they had all the power of God. It is they who answer prayers (St. Anthony himself finds and returns lost objects, etc.). And this is the official position of the Roman Catholic Church: Prayers are in fact offered to the "saints." Both Vatican II[37] and the new universal *Catechism of the Catholic Church* refer to Mary as "Mother of God, to whose protection the faithful fly in all their dangers and needs."[38] (EWTN informs us that "Mary" came to chase the devil away when he was pummeling Padre Pio.)

Mary is the mother of the body that Jesus took when He, the eternal Son of God, became a man to die for our sins. She is not the mother of Jesus *as God,* who is her Creator! And why fly to Mary for protection when God's and Christ's protection is available? To protect all Catholics from all dangers and to provide for all their needs, "Mary" would have to be omnipotent, omniscient, and omnipresent. Though denied in theory, in practice Catholicism has replaced both the Father and the Son with Mary and other "saints."

Catherine of Siena, Padre Pio, and other "suffering saints" are revered for having suffered for the sins of others, and are prayed to by millions of Catholics, including the current Pope. They are greater than Christ, whose suffering upon the cross leaves good Catholics in purgatory. But Padre Pio's and Catherine of Siena's suffering (and that of other special "saints") releases multitudes to heaven. On EWTN recently, Frs. Kosicki and Cohen urged viewers to make their suffering available "for salvation for souls" and to pray, "We offer our suffering for salvation of souls."

The highest Roman Catholic authority explains that Christ's payment of the penalty of sin leaves the repentant sinner under the obligation to purge himself by his own suffering.[39] Thus the suffering of others can accomplish what Christ's could not; and the sacrifice of the Mass can accomplish what was left undone by Christ's sacrifice on the cross. Vatican II blasphemously declares that believers have always "carried their crosses to make expiation for their own sins and the sins of others . . . [to] help their brothers obtain salvation from God. . . ."[40]

The Roman Catholic dogma that what Christ did on the cross was insufficient is shared by the Orthodox Church. As only one example, consider the annual 170-kilometer Russian "Sinners' March" across wilderness terrain to the village of Vyelikoryetskaya, about 1000 kilometers northeast of Moscow. Carrying the icon of St. Nikolai the Miracle Worker, the marchers "plod forward as much as 20 hours a day," exulting in the suffering they endure for their own and others' salvation. Explained one young man in the 1996 march, "Our aim in life is to carry a cross in order to gain eternal salvation."[41]

The "Miracles" of the "Saints"

Miraculous powers which only God possesses are attributed not only to Catholicism's Mary but to many other alleged saints. Catholics have their favorite saint or saints with whom they feel a special relationship and in whom they have special confidence. *The Hem of His Garment,* a new book by Fr. Lawrence Gesy, tells the stories of alleged healings attributed to "saints." For example, a woman "crippled in an auto accident [who] suffered 10 years of chronic pain and multiple surgeries" claimed a complete cure through St. Anne.[42]

To be voted into sainthood after death, one must have done miracles in life. Stories of apparitions of the "saints" and their continuing "miracles" are promoted along with the belief that they watch over and protect those who pray to them. The following is a recent newspaper account of the "making of a saint":

> Ten years ago, a little girl named after a Jewish-born nun killed by the Nazis lay dying in a Boston hospital. . . . Her parents prayed to her namesake, Edith Stein, who was known as Sister Teresia Benedicta.
>
> Their prayers were answered and the girl lived. . . . She believes Stein is still watching over her. . . .
>
> Now, the Vatican has ruled that her recovery was a miracle attributable to the nun and moved Stein a step closer to becoming a Roman Catholic saint. . . .
>
> The Vatican announced April 8 [1997] that Pope John Paul II had officially recognized the miracle, the final step before canonization.[43]

Padre Pio is another saint-in-the-making whom the Vatican is about to canonize. A "Prayer to Padre Pio" includes "Padre Pio, may the healings of the sick become the testimony that the Lord has invited you to join the holy company of Saints. In your kindness, please help me with my own special request. . . ."[44] There are far more testimonies of occult miracles involving Padre Pio than he needs to be voted a saint. The following is a typical account:

> While I was praying, I looked at the statue. Just as it often does, it started to transform . . . like a bright light on it. . . . The statue of the Sacred Heart of Jesus changes. Sometimes it is the Holy Mother, sometimes Jesus or the saints.
>
> But today, I could not make out who it was . . . when he got closer, there was a golden light around him. I could see him clearly. I said, "Padre Pio." He said, ". . . I want to share myself with you."
>
> After awhile, I . . . asked if he would help Dorothy [a friend with cancer]. He said, "Yes, tell her to pray to the Sacred Heart of Jesus, and to me, for three days. . . ."
>
> A few days later . . . he came to me, and told me not to worry. . . . I asked about Dorothy. He said, "I will be with her. . . ."[45]

The above involves classic occultism: the transformation of a statue into apparitions of Mary, Jesus, and other alleged saints accompanied by the bright light which the Bible associates with Satan. Whether Pio is in heaven or in hell, he is not free to appear on this earth. The Bible rejects the suggestion of such appearances even for a good purpose (Luke 16:27-31). And the omnipresence of God attributed to Pio and seemingly manifest can only be demonic.

That the person relating the story later "saw" Pio with Dorothy in her car as she drove away from Mass only adds to the demonic delusion. Yet such appearances are the authenticating factors that cause the Catholic hierarchy to vote a candidate into sainthood. The present Pope "became a spiritual son of Padre Pio at their first meeting in 1947,"[46] and has visited Pio's grave to pray there. In 1954, Pope Pius XII called Padre Pio "The Confessor of Europe."[47]

In Catholicism there is no assurance of salvation, so even the saints often expressed the fear that they might not attain heaven. Their salvation depends upon their good deeds, their suffering, and their sacrifices for others instead of upon the finished work of Christ. Conscience rightly denies that any of us is "good enough" to meet God's standard.

The *Padre Pio Gazette* recently referred to the many attacks that Pio suffered (or so he believed) at the hands of Satan, attacks that left him "bloodied, bruised and swollen." Again, no such account is found in the Bible. To be beaten by demons (a common occurrence for the monks at Mt. Athos, the Vatican of Greek Orthodoxy) is an occult manifestation. The *Gazette* told of the doubts that plagued Pio:

> Not so evident, but even more devastating, however, were the attacks on his *soul*. Those "thoughts of despair, distrust in God...."[48]

Relics and "Miracles"

Not only images of the saints and their tombs are seen as points of special power, but especially their relics: a mummified finger, a lock of hair, a bone, a bottle of alleged tears, or some other item. Such relics are on display in Catholic and orthodox cathedrals and shrines all over the world. "Miracles" are attributed to these objects just as they are to the similar objects venerated in voodoo and other pagan religions.

Roman Catholics by the millions have made pilgrimages to holy sites to view supposed relics of the saints. We cannot even begin to make a survey of the miracles allegedly taking place around the world: the "Eucharistic miracle" (alleged transformation of bread into Christ's flesh) "involving a Korean seer... during a private Mass celebrated by Pope John Paul II at the Vatican in 1995; Turin's fourteenth-century "Great Madonna statue," seen to weep by parish priest Fr. Cavallo; etc., etc.

One of the newest "miracles" is the "tears of blood" which have been seen coming from the eyes of a "small white plaster statue of Our Lady" purchased originally in Medjugorje. Located in the city of Civitavecchia, about 50 miles northeast of Rome on the Italian coast, the statue is attracting as many as 30,000 pilgrims in one day. In their impatience to get close enough to the statue "to see, to beseech, to reflect, to pray," the crowd often becomes unruly. A team of ten experts was sent from Rome to investigate and reported:

(1) The eyewitnesses were credible . . . ;
(2) The red liquid [coming from the eyes] was in fact . . . male human blood;
(3) There was no mechanism or trick . . . which could explain the flow of blood from the statue's eyes . . . no evidence of fabrication or hoax.[49]

Male blood from a statue of *Mary?* Fr. Aristide Serra, a professor at Rome's "Marianum," suggests that this "points to the blood of Christ shed for the world. . . ."[50] It also points to the unbiblical belief which the Pope is hoping to announce as a new dogma, that Mary is "Co-Redemptrix" with Christ. Again we see the exaltation of Mary through occult means.

The Rosary is also an instrument of the occult. It involves vain repetitions which Christ forbade: "But when ye pray, use not vain repetitions, as the heathen do; for they think that they shall be heard for their much speaking" (Matthew 6:7). Yet in Roman Catholicism miracles are created through such repetition, and the apparitions agree. On June 25, 1985, Our Lady of Medjugorje declared, "I urge you to ask everyone to pray the Rosary. With the Rosary you will overcome all the troubles which Satan is trying to inflict on the Catholic Church."[51]

The late Mother Teresa continually prayed the Rosary for her salvation. Padre Pio relied on the Rosary as his "weapon" against Satan.[52] We have previously quoted Pope John Paul II in his declaration that the Rosary is "the medicine" against all the evil with which Satan tries to inflict us. Said the Pope, "Pray, pray [the Rosary] . . . leave everything else up to the Madonna."[53] To attribute magic power to the repetition of a formula is to invite the occult into one's life.

All of this seeking for salvation and forgiveness through "saints," images, relics, scapulars, medals, formulas and repetition of the Mass denies the efficacy of Christ's completed ("It is finished!") sacrifice on the cross. To look to anyone or anything in addition to Christ (which is the very essence of Roman Catholicism) is to reject the salvation He offers as a gift of God's grace.

The High Fraud of Indulgences

In their eagerness to pretend either that the Reformation never occurred or that the issues raised were of no consequence, leading evangelicals suppress the truth about Roman Catholicism. Typical of the misinformation promoted to justify an unprecedented ecumenical madness is the following false statement from Charles Colson: "The Reformers, for example, assailed the corrupt practices of indulgences; today they are gone (save for the modern-day equivalent practiced by some unscrupulous television hucksters, ironically mostly Protestants, who promise healing and blessing for contributions)."[54]

In fact, Vatican II contains 17 pages and 20 complex rules providing instructions regarding indulgences (which this author has sent to Colson), reinforcing what the Church has always taught and practiced. Here is rule 17, for example:

> The faithful who use with devotion an object of piety (crucifix, cross, rosary, scapular or medal) after it has been duly blessed by any priest, can gain a partial indulgence.
>
> But if this object of piety is blessed by the Pope or any bishop, the faithful who use it with devotion can also gain a plenary indulgence on the feast of the Apostles Peter and Paul, provided they also make a profession of faith using any approved formula.[55]

What "god" grants forgiveness of sins through the magical use of some physical object and the recitation of a formula? What about justice? We're back to voodoo again! And why would any Christian church indulge in such delusion when Christ has provided full and free pardon from sin? The whole idea of indulgences is a rejection of the biblical teaching that God grants forgiveness only on the righteous basis of the full penalty having been paid by His Son, Jesus Christ, and that forgiveness comes freely by His grace, directly from Him.

It is a blatant denial of the sufficiency of Christ's death on the cross and a perversion of God's righteous forgiveness by grace to pretend that some physical object has any efficacy whatsoever. Clearly, those who wear a scapular (as the Pope has done since childhood), in reliance upon its promise that those who die wearing it "shall not suffer eternal fire," have not believed Christ's promise of eternal life as a free gift of His grace or they would not feel the need of such a magical object. In fact, they have rejected Christ's salvation and will find, to their sorrow, that indulgences are a fraud. A scapular or medal around the neck is of no more benefit in escaping hell than a rabbit's foot in the pocket!

By making the rules and regulating and dispensing the alleged graces through the usage of "holy objects," the Church enslaves its members, who must look to it for salvation. Such objects must be used repeatedly to obtain further installments toward eternal life. There is no end of the objects in which Roman Catholics place their hope for eternity. Consider the following from one of the most prestigious Catholic magazines, *Inside the Vatican:*

> Pope Celestine V gave a Holy Door to the Cathedral of Maria Collemaggio in his Bull of 29 September, 1294. To obtain this "perdonanza" indulgence, it's necessary to be in the Cathedral between 18:00 (6 P.M.) 28 August and 18:00 (6 P.M.) 29 August, to truly repent of one's sins, and to confess and go to mass and communion within 8 days of the visit. The Holy Door is open [for 24 hours] every year, but this year, 1994, is the *700th anniversary* of the Bull of Pardon. Go there! (emphasis in original).[56]

It is tragic that millions of Roman Catholics rely upon such fraudulent promises—promises which undermine God's justice and deny the full efficacy of Christ's death on the cross. Why journey to Rome to obtain a plenary indulgence (forgiveness of all sin to that point) when the next sin will put one in need of a further indulgence? Indulgences are not biblical. Yet the Roman Catholic Church unashamedly promotes such heresy and *anathematizes those who object.* Contradicting Colson's statements, Vatican II, quoting the Council of Trent, sternly declares:

> The Church . . . "teaches and commands that the usage of indulgences—a usage most beneficial to Christians and approved by the authority of the Sacred Councils—should be kept in the Church; and it condemns with anathema those who say that

indulgences are useless or that the Church does not have the power to grant them."[57]

Many Catholics reject indulgences. Yet they attend Mass and imagine that they are in good standing with their Church. In fact, they have been anathematized by the highest Church authority—i.e., excommunicated and damned. Their only escape from hell (according to their Church) is to repent and confess their rejection of indulgences.

The Magic of the Mass

The sacraments (liturgy and ritual) are the very heart of Roman Catholicism and essential to the salvation it purports to offer. At the heart of the liturgy is the sacrifice of the Mass. (Anyone who desires to observe the Roman Catholic Mass will find it enacted on EWTN.) Pope John Paul II has said, "Holy Mass is the absolute center of my life and of every day of my life . . . the most important and the most sacred moment for me is the celebration of the Eucharist."[58]

Yet in that which he considers most sacred, the Pope continues the compromise with pagan occultism begun by Constantine. During a 1984 visit to New Guinea, Pope John Paul II presided over an outdoor celebration of the "New Mass" involving "dancers who pranced to the altar for the offertory procession, throwing up clouds of orange and yellow smoke, a pagan custom to ward off evil spirits . . . [while] an 18-year-old college student read a passage of Scripture at the papal altar wearing her traditional clothes [nude above the waist]." The *New York Times* said the Mass was indicative of

> . . . the Roman Catholic Church's efforts to make its services more universal by integrating into its ritual and liturgy elements of the cultures of the peoples to whom Western missionaries brought their religion.[59]

The Mass and all Roman Catholic ritual is a form of magic. The sacraments are not intended as mere symbols of a spiritual reality, but, like voodoo and ritual magic, they are perceived as possessing intrinsic power. Their very performance transmits grace. To deny that is to be anathematized. The Council of Trent decreed and Vatican II reconfirmed that—

> If anyone says that by the sacraments of the New Law [i.e., the Roman Catholic *Code of Canon Law*] grace is not conferred *ex opere operato* [i.e., in the very act itself], but that faith alone in the divine promise is sufficient to obtain grace, let him be anathema.[60]

Nor does Catholic ritual confer some minor "grace" to help one through a difficult day. It is *salvation* that is conferred:

> If anyone says that the sacraments of the New Law are not necessary for salvation but . . . that without them . . . men obtain from God through faith alone the grace of justification . . . let him be anathema.[61]

Vatican II declares, "For it is the liturgy through which, especially in the divine sacrifice of the Eucharist, 'the work of our redemption is accomplished. . . .' "[62] In contrast, the Bible says that our redemption was accomplished on the cross alone (Romans 3:24; Ephesians 1:7; Colossians 1:14; Hebrews 9:12, etc.). Rome's greatest heresy is the denial of the full efficacy of Christ's sacrifice as a completed transaction for all time, and its claim that the Mass is a continuation of that sacrifice:

> Finally the Mass is the divinely ordained means of applying the merits of Calvary. Christ won for the world all the graces it needs for salvation and sanctification. But these blessings are conferred *gradually and continually* . . . mainly through the Mass.
>
> Consequently, the Mass is a truly propitiatory sacrifice, which means that by this oblation "the Lord is appeased, He grants grace . . . and He pardons wrongdoings and sins, even grave ones."[63]
>
> If anyone says that the sacrifice of the mass . . . is a mere commemoration of the sacrifice consummated on the cross but not a propitiatory one . . . and ought not to be offered for the living and the dead, for sins, punishments, satisfactions, and other necessities, let him be anathema.[64]

Catholicism says that Christ is continually being offered on its altars; the Bible says, "nor yet that he should offer himself often . . . but now once . . . hath he appeared to put away sin by the sacrifice of himself. . . . So Christ was once offered to bear the sins of many" (Hebrews 9:25-28). Catholicism says that the Mass is no mere commemoration of Calvary but a real and propitiatory sacrifice; the Bible says, "There is no more offering [sacrifice] for sin" (Hebrews 10:18). Catholicism says that the wafer is Christ present on its altars as sacrifice, and Catholics sit before the wafer host displayed in the monstrance, believing they are in His presence (EWTN recently challenged viewers to "spend an hour with Him in Eucharistic adoration"); the Bible says that "after he had offered one sacrifice for sins forever, [He] sat down on the right hand of God" (Hebrews 10:12).

It was that mass murderer of Christians and Jews, Pope Innocent III, who by decree in A.D. 1215 made the Mass as a "sacrifice" an official dogma. For that to be so, Catholicism relies upon its central magic: transubstantiation. "The priest is indispensable, since he alone by his powers can change the elements of bread and wine into the body and blood of Christ."[65]

Catholicism boasts that it takes Christ literally when He said, "Except ye eat the flesh of the Son of man and drink his blood, ye have no life in you" (John 6:53). Yet He is not taken literally when He calls Himself "the true vine" and His followers "branches" (John 15:1,5); or when He says He is "the shepherd" and "the door" and his followers "sheep" (John 10:9,14, etc.). If He is speaking literally, then those who eat His flesh and drink His blood will literally "never hunger [or] thirst" again (John 6:35). EWTN told of Teresa Newman, who "from 1926 to 1962 never ate anything except the Eucharist," thus "proving what Jesus said." However, that promise was for anyone, not a few "saints." Christ's words make sense only if by eating He meant *believing* and if he referred to *spiritual and eternal* life, not a mere flesh-and-blood physical life on this earth.

Roman Catholicism has perverted the gospel. Salvation no longer comes through the once-for-all sacrifice of Christ upon the cross in which He fully paid the penalty which His own infinite justice demanded for sin. It now comes through a form of ritual magic whereby bread and wine are transformed into the body and blood of Christ, to be sacrificed for partial forgiveness of sins—a sacrifice that must be repeated endlessly.

The New Age and Catholicism

One finds every shade of New Age, occult and mystical belief inside the Roman Catholic Church itself. *Catholic World* had an entire issue affirming the New Age movement as a "genuine spiritual awakening," without a word of reproof. The articles were all sympathetic, including favorable quotes from the Pope.[66] Another issue was dedicated to Buddhism, with one article titled "The Buddha Revered As a Christian Saint."[67]

Millions of Roman Catholics, including thousands of priests and nuns, are openly involved in various occult practices, with no apparent disapproval from the Church hierarchy. The following is a typical ad in a Catholic publication: *Wholistic Growth Resources* operating since 1982 by the Franciscan Sisters of Little Falls, MN, offers women religious wholistic experiences through a transformational journey: weekly individual counseling, group process, body therapy, enneagram, art therapy, parental synthesis... Holotropic Breathwork, ritual, psychosynthesis, foods/nutrition, feminine spirituality, journaling, Myers-Briggs, and more."[68]

A typical brochure from another source offers "Wholistic Therapeutic Massage by: Fran Rees, SP (Sisters of Providence)... [who] blends this ancient healing art of massage into ministry for the mind, body and spirit... [offering complete] understanding of one's body, mind and spirit...." The brochure goes on to promise that wholistic massage enhances spiritual development...." Obviously something more is going on than mere massage of the body!

The brochure explains that "Fran's office is located at The Hermitage in Indianapolis... a [Franciscan] healing center dedicated to the spiritual, emotional, intellectual and professional growth of people. Fran... is certified in... spirituality and worship." How and by whom does one become "certified in spirituality"? The hype continues: "Fran has facilitated numerous workshops dealing with topics of spirituality, psychology, stress reduction, yoga and nutrition. Through her ministry in Wholistic Therapeutic Massage, she continues her interest in helping people develop body, mind and spirit."[69]

The door that Constantine opened has allowed an incredible mix of occultism to be embraced by Catholicism. A recent article in *National Catholic Reporter* is typical. The author referred to Chicago Bulls coach Phil Jackson approvingly as a "Zen Christian" and commended his spirituality:

> Not long ago, Jackson spoke at Old St. Patrick's Church in Chicago's loop. . . . He told the crowd of the power of prayer. . . . "I was far more effective when I balanced the masculine and feminine side of my nature," he wrote in his book. . . .
> Study Pastor Jackson. He will free you up to lead others—and control yourself.[70]

The centuries-long involvement of Roman Catholicism in pagan/occultic practices has led naturally to its more recent marriage to the New Age. Matthew Fox, a Dominican priest and prolific writer, was a blatant New Ager. In 1977 Fox founded the Institute for Culture and Creation Spirituality. It was located at Holy Names College in Oakland, California, since 1983. Its faculty included: Starhawk the witch; Buck Ghost Horse, a North American shaman; Luish Teish, a voodoo priestess; and Robert Frager, a Sufi mystic.

Fox's "Cosmic Christ" is everyone and everything. The Vatican silenced Fox for one year, ending December 15, 1989. Yet the Church made it clear that the disciplining of Fox was for his failure to submit to the hierarchy, not for his horrendous heresies.[71] Dismissed from the Dominican Order for insubordination, Fox continued as a priest until he defected to the Episcopalian Church. He still retains a huge following among Catholics. The Dominican Province of the Netherlands protested that the dismissal of Matthew Fox from the Dominican Order was "a disgrace for an order searching for truth. . . ."[72]

Early in 1997, Fox founded the University of Creation Spirituality (UCS) in Oakland, California, which he calls "the first and only university in spirituality." UCS offers courses in a broad range of occultism such as "Mystics East and West, African American Spirituality . . . Indigenous Peoples' Rituals, Dreams and Myths . . . Urban Shamanism, Shabda Yoga," etc.[73] The first conference (attended by many Catholics) was held June 22-29, 1997, and offered workshops (in addition to the courses above) in "The Spell of the Sensuous, Urban Spirituality . . . Ancestral Voices . . . Native American Ritual," etc.[74]

Assurance of Eternal Life

An obvious reason for the involvement of so many Roman Catholics in the occult is the fact that, having no assurance of salvation through Christ alone, they look to many other sources for help in getting to heaven. The Council of Trent made it a mortal sin for anyone to claim assurance of heaven:

> If anyone says that he will for certain, with an absolute and infallible certainty, have that great gift of perseverance even to the end, unless he shall have learned this by a special revelation, let him be anathema.[75]

Christ promised eternal life as a free gift to all who believe in Him. He declared unequivocally, "He that believeth on the Son hath everlasting life" (John 3:36) and "shall not come into condemnation, but is passed from death to life" (John 5:24); "My sheep hear my voice . . . I give unto them eternal life, and they shall never perish" (John 10:27,28). Paul proclaimed that "the gift of God is eternal life through Jesus Christ our Lord" (Romans 6:23). A gift can neither be merited nor earned but is by grace, the manner in which all of Scripture assures us salvation is received. John writes, "And this is the promise that he hath promised us, even eternal life" (1 John 2:25).

John assures: "These things have I written unto you . . . that ye may know [present knowledge] that ye have [present possession] eternal life" (1 John 5:13). With such clear promises it is the height of unbelief to say that a "special revelation" is needed. Yet that continues to be the tragic state of those in the Roman Catholic Church. John Cardinal O'Connor said:

> Church teaching is that I don't know, at any given moment, what my eternal future will be. I can hope, pray, do my very best—but I still don't know. Pope John Paul II doesn't know absolutely that he will go to heaven, nor does Mother Teresa of Calcutta. . . .[76]

If the pope, Cardinal O'Connor and Mother Teresa cannot know whether they are going to heaven, what hope is there for the average Catholic!

Satan Within the Church?

Pope John XII was not only a murderer and womanizer (like so many other popes), but even toasted Satan at St. Peter's altar. The charge of Satanism within the Church is being renewed today, and from some very credible sources, as the quotations at the beginning of the chapter attest. Yet the media are reluctant to deal with the subject.

World media gave little attention to Archbishop Emmanuel Milingo's recent charge of Satanism being practiced by Roman Catholic clergy. When interviewed on this subject, Malachi Martin, church historian and bestselling author who formerly taught at the Vatican, declared: "Archbishop Milingo is a good bishop and his contention that there are Satanists in Rome is completely correct.[77]

Milingo, a church exorcist presently stifled by the Vatican, made the accusation in an address on November 1996 at Rome's Fatima 2000 International Congress on World Peace. In contrast to the silence elsewhere, the Italian press made much of the story. *Il Messaggero,* Rome's largest daily, headlined it on the front page. Milingo told the Fatima Congress:

> The devil in the Catholic Church is so protected now that he is like an animal protected by the government . . . on a game preserve that outlaws anyone . . . from trying to capture or kill it . . . so that the exorcist today is forbidden to attack the devil.[78]

In his latest book, *Windswept House,* a novel published by Doubleday and based upon thinly disguised facts known to Malachi Martin, he depicts satanic rituals being practiced by high-level Roman Catholic officials and even within the Vatican itself. When asked whether some of the events contained in the novel, including the very enthronement of Satan himself within the Church, reflected fact, Martin replied:

> Oh, yes, it is true; very much so. But the only way I could put that down into print is in novelistic form.[79]

The shaman . . . can be viewed as an early psychotherapist.
                              —Herbert Benson, M.D., Harvard professor

*The basic model of man that led to the development of [Eastern]
meditational techniques is the same model that led to humanistic
psychotherapy.*
                              —Lawrence LeShan, past president of the
                              Association for Humanistic Psychology (AHP)[1]

*The discussion of [C.G.] Jung's psychic participation must begin with
taking a deep breath. It is a story so unbelievable . . . that—ever since
it was fully revealed—analytic psychologists have been staggering under
the impact, psychoanalysts have ignored it as a fairy tale, and parapsychologists have found it a diet so rich that up to now they have not
been able to digest it. . . .*

   Jung's . . . doctoral thesis of 1899 [was] on The Psychology and
Pathology of So-Called Occult Phenomena. *. . .*
                              —Nandor Fodor in *Freud, Jung and Occultism*[2]

*The core of the problem, which psychological and psychiatric research has
not resolved yet, and is unlikely to resolve, consists in a correct distinction
between pathological behaviour of a psychic nature and demonic invasion.*
                              —Eugenio Fizzoti, professor of The Psychology of Religion,
                              School of Education, Pontifical Salesian University, Rome[3]

*When we think of religion, we usually think of a large institution . . .
prescribed doctrines . . . a power structure . . . dogmas. . . . When I say
"spiritual," however, I'm trying to get back to the original experience
that led to the development of religion in the first place . . . [through]
altered states of consciousness. . . .*

   *The exciting thing about transpersonal psychologies . . . you don't
have to believe . . . some religious tract written hundreds or thousands
of years ago [such as the Bible]. Techniques can be developed—whether
they be meditation techniques or psychotherapeutic techniques or
whatever—that lead people back to the experiential basis that gave
rise to religion in the first place.*
                              —Charles Tart, University of California professor of psychology[4]

*There is abundant evidence that in many forms of modern thought—
especially the so-called "prosperity" psychology, "will-power building"
. . . and systems of "high-pressure" salesmanship—black magic has
merely passed through a metamorphosis, and although its name may be
changed, its nature remains the same.*
                              —Manly P. Hall, occult authority/historian[5]

* * *

21

* * *

Psychology and
the Occult

The great physicist David Bohm accepted reluctantly "the impossibility of final knowledge" through science. As a student of the Indian mystic Krishnamurti, Bohm was heavily influenced by Hinduism and its reliance on mystic revelation.[6] Similar conclusions on the part of other leading thinkers and scientists are presented in an irreverent and godless though thought-provoking book by *Scientific American* senior staff writer John Horgan titled *The End of Science: Facing the Limits of Knowledge in the Twilight of the Scientific Age.*

Nobelist Richard Feynman (with other leading physicists) has held a dim view about the future of physics. It is frustrating to scientists to admit that underlying everything is something man can never understand. Of course, this is exactly what one would expect of a universe created by God. Long before modern physics came along, the Bible informed us:

> Through faith we understand that the worlds were framed by the word of God, so that things which are seen were not made of things which do appear (Hebrews 11:3).

There are some things that we can only understand by believing what God tells us. He doesn't say that the visible universe was made of *something invisible,* or that it was made out of *nothing*—only that it was not made of anything that man can see, even with his most sophisticated electron microscopes or any other instrument he may invent. We are informed that the universe came into existence by "the word of God" and is sustained, or held together, "by the word of his power" (Hebrews 1:3). More than that we cannot and need not know.

Man will never unravel the mystery underlying the existence of space, time, and matter. Each door that science opens reveals ten more unopened doors on the other side. The unknown explodes ahead of us with each new discovery like receding images in a hall of mirrors. Nobelist Niels Bohr said of quantum mechanics, "If you think you understand it, that only shows you don't know the first thing about it."[7] Indeed, we don't know what anything is—gravity, energy, the electron, or anything else. Science has given up the once-proud hope of exploring final reality. We earlier quoted Sir James Jeans:

> The outstanding achievement of twentieth-century physics is not the theory of relativity . . . or the theory of quanta . . . or the dissection of the atom . . . [but] it is the general recognition that we are not yet in contact with ultimate reality. . . .[8]

At what point the physical interfaces with the spiritual we do not know. But somewhere out there (or in there?) is another *nonphysical* universe (or universes?) entirely beyond our grasp. Whether the spiritual underlies the physical, is an extension thereof, or is something entirely different cannot be determined by any scientific methods or instruments.

The imposing reality of this "spiritual" dimension can no longer be denied. Joan Borysenko, cancer cell biologist and New Age leader, talks of "psychology and medicine and spirituality all [coming] together."[9] With the failure of science to provide the answers the heart seeks, the world, instead of turning to God and to His sure Word, has turned back to mysticism and occultism, now supported by psychology. And even the prestigious *American Journal of Psychiatry* admitted that often the former works better than the latter:

> Patients given conventional mental-health treatment in Puerto Rico reported less improvement than those who went to spiritist healers. . . .
>
> [In] spiritist healing . . . mediums receive spirit messages or become possessed by spirits in order to diagnose, counsel or prescribe herbal and ritual remedies.[10]

Life, Soul, and Spirit

If the physical universe is an unsolvable mystery, life itself is even more mysterious. We don't know what life is—only that it comes from God and is not physical. Life animates physical bodies, yet is not part of the body. Physical life has something to do with a soul: God "breathed into man's nostrils the breath of life, and man became a living soul" (Genesis 2:7). The Bible doesn't define soul, but it seems to be present within creatures that breathe.

Whereas lower creatures are said to have a soul, never is spirit associated with animal life. Man is created "in the image of God" (Genesis 1:26,27; 9:6; etc.), who is a spirit. Not so with animals. Without defining either, the Bible distinguishes between soul and spirit: "your whole spirit and soul and body" (1 Thessalonians 5:23); "the dividing asunder of soul and spirit" (Hebrews 4:12; see also 1 Corinthians 15:45).

Man is a spirit living in a body through which he participates in physical events. The spirit in man distinguishes him from animals and makes it possible for him to know God. Neither man's body nor soul is in God's image, for God has neither. Man's *spirit* is in the image of God. Separation of man's spirit from God's Spirit brings spiritual death to man. God declares, "Your iniquities have separated between you and your God" (Isaiah 59:2); and you are "dead in trespasses and sins" (Ephesians 2:1; etc.).

Separation of the spirit from the body brings death to the body: "As the body without the spirit is dead" (James 2:26). At death the body goes into the grave and "the spirit shall return unto God who gave it" (Ecclesiastes 12:7). Taking the Bible as a whole, this can only mean that man's spirit is at God's disposal to be sent either to heaven or to hell. The spirit of a dead person would not be floating about, haunting or appearing to those on earth, as the world of the occult would have us believe. "Ghosts" can only be masquerading demons.

The spirit separated from the body remains conscious, whether in heaven or hell. We have already noted that the brain does not think. Thought originates in the spirit, which then uses the brain to cause the body to say or do its will. The rich man, whose body was in the grave, was certainly conscious in hell (Luke 16:23-31), and so are those in heaven who have been separated from their bodies: "I saw under the altar [in heaven] the souls of them that were slain for the word of God. . . . And they cried with a loud voice" (Revelation 6:9,10).

Psychology, the Religious Science

While the very term "psychology" acknowledges the psyche, there was a stubborn insistence that the psyche was merely the sum total of purely physiological reactions to physical stimuli. For nearly a century, psychologists and psychiatrists clung to Freud's medical model and B.F. Skinner's behavioristic theories, both of which stubbornly (and against common sense) tried to explain thought, emotions, and personality in terms of the physical body alone.

This delusion held on longer than it should have due to the proud determination to establish psychology as a science. There can be no science of the spirit, for science has no means of observing spirits. Nevertheless, the Mind Science cults, as we have seen (Christian Science, Religious Science, Science of Mind, et al.), tried to make a science out of spirituality and have thereby fallen deeply into the occult.

In his latest book, *Worldwide Laws of Life*, John Marks Templeton (of the Templeton Prize for Progress in Religion) reiterates his dream of a "new Renaissance in human knowledge" through "the scientific exploration of spiritual subjects. . . . I hold a vision of the establishment of a new branch of science: the science of spiritual information and research."[11] This, as we have seen, is precisely what occultism is: religious science. Occultism purports to utilize a spiritual power that works by certain laws, making it possible to elicit a predictable response from the spirit world.

A hundred years ago William James wrote, "I wish by treating Psychology like a natural science, to help her become one."[12] Post-World-War-II society believed the lie and eagerly submitted to each new experiment and theory. "The scientism of psychology made grand promises: solutions to societal and international problems, understanding and change of individual and social

behaviour, and the creation of a safer and better world by elim-
inating the destructive forces that had brought about the war.
. . ."[13] The delusion took over that "the social world is know-
able, predictable, and controllable and . . . that breakthroughs
in understanding the individual human mind would be basic
building blocks for a better society."[14]

In fact, a lengthy study appointed by the American Psychological Association (subsidized by the National Science Foundation and involving 80 eminent scholars) concluded in 1979
that psychology is not and cannot be a science.[15] Karl Popper,
one of the greatest philosophers of science, declared that psychological theories have "more in common with primitive
myths than with science. . . ."[16] The famous Jewish psychiatrist
Thomas Szasz called psychology "the clever and cynical destruction of the spirituality of man, and its replacement by a
positivistic 'science of mind.' "[17] The attempt to deal with human behavior scientifically has opened the door to occult
seduction.

Man's problem is that he is separated from God by sin.
Psychology has turned sin into sickness, a sickness of the mind
that requires not repentance and reconciliation with God, but
therapy and reconciliation with one's "inner truth." Templeton
promotes it as "learn[ing] to tap . . . the resources of our inner
being.[18] This is nothing but shamanism/occultism.

While most psychologists still profess to be involved in a science, many others would admit that there can be no science of
human behavior. The human guinea pig hops about capri-
ciously making choices which could not possibly be predicted
on any purely scientific basis. The very term "social science"
has wasted much time and has led to grave errors.

Freud said that religion is the "enemy."[19] Yet he established a
new destructive religion with man as god. In fact, like Jung, Freud
was heavily involved in the occult. In their new book *The End of
"Christian Psychology,"* Martin and Deidre Bobgan point out:

> Freud . . . collected a large number of ancient Greek, Roman,
> Oriental, and Egyptian artifacts . . . rows of statuettes arranged on
> his desk and around his office.
> One person who knew the family said that for Freud, "The artifacts
> weren't only decorative. He used some of them to help him to write."[20]

One writer suggests . . . [that] Freud may have been practicing. . . . an ancient form of magic in which consecrated statues representing spirits or transpersonal powers would engage the magician in imaginal dialogues and supply him with invaluable knowledge.[21]

A Subtle Takeover in Process

Posing as scientists of the psyche, or soul, psychologists and psychiatrists have taken over as the experts who alone can define normal behavior. Martin L. Gross explains:

> As the Protestant ethic has weakened in Western society, the confused citizen has turned to the only alternative he knows: the psychological expert who claims there is *a new scientific standard of behavior* to replace fading traditions. . . .
>
> The citizen-patient has been told, and usually believes, that his tormenting doubts about love, sex, work, interpersonal relations, marriage and divorce, child raising, happiness, loneliness, even death, will yield to the new technology of the mind. Mouthing the holy name of *science,* the psychological expert claims to know all.[22]

The result has been destructive to society and the family. The explosion of crime, rebellion, and immorality has coincided with the exponential growth of psychology since the early 1950s. There was a 43 percent increase in the number of Americans in the 10–19 age bracket committed to psychiatric hospitals from 1980 to 1987, while the number of private psychiatric beds per 100,000 persons more than doubled in the five years from 1983 to 1988. What a growth industry! Psychology has been rightly called the only profession that "creates the diseases which it claims to cure."

Public trust and media support for this profession continue in spite of the fact that its ranks shelter more moral, emotional, and behavioral problems than any other. One out of four psychologists has suicidal feelings at times. Bruno Bettelheim, Paul Federn, Wilhelm Stekel, Victor Tausk, Lawrence Kohlberg, and Sigmund Freud are some of the prominent "mental health professionals" who have committed suicide.[23] A report by the American Psychiatric Association Task Force on Suicide Prevention revealed that "psychiatrists commit suicide at rates about twice those expected [of physicians]. . . ."[24]

Freud was a basket case who often fainted, could not control his own sexual impulses, couldn't stop smoking even after 30 operations, and was haunted by superstitions.[25] Freud said, "Patients are nothing but riff-raff. The only useful purposes they serve are to help us make a living and to provide learning material. In any case, we cannot help them."[26] Dr. Al Parides, Professor of Psychiatry at UCLA, observed:

> If you look at the personal lives of all Freud's . . . initial disciples . . . [they] have an unbelievable amount of particular problems in the sexual area. . . . The amount of deviancy as far as their sexual behavior and so forth is enormous.[27]

In spite of the growing mass of evidence against psychology, it has been embraced as the new truth and new hope. Such public trust has given psychologists enormous power. It is frightening to see where they would like to take society. Leading psychologists have suggested that "parents be licensed to have children only upon demonstrating a sound understanding . . . of truths dispensed by psychologists"[28] and that political and military leaders should be given psychological tests to make certain they don't harbor the fundamentalist belief that Armageddon is inevitable.[29] In 1971 the president of the American Psychological Association proposed that psychologists administer behavior modification drugs to civil and military leaders to reverse their aggression impulses.

A Dangerous Pseudoscience

Psychological theories come and go in a merry-go-round of confusion. For example, *drapetomania* was the official psychiatric diagnosis of a "mental illness" that was epidemic in early America. Afflicting only slaves, it was marked by a compulsion to escape the plantation—a mental illness that was cured by the Civil War. Today, "mental illnesses" are created or cured by vote. In previous decades homosexuality was always recognized as unnatural behavior. In 1974, however, on the basis of a vote by members of the American Psychiatric Association (5854 to 3810), homosexuality was changed from deviant/abnormal behavior to a "sexual preference." Finally it was removed from the diagnostic manuals altogether. This is not science.

A similar vote decides which newly invented mental illnesses will be included in the latest Diagnostic and Statistical Manual. One psychologist who attended the DSM-III-R hearing remarked sadly:

> The low level of intellectual effort was shocking. Diagnoses were developed by majority vote on the level we would use to choose a restaurant. You feel like Italian, I feel like Chinese, so let's go to a cafeteria. Then it's typed into the computer. It may reflect on our naivete, but it was our belief that there would be an attempt to look at things scientifically.[30]

In her excellent expose of psychology, *Manufacturing Victims,* Dr. Tana Dineen points out that "what the Psychology Industry has persuaded people to believe and what has actually been proven are quite different." She suggests that if psychologists "were to look honestly at what they are doing it would cause them to have doubts about their effectiveness, their worth, their self-image and their career."[31] In fact, she points out that scientific studies show that therapy is ineffective and unnecessary, and can actually be harmful.[32]

Psychologists have developed several hundred rival theories and several thousand therapies. Any primitive superstition or newly invented scam, from Primal Scream to Rebirthing and Past Life Regression, becomes legitimate when it is labeled "therapy." In an article titled "Psychology Goes Insane, Botches Role As Science," psychologist Roger Mills writes: "I have personally seen therapists convince their clients that all of their problems come from their mothers, the stars, their biochemical make-up, their diet, their life-style and even the 'karma' from their past lives." A brochure put out by former Dominican nun Kathleen A. FitzGerald, Ph.D., reads:

> Sacred Psychology... [is] exploring and understanding the unique nature, color and feel of our individual souls. It is about Soul Loss, Soul Retrieval, Soul Care and Soul Celebration. . . .
> The Inner Child sends her/his Soul into exile until it is safe to return. . . . In Native American Spirituality, shamans journey to Retrieve Soul. . . .[33]

This is mythology! Carnegie-Mellon University professor Robyn M. Dawes wrote *House of Cards: Psychology and Psychotherapy*

Built on Myth out of "anger, and a sense of social obligation." Professor Dawes cites the example of a female Harvard psychiatrist whose patient committed suicide. The concern expressed by the professional board of inquiry was whether she had had sex with her patient. The fact that she had "regressed" him "to an infantile state so that she could 'reparent' him" was ignored—for who could say that such nonsense was not legitimate therapy?[34]

Dawes indicts the field of psychology with "espousing principles that are known to be untrue and [with] employing techniques known to be invalid."[35] Indeed, in the famous Cambridge-Sommerville Youth Study, involving 650 underprivileged boys six to ten years of age (divided equally into two groups), follow-up 30 years later revealed that those who received therapy had more problems with "alcoholism, mental illness, job dissatisfaction and stress-related diseases" and committed significantly more serious crimes than those who were not given the "benefit" of psychological counseling.[36] Any scientific evidence we have been able to compile proves that psychotherapy is at best ineffective and is even harmful in many cases.

Defining the Spiritual

In his 1992 book, *Consciousness Explained*, Tuft University philosopher Daniel Dennett contended that "consciousness—and our sense that we possess a unified self—was an illusion arising out of the interaction of many different 'subprograms' run on the brain's hardware."[37] There is just as much scientific evidence for Santa Claus and the tooth fairy. While some psychologists still cling to such madness, psychology as a whole has moved on—forced to do so by the phenomena it faces. It is no longer embarrassing to admit that the human spirit and/or soul exist and that they cannot be measured or defined.

It was the new discipline of parapsychology (the investigation of psychic phenomena) that forced reluctant researchers to admit man's nonphysical side. Experiments seemed to indicate that the human mind could influence physical matter at distances far beyond the range of any detectable emanations from the brain. In fact, from the days of Anton Mesmer it had been noted that some hypnotized subjects could "see" events occurring many miles away. There was no physical explanation. The mind had to be a nonphysical entity distinct from the brain.

Even that admission, however, failed to explain the phenomena. The human mind alone cannot account for remote viewing, and it certainly cannot be responsible for visitations from spirit entities or glimpses into the future or the ability to speak languages to which one has never been exposed. The phenomena could only be explained if the human mind was in contact with another source of information and power.

Much psychotherapy involves hypnotizing the patient for regression into the past, or some other means of placing the patient in a highly suggestible state. While the therapist exercizes verbal control, other minds could exert mental control. Edgar Mitchell engaged in seemingly successful experiments communicating with earth through telepathy during his Apollo 14 moon mission. Both the KGB and CIA have experimented with telepathically influencing the behavior of a subject at a distance. As we shall see, only the influence of minds other than the therapist's could explain much that occurs in therapy.

In Search of Other Minds

The Bible tells us, and all cultures in history have always believed, that spirits exist—intelligent beings without bodies. Yet some (whether angels or demons) can take bodily form in a manner which we do not understand. They can even impact the physical dimension in which our bodies function and seemingly "possess" a human body and personality. Again, how this takes place (even with the assent of the possessed), we don't know. Nor are we to attempt to understand, much less to interact with, these beings:

> The soul that turneth after such as have familiar spirits, and after wizards, to go a whoring after them, I will . . . cut him off from among his people (Leviticus 20:6).
>
> There shall not be found among you . . . a consulter with familiar spirits, or a wizard, or a necromancer. For all that do these things are an abomination unto the Lord . . . (Deuteronomy 18:10-12).
>
> Let no man beguile you . . . worshipping . . . angels, intruding into those things which he hath not seen (Colossians 2:18).

Carl Jung's occult beliefs have had a staggering impact upon psychology. His personal spirit guide, Philemon, like the "ghosts" that haunted Jung, could appear out of thin air and just as suddenly disappear. Yet he seemed to have a tangible form and to be a real and independent entity whom Carl Jung eventually looked up to as his guru. And it was from such demonic sources that Jung learned his major theories, theories which heavily impact psychology today.

Researchers have settled upon four possibilities to explain the phenomena: 1) We are all part of a universal mind and thus potentially have all knowledge and power at our disposal; 2) the discarnate spirits of the dead are able to communicate and interact with the living; 3) the "other minds" out there belong to extraterrestrials, some of whom may even have evolved beyond the need of bodies and can influence or even take over human thinking; 4) there are other minds belonging to demons and angels, both of whom seek to influence mankind, the first under the direction of Satan, the second directed by God.

The first theory falls of its own weight, attributing to mankind a readily available source of infinite wisdom and power. That hardly squares with normal human experience. That one must get into an altered state of consciousness to contact and tap into this alleged universal mind seems rather lame. We are either part of it and thus it should be readily available, or we are not. The latter is clearly the case.

As for the second alternative (that the spirits of the dead are able to contact the living), the Bible contradicts it, as does common sense. Why should Aunt Jane (for example), who was a very ordinary person in life, become so all-knowing on the "other side"? Moreover, the alleged discarnates, as we have seen, unanimously peddle Satan's lies from the Garden. They may have claimed to be Christians or atheists or just indifferent in life, but after death they have become articulate and convincing spokespersons for Satan. It is more likely that demons are masquerading as discarnates.

Concerning the third alternative (of highly evolved extraterrestrials), we have already seen the impossibility of evolution and that the facts eliminate the ETI hypothesis. Author Robert A. Baker points out that no one has been able to produce a "material artifact that unquestionably proves alien spaceships exist, or that alien forms of life—intelligent or otherwise— exist," and until then one must remain "unconvinced of any and all reports of aliens, alien spaceships, and alien abductions."[38] California clinical psychologist Terence Sanbek raises another obvious common-sense objection:

> To go to the nearest star is going to take years . . . [even] if you travel at the speed of light, which you can't. When you got there, would you talk to a drunken fisherman from Mississippi or would you talk to a head of state? If you're that intelligent, you couldn't act that stupid.[39]

We are left with the only other choice: that demons are behind occult phenomena. All the evidence we have examined thus far indicates that we have been invaded by personal beings of great cunning whose ultimate goal is to pull mankind down to the destruction which they themselves face for their rebellion. Yes, their goal was betrayed by Satanist Marilyn Manson's "I'm on my way down and want to take you with me." That sort of insane bravado appeals to certain people. But in laying the trap for most of mankind, demons masquerade as ETIs, Ascended Masters, splits of the psyche, multiple personalities, or whatever else appeals most to those with whom these evil entities have been able to establish contact. And their game is made that much easier by mankind's amazing reluctance to face the truth—and by psychotherapists' eagerness to play right along with their lies.

The Mecca of Human Potential

During the 1960s and 1970s many of the leading lights in the blossoming field of humanistic psychology used to gather to share their theories at Esalen Institute, in the Big Sur area south of San Francisco. In 1962 Abraham Maslow and his wife, Bertha, stumbled upon it almost by chance and thereafter enjoyed a long relationship with Esalen. Many celebrities, including Aldous Huxley, Paul Tillich, Arnold Toynbee, Joan Baez, Simon and Garfunkel, some of the Beatles, B.F. Skinner, Linus Pauling, and Jerry Brown, dropped in for discussions.[40]

Esalen became the New Age center on the West Coast before the term "New Age" became known. Esalen was into "channeling" spirit entities long before it became popular. Esalen had its own resident "channeler," a young English woman named Jenny O'Connor. By means of automatic writing, a group of nonhuman entities calling themselves "The Nine" (and allegedly based on the star Sirius), delivered regular messages through Jenny and were at times quite remarkable for their uncanny precognitive accuracy. Cofounder Richard Price, prior to his macabre death in 1985, was so impressed that he began to involve The Nine in his Gestalt therapy sessions. For several years the Esalen Catalog offered a course in Gestalt which it promised would be facilitated by "The Nine, a paranormal intelligence. . . ."[41]

There was even a biographical entry in the catalog for The Nine, which described them as "giant reflectors of yourselves, gestalt practitioners, marriage counselors—pure energy of emergence quality available to all." Price expressed the opinion that it didn't matter whether the material channeled through Jenny from The Nine "came from Sirius or from Jenny's unconscious." The Nine were even consulted by Esalen's senior directors in a famous meeting that resulted in a shakeup of the top leadership.[42]

Of interest to our study is the fact that The Nine have communicated through other mediums and with other organizations and people involved in the occult. They contacted Andrija Puharich in his laboratory, drawing him into the occult. The late Gene Roddenberry hoped to get in touch with The Nine and created a script called "The Nine."[43] Books have been dedicated to them, such as *The Only Planet of Choice*, dedicated to "Tom and the Council of Nine," "Tom" being the alleged spokesman for the Council. Paul identified the Nine (archons) 1900 years ago as demonic enemies of mankind wielding "spiritual wickedness" (Ephesians 6:12).

Humanistic and Transpersonal Psychology

The Association for Humanistic Psychology (AHP) has been deeply penetrated by the most flagrant occultism. As early as

1986, practicing shamans were among key speakers at the AHP's 24th annual meeting, held at San Diego State University. Participants were given the opportunity to experience and learn to develop in others the shamanic altered state conducive to contact with spirits. There were mediumistic seances for exploring communications with "spirit guides and other spiritual friends." In its report on the convention, the *Los Angeles Times* included a photo of Durchback Akuete, an African witch doctor, "inducing a trance in AHP co-president Lonnie Barbach."[44]

The AHP, which claims to be involved in the *science* of psychology, advertised that 1986 convention in *Shaman's Drum: A Journal of Experiential Shamanism*. A glance at any issue of *Shaman's Drum* reveals the heavy involvement of psychologists. A typical issue of *Shaman's Drum* contains such articles as "Learning to Trust the Spirits"[45] and promotes the most primitive and demonic occultism as liberating truth. Consider the following descriptions beneath the illustrations in a recent article titled "Handling Hungry Spirits: Shamanic Rituals of the Embera":

> A young *haibana* . . . chants to invoke the *hai* [spirits]. . . .
> A girl is painted in the snake design . . . who will serve as hostess for the *hai* [spirits] during a curing.
> Dressed in beads and a traditional loincloth, the *haibana* holds one of his shamanic staffs as he offers the spirits commercial alcohol and imported Marlboro cigarettes.
> Aceite passes a live snake three times over a patient so that it will absorb her disease.[46]

By advertising in *The Shaman's Drum,* the AHP clearly hoped to attract to its ranks more practicing shamans through the relationship between psychotherapy and their ancient religion. The implication was also clear that psychologists may be able to teach shamans a few new tricks. The ad read in part:

> An unforgettable opportunity to learn from some of the most important healers and spiritual leaders in West Africa and Brazil—
> Journey into altered states of consciousness where one can meet one's higher spirit teachers and the "gods" themselves. . . .
> Topics Include: Ritual, Meditation . . . Altered States of Consciousness, Shamanism and Spirit Healing, Mediumship. . . .[47]

What do "scientific" psychologists mean by "higher spirit teachers," by "gods," or by "Spirit Healing" and "Mediumship"? Transpersonal psychology is even more open about its occult involvement. A newspaper reported:

> Seeing visions. Speaking in tongues. Walking and talking with Jesus. Blissed out on Buddha. Wrestling with Satan. Sighting UFOs. It reads like a litany of psychological afflictions . . . of people who have . . . become card-carrying crazies. Or have they?
>
> At the Institute for Transpersonal Psychology in Menlo Park [California] . . . the psychiatrists, psychologists and counselors . . . are dedicated to recognizing spirituality . . . as an important element of the human condition.[48]

Professor Charles Tart considers transpersonal psychology to be spiritual psychology. He has been called "one of this country's leading scholars on transpersonal psychology, the psychology of spiritual growth. His anthologies, *Altered States of Consciousness* and *Transpersonal Psychologies*, are generally considered classics." Tart writes:

> Spiritual psychologies . . . that show you how to grow spiritually, can be found embedded in Sufism, in various forms of Buddhism such as Zen, within traditional yogic practices . . . [etc.]
>
> They usually . . . [teach] that our true destiny is to evolve toward some higher spiritual nature. . . .[49]

Writing in the *Journal of Humanistic Psychology*, psychologist John Heider acknowledges that a major catalyst in the development of transpersonal psychology was "the widespread use and abuse of psychedelic or mind-manifesting substances such as marijuana, LSD and mescaline. . . . The psychedelic drugs gave incontrovertible proof that altered states of consciousness had reality and that paths toward transcendent experience existed."[50]

Sigmund Freud's Legacy

Freud has been exposed as a fraud. His work was not scientific. Some of the case studies he offered to support his theories are disguised autobiographical sketches. His "discoveries" reflect his own perverted sexual obsessions, as did Jung's. Early correspondence between them involved Jung's efforts to have Freud advise him regarding his seduction of a patient, Sabina Spielrein. Jung had other mistresses, just as Freud was not limited to his sister-in-law, Minna Bernays. Modern psychology springs in large part from sexual depravity and rebellion against God on the part of its honored "discoverers."

Freud's theories were founded upon his warped view that all thought, feeling, and motivation have their roots in sexual cravings. His "Oedipus Complex," for which no evidence can be found in the general population, clearly reflected his own obsession with incest. The evil that has resulted from Freud's and Jung's influence is beyond calculation. Even the well-known German magazine *Der Spiegel*, in a July 1994 feature article, raised the possibility of demonic involvement through Freudian and Jungian psychology.

Even though he has been discredited, two of Freud's theories remain as the major underpinnings of most psychology and psychotherapy: the unconscious and psychic determinism. Freud claimed to have discovered that human behavior is driven by urges arising out of childhood traumas and which lie hidden in a region called the unconscious and can only be accessed and cured by psychotherapy. Professor Dawes expresses his outrage:

> The most pernicious of these beliefs is that adult behavior is determined mainly by childhood experiences, even very subtle ones, and particularly those that enhance or diminish self-esteem.[51]

The obvious effect of such theories is to exonerate the offender no matter what he or she may have done. In the index for Freud's works, which fills an entire volume, one word is missing—*responsibility*.

Without responsibility, no one is guilty. "Alcoholism and drug addictions became 'diseases,' criminality became a 'byproduct' of the social environment in which people were raised, and so on.' "[52] Instead of being guilty, we are all victims—not only of what others have done to us but also victims of our own feelings and therefore not accountable. Thus the District of Columbia Court of Appeals decision in 1954 that a person "could be ruled not guilty of a crime by reason of irresistible impulse . . . later led to the acquittal of John Hinckley in the attempted assassination of then President Reagan."[53]

Recovering "Repressed" Memories

If the problem lies in the past, then, decided Freud, one must go into the past to uncover and deal with the trauma. This process is called "regression therapy," and it raises many questions. Memory is far from infallible and often mistaken and self-serving, as proved by numerous scientific tests.

Then there is the way memories are extracted in therapy. The client is subtly led into a highly suggestible state of mind, then plied with leading suggestions in an attempt to assist the "memory." The suggestions very often take hold and become the trigger to "remember" what never happened. Events are thus created in much the same way that a shaman operates.

Often the therapist has his own agenda and pressures the patient to "remember" what the therapist (without any evidence) has already concluded is the problem. If the patient can't remember what the therapist wants him to, he is accused of suppressing the memory or of being in denial. Freud's modus operandus continues to this day. Freud wrote:

> We must not believe what they [patients] say [when they deny having memories], we must always assume, and tell them, too, that they have kept something back. . . .
> We must insist on this, we must repeat the pressure and represent ourselves as infallible, till at last we are really told something. . . the pressure technique, in fact, never fails.[54]

This kind of therapy has repeatedly led to false memories. Thousands of families across America have been destroyed by false memories of alleged sexual and satanic ritual abuse (SRA) that never happened. The accused (most often fathers) are striking back and the courts have been awarding large judgments in some cases against the therapists responsible.

Most "memories" of alleged past sexual abuse and SRA are uncovered under hypnosis. Freud himself used this technique. Hypnosis has been proved to create false memories. Therefore testimony thus gained is unacceptable in court in most states. Yes, factual memories also have been known to come forth under hypnosis, but here we confront a serious problem.

Hypnotized subjects "regressed" back into the womb "remember" details (including conversations they couldn't have understood) involving their own birth. Yet the scientific fact is that the myelin sheathing of the brain is too underdeveloped at the time of birth to carry memories. Obviously, the "memories" didn't come from the brain. We can only conclude that some other mind is providing the "memory" as a deception.

We have already seen the connection between the occult and reincarnation, a basic belief in Eastern mysticism and witchcraft. Under hypnotherapy, factual "memories" of the locale and events of alleged past lives and even the foreign language spoken are also produced. Again we are forced to the inescapable conclusion that some other mind is providing the data which is surely beyond the knowledge of the hypnotized subject. Using their spirit guides, shamans have engaged in precisely this technique for thousands of years.

Multiple Personalities?

Another delusion spawned by Freud's theories of the unconscious and psychic determinism is the belief that one can be "inhabited" by numerous personalities. Such a patient is said to be afflicted with a "multiple personality disorder" (MPD). Scarcely anyone had heard of MPD prior to the publication in 1957 of *The Three Faces of Eve*. It tells the story of Christine Costner Sizemore, who, after much therapy, allegedly manifested 22 different personalities. The 1973 book *Sybil* (and its movie in 1977) caused this belief to explode, and MPD became associated with sexual abuse. The 1980 publication of *Michelle Remembers* added the dimension of SRA to MPD.

In 1980 MPD was recognized in DSM-III as a psychiatric disorder. Some psychologists now theorize that we all have multiple personalities and that mankind could take a great evolutionary leap forward by learning to harness this power within. Others point out MPD's connection to occult experiences and the relationship of "multiples" to the "higher self" discovered in yogic trance.[55] New York City clinician Armand DiMele's description makes the occult connection very clear:

> In dealing with multiples you ... actually invite that thing in through a hypnotic state. . . .
>
> *I have spoken to "spirit voices"* who have come through multiples that have told me things about my childhood. Specifics, like things that hung in the house. There's some undeniable evidence... [of] something we don't understand and can't measure (emphasis in original).[56]

California psychiatrist Ralph B. Allison, one of the leading authorities on MPD, is a firm believer in and practitioner of the higher Self. Says Allison: "We each have access to it. We don't have to go to ... [a channeler]. We can do it privately, quietly. . . ." Allison sometimes refers to his own higher Self as "Mike," reserving final judgment on who or what Mike might ultimately be. MPD patients, according to Allison, don't listen to higher helpers, so they suffer. Therapy involves teaching them to listen.[57] This is *science?*

In classic occult terminology, Dr. Allison refers to these entities as "Ascended Masters," who, he believes, are related to our own higher Selves. Based upon his experience with MPDs, this psychiatrist has come to believe in the existence of *disembodied minds.* In his conversations with these entities, some say to him, "Don't worry about where we come from or what's our address, or where we've lived before." Others say such things as, "I had my last life as a Sioux Indian in the Dakotas and I was a multiple then, and now I've been sent by God here to help her [the client] with her troubles—I'm an expert at it."

In typical fashion for a psychiatrist, Dr. Allison says,"Who am I to argue ... ? I'm in the business of helping people, and I could care less where the information comes from. Does it work?"[58] In fact, the identity of these entities ought to be of great concern. It sounds like demonic possession.

Among the many cases that would be laughable were they not so tragic is that of Nadean Cool, who sued her former psychiatrist for malpractice, "saying he convinced her she had 120 personalities and then charged her insurance company for group therapy." Blue Cross, which paid about 113,000 dollars

to the psychiatrist, Dr. Kenneth Olson, and 114,000 dollars to
St. Elizabeth Hospital in Wisconsin, joined Cool in the suit,
complaining that Olson had billed for group sessions, claiming
he was counseling more than one person.[59] What science is
this? Common sense recoils from the delusion.

Extraterrestrials and Psychology

Whether UFO cultism is myth, magic, or madness, its high
priests are psychiatrists, and the religious ritual they employ is
hypnosis. This ancient shamanic practice provides a link between UFOs, NDEs, and the occult. Few, if any, abductees ever
have a conscious memory of the alleged experience. In the
process of being regressed back in time under hypnosis (with
the help of some leading suggestions), the "memory" of the
"abduction" and of being physiologically analyzed and sometimes sexually assaulted is uncovered by the therapist—exactly
like the memories of alleged childhood sexual abuse have been
"uncovered" by the thousands.

Jacques Vallee refers to regression under hypnosis to recover memories as "a highly questionable method, which has
unfortunately become one of the standards of UFO research.
. . ."[60] In fact, any hypnotized subject can, with a minimum of
suggestion, "remember" UFO abductions that conform in detail to those described by supposed genuine abductees.[61] The
experience of so-called clinical death is also duplicated under
hypnosis, revealing an occult link to the UFO phenomena.[62]

Across America, hundreds of groups of those who believe
they have encountered aliens or have been abducted meet regularly, usually under the guidance of a psychotherapist. Typical
is the group in suburban Los Angeles led by hypnotherapist
Yvonne Smith "for people who think their sexual and repro-
ductive behavior is being monitored by aliens."[63]

The chief priest of UFO abductions is Dr. John E. Mack, professor of psychiatry at the Cambridge Hospital, Harvard
Medical School, and a Pulitzer-Prize-winning author. He has interviewed more than a hundred people who claim to have
been abducted by aliens aboard UFOs. Much of what he claims
to have learned through these encounters is revealed in his

book *ABDUCTION: Human Encounters with Aliens.* James S. Gordon reviewed the book in the *New York Times:*

> For four years this noted psychiatrist . . . has been recording the strange and striking stories of ordinary men and women who believe they have been abducted from their homes and cars and transported, through walls and on beams of light, to spaceships. . . .
>
> These articulate, sensitive and well-educated men and women were not, it seemed to Dr. Mack, psychotic, delusional or self-promoting. . . . Their experiences with U.F.O. abductions seemed to be the source, not the symptom, of their troubles.
>
> As Dr. Mack listened, he began to believe that their experiences were in some sense quite "real" and . . . under hypnosis, their fragmentary memories became crystals around which complicated scenes of abduction, violation and instruction formed. . . .
>
> As his book reveals . . . Dr. Mack [began] to make other connections—between abductions, near-death experiences and "past-life regressions." All of these experiences are, Dr. Mack suggests, vehicles for recovering perennial [occult] wisdom. . . .
>
> Unfortunately . . . the abductees' accounts . . . lack the weight of authority that Dr. Mack and a sympathetic reader would like to give it. . . . It is here, precisely on the clinical and scientific ground . . . that his book is most vulnerable to criticism. . . .
>
> Equally disturbing is the dearth of material about Dr. Mack's methodology . . . how he induces a hypnotic trance or how he questions his subjects under hypnosis . . . [and] his statement that he and the abductees are "co-creating" their reality.[64]

Dr. John Mack refers to "phenomena that seem to come from another dimension; information obtained by telepathy; clairvoyance and the whole psi [psychic] realm; out-of-body experiences; near-death experiences; telekinesis and the alien abduction phenomenon itself—i.e., phenomena that may manifest in the physical world, but seem to originate in another dimension, to come from a place unseen. . . ."[65] He is describing the world of the occult, in which he has now become a staunch believer.

Carl Jung lived in continual confusion, a state which had haunted him since childhood. He was torn between whether the conscious state or the unconscious was the real one. That ambivalence is reflected in the following account of a dream, which also reveals his view of UFOs and the fact that he had deeper problems than many of his patients:

I caught sight from my house of two lens-shaped metallically gleaming disks, which hurtled in a narrow arc over the house . . . two UFOs. Then another body came flying . . . through the air: a lens with a metallic extension which led to a box—a magic lantern [film strip projector]. At a distance of sixty or seventy yards it stood still in the air, pointing straight at me.

I awoke with a feeling of astonishment . . . the thought passed through my head: "We always think that the UFOs are projections of ours. Now it turns out that we are their projections. I am projected by the magic lantern as C.G. Jung. But who manipulates the apparatus?"[66]

The Amazing Products of Hypnotic Trance

The mysterious effects accompanying hypnosis leave modern scientific investigators thoroughly puzzled. Spontaneous "memories" of past and future lives (about one-fifth involving existence on other planets) often surface.[67] Hypnotic trance also duplicates the experiences common under the stimulation of psychedelic drugs, TM, and other forms of yoga and Eastern meditation.[68] Moreover, hypnotized subjects spontaneously manifest psychic powers, clairvoyance, out-of-body experiences, and the whole range of occult phenomena.[69]

Consider the case of William, an intelligent, well-adjusted, 21-year-old college student hypnotized by Professor Charles Tart. William experienced the same cosmic consciousness and self-realization induced by yoga and clinical death. He experienced a deep peace, then detachment from his body, then release from his own identity to merge with the universe, the feeling that he was everything and had no limitation upon what he could experience or become. He sensed the fullness of God-consciousness "in which time, space, and ego are supposedly transcended, leaving pure awareness of the primal nothingness from which all manifested creation comes."[70]

Accepted only in 1958 by the American Medical Association as a therapeutic technique, hypnosis seems to demonstrate the power of the mind to influence the body. It is the placebo effect under precise direction. There is evidence even that "cellular changes take place in the body, alongside attitude changes."[71] Martin and Deidre Bobgan write:

Compounding the word *hypnosis* with the word *therapy* does not lift the practice from the occult to the scientific. . . .

The white coat may be a more respectable garb than feathers and face paint, but the basics are the same. Hypnosis is hypnosis, whether it is called medical hypnosis, hypnotherapy, autosuggestion, or anything else.

Hypnosis in the hands of a medical doctor is as scientific as a dowsing rod in the hands of a civil engineer.[72]

Some doctors use hypnosis as an anesthetic. When the suggestion is given to some hypnotized subjects that no pain will be felt or even that there will be no bleeding during the operation, that becomes the patient's reality in many cases. A posthypnotic suggestion (that cigarettes will taste horrible, for example, to help a smoker quit) often becomes the new reality when the person is brought back to normal consciousness.

Yoga and other types of Eastern meditation are a form of self-hypnosis or autosuggestion. Various other forms of self-hypnosis are practiced. Based upon years of research, medical doctor William Kroger and psychologist William Fezler warn against being "confused by the supposed differences between hypnosis, Zen, yoga and other Eastern healing methodologies. Although the ritual for each differs, they are fundamentally the same."[73]

Self-hypnosis is widely practiced in the holistic health movement and on the success-seminar circuit for producing success and enhancing one's self-image. The results of hypnosis cannot be explained by any capacity of the human brain or mind. Hypnosis is a major doorway to the occult and has played a key role in the occult invasion of Western society. Self-hypnosis, learned from his elder brother Joe, played a large part in Phil Jackson's introduction to the occult.[74]

Two conclusions that most investigators find very distasteful seem nevertheless to be inescapable: 1) There is a common source behind all occult phenomena, including UFOs, which seems to be intelligently and deliberately orchestrating a clever deception for its own purposes; and 2) hypnosis, or the power of suggestion, is at the very heart of this scheme. If these two conclusions are rejected, then nothing makes sense. The researcher is left, like Professor Alvin H. Lawson of California State University at Long Beach, to mutter, "The nature of the stimulus here is a very spooky thing!"[75]

Psychology and psychiatry . . . offer . . . scientific adjustment of the psyche . . . [to replace] Christianity . . . confession . . . mystical workings . . . a trained priesthood . . . devoted to servicing the paying-by-the-hour communicants.

The medico-psychological concept of sick has replaced [sin] almost intact. We now speak glibly of murderers . . . as being "sick.". . . Freud's atheistic ideas have paradoxically [influenced] ministers, priests and rabbis [who] now flock to courses in pastoral counseling, *making many members of the cloth seem more Freudian than Christian.*

—Martin L. Gross[1]

In cases of difficult diagnosis I usually get a horoscope.

—Carl Jung[2]

A surprising number of today's psychotherapists are following Jung's advice [about consulting a horoscope].

—Wholemind Newsletter[3]

Although few psychologists accept all of Freud's theorizing, his views on the presence of unconscious thoughts, wishes, and feelings are now nearly universally accepted.

—Bruce Narramore, leading Christian psychologist[4]

Under the influence of humanistic psychologists like Carl Rogers and Abraham Maslow, many of us Christians have begun to see our need for self-love and self-esteem. This is a good and necessary focus.

—Bruce Narramore[5]

Today the M.D. psychiatrist and . . . Ph.D. psychologist have appointed themselves the undisputed Solomons of our era. . . . The new seer delivers his pronouncements with the infallible air of a papal bull, a stance which intimidates even the most confident of laymen.

—Martin L. Gross[6]

It is indeed shocking that many, if not most forms of psychotherapy currently offered to consumers are not supported by credible scientific evidence.

—R. Christopher Barden, psychologist, lawyer, and president of the National Association for Consumer Protection in Mental Health Practices[7]

Psychiatry has been willing to sanctify its values with the holy water of medicine and offer them up as the true faith of "Mental Health." It is a false Messiah.

—E. Fuller Torrey, internationally respected psychiatrist[8]

22

* * *

"Christian" Psychology

There is nothing Christian about psychology. Its use of terms like soul, spirit, and even God, deceive many Christians into believing that psychology is somehow compatible with Christianity. However, psychology's meaning for such words comes from the occult, is contrary to the Bible and is irretrievably anti-Christian.

Psychology is, in fact, a rival religion with its own anti-Christian gospel which offers an unbiblical diagnosis and godless cure for the human condition. Even Rollo May expressed concern about psychology's link to religion. Other secular psychologists such as Sam Keen and Philip Reiff have "described psychotherapy as a kind of national religion, with a gospel of self-fulfillment and with therapists as the new priests."[9]

One psychologist says that "certain of the most influential pioneers in American psychology found in it an ideal vehicle for renouncing their own Christian upbringing in the name of science."[10] Professor of psychiatry Thomas Szasz, a nonpracticing Jew, declares, "One of Freud's most powerful motives in life was . . . to inflict vengeance on Christianity. . . ."[11] Szasz called psychotherapy "not merely a religion that pretends to be a science . . . [but] a fake religion that seeks to destroy true religion."[12]

But isn't *Christian* psychology something else? No, it is not. Whether a psychiatrist or psychologist is a Christian or an atheist, he must have passed the same exams and met the same standards in order to be licensed by the state. For example, Fuller Graduate School of Psychology of Fuller Seminary in Pasadena, California, is credentialed by the American Psychological Association and must meet its godless standards like any secular school of psychology.

"*Christian*" Psychology Doesn't Exist

The simple truth is that no such thing as *Christian* psychology exists. Look at the index of any psychology textbook. There are listings for Freudian, Jungian, Behavioristic, Existential, Humanistic, Transpersonal, and many other psychologies, but no listing for *Christian* Psychology. The reason is simple: There is no Christian who is the founder of a distinct school of psychology known as "Christian."

In a paper they presented at a professional gathering of their colleagues, two Christian psychologists stated, with the agreement of the listeners:

> . . . there is no acceptable Christian psychology that is markedly different from non-Christian psychology.
>
> It is difficult to imply that we function in a manner that is fundamentally distinct from our non-Christian colleagues. . . . As yet there is not an acceptable theory, mode of research or treatment methodology [in psychology] that is distinctly Christian.[13]

Then what is meant by "Christian psychology"? Most laypersons imagine that there is indeed a psychology which is distinctly Christian. The professionals know, however, that they are involved in an *attempted integration* of atheistic and anti-Christian theories into Christian theology. Psychology is part of that very "wisdom of this world" taught by "the spirit of the world" which Paul rejected (1 Corinthians 2:5-14). Rapha founder Robert McGee frankly confesses that he joins the Holy Spirit in partnership with atheist Albert Ellis, who considers Christianity a cause of mental illness:

> Changing how we think, feel, and act is a process that involves the supernatural work of the Holy Spirit. . . . As a starting point, however, we will use a model adapted from psychologist Albert Ellis's Rational Emotive Therapy.[14]

Psychology comes out of the occult, is not scientific, and many of its leading professionals admit that it is destructive. The same legitimate criticisms that can be leveled against secular psychology apply equally to so-called "Christian" psychology. Yet it has invaded the best pulpits and is a large part of the curriculum in Christian universities and even seminaries. Several years ago Jerry Falwell notified his mailing list:

Next Sunday I will announce on National Television an historical breakthrough to the Body of Christ. The impact . . . will excite the Christian world, and launch us into a new era of ministry. . . .

There are simply not enough trained Christian Psychologists, Psychiatrists and Pastors to meet the counseling needs of the teeming masses who are crying out for help.

Liberty Institute for Lay Counseling will provide the necessary training. . . . You can be one of these . . . !

Picture this . . . ! Dr. Gary Collins and his staff . . . are there [in your home] with you via audiocassette. . . .[15]

A George Fox University ad is headlined "Our Psychology Doctorate Comes With Something Special. A Christian Worldview."[16] A Fuller Theological Seminary brochure boasts, "As a profession, Christian psychology isn't just new. It's Fuller. . . . Fuller's School of Psychology has it all . . . from an M.S. in Marital and Family Therapy to a Ph.D. in Clinical Psychology."[17] The following excerpt from a full-page advertisement by Wheaton College Graduate School in *Christianity Today* presents the same integrationist picture:

Symbols for a new century in Psychology—Psy.D. and M.A. in Clinical Psychology . . . commitment to Scripture and the integration of psychological theory with Christian faith. . . .

The Wheaton ad fails to explain why the *theories* of anti-Christians are being *integrated* into Christianity. Nor is it explained why such an incongruous mixture would be desirable. One is reminded of the closing lines of a poem:

Who would leave the fountainhead
To drink the muddy stream,
Where men have mixed what God has said
With every dreamer's dream!

The Seminal Influence of Norman Vincent Peale

It was Norman Vincent Peale, a 33rd-degree Mason who called the virgin birth of Christ "some theological idea,"[18] who pioneered the integration of theology and psychology which became "Christian" psychology.[19] In 1937, "Peale established a one-psychiatrist clinic at his church [which] grew to more than a score of doctors and ministers. . . ."[20] That became the inspiration for the thousands of similar clinics today.

Peale's chief disciple, Robert Schuller, became a major factor in bringing acceptability to this and many other of Peale's destructive beliefs among evangelicals. In reporting upon his attendance at the World Psychiatric Congress in Madrid in 1967, Schuller gave the impression that psychology and psychiatry were right in line with Christianity,[21] and he continued to promote that delusion in his many books and popular television ministry. On his October 5, 1997 "Hour of Power," Robert Schuller accepted the International Viktor Frankl Logotherapy Award. Logotherapy encourages the patient to recognize an existential meaning to his life on earth (with no regard for heaven or hell) involving "spiritual" values minus any "religious connotations" and based upon "the Good, the True, and the Beautiful"—but not God.[22] Logotherapy is humanistic and anti-Christian.[23] Yet in accepting the award, Schuller said it was "the greatest honor" and that "Viktor Frankl stands second only to Jesus Christ in teaching me. . . ."[24]

Today, most of the evangelical church follows Peale's example, and Schuller's "Hour of Power" has the largest audience of any televangelist each Sunday morning. The fact that Billy Graham has given his wholehearted endorsement of both Peale and Schuller has undoubtedly been a large factor in their growing influence. Those few pastors who still resist this occult invasion are looked down upon as lagging behind the times. In their book *The Integration of Psychology and Theology*, Christian psychologists John D. Carter and Bruce Narramore write:

> The typical conservative minister [is] 20 or 30 years behind his liberal colleague in being aware of the contributions of psychology to the understanding of personality.[25]

Peale was worse than a liberal. He openly acknowledged that many of his ideas came from two leading occultists, Religious Science founder Ernest Holmes[26] and Unity cult cofounder Charles Fillmore.[27] Two ministers (one a former Peale protege) have recently traced some of Peale's teachings to a further occult source, Florence Scovel Shinn.[28] After comparing Peale's books to hers, they—

> cite scores of specific instances in which Peale and Shinn not only think alike, but use similar or identical phrases. . . .

Shinn, who died in 1940, drew on mystical sources dating to the ancient Egyptian philosopher Hermes Trismegistus and the secrets of Freemasonry as delineated in The Kybalion. . . .

Shinn's . . . works, reissued by both Simon & Schuster and the Church of Religious Science, are available in New Age bookstores. Peale penned the introduction to the Simon & Schuster edition, indicating he had "long used" Shinn's teachings.[29]

The Impossible Profession

Christian psychologist James Dobson writes, "Christian psychology is a worthy profession for a young believer to pursue, *provided* his faith is strong enough to withstand the humanistic concepts to which he will be exposed. . . ."[30] Why must one be exposed to *humanistic concepts* in order to learn *Christian* psychology? Psychology was invented by humanists and cannot be separated from the humanism upon which it is founded.

On his nationwide radio program, Dobson and leading Christian psychologist Gary Collins (whom he was interviewing) agreed that psychology is founded upon the same five principles as humanism. They then went on to say that, of course, psychology (humanism) could be *integrated* with Christianity. One must ask why such a godless partnership!

In one of his books Gary Collins writes, "It is too early to answer decisively if psychology and Christianity can be integrated."[31] Since by his own admission it has not yet been integrated, the term *Christian psychology* was from the very beginning a misrepresentation foisted upon the church! Its influence, tragically, continues to grow. Upon visiting a Christian bookstore recently, one reporter made this comment:

> In the section devoted to the "Christian life," once the province of books on prayer and devotions, you can now find guides on how to stop worrying, overcome codependency, manage stress and live free of guilt.[32]

Again we ask, Why attempt to integrate theology with humanism? Can the wisdom of this world enhance Christianity? Is Christianity defective? And is psychology, invented by anti-Christians, what Christianity lacks? Was the church shortchanged for 1900 years? The very idea of *Christian* psychology is both illogical and unbiblical.

Yes, Christians can and do benefit from the wisdom of this world in some fields—physics, chemistry, medicine, and other secular disciplines—so why not from psychology? There are a number of reasons. To begin with, it would be ludicrous to speak of *Christian* physics or *Christian* chemistry because these vocations have nothing to do with Christianity. But psychology, unlike any other profession, claims to deal with the very matters which the Bible deals with: the soul and spiritual side of man. That claim is legitimate only if the Bible is insufficient.

Where Shall We Look for Counsel?

But don't we all need counsel? Indeed we do. The question is, What kind of counsel and from whom? Would one seek counsel concerning a heart ailment from an auto mechanic? Or investment counsel from a man who has gone bankrupt repeatedly? Or help in getting to heaven from a person who doesn't know the way and expects to go to hell? One should look for counsel to the best-qualified expert on the subject.

Man did not create himself nor can he understand himself. He certainly doesn't know what life is. How then can he understand the inner workings of his soul and spirit, his mind and emotions? Psychology is the study of the soul (psyche). But Jung admitted that "no one knows what the 'psyche' is." Only a fool, then, would accept Jung's psychological theories—yet they are followed by hundreds (if not thousands) of Christian psychologists.[33]

Psychology is man's futile attempt to understand himself, and to adjust his behavior. Christian psychology has brought this wisdom of the world, which is foolishness with God (1 Corinthians 1:20), into the church. It is offered as a supplement to Scripture.

Does the Scripture need such help, and would a partnership with humanism enhance biblical theology? If so, then we have an inadequate Bible. Of course the Bible is inadequate when it comes to space technology, engine repairs, kidney transplants, etc. It was not written about such matters. It would be folly to "go only by the Bible" in constructing a high-rise office building. But when it comes to the subjects it treats, the Bible is the highest authority. We don't need anything else.

The Bible is God's Word and is infallible. Therefore it does make good sense to "go only by the Bible" with regard to those matters in which the Bible instructs us. The Bible is concerned with the "things that pertain unto life and godliness," and it claims to have given us in Christ *all* that we need in that regard (2 Peter 1:3,4). The secret of the Christian life is "Christ in you" (Colossians 1:27). Surely Christ, "who is our life" (Colossians 3:4), needs no psychological counseling. We only need to obey Him and trust Him to live His life through us, and for this the Bible gives us full instructions.

God tells us, "The heart is deceitful above all things, and desperately wicked; who can know it? I the LORD search the heart" (Jeremiah 19:9,10). The wise man says with David:

> Search me, O God, and know my heart: try me and know my thoughts, and see if there be any wicked way in me, and lead me in the way everlasting (Psalm 139:23,24).

What could be better than for God to analyze our lives and motives and to guide us? One of the names of our Lord Jesus Christ is "Counselor" (Isaiah 9:6). Could we desire any better counsel than that which He provides in His Word and by His Holy Spirit? What an affront to our heavenly Counselor to look elsewhere for supplemental help!

Christian psychology claims to provide additional expertise which the Bible lacks. That claim contradicts the clear testimony of Scripture. The true church, without Christian psychology, withstood the Roman arena and the Inquisition and, by the blood of her martyrs, left the stamp of victorious Christian living upon the pages of history long before Freud or his "Christian" successors came upon the scene.

Is the Bible Sufficient?

The Bible *claims* to be sufficient for all our spiritual, emotional, and behavioral needs. God does not lie (Numbers 23:19). Were those whom God inspired to write the Bible limited by their own knowledge and therefore suffering from the lack of that deeper understanding of man which has lately been provided by Freud, Jung, Maslow, et al.? Blasphemy!

Psychotherapy consists of hundreds of conflicting and un-proved theories, so no one need be concerned about lacking its counterfeit wisdom. Furthermore, one of the great evidences that the Bible is God's Word is the fact that the times and cultures in which it was written had not the least influence upon it. The Bible is not limited by the wisdom or knowledge of those who were inspired to write it, but is the Word of God and is perfect.

Paul says that through Scripture alone the man or woman of God is made "perfect [mature, complete], throughly furnished unto *all* good works" (2 Timothy 3:17). For a person to live up to God's standards and to be all that God desires, all the coun-sel he needs is found in the Bible. Christian psychology, in ef-fect, says Paul was wrong and the Bible is insufficient. Clinical psychologist Bernie Zilbergeld writes:

> Those whose ancestors took comfort from the words of God and worshiped at the altars of Christ and Yahweh now take solace from and worship at the altars of Freud, Jung, Carl Rogers . . . and a host of similar authorities.[34]

Simple logic tells us that if Christian psychology has anything of value to offer, then the biblical claim of sufficiency is false; and in reliance upon the Bible alone the church has failed to meet the spiritual and emotional needs of Christians for the last 1900 years. Christian psychology claims that the Bible lacks insights which have lately been provided by atheistic humanists coming to the rescue.

The Bible has rightly been called "the Manufacturer's hand-book." God our Maker (Psalm 95:6; Proverbs 22:2; Isaiah 17:7; 45:11; 51:13; Hebrews 11:10; etc.) intended the creatures He made to continually consult that Handbook in confidence and to respond with obedience. Surely our Maker included in His operating manual every instruction needed for His creatures to function holily (Leviticus 11:44,45; 19:2; 1 Thessalonians 2:10; 1 Peter 1:16), happily (Job 5:17; Psalm 128:2; 144:15; 146:5; Proverbs 3:13,18; 14:21; 16:20; 28:14; 29:18; John 13:17; 1 Peter 3:14; 4:14), and fruitfully (Genesis 1:28; John 15:4,8; Colossians 1:10). Surely God has not overlooked any possible problem or malfunction which might befall us, nor has He failed to provide complete instructions and the appropriate remedy.

Suppose the descendants of Adam become angry, frustrated, fearful, anxious, insecure, or lonely. Suppose they feel misused and abused or useless and lacking in purpose or meaning. Let them turn for counsel and help to their Maker, who created them for His own good purpose and knows everything about them. Let them seek counsel from the Manufacturer's handbook, in which their Maker has provided complete operating instructions. Let them turn to Christ, who saves from the penalty and power of sin, who indwells and empowers and to whom the saints and martyrs throughout history turned and whom they always found sufficient. As David said, "What time I am afraid, I will trust in thee" (Psalm 56:3). What more do we need?

What Did God's People Do Before Psychology?

Until very recently the people of God looked to Him alone for their spiritual and emotional needs—and triumphed gloriously! Read again Hebrews 11. Mark the suffering and the triumph. None of these heroes and heroines of the faith had access to (or felt in the least the need of) any help from Steve Arterburn's New Life Clinics (previously Minirth-Meier New Life) or any other Christian psychology programs.

Consider the suffering Job endured without any therapy from a RaphaCare Program or one of the 17,500 members of the American Association of Christian Counselors. If Job didn't need such psychological counseling, then surely those who suffer far less today don't need this newly invented help either! Job teaches us that trials must be endured for our own good, to refine and mature us; and that God Himself will be with us and is all we need to carry us through.

Or consider Joseph. Misunderstood and criticized by his parents and hated by his brethren, who wanted to kill him, he was sold into Egypt. There he was falsely accused and wrongly imprisoned, to languish as a criminal. How could he have emotionally survived with no Christian psychologists or inner healers to provide the help that so many people now consider to be essential? A foolish question!

Consider what Paul endured: "In labors more abundant, in stripes [scourgings] above measure, in prisons more frequent, in deaths oft. Of the Jews five times received I [39] stripes. . . . Thrice was I beaten with rods, once was I stoned, thrice I suffered shipwreck, a night and a day have I been in the deep; in journeyings often, in perils of waters, in perils of robbers, in perils by mine own countrymen, in perils by the heathen, in perils in the city, in perils in the wilderness, in perils in the sea, in perils among false brethren; in weariness and painfulness . . . hunger and thirst, in fastings often, in cold and nakedness . . . [and] that which cometh upon me daily, the care of all the churches" (2 Corinthians 11:23-28).

Paul testified, "Nay, in all these things we are more than conquerors through him that loved us" (Romans 8:37). In spite of the grievous sufferings and trials he endured, Paul could exult, "Now thanks be unto God, which always causeth us to triumph in Christ" (2 Corinthians 2:14). He could write from prison to encourage others: "But my God shall supply all your need according to his riches in glory by Christ Jesus" (Philippians 4:19).

Tragically, the Bible is neglected by many Christians. Charismatics often seek experiences rather than sound biblical teaching, and evangelicals seek the superficial escape through therapy of trials that are intended to refine and strengthen them (1 Peter 1:7)—psychological counseling rather than the humility and repentance that comes from biblical counseling. As the Bobgans point out in a recent newsletter:

> Prior to the advent of psychoheresy in the church, preachers taught people about the powerful, sufficient grace of God during times of trial and affliction. But now many seem to assume that people are "hurting" and thus needing some kind of psychological wisdom and help.
>
> Rather than preaching the power of the Gospel both to save and to sanctify, they offer an insipid solution to the latest trend of psychological ills that surely must be debilitating the flock.[35]

This is a "*yes, but*" generation. Isn't the Bible God's inerrant Word? *Yes, but . . . for me it doesn't work.* Don't we have the Holy Spirit? *Yes, but. . . .* Hasn't Christ come to live in our hearts and won't He guide and empower us? *Yes, but. . . .* Was not the Word of God, the comfort and guidance of the Holy Spirit, and the indwelling Christ enough for suffering and martyred Christians during the first 19 centuries of the church? *Yes, but . . . the world is more complex today and we need additional help.* The heroes and heroines of the faith mentioned in Hebrews 11 triumphed amidst fierce persecution without psychology. *Yes, but . . . you don't understand my situation . . . my children, my husband, my wife, my boss, the abuse I suffered as a child. . . .*

Occultism and Selfism

By turning the focus inward, the Freudian/Jungian obsession with the unconscious spawned a menagerie of selfisms that invaded not only the world but the church: self-love, self-acceptance, self-improvement, self-worth, self-confidence, self-esteem, self-ad nauseam. Selfism is at the heart of the occult. Self is the sanctuary of human potential. It is self and pride that seeks psychic power. Jesus said a man must "deny himself" (Mark 8:34) and Paul denounced any confidence in self (Philippians 3:3-7). In contrast, Robert Schuller praises self:

> Self-love is a crowning sense of self-worth. It is an ennobling emotion of self-respect . . . an abiding faith in yourself. It is sincere belief in yourself.
> It comes through self-discovery, self-discipline, self-forgiveness and self-acceptance. It produces self-reliance, self-confidence and an inner security, calm as the night.[36]

Only 40 years ago, self-centeredness was considered a human failing, and an ugly one. Today self is the center of most psychotherapies, the god at whose altar one bows to beg favors. Rapha founder Robert McGee suggests that Christ's statement "*the truth shall make you free*" (John 8:32) includes "the application of truth in . . . our sense of self-worth."[37] He writes:

> Whether labeled "self-esteem" or "self-worth," the feeling of significance is crucial to man's emotional, spiritual, and social stability, and is the driving element within the human spirit.[38]

What a debt self owes psychology! Instead of being denied, self is now loved, esteemed, and promoted. We are being told repeatedly from pulpit, radio, television, books, magazines, and seminars that the greatest need facing the church is for

Christians to develop their self-love, self-esteem, self-worth, and positive self-image. James Dobson writes:

> In a real sense, the health of an entire society depends on the ease with which the individual members gain personal acceptance. *Thus, whenever the keys to self-esteem are seemingly out of reach for a large percentage of the people, as in twentieth-century America, then widespread "mental illness," neuroticism, hatred, alcoholism, drug abuse, violence, and social disorder will certainly occur* . . . (emphasis in original).[39]

It was in the Garden of Eden that self had its awful birth through heeding Satan. Self was born of the desire to be one of the gods. And the promotion of self within the church is part of the occult invasion.

A Flagrant Contradiction of Scripture

The self-esteem delusion has swept the church. Jerry Falwell's Liberty University promotes self-esteem. Robert Schuller has called self-esteem "the single greatest need facing the human race today.[40] Calling this lie from psychology the basis for a "new reformation," Schuller writes:

> Where the sixteenth-century Reformation returned our focus to sacred Scriptures as the only infallible rule for faith and practice, the new reformation will return our focus to the sacred right of every person to self-esteem.[41]

Such destructive folly comes from psychology and contradicts the Bible. We are exhorted, ". . . in lowliness of mind let each esteem other[s] better than themselves" (Philippians 2:3). Romans 12:3 warns us not to think of ourselves "more highly than [we] ought to think." Nowhere does the Bible warn us against thinking too poorly of ourselves. Samuel Yochelson, a psychiatrist, and Stanton Samenow, a clinical psychologist, spent six-and-a-half years investigating hundreds of hardened criminals and could not find even one who did not think highly of himself even when plotting a crime.[42]

No wonder the Bible frequently reminds us that we are sinners and unprofitable to God in and of ourselves. Yet Christian psychology is designed to help us escape such "negativity." We must always be "positive."

"As a man thinketh in his heart" is a misquotation of Scripture that is used by Christian psychologists to encourage positive self-talk and to teach an ancient occult belief: that we can make ourselves into whatever we desire by our thoughts. But the Bible doesn't say, "As a man thinketh in his heart, so he becomes." Solomon is warning his son that when he becomes king other rulers may invite him to a feast, but their pretence of friendship may not be sincere. Don't be deceived, for "As he thinketh in his heart, so is he: Eat and drink, saith he to thee; but his heart is not with thee" (Proverbs 23:7). It is a warning that a man's warm words may not reflect his true feelings.

The Truth About Self

When Christ said, "Love your neighbor as yourself," He wasn't telling us (as Christian psychologists insist) that we need therapy or seminars to teach us to love ourselves. If so, He would have been saying, "Love your neighbor as you inadequately love yourself," which makes no sense. Christians always believed (until the advent of psychology) that Christ was correcting our natural obsession with self. He was saying, "Give some of the love and attention and care to your neighbor that you give to yourself!" And we need that exhortation!

Today's new interpretation was given to the church by a godless psychologist named Erich Fromm, who called "belief in God . . . a childish illusion."[43] He claimed that when Christ said, "Love your neighbor as yourself," He meant that we had to learn to love ourselves before we could love our neighbors or God. That false view was promoted by Robert Schuller in his book *Self-Love, the Dynamic Force of Success;* and from there the lie spread throughout the church. The new men's movement, Promise Keepers, has been flagrantly promoting the lies of Christian psychology. A PK newsletter stated:

> Many Christian single men have fought the battle to build their own self-worth, self-esteem, and self-love . . . it is impossible to have a healthy relationship with others while having an unhealthy relationship with one's self. Jesus recognized this when He challenged us to love our neighbor as we would love ourself (Mark 12:31).[44]

Yes, some people say, "I hate myself!" How do we reconcile that statement with "No man ever yet hated his own flesh" (Ephesians 5:29)? What that person actually hates may be his appearance, clothes, job, salary, the way people look down upon him, etc. But he doesn't hate *himself*. If he did, he would be *glad* he was homely, had poor clothes, low income, and was abused by others. That he complains about these things proves that he loves himself, exactly as the Bible says.

It was surely not a "negative self-image" that was Lucifer's downfall, but a very "positive" one. More than 200 years ago, William Law expressed what Christians had always understood:

> Self-love, self-esteem, and self-seeking are the essence and the life of pride; and the Devil, the father of pride, is never absent from these passions, nor without an influence in them. . . .[45]

Unfortunately, the lies of psychology have infected not only Christian psychologists but many pastors and Christian authors. Josh McDowell, who has done so much good otherwise (his book *Evidence That Demands a Verdict* has blessed many), has devoted two books to building self-image, self-esteem, and self-worth: *Building Your Self-Image* (Tyndale, 1978) and *His Image, My Image* (Here's Life, 1984).

Biblical Examples Refuting the Lie

In *His Image,* Josh presents three psychological essentials for a well-integrated personality: 1) a sense of belonging (acceptance by others); 2) a sense of worthiness (feeling good about oneself); and 3) a sense of competence (confidence in oneself). In fact, most if not all of the heroes and heroines in the Bible lacked all that Josh says one needs.

Moses, for example, was rejected by his own people and considered himself to be both unworthy and incompetent (Exodus 3:11; 4:10-13). If there were ever a man with an abysmal self-image and self-esteem, it was Moses. But instead of prescribing months of Christian psychological counseling to raise his self-image, God said, "I will be with you!" In fact, God chose Moses *because he lacked self-esteem.* God chose the meekest man on earth (Numbers 12:3) to confront its mightiest emperor to deliver

His people from that tyrant's grip so that God alone would have all the glory.

Look at Paul. Hated by the Jews and rejected by most of the church ("no man stood with me"—2 Timothy 4:16; "all they . . . in Asia be turned away from me"—2 Timothy 1:15), he considered himself the chief of sinners (1 Timothy 1:15) and "less than the least of all saints" (Ephesians 3:8). Instead of building up Paul's self-image and self-esteem, Christ declared that His strength was made perfect in Paul's weakness (2 Corinthians 12:9). Try to reconcile Paul's "when I am weak, then am I strong" (verse 10) and "in me . . . dwelleth no good thing" (Romans 7:18) with psychology's three essentials!

Left Holding the Self-Esteem Bag

Christian psychology has promoted the lie that God loves us because of some value He sees in us; and even that Christ's death proves we are of infinite value to God. Bruce Narramore exults: "What a foundation for self-esteem . . . ! What a sense of worth and value this imparts. The Son of God considers us of such value that He gave His life for us."[46] How self-centered! The price He paid was because of our sin and the requirements of his justice. Nor is love based upon value. Spurgeon said it well:

> Jesus did not die for our righteousness, but he died for our sins. He did not come to save us because we were worth saving, but because we were utterly worthless, ruined, and undone.
>
> He did not come to earth out of any reason that was in us, but solely . . . because of reasons which He took from the depths of His own divine love. In due time He died for those whom He describes . . . as *ungodly*, applying to them as hopeless an adjective as He could. . . .[47]

Christian psychologists are left holding the self-esteem bag. Even youth are fed up with the phoniness. As one student put it, "Being praised for everything makes you feel worse. You ask yourself, if everything is getting praised, what is worth doing?" A *Washington Post* reporter wrote:

> You know those self-esteem champions . . . who preach children should be told over and over again how wonderful they are? Close

your eyes and imagine that you are perfect, goes one of their exercises. Write down five things that make you special, goes another.

Boost the self-esteem of a child, self-esteem proponents say, and you will see achievement soar. Teach self-esteem and youth won't be tempted to pop drugs or have babies. "Self-esteem can save lives" . . . [and] scientists have designed more than 200 measurements and made more than 10,000 studies in an attempt to prove this. The data, however, have not complied. . . .

But new voices are emerging, saying teaching self-esteem is a waste of time and resources, a dangerous distraction from truly significant tasks of building knowledge, skills and character. . . .[48]

"Welcome to California, the state of self-esteem." That was the title of a preposterous 1990 California Self-Esteem Task Force report asserting that "the lack of self-esteem is central to most personal and social ills plaguing our nation." However, after many years of study, California's Task Force failed to find evidence to support its claims. The Minneapolis *Star Tribune* documented that sex offenders who received the state's psychological treatment (much of it emphasizing the building up of self-esteem) were "more likely to commit new sex crimes than those who did not receive treatment."[49] Roy Baumeister, a professor of psychology at Case Western Reserve University who has spent decades studying the subject, says:

The [claims of the self-esteem movement] range from fantasy to hogwash. . . .[50]

It's alarming to think what will happen when this generation of schoolchildren grows up thinking they're smarter than the rest of the world. America will be a land of conceited fools.[51]

Numerous studies by secular psychologists and psychiatrists have demonstrated that the higher one's self-esteem, the more likely one is to be immoral, violent, and prone to trample on the rights of others. The self-esteem movement is being indicted with having caused much harm. *Newsweek's* cover announced its feature article in large letters: "THE CURSE OF SELF-ESTEEM: WHAT'S WRONG WITH THE FEEL GOOD MOVEMENT."[52] A feature story in newspapers across America by a professor/researcher was titled "Note to California: Drop self-esteem, self-control is most important. . . ." Based upon years of research, the author declares: "If we could cross out self-esteem and put in self-control, kids would be better off and society in general would be much better off."[53]

Yet the fallacious and destructive self-esteem theory continues to be the very bread and butter of Christian psychology. The Christian leaders who have promoted the self-esteem delusion owe the church an apology and ought to diligently pursue undoing the harm they have caused for years.

Heaven's joy fills repentant sinners. In contrast to Simon the Pharisee, who had plenty of self-esteem but gave Jesus neither water nor towel, a sinful woman washed His feet with her tears and dried them with her hair. Jesus used her example to show Simon that the love which will eternally radiate in heaven comes from the recognition of our unworthiness, a recognition which magnifies His love in saving us (Luke 7:36-50). The more we realize our guilt and wretchedness, the greater will be our gratitude and love to the One who stooped so low to rescue us.

Multiple Personality Disorder (MPD) in the Church

One of the latest delusions in the world which has invaded the church is called Multiple Personality Disorder (MPD), a recent "discovery." Christian psychologist James G. Friesen, a leader in this growing field, writes in a Here's Life Publishers book: "The incidence is turning out to be much higher than anyone expected. The number of MPD therapists is lagging far behind the growing demand. . . ."[54]

Friesen glibly tells us that the secret of dealing with MPD (of which the Bible says nothing) is the "perplexing" necessity of "uncovering . . . hidden memories." He admits that these alleged "memories" are "forgotten" and "usually are unbelievable":

> They are awful, painful, and even grotesque events that nobody wants to discover. "That didn't happen to me!" is a common response. . . . Friends and family can be in denial too. We all would like to believe those things didn't happen, but *maybe* they did.[55]

"*Maybe*" they happened? Common sense would give no credence to memories that didn't exist until therapy "uncovered" them and which seem unreal to the patient and involve unbelievable events which family and friends insist never happened!

Friesen goes on, "Distinguishing between [multiple] selves and demons is crucial. . . ." One wonders why Jesus never followed this procedure (nor did Paul) in casting out of many demons.

Friesen insists that demons "are not removable until those [hidden] memories are uncovered."[56] Yet Jesus never engaged in uncovering memories, nor did Paul when casting out demons. Friesen adds that exorcism must be "carried out by people with experience in both the Christian and the psychological arenas."[57] Yet Christ and His apostles were very successful at casting out demons 1900 years before psychology invaded the church! If Christian psychology is true, the Bible is not!

Some Christian psychologists labor to win each "multiple" to Christ. Friesen suggests that the therapist "teach the client to live life from the strong [multiple] selves, and reserve work with the injured selves to be carried out in therapy. . . . Get every self to work for the common good . . . having the adult selves stay in charge most of the time, while the child selves are safely kept away from the stresses of adult living."[58] It sounds more like the inmates running the asylum than a cure! One wonders why these vital instructions are missing from the "Manufacturer's Handbook" and why Paul would say, "I kept back nothing that was profitable unto you . . . I have not shunned to declare unto you all the counsel of God" (Acts 20:20,27) when he left out essential help for MPDs! Either Paul was wrong or Christian psychology is a fraud.

A Menagerie of Occultism

We dealt somewhat with hypnosis in the previous chapter. It has been part of the stock-in-trade of witch doctors for thousands of years. Michael Harner lists it as one of the major elements of shamanism being revived in Western society. Amazingly, hundreds of Christian psychologists use hypnosis.

An equally deadly form of shamanism now part of the occult invasion through "Christian" psychology is visualization. In fact, it is the most powerful occult technique known and is the method used by most shamans for acquiring spirit guides. Will Baron learned it in the New Age cult to which he belonged:

We finally imagined ourselves seated under a tree in a beautiful garden called the garden of the soul. These techniques were to balance the mind, body, and emotions and to open us to the higher self and receive communication from the masters.

After about five minutes of silent meditation, Muriel spoke again. "We invite the presence and the energy of our beloved master, Djwhal Khul. . . . Do not use your minds. . . . Listen to the voice of God."

After a time of silence, Muriel spoke again, "We are going to go around the light circle in sequence and channel Master Jesus."[59]

To Will's amazement, the members of the group began to receive transmissions from "Jesus." Of course, this was not the Jesus of the Bible. A spirit masquerading as Jesus appears to those who visualize him, whether Christians or New Agers.

Eastern mysticism and shamanism converge in visualization at the center of the occult world. This is the essence of all mysticism, whether practiced by yogis or Roman Catholic "saints." It is the heart of the spiritual exercises of Ignatius of Loyola, the founder of the Jesuits. Yet it is used by hundreds of Christian psychologists and even evangelical leaders. We have introduced it earlier and will deal with it in more depth in the next chapter.

Richard Foster advocates the visualization of Jesus, as do David Seamands, H. Norman Wright, and other Christian psychologists. Christians are badly deceived when they imagine that Christ will forsake the Father's right hand to appear to them when they visualize Him. Instead of admitting the occult practices within Christian psychology and warning his readers, Gary Collins debunks concerns:

> . . . many who fear the entrance of occult practices into psychology nevertheless draw invalid and illogical conclusions about current counseling practices. In their often sincere desires to purge occult influences from counseling, some writers have condemned visualization, self-talk, the healing of memories and other frequently used therapeutic methods.[60]

He goes on to say, "Visualization, imagination and guided imagery are related words that describe the use of mental pictures to bring increased understanding, relaxation or self-confidence."[61] Self-confidence is contrary to the Bible, but he promotes it as desirable. While agreeing "that some counselors misuse visualization and guided imagery," he never explains what might be wrong nor does he warn against the occult uses of visualization.

Recovering "Suppressed" Memories

A plague of false memories of alleged sexual abuse "revealed in therapy" is destroying literally thousands of families across the country, many of them Christian. This author received a call from a disturbed pastor. "I need some advice," he began. "A young woman in our church has been going to a respected Christian psychologist and has discovered that her father abused her sexually between the ages of two and five and even involved her in satanic rituals! And he's the head of our board of elders! What do we do?"

When asked how this "abuse" was discovered, the pastor replied: "The psychologist regressed her back into her childhood, and the memories surfaced. Of course, the father denies the accusation and the mother swears it never happened. Brothers and sisters, some older and some younger, also say it couldn't have happened. But these 'memories' are so real, she says we've got to do something."

Such cases, rare in the past, are now proliferating as increasing numbers of psychologists and psychiatrists regress patients into the past in search of abuse. Some therapists are convinced—and convincing a growing audience—that rare indeed is the person who has not been sexually (and probably satanically) abused. It has been estimated that if the stories being uncovered by therapists are indeed true, "as many as 50,000 human sacrifices are being carried out each year in the United States."[62] That is clearly preposterous. Yet on the basis of these false memories, many of them being uncovered by Christian psychologists, families are being destroyed and lives are being ruined.

The falsely accused, some of whom have been sent to prison, are beginning to strike back, suing the therapists involved. And the courts are hearing their cases, weighing the evidence and awarding large judgments. Washington State University professor Elizabeth Loftus, one of the foremost experts on memory, warns of the inaccuracy of memory in general, let alone those "recovered" under therapy. She tells, for example, of a rape victim who became hysterical when viewing the man she identified as the rapist. He was convicted on her testimony—but another man later confessed to the crime.

Moody magazine promoted this delusion in a cover story about a young woman who, through therapy, "uncovered memories" of alleged incidents of incest and satanic ritual abuse (SRA). She had previously had no such "memory"; it all came out in therapy. After two more years of therapy the patient began to manifest multiple personalities—again *created* in therapy. The article concluded that several more years of therapy would be required to "cure" the patient, and that it would be extremely dangerous to leave such persons to the usual Christian remedies of prayer, Bible study, and submission to the Lord.

We are not suggesting that sexual abuse never occurs; it is all too prevalent. However, "memories" allegedly restored through hypnotherapy are almost certain to be false. "What *really happened,* happened in therapy," says Sherrill Mulhern of the University of Paris, after an extensive study. As Columbia University psychiatrist Richard Gardner, author of *Sex Abuse Hysteria,* says, "It's unlikely that a patient *wouldn't* remember a traumatic event such as rape or forced intercourse. Amnesia is not a common thing in post-traumatic stress disorder. The opposite is the case: There's a preoccupation with the event."[63]

Fred and Florence Littauer's book *Freeing Your Mind from Memories That Bind* presents the thesis that uncovering hidden memories is the key to emotional and spiritual well-being. They suggest that if one has any "memory gaps" from childhood it indicates that he or she has probably been abused (and very likely, sexually).[64] By that definition we've all been abused. Such a theory is contrary to common sense and is without scientific verification or biblical support.

Why must one uncover memories (even if accurate) of past abuse suffered in order to have a right relationship with God? Where does the Bible suggest this? And if remembering the past is really the key, then we would have to uncover every detail. That task would be hopeless. Yet once the theory is accepted one can never be certain that some trauma is not still hidden in the unconscious, a trauma holding the key to emotional and spiritual well-being!

Paul, in contrast, *forgot* the past and pressed on toward the prize (Philippians 3:13,14) which is promised to all those who love Christ's appearing (2 Timothy 4:7,8). The past is of little consequence if Christians truly are new creations in Christ, for whom "old things are passed away [and] all things are become new" (2 Corinthians 5:17). Though searching the past in order to find an "explanation" for one's present behavior may seem to help for a time, it introduces uncertainty ("have I uncovered it all?") and robs one of the biblical solution through Christ. What matters is not the past but one's personal relationship to Christ right now.

The Littauers, like many Christian psychologists, rely heavily upon the so-called Four Temperaments. This long-discredited personality theory evolved from the ancient Greek belief that the physical realm was composed of four elements: earth, air, fire, and water. Empedocles related these to four pagan deities, while Hippocrates tied them to what were considered at that time to be the four bodily humors: blood (sanguine), phlegm (phlegmatic), yellow bile (choleric), and black bile (melancholy). These characteristics were further connected to the signs of the zodiac.

There is no scientific basis for Four Temperaments. Yet many Christian psychologists and lay "healers" make them the basis of "personality classification" and the key to behavioral insights. As the Bobgans point out in their excellent book *Four Temperaments, Astrology & Personality Testing:*

> The word temperament itself comes from the Latin word *temperamentum,* which meant "proper mixing." The idea was that if the bodily fluids were tempered . . . by balancing the humors with each other, then healing would occur. . . . Even the positions of various planets were thought to alter the fluids for better or worse. . . .
>
> The four temperaments had virtually been discarded after the Middle Ages . . . until a few lone souls . . . marketed them in twentieth-century language. . . . [They] have been enjoying a revival . . . among astrologers and evangelical Christians. . . . [65]

What Is Truth?

"All truth is God's truth." This is the major rationale given by Christian psychologists for integrating the theories of godless anti-Christians into Christian theology. They argue that Freud, et al. had some of God's truth and this is all that Christian psychology has borrowed from them. This thesis has deceived multitudes. Its validity depends upon two factors: 1) What is true in psychology? and 2) What is *God's truth?*

Psychologists can't agree among themselves. There are hundreds of conflicting theories and many opposing schools of psychology. Because it is not scientific, there is no objective standard by which to measure truth in psychology. But even if it were, science, no matter how well established, is not *God's truth.*

Many people have the mistaken notion that anything factual is *part* of God's truth. It logically follows, then, that the Bible does not contain all of God's truth. That idea, however, is contradicted by what the Bible says about truth.

Jesus said of Himself, "I am the truth." He doesn't say He is one truth among many truths, or part of the truth, but that He *is the truth.* That statement alone separates God's truth from science and from the theories of psychology.

Does God's truth exist outside the Bible? Not according to Jesus. He declared, "Thy [God's] word is truth." Not part of, but *truth.* He said, "If ye continue in my word ... ye shall know the truth, and the truth shall make you free" (John 8:31,32). Again not *part* of the truth, but *the truth. All* of God's truth is in His Word, and it sets free from sin.

Couldn't Freud and other secular psychologists have stumbled independently upon some of the truth that is in God's Word? God has written His law in every conscience (Romans 2:15), and thus to the extent they heeded their consciences they knew something of God's truth. But even if psychologists have some of God's truth, what is the point of dredging through the muck and mire of their false teachings for a truth which can be found clean, clear, and readily available in God's Word?

Jesus promised that after His ascension he would send to the disciples a Comforter, "even the Spirit of truth, whom the world cannot receive because it seeth him not neither knoweth him" (John 14:17). That eliminates Freud et al. And the Holy Spirit "leads into *all* truth" (John 16:13). Clearly, God's truth is revealed *only* in His word by His Spirit to His own.

Paul confirms this fact: "... the things of God knoweth no man but [by] the Spirit of God" (which eliminates all unsaved); "But the natural [unsaved] man receiveth not the things of the Spirit of God, for they are foolishness unto him" (1 Corinthians 2:11,14). Again, Freud and his followers don't qualify. Thus they could hardly be giving us some of God's truth.

Discerning the Truth

In spite of the clarity of what Jesus and Paul said, Christian psychologists and their defenders continue to justify integration. In the Christian Research Institute *Journal*, Bob and Gretchen Passantino attempted to show that any fact is part of God's truth. They said, "100 times 100 equals 10,000, and we can count on that as 'God's truth' because it corresponds to reality, including the laws of logic." On the contrary, it doesn't meet the biblical criteria for God's truth: of setting people free, being contained in God's Word, being revealed by the Spirit of truth, not known by the natural man, etc.

Jesus said to the Jews, "Because I tell you the truth you believe me not" (John 8:45). The Jews would have acknowledged that 100 times 100 equals 10,000—yet Christ said they would not believe *the truth*. Clearly, the Passantinos, in common with Christian psychologists whom they seek to justify, have a false view of God's truth. The Passantinos declared:

> The Biblical Counseling Movement (BCM) ... falls short of a comprehensive program [quite an indictment of the Bible!]. . . . Hunt and some other BCM advocates take 1 [sic] Peter 1:3 out of context. . . . The verse reads, "His divine power has given us everything we need for life and godliness . . ." [2 Peter 1:3]. Its context is salvation, not the details of daily human living.[66]

On the contrary, Peter is not telling us how to get saved but how we are to live as Christians. Surely "godliness" involves our behavior here on earth. The *context* deals with this life. Peter exhorts to diligence, virtue, knowledge, temperance, patience, godliness, and brotherly kindness, which are to characterize the very "daily human living" here on earth, which the Passantinos claim is not Peter's subject.

Inasmuch as all of God's truth is contained in God's Word, Christian psychology has nothing to offer and leads into gross error. Preventing God's people from believing in the sufficiency of Scripture is essential for Christian psychologists if they hope to remain in business.

Paul was very clear that what he preached was "not the wisdom of this world . . . [but] the wisdom of God" and that he carefully spoke "not in the words which man's wisdom teacheth, but which the Holy Ghost teacheth" (1 Corinthians 2:5-13). In contrast to Paul, the Passantinos (along with the entire Christian psychology movement) consider at least some of "the words which man's wisdom teacheth" to be an essential supplement to *the truth* of God's Word. We ought rather to believe God's promise that "love, joy, peace, longsuffering, gentleness, goodness, faith, meekness, temperance" are indeed the "fruit of the Spirit" (Galatians 5:22,23) and not at all the fruit of *therapy*.

Imagination—It is that deceitful part in man, that mistress of error and falsity . . . impressing the same character on the true and the false. I do not speak of fools, I speak of the wisest men; and it is among them that the imagination has the great gift of persuasion. Reason protests in vain. . . .

—Blaise Pascal[1]

We of the New Age can risk going against the tide. Let us with abandon relish the fantasy games of children. Let's see visions and dream dreams. Let's play, sing, laugh. The imagination can release a flood of creative ideas, and exercising our imagination can be lots of fun. Only those who are insecure about their own maturity will fear such a delightful form of celebration.

—Richard Foster[2]

The best way to interact with God and one another is to use your imagination. And music is very effective in opening up your imagination.

—Roman Catholic musician John Michael Talbot[3]

My warm friend Billy Graham dedicated Oral Roberts University before 18,000 people on April 2, 1967.

—Oral Roberts[4]

And you can perform miracles if you but understand the power of God and the laws . . . that unlock God's power . . . the basic principles that enable you to understand and experience the flow of God's energy.[5] In short, God uses the spoken word [spoken by us] to translate spiritual energy—sheer power—into the material. . . . We speak to money, and it comes. We speak to storms, and they cease . . . when you confess blessing . . . and success, those things will come to you.

—Pat Robertson[6]

On October 6, 1979 . . . CBN Center was dedicated. Billy Graham came to give the keynote address. And with him came . . . Bill Bright . . . Jim Bakker . . . Demos Shakarian . . . Rex Humbard, and many others.

—Pat Robertson[7]

Finally, the believer is called "Christ." . . . That's who we are; we're Christ! *(emphasis in original).*

—Kenneth Hagin[8]

23

* * *

Charismatic/
Evangelical Occultism

When His disciples asked Jesus what the signs would be of the nearness of His return and the end of the world, the first sign He gave them was *religious deception:* "Take heed that no man *deceive* you" (Matthew 24:4). His reply came as a *warning.* He went on to explain the nature of the deception, repeating this first and most important sign three times:

> For many shall come in my name, saying, I am Christ; and shall *deceive* many. . . . And many false prophets shall rise, and shall *deceive* many. . . . For there shall arise false Christs, and false prophets, and shall show great signs and wonders, insomuch that, if it were possible, they shall *deceive* the very elect. Behold, I have told [warned] you before (verses 5,11,24,25, emphasis added).

Obviously, Christ's warning is not about atheists or rank unbelievers or leaders of some opposing non-Christian religion. There is no deceit involved in such frontal assaults. Christ's warning is about a deception which is all the more subtle because it comes from within the church—and *in His name!*

Seduction from Within

Jude also warns about "certain men [who have] crept in unawares" (Jude 4). Crept in where? Obviously, into the church. That these are not Satanists or deliberate occultists who are insidiously at work in the church, but "Christian leaders," is clear from Christ's description:

Many will say to me in that day, Lord, Lord, have we not prophesied in thy name, and in thy name have cast out devils, and in thy
name done many wonderful works? (Matthew 7:22).

These enemies who oppose Christ *in His name* are clearly
occultists. Some power is at work that is not of God. Christ is
not describing mere trickery, though these men are not above
that. Their signs and wonders are so impressive that even the
elect are in danger of being deceived. Moreover, the "power"
convinces these false prophets themselves, for they ask, seemingly surprised, "Lord, have we not...?" It is the display of
such power that attracts revival seekers today.

The lust for health and wealth and especially godlike power
opens the door to occult bondage. This is a major problem in
the charismatic movement: A desire for power and at the same
time a denigration of biblical doctrine, with the resultant loss
of the very guidelines which would protect one from occult involvement. Benny Hinn admits that when he first saw the
power flowing through Kathryn Kuhlman he determined, "I've
got to have this...I want...it with every fiber of my being."[9]

Consider Benny Hinn on TBN (with Paul and Jan Crouch
laughing uproariously) telling with much merriment of a
man's wig flying off when he fell "under the power" after Hinn
touched his forehead. The man pulled the wig back on, a bit
askew, and got up; Hinn touched him again *just to see him fall
and the wig fly off.* He did this *five times,* admitted Hinn, laughing
impishly. Was this *God's* power on display, the Holy Spirit at
work? Surely not! Then what power caused the man to fall
repeatedly, this strange force that Hinn claims to have picked
up at the graves of Kathryn Kuhlman and Aimee Semple
McPherson? Such questions must be faced seriously!

A False "Signs and Wonders" Movement

Tragically, the Hinns, Hagins, Copelands, et al. convince themselves and others that the supposed miracles they perform are
proof that they belong to Christ. Will some of today's charismatic leaders be among those who will say, "Lord, Lord, did we
not..." and to whom the Lord will reply, "I never knew you;
depart from Me..." (Matthew 7:23)? If not, then who? Very

clearly, Christ is warning (as do other Scriptures) of a *false* "signs-and-wonders" movement in the last days. Paul was even more specific:

> This know also, that in the last days perilous times shall come. For men shall be . . . ever learning, and never able to come to the knowledge of the truth. Now as Jannes and Jambres withstood Moses, so do these also resist the truth: men of corrupt minds, reprobate concerning the faith (2 Timothy 3:1,7,8).

Jannes and Jambres were occultists—magicians in Pharaoh's court. By the power of Satan, they duplicated some of the miracles that God performed through Moses and Aaron. Paul declares that resistance to the truth in the last days will come from those who produce by the power of Satan what seem to be miracles of God and thereby pervert the faith.

Many false prophets will arise and will deceive *many.* Christ is not describing something small. The false revival will be worldwide. In fact, such a movement is here and it is growing with the support of those who ought to know better.

Bill Bright speaks and writes with enthusiasm that we are about to experience the "greatest revival in the history of the church."[10] Pat Robertson agrees, referring to "the most extraordinary time of revival mankind has ever known."[11] Others describe it similarly. Unfortunately, what they praise is characterized by a neglect of sound doctrine and tolerance for false prophets. Such gullibility and the rejection of biblical guidance open the door to the occult.

False Prophecies by the Dozen

Satan's power is limited. Jannes and Jambres could duplicate God's miracles only to a point. When Satan's power fails, the false prophet is left to his own foolish devices. Yet even when these impostors make the most obvious blunders, their gullible supporters continue to honor and follow them.

Each month millions of letters go out to those on the mailing lists of numerous ministries. Many of them are computer-generated with the recipient's name inserted at several strategic places to personalize the letter. Our files contain countless letters from televangelists. Many have told how the writer was up much of the night praying for the addressee; or the writer has received a special word from the Lord just for him, etc. Such claims are beyond belief except to the most gullible. It is humanly impossible for any person to pray individually for the many thousands of people on a televangelist's mailing list, let alone to keep track of individual needs and requests and receive individual prophecies for each one.

In one letter mailed to supporters, Oral Roberts declared, ". . . the gift of prophecy came on me . . . and 33 predictions were given me concerning you [here the person's name has been inserted by the computer]."[12] False prophets count on the gullibility of their followers. Doubtless many of those receiving this letter were flattered that a "man of God" had received 33 prophecies specifically for them—not knowing that the identical letter went to hundreds of thousands.

Is Oral deliberately deceiving his followers in order to receive a "seed-faith" offering from them, or is he truly deluded into thinking he is getting revelations from God? The *News-Sentinel* of Knoxville, Tennessee, published this letter to the editor:

> Upon the urging of my terminally ill wife I poured hundreds of dollars into the Oral Roberts Empire. She was brainwashed into the belief that he and God would restore her. . . .
>
> Approximately one year after her death, she received a letter over the signature of Oral Roberts in which he claimed that he had a talk with God the previous night who had assured him that my wife would be made whole. . . .
>
> This so much incensed me that I turned the letter over and replied in substance that he was a liar; that God never told him any such thing; that God knew she had been in heaven for about a year. . . . I received no reply.
>
> When are we gullible people going to stop channeling monies to these (whatever); providing them Cadillacs . . . etc.?[13]

In Johannesburg, South Africa, early in 1996, a man collapsed to the floor during a Benny Hinn revival and was carried out. Benny assured the audience that the Lord had told him the man would be all right. In fact, he died in the ambulance on the way to the hospital. In the 1989 New Year's Eve service at his church in Orlando, Florida, Benny made a number of false prophecies. Here is just one: "The Lord also tells me to tell you . . . about '94 or '95, *no later than that,* God will destroy the homosexual community of America . . . He will destroy it with fire."[14] It didn't happen. Yet Hinn's following grows larger.

Kenneth Copeland has likewise given numerous false prophecies, many so outrageous that only the heavily deluded could have taken them seriously. Again, only one example:

> As you move into the month of January [1976] you shall see more of the outpouring of God's glory than you've ever seen in the history of this world . . . limbs that have been amputated put back on by the power of God . . . eyeballs replaced where there were no eyeballs . . . God will cause your automobile, that you are driving and getting 10 miles to the gallon, to get 70 miles to the gallon—the same old car![15]

None of it happened. Israel was instructed to stone such false prophets, but today's Christian leaders heap honor on them, and their followers eagerly anticipate the next "word from the Lord." Pastor John Hinkle (unheard of until then) said on TBN in 1993 that God had told him, "On Thursday, June 9 [1994], I will rip the evil out of this world." Evil is not a *thing* that can be "ripped out of the earth"; it resides in the human heart. Jesus said, "For out of the heart proceed evil thoughts, murders, adulteries," etc. (Matthew 15:19). Antichrist, the very embodiment of evil (2 Thessalonians 2:4-10), is yet to come, and his reign by the power of Satan (Revelation 13:2,4) will unleash the culmination of all that is evil in unfettered fury upon this earth.

In complete disregard of the Scriptures and common sense, Hinkle's prophecy was greeted with applause by the studio audience and promoted enthusiastically on TV by Paul Crouch, and later by Pat Robertson as well. Crouch also backed this ludicrous prophecy to the hilt in at least three newsletters. Youth With A Mission (YWAM) "prophets" allegedly verified it. June 9, 1994, came and went and evil flourished unabated on the earth. Undaunted, Crouch claimed the prophecy had been fulfilled—and he is still on the air!

Charismatics' desire to receive extrabiblical revelations opens the door to the occult. Pat Robertson had a "word from the Lord" that he was to run for President of the United States in 1988. When questioned about this "revelation," here was his shocking response:

> Bob Slosser: "If God called you to run, then why did you fail to get the Republican presidential nomination?"
>
> Pat Robertson: "I suppose we could ask the same question of Jesus. God sent Him to be the Messiah of Israel and King of Israel; why did He fail the first time around and get crucified?"[16]

Deceiving and Being Deceived

When we name those who have led or are leading the church into occultism, we are not suggesting that this is necessarily deliberate on their part. Few people, even atheists, intentionally go into the occult. Even Luke Skywalker, in the *Star Wars* film series, didn't intend to be involved in something evil. He thought that he was using the "light side" of the Force. But he was drawing guidance and power not from the true God who created this universe but from a "force" which could only be a front for Satan.

For three years Paul warned the Ephesian elders night and day with tears that even some of them would speak "perverse things to draw away disciples after them" (Acts 20:28-31). The charismatic movement in particular follows after men and women who speak perverse things and promise signs and wonders, among them Kenneth Hagin, Kenneth and Gloria Copeland, Marilyn Hickey, Frederick K.C. Price, Oral Roberts, Pat Robertson, Benny Hinn, Yonggi Cho, and others.

The above-named individuals may sincerely believe they are serving Christ, but they have perverted the Scriptures. The power of the Holy Spirit is emphasized and sought with little regard to the fact that He is the *Holy* Spirit and the Spirit of *truth*. But the occult power manifest through false prophets causes their followers to overlook all else.

The Power of Imagination

The key element in occultism is imagination. This amazing capability which God has given man can be used for good or evil. Unhappily, the heart of man being the slave of evil because of his rebellion against God, his imagination most often carries him in the direction dictated by his selfish ambitions. God's pronouncement is unequivocal:

> And God saw that the wickedness of man was great in the earth, and that *every imagination* of the thoughts of his heart was *only evil continually* (Genesis 6:5, emphasis added).
>
> . . . for the imagination of man's heart is *evil from his youth* . . . (Genesis 8:21, emphasis added).
>
> This *evil people,* which refuse to hear my words, which *walk in the imagination of their heart* . . . (Jeremiah 13:10, emphasis added).

Any mother or father knows that no child has to be taught to be selfish or envious or unkind. These natural traits manifest themselves before the child is out of diapers and long before society has had any influence upon him. The restraint of discipline in the home (little known these days), the restraint of the conscience which God has placed within us all, the restraint of knowing that others would disapprove, and the restraint of teachers, friends, and government all work to keep outward evil somewhat in check.

There is no restraint, however, upon imagination except conscience. There self reigns and fantasies may be enjoyed that one would be ashamed of in the real world. In the imagination one can indulge the basest passions—and the world of the occult can be easily entered.

Television was a quantum leap beyond radio in assisting the imagination of man to visualize the desires of his heart. Through television a flood of lust and evil beyond the conception of past generations has been poured into homes around the world. Yes, there are some good and worthwhile programs, but they are overwhelmed by a flood of evil. Video games were another quantum leap. Youth easily become completely absorbed hour after hour in fighting, killing, facing demons, and using occult powers. The imagination has been opened to the occult. Eventually the video and real worlds merge into one.

And now the new technology of virtual reality is upon us and it will take the imagination another quantum leap, making it possible to engage "legitimately" in evil of all kinds in what will indeed seem to be the real world. One will be able to enjoy a realistic vacation without leaving home, or make love to a beautiful woman (or handsome man) without the restraint of conscience or law, for it will only be fantasy, not *really* real, just *virtual* reality. All of this, however, is the subject for a different book.

The imagination may not be used for contact with God, as Calvin Miller,[17] Richard Foster and others are now teaching. It is instead the doorway to the occult. The imagination makes hypnosis possible and establishes the false memories which are destroying so many lives. Somehow imagination is the vehicle used by apparitions, and it opens the door to unlimited additional delusions, some of which are rampant in the charismatic movement through the emotionalism which characterizes so much of the eager seeking for signs and wonders.

A famous case revealing the power of imagination to open the door to the occult was the Philip Experiment. It has been duplicated a number of times around the world. Members of the Canadian Toronto Society of Psychical Research made up a history of a "ghost" they named Philip. They then tried to believe that "Philip" was real and sought to contact him. An entity identifying itself as Philip communicated through rappings emanating from the table around which they sat. It corrected the history they had invented, and levitated the table so forcefully that they could not hold it down and had to run around the room to keep up with it.[18]

Never do we find in the Bible that God uses the imagination of man for His purposes, but only that man is led astray by his imagination and that it caters to his lusts. False prophets imagine God is speaking to them, when it is the deceit of their own hearts saying what they want to hear.

"Prophets" with Undeserved Honor

Today's false prophets boast of their power and use it to threaten those who would reprove them with God's Word. To escape correction, they warn critics, "Touch not the Lord's anointed," and threaten that those who question them will suffer God's judgment. With Paul Crouch backing him, Benny Hinn threatened on TBN that if critics dared to "touch the Lord's anointed" (meaning him), their children would die.[19] In one of the many visions of Jesus which Kenneth Hagin says he has received, he was told ("The Lord said to me") that there would be ministers who rejected him as a prophet who, as a result, would "fall dead in the pulpit."[20] They should have been falling like flies, for there are thousands of ministers who have rejected Hagin's message.

This perverted interpretation of Scripture is widely used to defend charismatic leaders from the correction they desperately need. The phrase is first found in Scripture when Saul had been twice in David's hands and his men urged him to kill Saul. David refused, saying, "I will not put forth mine hand against... the LORD's anointed" (1 Samuel 24:10; see also 26:9,16; 2 Samuel 1:14-16; Psalm 105:15).

"Touching the Lord's anointed" always means to harm *physically* or even to kill. David would not do that—but he rebuked Saul publicly before his own men and Saul's army (1 Samuel 24:9-15), and Saul repented (verses 16-21). One may not use this phrase to guarantee immunity from criticism to church leaders.

This author watched in astonishment as Paul Crouch lashed out for about ten minutes on international television against his favorite target, "heresy hunters." He called them a "rotten sanhedrin crowd... damned and on their way to hell... [no] redemption for them.... To hell with you.... God's going to shoot you if I don't!"[21] Similarly, in a Sunday morning service, John Kilpatrick, Brownsville Assembly of God pastor, declared:

> I want to say something this morning to Hank Hanegraaff... you may criticize other people and other moves of God and other ministries, but you'd better leave your hands off of this one....
>
> I'm going to prophesy to you that if you don't... within 90 days the Holy Ghost will bring you down. I said, within 90 days the Holy Ghost will bring you down, and I speak that as a man of God... this is a move of God and you better leave it alone....
>
> Mr. Hanegraaff and all other devils, listen up.... I'm saying this as a man of God from behind this holy desk in this holy environment of a great outpouring of the Holy Ghost... this revival shall not diminish and this revival shall turn into a national awakening.[22]

Several weeks before the prophesied 90 days would have expired (July 5, 1997), pastor Kilpatrick issued an apology to Hank on the internet. He said he had been in the flesh when he had pronounced that judgment. Try to imagine Isaiah or

Jeremiah saying, "Sorry, but I was in the flesh when I wrote chapters 3, 11, and 24, so disregard them."

Today's avowed revival is led by false prophets who dare to say that it is legitimate for prophets *in training* to make mistakes. But according to the Scriptures, if someone says "Thus saith the Lord" and is wrong, that is no mere mistake to apologize for; that is blasphemy! John Wimber, until his recent death, taught how to do signs and wonders and how to prophesy, and charged a stiff fee for attendance at such seminars. And some of the techniques the Vineyards still use, such as moving one's hands slowly back and forth a few inches from a subject's body to feel for hot spots to see where God is at work, or letting one's mind go blank and speaking forth whatever thoughts come, open the door to the occult. Biblical prophets never *learned techniques.*

Pat Robertson and CBN

Pat Robertson is both a Southern Baptist and a leading charismatic. His biographer says, "While Southern Baptists do not openly endorse 'charismatics,' they have not shunned Robertson. In fact, Adrian Rogers, president of the Southern Baptist Convention, was the featured speaker at CBN's 25th anniversary."[23] Pat began the network with 70 dollars. He tells of the miracles God did to create a Christian TV empire, including the Family Channel network, with funds provided by tens of thousands of Christian donors.

One wonders how it was that Pat and his family ended up owning controlling interests in the Family network and selling it in 1997 for 1.9 billion dollars to Ruppert Murdoch's Fox network. Did Christians give their money to make Pat's family wealthy, and so that a TV network acquired for spreading the gospel would eventually fall into godless hands?[24] All of the "miracles" Pat tells about concerning CBN's great success story now have a hollow ring.

Much of Pat's dream for CBN came out of a false prophecy going all the way back to May 1968. Pat tells the story:

> It was dedication week of our new Portsmouth facility. . . . I'd just given a short talk on the bright future ahead of us at CBN, when all at once Harald Bredesen, our long-time Christian

friend, came forward, placed his hand on my head, and began to speak a word of prophecy so powerful, I will never forget it as long as I live. For I knew God Himself was speaking to us that very moment:

> The days of your beginning seem small in your eyes in light of where I have taken you . . . but these days shall seem small in light of where I am going to take you . . . for I have chosen you to usher in the coming of My Son.

Electric excitement shot through the assembly! Applause burst forth from every corner of the room. I was absolutely awestruck. God had assigned to CBN, in these last days, a ministry of John the Baptist—to prepare the way for Jesus' second coming![25]

This preposterous prophecy also plays a part in Pat's view of the kingdom and the last days, to which we will refer in a later chapter. The prophecy, of course, was used for fundraising, with phrases such as "The time had arrived to usher in the second coming of Jesus! And I'd like to invite you now to be part of the greatest spiritual breakthrough the world has ever known, through your faith-stretching gift today. And I'm asking you to give today as you've never given before, to prepare the way of the Lord Jesus Christ." Who could refuse such an appeal? The gift response sheet was headlined in large, bold letters "USHER IN THE COMING OF THE LORD" and said in part:

> Jesus is coming back . . . and it may be sooner than we think! And today I'm urging you to help usher in the coming of the Lord. Please respond immediately by sending your gift with your reply card today.
>
> Yes, Pat! I want to help usher in the coming of Jesus by preparing Israel and the world for Christ's return to earth! [Note, this is not the rapture.][26]

Nearly 30 years later we ask sincerely what CBN has done to create "the greatest spiritual breakthrough the world has ever known," and to "usher in the coming of the Lord"? In addition to false prophecy, there has been other occultism, though no doubt unwitting, from the very beginning. Robertson describes the new Portsmouth studios that were dedicated on May 3, 1968:

> The beautiful prayer chapel was dedicated to the memory of my mother . . . [and] was alive with symbolic meaning. Everything in

the room forced attention heavenward. A hand-carved cross was suspended in the middle of the room over an uncut boulder of white crystal rock.[27]

Crystals are used in the New Age as a focus of the universal "force." Stones have been used in pagan worship from time immemorial. Why would Christians gather around a stone for prayer? And how can an "uncut boulder" turn one's "attention heavenward"? Pat has some further explaining to do.

Charismatic Christian Science

Furthermore, Pat's book *The Secret Kingdom,* in which he reveals the secrets of success that built CBN, reads like an occult manual. While it contains many inspiring stories of miracles God did in people's lives and of many who came to Christ, there are serious problems. We have noted that the occult is built upon laws governing powers allegedly innate within the universe which even the spirit world must obey. The same lie deludes charismatic leaders and their followers.

Kenneth Hagin talks about God's "law of faith."[28] Yonggi Cho teaches the same, admitting that the "Laws of the Fourth Dimension" will work miracles for occultists as well as for Christians. In fact, he faults the Christians for not using these laws for success, while the occultists have been doing so.[29] Pat tells us the eight "laws of the kingdom." As with Cho, Hagin, and others, Robertson sees these laws as applying to anyone, even the ungodly. We are back to Christian Science and its occult connection! Pat explains:

> I began to realize there are principles in the kingdom . . . as valid for our lives as the laws of thermodynamics or the law of gravity. . . .
>
> Once we perceive this secret, we realize anew that the Bible is not an impractical book of theology, but rather a practical book of life containing a system of thought and conduct that will guarantee success. . . . He said in effect, "Seek the kingdom, understand the way it works, and then, as day follows night . . . the evidences of earthly success will follow you. . . ."
>
> These were principles so universal they might better be considered as laws, in the same sense as the natural laws established by God. . . . Jesus . . . said bluntly, "If you do these things, this is what will happen." If applied, the principles would *simply work.* . . .

Unfortunately, such people as Napoleon Hill, who wrote *Think and Grow Rich,* have gleaned only a few of the truths of the kingdom of God. . . . Some of the metaphysical principles of the kingdom, taken by themselves, can produce fantastic temporal benefits. . . .[30]

So God's kingdom runs on metaphysical principles that Napoleon Hill used and will work for anyone! The Bible isn't about *theology* (the knowledge of God), which is impractical, but it is about principles and laws that work for and will bring *earthly success* to anyone! The occult formula works!

The Bible makes it clear that one does not get an automatic response from God in this manner; but Satan will oblige. Yes, Pat talks at times about knowing and submitting to God's will. Yet he says these *metaphysical* principles and laws work even for a Napoleon Hill, who doesn't know God.

According to Pat, one of the eight laws ruling the secret kingdom is "The Law of Miracles." On the one hand he admits that a miracle represents a "contravention of the natural laws" by God.[31] Yet he claims there is another law, the Law of Miracles, that God cannot override but must obey in order for a miracle to occur. He says that the power of God is at our disposal "if we know the *rules of miracles.*"[32] Says Pat, "The magnificent [CBN] center standing on that property today is eloquent testimony to the power of God and the operation of the Law of Miracles."[33]

Oral Roberts and the City of Faith

Pat Robertson claimed that God had chosen him to usher in the coming of His Son and thereby persuaded his supporters to send in money to finance that incredible project. Oral Roberts claimed that Jesus appeared to him and told him God had chosen him to find the cure for cancer. This "revelation" came during a "seven-hour-long conversation" between Jesus and himself with "a 900-foot-tall Jesus . . . who told him [Oral] to ask his hundreds of thousands of 'prayer partners' to send in $240 each to complete the [medical] center [a 60-story diagnostic clinic and 30-story hospital] so researchers there can find cures for cancer and 'other dread diseases.' "[34] Oral's "prayer partners" funded the more than 200-million-dollar project.

That this was a false vision and prophecy is now history. There were no miracles, no cure for cancer, and the hospital that "Jesus" told him to build soon went bankrupt. In his autobiography, *Expect a Miracle: My Life and Ministry*, Oral tries to make it appear that this was exactly what God had planned and there was no failure at all: "It was God's time to close the City of Faith and medical and dental schools."[35] The media, however, unlike Roberts' followers, were not deceived:

> Oral Roberts' dream of a hospital combining religious faith and medical technology is coming to an end. The evangelist, sued over past-due bills, is selling his City of Faith medical complex, which he said God told him to build. He began shutting down the complex—three towering buildings . . . in 1989. . . .
> The 777-bed hospital, opened in 1981, reached a peak of only 148 patients in 1984.[36]

Was Oral hallucinating, or lying, about this 900-foot-tall Jesus and the seven hour conversation? It is certain that Jesus did not appear to Oral and tell him to build a hospital that wasn't needed and promise miracles that never came to pass! Yet Oral is still highly regarded by millions, including many church leaders, especially among charismatics. In 1989 he was named "Christian Leader of the Year by the International Christian Business Leaders organization."[37]

The secrets of success which Napoleon Hill received from the spirit world have been embraced by the charismatic movement and much of the evangelical church as well. The "Supreme Secret" given to Hill by demonic entities was that "anything the human mind can believe, the human mind can achieve."[38] Oral Roberts claims that God revealed basically the same principle to him: "Whatever you can conceive and believe, you can do!"[39]

Roberts, like other charismatic leaders, is clearly referring to what Hill called "The Magic Power of Belief."[40] Norman Vincent Peale called it the Power of Positive Thinking and Robert Schuller calls it the power of Possibility Thinking.

Oral Roberts claims to have discovered that the sick were healed when he touched them with his right hand, not with his left. Again this is occultism—and few, if any, were actually healed. Nowhere in the Bible can this "sign" be found, but it has occurred among a number of occultists and false prophets, such as William Branham, who himself was never sure whether it was God or Satan who gave him his power, but "felt God" in his left hand.[41] Said Roberts:

> I was hearing God say to me that henceforth I would experience His presence in my right hand. . . . For sure, God's presence coming in my right hand was a sign to great numbers of sick people that there is a God and it is His nature to heal.
>
> When it came, it was unmistakable. I mean, it was there! When it was not there, I was so ordinary, everyone knew it was not there.[42]

Money, Money, Who's Got the Money?

Money is a major focus in the occult. Kenneth Copeland unashamedly declares that God called him to preach the unbiblical "gospel of prosperity." Marilyn Hickey, author of *God's Seven Keys to Make You Rich,* is chairman of the board of regents of Oral Roberts University. In the *Miracle of Seed Faith,* Oral claims God revealed to him that the great principle of sowing and reaping so evident in the physical world also held true in the spiritual realm. One could "plant" a monetary gift in a ministry and "reap" miracles. In response to this claim, hundreds of millions of dollars from sincere but deceived Christians have poured into the ministries of numerous "faith teachers," making the latter wealthy. Simple souls have been enticed by the promise of a "hundredfold return" on their gifts.

This false teaching panders to a desire for riches, one of the basest human lusts. "Jesus was rich," say Frederick Price and other "faith teachers,"[43] and therefore His followers must be rich. Kenneth Hagin says that to drive an old car instead of a new Cadillac isn't "being humble, that's being ignorant [of God's laws of prosperity]."[44] Frederick Price agrees: "I drive a Rolls Royce . . . following Jesus' steps."[45] Gloria Copeland writes, "You give [us] . . . $1,000 and receive $100,000. . . . Mark 10:30 is a very good deal."[46] Oral Roberts promises "PROSPERITY MIRACLES" for those who "take advantage of the hundredfold return. . . ." How does this differ from Catholicism's sale of indulgences? Each is simply a different form of running "greedily after the error of Balaam for reward" (Jude 11). How does Pat Robertson's statement that when you "confess blessing . . . and success, those things will come to you"[47] differ from John Marks Templeton's statement that "your spiritual principles attract prosperity to you... material success... comes... from being in tune with the infinite..."?[48]

Gloria Copeland tells how she learned to take authority over money and command it to come to her "in Jesus' Name."[49] In the quote at the beginning of the chapter Robertson says the same. Yes, Pat does say that prayer "does not consist merely of asking for what we want. To pray in the truest sense means to put our lives into total conformity with what God desires." And he points to Jeremiah's warning against "those prophets who were speaking visions of their own imaginations...."[50] Such cautions, however, are like isolated contradictory parentheses in a book that overwhelmingly emphasizes how to wield power through automatic "principles" available to anyone.

Patti Roberts, divorced first wife of Richard Roberts, tells how, as they were leaving for their honeymoon, Oral took her and Richard into his study. He warned them that if they ever left Oral's ministry they would be "killed in a plane crash."[51] She tells of growing disillusionment, which led to clashes with Oral. It seemed to her that "all of our efforts revolved around fund-raising... sophisticated techniques to sell Jesus... so more people would... support" the ministry.

The disillusionment reached a crisis when Patti called Al Bush, longtime president of Oral Roberts Evangelical Association. The conversation as she recalls it went like this:

> Al, in the forty shows that we taped last year, how many times did we give people the plan of salvation?
>
> The plan of salvation? Gosh, Patti, I don't know. I'm sure we must have given it to them at least once.
>
> And how many times did we give them the principles of Seed-Faith?
>
> He laughed. Patti, you know the answer to that. We give the principles of Seed-Faith on every show. What's this all about?
>
> Al, in the letters that you received from viewers, how many of them thought that maybe if they gave money to Oral, they had bought a little place in the Kingdom? How many may have thought that swayed God's opinion about their eternal destiny?

He didn't answer for a long time. When he finally replied he lowered his voice and said soberly and a bit hesitantly, A whole lot of them did, Patti.[52]

Occult Money-Raising Schemes

Oral Roberts is continually dreaming up new schemes for raising money from his prayer partners, many of whom live on low incomes and sacrifice to support his lavish lifestyle. In one appeal, Oral asked "more than a million regular contributors for $500 each to stop a 'satanic conspiracy. . . .' 'I am unable to tell you . . . this problem on television because of the enemies of this ministry,' a fund-raising letter said."[53]

Some of Oral's ingenious money-raising gimmicks involve outright occultism. For example, he mailed two tiny "miracle candles," one red and one green, to his "prayer partners" to be used in a "miracle candlelight service." The instructions provided along with the candles read in part:

> Your miracle candlelight service is set for December 24th. Return the red candle to me today. Keep the green candle and light it on December 24th, as we agree for your miracle.
>
> I believe that God has a Christmas miracle in store for you!
>
> As I wrote those words, "GOD HAS A CHRISTMAS MIRACLE IN STORE FOR YOU," what a tremendous outburst of the Holy Spirit came through me for you. I do believe that you are on the eve of a truly great Christmas miracle . . . !
>
> I truly believe that the Holy Spirit is leading me to take some very specific steps for you, and that is why I have sent you two miracle Christmas candles. . . .
>
> What I feel the Lord is asking me to do . . . could bring a priceless miracle from God for you. He has asked me to light a candle and ignite my faith for your miracle needs. AND I'M GOING TO DO IT IN JESUS' NAME.
>
> In fact, I have asked Richard to join me in this . . . as we together conduct a private personal Miracle Candlelight Service for you and your miracle needs. Together, we are going to light a candle (as our miracle point of contact with you) and release our faith for your Christmas miracle.[54] (Emphasis in original.)

What blasphemy to claim God's leading for their occult charade! The red candle was to be returned to Oral and the green candle was to be kept for lighting on Christmas Eve, when Oral and his son Richard would light the red ones they had received. Of course, there was the inevitable plea for money, presented as though it were the secret to miracles:

> When you send your Candlelight Miracle Request Sheet and the red candle to me, INCLUDE A MIRACLE SEED OF FAITH— a Christmas gift to God's work... for your miracle Christmas need....
>
> I count it a personal privilege to minister to you and light a candle of miracle faith (as our point of contact together for your needs to be met)....
>
> Now... RUSH me your Candlelight Miracle Request Sheet— along with the red miracle candle AND THE BEST CHRISTMAS GIFT OF FAITH THAT YOU POSSIBLY CAN GIVE RIGHT NOW. I cannot think of a better way to celebrate this Christmas.
>
> [Person's name]—I am really speaking from my heart when I tell you that I don't want you to miss out on this miracle day! Words fail to adequately describe just how strongly I sense the presence of God in this....
>
> [Person's name], let me remind you again to act immediately. When we begin to light the red miracle candles on December 24th—I WANT YOURS TO BE THERE—AND I WANT YOU TO RECEIVE YOUR CHRISTMAS MIRACLE (emphasis in original).[55]

Does he have no conscience? This is pure witchcraft. Included in the envelope was a large poster showing Oral and Richard lighting red candles, Oral holding a bundle of "Miracle Request Sheets" in his hands, and Richard with hands extended over stacks of such sheets, both men showing expressions of great concern and earnest zeal.

The Point of Contact

Man has always found it helpful to have something tangible in which to believe. The magician's wand is an instrument of magic that seems to make miracles happen. A divination device can be any physical object that becomes the point of contact with the spirit world. Fetishes and charms and Roman Catholic scapulars, crucifixes, medals, and images, as well as Orthodox icons, play the same role.

Other divination devices are Ouija boards, pendulums, dowsing rods, crystal balls, tarot cards, signs of the zodiac, etc. They provide something visible to arouse expectancy in those who believe in them. Witchcraft utilizes magic potions, candles, and other tangible objects as the bridge into the spirit world. All of these objects, of course, work according to what Pat Robertson calls the metaphysical laws of the secret kingdom.

In the same category as the occult devices named above is the charismatics' "point of contact." Oral Roberts has called this his "greatest discovery."[56] In the fund-raising letter quoted above candles were the "point of contact." W.V. Grant has sent an outline of his feet for recipients to stand upon as the point of contact. Oral has several times sent an outline of his hand for followers to place their hands upon as the point of contact. Other "faith teachers" have their own variations of this occult technique—and over television, the TV screen itself for viewers to touch. In a fund-raising letter, Roberts said:

> Begin right now: Take the enclosed point-of-contact reminder poster and put it . . . where you will not be able to miss seeing it every day. Place your hand over mine and say out loud, "I'm joining my faith with Oral Roberts . . . I'm expecting my miracle. . . .
>
> Take your prayer sheet and be sure to . . . TRACE YOUR RIGHT HAND on the prayer sheet . . . then write down your needs on the hand. I WANT TO ANOINT YOUR REQUESTS IN THE PRAYER TOWER ON JULY 28TH AND PLACE MY HAND OVER THE TRACING OF YOUR HAND, AS I RELEASE THIS EXPLOSIVE FAITH FOR A MIRACLE SUPPLY FOR YOU!
>
> Don't forget to check the square that lets me know that you want to receive a personal vial of anointing oil . . . when you receive it . . . apply that oil, in the Name of Jesus, to every area of need that you have . . . [emphasis in original].[57]

This "point of contact" delusion comes from a misunderstanding of Christ's statement, "If two of you shall agree on earth as touching anything that they shall ask, it shall be done for them of my Father which is in heaven" (Matthew 18:19). The phrase "as touching anything" is taken to mean that the two parties must literally touch some common object in order to activate the power of God.

The old English expression "as touching," found in the King James Bible, has nothing at all to do with physically "touching" anything. The Greek word translated "touching" is *peree*, which means "about, concerning, regarding, or with respect to" and is so rendered in modern translations. For example, the New King James Version says, "If two of you agree on earth concerning anything that they ask. . . ."

Simple ignorance has created the fallacy about a "point of contact" as the key to getting miracles. Faith teachers have thereby led millions of their followers into one more form of occultism. According to John Goodwin, former Vineyard pastor and close associate of John Wimber:

> Wimber talked about the use of relics to heal people. He believed that is legitimate . . . relics are things the saints have either touched or owned, their bones, a lock of hair, having been imbued with the healing power of the saint and someone comes into contact with that relic and they get healed.
>
> [Wimber] encouraged that. He says, "That's been going on in the Catholic Church for 1200 years. . . . We Protestants have a problem with that, don't we . . . but we healers shouldn't."[58]

"Inner Healing"

Regression therapy, which creates false memories, is carried on within the church by Christian psychologists. There is another form of the same delusion, called "inner healing." It was introduced to Christians by one of the most astonishing occultists to infect the church, Agnes Sanford, to whom we have earlier referred briefly. She is the "Mary Baker Eddy" of the charismatic movement and her occult teachings have affected multitudes of noncharismatics. John Wimber was a major factor in spreading her teachings as well as those of other occultists such as Sanford's pastor, Morton Kelsey.

The occult technique of visualization is the key to inner healing. One visualizes a situation in the past, then visualizes Jesus coming into the scene and solving the problem. Often this "Jesus" comes alive and moves and speaks on its own. Contact has not been made with the Lord Jesus Christ but with a masquerading demon.

Since Sanford's death, inner healing has been carried on by those she trained and/or influenced, such as Ruth Carter Stapleton, Rosalind Rinker, John and Paula Sandford, William Vaswig, Rita Bennett, and others. Initially most prevalent among charismatics and liberal churches, inner healing has now spread widely in evangelical circles. There it is practiced in a more sophisticated form by psychologists such as David Seamands, H. Norman Wright, and James G. Friesen and by a number of lay therapists like Fred and Florence Littauer.

John and Paula Sandford confess that Agnes Sanford was "for all of us the forerunner in the field of inner healing . . . [and] our own first mentor in the Lord, our friend and advisor. . . ." They call her "a sound church woman . . . [who] founded the School of Pastoral Care. . . ." Those trained by Sanford included Roman Catholic leader Francis MacNutt. This "mentor" of today's inner healers taught that

> God's love was blacked out from man by the negative thought-vibration of this sinful . . . world. . . . So our Lord . . . lowered His thought-vibrations to the thought-vibrations of humanity . . . [and] cleansed the thought-vibrations that surround this globe. . . .
> Therefore since He became a very part of the collective unconscious of the race, when He died upon the cross a part of humanity died with him . . . [and] an invisible and personalized energy of our spirits has already ascended with Him into the heavens. . . .
> His blood, that mysterious life-essence . . . remains upon this earth, in plasma form, blown by the winds . . . to every land . . . exploding in a chain reaction of spiritual power. . . .
> We direct this great flow of life into a closed mind . . . by doing penance for the sins of the world, or for [a] particular [person]. . . . And by taking that one [by visualization] to the cross of Christ and there receiving for him forgiveness, healing and life. . . .
> I have learned to combine the sacramental with the metaphysical approach . . . the metaphysical methods.[59]

Sanford's books are so blatant in their occultism that their acceptance stands as an indictment of the entire charismatic movement. Indeed, after her occultism was exposed in *The Seduction of Christianity*, Sanford was defended by charismatic leaders, and this author and T.A. McMahon were castigated for having written that book. John Sandford later claimed that he had cast a demon out of Sanford and led her to Christ—after she had mentored him and other inner healers!

For Sanford, anything was acceptable that enabled one to tap into what she called "this flow of energy,"[60] this "high voltage of God's creativity."[61] Claiming that "we are part of God,"[62] Sanford also called God "primal energy"[63] and Jesus "that most profound of psychiatrists."[64] She taught that one could forgive another's sins through visualization.[65]

Richard Foster wrote, "I have been greatly helped in my understanding of the value of the imagination in praying for others by Agnes Sanford. . . . This advice . . . [of] prayer through the imagination . . . pictur[ing] the healing . . . and much more, was given to me by Agnes Sanford."[66] She taught:

> In the healing of the memories one must firmly hold in the imagination the picture . . . of this person . . . [though evil, as] a saint of God, and turn in the imagination the dark and awful shadows of his nature into shining virtues and sources of power.
> Indeed, they can be thus turned. This is redemption![67]

Foster endorsed Sanford and her books and wrote, "I have discovered her [Sanford] to be an extremely wise and skillful counselor. . . ."[68] Yet she openly taught Eastern mysticism and occultism. She taught that humans existed in heaven prior to coming to earth, trailing "a cloud of glory . . . [with] an unconscious memory" of that pre-earth existence.[69] The following excerpts from Sanford's books stand as an indictment of those who endorse her:

> Now in speaking in tongues . . . the unconscious may make rapport with the unconscious mind of someone else living . . . or of someone who has lived before or of someone who will live in the future or even of someone from heaven. . . .
> I cannot tell what my spirit does and whither it goes. But that it does travel and that God does work through my spiritual body even when my mind is quite unaware of it, becomes more and more apparent.
> Therefore, simply call in your mind to me, or to someone else as a human channel for the love of Christ.[70]

Rebecca Brown also teaches that when one wakes up tired in the morning it is because God has been using one's "spirit body" all night in spiritual warfare. Much of Sanford's occultism was undoubtedly learned from her pastor, Morton T. Kelsey, who studied at the C.G. Jung Institute near Zurich, Switzerland, and who became a Jungian psychologist, as did also Sanford's son, John Sanford, whose many books continue to spread similar occult practices. Kelsey's books are very popular and have brought much occultism into the church.

Kelsey equates shamanistic powers with the gifts of the Holy Spirit,[71] believes that his mother died for him "as did our Lord,"[72] and declared that a shaman or witch doctor is "one in whom the power of God is concentrated and can thus flow out to others."[73] Kelsey writes:

> There is nothing intrinsically evil about . . . psi [psychic power] or its use. . . . Psi experiences . . . are simply natural experiences of the human psyche. . . .
>
> Clairvoyance, telepathy, precognition, psychokinesis, and healing have been observed in and around the lives of many religious leaders and nearly all Christian saints. . . .[74]
>
> My students begin to see the role Jesus was fulfilling when they read Mircea Eliade's Shamanism and Carlos Castaneda's Journey to Ixtlan [glorifying shamanistic powers]. . . .[75]

The Denigration of Doctrine

Biblical doctrine is the container of truth and our shield against error. A mark of the last days prior to Christ's return is the refusal to test all things against the Bible. Wimber went by experience, and it is experience that is sought above all else at the current "revivals." No one goes to the Toronto laughing revival or to the Pensacola revival to hear biblical exegesis; they go there to *experience* what they call "a fresh touch of the Holy Spirit." And how does one know such a touch has been received? Only by feelings and by physical manifestations, often of the most bizarre kind.

The teaching one hears at such meetings is often confused and perverted. At the Airport church in Toronto, this author heard a message on how inadequate Jesus felt at the wedding in Cana of Galilee, how it was His mother's encouragement that made Him realize that if He only tried He could do a miracle, and how this should be an encouragement to the rest of us in our feelings of inadequacy.

We watched as a man writhed in agony on the platform in the Brownsville Assembly of God in Pensacola and Steve Hill expressed this heresy to the audience, "He is giving birth, spiritual birth to you . . . he is dying that you might have life." The following letter came recently:

> My pastor and some others from my church went to Pensacola and the result has been division and devastation in the church. Now the pastor is saying doctrine doesn't matter and [is] concentrating on manifestations and gifts of the Spirit. He has totally changed and shuns the members who haven't had the "Pensacola experience."

Defending Occultism

One of today's heroes among charismatics and Pentecostals is William de Arteaga, who is honored (such as on Crouch's TBN) for having written a book titled *Quenching the Spirit* in opposition to *The Seduction of Christianity*. That de Arteaga defends occult visualization, a pre-earth existence of human souls, past-life regressions under hypnosis, and Eastern mysticism's karma and reincarnation does not inhibit his wide acceptance among charismatics.

The basic thesis of *Quenching the Spirit* is both preposterous and heretical: that God brings new truth to the church through first revealing it to cults and occult groups. Therefore, the fact that unbiblical practices such as visualization, inner healing, Positive Thinking, and Positive Confession came out of the occult is really in their favor because that's how God works! Charismatics love the book because it opposes *The Seduction of Christianity*, which exposes their errors. Of course, the book is highly recommended by almost everyone in that camp, from Jack Hayford to Oral Roberts. Fuller Seminary professor C. Peter Wagner calls it "a valuable picture of opposition to new and unusual works of the Holy Spirit, from John Calvin to Dave Hunt. . . ."

De Arteaga validates occult mind-over-matter techniques by arguing that quantum physics proves that "mind-observation" affects subatomic particles. This is a myth invented by New Age physicists. Something must make contact with any object for human observation to take place. Ordinarily, light photons bounce off an object and create an image in the eye and brain. Light bouncing off a car does not move it. However, to bounce a photon off a subatomic particle in order to "observe" it is like bouncing a car off a car—so of course observation (not the observer's *mind*) affects a subatomic particle.

From this misunderstanding of quantum physics, de Arteaga reasons that "by faith the mind acts in the power of God and can move mountains."[76] God's power is seen as a force which our minds operate when we obey "spiritual laws." This principle, he says, was opened by "the Logos" to the metaphysical cults and from there came into the church. In fact, the source was Satan and the biblicized "Science of Mind" which de Arteaga promotes is pure occultism.

The thesis of *Quenching* was previously presented by de Arteaga in *Past Life Visions* (1983): "The Holy Spirit will flow into occult groups if it [sic] is blocked out by Orthodox Christians" (page 17). He lauds Agnes Sanford's incredibly heretical *The Healing Light* (page 132); defends her belief in a pre-earth human existence (pages 145–146); seems to embrace evolution of man from lower species (page 126); declares that "ghosts" are "earthbound souls" (page 187) who may legitimately communicate with the living (page 182); and claims that the dead should be ministered to by the church (page 183). He argues that reincarnation is biblical and was even "validated by Jesus" (pages 197–209) and that such a gospel is helpful for India because it allows "the Hindu to maintain . . . the concept of karma-reincarnation" (page 215). He also recommends regression into past lives as a standard method of spiritual healing (pages 151-163). Leading charismatics take comfort in having the support of such a heretic!

What grief such departures from the sound doctrine of God's grace must cause the One who said, "The truth shall make you free" (John 8:32). And what bondage many in the church have embraced for want of a proper regard for truth. Let us not be taken in by those who have "crept in unawares" (Jude 1:4).

*Without a clear scriptural position, then, we need to consult those
with experience. . . . Those who work with cancer patients know that
Christians can and do develop cancer. Likewise, those with clinical
experience with Christians having demonic symptoms have overcome
their doubts and concluded that Christians can and regularly do carry
demons.*
— Fuller Seminary professor Charles Kraft[1]

*As we're in worship, people see visions, they see pictures. Through
watching other people in worship sometimes, the Spirit will reveal to
them what they are interceding over. . . . And then the Lord just identifies to us what the direction is for the evening.*
— Craig Howell, intercessory team captain at
Brownsville Assembly of God, Pensacola, Florida[2]

*Holy Trinity Church in Brompton had imported the Toronto Blessing to
England. [Steve] Hill, while visiting Holy Trinity, received a touch from
the pastor, Sandy Millar, and brought the anointing to Pensacola.*
— Albert James Dager, reporting on interview[3]

*I'd rather be in a church where the devil and the flesh are manifesting
than in a church where nothing is happening because people are so
afraid to manifest anything . . . and if the devil manifests, don't worry.
. . . Rejoice, because at least something is happening.*
— Rodney Howard-Browne[4]

*There are those involved in the Toronto Blessing who . . . think the
Holy Spirit is a power that they can pump, scoop, blow, and press into
others. There may be such a power present. But it is not the Holy
Spirit. . . .*
— Pastor George Byron Koch[5]

*Lausanne II was the seedbed for the subsequent development of the
Spiritual Warfare Network. While in Manila, the Lord spoke to me . . . :
"I want you to take leadership in the area of territorial spirits. . . ." I
became the coordinator of the International Spiritual Warfare Network.*
— C. Peter Wagner[6]

*Why should you [Christians] fear? Why should you be afraid? Do you
not know that the prince of this world [Satan] has been judged? He
is no lord, no prince any more. You have a different, a stronger Lord,
Christ, who has overcome and bound him. Therefore, let the prince and
god of this world look sour, bare his teeth, make great noise, threaten
. . . he can do no more than a bad dog on a chain. . . .*
— Martin Luther[7]

24

* * *

Spiritual Warfare
and Revival

"Spiritual warfare," one of the hottest topics at the 1989
Manila Conference (Lausanne II), attended by 4000
evangelical leaders from around the world, is the resounding
cry in the church today. From radio, TV, Christian books and
magazines, and some of the most popular pulpits we are being
told that taking the offensive against Satan and "binding"
the various evil spirits that dominate this earth are the secret
to world evangelization and personal victory and prosperity. Even Our Lady of Medjugorje has declared, "Christians can stop war and even natural calamities by prayer and
fasting."

If so, then Christians are to blame for all the world's natural
calamities and wars. If evil rules in this world and people go to
hell, it is because Christians have not prayed enough. But that
is neither reasonable nor biblical. No matter the degree of
prayer and fasting by Christians, individuals must still make
a personal choice whether to follow God or Satan, whether to
believe the gospel and receive God's forgiveness or to reject
Christ and suffer His just judgment. The battle between God
and Satan is fought in each individual heart.

Yes, Paul said that we "wrestle . . . against principalities,
against powers, against the rulers of the darkness of this
world" (Ephesians 6:12). But what did he mean? He urged us
to "stand against the *wiles* of the devil," not *attack* him, and
he promised that with the "shield of faith" we could "quench"
Satan's "fiery darts," not return his fire. *Faith* is a personal
matter, and its shield protects the individual *believer.* It cannot

be spread over unbelievers. Clearly this is a *personal* battle against *wiles*—that is, the deceitful trickery of lies and lusts fought within the heart and mind. For such resistance the individual Christian is well-equipped. And the battle is won through *believing the truth of God's Word,* which is the "sword of the Spirit" (verse 17) with which we "fight the good fight of *faith*" (1 Timothy 6:12).

The Bible says nothing about going on the offensive against demonic strongholds. Nor did the apostles and early church ever engage in such a practice. When Paul cast the demon out of the "damsel possessed with a spirit of divination" (Acts 16:16), it was only after she had followed Paul "many days" and he was at last "grieved" by the continued attempt of Satan to identify his ministry with divination. Paul did not travel about on the offensive against demons—*ever.* The details in Acts demonstrate the living-out of what Christ meant by the following:

> Or else how can one enter into a strong man's house and spoil his goods, except he first bind the strong man? . . .
> Verily I say unto you, Whatsoever ye shall bind on earth shall be bound in heaven, and whatsoever ye shall loose on earth shall be loosed in heaven. . . .
> All power [authority] is given unto me in heaven and in earth (Matthew 12:29; 18:18; 28:18).
> Now is the judgment of this world; now shall the prince of this world be cast out. And I, if I be lifted up from the earth, will draw all men unto me (John 12:31,32).

Christ is the One who bound Satan the strong man. And He did it not by His *power* as God, but through paying the penalty for our sins on the cross. Satan is defeated and Christ has all authority. Yet evil continues on this earth because men reject Christ to follow self and Satan. We still pray, "Thy kingdom come; thy will be done in earth, as it is in heaven" (Matthew 6:10). Clearly God's will is not yet done throughout the whole earth, or else He would be to blame for all the evil on this planet. And we are to combat that evil not by a magical binding of Satan (whom Christ has already bound), but with faith and the gospel of salvation.

Today's Unbiblical "Spiritual Warfare"

A *Charisma* magazine cover pictures Youth With A Mission's John Dawson with this quote: "Battles against evil spiritual forces controlling our cities can be waged and won." According to Fuller Theological Seminary's C. Peter Wagner, Dawson's book *Taking Our Cities for God: How to Break Spiritual Strongholds* is "the most important book on the subject ever written." In the foreword, Pastor Jack Hayford writes: "This is a book of Holy Spirit insight . . . [into] the toughest problems we face on this planet today. . . ."[8] In that book Dawson writes:

> The [demonic] strongholds that bind our urban populations have power, but . . . we can overthrow them. This section lays out a fivefold approach to bringing down our cities' strongholds.[9]

One wonders why Christ, the apostles, and the early church never engaged in "bringing down" demonic strongholds in their day. That they didn't seems not to trouble today's advocates of an appealing ambition for which there is not one biblical precedent. The exciting prospect of victory through "spiritual warfare" has caught fire in the minds of Christians. The principles of Dawson's book (and of many similar ones) have been enthusiastically and expectantly followed by many pastors, churches, and individuals during the eight years since Dawson wrote it. Yet *not one* city anywhere in the world has been "taken for God." In fact, evil has increased.

Such is the case in spite of the many seminars held at Jack Hayford's Church on the Way in Southern California (speakers included Bill and Vonette Bright, Yonggi Cho, and Joy Dawson) and elsewhere, which train attendees to take their cities for God. Still, the enthusiasm for this delusion has not waned. We have great concern for the gospel to go to the ends of the earth, as Christ commanded. Why not follow the biblical program which the early church used with such great success? Why invent new methods and schemes which only divert energy from God's biblical plan?

The April 2, 1995, cover story of the *Pentecostal Evangel* (official magazine of the Assemblies of God) was titled "This City Belongs to God." The caption for the photo (of five pastors) read: "Detroit Pastors Stake Claim to Their City." Praise God that churches are stirred to bring the gospel to Detroit, but that city won't belong to God until Christ's millennial reign. To think otherwise is to be deceived.

In 1989, more than 1300 pastors from many denominations, led by Lloyd Ogilvie and Jack Hayford, began meeting quarterly in prayer at the Hollywood Presbyterian Church to wage spiritual warfare for the "deliverance" of Los Angeles.[10] In the years that followed evil has increased. There is *not one* example in the Bible to support such "deliverance." One pastor wrote to us: "We meet and fast and pray and bind the spirits and as soon as we leave the meeting they're on the loose again!" One of the leading pastors involved in the meetings had to leave his pastorate for sexual improprieties. While they were battling territorial spirits to deliver Los Angeles, one of their leaders was losing the battle in his own heart.

Who's to Blame for Not Telling Us Sooner?

These meetings, called *Love LA,* were inspired by Larry Lea, who declared: "This is a day to wage nothing less than militant warfare in the spirit realm. . . . Demonic strongholds keeping the greater Los Angeles area and our country in bondage will be . . . pulled down." *Charisma* showed Larry Lea, the "Apostle of Prayer," in combat fatigues calling for 300,000 "prayer warriors" to join him in taking America for God. Yet America and Los Angeles continue to worsen morally.

Introducing a book he edited titled *Breaking Strongholds in Your City: How to Use Spiritual Mapping to Make Your Prayers More Strategic, Effective and Targeted,* C. Peter Wagner writes:

> This book uncovers the wiles of the devil and exposes the prayer targets that will force the enemy to release millions of unsaved souls now held captive. I am excited that God has given us a marvelous new tool for effective spiritual warfare![11]

Does it not seem incongruous to boast of a "new tool" which will at last "release millions of unsaved souls"—a tool unmentioned in the Bible and unknown to Christ, the apostles, and the early church? Why didn't the Holy Spirit reveal these vital methods sooner? Can millions have gone to hell for nineteen centuries for lack of these new techniques? Or could it be that Wagner, Dawson, Lea, Hayford, and the other leaders in this new movement are deluding themselves and their followers?

On November 10, 1989, the Miami Arena rang with the songs, prayers, and victory shouts of 10,000 enthusiastic Christians. They had been promised a "spiritual breakthrough" by Larry Lea. Backed by 430 local pastors demonstrating an essential unity, Lea identified specific spirits of violence, drugs, witchcraft, greed, etc. that dominated Miami and vowed, "These spirits will not dominate this area." He declared that God showed him "the Strongman of Greed" holding back the wealth of the wicked, wealth which belonged to Christians, and that "if we bind the Strongman of Greed, the wealth of the nations will be given to the church" and to individual Christians. The excited audience joined Lea in wielding an "imaginary sword" and hacking this demon to pieces.

There has been no noticeable reduction in violence, drugs, etc. in the Miami area, nor a transfer of the "wealth of the wicked" to Christians. Nor has there been any detectable drop in homosexuality in San Francisco since Lea led Christians there, years ago, in binding the spirit of that sin.

Experience Produces Theology!

If these ideas are not biblical, how are so many Christians deceived by them? They are following men without checking their teaching against the Word of God. What these leaders say is more often based upon experience than upon Scripture.

Charisma interviewed "a panel of experts" concerning "the church's battle against the forces of darkness." In their answers, Scripture played a minimal role, while experience and opinion were predominant. In one of the major books on this subject, author C. Peter Wagner (one of the foremost "spiritual warfare" experts) makes this revealing statement:

> One fundamental thesis will control this discussion . . . of us coming to grips with some of the relatively new and at times somewhat radical ideas surrounding strategic-level spiritual warfare, spiritual mapping, identificational repentance and other such issues . . . the thesis that ministry [experience] precedes and produces theology, not the reverse.[12]

Wagner calls Wimber "my mentor."[13] Wimber said, "We are cataloguing all of our experiences so we can develop a theology."[14] What happened to the Bible? Don Lewis of Regent College rightly points out that Wimber's insistence that "critical thinking must be laid aside" is "nothing less than dangerous."[15] On more than one tape this author has heard Wimber say, "When are we going to see a generation that doesn't try to understand this book [the Bible] and just believes it?" But one cannot believe what one does not understand. The biblical emphasis is upon *understanding*, not feelings and experiences (Jeremiah 9:24; Matthew 13:19; 1 John 5:20; etc.).

The *Charisma* article cited above referred to "a select group of intercessors [who] convened in Southern California [early in 1990] to discuss the role of prayer in overcoming territorial spirits and winning the lost." The group included "C. Peter Wagner, John Dawson, Cindy Jacobs, Jack Hayford, Larry Lea, Gwen Shaw, Dick Bernal, Tom White, Joy Dawson, and Dick Eastman." (Other members include Ed Murphy, Charles Craft, and Frank Peretti.) They formed the Spiritual Warfare Network, which plays a significant role in the United Prayer Track of the A.D. 2000 Movement. Referring to these "foremost experts in the spiritual warfare movement," *Charisma* said:

> Their insights on the subject of spiritual warfare were not derived solely through Bible study, but also through personal experiences of challenging the forces of darkness.[16]

One of the "experts," Francis Frangipane, stated that the "sword of the Spirit" has two edges: One edge is Scripture and the other edge is "the living Word of God: what the Spirit is saying *now* to the church [i.e., by new revelation through new prophets]." Frangipane was an apostle, along with founder John Robert Stevens, of the heretical Church of the Living Word, which was infamous for its new revelations through false prophets and its unabashed occultism and immorality. Frangipane has never renounced his involvement, and here he is in *Charisma* promoting the same error. Of course, "new revelations" have made the charismatic movement what it is today, and they are foundational to the new doctrine of spiritual warfare/territorial spirits.

The examples given of successful spiritual warfare are generally weak. Cindy Jacobs tells of a witch in Mar del Plata, Argentina, who apparently "dropped dead—at the same moment we began praying."[17] But what of the hundreds of other witches who remained alive? This was no taking the city for God. They are grasping at experiential straws while ignoring the testimony of Scripture. Wagner tries to provide examples from church history, but examples from the Bible are conspicuous by their absence.

There was, says Wagner, "Gregory the Wonderworker," whose presence (according to *tradition*) shut down an idol in a pagan temple. Yet, as the story goes, upon the plea of the pagan priest, Gregory gave permission for the demon to function through the idol again.[18] What a contradictory myth! Wagner then quotes a historian to the effect that it was the "manhandling of demons—humiliating them, making them howl, beg for mercy, tell their secrets" that drew converts into the church.[19] Humiliating and making demons howl hardly sounds biblical—and it was an apostate church these "converts" entered. Remember, St. Augustine said that this church was filled with "people wearing amulets... clients of sorcerers, astrologers ... [who] fill the theatres on pagan holidays."[20] It sounds as though Satan had the last laugh.

Territorial Spirits?

Dawson writes, "The Bible usually identifies an evil spirit by its territory... for example, 'The prince of the kingdom of Persia' (Daniel 10:13). ..." *Usually?* Here is the *one* example proponents can find to justify the "territorial spirit" fad. But it doesn't fit. Daniel was not praying for Persia but for prophetic insight concerning the last days. That *insight* (being brought by Gabriel) was what this "prince" opposed. Neither Daniel nor Gabriel "bound" this "prince"; nor is there any hint that to do so would have resulted in some spiritual breakthrough for Persia. Were Daniel and Gabriel simply ignorant of today's new strategies and thus failed to apply them?

Wagner argues, "The existence, identity and activities of territorial spirits are particularly well known by those who live in or travel frequently to the Third World." This is their opinion, but again it has no scriptural basis. Timothy M. Warner, professor in the School of World Mission and Evangelism at Trinity Evangelical Divinity School and a specialist in "spiritual warfare," also relies upon experience rather than Scripture:

> I have come to believe that Satan does indeed assign a demon or a corps of demons to every geopolitical unit in the world and that they are among the principalities and powers against whom we wrestle. For me, this concept first came up in a missionary context [not from biblical exegesis]....[21]

Very simply, if this new teaching is true, then Paul and the other apostles (and Jesus Himself) were remiss in not binding the territorial spirits in their day. Wagner quotes an "expert" that Kali "is the goddess of darkness, evil and destruction . . . to whom the entire city [of Calcutta] is dedicated."[22] That does not mean, however, that Kali can be bound and the entire city of Calcutta thereby set free. Breaking free from any demon, whether or not represented by an idol, is a matter of individual faith in Christ through the preaching of the gospel.

Millions of people, including pagans in deepest demonic darkness and bondage, have come to Christ without anyone binding any spirits. The New Tribes Mission video, *Delivered from the Power of Darkness*,[23] documents the conversion of the Taliabo. These were pagans on a remote island in Indonesia who were in bondage to demons. There was no binding of spirits by the missionaries and no "spiritual warfare" of the type currently being advocated. Instead, through the straightforward presentation of the gospel, these people were converted and completely delivered. Furthermore, the missionaries walked right into the idol temples and held their meetings there without giving the demons any attention!

In contrast, the Brownsville Assembly of God in Pensacola, now alleged to be experiencing the greatest revival in the world, must be cleansed of demons continually. That fact alone discredits this "revival." Here is the procedure:

> We were instructed to grab the hands of two or three others and move through the auditorium and cleanse the house. During the revival services the lost come in by the hundreds and demonic spirits who have oppressed many are driven out by the power of God.

These prayer warriors go into action and little groups of three or four move thoughout the auditorium, cleansing every area of the house. They pray over every seat....[24]

New "Spiritual Technologies"?

We have seen the error of the "point of contact" and of physical objects of power such as fetishes, images of the saints, and holy water. The same error underlies the idea of territorial spirits and the belief that to engage in strategic praying one must go to the place of power (or pray over every seat). In their book *Prayerwalking: Praying on Site with Insight,* Steve Hawthorne and Graham Kendrick write, "Prayerwalking is on-site prayer. On-site praying is simply praying in the very places where you expect your prayers to be answered."[25] Wagner states approvingly:

> The Catholic Church uses rites [rituals] of exorcism to remove demons from buildings.[26]
>
> On the Day to Change the World in 1993, for example, YWAM and others recruited and deployed prayer journey teams that traveled to the 24 cardinal points of the world (the northernmost, southernmost, easternmost and westernmost points of six of the continents) to pray that the strongholds over the continents would be pulled down and the fullness of God's kingdom would come.[27]

The world didn't change—except for the worse. The time and expense of traveling to these allegedly strategic points was wasted. No strongholds over continents were pulled down. The spiritual condition on all continents only worsened and will continue to do so: "Evil men and seducers shall wax worse and worse, deceiving and being deceived" (2 Timothy 3:13). This unbiblical "warfare" becomes an obsession with Christians that wastes their time, energy, and resources. Charles Kraft says, "I think one of the challenges of the '90s is to work as quietly as possible within evangelicalism to move them into these areas."[28] Unfortunately, evangelicals are increasingly embracing this delusion.

Wagner heads this section in his book "SPIRITUAL TECHNOLOGY FOR THE 1990s." Again we are moving into the occult. God's power does not depend (as occult power does) upon some "spiritual technology" (biblically there is no such thing) nor upon *where* a prayer is offered. Who decided that to pray from these 24 points would be "strategic"? And what does that mean? Where does the Bible inform us, by example or doctrine, that prayer is more effective if done "on-site"? When one begins to believe that *techniques* are essential to the release of spiritual power, one is being set up for occult delusion. This is no different from lighting candles and making the sign of the cross. At an "Academic Symposium on Power Evangelism" at Fuller Theological Seminary, referring to a British psychiatrist, Wagner endorses an occult delusion:

> As an Anglican he is very much in tune with the power of God channeled through the sacrament of the Eucharist.[29]

Demons are blamed for human unbelief and disobedience: It is not the fault of Christ-rejectors that they are on their way to hell, but the fault of Christians who haven't bound the territorial spirits or used the right prayer techniques! The same delusion permeates today's "deliverance" scene. Bill had the "spirit of lust" cast out Friday night, and things went well until the following Wednesday, when he committed fornication. Obviously that "spirit of lust" got back into him and must be cast out again. Self is exonerated.

Here is John Avanzini (TBN's favorite fund-raiser) on TV making false promises to entice people to give to his ministry: "If you will stay with me in this seminar, I promise you . . . the power of the *spirit of debt* will be broken in your life . . . a supernatural power to get wealth will be loosed into your hands." It is the twin to the lie of Christian psychology. The one blames failings upon past traumas; the other blames a "spirit of debt." It is not that diligence, prudence, further training, or any other practical solution is needed. One need simply rebuke and bind the "spirit of debt" and money will magically start flowing into one's pockets!

Implications for the Gospel

C. Peter Wagner and his fellow Fuller professor Charles Kraft speak of "authoritative prayer." Instead of praying "Not my will but thine be done," this kind of prayer *commands* God to do certain things.[30] Satan and his minions are also *commanded* to take their hands off a church or person or situation. But Satan has been "rebuked" and "bound" countless times by those who imagine that this formula works, yet he seems to carry on his evil designs uninhibited by such bravado.

How must it affect the faith of youth who, week after week, see pastor and elders *command* healings in the name of Jesus, but none occur? Typical is Richard Roberts on TV with his second wife *commanding* the Word of God to go out and heal all illness and financial lack in everyone watching. No one really thought it would happen, nor did it. How can anyone deny that something is fundamentally wrong!

The relationship is evident between all of the above and John Wimber's popular "Power Evangelism" theory that "signs and wonders" *cause* people to believe the gospel. If so, then all of Israel should have been converted when Christ was here. Instead, "But though he had done so many miracles before them, yet they believed not on him" (John 12:37). Romans 1:16 assures us that "the *gospel* . . . is the power of God unto salvation to everyone that *believeth* [it]." Paul declared, "It pleased God *by the foolishness of preaching* to save them that *believe*" (1 Corinthians 1:21). Ah, but today the gospel needs help from "signs and wonders," and demons must be bound. John Dawson writes: "We need to overcome the enemy [Satan] *before* we employ other methods of ministry. . . ." *Experience* has replaced *truth*.

This teaching undermines the gospel. Consider Jack Deere, who left Dallas Theological Seminary after 12 years on its faculty to become the leading theologian in Wimber's Vineyard movement. He was interviewed by Graham Banister in Sydney, Australia, at a Spiritual Warfare Conference taught by Wimber and his team to 5500 church leaders (who paid 150 dollars each, over 800,000 dollars to attend). Peter told Simon the magician, who offered to pay for a course in signs and wonders, "Thy money perish with thee, because thou hast thought that the gift of God may be purchased with money" (Acts 8:20). But Vineyard teams are well paid for "teaching" signs and wonders. Banister reported:

> After introducing myself, I said to Dr. Jack Deere, "I wonder if you might tell me why you felt my explanation of the gospel was

defective yesterday?" To which he replied, "I'm really not very prepared to talk about that."

I was a little surprised . . . considering that he had just finished speaking to 5,500 people [and] . . . had informed us of the many ancient languages in which he had become proficient in order to fully understand the Bible. I wouldn't have thought that someone with such impressive credentials would need to do all that much preparation for a friendly discussion on the content of the gospel.

I then asked, "Well, just off the top of your head, what do you think the gospel is?" Jack Deere replied, "I'm not prepared to make a formal statement about that." So I asked, "Could you perhaps tell me informally what you believe to be the gospel?" Jack Deere answered, "I'm not sure."

Somewhat stunned, I said, "I find that quite surprising—that you're not sure what the gospel is." He replied, "I used to be just like you . . . thinking the gospel was simply justification by faith." I responded, "Are you saying it's more than that? . . . What would you add to it?"

"Deliverance," he said, ". . . things like demons and healing." I said, "You would add as an essential part of the gospel . . . the exorcising of demons and healing?" He nodded. I continued, ". . . like what John Wimber was saying last night . . . ?" "Yes," he said.

"But you're not sure exactly what should be included?" I asked. "No," he said, "not yet."

"Would it be fair to say," I asked, "that you're in a state of flux since you joined the Wimber thing?" He quickly responded, "We're always in a state of flux—you are. . . ."

"But on the gospel message?" I asked. . . . Continuing to be amazed, I said, "Are you saying that you couldn't go back into that pavilion and tell those people the gospel?" He replied, "No—not yet." I responded, "When do you think you could do it?" And he said, "Maybe five years, maybe ten. . . ."

I remained stunned that one of the leading minds, if not the leading theological mind in the Signs and Wonders Movement, did not know what was the gospel![31]

On TBN's "Praise the Lord" January 25, 1994, John Wimber said he thought that a demon in Hong Kong put a "Chinese cancer" upon him and said it would kill him. Somehow, with all of the binding of territorial spirits all over the world and claiming cities for God this one demon was not defeated by the spiritual warfare experts and their "mentor" succumbed to that demon's cancer in November 1997. Something doesn't add up!

The "Toronto Blessing"

Rodney Howard-Browne, who calls himself "the Holy Ghost bartender," brought the laughing revival to America from South Africa. At Howard-Browne's first meeting in Hinn's church, the latter seemed startled at the uncontrollable laughter that turned the sanctuary into a howling asylum. Hinn soon declared to his flock, however, "This is the Holy Ghost!"

This new phenomenon became known as holy laughter and spread everywhere Howard-Browne went. He came to Oral Roberts University and Oral testified that "at the end of his message he had the longest sustained applause in the history of ORU . . . he changed my life and my son's life."[32] The laughing revival, however, didn't catch the attention of the world until mid-January 1994, when it came to the Toronto Vineyard Church, pastored by John Arnott. Here one heard not only uncontrollable laughter, but horrible animallike sounds—and worse—from those in the throes of the "blessing."

In the months that followed, tens of thousands of seeking souls came from all over the world to "get it" at Toronto. Holy Trinity Brompton in London, as already mentioned, became the center of holy laughter for England and Europe. Toronto began to fade from prominence by mid-1996 and no longer experiences the crowds or as many manifestations as at its height.

Late in 1995 the Toronto Vineyard was removed by John Wimber from the Fellowship of Vineyard Churches and became the Toronto Airport Christian Fellowship (TACF). This action has been mistakenly taken as a sign that Wimber was maturing, and rejecting some of the excesses that he once embraced. On the contrary, many Vineyard churches continue their involvement in "holy laughter." Wimber was not opposed to the animal behavior and sounds; they have been part of the Vineyard movement from the beginning. What he objected to was the attempt on the part of the TACF leadership to justify these manifestations from the Bible, which Wimber believed was unnecessary.

In fact, it had been Randy Clark, pastor of the St. Louis Vineyard Christian Fellowship, who brought the laughing revival to Toronto. Clark "got it" from Rodney Howard-Browne at Kenneth Hagin, Jr.'s Rhema Bible Church in Tulsa and continues to promote the manifestation worldwide. Moreover, Clark was attracted to Howard-Browne because "people shaking, falling, laughing" reminded him of what he had seen "years earlier in the Vineyard revivals."[33] A featured speaker at the 25th International Lutheran Conference on the Holy Spirit in St. Paul, Minnesota, on August 6–10, 1997, Clark was described in the conference brochure as the one who "was used of God as the catalyst for the outbreak of the Spirit in Toronto. . . ."

Some who attend the Toronto services are so "drunk" that they are unable to drive home. Some are unable to board their plane home because of their bizarre and uncontrollable behavior. This is hardly glorifying to the Lord. An attempt to justify such madness is made on the basis of the disciples being accused of drunkenness on the day of Pentecost. However, the only strange thing about them was that, although they were "all Galileans," those from many different places each "heard them speak in his own language." The hearers could think of no other explanation than to say they were "full of new wine," but it wasn't because they were acting drunk (Acts 2:6-13).

John Goodwin was the pastor of a Vineyard church and a leader in the movement for a number of years. Prior to coming to Christ, he had been in the Hollywood music and drug and Eastern mysticism scene. It was his realization of the connection between the occultism he had experienced before he was saved and what he became involved in within the Vineyard movement that caused him to leave the Vineyard churches. Goodwin says with deep concern and warning:

> There's more to what's going on with the Vineyards, with Toronto, with Pensacola, Florida than meets the eye. It's not just an issue of some heresy, some false doctrine and strange experiences. When you see people barking like a dog, roaring like a lion, slithering on the floor like a snake. . . .
>
> Have you ever seen a person transformed into an ape before your very eyes? That will shake you up!
>
> We were in London and John Wimber was up teaching. . . . I'm up in the balcony . . . with Blaine Cook . . . and Carl Tuttle . . . now the pastor of the Vineyard in Anaheim. . . .
>
> All of a sudden out of the corner of my eye I saw this form leap out of a chair backwards, about five feet over the top of the back of

the chair into an aisle ... and he began to transform physically into an ape. ...

His face changed. ... You've seen these weird horror movies where suddenly a person changes into a werewolf? It was like that ... ! His arms lengthened, his shoulders changed ... they became like an ape's shoulders ... the total demonic manifestation of an ape!

People were extending their hands toward him saying, "Lord, we just bless the work of your Holy Spirit. ..."

I wanted to run out of the room, and I wasn't real close. ...

I only relate this to impress upon you [that] what we see going on with this group ... [are] totally demonic manifestations. And I can't tell you how many times I was in seminars and conferences where this sort of thing would take place. People would be screeching and howling. Animal noises? Forget it. You never heard animals make noises like this ... ! These are supernatural noises!

They're teaching that these are manifestations of the Holy Spirit upon the person's life. ... There's no Scriptural warrant for any of this. ...[34]

The Brownsville Assembly of God

The "revival" that has been underway for more than two years (since Father's Day 1995) at the Brownsville Assembly of God in Pensacola, Florida, has spread worldwide to become much larger and more influential than the Toronto laughing revival, of which it is an extension. It was preceded by more than two years of prayer and fasting, *for revival*, utilizing spiritual warfare techniques. They now sweep the sanctuary to drive out demons from every seat and corner. They believe that "spiritual warfare" plays an important role in the ongoing success of the meetings and protection of the church staff.

How odd that Paul, who "turned the world upside down" with the gospel (Acts 17:6), found no need for any of these procedures. He reasoned each Sabbath in the synagogues from the Scriptures (Acts 17:2,3) and was found disputing "in the market daily" and in the centers of learning such as Mars Hill (Acts 17:17-34). Within hours after his conversion, Paul "preached Christ ... that he is the Son of God." He "confounded the Jews ... proving that this is very Christ" and "disputed against the Grecians. ..." So powerfully did Paul preach the gospel that they either had to believe or to kill him—and they chose the latter (Acts 9:20-29).

A lack of such careful and clear enunciation of the gospel is one of the characteristics of today's so-called revival. This author met with Michael L. Brown, the Brownsville theologian who heads the Brownsville Revival School of Ministry. We told Brown that we had watched six different tapes of services at Brownsville, had seen hundreds of persons going forward, yet had not heard Steve Hill, the evangelist, clearly present the gospel. Brown maintains that the gospel is indeed presented, suggesting that perhaps the videos in question did not feature complete services, or that they might have been atypical.

The testimonies on the videotapes seemed to indicate that people were coming from all over the world to "get it." *Get what?* we wondered. There were jerking and shaking and collapsing and violent, unnatural motions such as the body could not endure normally and would look demonic to an unbiased observer. People literally had to be carried out of the baptismal tank to prevent them from drowning, while some were shaking so violently that it took several men to handle them. What the videos revealed violated Paul's admonition, "Let all things be done decently and in order" (1 Corinthians 14:40). Then there were the heretical statements, such as evangelist Steve Hill's comments about a young man writhing on the platform:

> God's put it on him . . . caused him to fall to the ground and experience "birth pains" . . . he's giving spiritual birth to you . . . he's dying for you . . . he's dying that you might have life.[35]

Michael Brown has written a book in defense of the Pensacola phenomena, with the subtitle *Confronting the Critics of Revival.* The book fails to take seriously the real problems at Pensacola and their undeniable relationship to Toronto. Brown accuses critics of having "the same negative, narrow, and nit-picking spirit that would have rejected Jesus—failing to hear Him out sympathetically, looking to accuse and disprove, disregarding the overall tenor of the scriptural message in the name of loyalty to the Word. . . ."[36] On the contrary, we do not doubt the sincerity of those involved nor that souls have been saved and lives changed. But there are manifestations which are not glorifying to the Lord and some that even appear to be demonic. These problems need to be honestly faced.

Revivalism and Dominionism

Another area of concern in relation to spiritual warfare proponents is that a number of them promote dominion theology (although Brown states that isn't the case at Brownsville, which he says believes in a standard dispensational theology). Dominion theology declares that when Adam sinned he lost to Satan the dominion God had given him, and that this dominion is restored in Christ. Christians are therefore to take dominion over the media, schools, and governments and are to rule earth, setting up God's kingdom.

Of course, it is spiritual warfare through which this takeover of the world is to be accomplished. When Christians are in control, so this teaching says, Christ will return to earth, not to rapture us to heaven, but to rule over the kingdom we have established. Here is how Gary D. Kinnaman, a leader in the spiritual warfare movement, explains and promotes it in his book *Overcoming the Dominion of Darkness:*

> Actually, the Great Commission . . . is a recommissioning to represent the authority of the King in every aspect of life. The Commission was first given in Genesis 1 . . . we were created to rule, to have dominion. . . .
>
> Jesus came to resurrect the Kingdom Commission: "Have dominion . . . upon the earth" (Genesis 1:28). . . . He destroyed the base of the kingdom of darkness and made it possible once again for God's people to fulfill the Genesis commission to have dominion.[37]

In fact, God gave Adam "dominion over the fish of the sea . . . the fowl of the air . . . the cattle, and over all the earth [to till the soil and produce food], and over every creeping thing that creepeth upon the earth" (Genesis 1:26). Nor did man lose that dominion: We still ride horses, eat chicken and beef, and swat mosquitoes. God says nothing about dominion over the media or schools or governments. That unbiblical goal is shared by many in the revival and spiritual warfare movements along with marches for Jesus and Promise Keepers, especially in relation to the year 2000. More of that in the next chapter.

What About Revival?

It comes as a shock to most Christians to discover that the word "revival" is not found in the entire King James Bible. "Revived" appears six times, but it always refers to the physical revival of an individual. "Revive" occurs eight times, mostly referring to Israel. Never is there even a hint in the entire Bible of a "spiritual revival" as Christians think of it today. Not once!

"Revival" *sounds* so biblical, so spiritual, and is the most sought-after goal among Christians in our time. Everyone remembers the great revivals in history: under Wesley, Whitefield, Edwards, Finney, Moody, and others. Surely it must be right to desire another such "visitation of the Holy Spirit." Isn't that every godly pastor's hope for his church, for our country, and for the world? And it isn't in the Bible? Impossible!

Legitimate questions come to mind. First of all, there are a number of expressions which have no biblical basis (in fact they contradict biblical teaching) but are associated with the idea of revival and are accepted without question. For example, Brownsville Assembly of God pastor John Kilpatrick declares with great authority: "Every minister of God in these days needs a mantle of the '90's. The '80's mantle won't work anymore. . . . Even the early and mid-'90's mantle won't work anymore. . . . You have to have a fresh mantle."[38] It sounds impressive, but what is this *mantle?* And how does it change? He doesn't explain. It is simply accepted revival terminology.

Presumably, Kilpatrick's "fresh mantle" is related to other revival terms such as a "fresh visitation of the Spirit" and a "fresh anointing." If the believer is indwelt by Christ (Romans 8:10,11; 2 Corinthians 13:5; Colossians 1:27; etc.) and by the Holy Spirit (John 14:17; Romans 8:9; 1 Corinthians 3:16; etc.), and has an abiding anointing of the Spirit (1 John 2:27), and if Christ is always in our midst when we meet, as He promised, then what could be the meaning of a "fresh visitation of the Spirit" or a "fresh anointing"? Leaders of this current revival habitually invite the Holy Spirit to be present and to work. But He *is* indwelling us and He *is* present and at work among us when we meet. So the idea of "revival" as some special anointing or visitation of the Holy Spirit is not biblical and could lead into error, as indeed it has done in the charismatic movment.

How would one recognize the arrival of a *fresh* visitation or anointing or mantle? By *unusual* manifestations, of course. Thus one is predisposed to look for such manifestations and they become the proof that God is at work. *Revival* is something *special* with unique signs. One can see this error at Toronto and at Pensacola, as we have pointed out above. Ed Roebert, pastor of the 6000-member Hatfield Christian Church in Pretoria, South Africa, declares unequivocally:

> God is taking us to the greatest outpouring of the Holy Spirit the world has ever known. I believe that as God takes us into the new millennium, He's going to take us in with signs and wonders and miracles and heavenly power. I will not back down from this.

If Christ is in us and with us, as He surely is, and we are being "filled with the Spirit" (Ephesians 5:18) as Paul indicates may be our continual experience (not something special), then we ought to be supremely happy, victorious, and fruitful. That being the case, what is this "outpouring of the Holy Spirit"? And if it takes a special "outpouring," then could we not blame God for withholding it? And if it only comes through prayer and fasting, then we are to blame for souls going to hell and Christians living in sin. The Bible advocates prayer and fasting for special needs (Daniel 9:3; Matthew 17:21; 1 Corinthians 7:5) but never to bring about a "fresh outpouring" of revival with special manifestations.

If the Holy Spirit is in and with us to convict sinners and to teach us from the Word, then we ought to be content and live in the light of that truth. Surely God's Word, the "sword of the Spirit" (Ephesians 6:17; Hebrews 4:12), is the means by which souls are convicted and saved. God's Word is sufficient to perfect us if we heed it (2 Timothy 3:15-17). Could it be possible that looking for a special anointing or outpouring or revival could prevent us from living in the fullness of what God has already given us, and could even provide us with an excuse for failure to do so?

Some Earnest Concerns

Our desire is not to be critical but to earnestly face the facts and the dangers. Whether one believes that revival is biblical or not, and whatever one's definition, surely one's desire is that through revival God would be exalted, Christ would be made known as He truly is, and His Word obeyed. What if that should not be the case? What if we had a revival of false teachings? Is that not a legitimate concern? Forty years ago, before the apostasy had reached its present proportions, A.W. Tozer warned:

> Wherever Christians meet these days one word is sure to be heard constantly repeated; that word is *revival.*
>
> In sermon, song and prayer we are forever reminding the Lord and each other that what we must have to solve all our spiritual problems is a "mighty, old-time revival. . . ."
>
> So strongly is the breeze blowing for revival that scarcely anyone appears to have the discernment or the courage to turn around and lean into the wind, even though the truth may easily lie in that direction. . . .
>
> It is my considered opinion that under the present circumstances we do not want revival at all. A widespread revival of the kind of Christianity we know today in America might prove to be a moral tragedy from which we would not recover in a hundred years.[39]

One would think that those who want what Tozer calls a "mighty, old-time revival" would be concerned about the occultism being embraced today to bring it about. And the revival they have brought is surely a far cry from the Christianity we read of in the New Testament.

For many, Christianity has become "signs and wonders," or "falling under the power," or laughing uncontrollably. Others offer a Christianity which is designed to appeal to the worldly minded and to be inoffensive to sinners, including church services and "Christian" TV that outglitz Hollywood, or the excitement of 50,000 men cheering Jesus in a football stadium. For others it's the quest for self-esteem and a "positive self-image," probing the unconscious for past abuses that excuse present unbelief and carnality; or quietly carrying on a conversation with an imaginary "visualized Jesus." We do not need a "revival" of that kind of Christianity. It is the proclamation of the gospel and sound doctrine which alone can counteract the growing apostasy, not signs and wonders.

As we observe today's scene, there is another concern. Revival is being pumped up through emotionalism and hype. The so-called "praise and worship team" plays a large part in most churches. It is a necessary feature at Toronto or Pensacola.[40] Much of its style comes from the Vineyard and is characterized by shallow, repetitive lyrics and a rocklike beat. This author has listened sadly to "We love to worship You, we love to worship You" or perhaps "We love to praise You" repeated again and again. But there is neither worship nor praise in such repetitive phrases.

It is as though we have fallen in love with love, we praise praise, and worship worship. The *emotion* is being worked up, but there is no content—just *feelings* without reason. True worship and praise require an *appreciation of who Christ is* and *what He has done,* which the old hymns present with deep understanding. This depth is largely missing from today's lyrics.

Even when there may be some worthwhile content to the lyrics, the rock beat dominates. Such "worship" goes on for more than an hour at Pensacola or Toronto, where the audience is standing, clapping, jumping, and dancing and is gradually worked into an emotional frenzy that is conducive neither to genuine worship nor to an understanding of the Word of God or the person of Christ.

Monkey See, Monkey Do

Observing a Benny Hinn or Rodney Howard-Browne at work, one notices the careful audience preparation for what follows. Four former leaders in the new revival from England authored a book that every Christian should read: *The Signs and Wonders Movement—Exposed.*[41] They were accomplished performers of the signs and wonders, and they explain that it was all a matter of learning how. The book lists "VINEYARD TIPS FOR LEADERS." Here is a sampling, which explains a great deal about how to work up a revival and is the same pattern followed at Toronto and Pensacola:

It is usually helpful to begin every time with worship [singing, clapping, dancing etc.] followed by testimonies of people who have been touched. Immediately after the testimonies, invite the Holy Spirit to come upon these individuals again and do a further work. . . . They often begin to experience the same outward manifestations again.

When ministry begins, look for . . . manifestations such as crying, shaking, laughing, etc. . . .

Encourage people not to be fearful of what God is doing. . . .[42]

Much of today's "deliverance" takes place in the emotionally charged atmosphere of Toronto and Pensacola and their offshoots. Pastor Don Matzat reminds us that a skeptical student informed Dr. Jean-Martin Charcot, chief physician at the Salpetriere Hospital in Paris in the 1880s, that he had "invented rather than discovered 'hystero-epilepsy.'" Because patients who were susceptible to suggestion were housed with genuine epileptics, they began to have what appeared to be seizures. Similar transference of behavior takes place in these revivals, as any sober observer can readily see.

The emotional manifestations seem to mimic one another in all those who "get it." While there is definitely a relationship between the two, there is a different style of behavior at Toronto from that at Pensacola. It seems clear that the behavior is learned in the local setting.

This raises another concern: That much of today's preaching of the gospel is characterized by emotional appeals to "make a decision for Christ" without clearly explaining the *GOSPEL!* Multitudes attracted to Christ because of His winsome personality and admirable character, or because "He changes lives" or heals bodies or prospers businesses, have not truly believed the gospel. Thus, sadly, they are not saved at all. How often have we witnessed a psychological, even hypnotic, manipulation of the audience to obtain "decisions." No one can do this more effectively than Steve Hill, the evangelist at Pensacola. He uses every trick for pulling people forward, and it all somehow passes for the leading of the Holy Spirit. Such manipulation was evident that famous Father's Day in 1995. Far from being a "spontaneous move of the Spirit" as claimed, the "revival" began with much coaxing and fleshly effort on Hill's part and with little comparative result.

A Deep Concern About Leadership

Another grave concern is the associations of those who are leading today's revival. This "revival" draws everyone together in the same manner that Promise Keepers does. Roman Catholics who do not know the gospel and whose Church, as we have thoroughly documented, is in fact opposed to the gospel, are being "revived" as well and embraced as brothers and sisters in Christ. A mixed multitude go to Toronto or Pensacola or elsewhere, "get blessed," and come back emotionally charged to carry on in their own churches.

Bill Bright claims that the Holy Spirit has revealed to him that the awakening now underway "will result in the greatest spiritual harvest in history."[43] In his speech at a Catholic church in Rome when accepting the Templeton Prize for Progress in Religion, Bill pledged that "all the proceeds [more than a million dollars] ... will go to that God-inspired purpose ... [of] fast[ing] and pray[er] for a worldwide spiritual awakening and the completion of the Great Commission ... by the end of the year 2000. ..."[44]

One must, however, question a prayer-and-fasting crusade for revival financed by acceptance of a prize for contributing to progress toward the establishment of a *new world religion!* It takes no prayer and fasting at all to recognize that ecumenism and compromise are increasingly infecting many leaders in the highest ranks among evangelicals. And it is disconcerting that those who lead the revival movement are contributing to this apostasy. Let us face the painful facts.

The Templeton Prize for "Progress in Religion"

We have already noted that one of the most anti-Christian men ever to be accepted as a Christian leader is wealthy money manager John Marks Templeton. He is so obviously an occultist that it is astounding that he could have "crept in unawares," yet he has. Templeton offers an annual religion prize larger than the Nobel Prize. He explains why:

Microbes slowly evolved into worms, fishes, reptiles, and mammals. Humans did not appear until forty thousand years ago ... the human mind is so potent ... that no one knows what may happen next. Evolution is accelerating ... traditional Judaism and Christianity are losing their powers to inform the contemporary mind. ...

Theologians ... must begin to explore the vast unseen dimensions of our evolving universe. ... The main purpose of the Templeton Foundations is to encourage enthusiasm for accelerating discovery and progress in spiritual matters. ...

The next stage of human divine progress on the evolutionary scale needs ... geniuses of the spirit ... [who] can develop a body of knowledge about God that doesn't rely on ancient revelations or scripture [such as the Bible] ... that is scientific ... and is not disputed because of divisions between religions or churches or ancient scripture or liturgy. ...

To encourage progress of this kind, we have established the Templeton Foundation Prizes for Progress in Religion.[45]

Templeton could not state more clearly that he hopes to establish the new world religion of Antichrist which will unite all religions! To that end he has formed a religious research center called the Humility Theology Information Center.[46] According to Templeton, "progress" is needed because the world's scriptures (including the Bible) "were written ... [by] men whose minds were limited by cosmologies long since discredited."[47] Nor does the Bible accurately record the words of Christ, because those who reported them "could write down only what they understood ... [as] ignorant and primitive ... Jews."[48]

On the contrary, Paul affirmed that every word in the Bible "is given by inspiration of God" (2 Timothy 3:16). Peter said of the Bible, "Holy men of God spoke as they were moved by the Holy [Spirit]" (2 Peter 1:21). The psalmist said, "Forever, O LORD, thy word is settled in heaven" (Psalm 119:89). But Templeton believes none of this.

Though Templeton honors all religions, he reserves his strongest praise for two of the most blatantly anti-Christian cults: The Unity School of Christianity and The Church of Religious Science. He commends them for viewing man as "an expanding idea in the mind of God" and for striving for "progress" in religion because "as mind advances, the old forms [of religion] die."[49] He writes:

> The doctrinal formulations of Christianity have changed and will change from age to age. . . . Christians think God appeared in Jesus of Nazareth two thousand years ago for our salvation and education. But we should not take it to mean that . . . progress stopped . . . that Jesus was the end of change. . . . To say that God cannot reveal Himself again in a decisive way [through other Messiahs] . . . seems sacrilegious. . . .[50]

In keeping with his idea of "progress" in religion, Templeton suggests, "Maybe one of the attributes of God is change."[51] That is obviously true of *his* "god," but the God of the Bible declares, "For I am the LORD, I change not" (Malachi 3:6). Templeton's god is clearly the god of pantheism, not the God of the Bible:

> God is billions of stars in the Milky Way and He is much more. . . . Time and space and energy are all part of God . . . God is five billion people on Earth . . . God is untold billions of beings on planets of millions of other stars . . . God is the only reality. . . . God is all of you and you are a little part of Him.[52]

The Humble Approach?

To suggest that Christianity is the one true faith and is unchangeable contradicts what Templeton calls *The Humble Approach* in religion. According to him, when people take a "humble attitude, they welcome new ideas about the spirit just as they welcome new scientific ideas. . . . Humility opens the door to the realms of the spirit, and to research and progress in religion" and "is the key to progress"[53] because it prevents the proud delusion that any one religion could be right:

> The truly humble should be so open-minded that they welcome religious views from any place in the universe that is peopled with intelligent life. Seekers following the humble approach . . . never . . . reject ideas from other nations, religions, or eras . . . the humble approach to theology is ongoing and constantly evolving. . . .
>
> In fact, at the heart of true religion is the willingness to see truths in other religions. The Persian scriptures claim, "Whatever road I take joins the highway that leads to Thee. . . . Broad is the carpet God has spread. . . ."[54]

Christ, too, spoke of the broad road; but far from commending it, He said it led to destruction (Matthew 7:13). Yet Templeton declares, "No one should say that God can be reached by only one path. Such exclusiveness lacks humility. . . . New, freer, more imaginative and adaptable creeds will have to be devised in order that man's God-given mind and imagination can help to build the kingdom of heaven."[55] He has clearly rejected Christ, who said, "I am the way, the truth, and the life; no man cometh unto the Father [God] but by me" (John 14:6).

The very idea of "progress in religion" denies the gospel of Jesus Christ. Christianity is not a religion, nor is it subject to progressive development. Jesus Christ is "the same yesterday and today and forever" (Hebrews 13:8). Neither does Christianity maintain a friendly, ecumenical relationship with the world's religions; it opposes all of them as devices of Satan. We are to "earnestly contend for the faith which was once [for all time] delivered unto the saints" (Jude 3). Every true Christian should be uncompromisingly opposed to Templeton's neopagan beliefs and the prize he offers.

Obviously, it would be dishonest for anyone to accept the Templeton Prize for Progress in Religion who was not in complete sympathy with its purpose and the beliefs behind it. The very acceptance of the prize constitutes an endorsement of all that the prize represents. Nor can any evangelical recipient claim ignorance, for Templeton's neopagan views have been widely published for years. Yet Billy Graham (1982), Charles Colson (1993), and Bill Bright (1996) have accepted it, joining leading Hindu, Buddhist, and Muslim recipients.

Try to imagine Elijah accepting an ecumenical prize from the prophets of Baal, or Paul from the pagan leaders of his day! Yet an editorial in *Moody* magazine said:

> Despite the concerns of his critics, Charles Colson was right to accept his award and the opportunities that came with it.[56]

In the February 17, 1993, news conference announcing him as the recipient, Colson said, "I salute Sir John for establishing this award and doing it in such a generous way. . . ." His acceptance speech was made in Chicago on September 2, 1993, at the Parliament of the World's Religions (of which Templeton is a board member and major donor). This scheduled plenary event[57] had to be moved to a special location to accommodate the crowds for that night, allowing Colson's office to deceitfully claim that it was not a Parliament event,[58] though the robed delegates to the Parliament representing the world's religions were seated on the platform with Colson.[59] The meeting was opened with "a prayer by an Islamic scholar and concluded with a meditation by a Buddhist monk."[60]

Tragically, Colson did not clearly present the gospel. Nor did Bill Bright in his acceptance speech at a Catholic Church in Rome, though he was not sparing in his praise of Templeton and his anti-Christian prize. Said Bright:

> The prestigious Templeton Prize, to me, because of the nature of its objective, is greater than any other prize that could be given for any purpose. So I am deeply humbled and greatly honored to be the recipient of this 1996 magnificent Templeton Prize. I would like to thank and commend Sir John Templeton for establishing this prize....[61]

The battle is between the truth of God and the lie of Satan. It is fought not through the foolish binding of territorial spirits but with God's word. Jesus said that it is *the truth of His Word* that sets people free (John 8:30,31). Tragically, all too many evangelical churches give little help to their congregants, especially the youth, who face daily at school, among their peers, and in the media the lies of Satan presented in their most enticing form. There is a high dropout rate from Christianity among those raised in evangelical churches when they leave home, attend university, and move out into the working world. And how can a genuine rebirth of biblical Christianity take place when those leading the revival are themselves engaged in unconscionable compromise with the enemies of Christ!

*At the United Nations plans are underway for the great global happen-
ing of the year 2000. . . . The planet is alive with excitement . . .
[awaiting] a global renaissance. . . .*
—Matthew Fox, New Age priest[1]

*The year 2000 is the most compelling symbol of the future in our
lifetimes.*
—John Nesbitt, *Megatrends 2000* New Age author[2]

*It is only three years until the Great Jubilee of the Year 2000. The
Church and civil community of Rome are called to play an important
role in this event. The common conviction is that it will put our city at
the centre of world attention, giving concrete expression to the name*
Caput mundi, *which it is commonly called. . . .*[3]
*In fact, preparing for the year 2000 has become as it were a herme-
neutical key of my pontificate.*
—Pope John Paul II[4]

*Pope John Paul II stands like a rock against all opposition in his clear
enunciation of the foundational principles of the Christian faith.*
—Pat Robertson[5]

*The Pope's a great guy, he's a real born-again, evangelical Charis-
matic. . . .*
—John Wimber[6]

*The Salem [Massachusetts] Religious Leaders Association has officially
welcomed a high priest witch into its ranks. . . . Randal Wilkinson,
priest at Saint Peter's Episcopal Church, says nobody in the interfaith
clergy support group "could think of any compelling reason" to forbid
Poirier from joining. . . . "We don't discriminate based on creed."*
—Associated Press[7]

*One of the most visible American "televangelists," the Rev. Robert
Schuller, will make a broad appeal for Christian-Muslim understanding
today, delivering a keynote address before a large gathering of
American Muslims at the Meadowlands.*
—The Times-Post Wire Service, August 31, 1997[8]

*The 2000th birthday of Christ could mark the end of the Reactionary
Age [resulting from the Reformation] in church history (1517–1999)
and . . . Christ's church born again!*
—Robert Schuller[9]

25

* * *

A.D. 2000:
Millennial Madness

Every day follows another, year after year and century after century. Logically, therefore, there is no basis for the excitement that builds in anticipation of the turn of each century, nor for Roman Catholicism's designation of the first year of each new century as a "Holy Year." Nevertheless, as the year 2000 approaches, there is a growing hope among the world's religious and political leaders that it will mark the dawning of a new era of peace and harmony for mankind.

The first week in September 1997, about 60 of the world's leading thinkers met in the Czech capital at the invitation of Czech President Vaclav Havel and Nobel Laureate Elie Wiesel to plan a new future in the new millennium. Among those attending were the Dalai Lama, former Israeli Prime Minister Shimon Peres, former South African President F.W. de Klerk, and Crown Prince Hassan of Jordan.[10]

Pope John Paul II is using his immense power and prestige to push bankers into forgiving Third World debt as a unique tribute to the year 2000, which—to whatever extent that may happen—would polish the Vatican's image. Pat Robertson has been promoting the same idea. In what the International Monetary Fund (IMF) called "a historic event," world financial leaders, including IMF managing director Michel Camdessus (a French Catholic) and World Bank president James Wolfensohn, met with Vatican officials and Catholic bishops from Third World countries in a closed-door session at the Vatican during June 9 and 10, 1997. An interfaith coalition backing the Pope argues that—

...the arrival of a new millennium provides a perfect occasion—and rationale—for a one-time forgiveness of debts owed by the world's most impoverished countries.[11]

The year 2000 does not represent a measure of time since the birth of Buddha or Confucius or Mohammed, but since the birth of Christ. The initials A.D. are short for anno Domini, meaning "in the year of our Lord." Christ's birth determines dates used all over the world, even in atheistic countries or those of a non-Christian religion. Behind every date on each calendar, coin, or document is the Person Jesus Christ and the great event of God's incarnation through the virgin birth in Bethlehem. The turn of the millennium, therefore, cannot escape its association with Jesus Christ.

Elaborate plans are being made by various Christian organizations to celebrate Christ's 2000th birthday—a celebration "not limited to Christians."[12] It is hoped that through participation in these festivities, non-Christians will be drawn to Christ. In fact, we passed the 2000th birthday at the latest in 1996 due to an error in the calendar. Christ's birth must have been in 4 or 5 B.C., inasmuch as Herod the Great, in whose days Jesus was born (Matthew 2:1), died in 4 B.C.[13] There is no special reason, however, to celebrate Christ's 2000th "birthday."

It is this author's carefully considered opinion that the celebration and events accompanying the eve of the year 2000 will generate a worldwide spiritual delusion beyond anyone's capacity even to imagine at this time. So great will be the confusion, and so all-inclusive the false religious unity created, that true Christianity may well be forced underground. Robert Muller, former U.N. Assistant Secretary-General and chancellor of the University for Peace, has said:

> We need a world or cosmic spirituality. . . . I hope that religious leaders will get together and define before the end of this century the cosmic laws which are common to all faiths. . . .
>
> We must hope also that the Pope will come before the year 2000 to the United Nations, speak for all the religions and spiritualities on this planet and give the world religious view of how the third millennium should be a spiritual millennium which will see the integration and harmony of humanity with creation, with nature, with the planet, with the cosmos and with eternity.[14]

A "Jesus" Under the Curse of the True Jesus

On New Year's Eve 1999, the entire world will celebrate a "new millennium" with high hopes for a rebirth of humanity into that very New Age of peace and prosperity prophesied by numerous occultists from Edgar Cayce to Alice Bailey. The fact, however, that the date being celebrated is a measure of time from the birth of Christ cannot be escaped even by non-Christians. Therefore, ecumenically minded Christians are planning to use the coming celebration for "evangelism." The late M.H. Reynolds pointed out somberly:

> There are several important facts God's people need to know about the dangers of A.D. 2000 evangelism.
>
> First, this new ecumenical evangelism requires the acceptance of Roman Catholics and liberal Protestants as partners in evangelism, not those in need of being evangelized. . . .
>
> Evangelicals have followed the path of compromise for so long that they have lost almost all spiritual discernment. Evangelical leaders have become "blind leaders of the blind" and those who follow their leadership are in danger of falling into the ecumenical ditch. . . .
>
> So successful has been the devil's plan to use "Evangelism" to forge an unscriptural Ecumenism that there has never been a time in history when a larger number of diverse groups are singing the same song, "We must get together to evangelize the world."[15]

In anticipation of the year 2000, plans are underway for the most spectacular and worldly commemoration of Christ in history. The *Los Angeles Times* reported, "From Vatican City to Anaheim Hills, plans are afoot for the biggest blowout Christmas celebration the world has ever seen."[16] If present plans by leading Christians (in cooperation with Roman Catholics and secularists) succeed, a false "Christ" will have become the world's hero, with true Christianity all but forgotten. Could this be what Christ meant when He asked, "When the Son of man cometh, shall he find [the] faith on the earth?" (Luke 18:8).

Much of the dangerous delusion surrounding the coming of the year 2000 is promoted in author Jay Gary's incredible book *The Star of 2000*. Here is an entire volume by a Christian leader which enthusiastically proposes and describes many ingenious plans for ushering in the year 2000 with worldwide parties and gala events in celebration of the birth of Jesus Christ. Yet the gospel giving the purpose of Christ's coming is not to be found anywhere in its pages! This book is endorsed by a veritable *Who's Who* of leading evangelicals, including:

> Joe C. Aldrich, president, Multnomah School of the Bible; Bill Bright, Campus Crusade founder; Paul E. McKaughan, president, Evangelical Fellowship of Mission Agencies; Dick Eastman, International president, Every Home for Christ; John Dawson, Youth With A Mission; Paul Cedar, president, The Evangelical Free Church of America; Paul Eshleman, The *JESUS* Project; David Bryant, president, Concerts of Prayer International; E. Brandt Gustavson, president, National Religious Broadcasters, and others.[17]

Backed by this impressive galaxy of leaders, Jay Gary writes ardently about "the tremendous glory, beauty and dignity the people of the world [saved and unsaved] have and can bring before God in honor of Christ."[18] In contrast, the Bible declares that the natural man has nothing to offer God, for "all our righteousnesses are as filthy rags" (Isaiah 64:6). Indeed, even "the sacrifice of the wicked is abomination . . ." (Proverbs 21:27).

Nevertheless, Gary and many Christian leaders are determined that all the world, saved and unsaved, will hail Jesus as the "Man of the Millennium."[19] If they succeed in this goal they will have created a false Jesus guilty of the very thing the true Jesus warned against: "Woe unto you when all men shall speak well of you!" (Luke 6:26). Gary promises that Christmas 1999 will be—

> . . . the most meaningful Christmas in 2,000 years. When that starts to happen, the whole world will experience a new awakening in light of the new millennium.[20]

Almost everyone is jumping on the bandwagon of this counterfeit Christ. Even former Soviet President Mikhail Gorbachev claims that "true socialism promotes the values preached by Christ . . . we promote the cause of Christ." After touring sites in Israel and recalling the life of Jesus, Gorbachev termed himself a "lifelong socialist, following in the footsteps of Jesus." He even affirmed that peace and social harmony between Palestinians and Israelis "would have to be founded on the spirit of Jesus."[21]

Such is the growing appeal of Ghandi's Jesus, whom the world is embracing through "Jesus celebrations" and marches.

A Generic "Jesus" Praised by All

At the same time that he has gained the confidence and backing of the top evangelical leadership, Jay Gary has also been working closely with New Agers such as Robert Muller and John Nesbitt. He has worked also with *World Goodwill*, which comes out of leading occultist Alice Bailey's Lucifer Publishing Company. Gary is founder and executive director of Bimillennial Global Interaction Network (BEGIN), which *World Goodwill* approvingly describes as "a group of world citizens who circulate information and ideas on celebrating the year 2000 as a planetary jubilee with an agenda of hope."[22]

BEGIN has advertised Nesbitt's *Megatrends 2000* and promoted the 1993 Parliament of the World's Religions.[23] *World Goodwill* published a letter by Gary in which he solicited participation in the celebration of Christ by its occultist readers, the vast majority of whom are enemies of Christ:

> One common project we are developing is an "International Year of Thanksgiving" in 2000, especially through the United Nations. Dr. Robert Muller has given leadership to this proposal. If any of your readers would like to bring definition to a World Thanksgiving Year in 2000 marked by reflection, reconciliation, and gratitude between nations, cultures and peoples [no mention of gratitude to Christ or God], please have them correspond with us.
>
> We are collecting articles and papers on these themes for an upcoming *Let's Talk 2000* Forum.[24]

Most of the celebrations that Gary proposes for the year 2000 involve sentimentality mixed with Disneyland-like glamor and fun calculated to appeal to non-Christians. How many will be deluded into thinking that by celebrating His advent they have achieved a relationship with Christ? Some of the ingenious possibilities exciting Gary include reenacting "the 2,000th anniversary of the journey of the Magi . . . with horses and camels over the original Middle East route!"[25] Also a 'Journey of the Magi' visitor's center in Bethlehem, complete with a planetarium!"[26]

Gary is offering the world a generic "Jesus" who "belongs to people everywhere, no matter what their race or creed . . . the hope of revolutionaries and evolutionaries, he fascinates intellectuals and anti-intellectuals. . . ."[27] The book proposes that Christ can be celebrated by *everyone* as "the Star of 2000 . . . the greatest religious genius that ever lived . . . the outstanding personality of all time . . . one of the greatest teachers humanity has ever had . . . the most important and influential person who has ever lived . . . the celebrity . . . history's most intriguing figure," etc.[28] Such humanistic praise appeals to mankind's fallen nature and natural inclination to worship heroes. The closer the world is drawn to this false Jesus, however, the further it will be removed from Jesus Christ and His gospel and mission.

Indeed, Gary suggests that one need not "embrace the theological Jesus" to find him "worthy of a momentous anniversary tribute." Instead of encouraging the "repentance toward God and faith toward our Lord Jesus Christ" (Acts 20:21) which Paul preached, he invites a godless and Christ-rejecting world to celebrate "the most meaningful Christmas in 2,000 years . . . the greatest [birthday] celebration in the history of civilization."[29] The world loves to party, and Gary promises that this will be the biggest and most fun-filled party in history.

Were the entire world to engage in the celebration Gary proposes, it would not be a triumph for Christ and His cross, but a tragic cover-up of the world's rejection of the salvation He offers. To propose this huge party in the name of Jesus is deception of the worst sort. That leading evangelicals would enthusiastically endorse this book speaks volumes about the condition of the church today and where the year 2000 could find her. M.H. Reynolds called the A.D. 2000 Evangelism movement—

> . . . the greatest and most deceptive push toward ecumenical apostasy the world has ever seen.[30]

National Prayer and Marches for "Jesus"

In a similar spirit of ecumenism, Shirley Dobson, wife of Christian psychologist James Dobson, has said that the National Day of Prayer, which she chairs, "belongs to all faiths and all people. And we're encouraging all people in their spheres of influence to come together to pray and intercede for our nation."[31] Did the Pope indeed have the right idea at Assisi? Are the prayers of everyone—even animists, witch doctors, Hindus, and Buddhists—efficacious? How can evangelicals encourage pagans, occultists, and members of false religions to join with them in prayer for "God's" blessing? Isn't that like Elijah asking the prophets of Baal to join him in prayer for God's blessing upon Israel, or Paul asking the priests at the temple of Diana in Ephesus and Stoics on Mars Hill to join the church in prayer for God's blessing upon the Roman Empire?

We watched the observance of the 1997 National Day of Prayer presented on TBN. There was no doubt about the sincerity and earnestness of those who participated. The prayers and speeches of those involved (Promise Keepers, the March for Jesus, etc.) evidenced a genuine passion for national unity and blessing upon America. But it was also clear that something was tragically amiss, for unity alone was the defining element.

Again and again participants expressed their longing for a moral and spiritual awakening in America that would unite families and communities. The longed-for unity and awakening, however, was to be centered in a generic "faith" and an ecumenism that finds no fault with false doctrine or occult practices. No distinction was made between God's truth and Satan's lie; no concern was expressed for the false beliefs that delude and damn mankind—only the desire for a unity without truth. How odd it is that those who crusade so vigorously against abortion and other evils in the world rarely express concern for the heresy and occultism in the church.

The annual March for Jesus (MFJ) has its origins in a London, England, charismatic group called Icthus Christian Fellowship. In cooperation with YWAM, it brings literally millions around the world into the streets to "celebrate Jesus." On June 25, 1994, according to reports—

> More than 20,000 inmates participated in March for Jesus events in prisons across the country. . . .
> In Sao Paulo, Brazil, 850,000 danced and sang in the streets in pouring rain. . . .
> An estimated 1 million people participated in a single prayer rally in Seoul, Korea.

For the first time, Christians were given permission to hold public marches in Mongolia and in Phnom Penh, Cambodia. . . .[32]

And so it went around the world. It sounds so good! But March For Jesus literature encourages everyone (including Catholics and even Hindus, Buddhists, and Muslims) to join together in a Jesus celebration. How can those who embrace religions and philosophies that *oppose* Christ express *appreciation* for Him? Does this not produce pseudofollowers of Christ who are as far from the truth as those alleged converts in John 2, 6, and 8—and as much opposed to the gospel? Gandhi admired Jesus but remained a Hindu whose very admiration for his false "Christ" prevented him from knowing the real Jesus.

Jay Gary has been the Midwest regional coordinator for MFJ. He is the founder of the AD 2000 Global Service Office and of Celebration 2000 and of the umbrella organization AD 2000, with which MFJ is affiliated. The 1994 MFJ brochure states, "March for Jesus is part of the AD 2000 network of international ministries. . . ."

Jay Gary boasts that "the March for Jesus is becoming the world's biggest street party"[33] and is helping to prepare the world for the biggest-ever celebration of Jesus. Is that really why Christ came, so that street parties could be held in His name? Marches let the politicians know that here is a large voting block to be appeased. Pat Robertson has said a number of times that "the Washington For Jesus Rally in April 1980 [which he co-chaired with Bill Bright] was a turning point in American politics."[34] Even so, America has continued to go downhill politically and morally.

Christianity is being subtly redefined to make it attractive to the world. Millions of "Christians" of all stripes, from evangelicals to Catholics to Mormons and Moonies, have joined together in various organizations (such as Pat Robertson's Christian Coalition) to Christianize America by calling it back to the "traditional moral values" upon which it was founded. Somehow, this "mission" has captured the imagination and loyalty of multitudes of evangelicals and has become confused in their hearts and minds with the biblical Great Commission. The new hope is that "America can be saved" with a compromised ecumenical gospel which has been watered down enough that it doesn't offend anyone.

The Sellout of Christianity

Roman Catholics have become the evangelicals' partners in evangelizing the world when in fact they ought to be a chief target of evangelism on the part of evangelicals—as millions of former Roman Catholics would testify. And those such as Graham, Bright and Colson, who have been foremost in embracing Catholics as "brothers and sisters in Christ," have compromised the gospel to do so.

Colson's office claimed that accepting the Templeton prize gave Colson "a marvelous opportunity, not unlike that of Paul on Mars Hill, to present the Gospel of Jesus Christ clearly and powerfully to . . . many who have perverted the truth."[35] Sadly, however, the gospel was not presented. In his acceptance speech at Chicago's 1993 Parliament of the World's Religions (as elsewhere), Colson began by saying that Jesus Christ had transformed his life and that He is God and "the Way, the Truth, and the Life." It was a good start, but he never got around to the essential explanation of what that meant. After all, Hindus believe that Jesus, along with everyone, is God; and New Agers believe that the way, truth, and life is within everyone. Colson ended by mentioning the cross and resurrection. But there was no explanation to distinguish the biblical meaning of these terms from the false beliefs of most in his audience.

Colson's speeches were classic exercises in the religious equivalent of political correctness. There were repeated references to "moral breakdown," "moral values," a "rising spiritual movement in America," and other vague terms open to differing interpretation. He spoke of "transcendent values . . . moral consensus . . . moral choices . . . spiritual awakening . . . moral revival and social renewal . . . moral uplift . . . human dignity . . . character and creed . . . traditional beliefs . . . Judeo-Christian heritage," etc. All religions were equally honored with phrases such as "religious influence . . . every religious tradition finds common ground . . . religious conviction . . . all our creeds . . . true religion and its humanizing values," etc.

While Colson did refer to "the love of Christ," the "reconciling power of Christ," and to a friend's "conversion to Christ," there was no explanation of who Christ is, why He came, and how one can be saved. Colson described his own conversion as calling out to God to "take me as I am," with the added comment that "from that moment to this, my life has never been the same. . . ." Followers of many religions give similar testimonies, and credit their gods with the same transforming powers. Nothing was said that would contradict the false beliefs of Templeton or offend the press corps or that would lead anyone to saving faith in Christ.

Worse yet, at the Parliament, Colson perverted the gospel with his final story of a crucifix in a prison cell to which a prisoner pointed and said, "He's doing time for all the rest of us." Christ is not "doing time" for us. He is no longer on the cross. The debt has been paid in full! Colson's promotion of this false Christ of Catholicism left unbelievers further from salvation than before.

The same was true of Colson's "Speech to the National Press Club" on March 11, 1993, when it was first announced that he had been awarded the Templeton Prize. Again, not only was the gospel missing but some of the terminology he used actually undermined it.

He suggested that placing nonviolent inmates in "work camps or community-based treatment centers" would be "redemptive for the individual" and that "religion [*any* religion?] provides a moral impulse to do good." Colson mentioned "the love of Christ," a "beautifully carved crucifix of Jesus hanging on the cross," but did not present the gospel. He hinted at it ("only the gospel of Christ can bring about moral reformation. . . . It is Jesus Christ who made a lasting difference in my life") but never explained how or why.[36]

Tragically, this same compromise and confusion also characterized Bill Bright's Templeton Prize acceptance speech at a Catholic church in Rome, to which we have already referred. He used similar religiously correct terms that would not offend Templeton or Catholic Church leaders (four cardinals were present) or representatives of other religions. The terminology Bright used was general enough to allow anyone present to attach his own meaning to the words.

In fact, the very acceptance of the prize by Graham, Colson, and Bright was a denial of the gospel and put them in a position where they had to continue to compromise. It would have been the height of hypocrisy and ingratitude to accept an award designed to promote all religions and at the same time to declare that Christ alone saves. No wonder the gospel was not made plain! Even *Moody* magazine admitted as much but also justified that failure in its editorial:

> Colson's critics are right in noting that his address focused more on morals than the gospel. Non-Christians probably didn't hear enough about the work of Christ to understand the way of salvation. But in a pluralistic setting, a speech on the social benefits of Christian ideals can serve a pre-evangelistic purpose.[37]

"Pre-evangelistic purpose"? Some of those present may have had no other opportunity to hear the gospel. Why not present it at this most unusual opportunity, as Colson promised he would? In fact, accepting that prize encouraged Templeton in his error. Graham, Colson, and Bright should rather have rejected his prize and presented the gospel to this deluded man in an attempt to rescue him from a Christless eternity. And what of the multitudes led astray by the acceptance of this prize and the commendation of it and of Templeton?

An Ecumenical Gospel for the Next Millennium

There is an almost wholesale acceptance by evangelicals of the growing ecumenical movement to evangelize the world by the year 2000. One of its leaders, Michael Green, has spoken at such prestigious gatherings as Billy Graham's 1983 International Conference for Itinerant Evangelists in Amsterdam. There he told these evangelists from around the world (who were looking to the speakers Graham had chosen for advice), "Don't talk about the new birth, talk about liberation. . . . Identify with and befriend secular society. Become one with them. . . ." In his book *The Futures of Christianity*, Green suggests that Christians "can be taught . . . about devotion to God by Muslims or Hindus, about detachment from the passions by Buddhists, about the sacredness of nature by animists, and about goodness by atheists . . ."![38] That the lost must be "born again," as Jesus said (John 3:3,7), is being exchanged for a humanistic gospel of self-righteousness.

The call for a return to morality is replacing the gospel. One need only promote "traditional morals" to be warmly welcomed among evangelicals. William J. Bennett, former U.S. Secretary of Education, though a leader in the Catholic Campaign for America, has become a popular speaker among evangelicals because of his stand for traditional values. Evangelicals have praised Bennett's *The Book of Virtues*. In his final chapter he presents this destructive delusion:

> There is nothing distinctively Christian . . . in recognizing that religious faith adds a significant dimension to the moral life. . . . Faith is a source of discipline and power and meaning in . . . any major religious creed. . . . What Paul cites as "the fruit of the Spirit" . . . has its parallels in all the major faiths. . . .

The ecumenical tide has reached irresistible proportions. The Pope's 1986 gathering for prayer at Assisi, where he welcomed snake worshipers, fire worshipers, spiritists, animists, Buddhists, Hindus, Muslims, and shamans, was supported and attended by representatives of the World Council of Churches and even evangelicals. Represented there were the YWCA and YMCA, the Mennonite World Conference, the Baptist World Alliance (which includes the Southern Baptist Convention), the World Alliance of Reformed Churches, and the Lutheran World Federation.[39] Even the Associated Press in its report seemed amused by the mixture:

> Chants, temple bells and pagan spells echoed around the Roman Catholic shrines of Assisi yesterday as Pope John Paul II and his 200 guests from the world's 12 main religions prayed for world peace. . . .
>
> The medicineman of the Crow Indians, Chief John Pretty-on-Top, offered to cast out evil spirits. Many came forward, among them a young Franciscan monk.
>
> In a chapel down the road, the head of the Zoroastrian church in Bombay prayed before a fire that symbolized his God. . . .
>
> The 14th Dalai Lama, exiled god-king of Tibet, headed the strong Buddhist contingent, mumbling sutras amid tinkling bells at the Basilica of St. Peter. . . .

African animists, their togas the envy of any designer, invoked the spirits of trees and plants to come to the aid of peace. . . .[40]

The 1993 Parliament of the World's Religions was sponsored not only by the American Buddhist Congress and Spiritual Assembly of Baha'is, but also by the Roman Catholic Archdiocese of Chicago, the Catholic Theological Union, Chicago's Lutheran School of Theology, the Evangelical Church in America, Chicago Synod, the United Methodist Church, Northern Illinois Conference, Presbyterian Church (USA), and the united Church of Christ, Ecumenical Affairs, Chicago. The Vatican's official representative to the Parliament was "His Excellency the Most Reverend Francesco Gioia, of the Pontifical Council for Interreligious Dialogue."

Jay Gary has been involved in leadership and planning with Billy Graham's Lausanne movement and Campus Crusade for Christ. He praises the World Council of Churches for bringing "unity in modern times" and he anticipates "the greatest Christian congress in 2,000 years . . . [with] all of Christianity's 160 major traditions . . . join[ing] together in celebration of the Eucharist"[41] in the year 2000.

Cardinal Edward Cassidy, head of the Vatican's Ecumenical Ministry, has also proposed "joint Christian celebrations for Easter in the year 2000."[42] Unlike Gary, however, Cassidy makes no mention of the Eucharist. For all its talk of unity, Rome forbids Catholics to partake of the Protestant communion and forbids Protestants to partake of the Roman Catholic Mass or Eucharist. The very first words of Bill Bright's Templeton Award acceptance speech in Rome recognized warmly the presence of this deceiver from the Vatican: "Your Eminence, Cardinal Cassidy. . . ."[43]

Gary praises Pope John Paul II and the Vatican's New Evangelization 2000 as well as Fr. Tom Forrest, who heads it, and suggests that the Roman Catholic "gospel" is the true gospel.[44] One of the endorsers of Gary's book is Fr. Tom Forrest.[45] To know what the Vatican means by evangelization and the dishonesty of its pretense of working with evangelicals, one need only consider the following excerpts from the speech Forrest gave to a Catholic-only audience at a typical "unity" conference of Catholic and Protestant charismatics:

Our role in evangelization is not just to make Christians . . . [but to] bring . . . them into the Catholic Church. . . . Now listen again to the words of Paul VI. . . . "The commitment of someone newly evangelized . . . must be given concrete and visible form through entry into . . . the Church, our visible sacrament of salvation."

I like saying those words . . . "Our visible sacrament of salvation" . . . and if that is what the Church is, we have to be evangelizing into the Church. . . .

No, you don't just invite someone to become a Christian. You invite them to become Catholics. . . . Why would this be so important? . . . First of all, there are seven sacraments, and the Catholic Church has all seven. . . .

On our altars we have the body of Christ, we drink the blood of Christ. Jesus is alive on our altars as offering. . . . And it [this offering of Jesus] . . . opens the doors of Paradise. . . .

As Catholics we have Mary. . . . And that Mom of ours, Queen of Paradise, is praying for us till she sees us in glory.

As Catholics we have . . . popes from Peter to John Paul II . . . the rock upon which Christ did build His Church. . . .

As Catholics—now I love this one—we have purgatory! Thank God! I'm one of those people that would never get to the Beatific Vision without it. It's the only way to go. . . .

So as Catholics . . . our job is . . . evangelizing everyone we can into the Catholic Church, into the body of Christ, and into the third millennium of Catholic history. . . .[46]

Roman Catholicism's Ecumenical Role

The Pope and the Roman Catholic Church expect to play a leading role in the bimillennial celebration. After a private meeting (their fifth) between the two leaders in Rome on December 19, 1996, Yasser Arafat told reporters that he had "invited the Pontiff to celebrate Christmas in Bethlehem in the year 2000, and the Pope had accepted the invitation. 'I have offered to His Holiness the invitation to celebrate with us the 2000th year of our Jesus Christ,' Arafat said. . . ."[47]

"*Our* Jesus Christ"? Celebrate the birth of Jesus with Muslims, who teach that Jesus is not the Son of God, who deny His deity and death upon the cross for our sins, and who claim that someone died in His place rather than He in ours? This is the direction Rome's ecumenism has taken. Vatican II identifies the Muslim's Allah, a pagan deity, as the God of the Bible.

In 1985, speaking to Muslims in Brussels, Belgium, the Pope said: "Christians and Moslems, we meet one another in faith in the one God . . . [and] strive to put into practice . . . the teaching of our respective holy books."[48] Islam's Allah (the moon god) was the chief idol in the Kaabah long before Mohammed was born. Allah is *not* the God of the Bible, nor could any Christian commend the teachings of the Koran, which calls for *jihad* (holy war) against all non-Muslims. The Koran declares that Allah is not a father and has no son.[49]

Matching the Pope's apparent blindness was the naive praise of Muslims by President Clinton, speaking from the White House on January 12, 1997: "By experiencing hunger during Ramadan, the followers of Muhammad learn true compassion for the poor of the world who go hungry every day. [But the Muslims feast each night!] By reflecting on God's teachings in the Koran, they learn humility and the beauty of forgiveness. [But the Koran commands to slay all non-Muslims!] And, by their example of devotion and self-discipline during Ramadan, Moslems remind us all that our true strength is derived, not from food and drink, but from closeness to God. As the crescent moon [Allah's symbol] marks the beginning of Ramadan again this year, Hillary and I extend our best wishes for a holy and memorable observance."[50]

Meeting with Muslim leaders in West Africa in 1993, the Pope "called on Christians, Muslims and animists . . . to respect one another's religious beliefs. . . ."[51] How can one respect beliefs that lead people astray and into occult contact with demonic entities? Far from asking us to "respect" pagan beliefs, the Bible condemns them. Of course, Catholicism has always been paganism's partner.

John Paul II takes a broad-minded view not only of Islam but of Buddhism and all other religions as well. He considers the Tibetan Buddhist deity yoga (whereby we each become god) of his good friend the Dalai Lama, along with the prayers of witch doctors, spiritists, and every other religion, to be generating "profound spiritual energies" that are creating a "new climate for peace."[52] According to a *Los Angeles Times* news report:

Pope John Paul II slipped off his shoes to sit quietly and solemnly with the supreme patriarch of Thailand's Buddhists at a Buddhist monastery in Bangkok. . . .

The Roman Catholic pontiff later praised the "ancient and venerable wisdom" of the Asian religion.[53]

Try to imagine Peter attending a Buddhist temple ritual and praising Buddhism's wisdom! Or the apostle Paul telling audiences of Hindus, as John Paul II did during his visit to India, that he had not come there to teach them anything but "to learn from [their] rich spiritual heritage," and that the world needs to heed India's "spiritual vision of man"![54] The early Christians would never have been martyred had they taken a similar approach to Rome's pagan practices.

Speaking to Shintoists and Buddhists in Tokyo in 1981, John Paul II commended the wisdom of their ancient religions which inspired them "to see a divine presence in each human being. . . . [As Christ's Vicar] I express my joy that God has distributed these [religious] gifts among you"[55]—an unthinkable statement in view of the errors and occultism practiced in Shintoism and Buddhism! In Togo in 1985 the Pope exulted that he had "prayed for the first time with animists."[56] How better to confirm them in their darkness! One wonders how the Pope would answer Paul's question:

> . . . what communion hath light with darkness? And what concord hath Christ with Belial? Or what part hath he that believeth with an infidel? And what agreement hath the temple of God with idols? (2 Corinthians 6:14-16).

John Paul II declared that "the Second Vatican Council . . . recognized that in diverse religious traditions there is something true and good, the seeds of the Word. It encouraged Christ's disciples to discover 'the riches which a generous God has distributed among the nations.' "[57] Try to imagine Moses suggesting that Israel "discover the riches" to be found in the religions of the idol-worshiping pagans around them! A Catholic critic of his Church's astonishing ecumenism writes:

> Originally, ecumenism was concerned with unity among Christians. But it is now, increasingly . . . seek[ing] the union of all religions, Christian or non-Christian. On May 19, 1964, Paul VI

officially launched a Secretariat for the non-Christians . . . [which] played an important role during the last two sessions of the Council [Vatican II]. . . . Some months later, Msgr. Wojtyla [who became Pope John Paul II] declared:

"Nostalgia for the unity of Christians makes common cause with that of unity for the whole human race. . . . This gives rise to the attitude of the Church towards the other religions, which is based on the recognition of their spiritual values . . . reaching out to such religions as Islam, Buddhism, Hinduism. . . ."[58]

Once again it must be stated that there is not one instance in the Bible of recognizing "spiritual values" in false religions! Instead, such religions are denounced as devices of Satan. The occultism and demonic darkness that blinds and binds the followers of the religions the Pope praises ought to be exposed and the gospel given to them rather than commending their error and thereby encouraging their doom. The desire for ecumenical union brings destruction wrought by compromise Tragically, evangelical leaders are praising the Pope and encouraging a partnership with Rome.

An Astonishing Partnership

Evangelicals have joined in partnership with Roman Catholicism's counterfeit gospel to evangelize the world together. In so doing, they have also joined with all of Rome's pagan and occultist partners. Popes John XXIII and Paul VI were among the original founders of The Temple of Understanding, which joins all of the world's religions in one vast ecumenical bond known as the United Nations of Religions. In keeping with that spirit, Pope Paul VI told Hindu leader Sri Chinmoy, "Your message and mine are the same." And now evangelical leaders are saying to the Pope, "Your message and ours are the same." James Dobson, who received an honorary doctorate from Steubenville's Franciscan University[59] and works with Mormons and Catholics,[60] has called the Pope "the most eminent religious leader who names the name of Jesus Christ."[61]

A lead article in *Inside the Vatican* concerning the coming "third millennium of Christianity" (a favorite phrase of the Pope), begins with the following paragraph:

A perite mihi portas institiae ("Open to me the doors of justice")
John Paul II will utter these words on Christmas Eve, 1999. Then
he will knock three times with a silver hammer on the holy door on
the right side of St. Peter's facade which was sealed shut at the end
of the last Holy Year. Once the wall that covers the door is removed, the Pope will cross the threshold. He will bear a candle in
his left hand and a cross in his right. Thus will begin the Great
Jubilee of the year 2000.[62]

Jay Gary (with the endorsement of leading evangelicals)
speaks favorably of this event as part of the tradition that each
century, "as the pope struck the holy door with a golden hammer, living streams of grace and pardon from Christ, the rock,
were released." Gary presents this as though that hammer's
blows really did release "grace and pardon." He tells readers
that it was Pope Boniface VIII who began this tradition, and
that "from all over Europe, pilgrims streamed to Rome to experience forgiveness and spiritual renewal."[63] An additional 10
million visitors in the year 2000 are expected to visit Rome to
receive further installments of salvation from the Church—and
Gary and his evangelical supporters approve!

Gary neglects to tell his readers that Pope Boniface VIII was
no less a murderous monster than were so many of his fellow
popes. He fought wars to gain and keep the papacy; he had
both a mother and her daughter as his mistresses; he sacked
Palestrina, Italy, massacring its entire populace of nearly 6000,
smashing everything but the cathedral and sowing its fields
with salt. So evil was he that Dante's *Inferno* buried Boniface
facedown in a rocky fissure in the depths of hell.

Yet Boniface holds a revered place on that long list of popes,
each of whom is honored with the title "His Holiness . . . Vicar
of Christ"! In reaffirming Boniface's 1302 papal bull, *Unam
Sanctam*, the Fifth Council of Lateran referred to him as "our
predecessor Pope Boniface VIII, of happy memory."[64] "*Happy
memory*"? Such is the cover-up engaged in by Rome century
after century—a cover-up which continues to the present and
with which evangelical leaders have now aligned themselves.
And what did Boniface's *Unam Sanctam* decree?

There is but one holy, Catholic and Apostolic Church, outside
of which there is no salvation or remission of sins . . . [and] it is

altogether necessary for salvation for every creature to be subject to the Roman Pontiff.

That papal bull, the supreme law for Roman Catholics, has been reconfirmed and is still in force. Such is the true belief of the Pope and his bishops and cardinals—behind the ecumenical smiles and cooperative facade which they now present to the world. Pretending that Catholicism is in full accord with Protestantism, Richard John Neuhaus, coarchitect of ECT with Charles Colson, deceitfully declares:

> The first order of business is Christian unity, or ecumenism. As the second millennium has been one of Christian division, so John Paul says that the third millennium must be one of Christian unity. During the pontificates of John Paul and his predecessor, Paul VI, dramatic steps have been taken toward healing the breach.[65]

That phrase "Third Millennium of Christianity" is in keeping with the fact that Roman Catholicism rejects the biblical teaching of the rapture. Neuhaus adds that "John Paul speaks of the next century as a 'springtime' of Christian mission and Christian unity. . . . The Catholic church has only begun to reach out to evangelicals. . . . At the same time, this pontificate [of John Paul II] has been intensively engaged in forging new cooperative relations with other world religions. . . ."[66] In a more candid moment, Cardinal Augustin Bea, president of the Vatican Secretariat for Promoting Christian Unity, declared:

> The Roman Catholic Church would be gravely misunderstood if it should be concluded that her present ecumenical adventuresomeness and openness meant that she was prepared to reexamine any of her fixed dogmatic positions. What the church is prepared to do is to take . . . a more imaginative and contemporary presentation of these fixed positions.

So we have an evangelical-Catholic partnership to "evangelize the world by the year 2000" while Rome engages in "more cooperative relations with other world religions." Boston College professor Peter Kreeft (an evangelical convert to Catholicism) admits that Catholics don't know the gospel. While promoting Catholicism as the only true faith, Kreeft inadvertently reveals that most Catholics are not Christians, though Kreeft

equates being an active Roman Catholic with being "in Christ."
Here are his own words:

> Over the past twenty-five years I have asked hundreds of
> Catholic college students the question: If you should die tonight
> and God asks you why he should let you into heaven, what would
> you answer? The vast majority of them simply do not know the
> right answer to this, the most important of all questions, the very
> essence of Christianity. . . .
>
> After twelve years of catechism classes . . . their answer to that
> question is usually something like "be sincere" or "try your best" or
> "don't hurt people" or "work for peace". . . . They usually do not
> even mention Jesus![67]

The blunt truth is that Roman Catholics need to be evangelized, from the Pope on down. Instead, evangelicals have
signed an agreement not to "proselytize" and, having accepted
Catholics as Christians, are joining forces with them to evangelize the world by the year 2000. We trust that the immensity of
this delusion is now clear to the reader.

ECT has now been revised using evangelical language and
signed again. Colson, Bright, Packer, Robertson, and the other
Protestant signatories hope thereby to gain the support of other
evangelical leaders. However, the fact that some Catholic leaders have signed ECT2 has not changed in the slightest official
Roman Catholic dogma with its false gospel of works and ritual,
nor has it changed Catholicism as practiced by one billion faithful worldwide. ECT2 is an exercise in futility and duplicity.

Replacement Theology

Jay Gary writes, "For on January 1, 2001, we will celebrate the
start of the third millennium of the Christian era. Truly kings
and prophets longed to see our day!"[68] What an astonishing
statement! In fact, kings and prophets and true Christians
through the centuries have longed for Christ to take them to
heaven as He promised, not to see the world continue for a
third millennium since Christ. That the early Christians were
watching and waiting and hoping for Christ to take them at any
moment to heaven is clear from many Scriptures in the New
Testament, among them the following:

Let your loins be girded about, and your lights burning, and ye yourselves like unto men that wait for their lord . . . that when he cometh and knocketh they may open to him immediately. . . . Be ye therefore ready also, for the Son of man cometh at an hour when ye think not (Luke 12:35,36,40).

And if I go and prepare a place for you, I will come again and receive you unto myself, that where I am, there ye may be also (John 14:3).

For our conversation [citizenship] is in heaven, from whence also we look for the Savior, the Lord Jesus Christ, who shall change our vile body [at the rapture and resurrection], that it may be fashioned like unto his glorious body . . . (Philippians 3:20,21).

. . . how ye turned to God from idols to serve the living and true God, and to wait for his Son from heaven, whom he raised from the dead, even Jesus, which delivered us from the wrath to come (1 Thessalonians 1:9-10).

For the Lord himself shall descend from heaven with a shout, with the voice of the archangel and with the trump of God, and the dead in Christ shall rise first; then we which are alive and remain shall be caught up together with them in the clouds, to meet the Lord in the air, and so shall we ever be with the Lord. Wherefore comfort one another with these words (1 Thessalonians 4:16-18).

Henceforth there is laid up for me a crown of righteousness . . . and not to me only, but unto all them also that love his appearing (2 Timothy 4:8).

Looking for that blessed hope, and the glorious appearing of the great God and our Savior Jesus Christ . . . (Titus 2:13).

. . . unto them that look for him shall he appear the second time without sin unto salvation (Hebrews 9:28).

. . . we know that, when he shall appear, we shall be like him; for we shall see him as he is. And every man that hath this hope in him purifieth himself, even as he is pure (1 John 3:2,3).

Set your affection on things above, not on things on the earth. For ye are dead, and your life is hid with Christ in God. When Christ, who is our life, shall appear, then shall ye also appear with him in glory (Colossians 3:2-4).

God promised Israel an earthly kingdom, and those promises will be fulfilled at the second coming, when Christ returns to rescue His earthly people from Antichrist's armies and establishes His millennial kingdom on the throne of His father David in Jerusalem. But instead of waiting for Christ to come from heaven to restore the kingdom to Israel (Acts 1:6; 3:19-21), the popes fought with armies and navies to build a vast empire of earthly wealth and power for themselves. As an eighteenth-century historian reminds us, "The territory under the immediate dominion of the Pope was enlarged whenever war or treaty could increase it; and the inhabitants had to pay the utmost taxes they could bear."[69]

The delusion grew that the church had replaced Israel. Rome began to call itself the "new Jerusalem" and the "new Zion," and to take unto itself the titles which God had given to Jerusalem: the "city of God" and the "holy city," titles which Rome retains to this day. Anti-Semitism became official church doctrine as more than 100 anti-Semitic documents were published by the Roman Catholic Church between the sixth and twentieth centuries. The rationale was that "Christ crucifiers" had no rights in God's holy kingdom. The land of Israel belonged to the Christians, not to the Jews. Crusades were fought under the popes to drive out the Turks from the Holy Land—not to give it back to the Jews but to possess it for Rome.

To raise an army for the First Crusade, Pope Urban II promised instant entrance into heaven for all who fell in that great cause. The knights and knaves who responded with enthusiasm to that unbiblical promise left a trail of mayhem, plunder, and murder, giving the Jews they encountered on the long trek to Jerusalem the choice of baptism or death. After "liberating" that city by slaughtering the Turks, one of the victors' first acts was to herd the Jews into the synagogue and set it ablaze.

The Catholic Church has rejected the Bible prophecies concerning the return of Jews to Israel and those of the Messiah returning to reign from the throne of His father David. In 1862, echoing a belief held for centuries, *La Civilta,* the semiofficial voice of the Vatican, declared, "As the Jews were *formerly* God's people, so are the Romans [Catholics] under the New Covenant."[70]

Rejection of the Rapture

This Roman Catholic teaching that the church has replaced Israel, by placing the focus on an earthly kingdom led to a rejection of the biblical teaching that heaven is the Christian's home and hope. A rejection of the teaching of the rapture of the church to heaven then followed naturally. Thinking it is the new Israel, the Roman Catholic Church conceives of its mission as establishing the kingdom of God on earth. Because many Roman Catholics do not understand this dogma, Scott Hahn, a professed evangelical convert to Catholicism and now one of its ablest apologists, declares earnestly, "I would do anything to get Catholics to believe that the Church is the rebuilt Kingdom of David, the new and true Israel."[71] In *Christifideles Laici,* John Paul II prays thus to Mary: "O Virgin Mother, guide and sustain us. . . . Enable us to do our part in helping to establish on earth the civilization of truth and love. . . ."[72]

The Roman Catholic belief that Christians must establish an earthly kingdom, and the accompanying rejection of a rapture of Christians to heaven, has been adopted by many Protestants. This belief is becoming a major factor among charismatics, and noncharismatics of Reformed persuasion such as the Reconstructionists, many of whom now ridicule the rapture as an "escape theory." Robert Schuller has said, "When we built this church [the Crystal Cathedral], our aim was to construct such a building that it would stand for centuries."[73] Obviously he does not entertain the hope of an imminent return of Christ to take him to heaven, as did the early church. Schuller imagines "a professor of church history teaching in a theological seminary in the year 2300 . . . outlin[ing] the history of Christianity":

> The sixteenth-century Reformation will be seen as a reactionary movement. . . . And the period from 2000 A.D. on will be labeled as the Age of Mission. . . .
>
> [When] we find healing from the self-esteem-destroying emotions . . . we shall see a new church emerge in the next century—a body of believers who are relaxed, confident, inwardly secure people.[74]

Schuller sees the church gradually growing stronger and apparently taking over the world, not leaving for heaven. Many of those involved in the new spiritual-warfare movement imagine that they are thereby helping to take over the world for Christ in the process of establishing His kingdom. Promise Keepers is part of that "warfare." Early in 1994, Bill McCartney's pastor, James Ryle, declared, "Yes . . . 300,000 men have come together so far this year under Promise Keepers.... Never in history have 300,000 men come together except to go to war. These men are gathered for War!"[75]

To justify what is known as Reconstructionist, Dominionist, or Kingdom Now teaching, Old Testament promises for Israel are applied to the church. That Joshua was told to go in and possess the Promised Land is now taken to mean that the church must possess America and the world, which stretches God's promise to Joshua far beyond that which Joshua was given. Even J.I. Packer confuses Christ's call to proclaim the gospel with a call "to re-Christianize the North American milieu ... [and] rebuild the ruins ... [of] North American culture...."[76]

Reconstructionist leader Gary North writes: "God wants Christians to control the earth on His behalf.... [We] want to see a biblical reconstruction of the United States, so that it can serve as an example to be followed all over the world."[77] David Chilton declares: "Our goal is world dominion under Christ's lordship, a 'world takeover.' ..."[78] George Grant agrees:

> The army of God [church] is to conquer the earth, to subdue it, to rule over it, to exercise dominion. Christians are called to war. And it is a war we are expected to win.[79]

On the contrary, when Christ returns at the second coming, the world will not be under the control of the church but of Antichrist, "whom the Lord shall ... destroy with the brightness of his coming ..." (2 Thessalonians 2:8). This will occur at Armageddon, when the armies of Antichrist will be in the process of destroying Israel and Christ will return to rescue His earthly people. Then at last they will recognize that He is their God and Messiah (Zechariah 12:8-10; 14:1-9). In direct opposition to the clear teaching of Scripture, it is now widely believed by many Christians that the church must take over the world and only then can Christ come back to rule over the kingdom which has been established in His name.

One of the most incredible false prophecies on record (to which we have earlier referred) has apparently caused Pat Robertson to embrace the idea that the church must somehow prepare the way for Christ's second coming. Through Harald Bredesen, God allegedly said to Pat, "I have chosen you to usher in the coming of my Son." Reminiscing, Robertson declares enthusiastically:

> CBN had a mandate to fulfill: That of spreading the gospel of his Kingdom . . . of being part of a great company that would help to usher in the very second coming of Jesus . . . this was to remain CBN's mission. . . .[80]

In keeping with this vision, Robertson writes, "There *can* be peace; there *can* be plenty; there *can* be freedom . . . the minute human beings accept the principles of the invisible world and begin to live by them in the visible world."[81] By "human beings," he also means unsaved. He adds, "We know the King is coming—now it is our task to prepare the world's people to receive him. Who could imagine a more breathtaking prospect . . . ? There is a great vision yet to fulfill. A great work yet to be done. That is why CBN must and will continue to strive, to bring the good news of Jesus and of his Kingdom to renew this nation and this earth."[82] That delusion could be costly.

The Bible declares that before Antichrist is revealed, Christ will raise the dead and catch them and living believers up from this earth to meet Him in the air, to be taken to heaven. Obviously, then, those who meet their "Christ" with their feet planted on earth and welcome him to take over the kingdom they have established for him have not been serving Christ, but Antichrist! The latter will establish a kingdom upon this earth after the rapture—a kingdom which Christ will destroy when He comes to establish His millennial reign.

The Phenomenon of Promise Keepers

Promise Keepers (PK) with its Seven Promises may well be the fastest-growing religious movement in history. Actually, the first promise keepers meeting was held at the base of Mount Sinai when God gave the Ten Commandments and Israel promised to obey them. These first "promise keepers" utterly failed to fulfill their pledge. There is nothing wrong with the Ten Commandments; mankind is simply unable to keep them. Obviously, then, seven more obligations are not what we need. Who invented the seven new ones? And by what authority?

PK (which James Dobson helped to launch with an early $10,000 gift)[83] claims that Christian growth "begins by making some promises ... we intend to keep." Then Christians didn't grow until PK came along? The Bible doesn't say so, nor are these "new seven" even found in the Bible. If the Bible is sufficient, why do we need these new man-made rules that neither Christ nor Paul knew anything about?

PK puts in one package Roman Catholic ecumenism with its occult connections, Reconstructionist/Kingdom Now dominionism, and spiritual warfare with its openness to the occult. This orientation stems from its Vineyard roots. Founder Bill McCartney attends a Vineyard church. His pastor, James Ryle, is on the PK board, while a former Vineyard pastor, Randy Phillips, is its president.[84] It was the Vineyard movement which gave us false prophets, the Toronto laughing revival, and much other heresy, along with the shallow, repetitive songs of the praise-and-worship movement—and PK is under that influence. One of the major false prophets who strongly influenced the Vineyards was Paul Cain.

Cain's first arrival in Anaheim to meet Wimber was supposedly announced by an earthquake he had predicted. Wimber was so impressed that (until they had a falling out several years later) Cain was at the top of Wimber's list of prophets. Here is an account of a key Paul Cain prophecy:

> About 30 years ago the Lord gave Paul [Cain] a vision that has occurred to Paul more than 100 times, and still reoccurs to this day. It is a vision of the last days when sports stadiums all over the United States are filled with thousands of people.
>
> In this vision, people are being healed and miracles are happening to thousands in the name of Jesus Christ. People are turning to the Lord in droves and the whole nation is in revival. It seemed the whole earth was turning to Christ.
>
> Television news reporters are broadcasting stories of resurrections and miracle healings. ... He hears a TV anchorman saying, "There are no sporting events to report tonight because all the stadiums, all parks and arenas are being used for large revival meetings and are filled with people crying, Jesus is Lord, Jesus is Lord."[85]

John Wimber and other Vineyard leaders often referred to this prophecy from Cain and made similar prophecies themselves.

The relationship between such prophecies and Bill McCartney's dream of Promise Keepers filling stadiums caused the latter to be greeted with enthusiastic support by Vineyard leaders, who have played a key part in PK since its inception.

And PK has filled stadiums with unprecedented numbers of men meeting to cheer for Jesus. (More than 1 million men attended its 22 regional rallies in 1996—and nearly 3 million had done so by the end of 1997.)[86] There is a danger of emotionalism in such a movement. The comments of an astute participant among the more than 82,000 men who attended the 1995 Promise Keepers gathering in Detroit's Silverdome are significant:

> It was a finely orchestrated brainwashing extravaganza geared to mesmerize your emotions. Using music, videos, and loud and fast motivational speakers, the crowd was taken on an emotional ride. At one point, the speaker said, "Welcome to Woodstock, right here. ... There's a lot of testosterone here ... !"
>
> By attending Promise Keepers, my emotions were worked into a high state but I was not fed the Word of God. I was not drawn closer to God or His Word. The appeal was to draw nigh to Promise Keepers. I had my emotions stimulated but my heart and mind were not spoken to. Everyone I talked with afterward said "it was great." But when I asked them what they got out of it they were speechless. It was symbolism over substance.[87]

PK, Ecumenism, and Catholicism

PK's Promise 6 speaks of ignoring "denominational barriers" (including those between Catholics and evangelicals). So urgently is "unity" pursued that there can be no correction of doctrine or of practice. A homosexual is not to be told that what he is doing is a sin; he is simply to be "accepted." In the Promise Keepers manual, *Brothers! Calling Men into Vital Relationships,* Geoff Forsuch and Dan Schaffer write: "The first job of men's small groups is to learn complete acceptance:no judgment, no 'I told you so' or 'you should have known better.' No hidden agendas! I'm not out to change you and you're not out to change me." And yet they hope to change the world!

Promise 5 is a pledge for men to go back and support their church. That pledge was publicly renewed by the million men who gathered in Washington, D.C. October 4, 1997. There are serious errors in many Protestant churches. Some are apostate and involved in occult practices. The Roman Catholic Church has been in apostasy and occultism (communication with the dead, fetishes and magic rituals, etc.) for 1500 years, and many Catholics attend the stadium events. Yet PK literally calls upon men to support whatever church they may come from, no matter how heretical or occult it may be. That Catholics are told to go back and to support their church puts PK solidly in support of Roman Catholicism and all it stands for. Al Dager writes:

> I can see the "Jesus" of Promise Keepers. There he is, standing on the mountainside, exhorting his listeners: "I want you all to go back to your homes, your synagogues, your pagan temples, and don't forget Pilate's Praetorium! I want you to take leadership roles in all those arenas and proclaim to your hearers that you are men of integrity who have learned how to be sensitive and in touch with your feelings! But be careful not to judge others on what they believe."[88]

PK leaders have avoided telling the truth about PK's relationship with Roman Catholicism. That truth, however, can no longer be hidden with the publication of the cover story in *Our Sunday Visitor* [a major Roman Catholic newspaper] for July 20, 1997. Here are some excerpts:

> Promise Keepers ... has taken steps to attract even more Catholic men to its events. . . .
> At its March meeting, Promise Keepers' board of directors welcomed Mike Timmis as a new member ... a longtime leader in the Catholic charismatic renewal.
> At several rallies this year, Promise Keepers has spotlighted Catholic evangelist Jim Berlucchi as a speaker.
> In June, Promise Keepers hosted a "Catholic summit" at its headquarters in Denver, sounding out Catholic volunteers and leaders from around the country.
> And earlier this year, Promise Keepers amended its statement of faith, revising the lines that Catholics had found offensive. . . .

When criticized for Catholic involvement, PK spokesmen have "explained" that Catholics are invited to attend in order to win them to Christ. The truth is that, *from the very beginning,*

Catholics have been accepted by PK as already being Christians. Roman Catholicism has been accepted as the true gospel, and the Roman Catholic Church has been fully supported. "Promise Keeper founder Bill McCartney told *Our Sunday Visitor* recently that full Catholic participation was his intention from the start."[89]

Full participation for Roman Catholics means there is no distinction made between them and evangelicals. Yet the differing doctrines deny the unity PK pretends exists. The Council of Trent, Catholicism's highest authority, pronounced more than 100 anathemas against those who reject Rome's false gospel—all of them renewed by Vatican II. Thus there are men at PK rallies cheering Jesus side by side and being told that they are in unity, when, in fact, the majority of them are anathema to large numbers of others and they are not united at all in the gospel or in many other foundational Christian doctrines! There are Catholics in attendance wearing occult fetishes such as scapulars and medals and PK gives them full approval. Catholic men are told to go back and support the very Church which has anathematized those whom they have hugged at the rallies and with whom they have professed unity! To ignore these facts undermines the very integrity PK wants to encourage in men.

If we are to face the challenge of this hour, we must return in repentance to the awesome God of the Bible who doesn't exist to bless our plans but demands conformity to His will. We must declare in word and by example that preparation for heaven is not in the Pharisee's "positive affirmation" but in the publican's cry, "God be merciful to me a sinner" (Luke 18:9-14). It is not in the vaunted prophecies, miracles and exorcisms of those to whom Christ will say, "I never knew you, depart from me" (Matthew 7:21-23), but in the assurance that "Christ Jesus came into the world to save sinners" (1 Timothy 1:15).

The gospel is being compromised by the very leaders who ought to be foremost in its defense. An emotional celebration of yet another thousand years of spiritual darkness and growing occultism with the rejection of the One who alone is the Way, the Truth, and the Life will only compound the condemnation which has been pronounced upon this world and all its hopeful schemes and dreams.

Already the high priests, prayers and temples of the universal cult are with us. Curriculums are being drafted to indoctrinate our children in what John Rockefeller, Jr. calls "The Church of all People."... The first step is to break down loyalty to a single religious faith....

—Edith Kermit Roosevelt

The Planetary Mass is ... for a new millennium.... By taking Communion, I was partaking of the life force that fuels Creation ... myself as part of the divine body of the universe receiving the energy of the "Cosmic Christ."

—Phil Catalfo, New Age leader[1]

The two main Christian traditions—Roman Catholic and Protestant— need to work together ecumenically on ... creating a new world order.

—Norbert Greinacher, Catholic theologian[2]

... a general convergence of religions upon a universal Christ who ... satisfies them all: that seems to me the only possible conversion of the world, and the only form in which a religion of the future can be conceived.

—Pierre Teilhard de Chardin, Jesuit priest[3]

The ultimate aim should be that Judaism, Christianity and all other religions should vanish and give place to one great ethical world religion, the brotherhood of man.

—Victor Gollancz, millionaire publisher[4]

Global education must prepare our children for the coming of an interdependent, safe, prosperous, friendly, loving, happy planetary age as has been heralded by all great prophets. The real, the great period of human fulfillment on planet Earth is only now about to begin.

—Secretary-General U Thant, United Nations[5]

If I am still alive in the year 2000 ... I expect to be addressing a group of young ministers and saying to them: "It's a thrilling thing to feel the power and the impact of the enormously strong church ... to look across America ... and see tremendous institutions in every significant city carrying out fantastic programs.... Any church that really wants to be a part of this vigorous and vital church of the Twenty-First Century can be.

—Robert Schuller in 1974[6]

He [Jesus] meant to establish a world religion that would embrace every soul and synthesize every creed, and his work will not be consummated until he has done just that.

—Rodney R. Romney, Pastor of Seattle's First Baptist Church[7]

26

* · * *

The Coming World Religion

We have seen that there is a massive but subtle occult invasion of today's world and church. Materialism is dead. No longer clinging to the view that nothing exists except matter, science now admits the reality of a nonmaterial dimension governed by mysterious forces and inhabited by nonmaterial intelligences which it can neither identify nor explain. Every facet of occultism is now being explored as the new hope in medicine, education, psychology, business, military intelligence, and space science. Contact is sought and advice is followed from spirit entities whose trustworthiness cannot be established by scientific means. Psychic powers mistakenly assumed to arise from an alleged inner human potential are being avidly cultivated in many fields, and their pursuit can only lead deeper into the occult.

The occult has always been the foundation of non-Christian religions, and it invaded Christianity when Constantine allegedly became a Christian and wedded the church with paganism. Catholicism, which had its birth under Constantine, has been involved in the occult ever since, not only in its adaptation of pagan practices wherever it has spread but now in the more overt ecumenism under Pope John Paul II. In their new partnership with Rome, evangelicals have opened themselves further to the occult invasion.

The Mind Science cults such as Christian Science, Science of Mind, Religious Science, and Unity School of Christianity openly embrace the occult. Their brand of occultism has invaded charismatic and Pentecostal churches through the Positive Confession movement of Hagin, Copeland, Cho, Wimber, Hinn, and other false prophets and healers. The same "positive" occultism has invaded the evangelical church through Peale and Schuller and their followers. "Christian" psychology and the related practices of inner healing or healing of memories and 12 Step programs have accelerated that invasion as well.

All of these streams are now coming together through the ecumenical movement. Its scope is unprecedented in human history. What we are seeing can only be the great apostasy which Paul said must come in order for the day of Christ to dawn and the Antichrist to be revealed. All that remains for the occult invasion to triumph is the establishment of a New World Religion in partnership with a world government. One would have to be blind not to see that this New World Order heralded by President Bush and the Pope is fast coming upon us.

Few are the voices sounding the alarm and few are those who heed warnings such as the following, voiced by former Vineyard pastor John Goodwin. Goodwin came to Christ out of the occult and eventually realized that the Vineyard was involved in the very occult practices he had abandoned:

> I was a Vineyard pastor, and according to John Wimber, in his words, I "could do the stuff...anywhere and any time...." I was tuned in...I was in lock-step with what John was teaching....I have literally been to hundreds of Vineyard conferences....
>
> I'm here to [explain] that this is part of the last days heresy that's bringing the church into the New Age and into the New World Order....It's all part of the Antichrist system of a one world church, a one world government and a one world economy.[8]

Preparation for Antichrist

It is often argued that Antichrist is not a person but a spirit. The Bible, however, makes it clear that while there is in fact a spirit of antichrist, and many lesser antichrists, there is also a specific *man* coming who will be *the* Antichrist and the very embodiment of evil. It is fruitless to speculate upon his identity because he can only be revealed in God's time. Consider the following:

And as ye have heard that antichrist shall come, even now are there many antichrists . . . (1 John 2:18).

. . . that man of sin [will] be revealed, the son of perdition, who opposeth and exalteth himself above all that is called God, or that is worshiped, so that he as God sitteth in the temple of God, showing himself that he is God . . . that he might be revealed in his time. . . . And then shall that Wicked [one] be revealed . . . whose coming is after the working of Satan with all power and signs and lying wonders . . . (2 Thessalonians 2:3-9).

And he opened his mouth in blasphemy against God, to blaspheme his name and his tabernacle, and them that dwell in heaven. And it was given unto him to make war with the saints, and to overcome them; and power was given him over all kindreds and tongues and nations. And all that dwell upon the earth shall worship him, whose names are not written in the book of life of the Lamb . . . (Revelation 13:6-8).

These verses clearly indicate that Antichrist will sit in the rebuilt Jewish temple on Temple Mount in Jerusalem, where he will declare himself to be God *and will receive the world's worship.* There is, however, another "temple," the human body, a "temple" meant to be indwelt by God (1 Corinthians 3:16). Today, for the first time in history, not only a few yogis and gurus in the East, but increasing millions in the West, through occult techniques, are looking within what ought to be the temple *of* God and concluding that they *are* God! Through altered states of consciousness, the very occult religion of Antichrist is being embraced by the world at large and within an apostate church.

Surely the world and church are being prepared for the Antichrist and his world religion. Aleksandr Solzhenitsyn identified the root cause of moral decline in the Western world as "self-deification of man as supreme . . . a rationalistic humanism . . . [that makes man] the center of everything."[9] Historian Herbert Schlossberg, warning of the consequences of this growing delusion, suggests that it is reaching a climax in our day:

Exalting mankind to the status of deity dates from the furthest reaches of antiquity, but its development into an ideology embracing the masses is a characteristic trait of modernity.[10]

Anti is a Greek prefix which is generally understood to mean "opposed to or against." It has, however, another meaning: "in the place of or a substitute for." Antichrist will embody both meanings, according to the Bible. He will indeed oppose Christ, but in the most diabolically clever way it could be done (anything less would not be worthy of Satan's genius), by posing as Christ and thus corrupting Christianity from within.

That being the case, Antichrist's followers will be "Christians." No wonder, then, that the apostasy must precede his ascension to power. A false, ecumenical, and antichrist "Christianity" must sweep the world in preparation for his takeover. True Christians will have been taken to heaven in the rapture, and Antichrist will be worshiped by those who are left—except for those who come to faith in Christ during this horrible time and are martyred for their faith.

A popular 1997 Christmas card was already in tune with the coming world religion: "May the spirit of the holidays give us faith in ourselves and help us to believe in each other's dreams so we can make this world a better place."

An Antichrist "Christianity" Sweeping the World

Already the label "Christian" has lost its true meaning and can now be attached to any anti-Christian belief. The latest poll identifies 26 percent of Mormons as "born-again Christians," yet their "God" is an exalted man and their "Christ" is the half-brother of Satan![11] Not only in Roman Catholicism, but in all denominations there are pastors, teachers, and other leaders who are spreading a false gospel. They misrepresent Christ and His teachings and lead entire congregations astray. They pretend to represent Christ, but do not accept all that He taught. The Christ they present is more like Antichrist. Such is the "Christianity" which the White House now seems to espouse.

President Clinton and Vice-President Gore (a self-confessed New Ager who honors pagan religions) both claim to be Christians (Southern Baptists). President Clinton took the verse that Robert Schuller quoted at Clinton's inauguration as the theme for his second term: "Thou shalt raise up the foundations of many generations; and thou shalt be called

The repairer of the breach . . ." (Isaiah 58:12). On *Nightline* Schuller said, "He [Clinton] was honest-to-God under the spell of that Bible verse."[12] Such hypocrisy belongs to the new world religion.

One looks in vain for a concern for sound doctrine on the part of Clinton's spiritual advisors, Schuller and Tony Campolo. Promoting forgiveness without repentance and change, Campolo says, "Oh, how we need to become forgivers across party lines, across religious lines, across national lines."[13] On the same program Chris Burry said, "Newt Gingrich, too, has recently called for peace in the name of God." Newt is a New Ager. We wonder what god he refers to? Said Jerry Falwell:

> I think the president has done great damage to the moral fiber of this country the past four years. I have great difficulty swallowing hook, line and sinker the Bible in hand and the prophetic role of Bill Clinton while he still promotes abortion, infanticide and he's even brought the gays and lesbians into his administration which, while we must lovingly reach out to people with moral problems, I don't think we need to be role modeling this to the kids as a way of life.[14]

Even former Soviet President Mikhail Gorbachev, an atheist turned pantheist, dares to say of socialists: "We promote the cause of Christ."[15] Articles too numerous to quote follow Gorbachev across the country as he meets with religious leaders such as Jesse Jackson and James Parks Morton, dean of New Age Episcopal Cathedral of St. John the Divine in New York, and praises the importance of "religion" in the New World Order. What he advocates sounds like Antichrist's coming world religion. Ominously, United States Secretary of State Warren Christopher has declared that the new united Europe will not recognize any religious divisions.

Christ was hated. The prophets foretold Christ's rejection and death as part of God's plan for our redemption. He declared, "My kingdom is not of this world" (John 18:36). He came to call out of this world disciples for heavenly citizenship: "Lay not up for yourselves treasures upon earth, where moth and rust doth corrupt . . . but lay up for yourselves treasures in heaven.... For where your treasure is, there will your heart be also" (Matthew 6:19-21). But Antichrist, Satan's false messiah, will be worshiped by the world.

Gorbachev, the Pope, and Delusion

Gorbachev is likely not the Antichrist, but he is a very good prototype of him. In Israel, a peace dove landed on Gorbachev's head on the occasion of his acceptance of "three honorary degrees for speeding up Jewish immigration ... [and] a special award—[a] potato named after him ... [and he] praised Jesus as 'the first socialist.' "[16] Gorbachev "is framing an 'Earth Charter' intended to fuse socialism and mysticism into a UN-approved new world religion. The Earth Charter is scheduled to be presented to the UN General Assembly sometime before the year 2000, and Gorbachev insists that its adoption is necessary ... to save the earth from its rapacious inhabitants."[17]

Gorbachev and Pope John Paul II are great friends and mutual admirers. Gorbachev professes an interest in spirituality (but without truth), and the Pope encourages him in this delusion. Gorbachev writes:

> I have carried on an intensive correspondence with Pope John Paul II since we met at the Vatican in December, 1989 ... we share a desire to move forward and complete what we began together. ... What I have always held in high esteem about the Pope's thinking and ideas is their *spiritual content*, their striving to foster the development of a *new world civilization.* ...
>
> Now it can be said that everything which took place in Eastern Europe in recent years [the demise of Communism] would have been impossible without the Pope's efforts and the enormous role, including the *political role*, which he played in the world arena (emphasis added).[18]

The "*spiritual content*" of the Pope's ideas and his powerful "*political role*" are agreeable to Gorbachev. They are partners in planning a new world. One cannot imagine Christ, who was and is hated by the world, playing a *political* role in partnership with this world's Caesars—but those who claim to be His Vicars have done it for centuries.

The Pope (who considers Gorbachev to be a "crypto-Christian"), said of Gorbachev, "He does not profess to be a believer, but with me I recall he spoke of the great importance of prayer and of the inner side of man's life. I truly believe that our meeting was prepared by Providence. I believe he is a man committed to principles and very rich in spiritual terms. . . ."[19]

One can only wonder what kind of prayer the Pope thinks Gorbachev would pray (and to whom), and how an atheist can be "very rich in spiritual terms." Gorbachev's "spirituality" can be embraced by anyone—precisely what is needed for the new world religion. The Pope approves and has promoted the idea of an international organization in which "Slavic spirituality" could assert itself and has suggested that Gorbachev would be the ideal man to head it.[20] An atheist heading an international *spiritual* organization with the Pope's approval sounds like Antichrist's coming world religion!

Far from repenting of convening that abominable gathering of pagans in Assisi, the Pope reaffirms it continually. On October 7–10, 1996, the Catholic Community of Sant'Egidio in Rome sponsored an ecumenical conference where "more than 400 representatives of different religions (Christians, Jews, Muslims, Buddhists, Hindus, Shintoists, as well as more obscure Japanese and Indian cults)" met in the same spirit that was manifest in Assisi in 1986 under Pope John Paul II's leadership "to pray for a world without war." Held in Trastevere, where a few months earlier Bill Bright had given his Templeton Award acceptance speech, the name of the conference was "Peace Is God's Name." John Paul II sent this message to the conference:

> I would have liked to be . . . present . . . [but] I will be with you in spirit with affection and gratitude towards those present who generously commit themselves to keeping the spirit of Assisi alive so that it reach a growing number of men and women. . . .
>
> In this world, like a global village, we desire that every religious tradition be like a fountain of peace. Now it is so, in this ancient place of Trastevere. We wish it were so in every place of the earth. . . .[21]

No one has done more to promote unity among the world's religions than Sir John Marks Templeton and his annual prize. Once again in 1997, the prize went to an occultist: "Pandurang Shastri Athavale, founder and leader of a spiritual self-knowledge movement in India that has impacted more than 100,000 villages. . . . The award ceremony was held on May 6, 1997 in historic Westminster Abbey and the cash prize, totaling $1,210,000, was presented by Prince Philip, the Duke of Edinburgh,"[22] who had handed similar checks from Templeton to Graham, Colson and Bright.

Playing Antichrist's Game

The willingness to accommodate any kind of spirituality (a necessary ingredient of the coming world religion) is a growing attitude even among those who call themselves evangelicals. Pat Robertson refers to members of his Christian Coalition (Catholics, Mormons, Moonies and followers of other religions) as *people of faith*, who he says "are under attack as never before . . . by forces which wish to destroy all religious values, all worship, and all freedoms. . . ." Therefore, says Robertson, "We must lay aside certain Protestant differences to join hands to support those things upon which we all agree. . . ."[23]

In fact, Coalition members hold many faiths whose "religious values" and "worship" are totally incompatible. It is deceitful to speak of "people of faith" standing together, when to do so individual faith must be abandoned. Nor is it honest to call an organization which includes those of other religions "the *Christian* Coalition." And for a Christian to stand only for the least common denominator that everyone can agree upon is to abandon Christ Himself, whom the world hates and its religions reject or redefine. Far more than "Protestant differences" must be overlooked for Christians to join hands with non-Christians! Pat's coalition sounds more like what occult leader and priest Matthew Fox proposes:

> Deep ecumenism is the movement that will unleash the wisdom of *all* world religions—Hinduism and Buddhism, Islam and

Judaism, Taoism and Shintoism, Christianity in all its forms, and native religions and goddess religions throughout the world. This unleashing of wisdom holds the last hope for the survival of the planet we call home.[24]

Robert Schuller, who was referred to by President Clinton in his January 1997 inaugural address as "one of America's best-known pastors,"[25] has supported occultism within the church for many years. In the foreword to Yonggi Cho's *The Fourth Dimension*, Schuller said of the occult technique of visualization which Cho promoted, "Don't try to understand it. Just start to enjoy it! It's true. It works. I tried it."[26] Schuller seems to affirm a world religion upon which all can agree:

> That's what sets me apart from fundamentalists, who are trying to convert everybody to believe how they believe. . . . We know the things the major faiths can agree on. We try to focus on those without offending those with different viewpoints, or without compromising the integrity of my own Christian commitment.[27]

"The things the major faiths can agree on"? In fact they don't even agree on who God is, much less regarding Jesus Christ (whom *all* of the world's religions reject). Thus, by that criterion Schuller (who claims to be a minister of the gospel) cannot present the gospel. One can only wonder what "Christian commitment" Schuller isn't compromising.

Paul persuaded men to believe the gospel (2 Corinthians 5:11) because of his concern for their eternal destiny. Not so Schuller—nor Peale, Schuller's mentor. Norman Vincent Peale declared: "I try to talk about what's basic in Catholicism, Protestantism and Judaism: *love.* Love, fellowship, esteem for human beings . . . they all understand that."[28] But true love of Christ and mankind would obey Christ's command to preach the gospel.

Similar compromise was found in the Oxford Movement, which became Moral Rearmanent and deeply influenced Alcoholics Anonymous, as we have earlier noted. Frank Buchman, MRA's founder, explained that "*he never touched any doctrine in any of his meetings, as he did not want to upset or offend anyone*" (emphasis in original).[29] Bill Wilson, A.A.'s founder, described the Oxford Group as

...a nondenominational evangelical movement, streamlined for the modern world ... They would deal in simple common denominators of all religions. . . .[30]

Schuller, who claims to deal in the same common denominators of all religions, has castigated preachers "who spew forth their angry, hate-filled sermons of fire and brimstone." Yet Jesus spoke often and firmly about hell, warning mankind without apology and in what Peale and Schuller would call "negative" terms. Schuller has taken the occult teaching of the Power of Positive Thinking from his mentor, Norman Vincent Peale, turned it into "Possibility Thinking," and attributed everything one could ever want to this occult power. For more than 20 years he has been saying, "Possibility thinking makes miracles happen. . . . The greatest power in the world is the power of possibility thinking."[31] What happened to God?

In a newspaper column (which we earlier quoted in part) Schuller said, "We can tell the good religion from the bad religion" by whether it is "positive." He called upon "religious leaders . . . whatever their theology . . . to articulate their faith in positive terms." He then called for a "massive, united effort by leaders of all [including pagan/occult] religions" to proclaim "the positive power . . . of world-community-building religious values."[32] Antichrist could hardly say it better!

When Pope John Paul II designated the last decade of this century for "world evangelization," John Wimber exclaimed, "This is one of the greatest things that has ever happened in the history of the church. . . . I am thrilled with the Pope and glad that he is calling the church to this goal. . . ."

Sponsored by the Billy Graham Evangelistic Association at a cost of 21 million dollars, more than 10,000 Christian leaders met at Amsterdam in 1986 to plan a strategy for evangelizing the world. At that conference Leighton Ford declared, "Preach the gospel but don't be so negative as to refuse to endorse or work with those who belong to a group that proclaims a different gospel." He praised the late Mother Teresa after visiting her in Calcutta, though she constantly prayed the Rosary for her own salvation and considered Buddhism, Hinduism, Islam, and other religions to be acceptable ways to God. Billy Graham waxed even more eloquent in his praise of Mother Teresa immediately after her death:

> As Princess Diana was a queen of the hearts of millions of people, so Mother Teresa was a queen of the spiritual hearts. . . . We admire both of them in different ways. . . .
>
> I have known her [Teresa] for a number of years, and it was my privilege to be with her on several occasions. The first time was at the Home for Dying Destitutes in Calcutta. I had a wonderful hour of fellowship in the Lord with her. . . . When she walked into the room to greet me, I felt that I was indeed meeting a saint. . . .
>
> She was one of the most humble and sweetest of God's servants that I have ever known . . . [and] of dedication to the person of Christ. . . .[33]

The Great Tragedy of Mother Teresa

There was no one more ecumenical nor anyone more honored by the world and by numerous evangelical leaders than Mother Teresa, founder of the Missionaries of Charity and its director until her death early in September 1997. On October 2, 1994, she received the U Thant Peace Award (U Thant is a Buddhist). The award was presented by Hindu leader and United Nations guru Sri Chinmoy at San Gregorio, the Missionaries of Charity convent in Rome, in recognition of Mother Teresa's "sleepless service to humanity."[34]

The whole world knows of that sacrificial service and admired her for picking derelicts from the gutters of Calcutta and elsewhere to care for them. But what a tragedy that these pitiful creatures were then launched from a clean bed into a Christless eternity without being told the gospel which alone could save them! It is a gospel which Mother Teresa, as a lifelong Catholic, sadly, didn't know. She often said that she wanted to help those she comforted to "become a better Hindu, a better Muslim, a better Catholic, a better whatever [they] are. . . ." In contrast to the Bible, which warns that, "Jesus Christ . . . is the true God and eternal life . . . keep yourselves from idols!" (1 John 5:20,21), Mother Teresa told everyone no matter what their religion, "What God is in your mind you must accept."[35]

Even the secular press at times questioned this ecumenical looseness. *Time* magazine asked Mother Teresa a number of questions in December 1989. Her answers were revealing.

> *Time:* Here in Calcutta, have you created a real change?
> *Teresa:* [We've] created a worldwide awareness of the poor.
> *Time:* Beyond showing the poor to the world, have you conveyed any message about how to work with the poor?
> *Teresa:* You must make them feel loved and wanted. They are Jesus for me . . . in disguise.
> *Time:* What do you think of Hinduism?
> *Teresa:* I love all religions. . . .[36]

One naturally wonders how poor one must be in order to become "Jesus in disguise," and how much money or how many possessions must one acquire to cease being "Jesus." In fact, at the time of her death, Mother Teresa's organization had multimillions of dollars in the bank which had not been spent on the poor. Worst of all, she concerned herself with caring for bodies while neglecting souls. Pastor John MacArthur visited Mother Teresa in Calcutta in August 1988 and, in contrast to Leighton Ford and Billy Graham, reported as follows:

> We asked her questions that might reveal her spiritual state. Her answers were troubling: "I love and respect all religions"—an unthinkable remark in light of the hellishness of India's dominant religions.
> "All my people die beautiful deaths," she told me. I am convinced Mother Teresa is providing false comfort to the dying.[37]

We do not question Mother Teresa's sincerity or the genuineness of the great personal sacrifices she made. Yet there are troubling facts involving even the medical/practical side of her ministry. Numerous former workers in her clinics and visiting medical doctors report that patients were not given proper medication and that the beds and furnishings and general conditions were unsuitable for a hospital or clinic. The reports, coming as they do from a variety of independent observers, seem beyond dispute. As one example, Mary Loudon, a volunteer in Calcutta, wrote concerning Mother Teresa's Home for the Dying:

My initial impression was of all the photographs and footage I've ever seen of Belsen [Nazi death camp] and places like that, because all the patients had shaved heads. No chairs anywhere, there were just these stretcher beds. They're like First World War stretcher beds.

There's no garden . . . nothing. And I thought what is this? This is two rooms with fifty to sixty men in one, fifty to sixty women in another. They're dying. They're not being given a great deal of medical care. They're not being given painkillers really beyond aspirin . . . for the sort of pain that goes with terminal cancer. . . .[38]

We are not indicting Mother Teresa with lacking compassion or with cruelty toward her patients. The problem was her Roman Catholic belief that personal suffering helps to earn one's salvation. She expressed this clearly regarding her own salvation at the 1993 Presidential Prayer breakfast:

One of the most demanding things for me is traveling everywhere—and with publicity. I have said to Jesus that if I don't go to heaven for anything else, I will be going to heaven for all the traveling with all the publicity, because it has purified me and sacrificed me and made me really ready to go to heaven.

Mother Teresa was only expressing Roman Catholic doctrine. Vatican II anathematizes anyone who dares to believe that one does not need (in addition to Christ's suffering on the cross) to suffer for one's own sins. To this day, many Catholic priests and nuns wear hair undergarments, put stones in their shoes, flagellate themselves, and otherwise try to merit heaven by suffering. Poverty and suffering were not simply endured by Mother Teresa but were sought and even created as a means of preparation for heaven. Consider this example:

Given use of a three-story convent with many large rooms . . . the sisters . . . pulled up all the carpeting in the rooms and hallways. They pushed thick mattresses out the windows and removed all the sofas, chairs and curtains. . . . People from the neighborhood stood on the sidewalk and watched in amazement.

The beautifully constructed house was made to conform to a way of life intended to help the sisters become holy. Large sitting rooms were turned into dormitories where beds were crowded together. . . . The heat remained off all winter in this exceedingly damp house. Several sisters got TB during the time I lived there.[39]

The heat was not left off for lack of funds. Mother Teresa had millions of dollars on deposit, so she could have afforded proper heating, furnishings, and all the medical attention ever needed. Yet she did without all of these "luxuries," enforced the same rule upon her "Sisters of Charity," and deprived her patients as well. No doubt, just as she hoped to earn her way to heaven through her own deprivation and suffering, so Mother Teresa hoped to help her patients reach heaven through the suffering she imposed upon them. The morgue in Calcutta has this inscription on a wall: "I am leaving for heaven today."

In Roman Catholicism, baptism is essential for salvation. Mother Teresa's nuns secretly "baptize" patients by placing a damp cloth on fevered brows and saying under their breath the magic formula that allegedly erases original sin and gives entrance into the kingdom of God. Of course, the Catholic's uncertain route leads through purgatory and additional suffering in its flames before one reaches heaven. As one investigative reporter has written concerning the operation in Calcutta:

> Bear in mind that Mother Teresa's global income is more than enough to outfit several first-class clinics in Bengal. The decision not to do so, and indeed to run instead a haphazard and cranky institution . . . is a deliberate one. The point is not the honest relief of suffering but the promulgation of a cult based on death and suffering and subjection.
>
> Mother Teresa (who . . . has checked into some of the finest and costliest clinics and hospitals in the West during her bouts with heart trouble and old age) once gave this game away in a filmed interview. She described a person who was in the last agonies of cancer and suffering unbearable pain. With a smile, Mother Teresa told the camera what she told this terminal patient: "You are suffering like Christ on the cross. So Jesus must be kissing you."[40]

Many people who worked for years with Mother Teresa consider themselves fortunate to have escaped a cult. Susan Shields, having spent more than nine years as a Missionary of Charity in the Bronx, Rome, and San Francisco, writes:

I was able to keep my complaining conscience quiet because we had been taught that the Holy Spirit was guiding Mother. To doubt her was a sign that we were lacking in trust and, even worse, guilty of the sin of pride. I shelved my objections and hoped that one day I would understand the many . . . contradictions.[41]

Contradictions abound, not the least being Mother Teresa's association with unsavory persons from whom she received large sums of money and to whom she gave her blessing and endorsement. There she was in 1981, in Port-au-Prince, Haiti, in a photo with Michele Duvalier, wife of the infamous dictator Jean-Claude ("Baby Doc") Duvalier. The occasion was Mother Teresa's reception of the Haitian *Legion d'honneur* award. In return, she praised the wonderful treatment of the poor in Haiti, when in actuality they were enduring a living hell. The Duvaliers had to flee Haiti to save their wealth and their lives.

Then we have the photo taken with John-Roger, whom at that time almost everyone had already recognized as the most obvious of frauds, leader of the "Insight" cult known as Movement of Spiritual Awareness (MSIA). The occasion was her acceptance of the "Integrity Award" along with a check for 10,000 dollars from this shameless charlatan who claimed to have a "spiritual consciousness" superior to that of Jesus Christ.

This tiny, much-admired woman, soon to be voted a saint by her Church, received more than a million dollars from Charles Keating of Lincoln Savings and Loan. He was sentenced to prison for having swindled hundreds of millions of dollars from simple folk. Keating, a staunch Roman Catholic, was visited by Mother Teresa whenever she was in California. She wrote to Judge Lance Ito requesting leniency for Keating. Here is an excerpt from the reply which Paul W. Turley, a Deputy District Attorney, wrote to Mother Teresa:

> I am writing to you to provide a brief explanation of the crimes of which Mr. Keating has been convicted, to give you an understanding of the source of the money that Mr. Keating gave to you, and to suggest that you perform the moral and ethical act of returning the money to its rightful owners. . . .
>
> Ask yourself what Jesus would do if he were . . . in possession of money that had been stolen. . . . I submit that Jesus would

promptly and unhesitatingly return the stolen property to its rightful owners. You should do the same. You have been given money by Mr. Keating that he has been convicted of stealing by fraud. Do not permit him the "indulgence" he desires. Do not keep the money. Return it to those who worked for it and earned it![42]

That letter was written more than five years before Mother Teresa's death. According to now Assistant District Attorney Turley, he never received a reply from Mother Teresa, who made no move to return those wrongfully acquired funds.

Vital Distinctions: The Meaning of Terms

Psychology has taught the world and the church to use language that is positive and inoffensive. In the desire for unity, be it political or religious, words are chosen (such as Colson and Bright used in their Templeton Prize acceptance speeches) which are acceptable to anyone because each person can attach his own meaning to them. Obviously, to arrive at an "agreement" when the parties hold diverse meanings for key words is to be deluded.

For example, both Catholics and evangelicals use the term "born again," but their meanings are diametrically opposed. The Catholic is "born again" when baptized as an infant; the evangelical, through personal faith in Christ. Thus to say that they both believe in being born again is misleading. Both agree that Christ died for their sins, was buried, and rose from the dead the third day and is coming back again. Yet to each the meaning of Christ's death and how its benefits are received is so different that millions of evangelicals were willing to die throughout the centuries rather than to embrace the Roman Catholic interpretation. And their Catholic persecutors were likewise convinced that the difference was so great as to warrant the death of those holding evangelical views.

We have pointed out some of those differences in meaning, differences so great that to this day the highest authority of the Roman Catholic Church retains more than 100 anathemas pronounced upon those holding evangelical beliefs. In summary, some of the anathemas we have previously quoted apply as follows to: anyone who believes that salvation is by grace through faith in Christ apart from the sacraments and the Roman Catholic Church; anyone who believes that he need not suffer for his sins because Christ's suffering was sufficient; anyone who denies that Christ is being continually and literally immolated upon Catholic altars as a sacrifice for sins, but who places his faith in a sacrifice consummated once for all time upon the cross; or anyone who claims to know for certain that he is saved and assured of heaven. In each case, a Roman Catholic anathema is pronounced upon such a person.

The differences between an evangelical and a Catholic gospel and understanding of salvation are as great as the distance between heaven and hell. Only one can be right. And to pretend they are the same because they use similar words while ignoring the vast differences in the meaning of those words is to engage in sophistry of the worst order.

Neither Roman Catholic nor evangelical doctrine has changed in the least since the days when both sides were at least honest enough either to die or to kill for their faith. Therefore, when Roman Catholics and evangelicals call one another "brothers and sisters in Christ" and claim they both believe the same gospel, there has to be a serious mistake. Either the martyrs died for a mere semantic misunderstanding which has suddenly been cleared up in our day, or else this new acceptance of each other with its profession of unity is a fraud.

The document to which we have referred, "Evangelicals and Catholics Together: The Christian Mission in the Third Millennium," as we have seen, is one example of how the failure to define terms has created an illusion of unity which in fact doesn't exist at all. Of course, when church leaders of the stature of J.I. Packer, Charles Colson, Pat Robertson, and Bill Bright lead the way, it is only to be expected that millions of Christians, trusting the judgment of such stalwarts of the faith, will follow. Trinity Broadcasting Network (TBN) has promoted for years the delusion that the Roman Catholic gospel is biblical. Bill Hybels is another leader who, as pastor of Willow Creek Community Church in South Barrington, Illinois (which has been called "the most influential church in North America and perhaps the world"),[43] has led multitudes astray in this same direction.

Bill Hybels, who was mentored by Robert Schuller,[44] "is leading a worldwide movement. Attending a recent Willow Creek training conference . . . were over 2,300 church leaders from Australia, the Bahamas, Canada, England, Holland . . . India, Japan, Korea . . . Norway, Scotland, Sweden, the United States. . . [and elsewhere]. . . . Willow Creek . . . [with] more than two hundred seventy full and part-time staff members . . . is currently shaping how church is 'done' for thousands of churches."[45] Schuller has said:

> I was the first person to introduce real church growth to the American Church. . . . He [Hybels] became the first guy to take these principles, refine them, maximize them to the ultimate length of their potential. . . .
> I am so proud of him. . . . I think of him as a son. I think of him as one of the greatest things to happen in Christianity in our time. . . . Bill Hybels is doing the best job of anybody I know![46]

Misinformation from Trusted Leaders

Pastor Hybels invited a Roman Catholic priest, Fr. Med Laz from Holy Family Church, into his Willow Creek Community Church pulpit to share with the congregation "What Protestants Can Learn from Catholics." In introducing Laz, Hybels told how at Laz's invitation he had spoken to a conference of Catholic leaders at Holy Family and that he had "developed this enormous respect and admiration for this man as a brother in Christ. . . ."[47] Yet Laz told of "really becoming a Christian" *after* he was already a priest and that it happened through going to a motel room at 2:00 A.M. to see a young female acquaintance. Tempted to go to bed with her, he resisted the temptation and felt so good at having done so that he knew he was now a Christian. This "testimony" was greeted with enthusiastic applause,[48] though it was hardly an example of what evangelicals call getting saved and it implied a priesthood made up of men who don't know Christ.

While he admitted that he and the priest didn't agree upon everything, any differences were too minor to mention. Hybels had only praise for Roman Catholicism and its false gospel. He told the congregation, which looks to him for leadership and guidance, "I believe there are some things we can learn from the Catholic Church and I'd like to ask Med . . . to tell us what are some of the praiseworthy things of the Roman Catholic Church that you think Protestants can learn from. . . ."[49]

Fr. Laz boasted that Mother Teresa was part of the Catholic Church and Hybels implied that Protestants were jealous of that fact. There was not a word concerning her own deficient testimony. Laz also boasted that Covenant House, America's largest crisis shelter for runaways (with six locations), was run by Catholic nuns. Again Hybel's only response was approval.

The tragic truth can be found in a book titled *Am I Going to Heaven?* written by Covenant House director Sister Mary Rose McGeady. The book's title comes from its first story in which Sister McGeady tells of a 17-year-old girl who is about to die:

> She tried to lift her head up from the hospital bed pillow . . . but she couldn't. . . .
>
> "Sister, I need to know something," she whispered. "Please, tell me something."
>
> "Anything, Michelle," I said. "What do you want to know?"
>
> "Sister . . . am I going to Heaven? Even a street kid like me . . . ?"
>
> I bent down and hugged her, and told her I knew God had a special place for her. I told her how much I loved her, and how much I believed in her. . . .
>
> She cried in my arms, and whispered a "thank you." The next day, Michelle died in her sleep.[50]

One weeps for Michelle, who wanted to know how she could be assured of heaven and wasn't told! One weeps, too, for the 31,000 broken lives that Covenant House seeks to mend each year, children and youth in desperate need of the answer that Michelle sought but who, like Michelle, are not given it because McGeady and her fellow Catholic nuns do not know the gospel. In McGeady's entire book of heartrending stories, there is no hint of the only solution to the problems she writes about: the gospel of Jesus Christ!

Laz also boasted of Rome's firm commitment to marriage, to which Hybels again gave his full assent. Not a word was said of the more than 60,000 annulments given (for a fee) by the Catholic Church in the United States each year and which make a mockery of marriage.[51] Many annulments are granted for "psychological" reasons such as being raised in a "dysfunctional" family or being "psychologically unprepared" for a marriage that occurred decades before and produced numerous children—the ultimate in hypocrisy and cynicism. Typical is the distress of a faithful Catholic woman whose Catholic husband was granted an annulment after a 30-year marriage and five children so he could marry again "in the Church."[52]

Sadly enough, some Catholics now file secret letters with their attorneys at the time of marriage, expressing doubts—just in case they later want an annulment. The "PrimeTime" television show of January 6, 1994, dealt with the issue of Catholic annulments. A Catholic priest, as guest, remembered hearing a Church canon lawyer tell him, "Charlie, there isn't a Catholic marriage in the United States that we couldn't annul." A number of women guests told of their ex-husbands, after a divorce, seeking annulments so they could remarry in the Church: Barbara Zimmerman, married 27 years and mother of five children; Pat Cadigan married 23 years; Sheila Rauch Kennedy, married for 12 years to Congressman Joseph P. Kennedy II (Bobby Kennedy's eldest son) and mother of his twin sons.[53] This is mockery and desecration of marriage yet Hybels had nothing but praise for the Catholic "commitment to the sacredness of matrimony."

God said, "My people are destroyed for lack of knowledge" (Hosea 4:6). Tragically, Christian leaders who ought to be providing, along with the truth of God's Word, the factual knowledge that would help to keep evangelicals from today's ecumenical delusion are withholding it.

An Astonishing Betrayal

It is sad how many people profess for years to be Christians and then denounce their "faith." No doubt this is, at least in part, because many churches are more interested in experience and in helping people cope and feel good about themselves than in sound doctrine that would give a solid foundation for faith. Christianity has become a feeling that easily fades, as the following news item indicates:

Mel White . . . dean of the 1200-member Cathedral of Hope in Dallas, the "world's largest gay and lesbian congregation" . . . a Fuller Seminary professor for 14 years . . . ghostwrote books with Billy Graham, Jerry Falwell and Pat Robertson and speeches for Oliver North. . . . He now . . . rejects the "Christian" label and says this word "now stands for the enemy."[54]

It is perhaps even more tragic when Christian leaders betray that faith while continuing to profess it. On the Phil Donahue program in 1984, Norman Vincent Peale said: "It's not necessary to be born again. You have your way to God; I have mine. I found eternal peace in a Shinto shrine . . . I've been to Shinto shrines, and God is everywhere." Shocked, Phil Donahue responded, "But you're a Christian minister; you're supposed to tell me that Christ is the way and the truth and the life, aren't you?" Peale replied, "Christ is one of the ways. God is everywhere."[55] Yet Peale, who, in addition to his many heresies, was deeply involved in the occult, has enjoyed the unremitting praise not only of his chief disciple, Robert Schuller, but of Billy Graham and other evangelical leaders.

Sadly, Billy Graham himself, though he has faithfully preached the gospel and many people have been saved as a result, has also betrayed the gospel. On the *Larry King Live* television program the day after the inauguration of President Clinton's second term, Larry had the famous evangelist as his guest. Once again Graham's disturbing ecumenism (even implying approval of Mormonism!) was revealed:

King: What do you think of the other [churches] . . . like Mormonism? Catholicism? Other faiths within the Christian concept?

Graham: Oh, I think I have a wonderful fellowship with all of them. For example . . .

King: You're comfortable with Salt Lake City? You're comfortable with the Vatican?

Graham: I am very comfortable with the Vatican. I have been to see the Pope several times. In fact, the night—the day that he was inaugurated, made Pope, I was preaching in his cathedral in Krakow. I was his guest . . . [and] when he was over here . . . in Columbia, South Carolina . . . he invited me on the platform to speak with him. I would give one talk, and he would give the other . . . but I was two-thirds of the way to China. . . .

King: You like this Pope?

Graham: I like him very much. . . . He and I agree on almost everything.

King: Are you . . . are you comfortable with Judaism?

Graham: Very comfortable. . . . Yitzhak Rabin was a great friend . . . [and] in New York, they have had me to the Rabbinical Council to meet with them and to talk with them and Rabbi Tannenbaum, who was a great friend of all of us, who died, he gave me more advice and more counsel, and I depended on him constantly, theologically and spiritually and in every way.

King: You knew Dr. [Martin Luther] King, too, did you not?

Graham: I did. I did. I certainly did. He and I took a trip to Brazil once together. And we had a wonderful time. . . .

King: You're a big admirer of [Hillary Clinton], right?

Graham: Yes.

King: On this program you have defended her.

Graham: I think a great deal of Hillary. . . . I like the Clintons very much. . . .

King: Mr. Graham, if you had 30 seconds during the halftime at the Super Bowl, what would you tell the audience?"

Graham: I would tell them to . . . think about another game . . . the game of life, and to be sure they're on God's side, that God loves them and God is interested in them, and they can pray to God, and He'll answer their prayers."[56] [No Christ, no cross, no gospel!]

Graham, Schuller, and Peale

Robert Schuller has said, "It was Dr. [Norman Vincent] Peale who got me to go to Los Angeles . . . and it was [Billy] Graham who first got me to go on TV." Recently Schuller interviewed Billy Graham on his "Hour of Power," which has the largest television audience of any Christian program, reportedly going into 20 million homes.[57] The following excerpts are from that nationally televised program:

Schuller: Tell me, do you remember how this television program called the "Hour of Power" got started?

Graham: Oh, I remember a few things . . . I was holding a meeting [in 1969] in Anaheim and you came night after night and would sit in the little trailer that I had there as an office, and we would talk and pray. . . .

Schuller: And you said, "Bob, you should think about televising your church service. . . . And I think it was you or Fred [Deinert] who said [to call it] the Hour of Power. That Hour of Power title came from you. . . .

Graham: Oh my. Well, I'm honored. . . .

Schuller: Billy, if you looked into the future, what challenges would you throw out to Christians or to pastors—thousands of pastors, and hundreds of rabbis, and they tell me over a million Muslims a week, watch this program. What challenge would you have to these listeners? This is your platform, you started the Hour of Power, you got me into this, now have the last word. Give them a message right from your heart!

Graham: Well, the message is that God loves you. Whoever you are, wherever you are, whatever your religious background, God loves you, He wants to come into your heart and change the direction of your life and give you a peace and a joy that you've never had before. And He will do that today, if you will make that commitment to Him. [Again, no Christ, no cross, no gospel!]

Schuller: Billy, my mentor was Norman Vincent Peale. And a great teacher to me was . . . Archbishop Fulton Sheen, a very dear friend. . . . You knew Fulton Sheen and you knew Norman Peale. Your comments on both of these men?

Graham: I knew both of them, as you did, and loved them both. And I have in my book a story of how Fulton Sheen came to my apartment on a train once and we had two or three hours together. . . . The Roman Catholic Church . . . open their arms and welcome us and we have the support of the Catholic Church almost everywhere we go. . . .[58]

In an exclusive interview with *Parade* Sunday supplement, Billy Graham said: "I fully adhere to the fundamental tenets of Christian faith for myself and my ministry. But, as an American, I respect other paths to God—and, as a Christian, I am called on to love them."[59] Unless Jesus was mistaken when He said, "I am the way . . . no man cometh unto the Father but by me" (John 14:6), there are no "other paths to God." An earnest New Zealand Christian writes:

This writer hurried forward to commit his life to Christ at Carlaw Park Stadium in Auckland, New Zealand, after a clear preaching of the gospel of Jesus Christ and an emotional plea from Dr. Billy Graham for "decisions for Christ."

That was 1957 and . . . I can still recall the power of that evening and the love this man had for God, His Word, and the Truth . . . !

The pressures of teenage life soon crowded in and I forgot about my "conversion" . . . I graduated . . . traveled the world, married, had a family, divorced and remarried. Then . . . God sovereignly drew me to Christ and sound conversion! I recalled my evening with Billy Graham in 1957 and . . . began to investigate what had become of Dr. Billy Graham, with strong feelings of nostalgia.

In 1985 Dr. Leighton Ford . . . visited Sydney with an evangelistic campaign and I signed up as an usher/counselor and attended the necessary training sessions—and the nightly meetings. . . .

A lot of what I saw, heard and read during that time contradicted what I had experienced in 1957! Something had changed. . . . The Billy Graham Evangelistic Association had become "politically correct." It was now the friend of politicians and governments worldwide, and a welcome guest at the Vatican! Further investigation proved depressing and alarming. . . . The decline from Evangelical orthodoxy to ecumenical apostasy has taken a mere 40 years. . . .

Sad to say, my journey into my spiritual past left me with a heaviness and great concern for the future. . . .[60]

Paganizing Christianity

Thomas Merton (1915-1968), Trappist monk and Catholic mystic, was one of the most highly regarded (by both Catholics and Protestants) Catholic leaders of this century. According to Harvey D. Egan, a Jesuit scholar, Merton "blended in his writings the scriptures, the Fathers of the Church, the Desert Fathers, the great Christian mystics, the Russian Orthodox mystics, contemporary Catholic and Protestant theology, modern psychology . . . existentialism, Taoism and Buddhism . . . with an incredible sensitivity for . . . social justice, urban violence, poverty, ecumenism, and the East-West dialogue." He was a "voice of authority in the American [Catholic] Church, and far beyond."[61]

Merton rejoiced "in Vatican II's openness to Oriental religions," and Merton himself "strongly identified with Eastern mysticisms, especially Zen [Buddhism]." He commended Hindu, Buddhist, and Islamic mystics as "those who had experienced . . . union with the God of truth and love."[62] Merton saw "no contradiction between Zen and Christianity."[63]

Though no theologian, Chicago Bulls coach Phil Jackson picked up the same idea. He writes, "Merging Zen and Christianity allowed me to reconnect with my spiritual core and begin to integrate my heart and mind. The more I learned about the similarities between the two religions, the more compatible they seemed. Was Christ a Zen master? That may be a stretch, but clearly he was practicing some form of meditation when he separated himself from his disciples and became one with 'the Father.' "[64] Of course, Christ did not "*become* one with the Father"; He *is* one with the Father from eternity past to eternity future. In prophesying the birth of the Messiah, Isaiah declared that it was "the mighty God, the everlasting Father" (Isaiah 9:6) who would be born into the world.

Tragically, Jackson has never understood Christianity. He says that his mother hung John 3:16 in his bedroom when he was four. He quotes the verse correctly, then says, "From then on I started being concerned with keeping the faith so that I, too, could find eternal life."[65] That is not what that verse or any other says. The Bible teaches that eternal life is a gift of God's grace that none can merit. It was not Christianity that Jackson rejected but his misconception of it.

Jackson often prays the so-called "Lord's Prayer" with his players.[66] It begins, "Our Father who art in heaven. . . ." To pray it honestly one must know God as Father by experiencing a new birth into the family of God through faith in Christ. By his own admission, Phil Jackson has rejected the Jesus Christ of the Bible, as have most of his players, so it is a contradiction for them to pray the Lord's Prayer. *It is this loose merging of Christianity with whatever spirituality one fancies that will characterize the coming world religion—and destroy Christianity.*

An evangelical pastor spent ten days at an ecumenical gathering of the World Council of Churches (WCC) and National Council of Churches (NCC), held under the auspices of New York City's Auburn Theological Seminary. He was shocked at the overt rejection of Christianity and its replacement by paganism. The occult was honored as though it were of God. Here is part of the report he filed:

> I knew we were in trouble when our first worship "celebration" found us outdoors at a garden pond offering prayers and water libations to the Seven Spirits of the seven directions of the Universe ("O Spirit of the North, blow upon us ... O Spirit of the East ... West ... South ...). What to any objective observer was sheer paganism, we were told was simply an exercise in discovering the ecumenical variety of spiritual expression and experience that we must learn to share if we are to be truly one. . . .
>
> [There] was the outright denial of the Doctrine of the Trinity. . . [as] an archaic *symbol* for God so loaded with classical Western sexism and images of oppression that it must be abandoned in favor of something more palatable to enlightened sensitivities ... [like] Sophia. . . .
>
> While some of us may prefer to relate to Jesus as our personal "Christ-figure," we dare not make him exclusive. We must be *inclusive* of all potential "Christ-figures," so that we can learn to see through them all and behind them all to that one Savior Spirit of Liberation working through all the various "Christ-figure" masks of the world's religions. . . .
>
> Clearly, the ideologues of Liberationism have taken over the direction of the WCC and NCC and are leading them into nothing short of syncretistic paganism. And the awful thing is that, judging from the participants at this conference, many of the ecumenical leaders of mainline Protestantism are happily following this primrose path to apostasy.[67]

Toward a World Religion

Just before becoming Vice-President of the United States, Senator Al Gore wrote a book in which he praises "the wisdom distilled by all faiths. This panreligious perspective may prove especially important where our global civilization's responsibility for the earth is concerned." He praises goddess worship and blames Christianity for wiping out "the last vestige of organized goddess worship. . . ." He praises Islam, Hinduism,

Sikhism, and Baha'i as well as New Age and occultist Catholic priest Teilhard de Chardin.[68] In his plenary address at the 1990 Global Forum in Moscow, Gore, who worships Earth as the mother goddess, Gaia, declared that ecological problems could only be solved through a "new spirituality" common to all religions.

That we are heading in that direction is clear. It would take an entire volume even to begin to report on the scope of this movement. A few examples must suffice. Pope John Paul II, along with Nikkyo Niwano, founder of the Buddhist movement called Rissho Koseikai, opened the Sixth World Assembly of the World Conference on Religion and Peace at the Vatican in late 1994.[69] "This Geneva-based international council is dedicated to promoting peace through building bridges of communication and trust among different world religions. Pope John Paul II is a firm supporter. . . ."[70]

This dream is being put into practice worldwide. Consider, for example, the interfaith liturgy to celebrate the diversity of the "five great faiths" which was held at St. Luke's Anglican Church in Auckland, New Zealand, in August 1996. The Anglican bishop of Auckland, the Right Reverend John Paterson, welcomed Hindus, Jews, Buddhists, Muslims, and Christians to the celebration.[71]

The year 1996 also saw a gathering in San Francisco of 60 religious leaders from around the world calling for the founding of a United Religions Organization similar to the United Nations. California's Episcopal bishop, William Swing, having returned from a trip around the world attempting to establish unity among all religions, declared, "I am convinced that the time is ripe for a global initiative to call the world's religions together. . . ."[72]

On June 23, 1997, "200 delegates from scores of religious bodies around the world" met at Stanford University under the leadership of Bishop Swing. Plans were laid to establish on June 26, 2000, the "United Nations for all religions" that has been Swing's dream. The United Religions Initiative "seeks to bring religions and spiritual traditions to a common table, a permanent, daily, global assembly. There, respecting each other's distinctness, they will seek to make peace among religions so that they might work together for the good of all life and the healing of the earth."[73] Says Swing, who has been traveling the world since 1993 to put this project together:

> I've spent a lot of time praying with Brahmins, meditating with Hindus or being silent or chanting with Buddhists. I feel I've been enormously enriched inwardly by exposure to these folks.[74]

At the Atlanta, Georgia, Promise Keepers conference that saw 39,000 clergy gathered together, PK founder Bill McCartney said, "This is a dream come true. . . . It is exciting to see the denominational barriers come down as we have Protestants and Roman Catholics [and Mormons] here together. The purpose of this meeting is to have the unity of the church." The conference brought together the World Council of Churches, National Council of Churches, Pentecostals, charismatics, evangelicals, Mormons, and Roman Catholics, including 600 priests. Promise Keepers Vice-President of Pastoral Ministry, Dale Schlafer, who organized the conference, declared that this new unity is not built upon doctrine but upon relationships. Texas pastor Tom Watson warns:

> Shouldn't it be of some concern to us that the call for unity at the expense of doctrine not only comes from evangelicals but also from the apostate WCC and from New Agers who gain their wisdom from discarnate entities? Doesn't the Scripture warn us that this day would draw near? (2 Timothy 4:3,4).[75]

Concern for morality and ecology becomes the excuse for compromising theology. Kenneth S. Kantzer, a senior editor of *Christianity Today* (*CT*), wrote: "With the spread of moral rot that destroys the roots of a free and just society, we evangelicals need to close ranks with our Catholic neighbors. And with Mormons, conservative Jews, and secularists who share our values. . . ."[76] Had Christ joined the rabbis in such a coalition for moral improvement, think of the great ethical reformer He could have become and the immense good He could have accomplished—all without going to the cross!

At the same time, Christianity is being confused with Americanism. Millions of "Christians" of all stripes, from evangelicals to Catholics to Mormons and Moonies, have joined together to Christianize America by calling it back to the "traditional moral values" upon which it was founded. Somehow this "mission" has captured the imagination and loyalty of multitudes of evangelicals and has replaced the biblical Great Commission in their hearts and minds.

There is a new optimism in the air, the determined hope that "America can be saved" by a compromised ecumenical gospel. Even J. I. Packer seems to have succumbed to this delusion. Writing in *CT*, he transmutes Christ's command to proclaim the gospel into a call "to re-Christianize the North American milieu ... [and] rebuild the ruins ... [of] North American culture ... "![77] Where does the Bible suggest that? Llewellyn Rockwell writes:

> Christianity is now thoroughly politicized. The [Catholic] bishops and [Ralph] Reed have no trouble speaking about the importance of pro-family legislation, or the glories of religious pluralism, but they are shy about such basics as the Christian teaching on salvation. The longer the process of politicization continues, the thinner the faith gets. Political ambition causes people to water down their beliefs for the sake of gaining favor. .... The first stage of sell-out comes with the exaltation of political pluralism above doctrinal truth, the second stage with the denial of doctrinal truth altogether for achieving political goals.[78]

The Bible indicates that the coming world religion will be the foundation of Antichrist's world empire. That will be a revival of the Roman Empire under Antichrist, with ten divisions signified by the ten toes of Nebuchadnezzar's image (Daniel 2:42-44), the ten horns of Daniel's fourth beast (Daniel 7:7), and the ten horns of the principal beast in John's vision (Revelation 12:3; 13:1; 17:3; 12). Some of the characteristics of ancient Rome's religion are specified, such as emperor worship with death the penalty for noncompliance (Revelation 13:8, 14,15). It is therefore a reasonable conclusion that the coming world religion will be the same blend of Christianity and paganism as took place under Constantine and continued thereafter as Roman Catholicism.

Evangelicals and Roman Catholics Together

The document "Evangelicals and Catholics Together: The Christian Mission in the Third Millennium" was not a sudden development but the inevitable result of much earlier preparation. Charismatic magazines (from *Voice to Charisma*) and leaders (from the late Kathryn Kuhlman to Rex Humbard) have heaped praise upon Pope John Paul II in spite of his false gospel. In praising the Pope as a Christian leader, Jack Hayford said, "You don't have to be a Catholic to stand tall and say, "I'm a Christian, too." Billy Graham has called John Paul II "the greatest religious leader of the modern world, and one of the greatest moral and spiritual leaders of the century."[79] James Dobson, America's foremost expert on the family and one of the world's most highly respected Christian psychologists, calls the Pope "the most eminent religious leader who names the name of Jesus Christ."[80]

The ecumenical partnership with Rome has long been promoted in the pages of *Christianity Today*. As early as 1985, Kenneth Kantzer referred, in a *CT* editorial, to Pope John Paul II as "the successor of Saint Peter" whom "God has called . . . to forge a united church . . . [and whose] priority to the Christian message . . . endear[s] him to the hearts of evangelicals."[81] A year later Kantzer declared that "traditional Roman Catholics. . . retain much of biblical Christianity and possess qualities that I admire and wish to imitate. For example . . . their frequent celebration of the Lord's Supper [Mass] and loyalty to the Bible. . . ." In fact, as we have already noted, Rome anathematizes all who partake of the Lord's Supper as evangelicals commemorate it:

> If anyone says that the sacrifice of the mass . . . is a mere commemoration of the sacrifice consummated on the cross but not a propitiatory one . . . and ought not to be offered for the living and the dead, for sins, punishments, satisfactions, and other necessities, let him be anathema.[82]

Ralph Reed (the director of Pat Robertson's Christian Coalition until his recent resignation) has said, "An emerging partnership of Catholics and Evangelical Protestants is going to be the most powerful force in the electorate beyond the 1990s ... [bringing together] people of faith" for the common good of the nation. Apparently any "faith" will do. It was out of such a joining in common cause that "Evangelicals and Catholics Together: The Christian Mission in the Third Millennium" (ECT) was spawned. As the *New York Times* reported:

> They toiled together in the movements against abortion and pornography, and now leading Catholics and evangelicals are asking their flocks for a remarkable leap of faith: to finally accept each other as Christians.[83]

John Wimber often praised the Pope and Catholicism. John Goodwin relates: "John Wimber actively promotes the reunification of the Protestants and the Catholics. I was there at a seminar, a pastors' conference in Anaheim [with about 5000 pastors in attendance]. The archbishop of the archdiocese was attending, sitting up in front with his robes on. . . . John asked him to stand up and said to him, 'I want to apologize to you on behalf of all Protestants for leaving the Catholic Church and for the things we've said about you and the Church.' "[84]

Televangelist Jack Van Impe is another evangelical leader who praises the Pope as an evangelist, praises Mother Teresa and even quotes the apparitions of "Mary" as though they were of God. A pastor writes:

> I was watching Jack Van Impe [on TV]. The show was devoted to praising Pope John Paul II for his fine "Christian" work, his ecumenism, his love and desire for Christian unity. . . .
>
> Three-fourths of the way through the show Van Impe points out the major obstacles to Christian unity are being raised by Fundamentalists. . . . He [showed how foolish this was] by pointing out that the Pope and all orthodox Catholics hold to the [same] fundamentals [of the faith as evangelicals]. . . .
>
> I cry when I see this unity-at-all-costs mentality. . . . There is no unity outside of truth. . . . No pronouncement of any Roman council has ever really been rescinded. You can sidestep the issue or ignore it if you want, but Protestants by the nature of their beliefs are still anathema to the Roman Church![85]

A Choice to Make

For all his inventions and modern developments, man has not changed. He is still the descendant of Adam, fallen into sin and in need of reconciliation to his Creator. He still needs love and purpose and meaning not only in this life but beyond. Eternity is all that matters, and it hasn't changed. God hasn't been renovating heaven to keep up with the ideas current upon earth, nor has He revised the entrance requirements to broaden the spectrum of belief among its citizens.

God doesn't hire a Madison Avenue advertising and promotion team to persuade us that heaven will be a nice place to retire to. "Repentance toward God, and faith toward our Lord Jesus Christ" (Acts 20:21), no longer popular even among evangelicals, is still the only entrance ticket to heaven. Those who do not love God wholeheartedly and desire Him to have His way with them would be miserable there.

Heaven and hell are not states of mind, as Templeton and his cohorts imagine, but the real and eternal destinations of every human soul and spirit. Hell is where people go who turn to occult powers in rejection of God, who are determined to have things their own way, to enjoy their own passions, to create their own universe with their thoughts. Its inhabitants are self-centered, utterly lonely souls. Self has become so all-consuming that there is room for nothing else.

Christ was born the Savior of sinners. How marvelous that He who is God, one with the Father and the Holy Spirit, loves us so much that He was willing to be born of a virgin, to grow up in a world that hated Him, to be despised, rejected, mocked, scourged, crucified—and more than the physical suffering, to bear our sins and to pay the infinite price of our redemption demanded by His own infinite justice! He is still mocked and rejected by the world and His gospel perverted even within the professing church.

Heresy and compromise on the part of those who claim to be His followers is perhaps the most painful mockery He endures. It rejects Him as He really is and undermines His real purpose in coming to earth. Every true Christian should be deeply offended and concerned that serious error is being promoted not only in the world but even in seemingly sound churches and by those who are looked up to as evangelical leaders. It is our love for Christ in response to His love for us, and our love for the lost whom He loves and for whom He suffered and died, which causes us to hate heresy, to denounce the occult invasion and to earnestly contend for the faith once for all delivered to the saints. May we remain true to Him until He takes us home!

We face some trying days ahead if the Lord tarries. Recently this author watched a John Bradshaw seminar series that lasted five days on Public Broadcasting TV. While talking about faith in God (Bradshaw had his own unbiblical definitions for both faith and God), he denounced those who claim to be saved and who thereby "destroy the self-image of others who don't believe exactly as they do." It was all extremely clever and persuasive. The audience was obviously convinced of all he said. One could easily see the day coming when such arguments would be used to stifle or muzzle evangelicals as a menace to society.

The Christian martyrs throughout history (and those being martyred today, particularly in Muslim countries) could have chosen an ecumenical path of compromise and of affirming the "common beliefs of all religions," and thus have escaped the flames or the sword. But they chose instead to stand firm for the truth, to contend earnestly for the faith. Dare we do otherwise?

For us, at this crossroads in history, the issues have broadened. The deadly tentacles of the occult in its many guises have invaded the world, but also the church. What will be our response? One day we will give an account before God for that choice. What joy there is now and eternally in being true to Him!

Notes

Chapter 1—Why This Book?

1. Max Planck, *Where Is Science Going?* (Norton, 1932), p. 160.
2. Quoted in Nandor Fodor in *Freud, Jung and Occultism* (University Books, 1971), pp. 129–30.
3. Carl Jung, *Collected Letters, Vol. 1, 1906–1950* (Princeton University Press, 1973), p. 43.
4. Carl Rogers, *A Way of Being* (Houghton Mifflin Company, 1980), pp. 99–102.
5. M. Scott Peck, *People of the Lie* (Simon & Schuster, 1983), p. 196.
6. *Quantum Questions: Mystical Writings of the World's Great Physicists,* ed. Ken Wilber (New Science Library, 1984), p. 170.
7. Erwin Schroedinger, cited in *Quantum Questions: Mystical Writings of the World's Great Physicists,* ed. Ken Wilber (New Science Library, 1984), pp. 81–83.
8. Sir John Eccles with Daniel N. Robinson, *The Wonder of Being Human—Our Brain and Our Mind* (New Science Library, 1985), p. 54.
9. *Research in Parapsychology 1972* (special dinner address by Arthur Koestler), p. 203.
10. Marilyn Ferguson, *The Aquarian Conspiracy: Personal and Social Transformation in the 1980s* (Los Angeles: J.P. Tarcher, 1980), inside jacket.
11. *The Tidings,* October 13, 1989.
12. Art Kunkin, "The Dalai Lama in Los Angeles: What Does Kalachakra Have to Do with World Peace?" in *Whole Life Times,* August 1979, p. 8.
13. *Time,* September 17, 1979, p. 96.
14. "In Brief," *New Covenant,* January 1993, p.6.
15. *Newsweek,* September 17, 1979, p. 115.
16. C. Peter Wagner, *Confronting the Powers: How the New Testament Church Experienced the Power of Strategic-Level Spiritual Warfare* (Regal Books, 1996), p. 16.
17. Ibid., pp. 15–37, etc.
18. Session 12, White Alpha Course.
19. *Plus,* April 1986, p. 3.

Chapter 2—Evolution and Its Role

1. Colby Dam, "Occult Contacts," in *The Occult Digest,* January 1931, p. 14.
2. Edgar D. Mitchell, "Implications of Mind Research," an address to members of Congress and Congressional staff on behalf of the Congressional Clearinghouse on the Future. Printed in *Institute of Noetic Sciences Newsletter,* Spring & Summer 1980, vol. 8, no. 5, p. 5.
3. Stephen F. Smith, "Is Darwinism a Religion?" in *The Catholic World Report,* December 1996, p. 50.
4. Pierre Teilhard de Chardin, *The Phenomenon of Man* (Harper and Row, 1965), p. 219.

5. Joel Belz, "Witness for the prosecution," in *World*, November 30/December 7, 1996, p. 18.
6. Michael J. Behe, *Darwin's Black Box: The Biochemical Challenge to Evolution* (Simon & Schuster, 1996), pp. 232–33, 252.
7. W.L. Wilmhurst, *The Meaning of Masonry* (Bell Publishing, 1980), pp. 47, 94, as cited in Alan Morrison, *The Serpent and the Cross* (K&M Books, 1994), p. 230.
8. Robert Muller, ed., *The Desire to Be Human: A Global Reconnaissance of Human Perspectives in an Age of Transformation* (Miranana, 1983), p. 17.
9. Robert Muller, "Decide to Be," in *Link-Up*, 1986, p. 2.
10. Barbara Brown, *Supermind* (Harper & Row, 1980), pp. 6–7, 19.
11. Theodore Roszak, *Unfinished Animal* (Harper & Row, 1980), pp. 74–75.
12. Michael J. Harner, *The Way of the Shaman: A Guide to Healing and Power* (Harper & Row, 1980), p. 57.
13. Dave Hunt and T.A. McMahon, *The New Spirituality* (Eugene, OR: Harvest House Publishers, 1988), p. 155.
14. Vatican II, *Vatican Council II, Divine Revelation* (Knights of Columbus paraphrase edition), III.11e.
15. Pope John Paul II, "Message to Pontifical Academy of Sciences," in *L'Osservatore Romano*, 30 October 1996, pp. 3, 7.
16. Father Edward Daschbach, S.V.D., "Catholics and Creationism," in *Visitor*, October 21, 1984, p. 3.
17. *New Catholic Encyclopedia* (McGraw-Hill, 1967), vol. 5, p. 689.
18. Daschbach, S.V.D., *Visitor*, p. 3.
19. Editorial, "The Pope, the Press, and Evolution," in *Christianity Today*, January 6, 1997, p. 18.
20. Belz, "Witness for the Prosecution," p. 18.
21. Charles Haddon Spurgeon, *The Greatest Fight in the World*.
22. John Tagliabue, "Pope says God and Darwin can co-exist happily," in *The Times-Picayune*, October 25, 1996, p. A-3.
23. "Fathers, faith and fossils," in *New Man*, July-August 1996, p. 54.
24. Anton Szandor La Vey, *Satanic Bible* (Avon, 1969), from the nine satanic affirmations with which the book begins.
25. *The American Atheist*, 1978, p. 19, as cited in *The Christian News*, November 11, 1996.
26. George W. Cornell, "Scientist calls Darwin evolution theory absurd," in *Times-Advocate*, December 10, 1982, p. A10.
27. *Teilhardism and the New Religion* (Tan Books, 1988), p. 242, as cited in *The Christian News*, November 11, 1996, p. 15.
28. Klaus Dose, "The Origin of Life: More Questions Than Answers," in *Interdisciplinary Science Reviews*, 1988, pp. 13, 348.
29. Thomas E. Woodward, "Doubts About Darwin," in *Moody*, September 1988, p. 20.
30. *Times-Picayune*, October 25, 1996, p. A-3.
31. Mary Beth Marklein, "Pope: Evolution, religion don't clash," in *USA Today*, October 25, 1996, p. 3A.
32. Stephen F. Smith, "Is Darwinism a Religion?" in *The Catholic World Report*, December 1996, p. 50.
33. William Bole, "Of biochemistry and belief," in *Our Sunday Visitor*, December 1, 1996, p. 6.
34. Richard Dawkins, *The Blind Watchmaker* (Longman, England, 1986), p. 1.
35. Behe, *Black Box*, pp. 46–47.
36. Ibid., pp. 114–15.
37. Dawkins, *Watchmaker*, p. 18.
38. Behe, *Black Box*, pp. 4–5.
39. Ibid., p. 97.
40. From an interview by AP correspondent George W. Cornell, quoted from *Times-Advocate*, Escondido, CA, December 10, 1982, pp. A10-11.
41. Behe, *Black Box*, pp. 78, 93-97.

42. Ibid., pp. 120, 122, 136, 139, 187.
43. Bole, "Biochemistry," pp. 6–7; Behe, *Black Box*, p. 173.
44. Ibid., pp. 188–93.
45. Charles Darwin, *Origin of Species* (New York University Press, 6th ed., 1988), p. 154.
46. Behe, *Black Box*, p. 39.
47. Ibid., pp. 142–51, 159–61.
48. Ibid., p. 176.
49. Ibid., pp. 177–78.
50. Ibid., pp. 185–86.
51. Ibid., pp. 22–25.
52. Donald Devine, in *Human Events*, December 13, 1996, p. 19.
53. *Los Angeles Times*, November 30, 1996, p. B13.
54. Richard Bozarth in *The American Atheist*, 1978, p. 19, as cited in *The Christian News*, November 11, 1996, p. 15.
55. Doug Bandow, "Fossils and Fallacies," in *National Review*, April 29, 1991, p. 47.
56. Russell Schoch, "The Evolution of a Creationist," in *California Monthly*, November 1991, p. 22.
57. *The Catholic World Report*, December 1996, p. 50.
58. Shepherd Bliss, "Jean Houston: Prophet of the Possible," in *Whole Life Times*, October/mid-November 1984, pp. 24–25.

Chapter 3—What Is the Occult?

1. *The Occult Digest*, January 1931, pp. 14, 27.
2. Archie Fire Lame Deer and Richard Erdoes, *Gift of Power: The Life and Teachings of a Lakota Medicine Man* (Bear & Company Publishing, 1992), pp. 153–54.
3. Phil Jackson and Hugh Delehanty, *Sacred Hoops* (Hyperion, 1995), pp. 11–12.
4. Robert Lindsey in *New York Times*, cited in *Los Angeles Herald Examiner*, September 29, 1986, p. B-8.
5. Napoleon Hill, *Grow Rich!—With Peace of Mind* (Fawcett Crest, 1967), pp. 158–59.
6. Mark Andrew Ritchie, *Spirit of the Rainforest* (Island Lake Press, 1996).
7. Christopher Bird, "Fruitful Searches," in *New Realities*, March 1982, p. 59.
8. "Interview: Dowsing, The Divining Hand in Action," in *Acres U.S.A.*, August 23, 1984, p. 24.
9. P.F. Kuypers, "Dowsing," in *Gold Prospector*, April 1987, p. 15.
10. Kenneth Roberts, *Henry Gross and His Dowsing Rod* (Doubleday & Co., 1953), pp. 256–57.
11. *New Realities*, March 1982, p. 56.
12. Ibid.
13. Alan Morrison, *The Serpent and the Cross* (Birmingham, England: K&M Books, 1994), Preface.
14. Howard Kerr and Charles L. Crow, eds., *The Occult in America* (University of Illinois Press, 1986), p. 2.
15. Morrison, *Serpent*, Preface.
16. *Li.F.E. Letter*, December 1996.
17. Testimonial letter of user on file.
18. W. Brugh Joy, *Joy's Way* (J.P. Tarcher, 1979), pp. 8–9.
19. Harner, *Shaman*, p. 136.

Chapter 4—The Death of Materialism

1. From an interview in *Our Sunday Visitor*, December 1, 1996, pp. 6–7.
2. Louisa E. Rhine, *Mind Over Matter, Psychokinesis: The astonishing story of the scientific experiments that demonstrate the power of the will over matter* (Macmillan, 1970) pp. 389–90.

3. Arthur C. Clarke, *Childhood's End* (Ballantine Books, 1953), p. 181.
4. Sir Arthur Eddington, *Science and the Unseen World* (Macmillan, 1937), pp. 53–54.
5. D. Scott Rogo, "Transpersonal Psychology and the Spiritual Path: Taking a Larger View of Ourselves, An Interview with Charles Tart, Ph.D.," in *Science of Mind*, December 1986, pp. 12-13.
6. Sir James Jeans, *The Mysterious Universe* (The MacMillan Company, 1930), p. 140.
7. Sir John Eccles and Daniel N. Robinson, *The Wonder of Being Human: Our Brain and Our Mind* (New Science Library, 1981), p. 38.
8. Rogo, "Psychology," pp. 12–13.
9. Michael Polanyi, *The Tacit Dimension* (Anchor, 1967), p. 37, cited by Lawrence LeShan, *The Science of the Paranormal: The Last Frontier* (The Aquarian Press, 1987), p. 31.
10. *Time*, January 13, 1997, p. 57.
11. Carl Rogers, "The New World Person," in *Life Times*, no. 3, p. 47.
12. *Life Times: Forum for a New Age*, no. 3, pp. 47–48, originally published in South Africa's New Age magazine, *Odyssey*.
13. Quoted in Herbert Benson, M.D., with William Proctor, *Your Maximum Mind* (Random House, 1987), p. 46.
14. C.G. Jung, *Memories, Dreams, Reflections* (Pantheon Books, 1963), p. 322.
15. *Time*, June 24, 1996, p. 67.
16. Professor Courtney Brown interview on Art Bell Show, late in 1996.
17. Ken Wilber, "Of Shadows and Symbols: Physics and Mysticism," in *ReVISION*, Spring 1984, pp. 6–7.
18. Charles Tart, "Science vs. scientism: Role seen for spirit," in *Brain/Mind & Common Sense*, February 1993, pp. 1, 6.
19. Rogo, "Psychology," pp. 12–13.
20. Walter Yeeling Evans-Wentz, *The Fairy Faith* (University Books, 1966), p. xii.
21. C.S. Lewis, *The Screwtape Letters* (Fleming H. Revell, 1976), pp. 45–46.
22. From the "Official Statement by Courtney Brown" on his website dated 20 January 1997.
23. From message titled "To Whom It May Concern" put out on The Farsight Institute's website January 20, 1997.
24. Cult member speaking on tape aired on CNN March 27-28, 1997.
25. From the statement "Our Position Against Suicide" posted on the cult's website.
26. Deborah Hastings, The Associated Press, "Former cult members hold to beliefs," in *Bulletin* (Bend, OR), March 31, 1997, p. 2.
27. Taken from website www. farsight.org.
28. *Essays Catholic and Critical*, ed. Edward Gordon Selwyn (Macmillan, 1926), pp. 74–77.
29. "GeoConversation," an interview with Robert Jastrow in *Geo*, February 1982, p. 14.
30. *MAGICAL BLEND: A Transformative Journey*, Issue 17, 1987, p. 13.
31. Carlos Castaneda, *The Power of Silence* (Simon and Schuster, 1987), Front fly of jacket, Foreword, etc.
32. Jon Klimo, *Channeling: Investigations on Receiving Information from Paranormal Sources* (Jeremy P. Tarcher, Inc., 1987), p. 249.
33. Ibid., interview with Tart, p. 253.
34. William James, "Report on Mrs. Piper's Hodgson Control," in *Proceedings of the English Society for Psychical Research*, 23:1–121.
35. Klimo, *Channeling*, p. 313.

Chapter 5—Remote Viewing

1. Cited in Russell Targ and Harold Puthoff, *Mind-Reach: Scientists Look at Psychic Ability* (Dell Publishing Co., 1977), opposite acknowledgments page.
2. "Researcher sees psi as refutation of 'scientism,'" in *Brain/Mind and Common Sense*, February 1993, p. 6.
3. Targ and Puthoff, *Mind-Reach*, p. xi.

4. Harner, *Shaman*, pp. 20, 42–44, 49.
5. Ernest Jones, *The Life and Work of Sigmund Freud* (Basic Books, 1953), vol. III, p. 381.
6. C.G. Jung, *Memories, Dreams, Reflections* (Pantheon Books, 1963), p. 155.
7. Bernard Gittelson, *Intangible Evidence* (Simon & Schuster, 1987), p. 213.
8. *Brain, Mind & Common Sense*, June 1993, pp. 1–2.
9. Targ and Puthoff, *Mind-Reach*, pp. ix–x.
10. Ibid., pp. xvi, xxv.
11. Ibid., p. 73.
12. Ibid., pp. 1–4.
13. Ibid., p. 10.
14. John J. Heaney, *The Sacred and The Psychic: Parapsychology and Christian Theology* (Paulist Press, 1984), p. 21.
15. Ibid., pp. 42–43.
16. Gil Gross Show, November 1, 1996.
17. R.D. Scott, *Transcendental Misconceptions* (San Diego, 1978), pp. 37–38, 115–29.
18. From a tape of Art Bell's "Coast to Coast," November 19, 1996.
19. From an undated tape of the program that originally aired some time in November 1996.
20. From a transcript of "Coast to Coast," Fall 1996.
21. From a tape of the "Gil Gross Show," November 1, 1996.
22. *The Urantia Book* (Chicago: URANTIA Foundation, 1955), p. 366.
23. Ibid., pp. 60, 75.

Chapter 6—A Dark and a Light Side?

1. Joan Halifax, *Shaman: The Wounded Healer* (Thames & Hudson, 1982), p. 9.
2. Richard Erdoes and Archie Fire Lame Deer, *The Gift of Power: The Life and Teachings of a Lakota Medicine Man* (Bear & Company Publishing, 1992), pp. 159–60.
3. Klimo, *Channeling*, p. 183.
4. Wade Davis, *The Serpent and the Rainbow* (Warner Books, 1985), p. 42.
5. Norman Vincent Peale, "What Does It Take to Be a Christian?" in *Plus: The Magazine of Positive Thinking*, April 1986, p. 3.
6. Kenneth Copeland, TBN interview with Paul and Jan Crouch, February 5, 1986; Kenneth Copeland, "Questions and Answers," in *Believer's Voice of Victory*, June 1986, p. 14.
7. Lambert Dolphin, "Physics and the Bible: What Holds the Universe Together?" in *Personal Update*, January 1997, p. 13.
8. Joseph Campbell with Bill Moyers, *The Power of Myth* (Doubleday, 1988), pp. 207–08.
9. *Los Angeles Times*, February 13, 1988, Part II, p. 1.
10. *Minneapolis Star and Tribune*, November 27, 1986, p. 6.
11. From a transcript of "Geraldo," March 22, 1988.
12. T.H. Fitzgerald, "Practical Problems," in *AHP Perspective*, December 1984, p. 13.
13. *The Urantia Book* brochure, 1955.
14. *Orange County Register*, April 25, 1993, p. L-1.
15. *Possibilities*, Summer 1986, pp. 8–12.
16. John Marks Templeton, *Discovering the Laws of Life* (The Continuum Publishing Company, 1994), inside front of jacket.
17. John Marks Templeton, *The Humble Approach: Scientists Discover God* (Continuum Publishing Company, 1995), p. 137.
18. Templeton, *Discovering*, jacket.
19. Ibid., pp. 6, 7, 208, etc.
20. Jack Underhill, "Some New Age Myths and Truths," in *The Source* (Koloa, HI 96756), January/February 1988, p. 19.
21. Sir Arthur Eddington, *The Nature of the Physical World* (MacMillan, 1953), p. 317.
22. *MAGICAL BLEND: A Transformative Journey*, Issue 17, 1987, p. 13.

23. Black Elk, *The Sacred Pipe* (University of Oklahoma Press, 1989), pp. 3–9.
24. Davis, *Serpent and Rainbow,* pp. 213–14.
25. Manly P. Hall, *The Secret Teachings of all Ages: An Encyclopedic Outline of Masonic, Hermetic, Qabbalistic and Rosicrucian Symbolical Philosophy* (Los Angeles: The Philosophical Research Society, Inc., 1969), sixteenth ed., pp. LXXXVII–LXXXVIII.

Chapter 7—Naturalism or Supernaturalism?

1. Frederick K.C. Price, *The Word Study Bible* (Harrison House, 1990), p. 1178.
2. "The Viewpoint in the Science of Mind Concerning Certain Traditional Beliefs" (Science of Mind Publications). See also Ernest Holmes, *The Science of Mind* (textbook), p. 30, and *Science of Mind* (magazine), September 1983, p. 47.
3. *Plus,* May 1986, p. 23.
4. Robert Schuller, "Possibility Thinking: Goals," Amway Corporation tape.
5. *Houston Chronicle,* August 2, 1986, Section 6, p. 2.
6. Sir James Jeans, *The Mysterious Universe* (The Macmillan Company, 1939), pp. 147–58.
7. Eccles and Robinson, *Wonder,* p. 37.
8. Cited in Heaney, *Sacred,* p. 61.
9. Eddington, cited in *Quantum Questions: Mystical Writings of the World's Great Physicists,* ed. Ken Wilber (New Science Library, 1984), p. 5.
10. Wolfgang Smith, *Teilhardism and the New Religion: A Thorough Analysis of the Teachings of Pierre Teilhard de Chardin* (TAN Books, 1988), p. 242.
11. Personal interview with Carolyn Poole.
12. Horatio W. Dresser, ed., *The Quimby Manuscripts* (Citadel, 1980), p. 9.
13. Charles S. Braden, *Spirits in Rebellion: The Rise and Development of New Thought* (SMU Press, 1966), p. 20.
14. Ernest Holmes, *The Science of Mind* (textbook), p. 30.
15. James Reid, *Ernest Holmes: The First Religious Scientist* (Science of Mind Publications, Los Angeles), p. 14.
16. From the brochure "What Is the Science of Mind?"
17. "The Plus Factor," published excerpts from a Peale talk on Schuller's "Hour of Power," copyrighted 1985 by Robert Schuller, p. 3.
18. Braden, *Spirits,* p. 390.
19. Reid, *Ernest Holmes,* p. 14.
20. Braden, *Spirits,* p. 186.
21. Ibid., p. 387.
22. Norman Vincent Peale, *Positive Imaging* (Fawcett Crest, 1982), p. 77.
23. Norman Vincent Peale, *Plus: The Magazine of Positive Thinking,* Vol. 37, no. 4 (Part II), May 1986, p. 23.
24. Norman Vincent Peale, *The Power of Positive Thinking* (Fawcett Crest, 1983), pp. 52–53.
25. Norman Vincent Peale, *The Power of Positive Thinking,* New Condensed Edition (Center for Positive Thinking, 1987), p. 17.
26. Taped interviews on file at the Holy Spirit Research Center, Oral Roberts University, cited in Daniel Ray McConnell, *The Kenyon Connection: A Theological and Historical Analysis of the Cultic Origins of the Faith Movement,* a thesis submitted to the Theological Faculty, Oral Roberts University, Tulsa, OK, May 1982, p. 11.
27. McConnell, *Kenyon Connection,* p. 11.
28. E.W. Kenyon and Don Gossett, *The Positive Confession of the Word of God* (Tulsa: Custom Graphics, 1981), pp. 133–37, 152–55.
29. John Coffee and Richard L. Wentworth, *A Century of Eloquence: The History of Emerson College, 1880–1980* (Alternative Publications, 1982).
30. Kenyon and Gossett, *Confession,* pp. 129–36, 152–55, 182–85, etc.
31. E.W. Kenyon, *What Happened from the Cross to the Throne?* (Kenyon, 1945, 5th ed.), pp. 62, 173–76.

32. E.W. Kenyon, *The Hidden Man: An Unveiling of the Subconscious Mind* (Kenyon, 1970), p. 98.
33. *The Word of Faith* magazine, November 1984, p. 3.
34. Kenneth Copeland on TBN interview with Paul and Jan Crouch, February 5, 1986.
35. Dr. David Yonggi Cho, *The Fourth Dimension* (Bridge-Logos International, 1979), pp. 30, 64.
36. Urban C. Lehner, "New Faithful: Static in Some Nations, Christianity is Surging Among South Koreans," in *The Wall Street Journal*, May 12, 1983.
37. Kenneth Hagin, *Having Faith in Your Faith* (Rhema, 1980), pp. 3–4.
38. Pat Robertson, *Beyond Reason* (William Morrow and Company, Inc., 1985), p. 20.
39. Pat Robertson, *The Secret Kingdom* (Thomas Nelson Publishers, 1982), p. 43.
40. Ibid., p. 69.
41. Ibid., pp. 180–181.
42. John and Paula Sandford, *The Elijah Task* (Logos International, 1977), pp. 142–43.
43. Agnes Sanford, *The Healing Gifts of the Spirit* (Fleming H. Revell, 1966), p. 22.
44. Ibid., p. 27.
45. *The Healing Light*, 1947 edition, pp. 21–22, 60, 75.
46. Hagin, *Faith in Faith*, pp. 3–5.
47. Charles Capps, *The Tongue—A Creative Force* (Harrison House, 1976), pp. 8–9, 17, 130–36.
48. David Y. Cho and R. Whitney Manzano, *The Fourth Dimension: More Secrets for a Successful Faith Life*, vol. 2 (Bridge-Logos Publishing, 1983), p. 38.
49. *Gold Prospector*, April 1987, p. 15.
50. Heaney, *Sacred*, p. 26.
51. Ibid., pp. 25–84.
52. Ibid., p. 43.
53. Ibid., p. 21.
54. Ibid., p. 66.

Chapter 8—Native, Indigenous, and Nature Religion

1. Jackson and Delehanty, *Sacred*, p.109.
2. Ibid.
3. Jean Houston, *Life Force: The Psycho-Historical Recovery of the Self* (Quest Books, 1993), p. xiii.
4. Hall, *Encyclopedic Outline*, p. CXCIV.
5. Black Elk, *The Sacred Pipe: Black Elk's Account of the Seven Rites of the Oglala Sioux*, recorded and edited by Joseph Epes Brown (University of Oklahoma Press, 1989), p. 121.
6. Leslie G. Desmangles, *The Faces of the Gods: Vodoun and Roman Catholicism in Haiti* (The University of North Carolina Press, 1992), p. 180.
7. "Aloha Ambassador," in *Hemispheres*, October 1996, p. 15.
8. *Stronghold '93*, as cited in Creation Safari Footprint, August 1993.
9. Walter Yeeling Evans-Wentz, *The Fairy-Faith in Celtic Countries* (University Books, Inc., 1966), p. 401.
10. Elk, *Sacred Pipe*, p. 45.
11. Ibid., p. 56.
12. Ibid., pp. 124–25.
13. Ibid., pp. 7, 45.
14. Evans-Wentz, *Fairy-Faith*, inside back of jacket.
15. Harner, *Shaman*, pp. 58–59.
16. Herbert Schlossberg, *Idols for Destruction* (Thomas Nelson, 1983), p. 171.
17. Eccles and Robinson, *Wonder*, p. 61.
18. Jackson and Delehanty, *Sacred*, p. 211.
19. Ibid., p. 110.
20. Ibid., p. 112.

21. Barbara Slavin, "Ancient cycle of vengeance and violence: African crisis born of centuries of ethnic passions," in *USA Today*, November 12, 1996, p. 10A.
22. R.B. Stratton, *Captivity of the Oatman Girls* (University of Nebraska Press, 1983).
23. Tamara Jones, "Fire Goddess Defended: Harnessing of Volcano Is Hot Hawaii Issue," in *Los Angeles Times*, February 9, 1988, Part I, pp. 1, 18.
24. Joseph Campbell with Bill Moyers, *The Power of Myth* (Doubleday, 1988), p. 56.
25. Copy of letter on file.
26. Shoefoot, "Ashamed to be a Shaman," in *Natural History*, January 1997.
27. Translated and introduced by Rev. H.J. Schroeder, O.P., *The Canons and Decrees of the Council of Trent* (Tan Books and Publishers, Inc., 1978), Seventh Session, Sacrament of Baptism, Can. 4., p. 52.
28. Augustine, *de cat. rud.*, XXV, 48.
29. Cited in Evans-Wentz, *Fairy-Faith*, pp. 427–28.
30. *The Chieftain*, Pueblo, CO, July 22, 1995, p. 4B.
31. *Native Reflections*, Wesleyan Native American Ministries newsletter, Fall 1997, p. 4.
32. *NZ Herald*, November 14, 1996.

Chapter 9—Spirit Communication and Possession

1. Lame Deer and Erdoes, *Gift of Power*, p. 154.
2. Harner, *Shaman*, pp. 20, 42–44, 49.
3. Douglas James Mahr and Francis Racey, Ph.D., "Tired of the Program? Change Your Channel," *Australia's New Age News*, September 1987, p. 9.
4. Lawrence LeShan, *The Science of the Paranormal: The Last Frontier* (The Aquarian Press, 1987), p. 31.
5. Joan Halifax, *Shaman: The Wounded Healer* (Thames & Hudson, 1982), p. 13.
6. Cited in Klimo, *Channeling*, p. 82.
7. Quoted in Klimo, *Channeling*, p. 317.
8. Ruth Montgomery with Joanne Garland, *Ruth Montgomery: Herald of the New Age* (Fawcett Crest, 1986), pp. 71–111.
9. Laurens van der Post, *Jung and the Story of Our Time* (Random House, 1974), pp. 266–68.
10. Heaney, *Sacred*, p. 40.
11. Ibid., p. 186.
12. Klimo, *Channeling*, p. 40.
13. Heaney, *Sacred*, p. 40.
14. Ibid., p. 192.
15. Rev. Donald Bretherton, "Psychical Research and Biblical Prohibitions," in *Life, Death and Psychical Research*, J.D. Pearce-Higgins, ed., p. 108.
16. Willis Harman and Howard Rheingold, *Higher Creativity* (Jeremy P. Tarcher, 1984), pp. 46–47; cited in Klimo, *Channeling*, p. 314.
17. P.E. Vernon, ed., *Creativity Selected Readings* (Penguin Books, 1970), p. 57.
18. Harman and Rheingold, *Higher Creativity*, p. 46.
19. Ibid.
20. Klimo, *Channeling*, pp. 314–15.
21. Ibid.
22. Jerry Hopkins and Daniel Sugerman, *No One Here Gets Out Alive* (Warner Books, 1980), pp. 158–60.
23. *The Playboy Interviews with John Lennon and Yoko Ono* (Berkeley, 1982), p. 169.
24. Ibid., p. 203.
25. *Saturday Evening Post*, August 6, 1964.
26. *Rolling Stone*, May 5, 1977, p. 55.
27. *Playboy Interviews*, p. 106.
28. *Circus*, January 31, 1984, p. 70.
29. Charles White, *The Life and Times of Little Richard* (Harmony Books, 1984), p. 206.

30. James Douglas Morrison, *The Lords and New Creatures* (Simon & Schuster, 1970).
31. *Time*, December 16, 1974, p. 39.
32. *Rock*, April 1984, p. 30.
33. Sound track from film *Jimi Hendrix*, interview with Fayne Pridgon (side 4).
34. Ibid.
35. Chester Carlson, *New Frontiers Center Newsletter*, Fall/Winter 1986, p. 9.
36. Andrija Puharich, *Uri: A Journal of the Mystery of Uri Geller* (New York, 1975), p. 213.
37. William F. Barrett, "On Some Experiments with the Ouija Board and Blindfolded Sitters," in *Proceedings of the American Society for Psychical Research*, September 1914, pp. 381–94, cited in Edmund C. Gruss, with John G. Hutchins, *The Ouija Board: Doorway to the Occult* (Moody Press, 1979), pp. 53–57.
38. William Kirk Kilpatrick, *The Emperor's New Clothes* (Crossway Books, 1985), pp. 176–77.
39. Irving Litvag, *Singer in the Shadows* (Popular Library, 1972), cited in *Gnosis* magazine, no. 5, Fall 1987, p. 11.
40. Loraine O'Connell, "Seeing dead via mirror-gazing the latest trend in grief therapy," in *Daily News* (Los Angeles), December 27, 1993, p. L.A. LIFE - 19.
41. Klimo, *Channeling*, from the author's interview with DiMele, p. 238.
42. Klimo, *Channeling*, pp. 5–6.
43. Ibid., pp. 150–51.
44. Ibid., p. 43.
45. "A Matter of Course: Conversation with Kenneth Wapnick," in *SPC Journal*, vol. 7, no. 1, 1987, pp. 9–17.
46. Klimo, *Channeling*, p. 48.
47. Meredith Lady Young, *Agartha: A Journey to the Stars* (Stillpoint Publishing, 1984), p. 31.
48. Neale Donald Walsch, *Conversations with God: An Uncommon Dialogue* (G.P. Putnam's Sons, 1996), Introduction.
49. Ibid., pp. 33–34.
50. Ibid., pp. 33–34, 78, 86, 192.
51. Ibid., pp. 85–86, 89.
52. Ibid., pp. 108–09.
53. Ibid., p. 90.
54. Ibid., pp. 14, 85.
55. Ibid., p. 149.
56. Ibid., pp. 148, 193–95, 205–06.
57. Ibid., pp. 151, 215, etc.
58. Ibid., p. 217.
59. Eccles and Robinson, *Wonder*, p. 37.
60. Klimo, *Channeling*, p. 249.
61. *MAGICAL BLEND: A Transformative Journey*, Issue 17, 1987, p. 9.
62. Loyd Auerbach, *ESP, Hauntings and Poltergeists: A Parapsychologist's Handbook* (Warner Books, 1986), p. 218.
63. Klimo, *Channeling*, p. 182.
64. Maya Deren, *Divine Horsemen: Voodoo Gods of Haiti* (Chelsea House, 1970), pp. 247–49.
65. Davis, *Serpent and Rainbow*, pp. 85–91.
66. Ibid., pp. 214–15.
67. Ibid., pp. 47–48.
68. Allen Spraggett, *The Unexplained* (New York, 1967), pp. 68–71.
69. Ibid.
70. Willis Harman in *Noetic Sciences* newsletter, Autumn 1987, p. 24.

Chapter 10—Drugs, Imagination, and the Occult

1. Peter R. Breggin, M.D., *Talking Back to Prozac: What Doctors Aren't Telling You About Today's Most Controversial Drug* (St. Martin's Paperbacks, 1994), pp. 37, 39–40.

2. Calvin Miller, *The Table of Inwardness* (InterVarsity Press, 1984), p. 93.
3. "Military lifts peyote ban for Indians: Guidelines forbid use on planes, ships," in *The Bulletin*, April 16, 1997, p. A-6.
4. Jay Stevens, *Storming Heaven: LSD and the American Dream* (The Atlantic Monthly Press, 1987), p. 345.
5. Morrison, *Serpent*, p. 117.
6. *Los Angeles Times*, July 3, 1993.
7. William J. Bailey, *Indiana Prevention Resource Center Fact Line on Non-Medical Use of Ritalin* (Indianapolis, IN: 1995).
8. Gary Kane, "Armed Forces Off-Limits for Ritalin-User," *Grand Rapids Press*, December 1, 1996.
9. Ibid.
10. Breggin, *Prozac*, p. 17.
11. Michael D. Lemonick, "The Mood Molecule," *Time*, September 29, 1997, p. 56.
12. Breggin, *Prozac*, pp. 34, 39.
13. Ibid., pp. 33, 34, 37, 38–40.
14. Ibid., p. 73.
15. From a tape recording of an interview.
16. From an undated copy of *MAGICAL BLEND: A Transformative Journey*, pp. 25–26.
17. Ibid., p. 25.
18. Jean Houston, *Life Force: The Psycho-Historical Recovery of the Self* (Quest Books, 1993), pp. 227–28.
19. Peale, *Imaging*, Introduction.
20. Network News, "Shamans with Ph.D.s and Private Practices," in *Common Boundary*, Mar./Apr. 1986, p. 12.
21. Bernie S. Siegel, M.D., *Love, Medicine & Miracles* (Harper & Row, 1986), pp. 147–49.
22. Jackson and Delehanty, *Sacred*, p. 121.
23. Norman Vincent Peale, *Plus*, February 1986, p. 10.
24. Miller, *Table*, p. 94.
25. Will Baron, *Deceived by the New Age* (Pacific Press Publishing Association, 1990), pp. 61–62.
26. Ibid., pp. 100–01.
27. Robert L. Wise, "Healing of the Memories: A Prayer Therapy for You," in *Christian Life Magazine*, July 1984, pp. 63–64.
28. Napoleon Hill and W. Clement Stone, *Success Through a Positive Mental Attitude* (Pocket Books, 1977), p. 44.
29. Napoleon Hill, *Grow Rich with Peace of Mind* (Fawcett Crest, 1967), pp. 218–19, etc.
30. Ibid., p. 159.
31. Napoleon Hill, *Think and Grow Rich* (Fawcett, 1979), pp. 215–19.
32. Robert Masters and Jean Houston, *Mind Games* (Dell Publishing Co., 1972), pp. 199–201.
33. Art Ulene, *Feeling Fine* (J.P. Tarcher, 1977), pp. 97–99.
34. Siegel, *Love*, pp. 19–20.
35. Houston and Masters, *Games*, pp. 70–71.
36. From a personal interview with Doug Glover.

Chapter 11—Ecology, Shamanism, Science, and Christianity

1. From the 1985 Foundation catalog.
2. *FWR Report*, July 1993, p. 3.
3. *Institute of Noetic Sciences Bulletin*, late 1987.
4. Harner, *Shaman*, p. xi.
5. *Earth and Spirit: The Spiritual Dimension of the Environmental Crisis*, International Conference brochure sponsored by Chinook Learning Center, October 19–21, 1990, Seattle, WA.

6. Ibid.
7. *Science Digest,* November 1981, p. 39.
8. Carl Sagan, *Cosmos* (Random House, 1980), p. 243.
9. *Noetic Sciences Bulletin,* April–May 1988, p. 5.
10. *Dallas Morning News,* September 26, 1992.
11. *Foundation,* July/August 1994, pp. 6–7.
12. *Christian News,* March 21, 1994, p. 8.
13. *O Timothy,* vol. 11, Issue 3, 1994.
14. *O Timothy,* vol. 9, Issue 1, 1992.
15. Campbell with Moyers, *Power of Myth,* p. 197.
16. From the NACRE brochure, "Inter-continental conference on caring for creation," May 16–19, 1990.
17. Ibid.
18. Laura Sessions Stepp, "Creation theories aside, they join forces to save the Earth," in *The Morning News Tribune,* May 24, 1992, p. A3.
19. "Religious Leaders Join Scientists in Ecological Concerns," in *Christianity Today,* August 19, 1991, p. 49.
20. Ibid.
21. Ibid.
22. *New York Times,* May 16, 1992.
23. *Tarrytown News,* November 1984, p. 5.
24. "Interfaith Project Aims to Protect Environment: Gore helps to launch partnership of Catholic, Jewish, and Protestant leaders. Grass-roots activity in thousands of congregations is among its goals," in *Los Angeles Times,* October 9, 1993, p. B5.
25. Ibid.
26. *Calvary Contender,* June 15, 1996.
27. *The Oregonian,* April 10, 1993, p. C1.
28. *The Morning News Tribune* (Tacoma, WA), May 24, 1992, p. A3.
29. *Shared Vision: Global Forum of Spiritual and Parliamentary Leaders on Human Survival,* Autumn 1987, p. 5.
30. From an official brochure of Global Forum of Spiritual and Parliamentary Leaders on Human Survival, 304 East 45th St., 12th Floor, New York, NY 10017.
31. "For Global Survival: The Final Statement of the Conference," in *Shared Vision* (newsletter of Global Forum), Summer 1988, p. 12.
32. The Moscow Plan of Action of the Global Forum on Environment and Development for Human Survival, January 1990, final draft, p. 9.
33. Ibid., p. 12.
34. From the Moscow Declaration, *Shared Vision,* vol. 4, no. 7, 1990, p. 16.
35. From a copy of Gorbachev's speech to the 1990 Global Forum, pp. 1–3.
36. Richard J. Foster, *Celebration of Discipline: The Path to Spiritual Growth* (Harper & Row, 1978), p. 25.
37. *Christian News,* March 21, 1994, p. 8.
38. *Parade,* March 1, 1992.
39. *National Catholic Reporter,* June 19, 1992.
40. Ibid.
41. Cited in *Ground Zero,* October/November 1996, p. 8, C.T. Communications, Box 612, Gladstone, MB R0J 0T0, Canada.
42. *Parade,* January 23, 1994, p. 5.
43. Sir Eccles and Robinson, *Wonder,* p. 71.
44. Campbell with Moyers, *Power of Myth,* p. 197.
45. From a brochure promoting the event and sent out by Marilyn Ferguson and her *Brain/Mind* Newsletter.
46. From the 1990 brochure for the *Earth & Spirit* conference, op. cit.
47. Deepak Chopra's *Infinite Possibilities for Body, Mind & Soul,* November 1996, p. 1.
48. Ibid.
49. Ibid.

50. Jeanne Achterberg, "The Wounded Healer: Transformational Journeys in Modern Medicine," in *Shaman's Drum*, Winter 1987, pp. 20, 24.
51. *Time*, May 10, 1993, cover and p. 3.
52. Robert A. Vetter, "Journey of Awakening," in *Shaman's Drum*, Winter 1987, pp. 47–48.
53. Ed McGaa, Eagle Man, *Rainbow Tribe: Ordinary People Journeying on the Red Road* (San Francisco: Harper, 1992), p. 3.
54. Jonathan Adolph, "What Is New Age?" in *The 1988 Guide to New Age Living*, p. 12.
55. Andrija Puharich, *Uri: A Journal of the Mystery of Uri Geller* (New York, 1975), p. 213.
56. Campbell with Moyers, *Power of Myth*, p. xvi.
57. Ibid.

Chapter 12—The Influence of Eastern Mysticism

1. As quoted in Baron, *Deceived*, p. 62.
2. Edgar D. Mitchell, "Implications of Mind Research," an address to members of Congress and Congressional staff on behalf of the Congressional Clearinghouse on the Future. Printed in *Institute of Noetic Sciences Newsletter*, Spring & Summer 1980, vol. 8, no. 5, p. 5.
3. Lawrence LeShan, *How to Meditate* (Boston, 1974), pp. 150–51.
4. *The New Age Magazine*, September 1981, pp. 54–55.
5. Cited in *Christianity Today*, April 8, 1991, p. 64.
6. Jerry Adler, "800,000 Hands Clapping," in *Newsweek*, June 13, 1994, p. 46.
7. *Raleigh News and Observer*, March 1, 1989.
8. Campbell with Moyers, *Power of Myth*, p. 208.
9. Copy of confidential report on file.
10. Marilyn Ferguson, *The Aquarian Conspiracy: Personal and Social Transformation in the 1980s* (J.P. Tarcher, 1980), inside jacket.
11. Cited in *Christianity Today*, April 8, 1991, p. 64.
12. *Washington Post*, May 10, 1990.
13. *Seattle Times*, April 29, 1990.
14. Don Feder, " 'Omm' echoes from Harvard," in *Washington Times*, April 4, 1994.
15. Johannes Aagaard, "Hinduism's World Mission," in *Update*, September 1982.
16. Adler, "800,000 Hands," p. 46.
17. Bill Higgins, "Hollywood Elite Says Hello, Dalai," in *Los Angeles Times*, August 5, 1996, p. E3.
18. Jean Houston, *Life Force: The Psycho-Historical Recovery of the Self* (Quest Books, 1993), pp. 254–56.
19. Ibid., pp. 211–42.
20. C.G. Jung, *Memories, Dreams, Reflections* (Pantheon Books, 1963), pp. 323–24.
21. "The World According to Ram," *The Utne Reader*, July/Aug. 1988, p. 80, abridged from Martin Gardner, *The New Age: Notes of a Fringe Watcher* (Prometheus Books, 1988).
22. Robert Masters and Jean Houston, *Mind Games* (Dell Publishing, 1972), pp. 13, 229–30; see also Houston, *Life Force*.
23. Georg Feuerstein, "A Brief History of Hatha Yoga, Part II," in *Yoga Journal*, September/October 1987, p. 67.
24. Catherine Ingram, "Ken Wilber: The Pundit of Transpersonal Psychology," in *Yoga Journal*, September/October 1987, p. 43.
25. Naomi Steinfeld, "Passages In: For People in Spiritual Crisis," in *AHP Perspective*, February 1986, p. 9.
26. *Brain/Mind Bulletin*, July 12, 1982, p. 3.
27. Stanislav and Christina Grof, "Holotropic Therapy: A Strategy for Achieving Inner Transformation," in *New Realities*, March/April 1987, p. 11.
28. Art Kunkin, "Transcendental Meditation on Trial, Part Two," in *Whole Life Monthly*, September 1987, pp. 14, 17.

29. Ibid., p. 17.
30. Ibid., pp. 15–17.
31. R.D. Scott, *Transcendental Misconceptions* (San Diego, 1978), pp. 37–38, 115–29.
32. Ibid., p. 119.
33. Ken Carey, *The Starseed Transmissions: Living in the Post-Historic World* (Harper Collins, 1991), pp. 54–55.
34. Maurice Cooke, *The Nature of Reality: A Book of Explanations* (Marcus Books, 1979), p. ix.
35. Lyssa Royal and Keith Priest, *Preparing for Contact: A Metamorphosis of Consciousness* (Royal Priest Research Press, 1994), pp. vii–viii.
36. Royal and Keith, *Contact*, pp. viii–ix.
37. Robert Schuller, *Peace of Mind Through Possibility Thinking* (Fleming H. Revell, 1977), pp. 131–32.
38. Herbert Bruce Puryear, *Why Jesus Taught Reincarnation: A Better News Gospel* (New Paradigm Press, 1992), p. xii.
39. Ibid., p. v.
40. Ibid., pp. v, xii.
41. Herbert Benson with William Proctor, *Your Maximum Mind* (Random House, 1987), pp. 16–22.
42. Yogananda, *Autobiography*, p. 489.
43. Jonathan Ellis, "Practicing Meditation: Basic Techniques to Improve Your Health and Well-Being," in *Deepak Chopra's Infinite Possibilities for Body, Mind and Soul*, October 1996, p. 4.
44. Jackson and Delehanty, *Sacred*, p. 173.
45. Ibid., pp. 48–49.
46. Adler, "800,000 Hands," p. 46.
47. Edgar Mitchell with Dwight Williams, *THE WAY OF THE EXPLORER: An Apollo Astronaut's Journey Through the Material and Mystical Worlds* (Putnam, 1996), as cited in *Brain/Mind*, August 1996, p. 4.
48. Ibid.
49. Undated letter from Edgar Mitchell on Institute of Noetic Sciences letterhead, 600 Stockton Street, San Francisco, CA 94108, (415) 434-0626.
50. *Noetic Sciences Review*, date unknown, p. 6.
51. Bill Thomson, "Spiritual Values in the Business World," in *Yoga Journal*, January/February 1988, p. 52.
52. Bill Friedman, Ph.D., "Interview with Gerald Jampolsky, M.D.," in *Orange County Resources*, p. 3, from Jampolsky's book, *Teach Only Love*.
53. Jon Klimo, *Channeling* (Jeremy P. Tarcher, 1987), p. 149, quoted from Klimo's interview with Skutch.
54. "The World According to Ram," *Utne*, p. 80.
55. "The Guru and the FAA," in *Newsweek*, March 6, 1995, p. 32; see also Ruth Larson, "Unethical conduct found in FAA probe," in *Washington Times*, March 29, 1995, pp. A1, A18.
56. "World According to Ram," *Utne*, p. 80.
57. Jeane Dixon with Rene Noorbergen, *Jeane Dixon, My Life and Prophecies, Her Own Story As Told to Rene Noorbergen* (William Morrow and Company, 1969), pp. 160–61.
58. Ibid., p. 166.

Chapter 13—New Respectability in a New Age

1. M. Scott Peck, *The Different Drum* (Simon & Schuster, 1987), pp. 205–06.
2. Marion Long, "In Search of a Definition," in *Omni*, October 1987, p. 160.
3. Mary B.W. Tabor for *The New York Times News Service*, "Publishers spread wings with spiritual books; reap benefits," in *The Daily Astorian*, August 11, 1995, p. 9A.
4. Walter Bromberg, *From Shaman to Psychotherapist* (Henry Regnery Co., 1975), p. 336.

5. *The Occult Digest,* January 1931, p. 27.
6. Robert Lindsey, *New York Times,* cited in *St. Petersburg Times,* December 6, 1986, p. 7E.
7. Tabor, "Publishers spread wings," p. 9A.
8. Dick Sutphen, "Infiltrating the New Age Society," in *What Is,* Summer 1986, p. 14.
9. Joan Connell, "The New Age Spiritualist and the Old School Scholars; Academics Take Their Measure of Longtime Channeler JZ Knight," in *The Washington Post,* March 8, 1997, pp. B7–8.
10. Ibid.
11. Ibid.
12. Gene Edward Veith, "Heroin Chic," in *World,* November 9, 1996, pp. 13–15.
13. Ibid., p. 15.
14. M. Scott Peck, *The Road Less Traveled* (Simon & Schuster, 1978), p. 282.
15. M. Scott Peck, *People of the Lie* (Simon & Schuster, 1983), p. 201.
16. Brenda Scott and Samantha Smith, *Trojan Horse: How the New Age Movement Infiltrates the Church* (Huntington House Publishers), p. 133.
17. Matthew Fox, *The Coming of the Cosmic Christ* (San Francisco: Harper, 1988), pp. 6, 7, 32.
18. *Today in the Word,* April 1996, pp. 35, 37.
19. Scott and Smith, *Trojan,* p. 135.
20. Fox, *Cosmic,* p. 7.
21. Karen Burton Mains, *Lonely No More* (Word Publishing, 1993), inside back jacket.
22. Ibid., pp. 89–91, etc.
23. Ibid., pp. 92, 120–22, etc.
24. Ibid., pp. 129–31.
25. Ibid., p. 119.
26. Ibid., p. 114.
27. Ibid., p. 119.
28. Ibid., p. 115.
29. Debbie Warhola, "Spiritual Directors: An old tradition is rekindled," in *The Orange County Register,* August 17, 1995, NEWS 14.
30. Ibid., pp. 122–24.
31. *Christianity Today,* May 16, 1994.
32. Philip Yancey, "Christian McCarthyism," in *Christianity Today,* July 18, 1994, p. 72.
33. Richard Foster, *Celebration of Discipline* (Hodder & Stoughton, 1984), pp. 20–29.
34. Tony Campolo, *Carpe Diem: Seize the Day* (Word Publishing, 1994), pp. 85–88.
35. Richard W. Carlson, "The New Age: A Weather Report," in *The Covenant Companion,* January 1991, pp. 6, 7, 45.
36. Peter L. Berger, "The Other Face of Gaia—From a lecture given at the Harvard Divinity School by Aglaia Holt, Professor of Wymyns Studies, California State University at Poco, in *First Things,* August/September 1994, pp. 15–17.
37. *Scottish Rite Journal,* May 1992.
38. *The Miami Herald,* July 28, 1995, p. 1F.
39. Albert G. Mackey, *Manual of the Lodge* (Macoy and Sickles, 1802), p. 96.
40. Albert G. Mackey, 33rd degree, and Charles T. McClenachan, 33rd degree, *Encyclopedia of Freemasonry* (The Masonic History Company, 1921), revised ed., vol. II, p. 564.
41. Albert Pike, *Morals and Dogma of the Ancient and Accepted Scottish Rite of Freemasonry* (Supreme Council of the Thirty-Third Degree, 1964), pp. 104–05.
42. Ibid., p. 819.
43. Manly Palmer Hall, *The Lost Keys of Freemasonry* (Macoy Publishing, 1976), p. 48.
44. Lynn F. Perkins, *The Meaning of Masonry* (CSA Press, 1971), p. 53.
45. *Little Masonic Library,* vol. 4 (Macoy Publishing, 1977), p. 32.
46. Pike, *Morals,* pp. 219, 525.
47. Found in any official manual of Masonic rites.
48. Joseph Fort Newton, *The Religion of Masonry: An Interpretation* (Macoy Publishing and Masonic Supply Co., Inc., 1969), p. 11.

49. Joseph Fort Newton, *The Holy Bible: The Great Light of Masonry* (A.J. Holman, 1940), pp. 3–4.
50. Pike, *Morals*, p. 226.
51. Hall, *Lost Keys*, pp. 64–65.
52. "A Report on Freemasonry" (6 pages) published by the Home Mission Board, Southern Baptist Convention, March 17, 1993, in summary of the 75-page analysis "A Study of Freemasonry," which the Southern Baptist Convention in annual session June 9–11, 1992, directed the Interfaith Witness Department of the Home Mission Board to undertake. This quote is from pp. 4–5.
53. Paul Hawk in *The Magic of Findhorn* (Bantam Books, 1976), pp. 103–04.
54. "Stan Grof Interview," in *Sounds True Audio Catalog*, 1989090, pp. 21, 24.
55. Baron, *Deceived*, p. 44.
56. Ibid., pp. 47–48.
57. Campbell with Moyers, *Power of Myth*, p. xviii.
58. Tabor, "Publishers spread wings," p. 9A.
59. James Redfield, *The Celestine Prophecy: An Adventure* (Warner Books, Inc., 1993), from the jacket.
60. Baron, *Deceived*, p. 31.
61. Sue Browder, "Basic instincts," in *All Together: The Women's Newsletter from SEARS*, first edition October 1994, p. 6.
62. *Innerself*, November 1994, p. 34.
63. Paul McGuire, "Hooked on Hollywood Religion," in *Charisma*, November 1996, p. 61.
64. Virginia Smith, "Oprah Winfrey reveals secret of her incredible success," in *Examiner*, July 14, 1987, p. 29.
65. McGuire, "Hooked," p. 62.
66. December 1995, http://www.mindspring.com/biomind/pages/database.html, 4/3/97.
67. Patrick Tierney, "The Soviets' Peace Program," in *Omni*, December 1986, p. 89.
68. Alex Heard, "Rolfing with Yeltsin," in *The New Republic*, October 9, 1989, pp. 11–13.
69. *Psychology Today*, September/October 1996, p. 52.
70. Bob Ortega, "Research Institute Shows People a Way Out of Their Bodies," in the *Wall Street Journal*, September 20, 1994, pp. A1, A8.
71. *The Arizona Republic*, August 13, 1989, p. C5.
72. *Bulletin* (AP), December 28, 1995, front page.
73. *Chicago Tribune*, January 11, 1995, p. 4, Section 1.
74. Outlook, "The Bill-and-Newt Gurus," in *U.S. News & World Report*, January 23, 1995.
75. Shyam Bhatia, "Belief in the occult rules Saudi rulers," in *The Toronto Star*, March 31, 1995, p. A17.
76. Tart, *Science of Mind*, December 1986, pp. 81–88.
77. Jon Spiegel, "AHP Leadership in the Profession," Association for Humanistic Psychology *Newsletter*, February 1984, p. 22.
78. *The Bulletin*, Bend, OR, March 7, 1997, p. A-10.
79. Jackson and Delehanty, *Sacred*, p. 3.
80. Ibid.
81. *Daily Telegram* (London), October 1, 1994.
82. *The Christian News*, December 25, 1994, citing Calvary Contender, October 1, 1993.

Chapter 14—Holistic Medicine

1. *Time*, June 24, 1996, pp. 58–59.
2. Ibid., p. 59.
3. *Jerusalem Post, International Edition*, week ending November 28, 1996, Advertising Supplement, p. 14.
4. *Jerusalem Post International Edition*, week ending November 21, 1996, p. 21.
5. *Time*, June 24, 1996, p. 62.

6. Paul C. Reisser, T.K. Reisser, and John Weldon, *New Age Medicine* (InterVarsity Press, 1987), p. 158.
7. "Borysenko sees the spirit seeping into medicine," in *Brain/Mind and Common Sense,* June 1993, p. 5.
8. Charles Mackay, *Extraordinary Popular Delusions and the Madness of Crowds* (London, 1841), title page.
9. *Time,* June 24, 1996, p. 60.
10. *Washington Post,* February 5, 1993.
11. *Time,* June 24, 1996, p. 65.
12. "Why med schools teach meditation," in *USA Weekend,* February 21–25, 1997, p. 8.
13. Martha Brant, "Hopeful in Tijuana: A booming medical bazaar offers new lures," in *Newsweek,* June 2, 1997, p. 43.
14. "Why med schools teach," p. 8.
15. *UC Berkeley Wellness Letter,* September 1995, pp. 4–5.
16. *Jerusalem Post International Edition,* week ending November 21, 1996, p. 21.
17. Harner, *Shaman,* p. 136.
18. *Los Angeles Times,* September 19, 1994, p. A3.
19. "Borysenko sees," p. 5.
20. *Time,* June 24, 1996, p. 62.
21. Ibid., p. 61.
22. Colleen Smith, "The potent medicine of prayer," in *Our Sunday Visitor,* February 9, 1997, p. 10.
23. Ibid., p. 28.
24. Members are listed inside the cover of each issue of *Progress in Theology, the Newsletter of the John Templeton Foundation's Humility Theology Information Center.*
25. Gary Thomas, "Doctors Who Pray: How the medical community is discovering the healing power of prayer," in *Christianity Today,* January 6, 1997, pp. 20–30.
26. *Time,* June 24, 1996, pp. 60–61.
27. Ibid.
28. Breggin, *Prozac,* p. 42.
29. *Time,* June 24, 1996, p. 59.
30. *Christianity Today,* January 6, 1997, p. 29.
31. Thomas, "Doctors Who Pray," pp. 20–30.
32. Ibid.
33. Ibid., p. 30.
34. John Goodwin, "Testing the Fruit," Tape 2, Toronto, Canada, April 1997, Discernment Ministries, P.O. Box 129, Lapeer, MI 48446-0129.
35. Baron, *Deceived,* pp. 25–28.
36. *Time,* June 24, 1996, pp. 64–65.
37. Deepak Chopra, M.D., *Ageless Body, Timeless Mind: The Quantum Alternative to Growing Old* (Harmony Books, 1993), from the special page of testimonials just inside the front cover.
38. Ibid., pp. 35–37.
39. Ibid., pp. 280–82.
40. *Time,* June 24, 1996, p. 68.
41. Ibid., pp. 67–68.
42. Schuller, *Possibilities,* pp. 8–12; Templeton, *Discovering,* pp. 16–19, 59, 78, 124–25, etc.
43. *Deepak Chopra's Infinite Possibilities for Body, Mind and Soul,* November 1996, p. 4.
44. Ibid., pp. 2–3.
45. *Time,* June 24, 1996, p. 68.
46. *Chopra's Infinite,* p. 3.
47. Tony Perry, "Alternative Care Edges into Medical Mainstream," in *Los Angeles Times,* September 19, 1994, pp. A3, A19.
48. Ibid., p. 19.
49. *Time,* June 24, 1996, p. 62.
50. Ibid., p. 67.

51. *Washington Post*, October 2, 1989.
52. Testimonies on file.
53. *Christianity Today*, January 6, 1997, pp. 23–24.
54. *Time*, June 24, 1994, p. 59.
55. "Borysenko sees," p. 5.
56. *Chopra's Infinite*, November 1996, p. 8.
57. Henri F. Ellenberger, *The Discovery of the Unconscious: The History and Evolution of Dynamic Psychiatry* (Basic Books, Inc., 1970), pp. 10–12; Frank Boas, "The Religion of the Kwakiutl Indians," Part II, in *Columbia University Contributions to Anthropology* (New York University Press, 1930), pp. x, 1–4.
58. Davis, *Serpent and Rainbow*, pp. 222–23.

Chapter 15—Twelve Steps with "God As You Conceive Him"

1. Tim Stafford, "The Hidden Gospel of the 12 Steps," in *Christianity Today*, July 22, 1991, p. 14.
2. Ibid.
3. Ibid., pp. 14–19.
4. Michael G. Maudlin, "Addicts in the Pew," in *Christianity Today*, July 22, 1991, pp. 19–21.
5. Ibid.
6. Stafford, "Hidden Gospel," pp. 14–21.
7. Ibid., p. 18.
8. Ibid., p. 15.
9. Ibid., p. 18.
10. Ibid.
11. G.A. Pritchard, *Willow Creek Seeker Services* (Baker Books, 1996), inside front cover opposite title page, a quotation of author Lyle E. Schaller.
12. Ibid., p. 273.
13. Stafford, "Hidden Gospel," p. 18.
14. Pritchard, *Willow Creek*, p. 273.
15. Stafford, "Hidden Gospel," p. 18.
16. Pritchard, *Willow Creek*, p. 273.
17. *Twelve Steps and Twelve Traditions* (Alcoholics Anonymous World Services, Inc., 1953), pp. 26–27.
18. *Not-God: A History of Alcoholics Anonymous* (Hazelden Educational Services, 1979), p. 125.
19. Stafford, "Hidden Gospel," p. 19.
20. Ibid., p. 18.
21. Martin and Deidre Bobgan, *12 Steps to Destruction: Codependency Recovery Heresies* (East Gate Publishers, 1991), p. 72.
22. *Pass It On: The story of Bill Wilson and how the A.A. message reached the world* (Alcoholics Anonymous World Services, Inc., 1984), p. 102; as cited in Bobgan, *12 Steps*, p. 72.
23. Herbert Fingarette, *Heavy Drinking: The Myth of Alcoholism As a Disease* (University of California Press, 1988).
24. Herbert Fingarette, "Alcoholism: The Mythical Disease," in *Utne Reader*, November/December 1988, pp. 64–65.
25. Herbert Fingarette, "We Should Reject the Disease Concept of Alcoholism," in *The Harvard Medical School Mental Health Letter*, February 1990, p. 4.
26. Ibid., p. 68.
27. Stanton Peele, *Diseasing of America: Addiction Treatment Out of Control* (Heath and Company, 1989), p. 27.
28. *Twelve Steps and Twelve Traditions*, p. 22.
29. "Alcohol Abuse and Dependence," in *Harvard Medical School Mental Health Review*, Number Two Revised, p. 10.

30. Stafford, "Hidden Gospel," p. 19.
31. *Pass It On,* pp. 275–76.
32. Ibid., pp. 276, 278.
33. Ibid., pp. 275–279.
34. Ibid., p. 198.
35. Ibid., p. 375.
36. Ibid., p. 374.
37. Stafford, "Hidden Gospel," p. 14; see also *Pass It On,* p. 121.
38. Helen Smith Shoemaker, *I Stand at the Door: The Life of Sam Shoemaker* (Word Books, 1978), p. 133.
39. Ibid., p. 138.
40. Roy Livesey, *Twelve Steps to the New Age* (Bury House Books, 1995—an unpublished manuscript), pp. 21–22.
41. Stafford, "Hidden Gospel," p. 16.
42. The Layman with a Notebook (anonymous pseudonym), *What Is the Oxford Group?* (Oxford University Press, 1933), pp. 68–69.
43. Oliver R. Barclay, *Whatever Happened to the Jesus Lane Lot?* (InterVarsity Press, 1977), pp. 98–100.
44. Dick B, *Anne Smith's Spiritual Workbook* (Good Book Publishing Co., 1992), p. 45.
45. John Wimber, *Power Evangelism* (Hodder & Stoughton, 1985), p. 74.
46. Alan Morrison, *The Serpent and the Cross: Religious Corruption in an Evil Age* (K&M Books, 1994), pp. 195–97.
47. Livesey, *Twelve Steps,* pp. 47–49.
48. *Christian News,* May 12, 1997, p. 11.
49. Mike R. Taylor, *A.J. Russell and the "Two Listeners"* (London, 1933), p. 3.
50. T. Willard Hunter, *The Man Who Would Change the World: Frank Buchman and Moral ReArmament* (unpublished manuscript, 1977), pp. 110–11, as cited in Livesey, *Twelve Steps,* pp. 88–89.
51. Livesey, *Twelve Steps,* p. 56.
52. Eileen Caddy and Liza Hollingshead, *Flight into Freedom* (Findhorn Press, 1988),p. 28.
53. Frank N.D. Buchman, *Remaking the World* (London, 1941), p. 147, cited by Livesey, *Twelve Steps,* p. 84.
54. Livesey, *Twelve Steps,* p. 84.
55. Tom Driberg, *The Mystery of Moral Re-Armament* (London, 1964), pp. 156–67, as cited in Livesey, *Twelve Steps,* p. 19.
56. Livesey, *Twelve Steps,* pp. 21–22.
57. Ibid.
58. *Ideology and Co-existence* (MRA, Toronto, Canada), p. 2, as cited in Livesey, *Twelve Steps,* p. 20.
59. Livesey, *Twelve Steps,* p. 21.
60. Ibid., pp. 63–64.
61. Ibid., pp. 90–91.
62. Ibid., pp. 94–99.
63. Ibid., pp. 105–07.

Chapter 16—The Seduction of Youth

1. *Forbes,* February 1, 1993.
2. Baron, *Deceived,* p. 19.
3. Masters and Houston, *Games.*
4. Letter on file.
5. Thomas Roder, Volker Kubillus, and Anthony Burwell, *Psychiatrists: The Men Behind Hitler, The Architects of Horror* (Freedom Publishing, 1994), p. 286.
6. "The State of the World," According to Gorbachev, in *Christian News,* October 28, 1996, p. 1.
7. *Denver Post,* April 19, 1987.

8. Linda Chavez, "Where's our moral outrage?" in *USA Today*, September 11, 1996, p. 15A.
9. Robert Muller, *New Genesis: Shaping a Global Spirituality* (Doubleday, 1982), inside front of jacket.
10. Ibid., pp. xii–xiii.
11. Ibid., p. 134.
12. Ibid.
13. *The Robert Muller School: World Core Curriculum Manual* (The Robert Muller School, 1986), p. 8.
14. *Christian News*, October 28, 1996, p. 18.
15. Duane Elgin, *Awakening the Earth* (William Morrow, 1993), p. 171.
16. *Christian News*, October 28, 1996, p. 18.
17. Muller, *Genesis*, p. 134.
18. Ibid., p. 135.
19. Published by Lucis Publishing Company, New York.
20. *Muller: Curriculum*, Preface.
21. Berit Kjos, *Brave New Schools: Guiding Your Child Through the Dangers of the Changing School System* (Harvest House, 1995), p. 235, from the author's phone conversation with Cuddy.
22. Jean-Francois Revel, *The Flight from Truth: The Reign of Deceit in the Age of Information* (Random House, 1991), p. 315.
23. Charlotte T. Iserbyt, "The History of OBE-Mastery Learning," in *The Christian Conscience*, vol. 2, no. 9, October 1996, pp. 31–32.
24. Ibid., p. 33.
25. *Christian News*, October 28, 1996, p. 17.
26. Malachi Martin, *The Keys of This Blood: The Struggle for World Dominion Between Pope John Paul II, Mikhael Gorbachev, and the Capitalist West* (Simon & Schuster, 1990), p. 391.
27. Roder, Kubillus, Burwell, *Psychiatrists*, p. 306.
28. Jackson and Delehanty, *Sacred*, p. 32.
29. Ibid.
30. Ibid., pp. 32–38.
31. See, for example, W.H. Bowart, *Operation Mind Control* (Dell Publishing, 1978); and Gordon Thomas, *Journey into Madness: The True Story of Secret CIA Mind Control and Medical Abuse* (Bantam Books, 1989); and others.
32. Jeffrey Kane, "Reflections on the Holistic Paradigm," in *Holistic Education Review*, Winter 1993, p. 3.
33. *Humanist Magazine*, January–February 1983, as cited in Martin, *Keys*, p. 295.
34. Kjos, *Schools*, p. 75.
35. Barbara Clark, *Growing Up Gifted* (Los Angeles), p. 100.
36. Martin, *Keys*, pp. 232–33.
37. Bruce Logan, "It's goodbye to 'virtues' and hello to 'values,' " in *NZ Herald*, October 29, 1996, p. A13.
38. David Guthrie, "We're no longer bound by tradition," in *NZ Herald*, October 29, 1996, p. A13.
39. *Reader's Digest*, November 1992.
40. "Gorbachev Speaks to 17,000 in St. Louis," in *Christian News*, October 28, 1996, pp. 18–19.
41. Revel, *Flight*, pp. 306–12.
42. "The Meaning of Life," in *Life*, December 1988, p. 78.
43. Martin L. Gross, *The Psychological Society: The impact—and the failure—of psychiatry, psychotherapy, psychoanalysis and the psychological revolution* (Random House, 1978), pp. 4–5.
44. *Reader's Digest*, May 1992, reprinted from the *Wall Street Journal*.
45. *World*, November 16, 1996, cited in Calvary Contender, February 1, 1997, p. 1.
46. Allen Bergen, "Psychotherapy and Religious Values," quoting Carl Rogers, in *Journal of Consulting and Clinical Psychology*, vol. 48, p. 101.

47. "Psychology Today, Psychology Tomorrow, Psychology Forever," in *Chronicles*, March 1986, p. 48.
48. Gross, *Psychological*, pp. 178–79.
49. Bruce Wiseman, *Psychiatry, The Ultimate Betrayal* (Freedom Publishing, 1995), pp. 357–58.
50. Gross, *Psychological*, pp. 4–5.
51. Wiseman, *Betrayal*, pp. 359–60.
52. "A Journey Beneath Your Feet," in *READ* (Weekly Reader Corporation), as cited in Kjos, *Schools*, p. 89.
53. Louise Derman-Sparks, *Anti-Bias Curriculum* (National Association for the Education of Young Children, 1989), p. 92, as cited in Kjos, *Schools*, p. 91.
54. Lamar Alexander, *Steps Along the Way: A Governor's Scrapbook* (Thomas Nelson Publishers, 1986), p. 85.
55. Kjos, *Schools*, pp. 99–100.
56. Deborah Rozman, *Meditating with Children: A Workbook on New Age Educational Methods* (University of Trees, 1975), from endorsements in front of book.
57. *Seattle Times*, September 22, 1992, p. B6.
58. *Philadelphia Gay News*, April 7–13, 1995.
59. Ibid.
60. *Baltimore Sun*, April 1, 1993.
61. *Catholic Family News*, April 1994, p. 45; *Denver Christian News*, February 1993, p. 10; *Concerned Women For America*, October 1993 special mailing; *What Homosexuals Do*, 1S1S, Inc. P.O. Box 6725, Lincoln, NE 68506.
62. *Atlantic Monthly*, April 1993.
63. Letter on file.

Chapter 17—Playing God: The Lust for Power

1. *Science of Mind*, December 1986, p. 8.
2. Davis, *Serpent and Rainbow*, p. 76.
3. Daniel B. Clendenin, ed., *Eastern Orthodox Theology, A Contemporary Reader* (Baker Books, 1995), p. 184.
4. *Catechism of the Catholic Church* (The Wanderer Press, 1994), par. 460, p. 116.
5. His Holiness John Paul II, *Crossing the Threshold of Hope* (Alfred A. Knopf, 1994), p. 195.
6. Morrison, *Serpent*, p. 229.
7. Kenneth Copeland, Trinity Broadcasting Network (TBN) interview on "Praise The Lord" with Paul and Jan Crouch on February 5, 1986.
8. Charles Capps, *God's Image of You* (Harrison House, 1985), p. 34.
9. Jon Klimo, *Channeling* (Jeremy P. Tarcher, 1987), p. 296.
10. *Science of Mind*, June 1985, p. 42.
11. *Time*, May 11, 1992.
12. Jill Neimark, "Do the Spirits Move You?" in *Psychology Today*, September/October 1996, p. 50.
13. *Plus, The Magazine of Positive Thinking*, May 1986, p. 23.
14. David Spangler, *Reflections on the Christ* (Findhorn, 1978), pp. 36–37.
15. "The Meaning of Life," in *Life*, December 1988.
16. Francis X. Clines, "An Unnamed 'Healing Force' Debuts on Soviet TV," in *New York Times International*, November 26, 1989.
17. Dennis Romero (*Los Angeles Times*), "Researchers once again looking at psychedelics," in *Seattle Times*, November 24, 1994; see also *Los Angeles Times*, April 16, 1993, pp. A3, A25.
18. Neimark, "Spirits," p. 52.
19. *Psychology Today*, September/October 1996, p. 54.
20. *World Goodwill Newsletter*, July/August/September 1982, p. 5.
21. "I Was a Psychic Spy," in *Psychology Today*, September/October 1996, p. 52.

22. Ibid.
23. E'louise Ondash, "Mindpower: The world's most famous spoon-bender says it's a positive, take-charge attitude that puts him on a higher plane . . ." in *North County Times* (San Diego, CA), November 10, 1996, pp. E-1, E-5.
24. John Randolph Price, *The Planetary Commission* (Quartus Books, 1980), Foreword, p. 173.
25. M. Scott Peck, *The Road Less Traveled* (Simon & Schuster, 1978), pp. 28–29, 269–70, 282–83.
26. *Plus,* April 1986, p. 3.
27. Alan Watts, *This Is It* (Random House, 1972), p. 90.
28. *Utne Reader,* July/Aug. 1988, pp. 80–81.
29. Walsch, *Dialogue,* pp. 85–86.
30. Ibid., p. 113.
31. *Self Discovery* newspaper, Fall 1983, front cover.
32. J.Z. Knight, "First Word," in *Omni,* March 1988, p. 8.
33. Finis J. Dake, *God's Plan for Man* (Dake Bible Sales, 1977), p. 35.
34. *Praise The Lord Show,* Trinity Broadcasting Network, December 26, 1991; as cited in G. Richard Fisher and M. Kurt Goedelman with W.E. Nunnally, Stephen F. Cannon, and Paul R. Blizard, *The Confusing World of Benny Hinn* (Personal Freedom Outreach, 1997), p. 134.
35. Robert Tilton, *God's Laws of Success* (Word of Faith Publishing, 1983), pp. 170–71; Kenneth E. Hagin, *Plead Your Case* (Tulsa, 1985), p. 3; Charles Capps, *God's Image of You* (Harrison House, 1985), p. 34; etc.
36. Charles Capps, *The Tongue—A Creative Force* (Harrison House, 1976), pp. 17, 26.
37. Kenneth Copeland, "Questions and Answers," in *Believer's Voice of Victory,* June 1986, p. 14.
38. Charles Capps, *Seedtime and Harvest* (Harrison House, 1986), p. 53.
39. Copeland, *Believer's Voice,* June 1986.
40. Kenneth E. Hagin, *ZOE: The God-Kind of Life* (Rhema Bible Church, 1981), p. 36.
41. Morris Cerullo, "The Endtime Manifestation of the Sons of God," audiotape 1; as cited in Hank Hanegraaff, *Christianity in Crisis* (Harvest House Publishers, 1993), p. 109.
42. From a written transcript of the "Oprah Winfrey Show," February 17, 1988.
43. Rodney R. Romney, *Journey to Inner Space: Finding God-in-Us* (Abingdon, 1986), p. 26.
44. Ibid., p. 121.
45. Ibid., pp. 138–39.
46. Rex R. Hutchens, 33rd degree, *A Bridge to Light.*
47. *Salt Lake City Tribune,* September 18, 1974; October 7, 1974.
48. *Christian News,* April 10, 1995, p. 24.
49. *Deseret News,* June 18, 1873.
50. Rollo May, *The Courage to Create.*
51. Spencer W. Kimball, *The Miracle of Forgiveness* (Bookcraft, 1981), pp. 5–6.
52. *Journal of Discourses,* vol. 6, p. 4.
53. *Deseret News,* February 9, 1980, Church Section, p. 11.
54. *Kentucky Monitor,* p. XX.
55. *World Goodwill Newsletter,* p. 5.
56. Lawrence LeShan, *The Science of the Paranormal* (The Aquarian Press, 1987), pp. 14–15, 70, etc.
57. A.S. Eddington, *Science and the Unseen World* (Macmillan, 1937), p. 53.
58. "The Viewpoint in the Science of Mind Concerning Traditional Beliefs" (Science of Mind Publications); Ernest Holmes, *The Science of Mind* (textbook), p. 30; cited in *Science of Mind,* September 1983, p. 47.
59. *Science of Mind,* March 1978, "Victim or Master," pp. 3–4.
60. Jane Roberts, *The Nature of Personal Reality* (Prentice Hall, 1974), p. 509.
61. Klimo, *Channeling,* p. 43.

62. Jackson and Delehanty, *Sacred,* p. 38.
63. Cho, *Fourth,* p. 43.
64. Ibid., pp. 39–44, 64, etc.
65. Jackson and Delehanty, *Sacred,* pp. 121–22.
66. *Chopra's Infinite,* November 1996, p. 5.
67. Jeremiah 10:10–11.
68. *Praise the Lord* newsletter, March 1993, p. 1.
69. Daniel B. Clendenin, *Eastern Orthodox Christianity* (Baker Books, 1994), p. 135.
70. Ibid., p. 136.
71. Ibid., p. 137.
72. His Holiness John Paul II, *Crossing the Threshold of Hope* (Knopf, 1994), p. 195.
73. Peter E. Gillquist, ed., *Coming Home: Why Protestant Clergy Are Becoming Orthodox* (Conciliar Press, 1992), p. 64.
74. Frank Schaeffer, *Dancing Alone: The Quest for Orthodox Faith in the Age of False Religion* (Holy Cross Orthodox Press, 1994), dedication.
75. Schaeffer, *Dancing,* pp. 123, 138–39, 203–08.
76. John Randolph Price, *Practical Spirituality* (Quartus), p. 21.
77. Margaret R. Stortz, "The Principle in Practice," in *Science of Mind,* December 1986, p. 9.
78. *Time,* June 24, 1996, p. 68.
79. *Time,* March 3, 1997, p. 17.
80. LeShan, *Science,* pp. 14–15.
81. Ibid., pp. 30–31.
82. Ira Progoff, *The Image of an Oracle;* see also F. LaGard Smith, *Out on a Broken Limb* (Harvest House Publishers, 1986), pp. 42–46.
83. Stoker Hunt, *Ouija: The Most Dangerous Game* (Harper & Row, 1985), p. 90.
84. Curtis Knight, *Jimi* (Praeger Publishers, 1979), p. 127.
85. W.E.R. Mons, *Beyond Mind* (Samuel Weiser, Inc., 1985), p. 228, etc.
86. Ibid., pp. 228–30.

Chapter 18—UFOs, ETIs, and Near-Death Experiences

1. Masters and Houston, *Games,* pp. 70–71.
2. Henry Gris and William Dick, *The New Soviet Psychic Discoveries* (Souvenir Press, 1979), p. 125, as cited in Morrison, *Serpent,* p. 241.
3. *Psychology Today,* September/October 1996, p. 50.
4. *When Cosmic Cultures Meet,* May 27–29, 1995, an international conference presented by The Human Potential Foundation, The Proceedings, pp. 9, 12.
5. Jacques Vallee, *Revelations: Alien Contact and Human Deception* (Ballatine Books, 1991), p. 7.
6. *The Bulletin,* March 28, 1997, front page.
7. Annie Gottlieb, "In the Cosmic Neighborhood," in *Time,* August 4, 1997, Letters page.
8. Jacques Vallee, *Revelations,* p. 259.
9. Ibid., p. 275.
10. Ibid., p. 259.
11. "GEOConversation, an interview with Robert Jastrow," in *GEO,* February 1982, p. 14.
12. Andrija Puharich, *Uri: A Journal of the Mystery of Uri Geller* (New York, 1975), p. 213.
13. Whitley Strieber, *Communion* (William Morrow, 1987), p. 13.
14. See also *Omni,* December 1987, pp. 53ff.
15. Courtney Brown, Ph.D., *Cosmic Voyage: A Scientific Discovery of Extraterrestrials Visiting Earth* (Dutton, 1996), pp. 4–7.
16. "An Interview with Hafez Assad," in *Time,* October 20, 1986, pp. 56–57.
17. "UFO era turns 50 this week," in *The Bulletin,* June 22, 1997, p. A-1.
18. Vallee, *Revelations,* pp. 52–57.

19. Ibid., inside back cover.
20. Ibid.
21. AP, "UFO explanations hid U-2 secrets," in *Bulletin* [Bend, OR], August 4, 1996, p. A-2.
22. See "Air Force Report on the Roswell Incident, Memorandum for Correspondents No. 255-M, Sept. 9. 1994" and "Top-Secret Balloon Project Looms over TV Movie on Roswell Incident," in *Skeptical Inquirer,* January/February 1995, pp. 22–23, 41–48.
23. Vallee, *Revelations*, pp. 252–53.
24. Robert Burns, The Associated Press, "Air Force's latest story 'closes case,'" in *The Bulletin,* June 24, 1997, p. A-2.
25. Daniel Ross, *UFOs and the Complete Evidence from Space: The Truth About Venus, Mars, and the Moon* (Pintado Publishing, 1987), pp. 58–59.
26. Vallee, *Revelations*, pp. 58–59.
27. Ibid., pp. 235–45.
28. *The Christian News,* December 9, 1996, p. 19.
29. *Moscow Tribune,* September 10, 1996.
30. Midge Dexter, "Farrakhan's Apology," in *The Weekly Standard,* July 29, 1996, p. 35.
31. Steve Elliott, The Associated Press, "Arizona buzzing over lights in sky," *The Bulletin,* June 22, 1997, p. A-10.
32. Copy of memorandum on file.
33. Vallee, *Revelations*, pp. 247–48, 283.
34. Ibid., pp. 259, 281.
35. Cited in John Ankerberg and John Weldon, "Behind the 'Alien Abduction Syndrome,'" in *After Dark* (undated), p. 9.
36. Vallee, *Revelations*, p. 290.
37. Royal & Priest, *Contact,* pp. xv–xvi.
38. Jacques Vallee, *Messengers of Deception* (Berkeley, 1979), pp. 204–05.
39. Vallee, *Revelations*, p. 75.
40. Ibid., p. 34.
41. Brown, *Cosmic,* p. 37.
42. Ibid., p. 43.
43. Ibid., pp. 28, 37.
44. Ibid., pp. 204–05.
45. Ross, *UFOs,* pp. 35, 59.
46. Brown, *Cosmic,* p. 43.
47. Ibid., p. 44.
48. Ibid., pp. 44–45.
49. Norman Vincent Peale, "When Loved Ones Leave Us," in *Plus: The Magazine of Positive Thinking,* March 1985, pp. 6–8.
50. *Arthur C. Clarke's Mysterious Universe,* Discovery Channel, March 2, 1995; as cited in Richard Abanes, *Journey into the Light* (Baker Books, 1996), p. 77.
51. Ibid., pp. 78–79.
52. Jonathan Rosen, "Rewriting the End: Elisabeth Kübler-Ross," in *New York Times Magazine,* January 22, 1995, p. 22.
53. Raymond L. Moody, Jr., *Life After Life* (Mockingbird, 1976), p. 68.
54. Raymond Moody, *Reunions: Visionary Encounters with Departed Loved Ones* (Villard Books, 1993).
55. John Marshall, "Through a glass, and beyond the grave, the dead speak," in *Seattle Post-Intelligencer,* November 16, 1993.
56. Ken R. Vincent, *Visions of God* (Larson Publications, 1994), p. 91; as cited in Richard Abanes, *Journey into the Light* (Baker Books, 1996), p. 180.
57. *20/20,* ABC TV, May 13, 1994.
58. *Standard-Examiner* [Ogden, UT], March 6, 1993.
59. Betty Eadie, *Embraced by the Light* (Gold Leaf Press, 1992), pp. 13, 90.
60. "The Oprah Winfrey Show," ABC, January 3, 1994.

61. Ben Winton, "Near-death survivor: God is light, love," in *Arizona Republic,* January 4, 1997, Religion, p. 2.
62. H.W. "Bunny" Austin, *Frank Buchman As I Knew Him* (Grosvenor Books, 1975), pp. 101–02, as cited in Roy Livesey, Twelve Steps to the New Age (Bury House, 1995), unpublished manuscript, p. 89.
63. William M. Alnor, *Heaven Can't Wait: A Survey of Alleged Trips to the Other Side* (Baker Books, 1996), pp. 45–46.
64. Richard Fisher, "Heaven Hopping," in *Personal Freedom Outreach Newsletter,* October–December 1985, p. 4.
65. Maurice Rawlings, *Beyond Death's Door* (Bantam Books, 1979); Maurice Rawlings, *To Hell and Back* (Thomas Nelson, 1993).

Chapter 19—Apparitions of Angels, Ghosts, and Mary

1. Wade Davis, *The Serpent and the Rainbow* (Warner Books, 1985), pp. 204–05.
2. *The Fatima Crusader,* Issue 49, Summer 1995, p. 2.
3. *Caritas of Birmingham,* December 1996 through February 1997, p. 1, special newsletter reporting what Our Lady of Medjugorje says each month.
4. His Holiness The Dalai Lama, *The Good Heart: A Buddhist Perspective on the Teachings of Jesus* (Wisdom Publications, Boston, 1996), p. 83.
5. Robert W. Morgan, "Guardian Angels," in *The New Age Magazine* (Official Publication of the Supreme Council, 33°, Ancient & Accepted Scottish Rite of Freemasonry of the Southern Jurisdiction, United States of America), September 1986, pp. 7–10.
6. *USA Today,* November 12, 1996, p. 3C.
7. *Caritas,* April 1996 through November 1996, p. 8.
8. "Messages from Our Lady," in *Our Lady of Medjugorje,* January 25, 1991, cited in the Medjugorje newsletter, *Caritas of Birmingham,* April 1996 through November 1996, p. 7.
9. *Inside the Vatican,* November 1996, p. 17.
10. John White, "An Interview with Nona Coxhead: The Science of Mysticism," in *Science of Mind,* September 9186, pp. 10–14, 70–78.
11. Taylor, *A.J. Russell,* pp. 2, 8; as cited in Livesey, *Twelve Steps,* p. 51. See also A.J. Russell, *One Thing I Know* (Hodder & Stoughton, 1933).
12. *Time,* December 4, 1972, p. 12.
13. Michael H. Brown, *The Final Hour* (Faith Publishing Company, 1992), pp. 1–2.
14. *Psychology Today,* September/October 1996, p. 50.
15. *Newsweek,* December 28, 1993.
16. *Time,* December 28, 1993, cover.
17. Ken Carey, *Vision* (UNI-SUN, 1985), p. vii.
18. Ken Carey/Raphael, *The Starseed Transmissions* (UNI-SUN, 1982), pp. 68–70.
19. "Praise the Lord," Trinity Broadcasting Network, December 3, 1993, as reported in *The Quarterly Journal* of Personal Freedom Outreach, July–September 1994, p. 4.
20. "Praise the Lord," Trinity Broadcasting Network, December 13, 1993, as reported in *The Quarterly Journal* of Personal Freedom Outreach, July–September 1994, p. 4.
21. From the videotape of Hinn's special 1989 New Year's Eve service at his church in Orlando, Florida, as cited in *The Quarterly Journal,* October–December 1996, p. 7.
22. "God and Television," Special Report, *TV Guide,* March 29–April 4, 1997, pp. 28, 42, 45.
23. Ibid., p. 45.
24. John Meroney, "Religion and the ratings game," in *Our Sunday Visitor,* February 16, 1997, p. 14.
25. Ibid., p. 56.
26. Paul Crouch, "Praise the Lord," October 1996, p. 1.
27. Ibid.

28. Dave Hunt, *Global Peace and the Rise of Antichrist* (Harvest House Publishers, 1990), pp. 153–54.
29. *The Daily Astorian,* August 11, 1995, p. 9A.
30. Rosen, *Times,* pp. 22, 23.
31. G. Richard Fisher, "Angels We Have Heard on High?—What Are We Really Hearing in the New Obsession with Angels?" *The Quarterly Journal,* July–September 1994, p. 11.
32. Padre Pio Foundation of America (24 Prospect Hill Road, Cromwell, CT 06416), 1993 Appointment Calendar with daily readings; the month of April has a picture of the Padre with his hands held up to show the stigmata with the caption: "The wounds of the crucifixion. Padre Pio bled daily for 50 years."
33. Newsletter, The Padre Pio Foundation of America and the Mass Association (Holy Apostles Seminary, Cromwell, CT 06416), August or September 1988.
34. *Vatican Council II, The Conciliar and Post Conciliar Documents,* Austin Flannery, O.P., gen. ed. (Costello Publishing Company, 1988 Revised Edition), vol. 1, pp. 62–79.
35. Ibid.
36. Ibid.
37. Ibid.
38. *The Padre Pio Gazette,* XI, pp. 10–11.
39. *Angels of the New Age,* by Lenny & Diana Goldberg, a brochure that is available free to anyone coming into their store in Ashland, OR.
40. Ibid.
41. Ibid.
42. Robert R. Holton, "Portrait of an unlikely visionary," in *Our Sunday Visitor,* September 22, 1996, p. 6.
43. Ibid.
44. Holton, *Visitor,* September 15, 1996, p. 10.
45. *Orange County Register,* December 11, 1995, pp. B1, B10; December 16, 1995, pp. B12, B13.
46. *Mary, Messenger of Peace* (Florida Center for Peace, August 1995), p. 4.
47. Will Baron, *Deceived by the New Age* (Pacific Press Publishing Association, 1990), pp. 61, 66.
48. *Inside the Vatican,* November 1996, p. 22.
49. *Our Sunday Visitor,* September 15, 1996, p. 11.
50. *Inside the Vatican,* November 1996, p. 24.
51. Ibid., p. 27.
52. Ibid., p. 25.
53. Brown, *Final,* pp. 164–67.
54. Daniel B. Clendenin, "Why I'm Not Orthodox," in *Christianity Today,* January 6, 1997, p. 37.
55. Paul M. Allen, *Vladimir Soloviev: Russian Mystic* (Steinerbooks, 1978), p. 36.
56. "John Paul Woos Straying Flock: Protestants object to being labeled as 'sects,'" in *Christianity Today,* April 8, 1996, p. 94.
57. Bobby Ripp, *End Time Deceptions* (True Light, 1995), unpublished manuscript, p. MARY 57.
58. *Fidelity* (July–August 1995), p. 4.
59. *Caritas,* December 1996–February 1997, p. 1.
60. Holton, *Visitor,* September 22, 1996, p. 7.
61. *Devotions in Honor of Our Mother of Perpetual Help* (Liguori, MO), Imprimatur John N. Wurm, Ph.D., S.T.D., Vicar General, Archdiocese of St. Louis, back cover.
62. *Caritas,* December 1996–February 1997, p. 1.
63. *Mary, Messenger of Peace* (Florida Center for Peace, August 1995), p. 3.
64. *Caritas of Birmingham: Messages from Our Lady,* December 1996 through February 1997, p. 7.

65. *Our Lady of Fatima's Peace Plan from Heaven* (Tan Books and Publishers, 1983), back cover.
66. St. Alphonsus de Liguori, *The Glories of Mary* (Redemptorist Fathers, 1931); p. 235.
67. Canon Barthas, *Fatima 1917–1968* (1969), pp. 211–12; Fr. Alonso, *Fatima and the Immaculate Heart of Mary* (1974), pp. 37–48, as reported in *The Fatima Crusader,* Summer 1995, p. 4.
68. From a tract titled "The Magnificent Promise for the Five First Saturdays," by Father Nicholas Gruner, published by The Fatima Center, Route 30, Box 281, Constable, NY 12926, (800) 263-8160.
69. *The Fatima Crusader,* Issue 49, Summer 1995, p. 2.
70. *The Fatima Crusader,* Summer 1995, pp. 8–9.
71. Michael H. Brown, *The Final Hour* (Faith Publishing Company, 1992), pp. 1–2.
72. Barthas, *Fatima 1917–1968,* pp. 211–12; Fr. Alonso, *Fatima and the Immaculate Heart of Mary* (194), pp. 37–48, as reported in *The Fatima Crusader,* Summer 1995, p. 4.
73. *Lucia Speaks on the Message of Fatima* (Ave Maria Institute, Washington, NJ 07882), pp. 26, 30–31, 47.
74. Ann Ball, "The Holy Infants of Mexico," in *Our Sunday Visitor,* December 29, 1996, p. 10.
75. Ibid., pp. 10–11.
76. Brown, *Final,* p. 21.
77. Ibid., p. 8.
78. Holton, *Visitor,* September 15, 1996, p. 10.
79. Liguori, *Devotions,* pp. 46–47.
80. Brown, *Final,* p. 104.
81. Ibid., p. 263.
82. *Il Giornale,* October 25, 1995, p. 15.
83. As cited in *Inside the Vatican,* November 1996, p. 17.
84. Fulton J. Sheen, "Mary and the Moslems," in *The World's First Love* (Garden City Books, 1952); see also Malachi Martin, *The Keys of This Blood: The Struggle for World Dominion Between Pope John Paul II, Mikhail Gorbachev and the Capitalist West* (Simon & Schuster, 1990), p. 285.
85. *The Fatima Crusader,* Winter 1992, front cover and p. 3.
86. *The Fatima Crusader,* Summer 1995, p. 31.
87. Quoted on back of official commemorative card published by The Blue Army of Our Lady of Fatima, Washington, NJ 07882. The face of the card contains a photo of the Pope praying to the statue of Our Lady of Fatima during his visit to Fatima, Portugal, on May 13, 1982, to offer thanks to "Mary" for her protection.
88. Antonio Maria Martins, S.J., *Documents on Fatima & the Memoirs of Sister Lucia;* Robert J. Fox, *Pictorial Documentary and Historical Update* (Fatima Family Apostolate, 1992), p. 91.
89. Carol Damien, "Who Is Pachamama?" in *LANCHILE,* November/December 1996, pp. 28–36.
90. Morrison, *Serpent,* pp. 149–50.

Chapter 20—Occultism and the Roman Catholic Church

1. *Inside the Vatican,* November 1996, p. 22.
2. *The Fatima Crusader,* Winter 1997.
3. Ibid.
4. Ibid.
5. *Brain/Mind Bulletin,* June 1987, p. 3.
6. *Time,* June 24, 1996, p. 65.
7. Mary DeTurris, "What's Your Favorite Scripture?" in *New Covenant,* August 1996, p. 11.
8. *Caritas of Birmingham,* April 1996 through November 1996, p. 8.
9. Peter de Rosa, *Vicars of Christ* (Crown Publishers, 1988), pp. 34, 45.

10. R.W. Southern, *Western Society and the Church in the Middle Ages* (Penguin Books, vol. 2 of Pelican History of the Church Series, 1970), pp. 24–25.
11. Walter James, *The Christian in Politics* (Oxford University Press, 1962), p. 47.
12. De Rosa, *Vicars*, p. 35.
13. R.W. Thompson, *The Papacy and the Civil Power* (New York: Harper and Brothers, 1876), p. 559.
14. Will Durant, *The Story of Civilization: Part III, Caesar and Christ* (Simon & Schuster, 1944), pp. 654–55.
15. De Rosa, *Vicars*, p. 35 and jacket.
16. Durant, *Civilization*, vol. IV, p. 784.
17. Augustine, *de cat. ru.*, XXV, 48.
18. Durant, *Civilization*, vol. V, p. 528.
19. Ibid.
20. Hughes, *History*, p. 198.
21. H. Chadwick, *The Early Church* (Wm B. Eerdmans, 1976), p. 243.
22. Durant, *Civilization*, vol. IV, p. 657.
23. Walter Yeeling Evans-Wentz, *The Fairy-Faith in Celtic Countries* (University Books, 1966), pp. 427–28.
24. Davis, *Serpent and Rainbow*, p. 93.
25. *National Catholic Reporter*, February 7, 1997, p. 3.
26. George Gurtner, "In the Temple of the Voodoo," in *Our Sunday Visitor*, October 15, 1995, pp. 10–11.
27. Leslie G. Desmangles, *The Faces of the Gods: Vodoun and Roman Catholicism in Haiti* (The University of North Carolina Press, 1992), p. 27.
28. Ibid., pp. 172–73.
29. Ibid., pp. 173, 178.
30. *Los Angeles Times*, February 5, 1993.
31. Ibid., p. 179.
32. Desmangles, *Faces*, p. 99.
33. Ibid., p. 4.
34. Letter on file.
35. "Icons Speak of Christian History," *The Pope Speaks*, March/April 1990, vol. 35, no. 2, pp. 130–31.
36. Cover story, *National Catholic Reporter*, February 7, 1997, p. 3.
37. Austin Flannery, O.P., gen. ed., *Vatican Council II: The Conciliar and Post Conciliar Documents*, rev. ed. (Costello Publishing, 1988), vol. 1, *Lumen Gentium*, 21 November 1964, 66., p. 421.
38. *Catechism of the Catholic Church* (Libreria Editrice Vaticana—In the USA, The Wanderer Press, St. Paul, MN, 1994), section 971, p. 253, *Imprimi Potest* Joseph Cardinal Ratzinger.
39. Flannery, *Vatican*, p. 63; Schroeder, *Trent*, p. 46, etc.
40. Flannery, *Vatican*, vol. 1, p. 65.
41. *The Moscow Times*, August 31, 1996, pp. INSIGHT 13–17.
42. Colleen Smith, "The potent medicine of prayer," in *Our Sunday Visitor*, February 6, 1997, p. 10.
43. Robert Estrin, Associated Press, "Vatican attributes recovery of deathly ill child to dead nun," in *Santa Barbara News Press*, April 20, 1997, p. B5.
44. *The Padre Pio Gazette*, XI, p. 2, Padre Pio Foundation of America, 24 Prospect Hill Rd., Cromwell, CT 06416.
45. *The Padre Pio Gazette*, XI, pp. 13–14.
46. *The Padre Pio Gazette*, VI, p. 12.
47. Ibid.
48. Ibid., p. 5.
49. *Inside the Vatican*, June 1997, pp. 58–59.
50. Ibid.
51. *Caritas of Birmingham*, April 1996 through November 1996, p. 8.
52. *Gazette*, VI, p. 5.

53. *Inside the Vatican,* November 1996, p. 17.
54. Charles Colson, *The Body: Being Light in Darkness* (Word Publishing, 1992), p. 271.
55. *Vatican II,* Flannery, vol. 1, pp. 77–78.
56. *Inside the Vatican,* April 1994, p. 55.
57. *Vatican II,* Flannery, vol. 1, p. 71.
58. Pope John Paul II, ". . . the absolute center of my life," in *Our Sunday Visitor,* October 27, 1996, p. 14.
59. Quoted in *The Roman Catholic,* June–July 1984, p. 32.
60. The Council of Trent, Seventh Session, Canon 8., from *Canons and Decrees of the Council of Trent,* English trans. by Rev. H.J. Schroeder, O.P. (Tan Books and Publishers, Inc., 1978), p. 52; Flannery, *Vatican,* vol. 1, p. 412.
61. Ibid., Canon 4.
62. "The Constitution on the Sacred Liturgy," in *Sacrosanctum Concillium,* 4 December, 1963, Introduction, 2., Austin Flannery, O.P., gen. ed., *Vatican Council II: The Conciliar and Post Conciliar Documents* (Costello Publishing Company, Inc., 1988 Revised Edition), vol. 1, p. 1.
63. John A. Hardon, S.J., *Pocket Catholic Dictionary* (Doubleday, 1985), pp. 248–49.
64. Schroeder, *Trent,* p. 149.
65. Hardon, S.J., *Pocket Catholic Dictionary,* p. 249.
66. *The Catholic World,* May/June 1989.
67. *The Catholic World: The New Age, a Challenge to Christianity,* May/June 1990.
68. *National Catholic Reporter,* February 19, 1993, classified ad section; January 12, 1996, etc.
69. Brochure on file.
70. Tim Unsworth, "Chicago Bulls head pastor, Phil Jackson," in *National Catholic Reporter,* January 24, 1997, p. 29.
71. *National Catholic Reporter,* March 19, 1993.
72. *National Catholic Reporter,* April 16, 1993.
73. From a brochure introducing UCS.
74. From the conference brochure.
75. *The Canons and Decrees of the Council of Trent,* trans. H.J. Schroeder, O.P. (Tan Books and Publishers, Inc., 1978), Sixth Session, Canon 16., p. 44.
76. *New York Times,* February 1, 1990, pp. A1, B4.
77. Ibid.
78. *The Fatima Crusader,* Winter 1997.
79. William F. Jasper, "Dark Dealings in the Vatican?" in *The New American,* March 3, 1997, p. 24.

Chapter 21—Psychology and the Occult

1. Lawrence Leshan, *How to Meditate* (Boston, 1974), pp. 150–51.
2. Nandor Fodor, *Freud, Jung and Occultism* (University Books, 1971), p. 86.
3. Eugenio Fizzoti, "Satanism from a psychological viewpoint," in *L'Osservatore Romano,* Weekly Edition, 12 February, 1997, p. 10.
4. D. Scott Rogo, "Transpersonal Psychology and the Spiritual Path: Taking a Larger View of Ourselves, An Interview with Charles Tart, Ph.D.," in *Science of Mind,* December 1986, pp. 13–14, 80–81.
5. Manly P. Hall, *Masonic, Hermetic, Qabbalistic and Rosicrucian Symbolical Philosophy* (The Philosophical Research Society, Inc., Los Angeles, 1969), pp. CI, CII.
6. John Horgan, *The End of Science* (Helix Books, 1996), pp. 84–90.
7. Ibid., p. 91.
8. Sir James Jeans, *The Mysterious Universe* (The MacMillan Company, 1930), p. 140.
9. *Visions* magazine, May 1990, p. 5.
10. *American Journal of Psychiatry* 144:56–61.
11. John Marks Templeton, *Worldwide Laws of Life: 200 Eternal Spiritual Principles* (Templeton Foundation Press, 1997), pp. 121–23.

12. William James, *Collected Essays and Reviews*, 1920, "A Plea for Psychology As a Natural Science" (1892).
13. Dr. Tana Dineen, *Manufacturing Victims* (Robert Davies Publishing, 1996), p. 116.
14. W. Kessen, "The American Child and Other Cultural Inventions," in *American Psychologist*, 34(10), 1979, p. 820, as cited in Dineen, *Manufacturing*, p. 116.
15. Sigmund Koch, "Psychology Cannot Be a Coherent Science," in *Psychology Today*, September 1969, p. 66.
16. Robert N. Beck, ed., *Perspectives in Philosophy* (Rinehart, Winston, 1975), Karl Popper, "Scientific Theory and Falsifiability," p. 343.
17. Thomas Szasz, *The Myth of Psychotherapy* (Doubleday, 1978), pp. 104–05.
18. Templeton, *Worldwide*, p. 120.
19. Peter Gay, *A Godless Jew* (Yale University Press, 1987), p. 6.
20. Shirley Nicholson, *Shamanism* (The Theosophical Publishing House), p. 58, as cited in Martin & Deidre Bobgan, *The End of "Christian Psychology"* (East Gate Publishers, 1997), p. 105.
21. Ibid., p. 59.
22. Martin L. Gross, *The Psychological Society* (Random House, 1978), pp. 3–5.
23. Robert Epstein, Ph.D., "Why Shrinks Have So Many Problems," in *Psychology Today*, July/August 1997, pp. 59, 62.
24. Ibid., p. 62.
25. Ibid.
26. Quoted in A. Haynal, *Controversies in Psychoanalytic Method* (New York University Press, 1989), p. 32, as cited in Martin and Deidre Bobgan, *The End of "Christian Psychology"* (East Gate Publishers, Santa Barbara, CA, 1997), ch. 7.
27. Bruce Wiseman, *Psychiatry, the Ultimate Betrayal* (Freedom Publishing, 1995), p. 12.
28. *Chronicles*, March 1986, "Psychology Today, Psychology Tomorrow, Psychology Forever," p. 51, citing a *Psychology Today* article.
29. *Journal of Humanistic Psychology*, Fall 1992.
30. Paula J. Caplan, Ph.D., *They Say You're Crazy* (Addison-Wesley Publishing Company, 1995), p. 90.
31. Dr. Tana Dineen, *Manufacturing Victims: What the Psychology Industry Is Doing to People* (Robert Davies, 1996), pp. 151–52.
32. Ibid., p. 154.
33. Dr. Kathleen FitzGerald, "An Introduction to Soul Work (Sacred Psychology)" (Institute for Recovery, Deerfield, IL 60015).
34. Robyn M. Dawes, *House of Cards: Psychology and Psychotherapy Built on Myth* (The Free Press/Macmillan, 1994), p. 9.
35. Dawes, *House*, p. vii.
36. Ibid., p. 159.
37. Horgan, *End*, p. 179.
38. Robert A. Baker, *Hidden Memories: Voices and Visions from Within* (Prometheus Books, 1992), p. 305.
39. *Santa Barbara News Press*, November 20, 1994, p. A-6.
40. *Los Angeles Times Magazine*, December 6, 1987, pp. 20, 22.
41. *Esalen Catalog*, January–June 1980, and subsequently.
42. Walter Truett Anderson, *The Upstart Spring* (Addison-Wesley, 1983), pp. 302–05.
43. Phyllis V. Schlemmer, ed. Mary Bennett, *The Only Planet of Choice: Essential Briefings from Deep Space* (Gateway Books, 1994), p. v.
44. *Los Angeles Times*, August 20, 1986, Part V, p. 1.
45. *Shaman's Drum*, Fall 1996, pp. 21–23.
46. Ibid., pp. 36–47.
47. *Shaman's Drum*, Summer 1986, p. 9.
48. Joan Cannell, "The Spiritual Frontier," in *San Jose Mercury News*, June 14, 1986, p. 1c.
49. Tart, *Science of Mind*, December 1986, pp. 10–12.
50. John Heider, "Catharsis in Human Potential Encounter," in *Journal of Humanistic Psychology*, No. 14, 1974.
51. Dawes, *House*, p. 9.

52. Gross, *Psychological*, p. 231.
53. Dawes, *House*, p. 229.
54. Freud, *Standard Edition*, vol. 2, pp. 279, 281; vol. 3, p. 269.
55. Ray Grasse, "The Crowd Within: Multiple Personality Disorder, and Traditional Esoteric Psychologies," in *The Quest*, Autumn 1994, pp. 38–44.
56. Klimo, *Channeling*, pp. 238–39.
57. Ibid., p. 177.
58. Ibid., p. 245.
59. *St. Petersburg, Florida Times*, February 12, 1997, p. 7A.
60. Vallee, *Revelations*, p. 78.
61. Joel Greenberg, "Close Encounters, All In The Mind?" in *Science News*, February 17, 1979, pp. 106–07; John DeHerrera, "Does Hypnosis Create Contactees?" in *Second Look*, May/June 1980, pp. 16–17.
62. Greenberg, *Encounter.*
63. John Vaughan, "UFO, space alien stories fill the ether once more," in *Santa Barbara News Press*, November 20, 1994, p. A-6.
64. James S. Gordon, "Someone to Watch Over Us," in *The New York Times Book Review.*
65. John E. Mack, M.D., "Studying Intrusions from the Subtle Realm: How Can We Deepen Our Knowledge?" in *When Cosmic Cultures Meet, the Proceedings: An international Conference Presented by the Human Potential Foundation*, May 27–29, 1995, pp. 225–26.
66. C. G. Jung, *Memories, Dreams, Reflections* (Pantheon Books, 1963), p. 323.
67. Martin and Deidre Bobgan, *Hypnosis and the Christian* (Bethany House Publishers, 1984), pp. 23–24.
68. Greenberg, *Encounters.*
69. Greenberg, "Close Encounters"; DeHerrera, "Hypnosis."
70. Bobgan, *Hypnosis*, pp. 28–29.
71. *The Jerusalem Post International Edition*, week ending November 23, 1996, p. 21.
72. Bobgan, *Hypnosis*, ch. 6.
73. Joel Greenberg, "Close Encounters, All in the Mind?" in *Science News*, February 19, 1979, pp. 106–07.
74. Jackson, *Sacred Hoops*, p. 32.
75. Greenberg, "Close Encounters."

Chapter 22—"Christian" Psychology

1. Martin L. Gross, *The Psychological Society: The impact—and the failure—of psychiatry, psychotherapy, psychoanalysis and the psychological revolution* (Random House, 1978), pp. 8–11.
2. *Wholemind Newsletter: A User's Manual to the Brain, Mind and Spirit*, vol. 1, no. 1, p. 5.
3. Ibid.
4. S. Bruce Narramore, "Unconscious," in David G. Benner, ed., *Baker Encyclopedia of Psychology* (Baker Book House, 1985), p. 1188.
5. Bruce Narramore, *You're Someone Special* (Zondervan, 1978), p. 22.
6. Gross, *Society*, pp. 56–57.
7. The National Association for Consumer Protection in Mental Health Practices Press Release, Office of the President, 4025 Quaker Lane North, Plymouth, MN 55441, phone 612-595-0566, FAX 612-595-0035.
8. E. Fuller Torrey, *The Death of Psychiatry* (Penguin, 1974), p. 107.
9. Miles Vich and Rollo May, "Debating the Legitimacy of Transpersonal Psychology," in *The Common Boundary*, July/August 1986, pp. 7–15.
10. Mary Stewart van Leeuwen, *The Sorcerer's Apprentice* (InterVarsity Press, 1982), p. 49.
11. Thomas Szasz, *The Myth of Psychotherapy* (Doubleday, 1978), pp. 139, 146.
12. Szasz, *Myth*, p. 28.

13. J. Sutherland and P. Poelstra, *Aspects of Integration,* a paper presented to the Western Association for Psychological Studies, Santa Barbara, CA, June 1976.
14. McGee, *Search,* p. 140.
15. Undated letter and brochure on file.
16. *Christianity Today,* October 2, 1995, p. 80.
17. Brochure on file.
18. *Family Weekly,* Ventura Free Press, April 15, 1984, cover story.
19. *Los Angeles Times,* June 5, 1988, Part VI, p. 1.
20. *Chronicle-Tribune,* December 26, 1993.
21. Robert H. Schuller, *Self-Esteem, The New Reformation* (Word Books, 1982), pp. 21–22.
22. Viktor E. Frankl, *The Doctor and the Soul: From Psychotherapy to Logotherapy* (Random House, 1973), pp. xi, xiii, etc.
23. Ibid., pp. 276–277.
24. From a tape of the October 5, 1997 "Hour of Power" television program.
25. John D. Carter and Bruce Narramore, *The Integration of Psychology and Theology* (Zondervan, 1979), p. 37.
26. James Reid, *Ernest Holmes: The First Religious Scientist* (Science of Mind Publications, Los Angeles), p. 14.
27. Charles Braden, *Spirits in Rebellion* (Southern Methodist University Press), pp. 392, 396.
28. *The Quarterly Journal* (Personal Freedom Outreach), January–March 1006, p. 3.
29. Elinor J. Brecher, "Inspired or pirated? 2 question Peale's works," in the *Miami Herald,* July 28, 1995.
30. *Focus on the Family,* December 1988.
31. Gary R. Collins, *Can You Trust Psychology?* (InterVarsity Press, 1988), p. 130.
32. Gustav Niebuhr, "Evangelical Christians see value of psychology," in *Santa Barbara NewsPress,* February 15, 1997, p. D2.
33. Originally published as "Seele und Tod" in Berlin, 1934; cited in C. G. Jung, *Psychology and the Occult* (Princeton University Press, 1977), p. 131.
34. Bernie Zilbergeld, *The Shrinking of America: Myths of Psychological Change* (Little, Brown and Company, 1983), p. 3.
35. *Psychoheresy Awareness Letter,* May–June 1997, p. 8.
36. Robert H. Schuller, *Self-Love, The Dynamic Force of Success* (Hawthorne, 1969), p.32.
37. McGee, *Search,* p. xiii.
38. Ibid., p. 15.
39. James Dobson, *Hide or Seek* (Fleming Revell, 1974), pp. 12–13.
40. Schuller, *Self-Esteem,* p. 19.
41. Schuller, *Reformation,* p. 38.
42. Stanton E. Samenow, *Inside the Criminal Mind* (Time Books, 1984).
43. Erich Fromm, *Man for Himself: An Inquiry into the Psychology of Ethics* (Bantam Books, 1963), p. 59.
44. *Promise Keepers Newsletter,* Winter 1993.
45. William Law, ed. Dave Hunt, *The Power of the Spirit* (Christian Literature Crusade, 1971), p. 141.
46. Narramore, *You're Someone Special,* pp. 25–26.
47. C.H. Spurgeon, *All of Grace* (Moody Press), pp. 68–69.
48. *The Bulletin* (Bend, OR), November 23, 1995.
49. As cited in *PsychoHeresy Update,* Winter/Spring 1992, pp. 1–2.
50. Roy Baumeister, "Should Schools Try to Boost Self-Esteem?" in *American Educator,* Summer 1996.
51. Linda Seebach, "Beware freeway drivers with self-esteem," in the *Orange County Register,* November 18, 1996, p. Metro 8.
52. *Newsweek,* February 17, 1992, front cover and major article.
53. *The Oregonian,* November 23, 1995, and many other papers across the country.
54. James G. Friesen, *More Than Survivors: Conversations with Multiple-Personality Clients* (Here's Life Publishers, 1992), p. 203.

55. Ibid., p. 17.
56. Ibid., pp. 145–46.
57. Ibid., p. 220.
58. Ibid., p. 219.
59. Baron, *Deceived,* pp. 41–43.
60. Collins, *Trust,* pp. 104–05.
61. Ibid.
62. *D Magazine,* October 1991, p. 68.
63. Ibid., p. 69.
64. Fred and Florence Littauer, *Freeing Your Mind from Memories That Bind* (Thomas Nelson, 1989), pp. 142–43.
65. Martin and Deidre Bobgan, *Four Temperaments, Astrology and Personality Testing* (East Gate Publishers, 1992), pp. 24, 50, 51.
66. *Christian Research Journal,* Winter 1995.

Chapter 23—Charismatic/Evangelical Occultism

1. Blaise Pascal, *Pensees* (Encyclopedia Britannica, 1952), *Great Books of the Western World* edition, vol. 33, p. 186.
2. Richard Foster, *Celebration of Discipline* (Harper & Row, 1978), p. 170.
3. *The Arizona Republic,* August 31, 1996.
4. Oral Roberts, *Miracle of Seed Faith* (Fleming H. Revell, 1970), p. 9.
5. Pat Robertson with William Proctor, *Beyond Reason: How Miracles Can Change Your Life* (William Morrow and Company, Inc., 1985), p. 20.
6. Pat Robertson with Bob Slosser, *The Secret Kingdom: A Promise of Hope and Freedom in a World of Turmoil* (Thomas Nelson Publishers, 1982), pp. 62, 65, 69.
7. Pat Robertson with Jamie Buckingham, *Shout It from the Housetops* (Bridge Publishing, 1972, CBN 25th Anniversary Edition 1961–1986), p. 154.
8. Kenneth E. Hagin, *Zoe: The God-Kind of Life* (Rhema Bible Church, 1081), p. 41.
9. Benny Hinn, *Good Morning, Holy Spirit* (Thomas Nelson, 1990), pp. 9, 11–12.
10. Bill Bright, *The Coming Revival* (New Life Publications, 1995), p. 155.
11. Robertson and Buckingham, *Shout,* p. 145.
12. Undated mailer as cited in Hanegraaff, *Crisis,* p. 197.
13. Letter signed by Harry Maggart of Knoxville, as cited in Crowder Blvd. Church of Christ Sunday Bulletin, February 22, 1987.
14. From a tape of that service as reported in G. Richard Fisher and M. Kurt Goedelman with W. E. Nunnally, Stephen F. Cannon, and Paul R. Blizard, *The Confusing World of Benny Hinn* (Personal Freedom Outreach, April 1997), p. 172.
15. *Believer's Voice of Victory,* prophecy given by Kenneth Copeland on November 7, 1975.
16. Bob Slosser, "The Election According to Pat Robertson," in *Charisma & Christian Life,* October 1988, p. 56.
17. Calvin Miller, *The Table of Inwardness: Nurturing Our Inner Life in Christ* (InterVarsity Press, 1984), p. 93.
18. Stoker Hunt, *Ouija: The Most Dangerous Game* (Harper & Row, 1985), pp. 107–12; *Psychic* magazine, October 1974; *New Horizons,* June 1977, and other books and publications.
19. "Praise the Lord" show, TBN, October 23, 1992. See also *Christian Sentinel,* Winter 1992–93.
20. Kenneth E. Hagin, *I Believe in Visions* (Fleming H. Revell Company, 1972), p. 115.
21. "Praise-a-Thon" on TBN, April 2, 1991.
22. From a videotape of the April 6, 1997, church service.
23. Neil Eskelin, *Pat Robertson: A Biography* (Huntington House, Inc, 1987), p. 160.
24. *Washington Times,* June 12, 1997, p. B9.

25. Newsletter dated April 1982 on letterhead of Pat Robertson, Virginia Beach, Virginia 23463.
26. Response card enclosed in April 1982 newsletter.
27. Robertson with Buckingham, *Shout*, p. 120.
28. Kenneth Hagin, *Having Faith in Your Faith* (Rhema, 1980), pp. 3–4.
29. David Yonggi Cho, *The Fourth Dimension*, vol. 2 (Bridge-Logos Publishing, 1983), p. 38; Cho, *Fourth*, pp. 39–44.
30. Pat Robertson with Bob Slosser, *The Secret Kingdom: A Promise of Hope and Freedom in a World of Turmoil* (Thomas Nelson Publishers, 1982), pp. 43–46, 69.
31. Robertson with Slosser, *Secret*, p. 181.
32. Ibid., p. 182.
33. Ibid., p. 196.
34. Russell Chandler, *Times* religion editor, "Talked with Jesus, Evangelist Says," in *Los Angeles Times*, January 18, 1983, p. A1.
35. Oral Roberts, *Expect a Miracle: My Life and Ministry, an Autobiography* (Thomas Nelson Publishers, 1995), p. 299.
36. *The Bulletin* (Bend, Oregon), March 20, 1992.
37. *Charisma & Christian Life*, January 1990, p. 22.
38. Napoleon Hill, *Grow Rich with Peace of Mind* (Ballantine Books, 1967), p. 176.
39. Oral Roberts, *Miracle of Seed Faith* (Fleming H. Revell, 1970), p. 7.
40. Hill, *Peace of Mind*, p. 176.
41. David Edwin Harrell, Jr., *All Things Are Possible: The Healing and Charismatic Revivals in Modern America* (Indiana University Press, 1975), pp. 27–38.
42. Roberts, *Expect*, pp. 92–96.
43. Frederick Price on TBN, November 23, 1990; and so says Oral Roberts and many others.
44. Kenneth E. Hagin, *The Believer's Authority* (Rhema Bible Church, 1984), p. 40.
45. On his "Ever Increasing Faith" program on TBN, December 9, 1990.
46. Gloria Copeland, *God's Will Is Prosperity* (Harrison House, 1978), p. 48.
47. Robertson with Slosser, *Secret*, p. 69.
48. *Possibilities*, Summer 1986, pp. 8–12.
49. Gloria Copeland, *God's Will*, p. 54.
50. Robertson with Slosser, *Secret*, pp. 61–62.
51. Patti Roberts, *Ashes to Gold* (Word Books, 1985), p. 69.
52. Ibid., p. 122.
53. *St. Louis Dispatch*, November 14, 1991, as cited in *The Christian News*, November 18, 1991.
54. Complete mailer on file.
55. Letter and materials described on file.
56. Oral has said this a number of times. See Hanegraaff, *Christianity*, p. 399, #35.
57. Undated letter on file.
58. John Goodwin, "Testing," tape 2.
59. Agnes Sanford, *The Healing Light* (Macalester, 1947), pp. 125–26, 165; Agnes Sanford, *The Healing Gifts of the Spirit* (Fleming Revell, 1982), pp. 140–41.
60. Sanford, *Gifts*, p. 48.
61. Sanford, *Light*, p. 146.
62. Ibid., pp. 10, 34–35.
63. Ibid., p. 30.
64. Ibid., p. 74.
65. Ibid., pp. 63–64, 68, 112.
66. Foster, *Celebration*, pp. 36, 136.
67. Sanford, *Gifts*, pp. 49, 131.
68. Foster, *Celebration*, p. 136.
69. Sanford, *Gifts*, p. 45.
70. Ibid., p. 30.
71. Morton T. Kelsey, *The Christian and the Supernatural* (Augsburg, 1976), pp. 120–43.

72. Ibid., p. 149.
73. Ibid., p. 93.
74. Kelsey, *Supernatural,* pp. 109, 113, 142.
75. Ibid., p. 93.
76. William de Arteaga, *Quenching the Spirit: Examining Centuries of Opposition to the Moving of the Holy Spirit* (Creation House, 1992), pp. 162–63.

Chapter 24—Spiritual Warfare and Revival

1. Charles Kraft, *Defeating Dark Angels* (Servant Publications, 1992), pp. 64–65.
2. Interviewed by Albert James Dager, as reported in "Special Report, Pensacola: Revival or Reveling?" in *Media Spotlight,* prepublication copy, August 1997, p. 2.
3. Ibid., p. 1.
4. Rodney Howard-Browne, *The Coming Revival* (1991), p. 6.
5. Cited in *Discerning the "Thing from Toronto,"* pp. 7–8.
6. C. Peter Wagner, *Confronting the Powers: How the New Testament Church Experienced the Power of Strategic-Level Spiritual Warfare* (Regal Books, 1996), p. 20.
7. Ewald Plass, *What Luther Says* (Concordia Publishing House, 1959), pp. 391–404.
8. John Dawson, *Taking Our Cities for God: How to Break Spiritual Strongholds* (Creation House, 1989), p. 11.
9. Ibid., p. 163.
10. "Leading Pastors Pray for Revival in Los Angeles: Spiritual warfare and unity mark meeting," in *Charisma & Christian Life,* November 1989, p. 19.
11. C. Peter Wagner, ed., *Breaking Strongholds in Your City: How to Use Spiritual Mapping to Make Your Prayers More Strategic, Effective and Targeted* (Regal Books, 1993), Introductory page inside front cover.
12. Wagner, *Confronting,* p. 43.
13. Ibid., p. 16.
14. Don Lewis, *Assessing the Wimber Phenomenon* (Regent College, June 1985), as cited in Eric E. Wright, *Strange Fire?: Assessing the Vineyard Movement and the Toronto Blessing* (Evangelical Press, 1996), p. 148.
15. Ibid.
16. "The Devil, Demons & Spiritual Warfare," in *Charisma,* February 1994, pp. 52–57.
17. *Charisma,* February 1994, p. 56.
18. Wagner, *Confronting,* pp. 103–04.
19. Ibid., pp. 100–02.
20. Augustine, *de cat. rud.,* xxv, 48.
21. Timothy M. Warner, *Spiritual Warfare: Victory over the Powers of This Dark World* (Crossway Books, 1991), p. 135.
22. Wagner, *Confronting,* pp. 171–72.
23. Available from The Berean Call, P.O. Box 7019, Bend, OR 97708, 1-800-937-6638.
24. Don Milam, "Intercessory Prayer, The Heat Behind the Fire in Pensacola," in *Destiny Image Digest,* Winter 1997, p. 35.
25. Steve Hawthorne and Graham Kendrick, *Prayerwalking: Praying on Site with Insight* (Creation House, 1993), p. 16.
26. "Evangelist plans 'spiritual warfare,'" in *The Flint Journal,* September 9, 1990, p. B12.
27. Wagner, *Confronting,* p. 31.
28. *Foundation,* July–August 1990, p. 12.
29. *Foundation,* October–December 1988, p. 8.
30. *Foundation,* July–August 1990, p. 11.
31. *John Wimber, Friend or Foe?* (St. Matthias Press, undated), a reprint from "The Briefing," April 1990, pp. 23–24.
32. Oral Roberts, message on Daniel at Melodyland Christian Center, Anaheim, California, January 8, 1995, as cited in Hank Hanegraaff, *Counterfeit Revival* (Word Publishing, 1997), p. 32.
33. *Charisma,* June 1944.

34. John Goodwin, "Testing the Fruit," Tape 2, Toronto, Canada, April 1997, Discernment Ministries, P.O. Box 129, Lapeer, MI 48446-0129.
35. From a videotape of the Brownsville service.
36. Michael L. Brown, *Let No One Deceive You: Confronting the Critics of Revival* (Destiny Image Publishers, Inc., 1997), p. 91.
37. Gary D. Kinnaman, *Overcoming the Dominion of Darkness: Personal Strategies for Spiritual Warfare* (Chosen Books, 1990), pp. 46–51.
38. Don Nori, Publisher, "Pastor John Kilpatrick: Pastoring the Revival," in *Destiny Image Digest*, Winter 1997, p. 9.
39. A.W. Tozer, *Keys to the Deeper Life* (The Sunday Magazine, 1971), pp. 7–8.
40. Mark Haville, Chris Hand, Philip Foster, and Peter Glover, *The Signs and Wonders Movement—Exposed* (Day One, Bromley, Kent, 1997), p. 64.
41. Offered by The Berean Call, P.O. Box 7019, Bend, OR 97708, 1-800-937-6638.
42. Haville, Hand, Foster, and Glover, *Movement—Exposed*, pp. 64, 70–73.
43. Bill Bright, *The Coming Revival* (New Life Publications, 1995), p. 155.
44. "Acceptance Speech by Dr. William R. Bright, Receiving the 1996 Templeton Prize for Progress in Religion," delivered in Rome, Italy, at The Church of St. Maria in Trastevere, May 9, 1996, pp. 8–9.
45. John Marks Templeton, *The Humble Approach* (The Continuum Publishing Company, 1995, New Revised Edition), pp. 7, 30–33, 41, 58, 60, 135–39.
46. Ibid., p. 130.
47. Ibid., p. 61.
48. Ibid., pp. 39–40.
49. Ibid., p. 60.
50. Templeton, *Humility*, pp. 48, 53.
51. Ibid., p. 52.
52. Ibid., pp. 37–38.
53. Ibid., pp. 2–3.
54. Ibid., pp. 35–36, 45.
55. Ibid., pp. 35, 46.
56. *Moody*, November 1993, p. 8.
57. According to the official schedule of the Parliament.
58. Letter on Prison Fellowship stationery dated May 21, 1993, signed by James W. Jewell, Senior Vice President, Marketing & Communications, on file.
59. Letters on file from Prison Fellowship.
60. Editorial, "Don't Shoot the Messenger," in *Moody*, September 1993, p. 8.
61. "Acceptance Speech by Dr. William R. Bright Receiving the 1996 Templeton Prize for Progress in Religion," delivered in Rome, Italy, at The Church of St. Maria in Trastevere, May 9, 1996, p. 1.

Chapter 25—A.D. 2000: Millennial Madness

1. Matthew Fox, *The Coming of the Cosmic Christ* (Harper, San Francisco, 1988), p. 246.
2. *World Goodwill Newsletter*, 1993, no. 3, p. 7.
3. Address by Pope John Paul II to Hon. Francesco Rutelli, Mayor of Rome, and to the members at the city's Capitoline Administration in audience at the Vatican, *L'Osservatore Romano*, Weekly Edition, 12 February 1997, p. 7.
4. From Article 23 of a 72-page papal letter released November 10, 1994, titled "The Coming of the Third Millennium: Preparation for the Jubilee of the Year 2000."
5. Pat Robertson, *The Turning Tide* (Word, 1993), p. 279.
6. John Goodwin, "Testing the Fruit," Tape 2, Toronto, Canada, April 1997, Discernment Ministries, P.O. Box 129, Lapeer, MI 48446-0129.
7. As reported in *Christianity Today*, September 13, 1993, p. 58.
8. As reported in *The Bulletin* (Bend, OR), August 31, 1997, p. A2.
9. Schuller, *Self-Esteem*, pp. 174–75.
10. *Tampa Tribune-Times*, August 31, 1997.

11. William Bole, "Forgive them their debts?—Inspired by the Pope, international moneylenders consider freeing the Third World from its crippling debt," in *Our Sunday Visitor,* August 17, 1997, pp. 12–13.

12. Jay Gary, *The Star of 2000: Our Journey Toward Hope* (Bimillennial Press, 1994), pp. 23, 91–93.

13. Will Durant, *The Story of Civilization, Part III: Caesar and Christ* (Simon & Schuster, 1944), p. 535.

14. *NRI Trumpet,* January 1990, p. 7.

15. *Foundation,* January–February 1989, p. 5.

16. Roy Rivenburg, "A Bash 2,000 Years in the Making: Pilgrimages, Multimedia shows, Block parties, Christians have big plans for their own millennium celebrations," in *Los Angeles Times,* May 2, 1995, p. E1.

17. Gary, *Star,* first two pages inside front cover, outside back cover.

18. Ibid., pp. 121–22.

19. Gary, *Star,* p. 51.

20. Ibid., p. 27.

21. *The Orange County Register,* September 5, 1992, p. E8.

22. *World Goodwill Newsletter,* 1993, no. 3, p. 7.

23. *Bimillennial Research Report,* March–April 1992.

24. *World Goodwill Newsletter,* 1993, no. 3, p. 7.

25. Gary, *Star,* p. 24.

26. Ibid.

27. Ibid., p. 33.

28. Gary, *Star,* pp. 15, 29, 32, 33, 40, 82, etc.

29. Ibid., p. 22.

30. *Foundation,* January–February 1989, p. 4.

31. John Lofton, "Christians Against Christianity," in *Chalcedon Report,* July 1992, p. 6.

32. *Charisma,* September 1994, pp. 88–89.

33. Gary, *Star,* pp. 112–15.

34. Eskin, *Pat,* p. 161.

35. Letters on file.

36. From the transcript of his speech provided by his office.

37. *Moody,* November 1993, p. 8.

38. *Foundation,* July–September 1995, p. 10.

39. *O Timothy,* Volume 11, Issue 3, 1994, p. 14.

40. *Christian Beacon,* December 25, 1986, p. 7.

41. Gary, *Star,* pp. 39, 46–47.

42. *Inside the Vatican,* November 1996, p. 21.

43. "Acceptance Speech by Dr. William R. Bright Receiving the 1996 Templeton Prize for Progress in Religion," delivered in Rome, Italy, at The Church of St. Maria in Trastevere, May 9, 1996," p. 1.

44. Gary, *Star,* pp. 41–42.

45. Ibid., third page inside front cover.

46. "Roman Catholic Double-Talk at Indianapolis '90," in *Foundation,* July–August 1990, pp. 14–16; taken from a transcript of his talk.

47. *The Catholic World Report,* February 1997, p. 7.

48. Abbe Daniel Le Roux, *Peter, Lovest Thou Me?* (Instauratio Press, Australia, 1989), p. 140.

49. Surah 4:171.

50. *SNS News Service,* Israel.

51. *National Catholic Reporter,* February 19, 1993, p. 11.

52. *Our Sunday Visitor,* November 13, 1988.

53. *Courier-Journal,* May 11, 1984, p. A7.

54. Pope John Paul II, "Spiritual Vision of Man," in *L'Osservatore Romano,* February 10, 1986, p. 5.

55. Le Roux, *Peter,* pp. 144–45.

56. *La Croix*, August 23, 1985.
57. *L'Osservatore Romano*, February 10, 1993, as reprinted in *The Christian News*, August 2, 1993, p. 22.
58. Le Roux, *Peter*, p. 45.
59. *Focus on the Family*, September 1988, p. 15.
60. *Focus on the Family*, January 1987, pp. 6, 7.
61. *Focus on the Family Citizen*, January 1990, p. 10.
62. Jesus Colina, "First Step Toward Jubilee," in *Inside the Vatican*, January 1997, p. 12.
63. Gary, *Star*, pp. 78–79.
64. Sidney Z. Ehler and John B. Morall, tr. and ed., *Church and State Through the Centuries* (London, 1954), p. 93.
65. "The Religious Century Nears," in *The Wall Street Journal*, July 6, 1995.
66. Ibid.
67. Peter Kreeft, *Fundamentals of the Faith: Essays in Christian Apologetics* (Ignatius Press, 1988), 129.
68. Gary, *Star*, p. 61.
69. G. T. Bettany, *A Popular History of the Reformation and Modern Protestantism* (London, 1895), p. 4.
70. *La Civilta*, vol. iii, p. 11, 1862.
71. *Inside the Vatican*, June 1997, p. 48.
72. *Christifideles Laici*, December 30, 1988, *John Paul II's Book of Mary*, compiled by Margaret R. Bunson (Our Sunday Visitor, Inc., 1996), p. 12.
73. Robert Schuller, *The Power of the Inner Eye*, p. 7.
74. Schuller, *Self-Esteem*, pp. 174–75.
75. Jewel van der Merwe, "LATTER RAIN and the Rise of Joel's Army," in *Discernment*, October–December 1994, p. 5.
76. *Christianity Today*, December 12, 1994, p. 36.
77. Gary North, *Liberating Planet Earth*, vol. 1 of Biblical Blueprint Series (Dominion Press, 1987), pp. 24, 178.
78. David Chilton, *Paradise Restored: An Eschatology of Dominion* (Reconstruction Press, 1985), pp. 214–19.
79. George Grant, *Bringing in the Sheaves* (American Vision Press, 1985), p. 98.
80. Robertson and Buckingham, *Shout*, pp. 157–58, emphasis in original.
81. Pat Robertson with Bob Slosser, *The Secret Kingdom: A Promise of Hope and Freedom in a World of Turmoil* (Thomas Nelson Publishers, 1982), p. 46.
82. Robertson and Buckingham, *Shout*, p. 163.
83. "God of Our Father," *Time*, October 13, 1997, p. 41.
84. John Dart, " 'Promise Keepers,' a Message to L.A. Men," *Los Angeles Times*, May 6, 1995, pp. B4–B5.
85. Terri Sullivant, "Paul Cain: A Personal Profile," in *Grace City Report*, Fall 1989, pp. 13, 16.
86. "God of Our Fathers," *Time*, October 13, 1997, p. 39; Ellis Case, "Promises, Promises," *Newsweek*, October 13, 1997, p. 40.
87. Travers van der Merwe, "Spiritual Deception, Part IV," in *Discernment*, July/August 1995, pp. 6–8.
88. Albert James Dager, "Promise Keepers Update: Mormons, Catholics Laud Men's Movement," in *Media Spotlight*, vol. 16, no. 1, p. 12.
89. Mike Aquilina, "Making new Catholic men?" in *Our Sunday Visitor*, July 20, 1997, pp. 10–11.

Chapter 26—The Coming World Religion

1. *New Age Journal*, February 1995.
2. *Foundation*, March–April 1996, p. 31.
3. Pierre Teilhard de Chardin, *Christianity and Evolution* (Collins, 1971), p. 130.
4. Malachi Martin, *Keys*, p. 299.

5. From his 1971 farewell address to the United Nations, cited in *Muller School,* op. cit., p. 8.
6. Robert Schuller, *Your Church Has Real Possibilities!* (Regal Books, 1974), pp. 1–2, foreword by C. Peter Wagner.
7. Romney, *Journey,* p. 31.
8. John Goodwin, "Testing the Fruit," Tape 2, Discernment Ministries, P.O. Box 129, Lapeer, MI 48446-0129.
9. Harvard University commencement address, June 9, 1978.
10. Herbert Schlossberg, *Idols for Destruction* (Thomas Nelson, 1983), p. 40.
11. The Baptist Standard, September 17, 1997.
12. ABC News, *Nightline,* March 4, 1997, p. 3.
13. Ibid.
14. Ibid.
15. *The Orange County Register,* September 5, 1992.
16. *Toronto Star,* June 16, 1992.
17. "Pagans of the World Unite!" in *The New American,* August 19, 1997, p. 22.
18. *The Toronto Star,* March 3, 1992.
19. *The Toronto Star,* March 9, 1992.
20. *U.S. News & World Report,* May 18, 1992.
21. *Inside the Vatican,* November 1996, pp. 18–20.
22. Templeton newsletter, "Progress in Theology," July/August 1997.
23. From a form letter sent out by Pat Robertson on The Christian Broadcasting Network, Inc. letterhead responding to inquiries concerning his signing of ECT. Letter on file.
24. Fox, *Cosmic,* p. 228.
25. James Brady, "In Step with Robert Schuller," in *Parade,* April 20, 1997, p. 18.
26. Paul Yonggi Cho, *The Fourth Dimension* (Logos, 1979), foreword.
27. *USA Today,* March 23, 1989.
28. Michael Ryan, "Dr. Norman Vincent Peale's recipe for living, DO THE BEST YOU CAN WITH WHAT YOU'VE GOT," in *Parade,* May 17, 1987, cover story.
29. William C. Irvine, *Heresies Exposed* (Loizeaux Brothers, Inc., 1921), p. 54, as cited in the Bobgan's *PsychoHeresy Awareness Letters,* September–October 1997, p. 1.
30. Wilson quoted in *Pass It On: The story of Bill Wilson and how the A.A. message reached the world* (Alcoholics Anonymous World Service, Inc., 1984), pp. 127–28; as cited in *PsychoHeresy Awareness Letter,* September–October 1997, pp. 1, 4.
31. Schuller, *Your Church,* p. 85.
32. *The Orange County Register,* April 25, 1993, p. L-1.
33. *The Baptist Standard,* September 10, 1997.
34. *Christian News,* October 31, 1994, p. 17.
35. Desmond Doig, *Mother Teresa: Her People and Her Work* (Harper & Row, 1976), p. 156.
36. *Time,* December 12, 1989, p.12.
37. *Masterpiece,* Winter 1988, p. 6.
38. Christopher Hitchens, *The Missionary Position: Mother Teresa in Theory and Practice* (London and New York: Verso, 1995), pp. 39–40.
39. Hitchens, *Teresa,* p. 45.
40. Ibid., p. 41.
41. Ibid., p. 44.
42. Ibid., pp. 49–58.
43. G.A. Pritchard, *Willow Creek Seekers Services: Evaluating a New Way of Doing Church* (Baker Books, 1996), back cover.
44. Ibid., pp. 49–58.
45. Ibid., p. 11.

46. Ibid., p. 56.
47. Transcribed from audiotape M9010, "What Protestants Can Learn From Catholics," Bill Hybels/Fr. Med Laz, 0304, Seeds Tape Ministry, 67 East Algonquin Road, South Barrington, IL 60010, A Ministry of Willow Creek Community Church.
48. Ibid.
49. Ibid.
50. Sr. Mary Rose McGeady, *Am I Going to Heaven?: The shocking story of America's street kids* (Covenant House, 1994), pp. 5–6.
51. *National Catholic Reporter,* August 27, 1993.
52. Letter on file.
53. From a transcript of the program.
54. *Calvary Contender,* August 15, 1993.
55. *Christian News,* May 12, 1997, p. 11.
56. *Larry King Live,* January 21, 1997, transcript obtainable from Federal Document Clearing House, 1100 Mercantile Lane, Suite 119, Landover, MD 20785.
57. ABC News, *Nightline,* March 4, 1997, from a transcript of the program, available from Federal Document Clearing House, Inc., p. 2.
58. From a transcript of the "Hour of Power," June 1 and 8, 1997.
59. Colin Greer, "The Rev. Billy Graham reflects on his faith, his country and his life," in *Parade,* October 20, 1996, p. 4.
60. Mike Claydon, *Billy Graham—A Panorama,* unpublished and undated treatise.
61. Harvey D. Egan, S.J., *Christian Mysticism, the future of a tradition* (Pueblo Publishing Company, 1984), pp. 215–16.
62. Ibid., pp. 238–39.
63. Ibid., p. 241.
64. Jackson, *Sacred Hoops,* p. 52.
65. Ibid., p. 27.
66. Ibid., p. 54, etc.
67. *The Christian News,* November 7, 1968, p. 22.
68. Al Gore, *Earth in the Balance* (Houghton-Mifflin, 1992), pp. 258–61, 263.
69. "Issues of Faith and Peace Draw Religious Leaders to Vatican," in *Christian News,* November 14, 1994, p. 19.
70. "World Conference on Religion and Peace given special audience by the Pope," in *The Toronto Star,* July 20, 1991.
71. *New Zealand Herald,* August 10, 1996.
72. *San Francisco Chronicle,* June 20, 1996.
73. *URI News Update,* December 1996, as reported in *Calvary Contender,* March 1, 1997, p. 1.
74. "Pagans of the World Unite!" in *The New American,* August 19, 1997, p. 21.
75. *The Day Drawing Near,* Fall 1996, p. 1, a publication of Countryside Bible Church, 250 Ravenaux Drive, Southlake, TX 76092.
76. *Christianity Today,* July 18, 1994, p. 17.
77. *Christianity Today,* December 12, 1994, p. 36.
78. *New Oxford Review,* June 1996, p. 17.
79. *Saturday Evening Post,* January/February 1980, pp. 72–75, 89.
80. *Focus on the Family Citizen,* January 1990, p. 10.
81. *Christianity Today,* September 6, 1985, editorial titled "A Man Under Orders."
82. Schroeder, *Trent,* p. 149.
83. *New York Times,* March 30, 1994.
84. John Goodwin, "Testing the Fruit," Tape 2, Discernment Ministries, P.O. Box 129, Lapeer, MI 48446-0129.
85. Letter on file.

Index

Subject

Persons and Organizations

Other Books by
Dave Hunt